SQL: The Complete Reference

SQL: The Complete Reference

James R. Groff
Paul N. Weinberg

Osborne/**McGraw-Hill**
Berkeley New York St. Louis San Francisco
Auckland Bogotá Hamburg London Madrid
Mexico City Milan Montreal New Delhi Panama City
Paris São Paulo Singapore Sydney
Tokyo Toronto

Osborne/**McGraw-Hill**
2600 Tenth Street
Berkeley, California 94710
U.S.A.

For information on translations or book distributors outside the U.S.A., or to arrange bulk purchase discounts for sales promotions, premiums, or fund-raisers, please contact Osborne/**McGraw-Hill** at the above address.

SQL: The Complete Reference

4567890 DOC DOC 9019876543210

ISBN 0-07-211845-8

Publisher
Brandon A. Nordin

Associate Publisher and Editor-in-Chief
Scott Rogers

Senior Acquisitions Editor
Wendy Rinaldi

Acquisitions Editor
Jane K. Brownlow

Project Editor
Heidi Poulin

Editorial Assistant
Monika Faltiss

Copy Editor
Nancy Crumpton

Proofreader
Rhonda Holmes

Indexer
Valerie Robbins

Computer Designer
Jani Beckwith
Michelle Galicia

Illustrators
Robert Hansen
Brian Wells
Beth Young

Contents at a Glance

Part IV Database Structure

Part V Programming with SQL

Part VI SQL Today and Tomorrow

Part VII Appendices

Contents

Part I
An Overview of SQL

Part II
Retrieving Data

Part III

Updating Data

Part IV

Database Structure

Part V

Programming with SQL

Part VI

SQL Today and Tomorrow

Part VII

Appendices

Acknowledgments

Special thanks to Matan Arazi for doing such an exceptional job assembling the Bonus CD-ROM. He pulled off a real miracle to squeeze all five SQL DBMS products onto a single CD, a technical feat that would not have been possible without his diligent tenacity.

Thanks also to everyone at Osborne for pulling it all together, including Jane Brownlow and Wendy Rinaldi for doing tag-team duty as our acquisitions editors, and to Heidi Poulin for her meticulous attention to detail.

Preface

S QL: The Complete Reference provides a comprehensive, in-depth treatment of the SQL language for both technical and non-technical users, programmers, data processing professionals, and managers who want to understand the impact of SQL in the computer market. This book offers a conceptual framework for understanding and using SQL, describes the history of SQL and SQL standards, and explains the role of SQL in the computer industry today. It will show you, step-by-step, how to use SQL features, with many illustrations and realistic examples to clarify SQL concepts. The book also compares SQL products from leading DBMS vendors—describing their advantages, benefits, and trade-offs—to help you select the right product for your application. The accompanying CD contains actual trial versions of five leading SQL databases, so you can try them for yourself and gain actual experience in using the major database products from Oracle, Microsoft, Sybase, Informix, and IBM.

In some of the chapters in this book, the subject matter is explored at two different levels—a fundamental description of the topic, and an advanced discussion intended for computer professionals who need to understand some of the "internals" behind SQL. The more advanced information is covered in sections marked with an asterisk (*). You do not need to read these sections to obtain an understanding of what SQL is and what it does.

How this Book Is Organized

The book is divided into six parts that cover various aspects of the SQL language:

- Part One, "An Overview of SQL," provides an introduction to SQL and a market perspective of its role as a database language. Its four chapters describe the history of SQL, the evolution of SQL standards, and how SQL relates to the relational data model and to earlier database technologies. Part One also contains a quick tour of SQL that briefly illustrates its most important features and provides you with an overview of the entire language early in the book.

- Part Two, "Retrieving Data," describes the features of SQL that allow you to perform database queries. The first chapter in this part describes the basic structure of the SQL language. The next four chapters start with the simplest SQL queries, and progressively build to more complex queries, including multi-table queries, summary queries, and queries that use subqueries.

- Part Three, "Updating Data," shows how you can use SQL to add new data to a database, delete data from a database, and modify existing database data. It also describes the database integrity issues that arise when data is updated, and how SQL addresses these issues. The last of the three chapters in this part discusses the SQL transaction concept and SQL support for multi-user transaction processing.

- Part Four, "Database Structure," deals with creating and administering a SQL-based database. Its four chapters tell you how to create the tables, views, and indexes that form the structure of a relational database. It also describes the SQL security scheme that prevents unauthorized access to data, and the SQL system catalog that describes the structure of a database. This part also discusses the significant differences between the database structures supported by various SQL-based DBMS products.

- Part Five, "Programming with SQL," describes how application programs use SQL for database access. It discusses the embedded SQL specified by the ANSI standard and used by IBM, Oracle, Ingres, Informix, and most other SQL-based DBMS products. It also describes the dynamic SQL interface that is used to build general-purpose database tools, such as report writers and database browsing programs. Finally, this part describes the popular SQL APIs, including ODBC, the ISO-standard Call-Level Interface, and Oracle Call Interface, and contrasts them with the embedded SQL interface.

- Part Six, "SQL Today and Tomorrow," examines the state of SQL-based DBMS products today, major database trends, the "hot" new applications, and the directions that SQL will take over the next few years. It describes the intense current activity in SQL networking and distributed databases, and the evolution of special features to support SQL-based OLTP, and SQL-based data warehousing. This part also discusses the impact of object technology on SQL and relational databases, and the emergence of hybrid, object-relational database models.

Conventions Used in this Book

SQL: The Complete Reference describes the SQL features and functions that are available in the most popular SQL-based DBMS products and those that are described in the ANSI/ISO SQL standards. Whenever possible, the SQL statement syntax described in the book and used in the examples applies to all dialects of SQL. When the dialects differ, the differences are pointed out in the text, and the examples follow the most common practice. In these cases, you may have to modify the SQL statements in the examples slightly to suit your particular brand of DBMS.

Throughout the book, technical terms appear in italics the first time that they are used and defined. SQL language elements, including SQL keywords, table and column names, and sample SQL statements appear in an uppercase monospace font. SQL API function names appear in a lowercase monospace font. Program listings also appear in monospace font, and use the normal case conventions for the particular programming language (uppercase for COBOL and FORTRAN, lowercase for C). Note that these conventions are used solely to improve readability; most SQL implementations will accept either uppercase or lowercase statements. Many of the SQL examples include query results, which appear immediately following the SQL statement as they would in an interactive SQL session. In some cases, long query results are truncated after a few rows; this is indicated by a vertical ellipsis (. . .) following the last row of query results.

Why this Book Is for You

SQL: The Complete Reference is the right book for anyone who wants to understand and learn SQL, including database users, data processing professionals, programmers, students, and managers. It describes—in simple, understandable language liberally illustrated with figures and examples—what SQL is, why it is important, and how you use it. This book is not specific to one particular brand or dialect of SQL. Rather, it describes the standard, central core of the SQL language and then goes on to describe the differences among the most popular SQL products, including Oracle, Microsoft SQL Server, IBM's DB2, Informix Universal Server, Sybase Adaptive Server, and others. It also explains the importance of SQL-based standards, such as ODBC and the ANSI/ISO SQL2 and evolving SQL3 standards.

If you are a new user of SQL, this book offers comprehensive, step-by-step treatment of the language, building from simple queries to more advanced concepts. The structure of the book will allow you to quickly start using SQL, but the book will continue to be valuable as you begin to use more complex features of the language. You can use the SQL software on the companion CD to try out the examples and build your SQL skills.

If you are a data processing professional or a manager, this book will give you a perspective on the impact that SQL is having in every segment of the computer market—from personal computers, to mainframes, to online transaction processing systems and data warehousing applications. The early chapters describe the history of

SQL, its role in the market, and its evolution from earlier database technologies. The final chapters describe the future of SQL and the development of new database technologies such as distributed databases, business intelligence databases, and object-relational database capabilities.

If you are a programmer, this book offers a very complete treatment of programming with SQL. Unlike the reference manuals of many DBMS products, it offers a conceptual framework for SQL programming, explaining the why as well as the how of developing a SQL-based application. It contrasts the SQL programming interfaces offered by all of the leading SQL products, including embedded SQL, dynamic SQL, ODBC and proprietary APIs such as the Oracle Call Interface, providing a perspective not found in any other book.

If you are selecting a DBMS product, this book offers a comparison of the SQL features, advantages, and benefits offered by the various DBMS vendors. The differences between the leading DBMS products are explained, not only in technical terms, but also in terms of their impact on applications and their competitive position in the marketplace. The DBMS software on the companion CD can be used to try out these features in a prototype of your own application.

In short, both technical and non-technical users can benefit from this book. It is the most comprehensive source of information available about the SQL language, SQL features and benefits, popular SQL-based products, the history of SQL, and the impact of SQL on the future direction of the computer market.

Part I

An Overview of SQL

The first four chapters of this book provide a perspective and a quick introduction to SQL. Chapter 1 describes what SQL is and explains its major features and benefits. In Chapter 2, a quick tour of SQL shows you many of its capabilities with simple, rapid-fire examples. Chapter 3 offers a market perspective of SQL by tracing its history, describing the SQL standards and the major vendors of SQL-based products, and identifying the reasons for SQL's prominence today. Chapter 4 describes the relational data model upon which SQL is based and compares it to earlier data models.

Chapter 1

Introduction

3

T   he SQL language and relational database systems based on it are one of the most
         important foundation technologies in the computer industry today. Over the last
         decade, the popularity of SQL has exploded, and it stands today as *the* standard
computer database language. Literally hundreds of database products now support
SQL, running on computer systems from mainframes to personal computers and even
handheld devices. An official international SQL standard has been adopted and
expanded twice. Virtually every major enterprise software product relies on SQL for its
data management, and SQL is at the core of the database products from Microsoft and
Oracle, two of the largest software companies in the world. From its obscure
beginnings as an IBM research project, SQL has leaped to prominence as both an
important computer technology and a powerful market force.

What, exactly, is SQL? Why is it important? What can it do, and how does it work?
If SQL is really a standard, why are there so many different versions and dialects? How
do popular SQL products like SQL Server, Oracle, Informix, Sybase, and DB2 compare?
How does SQL relate to Microsoft standards, such as ODBC and COM? How does
JDBC link SQL to the world of Java and object technology? Does SQL really scale from
mainframes to handheld devices? Has it really delivered the performance needed for
high-volume transaction processing? How will SQL impact the way you use
computers, and how can you get the most out of this important data management tool?

The SQL Language

SQL is a tool for organizing, managing, and retrieving data stored by a computer
database. The name "SQL" is an abbreviation for *Structured Query Language*. For
historical reasons, SQL is usually pronounced "sequel," but the alternate pronunciation
"S.Q.L." is also used. As the name implies, SQL is a computer *language* that you use to
interact with a database. In fact, SQL works with one specific type of database, called a
relational database.

Figure 1-1 shows how SQL works. The computer system in the figure has a *database*
that stores important information. If the computer system is in a business, the database
might store inventory, production, sales, or payroll data. On a personal computer, the
database might store data about the checks you have written, lists of people and their
phone numbers, or data extracted from a larger computer system. The computer
program that controls the database is called a *database management system*, or DBMS.

When you need to retrieve data from a database, you use the SQL language to
make the request. The DBMS processes the SQL request, retrieves the requested
data, and returns it to you. This process of requesting data from a database and
receiving back the results is called a database *query*—hence the name Structured
Query Language.

The name Structured Query Language is actually somewhat of a misnomer. First of
all, SQL is far more than a query tool, although that was its original purpose and

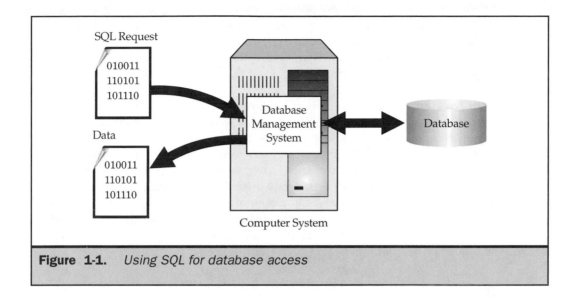

Figure 1-1. *Using SQL for database access*

retrieving data is still one of its most important functions. SQL is used to control all of the functions that a DBMS provides for its users, including:

- *Data definition*. SQL lets a user define the structure and organization of the stored data and relationships among the stored data items.

- *Data retrieval*. SQL allows a user or an application program to retrieve stored data from the database and use it.

- *Data manipulation*. SQL allows a user or an application program to update the database by adding new data, removing old data, and modifying previously stored data.

- *Access control*. SQL can be used to restrict a user's ability to retrieve, add, and modify data, protecting stored data against unauthorized access.

- *Data sharing*. SQL is used to coordinate data sharing by concurrent users, ensuring that they do not interfere with one another.

- *Data integrity*. SQL defines integrity constraints in the database, protecting it from corruption due to inconsistent updates or system failures.

SQL is thus a comprehensive language for controlling and interacting with a database management system.

Second, SQL is not really a complete computer language like COBOL, C, C++, or Java. SQL contains no IF statement for testing conditions, and no GOTO, DO, or FOR statements for program flow control. Instead, SQL is a database *sublanguage,* consisting of about forty statements specialized for database management tasks. These SQL statements can be *embedded* into another language, such as COBOL or C, to extend that language for use in database access. Alternatively, they can be explicitly sent to a database management system for processing, via a *call level interface* from a language such as C, C++, or Java.

Finally, SQL is not a particularly structured language, especially when compared to highly structured languages such as C, Pascal, or Java. Instead, SQL statements resemble English sentences, complete with "noise words" that don't add to the meaning of the statement but make it read more naturally. There are quite a few inconsistencies in the SQL language, and there are also some special rules to prevent you from constructing SQL statements that look perfectly legal, but don't make sense.

Despite the inaccuracy of its name, SQL has emerged as *the* standard language for using relational databases. SQL is both a powerful language and one that is relatively easy to learn. The quick tour of SQL in the next chapter will give you a good overview of the language and its capabilities.

The Role of SQL

SQL is not itself a database management system, nor is it a stand-alone product. You cannot go into a computer store and "buy SQL." Instead, SQL is an integral part of a database management system, a language and a tool for communicating with the DBMS. Figure 1-2 shows some of the components of a typical DBMS, and how SQL acts as the "glue" that links them together.

The *database engine* is the heart of the DBMS, responsible for actually structuring, storing, and retrieving the data in the database. It accepts SQL requests from other DBMS components, such as a forms facility, report writer, or interactive query facility, from user-written application programs, and even from other computer systems. As the figure shows, SQL plays many different roles:

- SQL is an *interactive query language*. Users type SQL commands into an interactive SQL program to retrieve data and display it on the screen, providing a convenient, easy-to-use tool for ad hoc database queries.

- SQL is a *database programming language*. Programmers embed SQL commands into their application programs to access the data in a database. Both user-written programs and database utility programs (such as report writers and data entry tools) use this technique for database access.

- SQL is a *database administration language*. The database administrator responsible for managing a minicomputer or mainframe database uses SQL to define the database structure and control access to the stored data.

- SQL is a *client/server language*. Personal computer programs use SQL to communicate over a network with database servers that store shared data. This client/server architecture has become very popular for enterprise-class applications.

■ SQL is an *Internet data access language*. Internet web servers that interact with corporate data and Internet applications servers all use SQL as a standard language for accessing corporate databases.

■ SQL is a *distributed database language*. Distributed database management systems use SQL to help distribute data across many connected computer systems. The DBMS software on each system uses SQL to communicate with the other systems, sending requests for data access.

■ SQL is a *database gateway language*. In a computer network with a mix of different DBMS products, SQL is often used in a *gateway* that allows one brand of DBMS to communicate with another brand.

SQL has thus emerged as a useful, powerful tool for linking people, computer programs, and computer systems to the data stored in a relational database.

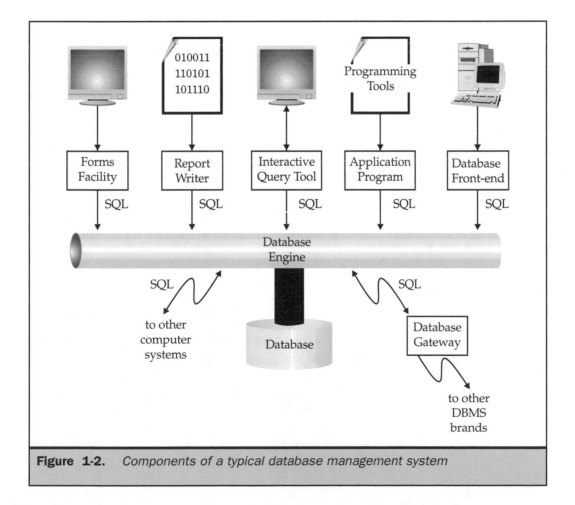

Figure 1-2. *Components of a typical database management system*

SQL Features and Benefits

SQL is both an easy-to-understand language and a comprehensive tool for managing data. Here are some of the major features of SQL and the market forces that have made it successful:

- Vendor independence
- Portability across computer systems
- SQL standards
- IBM endorsement (DB2)
- Microsoft commitment (ODBC and ADO)
- Relational foundation
- High-level, English-like structure
- Interactive, ad hoc queries
- Programmatic database access
- Multiple views of data
- Complete database language
- Dynamic data definition
- Client/server architecture
- Extensibility and object technology
- Internet database access
- Java integration (JDBC)

These are the reasons why SQL has emerged as the standard tool for managing data on personal computers, minicomputers, and mainframes. They are described in the sections that follow.

Vendor Independence

SQL is offered by all of the leading DBMS vendors, and no new database product over the last decade has been highly successful without SQL support. A SQL-based database and the programs that use it can be moved from one DBMS to another vendor's DBMS with minimal conversion effort and little retraining of personnel. PC database tools, such as query tools, report writers, and application generators, work with many different brands of SQL databases. The vendor independence thus provided by SQL was one of the most important reasons for its early popularity and remains an important feature today.

Portability Across Computer Systems

SQL-based database products run on computer systems ranging from mainframes and midrange systems to personal computers, workstations, and even handheld devices. They operate on stand-alone computer systems, in departmental local area networks, and in enterprise-wide or Internet-wide networks. SQL-based applications that begin on single-user systems can be moved to larger server systems as they grow. Data from corporate SQL-based databases can be extracted and downloaded into departmental or personal databases. Finally, economical personal computers can be used to prototype a SQL-based database application before moving it to an expensive multi-user system.

SQL Standards

An official standard for SQL was initially published by the American National Standards Institute (ANSI) and the International Standards Organization (ISO) in 1986, and was expanded in 1989 and again in 1992. SQL is also a U.S. Federal Information Processing Standard (FIPS), making it a key requirement for large government computer contracts. Over the years, other international, government, and vendor groups have pioneered the standardization of new SQL capabilities, such as call-level interfaces or object-based extensions. Many of these new initiatives have been incorporated into the ANSI/ISO standard over time. The evolving standards serve as an official stamp of approval for SQL and have speeded its market acceptance.

IBM Endorsement (DB2)

SQL was originally invented by IBM researchers and has since become a strategic product for IBM based on its flagship DB2 database. SQL support is available on all major IBM product families, from personal computers through midrange systems (AS/400 and RS/6000) to IBM mainframes running both the MVS and VM operating systems. IBM's initial work provided a clear signal of IBM's direction for other database and system vendors to follow early in the development of SQL and relational databases. Later, IBM's commitment and broad support speeded the market acceptance of SQL.

Microsoft Commitment (ODBC and ADO)

Microsoft has long considered database access a key part of its Windows personal computer software architecture. Both desktop and server versions of Windows provide standardized relational database access through Open Database Connectivity (ODBC), a SQL-based call-level API. Leading Windows software applications (spreadsheets, word processors, databases, etc.) from Microsoft and other vendors support ODBC, and all leading SQL databases provide ODBC access. Microsoft has enhanced ODBC support with higher-level, more object-oriented database access layers as part of its Object Linking and Embedding technology (OLE DB), and more recently as part of Active/X (Active/X Data Objects, or ADO).

Relational Foundation

SQL is a language for relational databases, and it has become popular along with the relational database model. The tabular, row/column structure of a relational database is intuitive to users, keeping the SQL language simple and easy to understand. The relational model also has a strong theoretical foundation that has guided the evolution and implementation of relational databases. Riding a wave of acceptance brought about by the success of the relational model, SQL has become *the* database language for relational databases.

High-Level, English-Like Structure

SQL statements look like simple English sentences, making SQL easy to learn and understand. This is in part because SQL statements describe the *data* to be retrieved, rather than specifying *how* to find the data. Tables and columns in a SQL database can have long, descriptive names. As a result, most SQL statements "say what they mean" and can be read as clear, natural sentences.

Interactive, Ad Hoc Queries

SQL is an interactive query language that gives users ad hoc access to stored data. Using SQL interactively, a user can get answers even to complex questions in minutes or seconds, in sharp contrast to the days or weeks it would take for a programmer to write a custom report program. Because of SQL's ad hoc query power, data is more accessible and can be used to help an organization make better, more informed decisions. SQL's ad hoc query capability was an important advantage over nonrelational databases early in its evolution and more recently has continued as a key advantage over pure object-based databases.

Programmatic Database Access

SQL is also a database language used by programmers to write applications that access a database. The same SQL statements are used for both interactive and programmatic access, so the database access parts of a program can be tested first with interactive SQL and then embedded into the program. In contrast, traditional databases provided one set of tools for programmatic access and a separate query facility for ad hoc requests, without any synergy between the two modes of access.

Multiple Views of Data

Using SQL, the creator of a database can give different users of the database different *views* of its structure and contents. For example, the database can be constructed so that each user sees data for only their department or sales region. In addition, data from several different parts of the database can be combined and presented to the user as a simple row/column table. SQL views can thus be used to enhance the security of a database and tailor it to the particular needs of individual users.

Complete Database Language

SQL was first developed as an ad hoc query language, but its powers now go far beyond data retrieval. SQL provides a complete, consistent language for creating a database, managing its security, updating its contents, retrieving data, and sharing data among many concurrent users. SQL concepts that are learned in one part of the language can be applied to other SQL commands, making users more productive.

Dynamic Data Definition

Using SQL, the structure of a database can be changed and expanded dynamically, even while users are accessing database contents. This is a major advance over static data definition languages, which prevented access to the database while its structure was being changed. SQL thus provides maximum flexibility, allowing a database to adapt to changing requirements while on-line applications continue uninterrupted.

Client/Server Architecture

SQL is a natural vehicle for implementing applications using a distributed, client/server architecture. In this role, SQL serves as the link between "front-end" computer systems optimized for user interaction and "back-end" systems specialized for database management, allowing each system to do what it does best. SQL also allows personal computers to function as front-ends to network servers or to larger minicomputer and mainframe databases, providing access to corporate data from personal computer applications.

Extensibility and Object Technology

The major challenge to SQL's continued dominance as a database standard has come from the emergence of object-based programming, and the introduction of object-based databases as an extension of the broad market trend toward object-based technology. SQL-based database vendors have responded to this challenge by slowly expanding and enhancing SQL to include object features. These "object/relational" databases, which continue to be based on SQL, have emerged as a more popular alternative to "pure object" databases and may insure SQL's continuing dominance for the next decade.

Internet Database Access

With the exploding popularity of the Internet and the World Wide Web, and their standards-based foundation, SQL found a new role in the late 1990s as an Internet data access standard. Early in the development of the Web, developers needed a way to retrieve and present database information on web pages and used SQL as a common language for database gateways. More recently, the emergence of three-tiered Internet architectures with distinct thin client, application server and database server layers, have established SQL as the standard link between the application and database tiers.

Java Integration (JDBC)

One of the major new areas of SQL development is the integration of SQL with Java. Seeing the need to link the Java language to existing relational databases, Sun Microsystems (the creator of Java) introduced Java Data Base Connectivity (JDBC), a standard API that allows Java programs to use SQL for database access. Many of the leading database vendors have also announced or implemented Java support *within* their database systems, allowing Java to be used as a language for stored procedures and business logic within the database itself. This trend toward integration between Java and SQL will insure the continued importance of SQL in the new era of Java-based programming.

The Complete Reference

Chapter 2

A Quick Tour of SQL

Before diving into the details of SQL, it's a good idea to develop an overall perspective on the language and how it works. This chapter contains a quick tour of SQL that illustrates its major features and functions. The goal of the quick tour is not to make you proficient in writing SQL statements; that is the goal of Part II of this book. Rather, by the time you've finished this chapter, you will have a basic familiarity with the SQL language and an overview of its capabilities.

A Simple Database

The examples in the quick tour are based on a simple relational database for a small distribution company. The database, shown in Figure 2-1, stores the information needed to implement a small order processing application. Specifically, it stores the following information:

- the *customers* who buy the company's products,
- the *orders* placed by those customers,
- the *salespeople* who sell the products to customers, and
- the *sales offices* where those salespeople work.

This database, like most others, is a model of the "real world." The data stored in the database represents real entities—customers, orders, salespeople, and offices. There is a separate table of data for each different kind of entity. Database requests that you make using the SQL language parallel real-world activities, as customers place, cancel, and change orders, as you hire and fire salespeople, and so on. Let's see how you can use SQL to manipulate data.

Retrieving Data

First, let's list the sales offices, showing the city where each one is located and its year-to-date sales. The SQL statement that retrieves data from the database is called SELECT. This SQL statement retrieves the data you want:

```
SELECT CITY, OFFICE, SALES
  FROM OFFICES

CITY          OFFICE      SALES
------------  -------  ------------
Denver            22  $186,042.00
New York          11  $692,637.00
Chicago           12  $735,042.00
Atlanta           13  $367,911.00
Los Angeles       21  $835,915.00
```

ORDERS Table

ORDER_NUM	CUST	PRODUCT	QTY	AMOUNT
112961	2117	2A44L	7	$31,500.00
113012	2111	41003	35	$3,745.00
112989	2101	114	6	$1,458.00
113051	2118	XK47	4	$1,420.00
112968	2102	41004	34	$3,978.00
113036	2107	4100Z	9	$22,500.00
113045	2112	2A44R	10	$45,000.00
112963	2103	41004	28	$3,276.00
113013	2118	41003	1	$652.00
113058	2108	112	10	$1,480.00
112997	2124	41003	1	$652.00
112983	2103	41004	6	$702.00
113024	2114	XK47	20	$7,100.00
113062	2124	114	10	$2,430.00
112979	2114	4100Z	6	$15,000.00
113027	2103	41002	54	$4,104.00
113007	2112	773C	3	$2,925.00
113069	2109	775C	22	$31,350.00
113034	2107	2A45C	8	$632.00
112992	2118	41002	10	$760.00
112975	2111	2A44G	6	$2,100.00
113055	2108	4100X	6	$150.00
113048	2120	779C	2	$3,750.00
112993	2106	2A45C	24	$1,896.00
113065	2106	XK47	6	$2,130.00
113003	2108	779C	3	$5,625.00
113049	2118	XK47	2	$776.00
112987	2103	4100Y	11	$27,500.00
113057	2111	4100X	24	$600.00
113042	2113	2A44R	5	$22,500.00

CUSTOMERS Table

CUST_NUM	COMPANY	CUST_REP	CREDIT_LIMIT
2111	JCP Inc.	103	$50,000.00
2102	First Corp.	101	$65,000.00
2103	Acme Mfg.	105	$50,000.00
2123	Carter & Sons	102	$40,000.00
2107	Ace International	110	$35,000.00
2115	Smithson Corp.	101	$20,000.00
2101	Jones Mfg.	106	$65,000.00
2112	Zetacorp	108	$50,000.00
2121	QMA Assoc.	103	$45,000.00
2114	Orion Corp.	102	$20,000.00
2124	Peter Brothers	107	$40,000.00
2108	Holm & Landis	109	$55,000.00
2117	J.P. Sinclair	106	$35,000.00
2122	Three-Way Lines	105	$30,000.00
2120	Rico Enterprises	102	$50,000.00
2106	Fred Lewis Corp.	102	$65,000.00
2119	Solomon Inc.	109	$25,000.00
2118	Midwest Systems	108	$60,000.00
2113	Ian & Schmidt	104	$20,000.00
2109	Chen Associates	107	$25,000.00
2105	AAA Investments	101	$45,000.00

SALESREPS Table

NAME	REP_OFFICE	QUOTA	SALES
Bill Adams	13	$350,000.00	$367,911.00
Mary Jones	11	$300,000.00	$392,725.00
Sue Smith	21	$350,000.00	$474,050.00
Sam Clark	11	$275,000.00	$299,912.00
Bob Smith	12	$200,000.00	$142,594.00
Dan Roberts	12	$300,000.00	$305,673.00
Tom Snyder	NULL	NULL	$75,985.00
Larry Fitch	21	$350,000.00	$361,865.00
Paul Cruz	12	$275,000.00	$286,775.00
Nancy Angelli	22	$300,000.00	$186,042.00

OFFICES Table

OFFICE	CITY	REGION	TARGET	SALES
22	Denver	Western	$300,000.00	$186,042.00
11	New York	Eastern	$575,000.00	$692,637.00
12	Chicago	Eastern	$800,000.00	$735,042.00
13	Atlanta	Eastern	$350,000.00	$367,911.00
21	Los Angeles	Western	$725,000.00	$835,915.00

Figure 2-1. *A simple relational database*

The SELECT statement asks for three pieces of data—the city, the office number, and the sales—for each office. It also specifies that the data comes from the OFFICES table, which stores data about sales offices. The results of the query appear, in tabular form, immediately after the request.

The SELECT statement is used for all SQL queries. For example, here is a query that lists the names and year-to-date sales for each salesperson in the database. It also shows the quota (sales target) and the office number where each person works. In this case, the data comes from SALESREPS table:

```
SELECT NAME, REP_OFFICE, SALES, QUOTA
  FROM SALESREPS

NAME            REP_OFFICE         SALES          QUOTA
-------------   ----------   ------------   ------------
Bill Adams              13   $367,911.00    $350,000.00
Mary Jones              11   $392,725.00    $300,000.00
Sue Smith               21   $474,050.00    $350,000.00
Sam Clark               11   $299,912.00    $275,000.00
Bob Smith               12   $142,594.00    $200,000.00
Dan Roberts             12   $305,673.00    $300,000.00
Tom Snyder            NULL    $75,985.00           NULL
Larry Fitch             21   $361,865.00    $350,000.00
Paul Cruz               12   $286,775.00    $275,000.00
Nancy Angelli           22   $186,042.00    $300,000.00
```

SQL also lets you ask for calculated results. For example, you can ask SQL to calculate the amount by which each salesperson is over or under quota:

```
SELECT NAME, SALES, QUOTA, (SALES - QUOTA)
  FROM SALESREPS

NAME                SALES          QUOTA    (SALES-QUOTA)
-------------   ------------   ------------  -------------
Bill Adams      $367,911.00    $350,000.00     $17,911.00
Mary Jones      $392,725.00    $300,000.00     $92,725.00
Sue Smith       $474,050.00    $350,000.00    $124,050.00
Sam Clark       $299,912.00    $275,000.00     $24,912.00
Bob Smith       $142,594.00    $200,000.00    -$57,406.00
Dan Roberts     $305,673.00    $300,000.00      $5,673.00
Tom Snyder       $75,985.00           NULL           NULL
Larry Fitch     $361,865.00    $350,000.00     $11,865.00
Paul Cruz       $286,775.00    $275,000.00     $11,775.00
Nancy Angelli   $186,042.00    $300,000.00   -$113,958.00
```

The requested data (including the calculated difference between sales and quota for each salesperson) once again appears in a row/column table. Perhaps you would like to focus on the salespeople whose sales are less than their quotas. SQL lets you retrieve that kind of selective information very easily, by adding a mathematical comparison to the previous request:

```
SELECT NAME, SALES, QUOTA, (SALES - QUOTA)
  FROM SALESREPS
 WHERE SALES < QUOTA

NAME                  SALES         QUOTA    (SALES-QUOTA)
--------------   ------------  ------------  -------------
Bob Smith         $142,594.00   $200,000.00    -$57,406.00
Nancy Angelli     $186,042.00   $300,000.00   -$113,958.00
```

The same technique can be used to list large orders in the database and find out which customer placed the order, what product was ordered, and in what quantity. You can also ask SQL to sort the orders based on the order amount:

```
SELECT ORDER_NUM, CUST, PRODUCT, QTY, AMOUNT
  FROM ORDERS
 WHERE AMOUNT > 25000.00
 ORDER BY AMOUNT

ORDER_NUM  CUST  PRODUCT   QTY      AMOUNT
---------- ----- --------  ----  -----------
   112987  2103  4100Y       11   $27,500.00
   113069  2109  775C        22   $31,350.00
   112961  2117  2A44L        7   $31,500.00
   113045  2112  2A44R       10   $45,000.00
```

Summarizing Data

SQL not only retrieves data from the database, it can be used to summarize the database contents as well. What's the average size of an order in the database? This request asks SQL to look at all the orders and find the average amount:

```
SELECT AVG(AMOUNT)
  FROM ORDERS

AVG(AMOUNT)
-----------
  $8,256.37
```

You could also ask for the average amount of all the orders placed by a particular customer:

```
SELECT AVG(AMOUNT)
  FROM ORDERS
 WHERE CUST = 2103

AVG(AMOUNT)
-----------
  $8,895.50
```

Finally, let's find out the total amount of the orders placed by each customer. To do this, you can ask SQL to group the orders together by customer number and then total the orders for each customer:

```
SELECT CUST, SUM(AMOUNT)
  FROM ORDERS
 GROUP BY CUST

CUST   SUM(AMOUNT)
-----  ------------
2101     $1,458.00
2102     $3,978.00
2103    $35,582.00
2106     $4,026.00
2107    $23,132.00
2108     $7,255.00
2109    $31,350.00
2111     $6,445.00
2112    $47,925.00
2113    $22,500.00
2114    $22,100.00
2117    $31,500.00
2118     $3,608.00
2120     $3,750.00
2124     $3,082.00
```

Adding Data to the Database

SQL is also used to add new data to the database. For example, suppose you just opened a new Western region sales office in Dallas, with target sales of $275,000. Here's the INSERT statement that adds the new office to the database, as office number 23:

```
INSERT INTO OFFICES (CITY, REGION, TARGET, SALES, OFFICE)
    VALUES ('Dallas', 'Western', 275000.00, 0.00, 23)

1 row inserted.
```

Similarly, if Mary Jones (employee number 109) signs up a new customer, Acme Industries, this INSERT statement adds the customer to the database as customer number 2125 with a $25,000 credit limit:

```
INSERT INTO CUSTOMERS (COMPANY, CUST_REP, CUST_NUM, CREDIT_LIMIT)
    VALUES ('Acme Industries', 109, 2125, 25000.00)

1 row inserted.
```

Deleting Data

Just as the SQL INSERT statement adds new data to the database, the SQL DELETE statement removes data from the database. If Acme Industries decides a few days later to switch to a competitor, you can delete them from the database with this statement:

```
DELETE FROM CUSTOMERS
 WHERE COMPANY = 'Acme Industries'

1 row deleted.
```

And if you decide to terminate all salespeople whose sales are less than their quotas, you can remove them from the database with this DELETE statement:

```
DELETE FROM SALESREPS
 WHERE SALES < QUOTA

2 rows deleted.
```

Updating the Database

The SQL language is also used to modify data that is already stored in the database. For example, to increase the credit limit for First Corp. to $75,000, you would use the SQL UPDATE statement:

```
UPDATE CUSTOMERS
   SET CREDIT_LIMIT = 75000.00
 WHERE COMPANY = 'First Corp.'

1 row updated.
```

The UPDATE statement can also make many changes in the database at once. For example, this UPDATE statement raises the quota for all salespeople by $15,000:

```
UPDATE SALESREPS
   SET QUOTA = QUOTA + 15000.00

8 rows updated.
```

Protecting Data

An important role of a database is to protect the stored data from access by unauthorized users. For example, suppose your assistant, named Mary, was not previously authorized to insert data about new customers into the database. This SQL statement grants her that permission:

```
GRANT INSERT
   ON CUSTOMERS
   TO MARY

Privilege granted.
```

Similarly, the following SQL statement gives Mary permission to update data about customers and to retrieve customer data with the SELECT statement:

```
GRANT UPDATE, SELECT
   ON CUSTOMERS
   TO MARY

Privilege granted.
```

If Mary is no longer allowed to add new customers to the database, this REVOKE statement will disallow it:

```
REVOKE INSERT
     ON CUSTOMERS
   FROM MARY

Privilege revoked.
```

Similarly, this REVOKE statement will revoke all of Mary's privileges to access customer data in any way:

```
REVOKE ALL
     ON CUSTOMERS
   FROM MARY

Privilege revoked.
```

Creating a Database

Before you can store data in a database, you must first define the structure of the data. Suppose you want to expand the sample database by adding a table of data about the products sold by your company. For each product, the data to be stored includes:

- a three-character manufacturer ID code,
- a five-character product ID code,
- a description of up to thirty characters,
- the price of the product, and
- the quantity currently on hand.

This SQL CREATE TABLE statement defines a new table to store the products data:

```
CREATE TABLE PRODUCTS
      (MFR_ID CHAR(3),
   PRODUCT_ID CHAR(5),
  DESCRIPTION VARCHAR(20),
        PRICE MONEY,
  QTY_ON_HAND INTEGER)

Table created.
```

Although more cryptic than the previous SQL statements, the CREATE TABLE statement is still fairly straightforward. It assigns the name PRODUCTS to the new table and specifies the name and type of data stored in each of its five columns.

Once the table has been created, you can fill it with data. Here's an INSERT statement for a new shipment of 250 size 7 widgets (product ACI-41007), which cost $225.00 apiece:

```
INSERT INTO PRODUCTS (MFR_ID, PRODUCT_ID, DESCRIPTION, PRICE,
                      QTY_ON_HAND)
   VALUES ('ACI', '41007', 'Size 7 Widget', 225.00, 250)

1 row inserted.
```

Finally, if you discover later that you no longer need to store the products data in the database, you can erase the table (and all of the data it contains) with the DROP TABLE statement:

```
DROP TABLE PRODUCTS

Table dropped.
```

Summary

This quick tour of SQL showed you what SQL can do and illustrated the style of the SQL language, using eight of the most commonly used SQL statements. To summarize:

- SQL is used to *retrieve* data from the database, using the SELECT statement. You can retrieve all or part of the stored data, sort it, and ask SQL to summarize the data, using totals and averages.

- SQL is used to *update* the database, by adding new data with the INSERT statement, deleting data with the DELETE statement, and modifying existing data with the UPDATE statement.

- SQL is used to *control access* to the database, by granting and revoking specific privileges for specific users with the GRANT and REVOKE statements.

- SQL is used to *create* the database by defining the structure of new tables and dropping tables when they are no longer needed, using the CREATE and DROP statements.

Chapter 3

SQL In Perspective

SQL is both a *de facto* and an official standard language for database management. What does it mean for SQL to be a standard? What role does SQL play as a database language? How did SQL become a standard, and what impact is the SQL standard having on personal computers, local area networks, minicomputers, and mainframes? To answer these questions, this chapter traces the history of SQL and describes its current role in the computer market.

SQL and Database Management

One of the major tasks of a computer system is to store and manage data. To handle this task, specialized computer programs known as *database management systems* began to appear in the late 1960s and early 1970s. A database management system, or DBMS, helped computer users to organize and structure their data and allowed the computer system to play a more active role in managing the data. Although database management systems were first developed on large mainframe systems, their popularity has spread to minicomputers, personal computers, workstations, and specialized server computers.

Database management also plays a key role in the explosion of computer networking and the Internet. Early database systems ran on laarge, monolithic computer systems, where the data, the database management software, and the user or application program accessing the database all operated on the same system. The 1980s and 1990s saw the explosion of a new, client/server model for database access, in which a user on a personal computer or an application program accessed a database on a separate computer system using a network. In the late 1990s, the increasing popularity of the Internet and the World Wide Web intertwined the worlds of networking and data management even further. Now users require little more than a web browser to access and interact with databases, not only within their own organizations, but around the world.

Today, database management is very big business. Independent software companies and computer vendors ship billions of dollars worth of database management products every year. Computer industry experts say that mainframe and minicomputer database products each account for about 10 to 20 percent of the database market, and personal computer and server-based database products account for 50 percent or more. Database servers are one of the fastest-growing segments of the computer systems market, driven by database installations on Unix and Windows NT-based servers. Database management thus touches every segment of the computer market.

Since the late 1980s a specific type of DBMS, called a *relational* database management system (RDBMS), has become so popular that it is *the* standard database form. Relational databases organize data in a simple, tabular form and provide many advantages over earlier types of databases. SQL is specifically a relational database language used to work with relational databases.

A Brief History of SQL

The history of the SQL language is intimately intertwined with the development of relational databases. Table 3-1 shows some of the milestones in its 30-year history. The relational database concept was originally developed by Dr. E.F. "Ted" Codd, an IBM researcher. In June 1970 Dr. Codd published an article entitled "A Relational Model of Data for Large Shared Data Banks" that outlined a mathematical theory of how data could be stored and manipulated using a tabular structure. Relational databases and SQL trace their origins to this article, which appeared in the *Communications of the Association for Computing Machinery*.

Date	Event
1970	Codd defines relational database model
1974	IBM's System/R project begins
1974	First article describing the SEQUEL language
1978	System/R customer tests
1979	Oracle introduces first commercial RDBMS
1981	Relational Technology introduces Ingres
1981	IBM announces SQL/DS
1982	ANSI forms SQL standards committee
1983	IBM announces DB2
1986	ANSI SQL1 standard ratified
1986	Sybase introduces RDBMS for transaction processing
1987	ISO SQL1 standard ratified
1988	Ashton-Tate and Microsoft announce SQL Server for OS/2
1989	First TPC benchmark (TPC-A) published
1990	TPC-B benchmark published
1991	SQL Access Group database access specification published
1992	Microsoft publishes ODBC specification
1992	ANSI SQL2 standard ratified
1992	TPC-C (OLTP) benchmark published
1993	First shipment of specialized SQL data warehousing systems
1993	First shipment of ODBC products
1994	TPC-D (decision support) benchmark published
1994	Commercial shipment of parallel database server technology
1996	Publication of standard API for OLAP database access and OLAP benchmark
1997	IBM DB2 UDB unifies DB2 architecture across IBM and other vendor platforms
1997	Major DBMS vendors announce Java integration strategies
1998	Microsoft SQL Server 7 provides enterprise-level database support for Windows NT
1998	Oracle 8i provides database/Internet integration and moves away from client/server model

Table 3-1.   *Milestones in the Development of SQL*

The Early Years

Codd's article triggered a flurry of relational database research, including a major research project within IBM. The goal of the project, called System/R, was to prove the workability of the relational concept and to provide some experience in actually implementing a relational DBMS. Work on System/R began in the mid-1970s at IBM's Santa Teresa laboratories in San Jose, California.

In 1974 and 1975 the first phase of the System/R project produced a minimal prototype of a relational DBMS. In addition to the DBMS itself, the System/R project included work on database query languages. One of these languages was called SEQUEL, an acronym for Structured English Query Language. In 1976 and 1977 the System/R research prototype was rewritten from scratch. The new implementation supported multi-table queries and allowed several users to share access to the data.

The System/R implementation was distributed to a number of IBM customer sites for evaluation in 1978 and 1979. These early customer sites provided some actual user experience with System/R and its database language, which, for legal reasons, had been renamed SQL, or Structured Query Language. Despite the name change, the SEQUEL pronunciation remained and continues to this day. In 1979 the System/R research project came to an end, with IBM concluding that relational databases were not only feasible, but could be the basis for a useful commercial product.

Early Relational Products

The System/R project and its SQL database language were well-chronicled in technical journals during the 1970s. Seminars on database technology featured debates on the merits of the new and "heretical" relational model. By 1976 it was apparent that IBM was becoming enthusiastic about relational database technology and that it was making a major commitment to the SQL language.

The publicity about System/R attracted the attention of a group of engineers in Menlo Park, California, who decided that IBM's research foreshadowed a commercial market for relational databases. In 1977 they formed a company, Relational Software, Inc., to build a relational DBMS based on SQL. The product, named Oracle, shipped in 1979 and became the first commercially available relational DBMS. Oracle beat IBM's first product to market by a full two years and ran on Digital's VAX minicomputers, which were less expensive than IBM mainframes. Today the company, renamed Oracle Corporation, is a leading vendor of relational database management systems, with annual sales of many billions of dollars.

Professors at the University of California's Berkeley computer laboratories were also researching relational databases in the mid-1970s. Like the IBM research team, they built a prototype of a relational DBMS and called their system Ingres. The Ingres project included a query language named QUEL that, although more "structured" than SQL, was less English-like. Many of today's database experts trace their involvement with relational databases back to the Berkeley Ingres project, including the founders of Sybase and many of the object-oriented database startup companies.

In 1980 several professors left Berkeley and founded Relational Technology, Inc., to build a commercial version of Ingres, which was announced in 1981. Ingres and Oracle quickly became arch-rivals, but their rivalry helped to call attention to relational database technology in this early stage. Despite its technical superiority in many areas, Ingres became a clear second-place player in the market, competing against the SQL-based capabilities (and the aggressive marketing and sales strategies) of Oracle. The original QUEL query language was effectively replaced by SQL in 1986, a testimony to the market power of the SQL standard. By the mid-1990s, the Ingres technology had been sold to Computer Associates, a leading mainframe software vendor.

IBM Products

While Oracle and Ingres raced to become commercial products, IBM's System/R project had also turned into an effort to build a commercial product, named SQL/Data System (SQL/DS). IBM announced SQL/DS in 1981 and began shipping the product in 1982. In 1983 IBM announced a version of SQL/DS for VM/CMS, an operating system that is frequently used on IBM mainframes in corporate "information center" applications.

In 1983 IBM also introduced Database 2 (DB2), another relational DBMS for its mainframe systems. DB2 operated under IBM's MVS operating system, the workhorse operating system used in large mainframe data centers. The first release of DB2 began shipping in 1985, and IBM officials hailed it as a strategic piece of IBM software technology. DB2 has since become IBM's flagship relational DBMS, and with IBM's weight behind it, DB2's SQL language became the *de facto* standard database language. DB2 technology has now migrated across all IBM product lines, from personal computers to network servers to mainframes. In 1997, IBM took the DB2 cross-platform strategy even farther, by announcing DB2 versions for computer systems made by Sun Microsystems, Hewlett-Packard, and other IBM hardware competitors.

Commercial Acceptance

During the first half of the 1980s, the relational database vendors struggled for commercial acceptance of their products. The relational products had several disadvantages when compared to the traditional database architectures. The performance of relational databases was seriously inferior to that of traditional databases. Except for the IBM products, the relational databases came from small "upstart" vendors. And, except for the IBM products, the relational databases tended to run on minicomputers rather than on IBM mainframes.

The relational products did have one major advantage, however. Their relational query languages (SQL, QUEL, and others) allowed users to pose *ad hoc* queries to the database— and get immediate answers—without writing programs. As a result, relational databases began slowly turning up in information center applications as decision-support tools. By May 1985 Oracle proudly claimed to have "over 1,000" installations. Ingres was installed in a comparable number of sites. DB2 and SQL/DS were also being slowly accepted and counted their combined installations at slightly over 1,000 sites.

During the last half of the 1980s, SQL and relational databases were rapidly accepted as the database technology of the future. The performance of the relational database products improved dramatically. Ingres and Oracle, in particular, leapfrogged with each new version claiming superiority over the competitor and two or three times the performance of the previous release. Improvements in the processing power of the underlying computer hardware also helped to boost performance.

Market forces also boosted the popularity of SQL in the late 1980s. IBM stepped up its evangelism of SQL, positioning DB2 as the data management solution for the 1990s. Publication of the ANSI/ISO standard for SQL in 1986 gave SQL "official" status as a standard. SQL also emerged as a standard on Unix-based computer systems, whose popularity accelerated in the 1980s. As personal computers became more powerful and were linked in local area networks, they needed more sophisticated database management. PC database vendors embraced SQL as the solution to these needs, and minicomputer database vendors moved "down market" to compete in the emerging PC local area network market. Through the early 1990s, steadily improving SQL implementations and dramatic improvements in processor speeds made SQL a practical solution for transaction processing applications. Finally, SQL became a key part of the client/server architecture that used PCs, local area networks, and network servers to build much lower cost information processing systems.

SQL's supremacy in the database world has not gone unchallenged. By the early 1990s, object-oriented programming had emerged as the method of choice for applications development, especially for personal computers and their graphical user interfaces. The object model, with its model of objects, classes, methods, and inheritance, did not provide an ideal fit with relational model of tables, rows, and columns of data. A new generation of venture capital-backed "object database" companies sprang up, hoping to make relational databases and their vendors obsolete, just as SQL had done to the earlier, nonrelational vendors. However, SQL and the relational model have more than withstood the challenge to date. Annual revenues for object-oriented databases are measured in the hundreds of millions of dollars, at best, while SQL and relational database systems, tools, and services produce tens of billions of dollars.

As SQL grew to address an ever-wider variety of data management tasks, the "one-size-fits-all" approach showed serious strain. By the late 1990s, "database management" was no longer a monolithic market. Specialized database systems sprang up to support different market needs. One of the fastest-growing segments was "data warehousing," where databases were used to search through huge amounts of data to discover underlying trends and patterns. A second major trend was the incorporation of new data types (such as multimedia data) and object-oriented principles into SQL. A third important segment was "mobile databases" for portable personal computers that could operate when sometimes connected to, and sometimes disconnected from, a centralized database system. Despite the emergence of database market subsegments, SQL has remained a common denominator across them all. As the computer industry prepares for the next century, SQL's dominance as *the* database standard is as strong as ever.

SQL Standards

One of the most important developments in the market acceptance of SQL is the emergence of SQL standards. References to "the SQL standard" usually mean the official standard adopted by the American National Standards Institute (ANSI) and the International Standards Organization (ISO). However, there are other important SQL standards, including the *de facto* standard SQL defined by IBM's DB2 product family.

The ANSI/ISO Standards

Work on the official SQL standard began in 1982, when ANSI charged its X3H2 committee with defining a standard relational database language. At first the committee debated the merits of various proposed database languages. However, as IBM's commitment to SQL increased and SQL emerged as a *de facto* standard in the market, the committee selected SQL as their relational database language and turned their attention to standardizing it.

The resulting ANSI standard for SQL is largely based on DB2 SQL, although it contains some major differences from DB2. After several revisions, the standard was officially adopted as ANSI standard X3.135 in 1986, and as an ISO standard in 1987. The ANSI/ISO standard has since been adopted as a Federal Information Processing Standard (FIPS) by the U.S. government. This standard, slightly revised and expanded in 1989, is usually called the "SQL-89" or "SQL1" standard.

Many of the ANSI and ISO standards committee members were representatives from database vendors who had existing SQL products, each implementing a slightly different SQL dialect. Like dialects of human languages, the SQL dialects were generally very similar to one another but were incompatible in their details. In many areas the committee simply sidestepped these differences by omitting some parts of the language from the standard and specifying others as "implementor-defined." These decisions allowed existing SQL implementations to claim broad adherence to the resulting ANSI/ISO standard but made the standard relatively weak.

To address the holes in the original standard, the ANSI committee continued its work, and drafts for a new more rigorous SQL2 standard were circulated. Unlike the 1989 standard, the SQL2 drafts specified features considerably beyond those found in current commercial SQL products. Even more far-reaching changes were proposed for a follow-on SQL3 standard. In addition, the draft standards attempted to officially standardize parts of the SQL language where different "proprietary standards" had long since been set by the various major DBMS brands. As a result, the proposed SQL2 and SQL3 standards were a good deal more controversial than the initial SQL standard. The SQL2 standard weaved its way through the ANSI approval process and was finally approved in October, 1992. While the original 1986 standard took less than 100 pages, the SQL2 standard (officially called "SQL-92") takes nearly 600 pages.

The SQL2 standards committee acknowledged the large step from SQL1 to SQL2 by explicitly creating three levels of SQL2 standards compliance. The lowest compliance level ("Entry-Level") requires only minimal additional capability beyond the SQL-89 standard. The middle compliance level ("Intermediate-Level") was created as an achievable major step beyond SQL-89, but one that avoids the most complex and most system-dependent and DBMS brand-dependent issues. The third compliance level ("Full") requires a full implementation of all SQL2 capabilities. Throughout the 600 pages of the standard, each description of each feature includes a definition of the specific aspects of that feature which must be supported in order to achieve Entry, Intermediate, or Full compliance.

Despite the existence of a SQL2 standard, no commercial SQL product available today implements all of its features, and no two commercial SQL products support exactly the same SQL dialect. Moreover, as database vendors introduce new capabilities, they are expanding their SQL dialects and moving them even further apart. The central core of the SQL language has become fairly standardized, however. Where it could be done without hurting existing customers or features, vendors have brought their products into conformance with the SQL-89 standard, and the same will slowly happen with SQL2. In the meantime, work continues on standards beyond SQL2. The "SQL3" effort effectively fragmented into separate standardization efforts and focused on different extensions to SQL. Some of these, such as stored procedure capabilities, are already found in many commercial SQL products and pose the same standardization challenges faced by SQL2. Others, such as proposed object extensions to SQL, are not yet widely available or fully implemented, but have generated a great deal of controversy. With most vendors far from fully implementing SQL2 capabilities, and with the diversity of SQL extensions now available in commercial products, work on SQL3 has taken on less commercial importance.

The "real" SQL standard, of course, is the SQL implemented in products that are broadly accepted by the marketplace. For the most part, programmers and users tend to stick with those parts of the language that are fairly similar across a broad range of products. The innovation of the database vendors continues to drive the invention of new SQL capabilities; some products remain years later only for backward compatibility, and some find commercial success and move into the mainstream.

Other SQL Standards

Although it is the most widely recognized, the ANSI/ISO standard is not the only standard for SQL. X/OPEN, a European vendor group, has also adopted SQL as part of its suite of standards for a "portable application environment" based on Unix. The X/OPEN standards play a major role in the European computer market, where portability among computer systems from different vendors is a key concern. Unfortunately, the X/OPEN standard differs from the ANSI/ISO standard in several areas.

IBM also included SQL in the specification of its bold Systems Application Architecture (SAA) blueprint, promising that all of its SQL products would eventually move to this SAA SQL dialect. Although SAA failed to achieve its promise of unifying the IBM product line, the momentum toward a unified IBM SQL continued. With its mainframe DB2 database as the flagship, IBM introduced DB2 implementations for OS/2, its personal computer operating system, and for its RS/6000 line of Unix-based workstations and servers. By 1997, IBM had moved DB2 beyond its own product line and shipped versions of DB2-Universal Database for systems made by rival manufacturers Sun Microsystems, Hewlett-Packard, and Silicon Graphics, and for Windows NT. With IBM's historical leadership in relational database technology, the SQL dialect supported by DB2 version is a very powerful *de facto* standard.

ODBC and the SQL Access Group

An important area of database technology not addressed by official standards is *database interoperability*—the methods by which data can be exchanged among different databases, usually over a network. In 1989, a group of vendors formed the SQL Access Group to address this problem. The resulting SQL Access Group specification for Remote Database Access (RDA) was published in 1991. Unfortunately, the RDA specification is closely tied to the OSI protocols, which have not been widely accepted, so it has had little impact. Transparent interoperability among different vendors' databases remains an elusive goal.

A second standard from the SQL Access Group has had far more market impact. At Microsoft's urging and insistence, SQL Access Group expanded its focus to include a call-level interface for SQL. Based on a draft from Microsoft, the resulting Call-Level Interface (CLI) specification was published in 1992. Microsoft's own Open Database Connectivity (ODBC) specification, based on the CLI standard, was published the same year. With the market power of Microsoft behind it, and the "open standards" blessing of SQL Access Group, ODBC has emerged as the *de facto* standard interface for PC access to SQL databases. Apple and Microsoft announced an agreement to support ODBC on Macintosh and Windows in the spring of 1993, giving ODBC "standard" status in both popular graphical user interface environments. ODBC implementations for Unix-based systems soon followed.

Today, ODBC is in its fourth major revision as a cross-platform database access standard. ODBC support is available for all major DBMS brands. Most packaged application programs that have database access as an important part of their capabilities support ODBC, range from multi-million dollar enterprise class applications like Enterprise Resource Planning (ERP) and Supply Chain Management (SCM) to PC applications such as spreadsheets, query tools, and reporting programs. Microsoft's focus has moved beyond ODBC to higher-level interfaces (such as OLE/DB) and more recently to ADO (Active Data Objects), but these new interfaces are layered on top of ODBC for relational database access, and it remains a key cross-platform database access technology.

The Portability Myth

The existence of published SQL standards has spawned quite a few exaggerated claims about SQL and applications portability. Diagrams such as the one in Figure 3-1 are frequently drawn to show how an application using SQL can work interchangeably with any SQL-based database management system. In fact, the holes in the SQL-89 standard and the current differences between SQL dialects are significant enough that an application must *always* be modified when moved from one SQL database to another. These differences, many of which were eliminated by the SQL2 standard but have not yet implemented in commercial products, include:

- *Error codes.* The SQL-89 standard does not specify the error codes to be returned when SQL detects an error, and all of the commercial implementations use their own set of error codes. The SQL2 standard specifies standard error codes.

- *Data types.* The SQL-89 standard defines a minimal set of data types, but it omits some of the most popular and useful types, such as variable-length character strings, dates and times, and money data. The SQL2 standard addresses these, but not "new" data types such as graphics and multimedia objects.

- *System tables.* The SQL-89 standard is silent about the system tables that provide information regarding the structure of the database itself. Each vendor has its own structure for these tables, and even IBM's four SQL implementations differ from one another. The tables are standardized in SQL2, but only at the higher levels of compliance, which are not yet provided by most vendors.

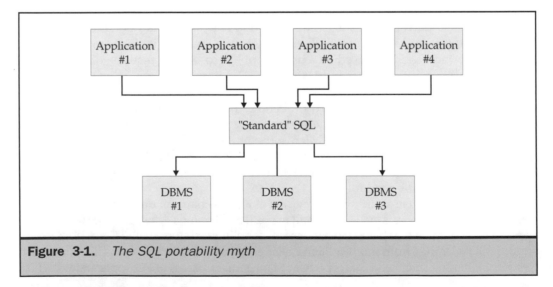

Figure 3-1.   *The SQL portability myth*

- *Interactive SQL.* The standard specifies only the *programmatic* SQL used by an application program, not interactive SQL. For example, the SELECT statement used to query the database in interactive SQL is absent from the SQL-89 standard. Again, the SQL2 standard addressed this issue, but long after all of the major DBMS vendors had well-established interactive SQL capabilities.

- *Programmatic interface.* The original standard specifies an abstract technique for using SQL from within an applications program written in COBOL, C, FORTRAN, and other programming languages. No commercial SQL product uses this technique, and there is considerable variation in the actual programmatic interfaces used. The SQL2 standard specifies an embedded SQL interface for popular programming languages but not a call-level interface.

- *Dynamic SQL.* The SQL-89 standard does not include the features required to develop general-purpose database front-ends, such as query tools and report writers. These features, known as *dynamic SQL*, are found in virtually all SQL database systems, but they vary significantly from product to product. SQL2 includes a standard for dynamic SQL, but with hundreds of thousands of existing applications dependent on backward compatibility, DBMS vendors have not implemented it.

- *Semantic differences.* Because the standards specify certain details as "implementor-defined," it's possible to run the same query against two different conforming SQL implementations and produce two different sets of query results. These differences occur in the handling of NULL values, column functions, and duplicate row elimination.

- *Collating sequences.* The SQL-89 standard does not address the collating (sorting) sequence of characters stored in the database. The results of a sorted query will be different if the query is run on a personal computer (with ASCII characters) and a mainframe (with EBCDIC characters). The SQL2 standard includes an elaborate specification for how a program or a user can request a specific collating sequence, but it is an advanced-level feature that is not typically supported in commercial products.

- *Database structure.* The SQL-89 standard specifies the SQL language to be used once a particular database has been opened and is ready for processing. The details of database naming and how the initial connection to the database is established vary widely and are not portable. The SQL2 standard creates more uniformity but cannot completely mask these details.

Despite these differences, commercial database tools boasting portability across several different brands of SQL databases began to emerge in the early 1990s. In every case, however, the tools require a special adapter for each supported DBMS, which generates the appropriate SQL dialect, handles data type conversion, translates error codes, and so on. Transparent portability across different DBMS brands based on standard SQL is the major goal of SQL2 and ODBC, and significant progress has been made. Today, virtually all programs that support multiple databases include specific "drivers" for communicating with each of the major DBMS brands, and usually include an ODBC driver for accessing the others.

SQL and Networking

The dramatic growth of computer networking over the past decade has had a major impact on database management and given SQL a new prominence. As networks became more common, applications that traditionally ran on a central minicomputer or mainframe moved to local area networks of desktop workstations and servers. In these networks SQL plays a crucial role as the link between an application running on a desktop workstation with a graphical user interface and the DBMS that manages shared data on a cost-effective server. More recently, the exploding popularity of the Internet and the World Wide Web has reinforced the network role for SQL. In the emerging "three-tier" Internet architecture, SQL once again provides the link between the application logic (now running in the "middle tier," on an application server or web server) and the database residing in the "back-end" tier. The next few sections in this chapter discuss the evolution of database network architectures and the role of SQL in each one.

Centralized Architecture

The traditional database architecture used by DB2, SQL/DS, and the original minicomputer databases such as Oracle and Ingres is shown in Figure 3-2. In this architecture the DBMS and the physical data both reside on a central minicomputer or mainframe system, along with the application program that accepts input from the user's terminal and displays data on the user's screen. The application program communicates with the DBMS using SQL.

Suppose that the user types a query that requires a sequential search of a database, such as a request to find the average amount of merchandise of all orders. The DBMS receives the query, scans through the database fetching each record of data from the

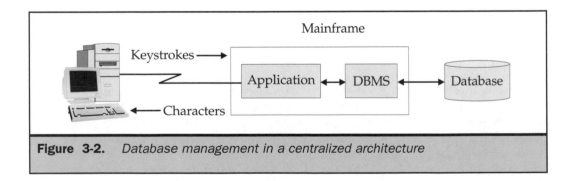

Figure 3-2. *Database management in a centralized architecture*

disk, calculates the average, and displays the result on the terminal screen. Both the application processing and the database processing occur on the central computer, so execution of this type of query (and in fact, all kinds of queries) is very efficient.

The disadvantage of the centralized architecture is scalability. As more and more users are added, each of them adds application processing workload to the system. Because the system is shared, each user experiences degraded performance as the system becomes more heavily loaded.

File Server Architecture

The introduction of personal computers and local area networks led to the development of the *file server* architecture, shown in Figure 3-3. In this architecture, an application running on a personal computer can transparently access data located on a file server, which stores shared files. When a PC application requests data from a shared file, the networking software automatically retrieves the requested block of the file from the server. Early PC databases, such as dBASE and later Microsoft's Access, supported this file server approach, with each personal computer running its own copy of the DBMS software.

For typical queries that retrieve only one row or a few rows from the database, this architecture provides excellent performance, because each user has the full power of a personal computer running its own copy of the DBMS. However, consider the query made in the previous example. Because the query requires a sequential scan of the database, the DBMS repeatedly requests blocks of data from the database, which is physically located across the network on the server. Eventually *every* block of the file will be requested and sent across the network. Obviously this architecture produces very heavy network traffic and slow performance for queries of this type.

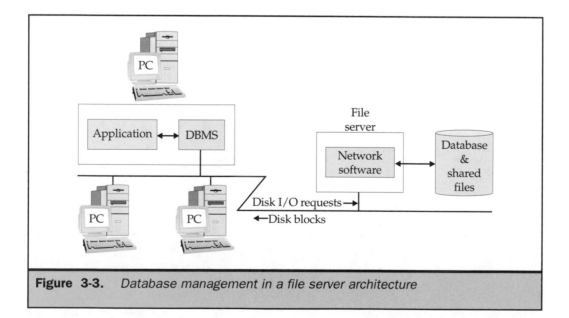

Figure 3-3.   *Database management in a file server architecture*

Client/Server Architecture

Figure 3-4 shows the next stage of network database evolution—the *client/server* database architecture. In this scheme, personal computers are combined in a local area network with a *database server* that stores shared databases. The functions of the DBMS are split into two parts. Database "front-ends," such as interactive query tools, report writers, and application programs, run on the personal computer. The back-end database engine that stores and manages the data runs on the server. As the client/server architecture grew in popularity during the 1990s, SQL became the standard database language for communication between the front-end tools and the back-end engine in this architecture.

Consider once more the query requesting the average order size. In the client/server architecture, the query travels across the network to the database server as a SQL request. The database engine on the server processes the request and scans the database, which also resides on the server. When the result is calculated, the database engine sends it back across the network as a single reply to the initial request, and the front-end application displays it on the PC screen.

The client/server architecture reduces the network traffic and splits the database workload. User-intensive functions, such as handling input and displaying data, are concentrated on the user's PC. Data-intensive functions, such as file I/O and query processing, are concentrated in the database server. Most importantly, the SQL

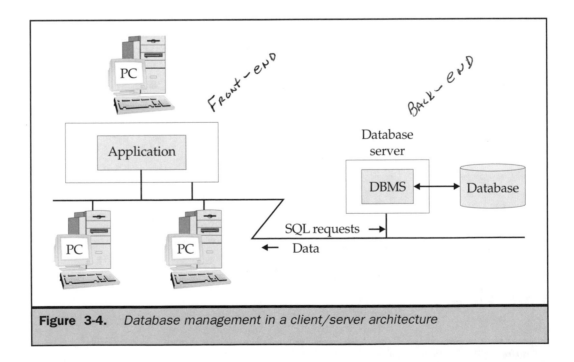

Figure 3-4. *Database management in a client/server architecture*

language provides a well-defined interface between the front-end and back-end systems, communicating database access requests in an efficient manner.

By the mid-1990s, these advantages made the client/server architecture the most popular scheme for implementing new applications. All of the most popular DBMS products—Oracle, Informix, Sybase, SQL Server, DB2, and many more—offered client/server capability. The database industry grew to include many companies offering tools for building client/server applications. Some of these came from the database companies themselves; others came from independent companies.

Like all architectures, client/server had its disadvantages. The most serious of these was the problem of managing the applications software that was now distributed across hundreds or thousands of desktop PCs instead of running on a central minicomputer or mainframe. To update an application program in a large company, the information systems department had to update thousands of PC systems, one at a time. The situation was even worse if changes to the application program had to be synchronized with changes to other applications, or to the DBMS system itself. In addition, with personal computers on user's desks, users tended to add new personal software of their own or to change the configuration of their systems. Such changes often disrupted existing applications, adding to the support burden. Companies developed strategies to deal with these issues, but by the late 1990s there was growing concern about the manageability of client/server applications on large, distributed PC networks.

Multi-Tier Architecture

With the emergence of the Internet and especially the World Wide Web, network database architecture has taken another step. At first, the Web was used to access ("browse") static documents and evolved outside of the database world. But as the use of web browsers became widespread, it wasn't long before companies thought about using them as a simple way to provide access to corporate databases as well. For example, suppose a company starts using the Web to provide product information to its customers, by making product descriptions and graphics available on its web site. A natural next step is to give customers access to current product availability information through the same web browser interface. This requires linking the web server to the database system that stores the (constantly changing) current product inventory levels.

The methods used to link web servers and DBMS systems have evolved rapidly over the last several years and have converged on the three-tier network architecture shown in Figure 3-5. The user interface is a web browser running on a PC or some other "thin client" device in the "front" tier. It communicates with a web server in the "middle tier." When the user request is for something more complex than a simple web page, the web server passes the request to an *application server* whose role is to handle the business logic required to process the request. Often the request will involve access to an existing ("legacy") application running on a mainframe system or to a corporate database. These systems run in the "back" tier of the architecture. As with the client/server architecture, SQL is solidly entrenched as the standard database language for communicating between the application server and back-end databases. All of the packaged application server products provide a SQL-based callable API for database access.

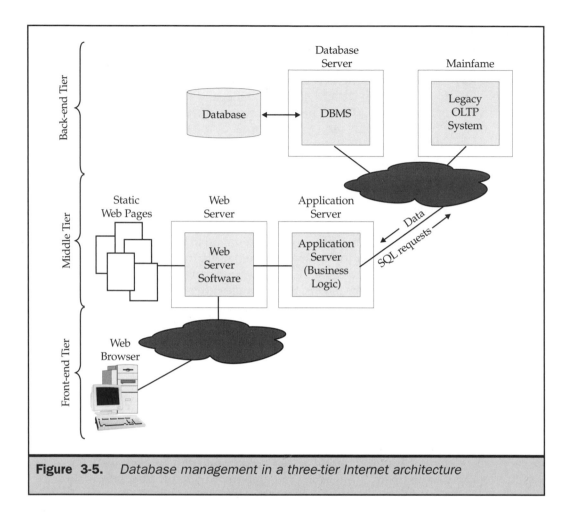

Figure 3-5. *Database management in a three-tier Internet architecture*

The Proliferation of SQL

As the standard for relational database access, SQL has had a major impact on all parts of the computer market. IBM has adopted SQL as a unifying database technology for its product line. SQL-based databases dominate the market for Unix-based computer systems. In the PC market, SQL databases on Windows NT are mounting a serious challenge to the dominance of Unix as a database processing platform, especially for departmental applications. SQL is accepted as a technology for online transaction processing, fully refuting the conventional wisdom of the 1980s that relational databases would never offer performance good enough for transaction processing applications. SQL-based data warehousing and data mining applications are helping companies to discover customer purchase patterns and offer better products and services. On the Internet, SQL-based databases are the foundation of more personalized products, services, and information services that are a key benefit of electronic commerce.

SQL and IBM's Unified Database Strategy

SQL plays a key role as the database access language that unifies IBM's multiple incompatible computer families. Originally, this role was part of IBM's Systems Application Architecture (SAA) strategy, announced in March 1987. Although IBM's grand goals for SAA were not achieved, the unifying role of SQL has grown even more important over time. The DB2 database system, IBM's flagship SQL-based DBMS, now runs on a broad range of IBM and non-IBM computer systems, including:

- *Mainframes.* DB2 started as the SQL standard-bearer for IBM mainframes running MVS and has now replaced SQL/DS as the relational system for the VM and VSE mainframe operating systems.

- *AS/400.* This SQL implementation runs on IBM's family of midrange business systems, targeted at small- and medium-sized businesses and server applications.

- *RS/6000.* DB2 runs under the Unix operating system on IBM's family of RISC-based workstations and servers, for engineering and scientific applications and as IBM's own Unix database server platform.

- *Other Unix platforms.* IBM supports DB2 on Unix-based server platforms from Sun Microsystems and Hewlett-Packard, the two largest Unix system vendors, and on Unix-based workstations from Silicon Graphics.

- *OS/2.* A smaller-scale version of DB2 runs on this IBM-proprietary operating system for Intel-based personal computers

- *Windows NT.* A PC-LAN server version of DB2 competes with Microsoft SQL Server, Oracle, and others on this fast-growing database server platform.

SQL on Minicomputers

Minicomputers were one of the most fertile early markets for SQL-based database systems. Oracle and Ingres were both originally marketed on Digital's VAX/VMS minicomputer systems. Both products have since been ported to many other platforms. Sybase, a later database system specialized for online transaction processing, also targeted the VAX as one of its primary platforms.

Through the 1980s, the minicomputer vendors also developed their own proprietary relational databases featuring SQL. Digital considered relational databases so important that it bundled a run-time version of its Rdb/VMS database with every VAX/VMS system. Hewlett-Packard offered Allbase, a database that supported both its HPSQL dialect and a nonrelational interface. Data General's DG/SQL database replaced its older nonrelational databases as DG's strategic data management tool. In addition, many of the minicomputer vendors resold relational databases from the independent database software vendors. These efforts helped to establish SQL as an important technology for midrange computer systems.

Today, the minicomputer vendors' SQL products have largely disappeared, beaten in the marketplace by multi-platform software from Oracle, Informix, Sybase, and others. Accompanying this trend, the importance of proprietary minicomputer operating systems has faded as well, replaced by widespread use of Unix on midrange systems. Yesterday's minicomputer SQL market has effectively become today's market for Unix-based database servers based on SQL.

SQL on Unix-Based Systems

SQL has firmly established itself as the data management solution of choice for Unix-based computer systems. Originally developed at Bell Laboratories, Unix became very popular in the 1980s as a vendor-independent, standard operating system. It runs on a wide range of computer systems, from workstations to mainframes, and has become the standard operating system for scientific and engineering applications.

In the early 1980s four major databases were already available for Unix systems. Two of them, Ingres and Oracle, were Unix versions of the products that ran on DEC's proprietary minicomputers. The other two, Informix and Unify, were written specifically for Unix. Neither of them originally offered SQL support, but by 1985 Unify offered a SQL query language, and Informix had been rewritten as Informix-SQL, with full SQL support.

Today, Oracle, Informix, and Sybase dominate the Unix-based database market and are available on all of the leading Unix systems. Unix-based database servers are a mainstream building block for both client/server and three-tier Internet architectures. The constant search for higher SQL database performance has driven some of the most important trends in Unix system hardware. These include the emergence of symmetric multiprocessing (SMP) as a mainstream server architecture, and the use of RAID (Redundant Array of Independent Disk) technology to boost I/O performance.

SQL on Personal Computers

Databases have been popular on personal computers since the early days of the IBM PC. Ashton-Tate's dBASE product reached an installed base of over one million MS-DOS-based PCs. Although these early PC databases often presented data in tabular form, they lacked the full power of a relational DBMS and a relational database language such as SQL. The first SQL-based PC databases were versions of popular minicomputer products that barely fit on personal computers. For example, Professional Oracle for the IBM PC, introduced in 1984, required two megabytes of memory—well above the typical 640KB PC configuration of the day.

The real impact of SQL on personal computers began with the announcement of OS/2 by IBM and Microsoft in April 1987. In addition to the standard OS/2 product, IBM announced a proprietary OS/2 Extended Edition (OS/2 EE) with a built-in SQL database and communications support. With the introduction, IBM again signaled its strong commitment to SQL, saying in effect that SQL was so important that it belonged in the computer's operating system.

OS/2 Extended Edition presented Microsoft with a problem. As the developer and distributor of standard OS/2 to other personal computer manufacturers, Microsoft needed an alternative to the Extended Edition. Microsoft responded by licensing the Sybase DBMS, which had been developed for VAX, and began porting it to OS/2. In January 1988, in a surprise move, Microsoft and Ashton-Tate (the PC database leader at the time with its dBASE product) announced that they would jointly sell the resulting OS/2-based product, renamed SQL Server. Microsoft would sell SQL Server with OS/2 to computer manufacturers; Ashton-Tate would sell the product through retail channels to PC users. In September 1989, Lotus Development (the other member of the "big three" of PC software at the time) added its endorsement of SQL Server by investing in Sybase. Later that year, Ashton-Tate relinquished its exclusive retail distribution rights and sold its investment to Lotus.

SQL Server for OS/2 met with only limited success. But in typical Microsoft fashion, Microsoft continued to invest heavily in SQL Server development and ported it to its Windows NT operating system. For a while, Microsoft and Sybase remained partners, with Sybase focused on the minicomputer and Unix-based server markets and Microsoft focused on PC local area networks (LANs) and Windows NT. As Windows NT and Unix systems became more and more competitive as database server operating system platforms, the relationship became less cooperative and more competitive. Eventually, Sybase and Microsoft went their separate ways. The common heritage of Sybase's and Microsoft's SQL products can still be seen in product capabilities and some common SQL extensions (for example, stored procedures), but the product lines have already diverged significantly.

Today SQL Server is a major database system on Windows NT. SQL Server 7.0, which shipped in late 1998, provided a significant step up in the size and scale of database applications that SQL Server can support. In addition to SQL Server's impact, the availability of Oracle, Informix, DB2, and other mainstream DBMS products has helped Windows NT to steadily make inroads into Unix's dominance as a database server platform. While Unix continues to dominate the largest database server installations, Windows NT and the Intel architecture systems on which it runs have achieved credibility in the midrange market.

SQL and Transaction Processing

SQL and relational databases originally had very little impact in online transaction processing (OLTP) applications. With their emphasis on queries, relational databases were confined to decision support and low volume online applications, where their slower performance was not a disadvantage. For OLTP applications, where hundreds of users needed online access to data and subsecond response times, IBM's nonrelational Information Management System (IMS) reigned as the dominant DBMS.

In 1986 a new DBMS vendor, Sybase, introduced a new SQL-based database especially designed for OLTP applications. The Sybase DBMS ran on VAX/VMS minicomputers and Sun workstations and focused on maximum online performance.

Oracle Corporation and Relational Technology followed shortly with announcements that they, too, would offer OLTP versions of their popular Oracle and Ingres database systems. In the Unix market, Informix announced an OLTP version of its DBMS, named Informix-Turbo.

In 1988 IBM jumped on the relational OLTP bandwagon with DB2 Version 2, with benchmarks showing the new version operating at over 250 transactions per second on large mainframes. IBM claimed that DB2 performance was now suitable for all but the most demanding OLTP applications, and encouraged customers to consider it as a serious alternative to IMS. OLTP benchmarks have now become a standard sales tool for relational databases, despite serious questions about how well the benchmarks actually measure performance in real applications.

The suitability of SQL for OLTP improved dramatically through the 1990s, with advances in relational technology and more powerful computer hardware both leading to ever higher transaction rates. DBMS vendors started to position their products based on their OLTP performance, and for a few years database advertising focused almost entirely on these "performance benchmark wars." A vendor-independent organization, the Transaction Processing Council, jumped into the benchmarking fray with a series of vendor-independent benchmarks (TPC-A, TPC-B, and TPC-C), which only served to intensify the performance focus of the vendors.

By the late 1990s, SQL-based relational databases on high-end Unix-based database servers had passed the 1,000 transactions per second mark. Client/server systems using SQL databases have become the accepted architecture for implementing OLTP applications. From a position as "unsuitable for OLTP," SQL has grown to be the industry standard foundation for building OLTP applications.

SQL and Workgroup Databases

The dramatic growth of PC LANs through the 1980s and 1990s created a new opportunity for departmental or "workgroup" database management. The original database systems focused on this market segment ran on IBM's OS/2 operating system. In fact, SQL Server, now a key part of Microsoft's Windows strategy, originally made its debut as an OS/2 database product. In the mid-1990s, Novell also made a concentrated effort to make its NetWare operating system an attractive workgroup database server platform. From the earliest days of PC LANs, NetWare had become established as the dominant network operating system for file and print servers. Through deals with Oracle and others, Novell sought to extend this leadership to workgroup database servers as well.

The arrival of Windows NT on the workgroup computing scene was the catalyst that caused the workgroup database market to really take off. While NetWare offered a clear performance advantage over NT as a workgroup file server, NT had a more robust, general-purpose architecture, more like the minicomputer operating systems. Microsoft successfully positioned NT as a more attractive platform for running workgroup applications (as an "application server") and workgroup databases.

Microsoft's own SQL Server product was marketed (and often bundled) with NT as a tightly integrated workgroup database platform. Corporate information systems departments were at first very cautious about using relatively new and unproven technology, but the NT/SQL Server combination allowed departments and non-IS executives to undertake smaller-scale, workgroup-level projects on their own, without corporate IS help. This phenomenon, like the grass roots support for personal computers a decade earlier, fueled the early growth of the workgroup database segment.

Today, SQL is well established as a workgroup database standard. Microsoft's SQL Server has been joined by Oracle, Informix, Sybase, DB2, and many other DBMS brands running on the Windows NT/Windows 2000 platform. Windows-based SQL databases are the second largest segment of the DBMS market and are the fastest growing. From this solid dominance in the workgroup segment, Windows-based server systems are mounting a continued assault on enterprise-class database applications, slowly but surely eating into low-end Unix-based database deployments.

SQL and Data Warehousing

For several years, the effort to make SQL a viable technology for OLTP applications shifted the focus away from the original relational database strengths of query processing and decision making. Performance benchmarks and competition among the major DBMS brands focused on simple transactions like adding a new order to the database or determining a customer's account balance. Because of the power of the relational database model, the databases that companies used to handle daily business operations could also be used to analyze the growing amounts of data that were being accumulated. A frequent theme of conferences and trade show speeches for IS managers was that a corporation's accumulated data (stored in SQL databases, of course) should be treated as a valuable "asset" and used to help improve the quality of business decision-making.

Although relational databases could, in theory, easily perform both OLTP and decision-making applications, there were some very significant practical problems. OLTP workloads consisted of many short database transactions, and the response time for users was very important. In contrast, decision-support queries could involve sequential scans of large database tables to answer questions like "What is the average order size by sales region?" or "How do inventory trends compare with the same time a year ago?" These queries could take minutes or hours. If a business analyst tried to run one of these queries during a time when business transaction volumes reached their peak, it could cause serious degradation in OLTP performance. Another problem was that the data to answer useful questions about business trends was often spread across many different databases, typically involving different DBMS vendors and different computer platforms.

The desire to take advantage of accumulated business data, and the practical performance problems it caused for OLTP applications, led to a new database trend called "data warehousing." The idea of the data warehouse is shown in Figure 3-6. Business data is extracted from OLTP systems, reformatted and validated as necessary, and then placed into a separate database that is dedicated to decision-making queries (the "warehouse"). The data extraction and transformation can be scheduled for off-hours batch processing. Ideally, only new or changed data can be extracted, minimizing the amount of data to be processed in the monthly, weekly, or daily warehouse "refresh" cycle. With this scheme, the time-consuming business analysis queries use the data warehouse, not the OLTP database, as their source of data.

SQL-based relational databases were a clear choice for the warehouse data store because of their flexible query processing. A series of new companies was formed to build the data extraction, transformation, and database query tools needed by the data warehouse model. In addition, DBMS vendors started to focus on the kinds of database queries that customers tended to run in the data warehouse. These queries tended to be large and complex—such as analyzing tens or hundreds of millions of individual cash-register receipts to look for product purchase patterns. They often involved

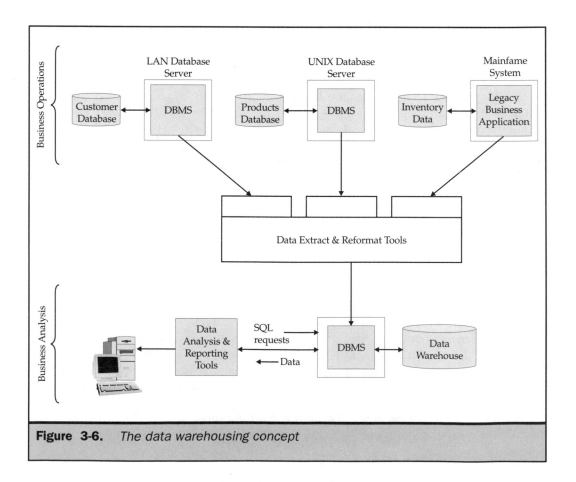

Figure 3-6. *The data warehousing concept*

time-series data—for example, analyzing product sales or market share data over time. They also tended to involve statistical summaries of data—total sales, average order volume, percent growth, and so on—rather than the individual data items themselves.

To address the specialized needs of data warehousing applications (often called "Online Analytical Processing" or OLAP), specialized databases began to appear. These databases were optimized for OLAP workloads in several different ways. Their performance was tuned for complex, read-only query access. They supported advanced statistical and other data functions, such as built-in time-series processing. They supported precalculation of database statistical data, so that retrieving averages and totals could be dramatically faster. Some of these specialized databases did not use SQL, but many did (leading to the companion term "ROLAP," for Relational Online Analytic Processing). As with so many segments of the database market, SQL's advantages as a standard proved to be a powerful force. Data warehousing has become a one-billion-dollar plus segment of the database market, and SQL-based databases are firmly entrenched as the mainstream technology for building data warehouses.

Summary

This chapter described the development of SQL and its role as a standard language for relational database management:

- SQL was originally developed by IBM researchers, and IBM's strong support of SQL is a key reason for its success.

- There are official ANSI/ISO SQL standards and several other SQL standards, each slightly different from the ANSI/ISO standards.

- Despite the existence of standards, there are many small variations among commercial SQL dialects; no two SQLs are exactly the same.

- SQL has become the standard database management language across a broad range of computer systems and applications areas, including mainframes, workstations, personal computers, OLTP systems, client/server systems, data warehousing, and the Internet.

Chapter 4

Relational Databases

Database management systems organize and structure data so that it can be retrieved and manipulated by users and application programs. The data structures and access techniques provided by a particular DBMS are called its *data model*. A data model determines both the "personality" of a DBMS and the applications for which it is particularly well suited.

SQL is a database language for relational databases that uses the *relational data model*. What exactly is a relational database? How is data stored in a relational database? How do relational databases compare to earlier technologies, such as hierarchical and network databases? What are the advantages and disadvantages of the relational model? This chapter describes the relational data model supported by SQL and compares it to earlier strategies for database organization.

Early Data Models

As database management became popular during the 1970s and 1980s, a handful of popular data models emerged. Each of these early data models had advantages and disadvantages that played key roles in the development of the relational data model. In many ways the relational data model represented an attempt to streamline and simplify the earlier data models. In order to understand the role and contribution of SQL and the relational model, it is useful to briefly examine some data models that preceded the development of SQL.

File Management Systems

Before the introduction of database management systems, all data permanently stored on a computer system, such as payroll and accounting records, was stored in individual files. A *file management system*, usually provided by the computer manufacturer as part of the computer's operating system, kept track of the names and locations of the files. The file management system basically had no data model; it knew nothing about the internal contents of files. To the file management system, a file containing a word processing document and a file containing payroll data appeared the same.

Knowledge about the contents of a file—what data it contained and how the data was organized—was embedded in the application programs that used the file, as shown in Figure 4-1. In this payroll application, each of the COBOL programs that processed the employee master file contained a *file description* (FD) that described the layout of the data in the file. If the structure of the data changed—for example, if an additional item of data was to be stored for each employee—every program that accessed the file had to be modified. As the number of files and programs grew over time, more and more of a data processing department's effort went into maintaining existing applications rather than developing new ones.

The problems of maintaining large file-based systems led in the late 1960s to the development of database management systems. The idea behind these systems was

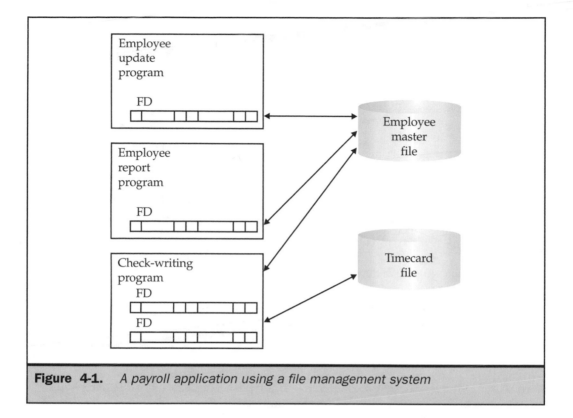

Figure 4-1.   *A payroll application using a file management system*

simple: take the definition of a file's content and structure out of the individual programs, and store it, together with the data, in a database. Using the information in the database, the DBMS that controlled it could take a much more active role in managing both the data and changes to the database structure.

Hierarchical Databases

One of the most important applications for the earliest database management systems was production planning for manufacturing companies. If an automobile manufacturer decided to produce 10,000 units of one car model and 5,000 units of another model, it needed to know how many parts to order from its suppliers. To answer the question, the product (a car) had to be decomposed into assemblies (engine, body, chassis), which were decomposed into subassemblies (valves, cylinders, spark plugs), and then into sub-subassemblies, and so on. Handling this list of parts, known as a *bill of materials*, was a job tailor-made for computers.

The bill of materials for a product has a natural hierarchical structure. To store this data, the *hierarchical* data model, illustrated in Figure 4-2, was developed. In this model,

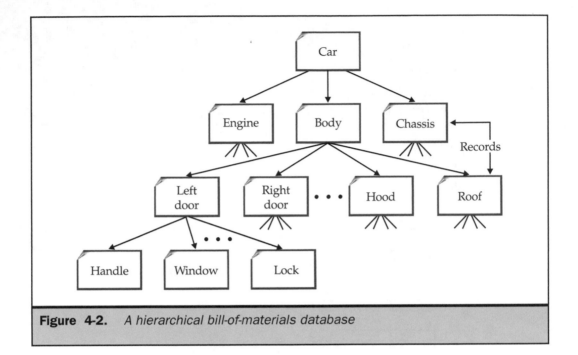

Figure 4-2. *A hierarchical bill-of-materials database*

each *record* in the database represented a specific part. The records had *parent/child relationships*, linking each part to its subpart, and so on.

To access the data in the database, a program could:

■ find a particular part by number (such as the left door),

■ move "down" to the first child (the door handle),

■ move "up" to its parent (the body), or

■ move "sideways" to the next child (the right door).

Retrieving the data in a hierarchical database thus required *navigating* through the records, moving up, down, and sideways one record at a time.

One of the most popular hierarchical database management systems was IBM's Information Management System (IMS), first introduced in 1968. The advantages of IMS and its hierarchical model follow.

■ *Simple structure.* The organization of an IMS database was easy to understand. The database hierarchy paralleled that of a company organization chart or a family tree.

■ *Parent/child organization.* An IMS database was excellent for representing parent/child relationships, such as "A is a part of B" or "A is owned by B."

- *Performance.* IMS stored parent/child relationships as physical pointers from one data record to another, so that movement through the database was rapid. Because the structure was simple, IMS could place parent and child records close to one another on the disk, minimizing disk input/output.

IMS is still a very widely used DBMS on IBM mainframes. Its raw performance makes it the database of choice in high-volume transaction processing applications such as processing bank ATM transactions, verifying credit card numbers, and tracking the delivery of overnight packages. Although relational database performance has improved dramatically over the last decade, the performance requirements of applications such as these have also increased, insuring a continued role for IMS.

Network Databases

The simple structure of a hierarchical database became a disadvantage when the data had a more complex structure. In an order-processing database, for example, a single order might participate in three *different* parent/child relationships, linking the order to the customer who placed it, the salesperson who took it, and the product ordered, as shown in Figure 4-3. The structure of this type of data simply didn't fit the strict hierarchy of IMS.

To deal with applications such as order processing, a new *network* data model was developed. The network data model extended the hierarchical model by allowing a record to participate in multiple parent/child relationships, as shown in Figure 4-4.

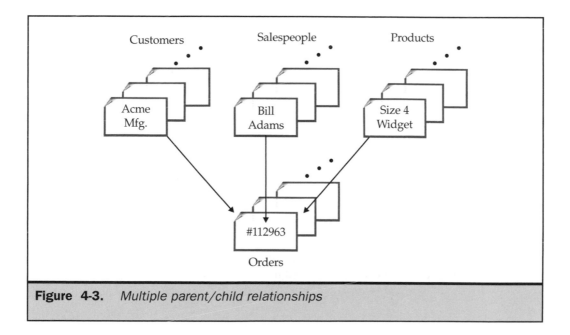

Figure 4-3.   *Multiple parent/child relationships*

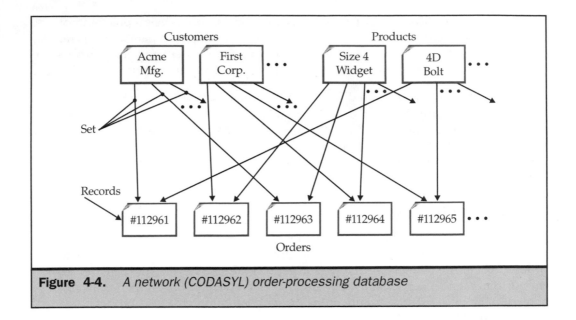

Figure 4-4.   *A network (CODASYL) order-processing database*

These relationships were known as *sets* in the network model. In 1971 the Conference on Data Systems Languages published an official standard for network databases, which became known as the CODASYL model. IBM never developed a network DBMS of its own, choosing instead to extend IMS over the years. But during the 1970s independent software companies rushed to embrace the network model, creating products such as Cullinet's IDMS, Cincom's Total, and the Adabas DBMS that became very popular.

For a programmer, accessing a network database was very similar to accessing a hierarchical database. An application program could:

- find a specific parent record by key (such as a customer number),
- move down to the first child in a particular set (the first order placed by this customer),
- move sideways from one child to the next in the set (the next order placed by the same customer), or
- move up from a child to its parent in another set (the salesperson who took the order).

Once again the programmer had to navigate the database record-by-record, this time specifying which relationship to navigate as well as the direction.

Network databases had several advantages:

- *Flexibility.* Multiple parent/child relationships allowed a network database to represent data that did not have a simple hierarchical structure.

- *Standardization.* The CODASYL standard boosted the popularity of the network model, and minicomputer vendors such as Digital Equipment Corporation and Data General implemented network databases.

- *Performance.* Despite their greater complexity, network databases boasted performance approaching that of hierarchical databases. Sets were represented by pointers to physical data records, and on some systems, the database administrator could specify data clustering based on a set relationship.

Network databases had their disadvantages, too. Like hierarchical databases, they were very rigid. The set relationships and the structure of the records had to be specified in advance. Changing the database structure typically required rebuilding the entire database.

Both hierarchical and network databases were tools for programmers. To answer a question such as "What is the most popular product ordered by Acme Manufacturing?" a programmer had to write a program that navigated its way through the database. The backlog of requests for custom reports often stretched to weeks or months, and by the time the program was written, the information it delivered was often worthless.

The disadvantages of the hierarchical and network models led to intense interest in the new *relational* data model when it was first described by Dr. Codd in 1970. At first the relational model was little more than an academic curiosity. Network databases continued to be important throughout the 1970s and early 1980s, particularly on the minicomputer systems that were surging in popularity. However, by the mid-1980s the relational model was clearly emerging as the "new wave" in data management. By the early 1990s, network databases were clearly declining in importance, and today they no longer play a major role in the database market.

The Relational Data Model

The relational model proposed by Dr. Codd was an attempt to simplify database structure. It eliminated the explicit parent/child structures from the database, and instead represented all data in the database as simple row/column tables of data values. Figure 4-5 shows a relational version of the network order-processing database in Figure 4-4.

Unfortunately, the practical definition of "What is a relational database?" became much less clear-cut than the precise, mathematical definition in Codd's 1970 paper. Early relational database management systems failed to implement some key parts of Codd's model, which are only now finding their way into commercial products. As the relational concept grew in popularity, many databases that were called "relational" in fact were not.

PRODUCTS Table

DESCRIPTION	PRICE	QTY_ON_HAND
Size 3 Widget	$107.00	207
Size 4 Widget	$117.00	139
Hinge Pin	$350.00	14
.		
.		
.		

ORDERS Table

ORDER_NUM	COMPANY	PRODUCT	QTY
112963	Acme Mfg.	41004	28
112975	JCP Inc.	2A44G	6
112983	Acme Mfg.	41004	6
113012	JCP Inc.	41003	35
.			
.			
.			

CUSTOMERS Table

COMPANY	CUST_REP	CREDIT_LIMIT
Acme Mfg.	105	$50,000.00
JCP Inc.	103	$50,000.00
.		
.		
.		

Figure 4-5. *A relational order-processing database*

In response to the corruption of the term "relational," Dr. Codd wrote an article in 1985 setting forth 12 rules to be followed by any database that called itself "truly relational." Codd's 12 rules have since been accepted as *the* definition of a truly relational DBMS. However, it's easier to start with a more informal definition:

A relational database is a database where all data visible to the user is organized strictly as tables of data values, and where all database operations work on these tables.

The definition is intended specifically to rule out structures such as the embedded pointers of a hierarchical or network database. A relational DBMS can represent parent/child relationships, but they are represented strictly by the data values contained in the database tables.

The Sample Database

Figure 4-6 shows a small relational database for an order-processing application. This sample database is used throughout this book and provides the basis for most of the examples. Appendix A contains a complete description of the database structure and its contents.

ORDERS Table

ORDER_NUM	ORDER_DATE	CUST	REP	MFR	PRODUCT	QTY	AMOUNT
112961	17-DEC-89	2117	106	REI	2A44L	7	$31,500.00
113012	11-JAN-90	2111	105	ACI		35	$3,745.00
112989	03-JAN-90	2101				6	$1,458.00
113051	10-FEB-90	2118					
112968	12-OCT-89	2102					
113036	30-JAN-90	2107					
113045	02-FEB-90	2112					
1129	17-DEC-89						

PRODUCTS Table

MFR_ID	PRODUCT_ID	DESCRIPTION	PRICE	QTY_ON_HAND
REI	2A45C	Ratchet Link	$79.00	210
ACI	4100Y	Widget Remover	$2,750.00	25
QSA	XK47	Reducer	$355.00	38
BIC	41672	Plate	$180.00	0
			$1,875.00	9
			$107.00	207
			$117.00	139
			$652.00	3
			$250.00	24
			$134.00	203
			$4,500.00	12
			$148.00	115
			$54.00	223

CUSTOMERS Table

CUST_NUM	COMPANY	CUST_REP	CREDIT_LIMIT
2111	JCP Inc.	103	$50,000.00
2102	First Corp.	101	$65,000.00
2103	Acme Mfg.	105	$50,000.00
2123	Carter & Sons	102	$40,000.00
2107	Ace International	110	$35,000.00
2115	Smithson Corp.	101	$20,000.00
2101	Jones Mfg.	106	$65,000.00
		108	$50,000.00

SALESREPS Table

NAME	AGE	REP_OFFICE	TITLE	HIRE_DATE	MANAGER	QUOTA	SALES
Bill Adams	37	13	Sales Rep	12-FEB-88	104	$350,000.00	$367,911.00
Mary Jones	31	11	Sales Rep	12-OCT-89	106	$300,000.00	$392,725.00
Sue Smith	48	21	Sales Rep	10-DEC-86	108	$350,000.00	$474,050.00
	52	11	VP Sales	14-JUN-88	NULL	$275,000.00	$299,912.00
					106	$200,000.00	$142,594.00
					104	$300,000.00	$305,673.00
					101	NULL	$75,985.00
					106	$350,000.00	$361,865.00
					104	$275,000.00	$286,775.00
					108	$300,000.00	$186,042.00

OFFICES Table

OFFICE	CITY	REGION	MGR	TARGET	SALES
22	Denver	Western	108	$300,000.00	$186,042.00
11	New York	Eastern	106	$575,000.00	$692,637.00
12	Chicago	Eastern	104	$800,000.00	$735,042.00
13	Atlanta	Eastern	105	$350,000.00	$367,911.00
21	Los Angeles	Western	108	$725,000.00	$835,915.00

Figure 4-6. *The sample database*

The sample database contains five tables. Each table stores information about one particular *kind* of entity:

- The CUSTOMERS table stores data about each customer, such as the company name, credit limit, and the salesperson who calls on the customer.

- The SALESREPS table stores the employee number, name, age, year-to-date sales, and other data about each salesperson.

- The OFFICES table stores data about each of the five sales offices, including the city where the office is located, the sales region to which it belongs, and so on.

- The ORDERS table keeps track of every order placed by a customer, identifying the salesperson who took the order, the product ordered, the quantity and amount of the order, and so on. For simplicity, each order is for only one product.

■ The PRODUCTS table stores data about each product available for sale, such as the manufacturer, product number, description, and price.

Tables

The organizing principle in a relational database is the *table,* a rectangular, row/column arrangement of data values. Each table in a database has a unique *table name* that identifies its contents. (Actually, each user can choose their own table names without worrying about the names chosen by other users, as explained in Chapter 5.)

The row/column structure of a table is shown more clearly in Figure 4-7, which is an enlarged view of the OFFICES table. Each horizontal *row* of the OFFICES table represents a single physical entity—a single sales office. Together the five rows of the table represent all five of the company's sales offices. All of the data in a particular row of the table applies to the office represented by that row.

Each vertical *column* of the OFFICES table represents one item of data that is stored in the database for each office. For example, the CITY column holds the location of each office. The SALES column contains each office's year-to-date sales total. The MGR column shows the employee number of the person who manages the office.

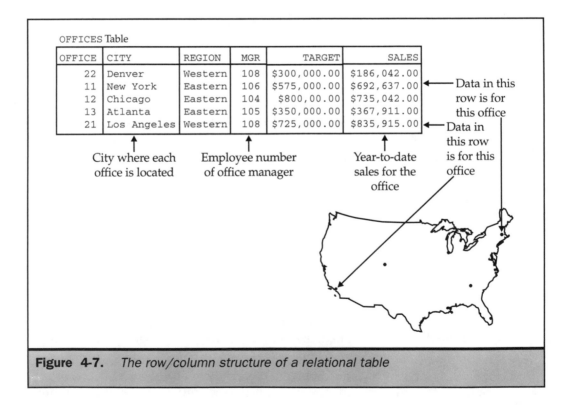

Figure 4-7.   *The row/column structure of a relational table*

Each row of a table contains exactly one data value in each column. In the row representing the New York office, for example, the CITY column contains the value "New York." The SALES column contains the value "$692,637.00," which is the year-to-date sales total for the New York office.

For each column of a table, all of the data values in that column hold the same type of data. For example, all of the CITY column values are words, all of the SALES values are money amounts, and all of the MGR values are integers (representing employee numbers). The set of data values that a column can contain is called the *domain* of the column. The domain of the CITY column is the set of all names of cities. The domain of the SALES column is any money amount. The domain of the REGION column is just two data values, "Eastern" and "Western," because those are the only two sales regions the company has!

Each column in a table has a *column name*, which is usually written as a heading at the top of the column. The columns of a table must all have different names, but there is no prohibition against two columns in two different tables having identical names. In fact, frequently used column names, such as NAME, ADDRESS, QTY, PRICE, and SALES, are often found in many different tables of a production database.

The columns of a table have a left-to-right order, which is defined when the table is first created. A table always has at least one column. The ANSI/ISO SQL standard does not specify a maximum number of columns in a table, but almost all commercial SQL products do impose a limit. Usually the limit is 255 columns per table or more.

Unlike the columns, the rows in a table do *not* have any particular order. In fact, if you use two consecutive database queries to display the contents of a table, there is no guarantee that the rows will be listed in the same order twice. Of course you can ask SQL to sort the rows before displaying them, but the sorted order has nothing to do with the actual arrangement of the rows within the table.

A table can have any number of rows. A table of zero rows is perfectly legal and is called an *empty* table (for obvious reasons). An empty table still has a structure, imposed by its columns; it simply contains no data. The ANSI/ISO standard does not limit the number of rows in a table, and many SQL products will allow a table to grow until it exhausts the available disk space on the computer. Other SQL products impose a maximum limit, but it is always a very generous one—two billion rows or more is common.

Primary Keys

Because the rows of a relational table are unordered, you cannot select a specific row by its position in the table. There is no "first row," "last row," or "thirteenth row" of a table. How then can you specify a particular row, such as the row for the Denver sales office?

In a well-designed relational database every table has some column or combination of columns whose values uniquely identify each row in the table. This column (or columns) is called the *primary key* of the table. Look once again at the OFFICES table in

Figure 4-7. At first glance, either the OFFICE column or the CITY column could serve as a primary key for the table. But if the company expands and opens two sales offices in the same city, the CITY column could no longer serve as the primary key. In practice, "ID numbers," such as an office number (OFFICE in the OFFICES table), an employee number (EMPL_NUM in the SALESREPS table), and customer numbers (CUST_NUM in the CUSTOMERS table), are often chosen as primary keys. In the case of the ORDERS table there is no choice—the only thing that uniquely identifies an order is its order number (ORDER_NUM).

The PRODUCTS table, part of which is shown in Figure 4-8, is an example of a table where the primary key must be a *combination* of columns. The MFR_ID column identifies the manufacturer of each product in the table, and the PRODUCT_ID column specifies the manufacturer's product number. The PRODUCT_ID column might make a good primary key, but there's nothing to prevent two different manufacturers from using the same number for their products. Therefore, a combination of the MFR_ID and PRODUCT_ID columns must be used as the primary key of the PRODUCTS table. Every product in the table is guaranteed to have a unique combination of data values in these two columns.

The primary key has a different unique value for each row in a table, so no two rows of a table with a primary key are exact duplicates of one another. A table where every row is different from all other rows is called a *relation* in mathematical terms. The name "relational database" comes from this term, because relations (tables with distinct rows) are at the heart of a relational database.

PRODUCTS Table

MFR_ID	PRODUCT_ID	DESCRIPTION	PRICE	QTY_ON_HAND
.				
.				
.				
ACI	41003	Size 3 Widget	$107.00	207
ACI	41004	Size 4 Widget	$117.00	139
BIC	41003	Handle	$652.00	3
.				
.				
.				

Primary
key

Figure 4-8. *A table with a composite primary key*

Although primary keys are an essential part of the relational data model, early relational database management systems (System/R, DB2, Oracle, and others) did not provide explicit support for primary keys. Database designers usually ensured that all of the tables in their databases had a primary key, but the DBMS itself did not provide a way to identify the primary key of a table. DB2 Version 2, introduced in April 1988, was the first of IBM's commercial SQL products to support primary keys. The ANSI/ISO standard was subsequently expanded to include a definition of primary key support.

Relationships

One of the major differences between the relational model and earlier data models is that explicit pointers, such as the parent/child relationships of a hierarchical database, are banned from relational databases. Yet obviously these relationships exist in a relational database. For example, in the sample database, each of the salespeople is assigned to a particular sales office, so there is an obvious relationship between the rows of the OFFICES table and the rows of the SALESREPS table. Doesn't the relational model "lose information" by banning these relationships from the database?

As shown in Figure 4-9, the answer to the question is "no." The figure shows a close-up of a few rows of the OFFICES and SALESREPS tables. Note that the REP_OFFICE column of the SALESREPS table contains the office number of the sales office where each salesperson works. The domain of this column (the set of legal values it may contain) is *precisely* the set of office numbers found in the OFFICE column of the OFFICES table. In fact, you can find the sales office where Mary Jones works by finding the value in Mary's REP_OFFICE column (11) and finding the row of the OFFICES table that has a matching value in the OFFICE column (in the row for the New York office). Similarly, to find all the salespeople who work in New York, you could note the OFFICE value for the New York row (11) and then scan down the REP_OFFICE column of the SALESREPS table looking for matching values (in the rows for Mary Jones and Sam Clark).

The parent/child relationship between a sales office and the people who work there isn't lost by the relational model, it's just not represented by an explicit pointer stored in the database. Instead, the relationship is represented by *common data values* stored in the two tables. All relationships in a relational database are represented this way. One of the main goals of the SQL language is to let you retrieve related data from the database by manipulating these relationships in a simple, straightforward way.

Foreign Keys

A column in one table whose value matches the primary key in some other table is called a *foreign key.* In Figure 4-9 the REP_OFFICE column is a foreign key for the OFFICES table. Although REP_OFFICE is a column in the SALESREPS table, the values that this column contains are office numbers. They match values in the OFFICE column, which is the primary key for the OFFICES table. Together, a primary key and

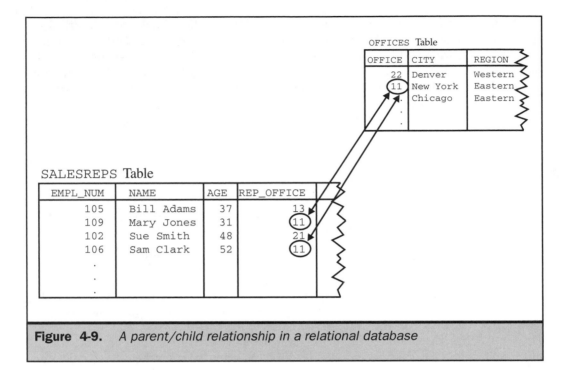

Figure 4-9. *A parent/child relationship in a relational database*

a foreign key create a parent/child relationship between the tables that contain them, just like the parent/child relationships in a hierarchical database.

Just as a combination of columns can serve as the primary key of a table, a foreign key can also be a combination of columns. In fact, the foreign key will *always* be a compound (multi-column) key when it references a table with a compound primary key. Obviously, the number of columns and the data types of the columns in the foreign key and the primary key must be identical to one another.

A table can contain more than one foreign key if it is related to more than one other table. Figure 4-10 shows the three foreign keys in the ORDERS table of the sample database:

- The CUST column is a foreign key for the CUSTOMERS table, relating each order to the customer who placed it.

- The REP column is a foreign key for the SALESREPS table, relating each order to the salesperson who took it.

- The MFR and PRODUCT columns together are a composite foreign key for the PRODUCTS table, relating each order to the product being ordered.

The multiple parent/child relationships created by the three foreign keys in the ORDERS table may seem familiar to you, and they should. They are precisely the same

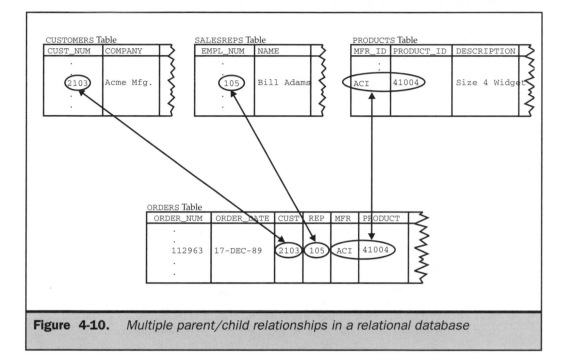

Figure 4-10.   *Multiple parent/child relationships in a relational database*

relationships as those in the network database of Figure 4-4. As the example shows, the relational data model has all of the power of the network model to express complex relationships.

Foreign keys are a fundamental part of the relational model because they create relationships among tables in the database. Unfortunately, as with primary keys, foreign key support was missing from early relational database management systems. They were added to DB2 Version 2, have since been added to the ANSI/ISO standard, and now appear in many commercial products.

Codd's Twelve Rules *

In his 1985 *Computerworld* article, Ted Codd presented 12 rules that a database must obey if it is to be considered truly relational. Codd's 12 rules, shown in the following list, have since become a semi-official definition of a relational database. The rules come out of Codd's theoretical work on the relational model and actually represent more of an ideal goal than a definition of a relational database.

1. *The information rule.* All information in a relational database is represented explicitly at the logical level and in exactly one way—by values in tables.

2. *Guaranteed access rule.* Each and every datum (atomic value) in a relational database is guaranteed to be logically accessible by resorting to a combination of table name, primary key value, and column name.

3. *Systematic treatment of null values.* Null values (distinct from an empty character string or a string of blank characters and distinct from zero or any other number) are supported in a fully relational DBMS for representing missing information and inapplicable information in a systematic way, independent of the data type.

4. *Dynamic online catalog based on the relational model.* The database description is represented at the logical level in the same way as ordinary data, so that authorized users can apply the same relational language to its interrogation as they apply to the regular data.

5. *Comprehensive data sublanguage rule.* A relational system may support several languages and various modes of terminal use (for example, the fill-in-the-blanks mode). However, there must be at least one language whose statements are expressible, per some well-defined syntax, as character strings, and that is comprehensive in supporting all of the following items:

   ■ Data definition

   ■ View definition

   ■ Data manipulation (interactive and by program)

   ■ Integrity constraints

   ■ Authorization

   ■ Transaction boundaries (begin, commit, and rollback)

6. *View updating rule.* All views that are theoretically updateable are also updateable by the system.

7. *High-level insert, update, and delete.* The capability of handling a base relation or a derived relation as a single operand applies not only to the retrieval of data but also to the insertion, update, and deletion of data.

8. *Physical data independence.* Application programs and terminal activities remain logically unimpaired whenever any changes are made in either storage representations or access methods.

9. *Logical data independence.* Application programs and terminal activities remain logically unimpaired when information preserving changes of any kind that theoretically permit unimpairment are made to the base tables.

10. *Integrity independence.* Integrity constraints specific to a particular relational database must be definable in the relational data sublanguage and storable in the catalog, not in the application programs.

11. *Distribution independence.* A relational DBMS has distribution independence.

12. *Nonsubversion rule.* If a relational system has a low-level (single record at a time) language, that low level cannot be used to subvert or bypass the integrity rules and constraints expressed in the higher-level relational language (multiple records at a time).

During the early 1990s, it became popular practice to compile "scorecards" for commercial DBMS products, showing how well they satisfy each of the rules. Unfortunately, the rules are subjective so the scorecards were usually full of footnotes and qualifications, and didn't reveal a great deal about the products. Today, the basis of competition for database vendors tends to revolve around performance, new features, the availability of development tools, the quality of vendor support, and other issues, rather than conformance to Codd's rules. Nonetheless, they are an important part of the history of the relational model.

Rule 1 is basically the informal definition of a relational database presented at the beginning of this section.

Rule 2 stresses the importance of primary keys for locating data in the database. The table name locates the correct table, the column name finds the correct column, and the primary key value finds the row containing an individual data item of interest. Rule 3 requires support for missing data through NULL values, which are described in Chapter 5.

Rule 4 requires that a relational database be self-describing. In other words, the database must contain certain *system tables* whose columns describe the structure of the database itself. These tables are described in Chapter 16.

Rule 5 mandates using a relational database language, such as SQL, although SQL is not specifically required. The language must be able to support all the central functions of a DBMS—creating a database, retrieving and entering data, implementing database security, and so on.

Rule 6 deals with views, which are *virtual tables* used to give various users of a database different views of its structure. It is one of the most challenging rules to implement in practice, and no commercial product fully satisfies it today. Views and the problems of updating them are described in Chapter 14.

Rule 7 stresses the set-oriented nature of a relational database. It requires that rows be treated as sets in insert, delete, and update operations. The rule is designed to prohibit implementations that only support row-at-a-time, navigational modification of the database.

Rule 8 and Rule 9 insulate the user or application program from the low-level implementation of the database. They specify that specific access or storage techniques used by the DBMS, and even changes to the structure of the tables in the database, should not affect the user's ability to work with the data.

Rule 10 says that the database language should support integrity constraints that restrict the data that can be entered into the database and the database modifications that can be made. This is another of the rules that is not supported in most commercial DBMS products.

Rule 11 says that the database language must be able to manipulate distributed data located on other computer systems. Distributed data and the challenges of managing it are described in Chapter 20.

Finally, Rule 12 prevents "other paths" into the database that might subvert its relational structure and integrity.

 # Summary

SQL is based on the relational data model that organizes the data in a database as a collection of tables:

- Each table has a table name that uniquely identifies it.

- Each table has one or more named columns, which are arranged in a specific, left-to-right order.

- Each table has zero or more rows, each containing a single data value in each column. The rows are unordered.

- All data values in a given column have the same data type, and are drawn from a set of legal values called the domain of the column.

Tables are related to one another by the data they contain. The relational data model uses primary keys and foreign keys to represent these relationships among tables:

- A primary key is a column or combination of columns in a table whose value(s) uniquely identify each row of the table. A table has only one primary key.

- A foreign key is a column or combination of columns in a table whose value(s) are a primary key value for some other table. A table can contain more than one foreign key, linking it to one or more other tables.

- A primary key/foreign key combination creates a parent/child relationship between the tables that contain them.

Part II

Retrieving Data

Queries are the heart of the SQL language, and many people use SQL as a database query tool. The next five chapters describe SQL queries in depth. Chapter 5 describes the basic SQL language structures that you use to form SQL statements. Chapter 6 discusses simple queries that draw data from a single table of data. Chapter 7 expands the discussion to multi-table queries. Queries that summarize data are described in Chapter 8. Finally, Chapter 9 explains the SQL subquery capability that is used to handle complex queries.

Chapter 5

SQL Basics

This chapter begins a detailed description of the features of SQL. It describes the basic structure of a SQL statement and the basic elements of the language, such as keywords, data types, and expressions. The way that SQL handles missing data through NULL values is also described. Although these are basic features of SQL, there are some subtle differences in the way they are implemented by various popular SQL products, and in many cases the SQL products provide significant extensions to the capabilities specified in the ANSI/ISO SQL standard. These differences and extensions are also described in this chapter.

Statements

The main body of the SQL language consists of about 40 statements, which are summarized in Table 5-1. Each statement requests a specific action from the DBMS, such as creating a new table, retrieving data, or inserting new data into the database. All SQL statements have the same basic form, illustrated in Figure 5-1.

Every SQL statement begins with a *verb*, a keyword that describes what the statement does. CREATE, INSERT, DELETE, and COMMIT are typical verbs. The statement continues with one or more *clauses*. A clause may specify the data to be acted upon by the statement or provide more detail about what the statement is supposed to do. Every clause also begins with a keyword, such as WHERE, FROM, INTO, and HAVING. Some clauses are optional; others are required. The specific structure and content vary from one clause to another. Many clauses contain table or column names; some may contain additional keywords, constants, or expressions.

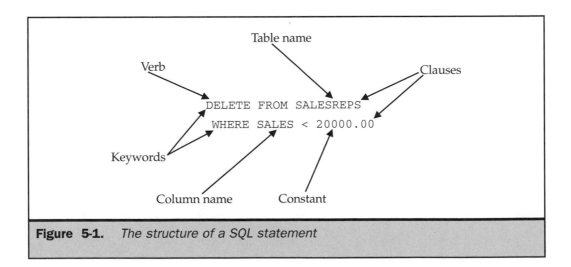

Figure 5-1. *The structure of a SQL statement*

Statement	Description
Data Manipulation	
SELECT	Retrieves data from the database
INSERT	Adds new rows of data to the database
DELETE	Removes rows of data from the database
UPDATE	Modifies existing database data
Data Definition	
CREATE TABLE	Adds a new table to the database
DROP TABLE	Removes a table from the database
ALTER TABLE	Changes the structure of an existing table
CREATE VIEW	Adds a new view to the database
DROP VIEW	Removes a view from the database
CREATE INDEX	Builds an index for a column
DROP INDEX	Removes the index for a column
CREATE SCHEMA	Adds a new schema to the database
DROP SCHEMA	Removes a schema from the database
CREATE DOMAIN	Adds a new data value domain
ALTER DOMAIN	Changes a domain definition
DROP DOMAIN	Removes a domain from the database
Access Control	
GRANT	Grants user access privileges
REVOKE	Removes user access privileges
Transaction Control	
COMMIT	Ends the current transaction
ROLLBACK	Aborts the current transaction
SET TRANSACTION	Defines data access characteristics of the current transaction

Table 5-1. *Major SQL Statements*

Statement	Description
Programmatic SQL	
DECLARE	Defines a cursor for a query
EXPLAIN	Describes the data access plan for a query
OPEN	Opens a cursor to retrieve query results
FETCH	Retrieves a row of query results
CLOSE	Closes a cursor
PREPARE	Prepares a SQL statement for dynamic execution
EXECUTE	Executes a SQL statement dynamically
DESCRIBE	Describes a prepared query

Table 5-1. *Major SQL Statements* (continued)

The ANSI/ISO SQL standard specifies the SQL keywords that are used as verbs and in statement clauses. According to the standard, these keywords cannot be used to name database objects, such as tables, columns, and users. Many SQL implementations relax this restriction, but it's generally a good idea to avoid the keywords when you name your tables and columns. Table 5-2 lists the keywords included in the ANSI/ISO SQL2 standard, which roughly tripled the number of keywords reserved by the earlier SQL1 standard. The SQL2 standard also includes a list of "potential keywords" that are candidates for becoming keywords in future revisions of the standard. These keywords are listed in Table 5-3.

Throughout this book, the acceptable forms of a SQL statement are illustrated by a syntax diagram, such as the one shown in Figure 5-2. A valid SQL statement or clause is constructed by "following the line" through the syntax diagram to the dot that marks the end of the diagram. Keywords in the syntax diagram and in the examples (such as DELETE and FROM in Figure 5-2) are always shown in UPPERCASE, but almost all SQL implementations accept both uppercase and lowercase keywords, and it's often more convenient to actually type them in lowercase.

Variable items in a SQL statement (such as the table name and search condition in Figure 5-2) are shown in *lowercase italics*. It's up to you to specify the appropriate item each time the statement is used. Optional clauses and keywords, such as the WHERE clause in Figure 5-2, are indicated by alternate paths through the syntax diagram. When a choice of optional keywords is offered, the default choice (that is, the behavior of the statement if no keyword is specified) is UNDERLINED.

ABSOLUTE	CROSS	GET	NEXT	SPACE
ACTION	CURRENT	GLOBAL	NO	SQL
ADD	CURRENT_DATE	GO	NOT	SQLCODE
ALL	CURRENT_TIME	GOTO	NULL	SQLERROR
ALLOCATE	CURRENT_TIMESTAMP	GRANT	OCTET_LENGTH	SQLSTATE
ALTER	CURRENT_USER	GROUP	OF	SUBSTRING
AND	CURSOR	HAVING	ON	SUM
ANY	DATE	HOUR	ONLY	SYSTEM_USER
ARE	DAY	IDENTITY	OPEN	TABLE
AS	DEALLOCATE	IMMEDIATE	OPTION	TEMPORARY
ASC	DEC	IN	OR	THEN
ASSERTION	DECIMAL	INDICATOR	ORDER	TIME
AT	DECLARE	INITIALLY	OUTER	TIMESTAMP
AUTHORIZATION	DEFAULT	INNER	OUTPUT	TIMEZONE_HOUR
AVG	DEFERRABLE	INPUT	OVERLAPS	TIMEZONE_MINUTE
BEGIN	DEFERRED	INSENSITIVE	PAD	TO
BETWEEN	DELETE	INSERT	PARTIAL	TRAILING
BIT	DESC	INT	POSITION	TRANSACTION
BIT_LENGTH	DESCRIBE	INTEGER	PRECISION	TRANSLATE
BOTH	DESCRIPTOR	INTERSECT	PREPARE	TRANSLATION
BY	DIAGNOSTICS	INTERVAL	PRESERVE	TRIM
CASCADE	DISCONNECT	INTO	PRIMARY	TRUE
CASCADED	DISTINCT	IS	PRIOR	UNION
CASE	DOMAIN	ISOLATION	PRIVILEGES	UNIQUE
CAST	DOUBLE	JOIN	PROCEDURE	UNKNOWN
CATALOG	DROP	KEY	PUBLIC	UPDATE
CHAR	ELSE	LANGUAGE	READ	UPPER
CHARACTER	END	LAST	REAL	USAGE

Table 5-2. *ANSI/ISO SQL2 Keywords*

CHAR_LENGTH	END-EXEC	LEADING	REFERENCES	USER
CHARACTER_LENGTH	ESCAPE	LEFT	RELATIVE	USING
CHECK	EXCEPT	LEVEL	RESTRICT	VALUE
CLOSE	EXCEPTION	LIKE	REVOKE	VALUES
COALESCE	EXEC	LOCAL	RIGHT	VARCHAR
COLLATE	EXECUTE	LOWER	ROLLBACK	VARYING
COLLATION	EXISTS	MATCH	ROWS	VIEW
COLUMN	EXTERNAL	MAX	SCHEMA	WHEN
COMMIT	EXTRACT	MIN	SCROLL	WHENEVER
CONNECT	FALSE	MINUTE	SECOND	WHERE
CONNECTION	FETCH	MODULE	SECTION	WITH
CONSTRAINT	FIRST	MONTH	SELECT	WORK
CONSTRAINTS	FLOAT	NAMES	SESSION	WRITE
CONTINUE	FOR	NATIONAL	SESSION_USER	YEAR
CONVERT	FOREIGN	NATURAL	SET	ZONE
CORRESPONDING	FOUND	NCHAR	SIZE	
COUNT	FROM	NULLIF	SMALLINT	
CREATE	FULL	NUMERIC	SOME	

Table 5-2. *ANSI/ISO SQL2 Keywords* (continued)

Names

The objects in a SQL-based database are identified by assigning them unique names. Names are used in SQL statements to identify the database object on which the statement should act. The most fundamental named objects in a relational database are table names (which identify tables), column names (which identify columns), and user names (which identify users of the database); conventions for naming these objects were specified in the original SQL1 standard. The ANSI/ISO SQL2 standard significantly expanded the list of named entities, to include schemas (collections of tables), constraints (restrictions on the contents of tables and their relationships), domains (sets of legal values that may be assigned to a column), and several other types of objects. Many SQL implementations support additional named objects, such as

AFTER	EQUALS	OLD	RETURN	TEST
ALIAS	GENERAL	OPERATION	RETURNS	THERE
ASYNC	IF	OPERATORS	ROLE	TRIGGER
BEFORE	IGNORE	OTHERS	ROUTINE	TYPE
BOOLEAN	LEAVE	PARAMETERS	ROW	UNDER
BREADTH	LESS	PENDANT	SAVEPOINT	VARIABLE
COMPLETION	LIMIT	PREORDER	SEARCH	VIRTUAL
CALL	LOOP	PRIVATE	SENSITIVE	VISIBLE
CYCLE	MODIFY	PROTECTED	SEQUENCE	WAIT
DATA	NEW	RECURSIVE	SIGNAL	WHILE
DEPTH	NONE	REF	SIMILAR	WITHOUT
DICTIONARY	OBJECT	REFERENCING	SQLEXCEPTION	
EACH	OFF	REPLACE	SQLWARNING	
ELSEIF	OID	RESIGNAL	STRUCTURE	

Table 5-3.   *ANSI/ISO SQL2 Potential Keywords*

stored procedures (Sybase and SQL Server), primary key/foreign key relationships (DB2), and data entry forms (Ingres).

The original ANSI/ISO standard specified that SQL names must contain 1 to 18 characters, must begin with a letter, and may not contain any spaces or special punctuation characters. The SQL2 standard increased the maximum to 128 characters.

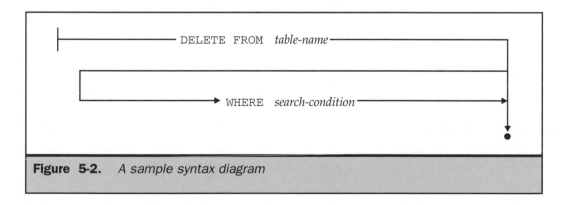

Figure 5-2.   *A sample syntax diagram*

In practice the names supported by SQL-based DBMS products vary significantly. DB2, for example, restricts user names to 8 characters but allows longer table and column names. The various products also differ in the special characters they permit in table names. For portability it's best to keep names relatively short and to avoid the use of special characters.

Table Names

When you specify a table name in a SQL statement, SQL assumes that you are referring to one of your own tables (that is, a table that you created). Usually, you will want to choose table names that are short but descriptive. The table names in the sample database (ORDERS, CUSTOMERS, OFFICES, SALESREPS) are good examples. In a personal or departmental database, the choice of table names is usually up to the database developer or designer.

In a larger, shared-use corporate database, there may be corporate standards for naming tables, to insure that table names do not conflict. In addition, most DBMS brands allow different users to create tables with the same name (that is, both Joe and Sam can create a table named BIRTHDAYS). The DBMS uses the appropriate table, depending on which user is requesting data. With the proper permission, you can also refer to tables owned by other users, by using a *qualified table name.* A qualified table name specifies both the name of the table's owner and the name of the table, separated by a period (.). For example, Joe could access the BIRTHDAYS table owned by Sam by using the qualified table name:

    SAM.BIRTHDAYS

A qualified table name generally can be used in a SQL statement wherever a table name can appear.

The ANSI/ISO SQL2 standard generalizes the notion of a qualified table name even further. It allows you to create a named collection of tables, called a *schema.* You can refer to a table in a specific schema using a qualified table name. For example, the BIRTHDAYS table in the EMPLOYEEINFO schema would be referenced as:

    EMPLOYEEINFO.BIRTHDAYS

Chapter 13 provides more information about schemas, users, and other aspects of SQL database structure.

Column Names

When you specify a column name in a SQL statement, SQL can normally determine from the context which column you intend. However, if the statement involves two columns with the same name from two different tables, you must use a *qualified column name* to unambiguously identify the column you intend. A qualified column name specifies both the name of the table containing the column and the name of the column, separated by a period (.). For example, the column named SALES in the SALESREPS table has the qualified column name:

```
SALESREPS.SALES
```

If the column comes from a table owned by another user, a qualified table name is used in the qualified column name. For example, the BIRTHDATE column in the BIRTHDAYS table owned by the user SAM is specified by the fully qualified column name:

```
SAM.BIRTHDAYS.BIRTH_DATE
```

Qualified column names can generally be used in a SQL statement wherever a simple (unqualified) column name can appear; exceptions are noted in the descriptions of the individual SQL statements.

Data Types

The ANSI/ISO SQL standard specifies the various types of data that can be stored in a SQL-based database and manipulated by the SQL language. The original SQL1 standard specified only a minimal set of data types. The SQL2 standard expanded this list to include variable-length character strings, date and time data, bit strings, and other types. Today's commercial DBMS products can process a rich variety of different kinds of data, and there is considerable diversity in the particular data types supported across different DBMS brands. Typical data types include:

- *Integers*. Columns holding this type of data typically store counts, quantities, ages, and so on. Integer columns are also frequently used to contain I.D. numbers, such as customer, employee, and order numbers.

- *Decimal numbers*. Columns with this data type store numbers that have fractional parts and must be calculated exactly, such as rates and percentages. They are also frequently used to store money amounts.

- *Floating point numbers*. Columns with this data type are used to store scientific numbers that can be calculated approximately, such as weights and distances. Floating point numbers can represent a larger range of values than decimal numbers but can produce round-off errors in computations.

- *Fixed-length character strings*. Columns holding this type of data typically store names of people and companies, addresses, descriptions, and so on.

- *Variable-length character strings.* This data type allows a column to store character strings that vary in length from row to row, up to some maximum length. (The SQL1 standard permitted only fixed-length character strings, which are easier for the DBMS to process but can waste considerable space.)

- *Money amounts.* Many SQL products support a MONEY or CURRENCY type, which is usually stored as a decimal or floating point number. Having a distinct money type allows the DBMS to properly format money amounts when they are displayed.

- *Dates and times.* Support for date/time values is also common in SQL products, although the details vary dramatically from one product to another. Various combinations of dates, times, timestamps, time intervals, and date/time arithmetic are generally supported. The SQL2 standard includes an elaborate specification for DATE, TIME, TIMESTAMP, and INTERVAL data types, including support for time zones and time precision (for example, tenths or hundredths of seconds).

- *Boolean data.* Some SQL products, such as Informix Dynamic Server, support logical (TRUE or FALSE) values as an explicit type, and some permit logical operations (comparison, AND/OR, and so on) on the stored data within SQL statements.

- *Long text.* Several SQL-based databases support columns that store long text strings (typically up to 32,000 or 65,000 characters, and in some cases even larger). This allows the database to store entire documents, product descriptions, technical papers, resumes, and similar unstructured text data. The DBMS usually restricts the use of these columns in interactive queries and searches.

- *Unstructured byte streams.* Several DBMS products allow unstructured, variable-length sequences of bytes to be stored and retrieved. Columns containing this data are used to store compressed video images, executable code, and other types of unstructured data. SQL Server's IMAGE data type, for example, can store a stream of up to 2 billion bytes of data.

- *Asian characters.* As databases grow to support global applications, DBMS vendors have added support for fixed-length and variable-length strings of 16-bit characters used to represent Kanji and other Asian characters. Searching and sorting on these GRAPHIC and VARGRAPHIC types is usually not permitted, however.

Table 5-4 lists the data types specified in the ANSI/ISO SQL standard.

Data Type	Description
CHAR (*len*) CHARACTER (*len*)	Fixed-length character strings
VARCHAR (*len*) CHAR VARYING (*len*) CHARACTER VARYING (*len*)	Variable-length character strings*
NCHAR (*len*) NATIONAL CHAR (*len*) NATIONAL CHARACTER (*len*)	Fixed-length national character strings*
NCHAR VARYING (*len*) NATIONAL CHAR VARYING (*len*) NATIONAL CHARACTER VARYING (*len*)	Variable-length national character strings*
INTEGER INT	Integer numbers
SMALLINT	Small integer numbers
BIT (*len*)	Fixed-length bit string*
BIT VARYING (*len*)	Variable-length bit string*
NUMERIC (*precision,scale*) DECIMAL (*precision,scale*) DEC (*precision,scale*)	Decimal numbers
FLOAT (*precision*)	Floating point numbers
REAL	Low-precision floating point numbers
DOUBLE PRECISION	High-precision floating point numbers
DATE	Calendar date*
TIME (*precision*)	Clock time*
TIMESTAMP (*precision*)	Date and time*
INTERVAL	Time interval*

*new data type in SQL2

Table 5-4. *ANSI/ISO SQL Data Types*

The differences between the data types offered in various SQL implementations is one of the practical barriers to the portability of SQL-based applications. These differences have come about as a result of innovation as relational databases have evolved to include a broader range of capabilities. The typical pattern has been:

- A DBMS vendor adds a new data type that provides useful new capability for a certain group of users.

- Other DBMS vendors add the same or similar data types, adding their own innovations to differentiate their products from the others.

- Over several years, the popularity of the data type grows, and it becomes a part of the "mainstream" set of data types supported by most SQL implementations.

- The standards bodies become involved to try to standardize the new data type and eliminate arbitrary differences between the vendor implementations. The more well-entrenched the data type has become, the more difficult the set of compromises faced by the standards group. Usually this results in an addition to the standard that does not exactly match *any* of the current implementations.

- DBMS vendors slowly add support for the new standardized data type as an option to their systems, but because they have a large installed base that is using the older (now "proprietary") version of the data type, they must maintain support for this form of the data type as well.

- Over a very long period of time (typically several major releases of the DBMS product), users migrate to the new, standardized form of the data type, and the DBMS vendor can begin the process of obsoleting the proprietary version.

Date/time data provides an excellent example of this phenomenon and the data type variations it creates. DB2 has long offered support for three different date/time data types:

- DATE, which stores a date like June 30, 1991,

- TIME, which stores a time of day like 12:30 P.M., and

- TIMESTAMP, which is a specific instant in history, with a precision down to the nanosecond.

Specific dates and times can be specified as string constants, and date arithmetic is supported. Here is an example of a valid query using DB2 dates, assuming that the HIREDATE column contains DATE data:

```
SELECT NAME, HIRE_DATE
  FROM SALESREPS
 WHERE HIRE_DATE >= '05/30/1989' + 15 DAYS
```

SQL Server provides a single date/time data type, called DATETIME, which closely resembles the DB2 TIMESTAMP data type. If HIRE_DATE contained DATETIME data, SQL Server could accept this version of the query (without the date arithmetic):

```
SELECT NAME, HIRE_DATE
  FROM SALESREPS
 WHERE HIRE_DATE >= '06/14/1989'
```

Since no specific time on June 14, 1989, is specified in the query, SQL Server defaults to midnight on that date. The SQL Server query thus *really* means:

```
SELECT NAME, HIRE_DATE
  FROM SALESREPS
 WHERE HIRE_DATE >= '06/14/1989 12:00AM'
```

If a salesperson's hire date was stored in the database as midday on June 14, 1989, the salesperson would not be included in the SQL Server query results but would have been included in the DB2 results (because only the date would be stored). SQL Server also supports date arithmetic through a set of built-in functions. Thus the DB2-style query can also be specified in this way:

```
SELECT NAME, HIRE_DATE
  FROM SALESREPS
 WHERE HIRE_DATE >= DATEADD(DAY, 15, '05/30/1989')
```

which, of course, is considerably different from the DB2 syntax.

Oracle also supports date/time data, with a single data type called DATE. Like SQL Server's DATETIME type, an Oracle DATE is, in fact, a timestamp. Also like SQL Server, the time part of an Oracle DATE value defaults to midnight if no time is explicitly specified. The default Oracle date format is different from the DB2 and SQL Server formats, so the Oracle version of the query becomes:

```
SELECT NAME, HIRE_DATE
  FROM SALESREPS
 WHERE HIRE_DATE >= '14-JUN-89'
```

Oracle also supports limited date arithmetic, so the DB2-style query can also be specified but without the DAYS keyword:

```
SELECT NAME, HIRE_DATE
  FROM SALESREPS
 WHERE HIRE_DATE >= '30-MAY-89' + 15
```

Finally, the ANSI/ISO SQL2 standard added support for date/time data with a set of data types that are based on, but not identical to, the DB2 types. In addition to the DATE, TIME, and TIMESTAMP data types, the standard specifies an INTERVAL data type, which can be used to store a time interval (for example, a timespan measured in days, or a duration measured in hours, minutes, and seconds). The standard also provides a very elaborate and complex method for dealing with date/time arithmetic, specifying the precision of intervals, adjusting for time zone differences, and so on.

As these examples illustrate, the subtle differences in data types among various SQL products lead to some significant differences in SQL statement syntax. They can even cause the same SQL query to produce slightly different results on different database management systems. The widely praised portability of SQL is thus true but only at a general level. An application can be moved from one SQL database to another, and it can be highly portable if it uses only the most mainstream, basic SQL capabilities. However, the subtle variations in SQL implementations mean that data types and SQL statements must almost always be adjusted somewhat if it is to be moved across DBMS brands. The more complex the application, the more likely it is to become dependent on DBMS-specific features and nuances, and the less portable it will become.

Constants

In some SQL statements a numeric, character, or date data value must be expressed in text form. For example, in this INSERT statement, which adds a salesperson to the database:

```
INSERT INTO SALESREPS (EMPL_NUM, NAME, QUOTA, HIRE_DATE, SALES)
     VALUES (115, 'Dennis Irving', 175000.00, '21-JUN-90', 0.00)
```

the value for each column in the newly inserted row is specified in the VALUES clause. Constant data values are also used in expressions, such as in this SELECT statement:

```
SELECT CITY
  FROM OFFICES
 WHERE TARGET > (1.1 * SALES) + 10000.00
```

The ANSI/ISO SQL standard specifies the format of numeric and string constants, or *literals,* which represent specific data values. These conventions are followed by most SQL implementations.

Numeric Constants

Integer and decimal constants (also called *exact numeric literals*) are written as ordinary decimal numbers in SQL statements, with an optional leading plus or minus sign.

```
21   -375   2000.00   +497500.8778
```

You must not put a comma between the digits of a numeric constant, and not all SQL dialects allow the leading plus sign, so it's best to avoid it. For money data, most SQL implementations simply use integer or decimal constants, although some allow the constant to be specified with a currency symbol:

```
$0.75  $5000.00  $-567.89
```

Floating point constants (also called *approximate numeric literals*) are specified using the E notation commonly found in programming languages such as C and FORTRAN. Here are some valid SQL floating point constants:

```
1.5E3   -3.14159E1   2.5E-7   0.783926E21
```

The E is read "times ten to the power of," so the first constant becomes "1.5 times ten to the third power," or 1500.

String Constants

The ANSI/ISO standard specifies that SQL constants for character data be enclosed in single quotes ('. . .'), as in these examples:

```
'Jones, John J.'   'New York'   'Western'
```

If a single quote is to be included in the constant text, it is written within the constant as two consecutive single quote characters. Thus this constant value:

```
'I can''t'
```

becomes the seven-character string "I can't".

Some SQL implementations, such as SQL Server and Informix, accept string constants enclosed in double quotes (". . ."):

```
"Jones, John J."   "New York"   "Western"
```

Unfortunately, the double quotes pose portability problems with other SQL products, including some unique portability problems with SQL/DS. SQL/DS allows column names containing blanks and other special characters (in violation of the ANSI/ISO standard). When these characters appear as names in a SQL statement, they must be enclosed in double quotes. For example, if the NAME column of the SALESREPS table were called "FULL NAME" in a SQL/DS database, this SELECT statement would be valid:

```
SELECT "FULL NAME", SALES, QUOTA
  FROM SALESREPS
 WHERE "FULL NAME" = 'Jones, John J.'
```

The SQL2 standard provides the additional capability to specify string constants from a specific national character set (for example, French or German) or from a user-defined character set. These capabilities have not yet found their way into mainstream SQL implementations.

Date and Time Constants

In SQL products that support date/time data, constant values for dates, times, and time intervals are specified as string constants. The format of these constants varies from one DBMS to the next. Even more variation is introduced by the differences in the way dates and times are written in different countries.

DB2 supports several different international formats for date, time, and timestamp constants, as shown in Table 5-5. The choice of format is made when the DBMS is installed. DB2 also supports durations specified as "special" constants, as in this example:

```
HIRE_DATE + 30 DAYS
```

Note that a duration can't be stored in the database, however, because DB2 doesn't have an explicit DURATION data type.

SQL Server also supports date/time data and accepts a variety of different formats for date and time constants. The DBMS automatically accepts all of the alternate formats, and you can intermix them if you like. Here are some examples of legal SQL Server date constants:

```
March 15, 1990   Mar 15 1990   3/15/1990   3-15-90   1990 MAR 15
```

and here are some legal time constants:

```
15:30:25   3:30:25 PM   3:30:25 pm   3 PM
```

Format Name	DATE Format	DATE Example	TIME Format	TIME Example
American	mm/dd/yyyy	5/19/1960	hh:mm am/pm	2:18 PM
European	dd.mm.yyyy	19.5.1960	hh.mm.ss	14.18.08
Japanese	yyyy-mm-dd	1960-5-19	hh:mm:ss	14:18:08
ISO	yyyy-mm-dd	1960-5-19	hh.mm.ss	14.18.08
TIMESTAMP format	yyyy-mm-dd-hh.mm.ss.nnnnnn			
TIMESTAMP example	1960-05-19-14.18.08.048632			

Table 5-5.   *IBM SQL Date and Time Formats*

Oracle dates and times are also written as string constants, using this format:

```
15-MAR-90
```

You can also use Oracle's built-in TO_DATE() function to convert date constants written in other formats, as in this example:

```
SELECT NAME, AGE
  FROM SALESREPS
 WHERE HIRE_DATE = TO_DATE('JUN 14 1989', 'MON DD YYYY')
```

The SQL2 standard specifies a format for date and time constants, based on the ISO format in Table 5-5, except that time constants are written with colons instead of periods separating the hours, minutes, and seconds.

Symbolic Constants

In addition to user-supplied constants, the SQL language includes special symbolic constants that return data values maintained by the DBMS itself. For example, in some DBMS brands the symbolic constant CURRENT_DATE yields the value of the current date and can be used in queries such as the following, which lists the salespeople whose hire date is still in the future.

```
SELECT NAME, HIRE_DATE
  FROM SALESREPS
 WHERE HIRE_DATE > CURRENT_DATE
```

The SQL1 standard specified only a single symbolic constant (the USER constant described in Chapter 15), but most SQL products provide many more. Generally, a symbolic constant can appear in a SQL statement anywhere that an ordinary constant of the same data type could appear. The SQL2 standard adopted the most useful symbolic constants from current SQL implementations and provides for CURRENT_DATE, CURRENT_TIME, and CURRENT_TIMESTAMP (note the underscores!) as well as USER, SESSION_USER, and SYSTEM_USER.

Some SQL products, including SQL Server, provide access to system values through built-in functions rather than symbolic constants. The SQL Server version of the preceding query is:

```
SELECT NAME, HIRE_DATE
  FROM SALESREPS
 WHERE HIRE_DATE > GETDATE()
```

Built-in functions are described later in this chapter.

Expressions

Expressions are used in the SQL language to calculate values that are retrieved from a database and to calculate values used in searching the database. For example, this query calculates the sales of each office as a percentage of its target:

```
SELECT CITY, TARGET, SALES, (SALES/TARGET) * 100
  FROM OFFICES
```

and this query lists the offices whose sales are more than $50,000 over target:

```
SELECT CITY
  FROM OFFICES
 WHERE SALES > TARGET + 50000.00
```

The ANSI/ISO SQL standard specifies four arithmetic operations that can be used in expressions: addition $(X + Y)$, subtraction $(X - Y)$, multiplication $(X * Y)$, and division (X / Y). Parentheses can also be used to form more complicated expressions, like this one:

```
(SALES * 1.05) - (TARGET * .95)
```

Strictly speaking, the parentheses are not required in this query because the ANSI/ISO standard specifies that multiplication and division have a higher precedence than addition and subtraction. However, you should always use parentheses to make your expressions unambiguous because different SQL dialects may use different rules. The parentheses also increase the readability of the statement and make programmatic SQL statements easier to maintain.

The ANSI/ISO standard also specifies automatic data type conversion from integers to decimal numbers, and from decimal numbers to floating point numbers, as required. You can thus mix these data types in a numeric expression. Many SQL implementations support other operators and allow operations on character and date data. DB2, for example, supports a string concatenation operator, written as two consecutive vertical bar characters (||). If two columns named FIRST_NAME and LAST_NAME contain the values "Jim" and "Jackson," then this DB2 expression:

```
('Mr./Mrs. ' || FIRST_NAME || ' ' || LAST_NAME)
```

produces the string "Mr./Mrs. Jim Jackson." As already mentioned, DB2 also supports addition and subtraction of DATE, TIME, and TIMESTAMP data, for occasions when those operations make sense. This capability has been included in the SQL2 standard.

Built-in Functions

Although the SQL1 standard doesn't specify them, most SQL implementations include a number of useful *built-in functions*. These facilities often provide data type conversion facilities. For example, DB2's built-in MONTH() and YEAR() functions take a DATE or TIMESTAMP value as their input and return an integer that is the month or year portion of the value. This query lists the name and month of hire for each salesperson in the sample database:

```
SELECT NAME, MONTH(HIRE_DATE)
  FROM SALESREPS
```

and this one lists all salespeople hired in 1988:

```
SELECT NAME, MONTH(HIRE_DATE)
  FROM SALESREPS
 WHERE YEAR(HIRE_DATE) = 1988
```

Built-in functions also are often used for data reformatting. Oracle's built-in `TO_CHAR()` function, for example, takes a `DATE` data type and a format specification as its arguments and returns a string containing a formatted version of the date. In the results produced by this query:

```
SELECT NAME, TO_CHAR(HIRE_DATE, 'DAY MONTH DD, YYYY')
  FROM SALESREPS
```

the hire dates will all have the format "Wednesday June 14, 1989" because of the built-in function.

In general, a built-in function can be specified in a SQL expression anywhere that a constant of the same data type can be specified. The built-in functions supported by popular SQL dialects are too numerous to list here. The IBM SQL dialects include about two dozen built-in functions, Oracle supports a different set of about two dozen built-in functions, and SQL Server has several dozen. The SQL2 standard incorporated the most useful built-in functions from these implementations, in many cases with slightly different syntax. These functions are summarized in Table 5-6.

Missing Data (`NULL` Values)

Because a database is usually a model of a real-world situation, certain pieces of data are inevitably missing, unknown, or don't apply. In the sample database, for example, the `QUOTA` column in the `SALESREPS` table contains the sales goal for each salesperson. However, the newest salesperson has not yet been assigned a quota; this data is missing for that row of the table. You might be tempted to put a zero in the column for this salesperson, but that would not be an accurate reflection of the situation. The salesperson does not have a zero quota; the quota is just "not yet known."

Similarly, the `MANAGER` column in the `SALESREPS` table contains the employee number of each salesperson's manager. But Sam Clark, the Vice President of Sales, has no manager in the sales organization. This column does not apply to Sam. Again, you might think about entering a zero, or a 9999 in the column, but neither of these values would really be the employee number of Sam's boss. No data value is applicable to this row.

SQL supports missing, unknown, or inapplicable data explicitly, through the concept of a *null value*. A null value is an *indicator* that tells SQL (and the user) that the data is missing or not applicable. As a convenience, a missing piece of data is often said to have the value `NULL`. But the `NULL` value is not a real data value like 0, 473.83, or "Sam Clark." Instead, it's a signal, or a reminder, that the data value is missing or unknown. Figure 5-3 shows the contents of the `SALESREPS` table. Note that the `QUOTA` and `REP_OFFICE` values for Tom Snyder's row and the `MANAGER` value for Sam Clark's row of the table all contain `NULL` values.

Function	Returns
BIT_LENGTH (*string*)	Number of bits in a bit string
CAST (*value* AS *data_type*)	The value, converted to the specified data type (e.g., a date converted to a character string)
CHAR_LENGTH (*string*)	Length of a character string
CONVERT (*string* USING *conv*)	String converted as specified by a named conversion function
CURRENT_DATE	Current date
CURRENT_TIME (*precision*)	Current time, with the specified *precision*
CURRENT_TIMESTAMP (*precision*)	Current date and time, with the specified *precision*
EXTRACT (*part* FROM *source*)	Specified part (DAY, HOUR, etc.) from a DATETIME value
LOWER (*string*)	String converted to all lowercase letters
OCTET_LENGTH (*string*)	Number of 8-bit bytes in a character string
POSITION (*target* IN *source*)	Position where the *target* string appears within the *source* string
SUBSTRING (*source* FROM *n*FOR *len*)	A portion of the *source* string, beginning at the *n*-th character, for a length of *len*
TRANSLATE (*string* USING *trans*)	String translated as specified by a named translation function
TRIM (BOTH *char* FROM *string*)	String with both leading and trailing occurrences of *char* trimmed off
TRIM (LEADING *char* FROM *string*)	String with any leading occurrences of *char* trimmed off
TRIM (TRAILING *char* FROM *string*)	String with any trailing occurrences of *char* trimmed off
UPPER (*string*)	String converted to all uppercase letters

Table 5-6. *Built-in SQL2 Functions*

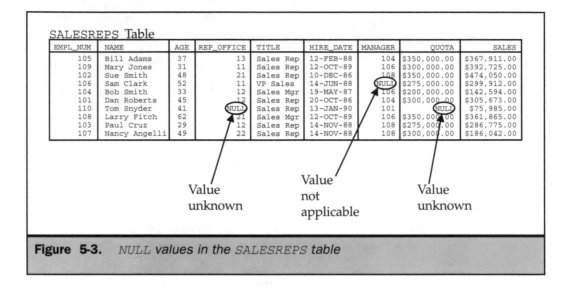

Figure 5-3.   *NULL values in the SALESREPS table*

In many situations NULL values require special handling by the DBMS. For example, if the user requests the sum of the QUOTA column, how should the DBMS handle the missing data when computing the sum? The answer is given by a set of special rules that govern NULL value handling in various SQL statements and clauses. Because of these rules, some leading database authorities feel strongly that NULL values should not be used. Others, including Dr. Codd, have advocated the use of multiple NULL values, with distinct indicators for "unknown" and "not applicable" data.

Regardless of the academic debates, NULL values are a well-entrenched part of the ANSI/ISO SQL standard and are supported in virtually all commercial SQL products. They also play an important, practical role in production SQL databases. The special rules that apply to NULL values (and the cases where NULL values are handled inconsistently by various SQL products) are pointed out in the relevant sections of this book.

Summary

This chapter described the basic elements of the SQL language. The basic structure of SQL can be summarized as follows:

- The SQL language that is in common use includes about 40 statements, each consisting of a verb and one or more clauses. Each statement performs a single, specific function.

■ SQL-based databases can store various types of data, including text, integers, decimal numbers, floating point numbers, and usually many more vendor-specific data types.

■ SQL statements can include expressions that combine column names, constants, and built-in functions, using arithmetic and other vendor-specific operators.

■ Variations in data types, constants, and built-in functions make portability of SQL statements more difficult than it may seem at first.

■ NULL values provide a systematic way of handling missing or inapplicable data in the SQL language.

Chapter 6

Simple Queries

In many ways, queries are the heart of the SQL language. The SELECT statement, which is used to express SQL queries, is the most powerful and complex of the SQL statements. Despite the many options afforded by the SELECT statement, it's possible to start simply and then work up to more complex queries. This chapter discusses the simplest SQL queries—those that retrieve data from a single table in the database.

The SELECT Statement

The SELECT statement retrieves data from a database and returns it to you in the form of query results. You have already seen many examples of the SELECT statement in the quick tour presented in Chapter 2. Here are several more sample queries that retrieve information about sales offices:

List the sales offices with their targets and actual sales.

```
SELECT CITY, TARGET, SALES
   FROM OFFICES

CITY              TARGET          SALES
------------   ------------   ------------
Denver         $300,000.00    $186,042.00
New York       $575,000.00    $692,637.00
Chicago        $800,000.00    $735,042.00
Atlanta        $350,000.00    $367,911.00
Los Angeles    $725,000.00    $835,915.00
```

List the Eastern region sales offices with their targets and sales.

```
SELECT CITY, TARGET, SALES
   FROM OFFICES
  WHERE REGION = 'Eastern'

CITY              TARGET          SALES
------------   ------------   ------------
New York       $575,000.00    $692,637.00
Chicago        $800,000.00    $735,042.00
Atlanta        $350,000.00    $367,911.00
```

List Eastern region sales offices whose sales exceed their targets, sorted in alphabetical order by city.

```
SELECT CITY, TARGET, SALES
  FROM OFFICES
 WHERE REGION = 'Eastern'
   AND SALES > TARGET
 ORDER BY CITY

CITY                TARGET          SALES
------------    ------------    ------------
Atlanta         $350,000.00     $367,911.00
New York        $575,000.00     $692,637.00
```

What are the average target and sales for Eastern region offices?

```
SELECT AVG(TARGET), AVG(SALES)
  FROM OFFICES
 WHERE REGION = 'Eastern'

 AVG(TARGET)    AVG(SALES)
------------    ------------
 $575,000.00    $598,530.00
```

For simple queries, the English language request and the SQL SELECT statement are very similar. When the requests become more complex, more features of the SELECT statement must be used to specify the query precisely.

Figure 6-1 shows the full form of the SELECT statement, which consists of six clauses. The SELECT and FROM clauses of the statement are required. The remaining four clauses are optional. You include them in a SELECT statement only when you want to use the functions they provide. The following list summarizes the function of each clause:

- The SELECT clause lists the data items to be retrieved by the SELECT statement. The items may be columns from the database, or columns to be calculated by SQL as it performs the query. The SELECT clause is described in later sections of this chapter.

- The FROM clause lists the tables that contain the data to be retrieved by the query. Queries that draw their data from a single table are described in this chapter. More complex queries that combine data from two or more tables are discussed in Chapter 7.

- The WHERE clause tells SQL to include only certain rows of data in the query results. A *search condition* is used to specify the desired rows. The basic uses of the WHERE clause are described later in this chapter. Those that involve subqueries are discussed in Chapter 9.

- The GROUP BY clause specifies a summary query. Instead of producing one row of query results for each row of data in the database, a summary query groups together similar rows and then produces one summary row of query results for each group. Summary queries are described in Chapter 8.

- The HAVING clause tells SQL to include only certain groups produced by the GROUP BY clause in the query results. Like the WHERE clause, it uses a search condition to specify the desired groups. The HAVING clause is described in Chapter 8.

- The ORDER BY clause sorts the query results based on the data in one or more columns. If it is omitted, the query results are not sorted. The ORDER BY clause is described later in this chapter.

The SELECT Clause

The SELECT clause that begins each SELECT statement specifies the data items to be retrieved by the query. The items are usually specified by a *select list*, a list of *select items* separated by commas. Each select item in the list generates a single column of query results, in left-to-right order. A select item can be:

- a *column name*, identifying a column from the table(s) named in the FROM clause. When a column name appears as a select item, SQL simply takes the value of that column from each row of the database table and places it in the corresponding row of query results.

- a *constant*, specifying that the same constant value is to appear in every row of the query results.

- a *SQL expression*, indicating that SQL must calculate the value to be placed into the query results, in the style specified by the expression.

Each type of select item is described later in this chapter.

The FROM Clause

The FROM clause consists of the keyword FROM, followed by a list of table specifications separated by commas. Each table specification identifies a table containing data to be retrieved by the query. These tables are called the *source tables* of the query (and of the SELECT statement) because they are the source of all of the data in the query results. All of the queries in this chapter have a single source table, and every FROM clause contains a single table name.

Query Results

The result of a SQL query is always a table of data, just like the tables in the database. If you type a SELECT statement using interactive SQL, the DBMS displays the query

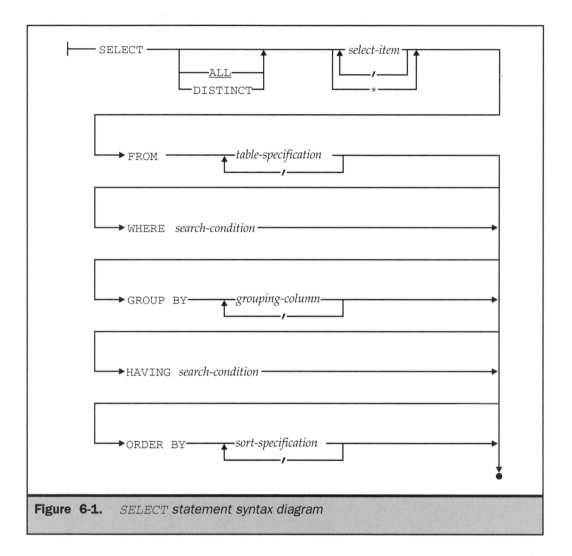

Figure 6-1. *SELECT statement syntax diagram*

results in tabular form on your computer screen. If a program sends a query to the DBMS using programmatic SQL, the table of query results is returned to the program. In either case, the query results always have the same tabular, row/column format as the actual tables in the database, as shown in Figure 6-2. Usually the query results will be a table with several columns and several rows. For example, this query produces a table of three columns (because it asks for three items of data) and ten rows (because there are ten salespeople):

List the names, offices, and hire dates of all salespeople.

```
SELECT NAME, REP_OFFICE, HIRE_DATE
  FROM SALESREPS

NAME            REP_OFFICE HIRE_DATE
-------------- ----------- ----------
Bill Adams             13 12-FEB-88
Mary Jones             11 12-OCT-89
Sue Smith              21 10-DEC-86
Sam Clark              11 14-JUN-88
Bob Smith              12 19-MAY-87
Dan Roberts            12 20-OCT-86
Tom Snyder           NULL 13-JAN-90
Larry Fitch            21 12-OCT-89
Paul Cruz              12 01-MAR-87
Nancy Angelli          22 14-NOV-88
```

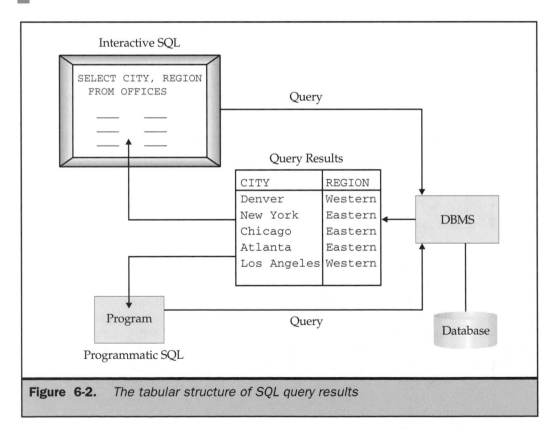

Figure 6-2. *The tabular structure of SQL query results*

In contrast, the following query produces a single row because only one salesperson has the requested employee number. Even though this single row of query results looks less "tabular" than the multi-row results, SQL still considers it to be a table of three columns and one row.

What are the name, quota, and sales of employee number 107?

```
SELECT NAME, QUOTA, SALES
  FROM SALESREPS
 WHERE EMPL_NUM = 107

NAME                    QUOTA         SALES
-------------- ------------ ------------
Nancy Angelli    $300,000.00   $186,042.00
```

In some cases the query results can be a single value, as in the following example:

What are the average sales of our salespeople?

```
SELECT AVG(SALES)
  FROM SALESREPS

  AVG(SALES)
  ------------
  $289,353.20
```

These query results are still a table, although it's a very small one consisting of one column and one row.

Finally, it's possible for a query to produce *zero* rows of query results, as in this example:

List the name and hire date of anyone with sales over $500,000.

```
SELECT NAME, HIRE_DATE
  FROM SALESREPS
 WHERE SALES > 500000.00

NAME            HIRE_DATE
------------ ----------
```

Even in this situation, the query results are still a table. This one is an empty table with two columns and zero rows.

Note that SQL's support for missing data extends to query results as well. If a data item in the database has a NULL value, the NULL value appears in the query results when the data item is retrieved. For example, the SALESREPS table contains NULL values in its QUOTA and MANAGER columns. The following query returns these NULL values in the second and third columns of query results:

List the salespeople, their quotas, and their managers.

```
SELECT NAME, QUOTA, MANAGER
   FROM SALESREPS

NAME                   QUOTA   MANAGER
--------------  ------------  --------
Bill Adams        $350,000.00      104
Mary Jones        $300,000.00      106
Sue Smith         $350,000.00      108
Sam Clark         $275,000.00     NULL
Bob Smith         $200,000.00      106
Dan Roberts       $300,000.00      104
Tom Snyder               NULL      101
Larry Fitch       $350,000.00      106
Paul Cruz         $275,000.00      104
Nancy Angelli     $300,000.00      108
```

The fact that a SQL query always produces a table of data is very important. It means that the query results can be stored back into the database as a table. It means that the results of two similar queries can be combined to form a larger table of query results. Finally, it means that the query results can themselves be the target of further queries. A relational database's tabular structure thus has a very synergistic relationship with the relational query facilities of SQL. Tables can be queried, and queries produce tables.

Simple Queries

The simplest SQL queries request columns of data from a single table in the database. For example, this query requests three columns from the OFFICES table:

List the location, region, and sales of each sales office.

```
SELECT CITY, REGION, SALES
   FROM OFFICES
```

CITY	REGION	SALES
Denver	Western	$186,042.00
New York	Eastern	$692,637.00
Chicago	Eastern	$735,042.00
Atlanta	Eastern	$367,911.00
Los Angeles	Western	$835,915.00

The SELECT statement for simple queries like this one includes only the two required clauses. The SELECT clause names the requested columns; the FROM clause names the table that contains them.

Conceptually, SQL processes the query by going through the table named in the FROM clause, one row at a time, as shown in Figure 6-3. For each row, SQL takes the values of the columns requested in the select list and produces a single row of query results. The query results thus contain one row of data for each row in the table.

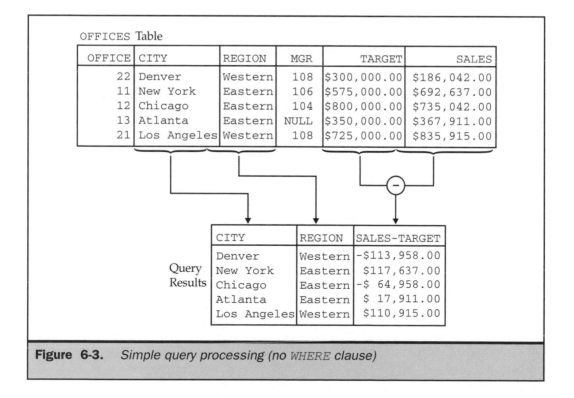

Figure 6-3. *Simple query processing (no WHERE clause)*

Calculated Columns

In addition to columns whose values come directly from the database, a SQL query can include *calculated columns* whose values are calculated from the stored data values. To request a calculated column, you specify a SQL expression in the select list. As discussed in Chapter 5, SQL expressions can involve addition, subtraction, multiplication, and division. You can also use parentheses to build more complex expressions. Of course the columns referenced in an arithmetic expression must have a numeric type. If you try to add, subtract, multiply, or divide columns containing text data, SQL will report an error.

This query shows a simple calculated column:

List the city, region, and amount over/under target for each office.

```
SELECT CITY, REGION, (SALES - TARGET)
  FROM OFFICES

CITY          REGION     (SALES-TARGET)
------------  --------   ---------------
Denver        Western      -$113,958.00
New York      Eastern       $117,637.00
Chicago       Eastern       -$64,958.00
Atlanta       Eastern        $17,911.00
Los Angeles   Western       $110,915.00
```

To process the query, SQL goes through the offices, generating one row of query results for each row of the OFFICES table, as shown in Figure 6-4. The first two columns of query results come directly from the OFFICES table. The third column of query results is calculated, row-by-row, using the data values from the current row of the OFFICES table.

Here are other examples of queries that use calculated columns:

Show the value of the inventory for each product.

```
SELECT MFR_ID, PRODUCT_ID, DESCRIPTION, (QTY_ON_HAND * PRICE)
  FROM PRODUCTS

MFR_ID  PRODUCT_ID  DESCRIPTION       (QTY_ON_HAND*PRICE)
------  ----------  ---------------   --------------------
REI     2A45C       Ratchet Link               $16,590.00
ACI     4100Y       Widget Remover             $68,750.00
```

```
QSA    XK47       Reducer            $13,490.00
BIC    41672      Plate                   $0.00
IMM    779C       900-lb Brace       $16,875.00
ACI    41003      Size 3 Widget      $22,149.00
ACI    41004      Size 4 Widget      $16,263.00
BIC    41003      Handle              $1,956.00
```

Show me the result if I raised each salesperson's quota by 3 percent of their year-to-date sales.

```
SELECT NAME, QUOTA, (QUOTA + (.03*SALES))
   FROM SALESREPS

NAME                 QUOTA   (QUOTA+(.03*SALES))
--------------    ------------    --------------------
Bill Adams        $350,000.00         $361,037.33
Mary Jones        $300,000.00         $311,781.75
Sue Smith         $350,000.00         $364,221.50
Sam Clark         $275,000.00         $283,997.36
Bob Smith         $200,000.00         $204,277.82
Dan Roberts       $300,000.00         $309,170.19
Tom Snyder               NULL                NULL
Larry Fitch       $350,000.00         $360,855.95
Paul Cruz         $275,000.00         $283,603.25
Nancy Angelli     $300,000.00         $305,581.26
```

As mentioned in Chapter 5, many SQL products provide additional arithmetic operations, character string operations, and built-in functions that can be used in SQL expressions. These can appear in select list expressions, as in this DB2 example:

List the name and month and year of hire for each salesperson.

```
SELECT NAME, MONTH(HIRE_DATE), YEAR(HIRE_DATE)
   FROM SALESREPS
```

SQL constants can also be used by themselves as items in a select list. This can be useful for producing query results that are easier to read and interpret, as in the example on the bottom of the next page.

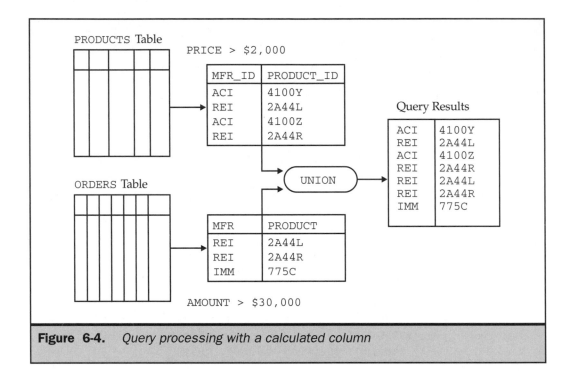

Figure 6-4. *Query processing with a calculated column*

List the sales for each city.

```
SELECT CITY, 'has sales of', SALES
  FROM OFFICES

CITY          HAS SALES OF           SALES
------------  -------------  ------------
Denver        has sales of    $186,042.00
New York      has sales of    $692,637.00
Chicago       has sales of    $735,042.00
Atlanta       has sales of    $367,911.00
Los Angeles   has sales of    $835,915.00
```

The query results appear to consist of a separate "sentence" for each office, but they're really a table of three columns. The first and third columns contain values from the OFFICES table. The second column always contains the same 12-character text string. This distinction is subtle when the query results are displayed on a screen, but it is crucial in programmatic SQL, when the results are being retrieved into a program and used for calculations.

Selecting All Columns (`SELECT *`)

Sometimes it's convenient to display the contents of all the columns of a table. This can be particularly useful when you first encounter a new database and want to get a quick understanding of its structure and the data it contains. As a convenience, SQL lets you use an asterisk (*) in place of the select list as an abbreviation for "all columns":

Show me all the data in the `OFFICES` *table.*

```
SELECT *
  FROM OFFICES

OFFICE CITY          REGION    MGR       TARGET        SALES
------ ------------  --------  ----  ------------  ------------
    22 Denver        Western   108   $300,000.00   $186,042.00
    11 New York      Eastern   106   $575,000.00   $692,637.00
    12 Chicago       Eastern   104   $800,000.00   $735,042.00
    13 Atlanta       Eastern   105   $350,000.00   $367,911.00
    21 Los Angeles   Western   108   $725,000.00   $835,915.00
```

The query results contain all six columns of the `OFFICES` table, in the same left-to-right order as in the table itself.

The ANSI/ISO SQL standard specifies that a `SELECT` statement can have either an all-column selection or a select list, but not both, as shown in Figure 6-1. However, many SQL implementations treat the asterisk (*) as just another element of the select list. Thus the query:

```
SELECT *, (SALES - TARGET)
  FROM OFFICES
```

is legal in most commercial SQL dialects (for example in DB2, Oracle, and SQL Server), but it is not permitted by the ANSI/ISO standard.

The all-columns selection is most appropriate when you are using interactive SQL casually. It should be avoided in programmatic SQL, because changes in the database structure can cause a program to fail. For example, suppose the `OFFICES` table were dropped from the database and then re-created with its columns rearranged and a new seventh column added. SQL automatically takes care of the database-related details of such changes, but it cannot modify your application program for you. If your program expects a `SELECT * FROM OFFICES` query to return six columns of query results with certain data types, it will almost certainly stop working when the columns are rearranged and a new one is added.

These difficulties can be avoided if you write the program to request the columns it needs by name. For example, the following query produces the same results as SELECT * FROM OFFICES. It is also immune to changes in the database structure, as long as the named columns continue to exist in the OFFICES table:

```
SELECT OFFICE, CITY, REGION, MGR, TARGET, SALES
  FROM OFFICES
```

Duplicate Rows (DISTINCT)

If a query includes the primary key of a table in its select list, then every row of query results will be unique (because the primary key has a different value in each row). If the primary key is not included in the query results, duplicate rows can occur. For example, suppose you made this request:

List the employee numbers of all sales office managers.

```
SELECT MGR
  FROM OFFICES

 MGR
----
 108
 106
 104
 105
 108
```

The query results have five rows (one for each office), but two of them are exact duplicates of one another. Why? Because Larry Fitch manages both the Los Angeles and Denver offices, and his employee number (108) appears in both rows of the OFFICES table. These query results are probably not exactly what you had in mind. If there are four different managers, you might have expected only four employee numbers in the query results.

You can eliminate duplicate rows of query results by inserting the keyword DISTINCT in the SELECT statement just before the select list. Here is a version of the previous query that produces the results you want:

List the employee numbers of all sales office managers.

```
SELECT DISTINCT MGR
  FROM OFFICES

 MGR
 ----
  104
  105
  106
  108
```

Conceptually, SQL carries out this query by first generating a full set of query results (five rows) and then eliminating rows that are exact duplicates of one another to form the final query results. The DISTINCT keyword can be specified regardless of the contents of the SELECT list (with certain restrictions for summary queries, as described in Chapter 8).

If the DISTINCT keyword is omitted, SQL does not eliminate duplicate rows. You can also specify the keyword ALL to explicitly indicate that duplicate rows are to be retained, but it is unnecessary since this is the default behavior.

Row Selection (WHERE Clause)

SQL queries that retrieve all rows of a table are useful for database browsing and reports, but for little else. Usually you'll want to select only some of the rows in a table and include only these rows in the query results. The WHERE clause is used to specify the rows you want to retrieve. Here are some examples of simple queries that use the WHERE clause:

Show me the offices where sales exceed target.

```
SELECT CITY, SALES, TARGET
  FROM OFFICES
 WHERE SALES > TARGET

CITY                 SALES        TARGET
------------  ------------  ------------
New York       $692,637.00   $575,000.00
Atlanta        $367,911.00   $350,000.00
Los Angeles    $835,915.00   $725,000.00
```

Show me the name, sales, and quota of employee number 105.

```
SELECT NAME, SALES, QUOTA
  FROM SALESREPS
 WHERE EMPL_NUM = 105
```

```
NAME                SALES        QUOTA
----------- ------------ ------------
Bill Adams    $367,911.00  $350,000.00
```

Show me the employees managed by Bob Smith (employee 104).

```
SELECT NAME, SALES
  FROM SALESREPS
 WHERE MANAGER = 104
```

```
NAME                SALES
----------- ------------
Bill Adams    $367,911.00
Dan Roberts   $305,673.00
Paul Cruz     $286,775.00
```

The WHERE clause consists of the keyword WHERE followed by a search condition that specifies the rows to be retrieved. In the previous query, for example, the search condition is MANAGER = 104. Figure 6-5 shows how the WHERE clause works. Conceptually, SQL goes through each row of the SALESREPS table, one-by-one, and applies the search condition to the row. When a column name appears in the search condition (such as the MANAGER column in this example), SQL uses the value of the column in the current row. For each row, the search condition can produce one of three results:

- If the search condition is TRUE, the row is included in the query results. For example, the row for Bill Adams has the correct MANAGER value and is included.

- If the search condition is FALSE, the row is excluded from the query results. For example, the row for Sue Smith has the wrong MANAGER value and is excluded.

- If the search condition has a NULL (unknown) value, the row is excluded from the query results. For example, the row for Sam Clark has a NULL value for the MANAGER column and is excluded.

Figure 6-6 shows another way to think about the role of the search condition in the WHERE clause. Basically, the search condition acts as a filter for rows of the table. Rows that satisfy the search condition pass through the filter and become part of the query results. Rows that do not satisfy the search condition are trapped by the filter and excluded from the query results.

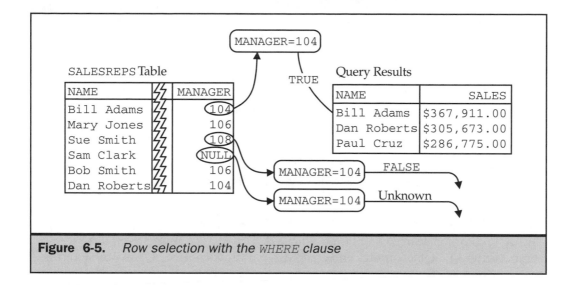

Figure 6-5. *Row selection with the* WHERE *clause*

Search Conditions

SQL offers a rich set of search conditions that allow you to specify many different kinds of queries efficiently and naturally. Five basic search conditions (called *predicates* in the ANSI/ISO standard) are summarized here and are described in the sections that follow:

■ *Comparison test*. Compares the value of one expression to the value of another expression. Use this test to select offices in the Eastern region, or salespeople whose sales are above their quotas.

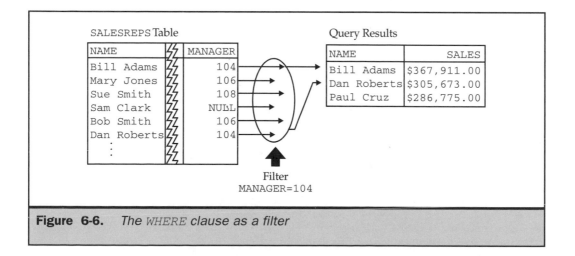

Figure 6-6. *The* WHERE *clause as a filter*

- *Range test.* Tests whether the value of an expression falls within a specified range of values. Use this test to find salespeople whose sales are between $100,000 and $500,000.

- *Set membership test.* Checks whether the value of an expression matches one of a set of values. Use this test to select offices located in New York, Chicago, or Los Angeles.

- *Pattern matching test.* Checks whether the value of a column containing string data matches a specified pattern. Use this test to select customers whose names start with the letter "E."

- *Null value test.* Checks whether a column has a NULL (unknown) value. Use this test to find the salespeople who have not yet been assigned to a manager.

Comparison Test (=, <>, <, <=, >, >=)

The most common search condition used in a SQL query is a comparison test. In a comparison test, SQL computes and compares the values of two SQL expressions for each row of data. The expressions can be as simple as a column name or a constant, or they can be more complex arithmetic expressions. SQL offers six different ways of comparing the two expressions, as shown in Figure 6-7. Here are some examples of typical comparison tests:

Find salespeople hired before 1988.

```
SELECT NAME
  FROM SALESREPS
 WHERE HIRE_DATE < '01-JAN-88'

NAME
------------
Sue Smith
Bob Smith
Dan Roberts
Paul Cruz
```

List the offices whose sales fall below 80 percent of target.

```
SELECT CITY, SALES, TARGET
  FROM OFFICES
 WHERE SALES < (.8 * TARGET)

CITY         SALES        TARGET
-------  ------------  ------------
Denver   $186,042.00   $300,000.00
```

List the offices not managed by employee number 108.

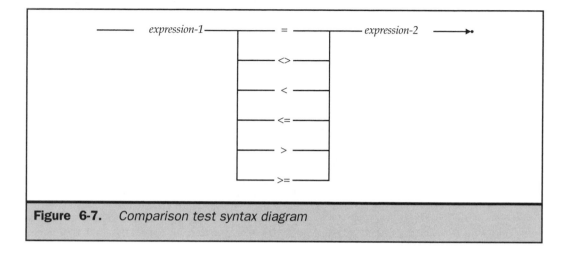

Figure 6-7.   *Comparison test syntax diagram*

```
SELECT CITY, MGR
  FROM OFFICES
 WHERE MGR <> 108

CITY        MGR
---------   ----
New York    106
Chicago     104
Atlanta     105
```

As shown in Figure 6-7, the inequality comparison test is written as "A < > B" according to the ANSI/ISO SQL specification. Several SQL implementations use alternate notations, such as "A != B" (used by SQL Server) and "A¬=B" (used by DB2 and SQL/DS). In some cases, these are alternative forms; in others, they are the only acceptable form of the inequality test.

When SQL compares the values of the two expressions in the comparison test, three results can occur:

- If the comparison is true, the test yields a TRUE result.
- If the comparison is false, the test yields a FALSE result.
- If either of the two expressions produces a NULL value, the comparison yields a NULL result.

Single-Row Retrieval

The most common comparison test is one that checks whether a column's value is equal to some constant. When the column is a primary key, the test isolates a single row of the table, producing a single row of query results, as in this example:

Retrieve the name and credit limit of customer number 2107.

```
SELECT COMPANY, CREDIT_LIMIT
   FROM CUSTOMERS
 WHERE CUST_NUM = 2107

COMPANY              CREDIT_LIMIT
------------------   -------------
Ace International       $35,000.00
```

This type of query is the foundation of forms-based database retrieval programs. The user enters a customer number into the form, and the program uses the number to construct and execute a query. It then displays the retrieved data in the form.

Note that the SQL statements for retrieving a specific customer by number, as in this example, and retrieving all customers with a certain characteristic (such as those with credit limits over $25,000) both have exactly the same form. These two types of queries (retrieval by primary key and retrieval based on a search of the data) would be very different operations in a nonrelational database. This uniformity of approach makes SQL much simpler to learn and use than earlier query languages.

NULL Value Considerations

The behavior of NULL values in comparison tests can reveal some "obviously true" notions about SQL queries to be, in fact, not necessarily true. For example, it would seem that the results of these two queries:

List salespeople who are over quota.

```
SELECT NAME
   FROM SALESREPS
 WHERE SALES > QUOTA

NAME
------------
Bill Adams
Mary Jones
Sue Smith
```

Sam Clark
Dan Roberts
Larry Fitch
Paul Cruz

List salespeople who are under or at quota.

```
SELECT NAME
  FROM SALESREPS
 WHERE SALES < = QUOTA

NAME
--------------
Bob Smith
Nancy Angelli
```

would include every row of the SALESREPS table, but the queries produce seven and two rows, respectively, for a total of nine rows, while there are ten rows in the SALESREPS table. Tom Snyder's row has a NULL value in the QUOTA column because he has not yet been assigned a quota. This row is not listed by either query; it "vanishes" in the comparison test.

As this example shows, you need to think about NULL value handling when you specify a search condition. In SQL's three-valued logic, a search condition can yield a TRUE, FALSE, or NULL result. Only rows where the search condition yields a TRUE result are included in the query results.

Range Test (BETWEEN)

SQL provides a different form of search condition with the range test (BETWEEN) shown in Figure 6-8. The range test checks whether a data value lies between two specified values. It involves three SQL expressions. The first expression defines the value to be tested; the second and third expressions define the low and high ends of the range to be checked. The data types of the three expressions must be comparable.

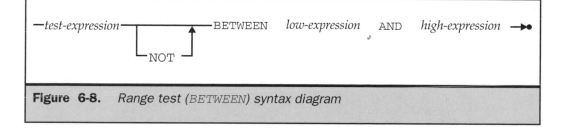

Figure 6-8. *Range test (BETWEEN) syntax diagram*

This example shows a typical range test:

Find orders placed in the last quarter of 1989.

```
SELECT ORDER_NUM, ORDER_DATE, MFR, PRODUCT, AMOUNT
  FROM ORDERS
 WHERE ORDER_DATE BETWEEN '01-OCT-89' AND '31-DEC-89'

ORDER_NUM ORDER_DATE  MFR  PRODUCT      AMOUNT
--------- ----------- ---- -------- -----------
   112961 17-DEC-89   REI  2A44L    $31,500.00
   112968 12-OCT-89   ACI  41004     $3,978.00
   112963 17-DEC-89   ACI  41004     $3,276.00
   112983 27-DEC-89   ACI  41004       $702.00
   112979 12-OCT-89   ACI  4100Z    $15,000.00
   112992 04-NOV-89   ACI  41002       $760.00
   112975 12-OCT-89   REI  2A44G     $2,100.00
   112987 31-DEC-89   ACI  4100Y    $27,500.00
```

The BETWEEN test includes the endpoints of the range, so orders placed on October 1 or December 31 are included in the query results. Here is another example of a range test:

Find the orders that fall into various amount ranges.

```
SELECT ORDER_NUM, AMOUNT
  FROM ORDERS
 WHERE AMOUNT BETWEEN 20000.00 AND 29999.99

ORDER_NUM      AMOUNT
--------- -----------
   113036  $22,500.00
   112987  $27,500.00
   113042  $22,500.00

SELECT ORDER_NUM, AMOUNT
  FROM ORDERS
 WHERE AMOUNT BETWEEN 30000.00 AND 39999.99

ORDER_NUM      AMOUNT
--------- -----------
   112961  $31,500.00
   113069  $31,350.00
```

```
SELECT ORDER_NUM, AMOUNT
  FROM ORDERS
 WHERE AMOUNT BETWEEN 40000.00 AND 49999.99

ORDER_NUM      AMOUNT
---------- -----------
   113045  $45,000.00
```

The negated version of the range test (NOT BETWEEN) checks for values that fall outside the range, as in this example:

List salespeople whose sales are not between 80 percent and 120 percent of quota.

```
SELECT NAME, SALES, QUOTA
  FROM SALESREPS
 WHERE SALES NOT BETWEEN (.8 * QUOTA) AND (1.2 * QUOTA)

NAME                 SALES        QUOTA
-------------- ------------ ------------
Mary Jones      $392,725.00  $300,000.00
Sue Smith       $474,050.00  $350,000.00
Bob Smith       $142,594.00  $200,000.00
Nancy Angelli   $186,042.00  $300,000.00
```

The test expression specified in the BETWEEN test can be any valid SQL expression, but in practice it's usually just a column name, as in the previous examples.

The ANSI/ISO standard defines relatively complex rules for the handling of NULL values in the BETWEEN test:

- If the test expression produces a NULL value, or if *both* expressions defining the range produce NULL values, then the BETWEEN test returns a NULL result.

- If the expression defining the lower end of the range produces a NULL value, then the BETWEEN test returns FALSE if the test value is greater than the upper bound, and NULL otherwise.

- If the expression defining the upper end of the range produces a NULL value, then the BETWEEN test returns FALSE if the test value is less than the lower bound, and NULL otherwise.

Before relying on this behavior, it's a good idea to experiment with your DBMS.

It's worth noting that the BETWEEN test doesn't really add to the expressive power of SQL, because it can be expressed as two comparison tests. The range test:

```
A BETWEEN B AND C
```

is completely equivalent to:

```
(A >= B) AND (A < = C)
```

However, the BETWEEN test is a simpler way to express a search condition when you're thinking of it in terms of a range of values.

Set Membership Test (IN)

Another common search condition is the set membership test (IN), shown in Figure 6-9. It tests whether a data value matches one of a list of target values. Here are several queries that use the set membership test:

List the salespeople who work in New York, Atlanta, or Denver.

```
SELECT NAME, QUOTA, SALES
  FROM SALESREPS
 WHERE REP_OFFICE IN (11, 13, 22)

NAME                   QUOTA          SALES
-------------- ------------ ------------
Bill Adams       $350,000.00  $367,911.00
Mary Jones       $300,000.00  $392,725.00
Sam Clark        $275,000.00  $299,912.00
Nancy Angelli    $300,000.00  $186,042.00
```

Find all orders placed on a Thursday in January 1990.

```
SELECT ORDER_NUM, ORDER_DATE, AMOUNT
  FROM ORDERS
 WHERE ORDER_DATE IN ('04-JAN-90', '11-JAN-90', '18-JAN-90', '25-JAN-90')

ORDER_NUM ORDER_DATE       AMOUNT
---------- ----------- ----------
    113012 11-JAN-90     $3,745.00
    113003 25-JAN-90     $5,625.00
```

Find all orders placed with four specific salespeople.

```
SELECT ORDER_NUM, REP, AMOUNT
  FROM ORDERS
 WHERE REP IN (107, 109, 101, 103)

ORDER_NUM   REP      AMOUNT
----------  ----  -----------
    112968  101    $3,978.00
    113058  109    $1,480.00
    112997  107      $652.00
    113062  107    $2,430.00
    113069  107   $31,350.00
    112975  103    $2,100.00
    113055  101      $150.00
    113003  109    $5,625.00
    113057  103      $600.00
    113042  101   $22,500.00
```

You can check if the data value does *not* match any of the target values by using the NOT IN form of the set membership test. The test expression in an IN test can be any SQL expression, but it's usually just a column name, as in the preceding examples. If the test expression produces a NULL value, the IN test returns NULL. All of the items in the list of target values must have the same data type, and that type must be comparable to the data type of the test expression.

Like the BETWEEN test, the IN test doesn't add to the expressive power of SQL, because the search condition:

```
X IN (A, B, C)
```

is completely equivalent to:

```
(X = A) OR (X = B) OR (X = C)
```

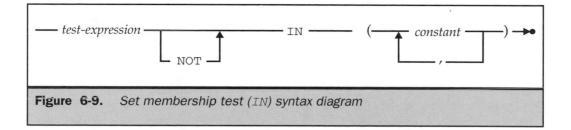

Figure 6-9.   *Set membership test (IN) syntax diagram*

However, the IN test offers a much more efficient way of expressing the search condition, especially if the set contains more than a few values. The ANSI/ISO SQL standard doesn't specify a maximum limit to the number of items that can appear in the value list, and most commercial implementations do not state an explicit upper limit either. For portability reasons, it's generally a good idea to avoid lists with only a single item, such as this one:

```
CITY IN ('New York')
```

and replace them with a simple comparison test:

```
CITY = 'New York'
```

Pattern Matching Test (LIKE)

A simple comparison test can be used to retrieve rows where the contents of a text column match some particular text. For example, this query retrieves a row of the CUSTOMERS table by name:

Show the credit limit for Smithson Corp.

```
SELECT COMPANY, CREDIT_LIMIT
  FROM CUSTOMERS
 WHERE COMPANY = 'Smithson Corp.'
```

However, you might easily forget whether the company's name was "Smith," "Smithson," or "Smithsonian." SQL's pattern matching test can be used to retrieve the data based on a partial match of the customer's name.

The pattern matching test (LIKE), shown in Figure 6-10, checks to see whether the data value in a column matches a specified *pattern*. The pattern is a string that may include one or more *wildcard* characters. These characters are interpreted in a special way.

Wildcard Characters

The percent sign (%) wildcard character matches any sequence of zero or more characters. Here's a modified version of the previous query that uses the percent sign for pattern matching:

```
SELECT COMPANY, CREDIT_LIMIT
  FROM CUSTOMERS
 WHERE COMPANY LIKE 'Smith% Corp.'
```

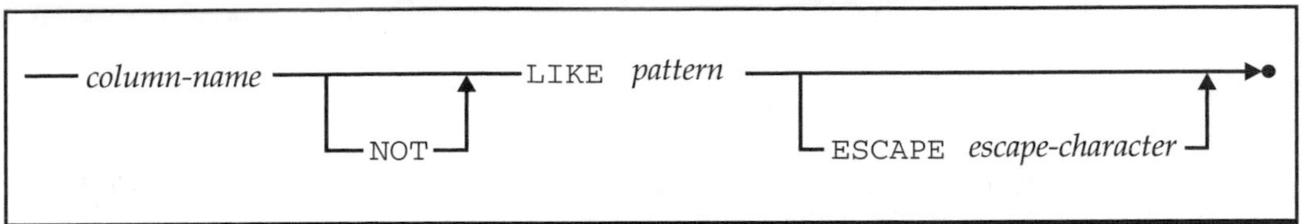

Figure 6-10. *Pattern matching test (LIKE) syntax diagram*

The LIKE keyword tells SQL to compare the NAME column to the pattern `"Smith%`
`Corp."` Any of the following names would match the pattern:

```
Smith Corp.    Smithson Corp.    Smithsen Corp.    Smithsonian Corp.
```

but these names would not:

```
SmithCorp     Smithson Inc.
```

The underscore (_) wildcard character matches any single character. If you are sure
that the company's name is either "Smithson" or "Smithsen," for example, you can use
this query:

```
SELECT COMPANY, CREDIT_LIMIT
  FROM CUSTOMERS
 WHERE COMPANY LIKE 'Smiths_n Corp.'
```

In this case, any of these names will match the pattern:

```
Smithson Corp.    Smithsen Corp.    Smithsun Corp.
```

but these names will not:

```
Smithsoon Corp.    Smithsn Corp.
```

Wildcard characters can appear anywhere in the pattern string, and several
wildcard characters can be within a single string. This query allows either the
"Smithson" or "Smithsen" spelling and will also accept "Corp.," "Inc.," or any other
ending on the company name:

```
SELECT COMPANY, CREDIT_LIMIT
  FROM CUSTOMERS
 WHERE COMPANY LIKE 'Smiths_n %'
```

You can locate strings that do *not* match a pattern by using the NOT LIKE form of the pattern matching test. The LIKE test must be applied to a column with a string data type. If the data value in the column is NULL, the LIKE test returns a NULL result.

If you have used computers through a command-line interface (such as the Unix shell), you've probably seen string pattern matching before. Frequently, the asterisk (*) is used instead of SQL's percent sign (%), and the question mark (?) is used instead of SQL's underscore (_), but the pattern matching capabilities themselves are similar in most situations where a computer application offers the ability to match selected parts of a word or text.

Escape Characters *

One of the problems with string pattern matching is how to match the wildcard characters themselves as literal characters. To test for the presence of a percent sign character in a column of text data, for example, you can't simply include the percent sign in the pattern because SQL will treat it as a wildcard. With some popular SQL products, you cannot literally match the two wildcard characters. This usually doesn't pose serious problems, because the wildcard characters don't frequently appear in names, product numbers, and other text data of the sort that is usually stored in a database.

The ANSI/ISO SQL standard does specify a way to literally match wildcard characters, using a special *escape character*. When the escape character appears in the pattern, the character immediately following it is treated as a literal character rather than as a wildcard character. (The latter character is said to be *escaped*.) The escaped character can be either of the two wildcard characters, or the escape character itself, which has now taken on a special meaning within the pattern.

The escape character is specified as a one-character constant string in the ESCAPE clause of the search condition, as shown in Figure 6-10. Here is an example using a dollar sign ($) as the escape character:

Find products whose product IDs start with the four letters "A%BC".

```
SELECT ORDER_NUM, PRODUCT
  FROM ORDERS
 WHERE PRODUCT LIKE 'A$%BC%' ESCAPE '$'
```

The first percent sign in the pattern, which follows an escape character, is treated as a literal percent sign; the second functions as a wildcard.

The use of escape characters is very common in pattern matching applications, which is why the ANSI/ISO standard specified it. However, it was not a part of the early SQL implementations and has been slowly adopted. To insure portability, the ESCAPE clause should be avoided.

Null Value Test (`IS NULL`)

NULL values create a three-valued logic for SQL search conditions. For any given row, the result of a search condition may be TRUE or FALSE, or it may be NULL because one of the columns used in evaluating the search condition contains a NULL value. Sometimes it's useful to check explicitly for NULL values in a search condition and handle them directly. SQL provides a special NULL value test (IS NULL), shown in Figure 6-11, to handle this task.

This query uses the NULL value test to find the salesperson in the sample database who has not yet been assigned to an office:

Find the salesperson not yet assigned to an office.

```
SELECT NAME
  FROM SALESREPS
 WHERE REP_OFFICE IS NULL

NAME
-----------
Tom Snyder
```

The negated form of the NULL value test (IS NOT NULL) finds rows that do not contain a NULL value:

List the salespeople who have been assigned to an office.

```
SELECT NAME
  FROM SALESREPS
 WHERE REP_OFFICE IS NOT NULL

NAME
--------------
Bill Adams
Mary Jones
Sue Smith
Sam Clark
Bob Smith
```

```
Dan Roberts
Larry Fitch
Paul Cruz
Nancy Angelli
```

Unlike the previously described search conditions, the NULL value test cannot yield a NULL result. It is always either TRUE or FALSE.

It may seem strange that you can't just test for a NULL value using a simple comparison search condition, such as this:

```
SELECT NAME
  FROM SALESREPS
 WHERE REP_OFFICE = NULL
```

The NULL keyword can't be used here because it isn't really a value; it's just a signal that the value is unknown. Even if the comparison test:

```
REP_OFFICE = NULL
```

were legal, the rules for handling NULL values in comparisons would cause it to behave differently from what you might expect. When SQL encountered a row where the REP_OFFICE column was NULL, the search condition would test:

```
NULL = NULL
```

Is the result TRUE or FALSE? Because the values on both sides of the equal sign are unknown, SQL can't tell, so the rules of SQL logic say that the search condition itself must yield a NULL result. Because the search condition doesn't produce a true result, the row is excluded from the query results—precisely the opposite of what you wanted

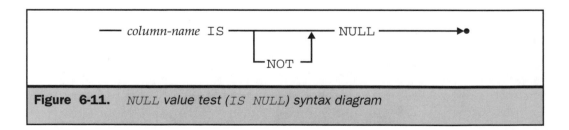

Figure 6-11. *NULL value test (IS NULL) syntax diagram*

to happen! As a result of the way SQL handles NULLs in comparisons, you must explicitly use the NULL value test to check for NULL values.

Compound Search Conditions (AND, OR, and NOT)

The simple search conditions described in the preceding sections return a value of TRUE, FALSE, or NULL when applied to a row of data. Using the rules of logic, you can combine these simple SQL search conditions to form more complex ones, as shown in Figure 6-12. Note that the search conditions combined with AND, OR, and NOT may themselves be compound search conditions.

The keyword OR is used to combine two search conditions when one or the other (or both) must be true:

Find salespeople who are under quota or with sales under $300,000.

```
SELECT NAME, QUOTA, SALES
   FROM SALESREPS
  WHERE SALES < QUOTA
     OR SALES < 300000.00
```

NAME	QUOTA	SALES
Sam Clark	$275,000.00	$299,912.00
Bob Smith	$200,000.00	$142,594.00
Tom Snyder	NULL	$75,985.00
Paul Cruz	$275,000.00	$286,775.00
Nancy Angelli	$300,000.00	$186,042.00

You can also use the keyword AND to combine two search conditions that must both be true:

Find salespeople who are under quota and with sales under $300,000.

```
SELECT NAME, QUOTA, SALES
   FROM SALESREPS
  WHERE SALES < QUOTA
    AND SALES < 300000.00
```

NAME	QUOTA	SALES
Bob Smith	$200,000.00	$142,594.00
Nancy Angelli	$300,000.00	$186,042.00

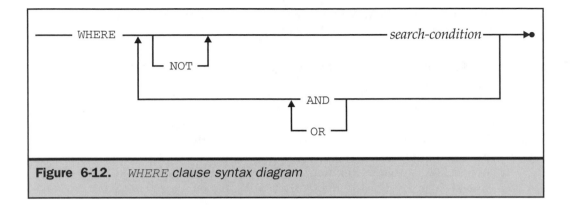

Figure 6-12.   *WHERE clause syntax diagram*

Finally, you can use the keyword NOT to select rows where a search condition is false:

Find all salespeople who are under quota, but whose sales are not under $150,000.

```
SELECT NAME, QUOTA, SALES
  FROM SALESREPS
 WHERE SALES < QUOTA
   AND NOT SALES < 150000.00

NAME                 QUOTA        SALES
-------------- ------------ ------------
Nancy Angelli    $300,000.00  $186,042.00
```

Using the logical AND, OR, and NOT keywords and parentheses to group the search criteria, you can build very complex search criteria, such as the one in this query:

Find all salespeople who either: (a) work in Denver, New York, or Chicago; or (b) have no manager and were hired since June 1988; or (c) are over quota, but have sales of $600,000 or less.

```
SELECT NAME
  FROM SALESREPS
 WHERE (REP_OFFICE IN (22, 11, 12))
    OR (MANAGER IS NULL AND HIRE_DATE >= '01-JUN-88')
    OR (SALES > QUOTA AND NOT SALES > 600000.00)
```

AND	TRUE	FALSE	NULL
TRUE	TRUE	FALSE	NULL
FALSE	FALSE	FALSE	FALSE
NULL	NULL	FALSE	NULL

Table 6-1.   *AND Truth Table*

Exactly why you might want to see this particular list of names is a mystery, but the example does illustrate a reasonably complex query.

As with simple search conditions, NULL values influence the outcome of compound search conditions, and the results are subtle. In particular, the result of (NULL OR TRUE) is TRUE, not NULL as you might expect. Tables 6-1, 6-2, and 6-3 specify truth tables for AND, OR, and NOT, respectively, and show the impact of NULL values.

When more than two search conditions are combined with AND, OR, and NOT, the ANSI/ISO standard specifies that NOT has the highest precedence, followed by AND and then OR. To ensure portability, it's always a good idea to use parentheses and remove any possible ambiguity.

The SQL2 standard adds another logical search condition, the IS test, to the logic provided by AND, OR, and NOT. Figure 6-13 shows the syntax of the IS test, which checks to see whether the logical value of an expression or comparison test is TRUE, FALSE, or UNKNOWN (NULL).

For example, the IS test:

```
((SALES - QUOTA) > 10000.00) IS UNKNOWN
```

OR	TRUE	FALSE	NULL
TRUE	TRUE	TRUE	TRUE
FALSE	TRUE	FALSE	NULL
NULL	TRUE	NULL	NULL

Table 6-2.   *OR Truth Table*

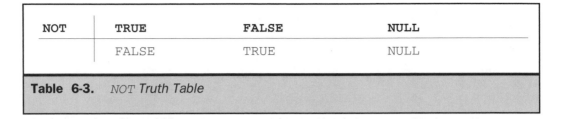

NOT	TRUE	FALSE	NULL
	FALSE	TRUE	NULL

Table 6-3.   *NOT Truth Table*

can be used to find rows where the comparison cannot be done because either SALES or QUOTA has a NULL value. Similarly, the IS test:

```
((SALES - QUOTA) > 10000.00) IS FALSE
```

will select rows where SALES are not significantly above QUOTA. As this example shows, the IS test doesn't really add to the expressive power of SQL, since the test could just as easily have been written:

```
NOT ((SALES - QUOTA) > 10000.00)
```

For maximum portability, it's a good idea to avoid the tests and write the expressions using only AND, OR, and NOT. It's not always possible to avoid the IS UNKNOWN form of the test.

Sorting Query Results (ORDER BY Clause)

Like the rows of a table in the database, the rows of query results are not arranged in any particular order. You can ask SQL to sort the results of a query by including the ORDER BY clause in the SELECT statement. The ORDER BY clause, shown in Figure

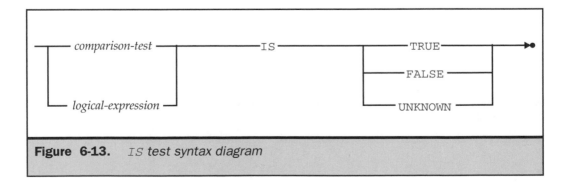

Figure 6-13.   *IS test syntax diagram*

6-14, consists of the keywords ORDER BY, followed by a list of sort specifications separated by commas. For example, the results of this query are sorted on two columns, REGION and CITY:

Show the sales for each office, sorted in alphabetical order by region, and within each region by city.

```
SELECT CITY, REGION, SALES
  FROM OFFICES
 ORDER BY REGION, CITY

CITY            REGION          SALES
------------   --------   ------------
Atlanta        Eastern    $367,911.00
Chicago        Eastern    $735,042.00
New York       Eastern    $692,637.00
Denver         Western    $186,042.00
Los Angeles    Western    $835,915.00
```

The first sort specification (REGION) is the *major* sort key; those that follow (CITY, in this case) are progressively more minor sort keys, used as "tie breakers" when two rows of query results have the same values for the more major keys. Using the ORDER BY clause, you can request sorting in an ascending or descending sequence, and you can sort on any item in the select list of the query.

By default, SQL sorts data in ascending sequence. To request sorting in descending sequence, the keyword DESC is included in the sort specification, as in the next example.

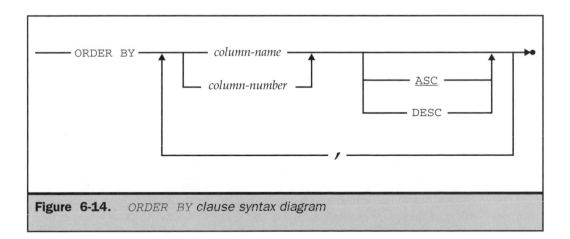

Figure 6-14.   *ORDER BY clause syntax diagram*

List the offices, sorted in descending order by sales, so that the offices with the largest sales appear first.

```
SELECT CITY, REGION, SALES
  FROM OFFICES
 ORDER BY SALES DESC

CITY           REGION         SALES
------------   --------   ------------
Los Angeles    Western    $835,915.00
Chicago        Eastern    $735,042.00
New York       Eastern    $692,637.00
Atlanta        Eastern    $367,911.00
Denver         Western    $186,042.00
```

As indicated in Figure 6-14, you can also use the keyword ASC to specify an ascending sort, but because that's the default sorting sequence, the keyword is usually omitted.

If the column of query results to be used for sorting is a calculated column, it has no column name to be used in a sort specification. In this case, you must specify a column number instead of a column name, as in this example:

List the offices, sorted in descending order by sales performance, so that the offices with the best performance appear first.

```
SELECT CITY, REGION, (SALES - TARGET)
  FROM OFFICES
 ORDER BY 3 DESC

CITY           REGION     (SALES-TARGET)
------------   --------   ---------------
New York       Eastern       $117,637.00
Los Angeles    Western       $110,915.00
Atlanta        Eastern        $17,911.00
Chicago        Eastern       -$64,958.00
Denver         Western      -$113,958.00
```

These query results are sorted on the third column, which is the calculated difference between the SALES and TARGET for each office. By combining column numbers, column names, ascending sorts, and descending sorts, you can specify quite complex sorting of the query results, as in the following final example:

List the offices, sorted in alphabetical order by region, and within each region in descending order by sales performance.

```
SELECT CITY, REGION, (SALES - TARGET)
  FROM OFFICES
 ORDER BY REGION ASC, 3 DESC

CITY          REGION    (SALES-TARGET)
-----------   --------  ---------------
New York      Eastern       $117,637.00
Atlanta       Eastern        $17,911.00
Chicago       Eastern       -$64,958.00
Los Angeles   Western       $110,915.00
Denver        Western      -$113,958.00
```

The SQL2 standard allows you to control the sorting order used by the DBMS for each sort key. This can be important when working with international character sets or to insure portability between ASCII and EBCDIC character set systems. However, this area of the SQL2 specification is quite complex, and in practice many SQL implementations either ignore sorting sequence issues or use their own proprietary scheme for user control of the sorting sequence.

Rules for Single-Table Query Processing

Single-table queries are generally simple, and it's usually easy to understand the meaning of a query just by reading the SELECT statement. As queries become more complex, however, it's important to have a more precise "definition" of the query results that will be produced by a given SELECT statement. The following steps describe the procedure for generating the results of a SQL query that includes the clauses described in this chapter.

As the next steps show, the query results produced by a SELECT statement are specified by applying each of its clauses, one-by-one. The FROM clause is applied first (selecting the table containing data to be retrieved). The WHERE clause is applied next (selecting specific rows from the table). The SELECT clause is applied next (generating the specific columns of query results and eliminating duplicate rows, if requested). Finally, the ORDER BY clause is applied to sort the query results.

To generate the query results for a select statement follow these steps:

1. Start with the table named in the FROM clause.

2. If there is a WHERE clause, apply its search condition to each row of the table, retaining those rows for which the search condition is TRUE, and discarding those rows for which it is FALSE or NULL.

3. For each remaining row, calculate the value of each item in the select list to produce a single row of query results. For each column reference, use the value of the column in the current row.

4. If SELECTED DISTINCT is specified, eliminate any duplicate rows of query results that were produced.

5. If there is an ORDER BY clause, sort the query results as specified.

The rows generated by this procedure comprise the query results.

These "rules" for SQL query processing will be expanded several times in the next three chapters to include the remaining clauses of the SELECT statement.

Combining Query Results (UNION) *

Occasionally, it's convenient to combine the results of two or more queries into a single table of query results. SQL supports this capability through the UNION feature of the SELECT statement. Figure 6-15 illustrates how the UNION operation can be used to satisfy the following request:

List all the products where the price of the product exceeds $2,000 or where more than $30,000 of the product has been ordered in a single order.

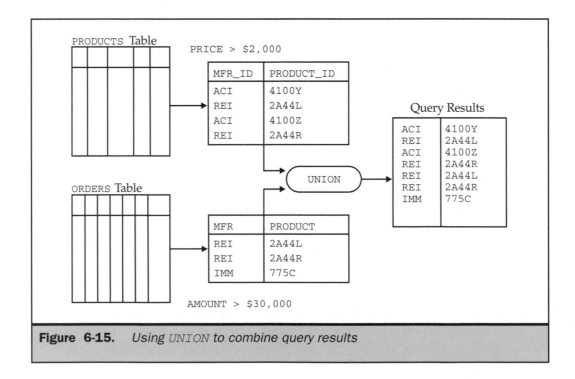

Figure 6-15. *Using UNION to combine query results*

The first part of the request can be satisfied with the top query in the figure:

List all the products whose price exceeds $2,000.

```
SELECT MFR_ID, PRODUCT_ID
  FROM PRODUCTS
 WHERE PRICE > 2000.00

MFR_ID   PRODUCT_ID
-------  -----------
ACI      4100Y
REI      2A44L
ACI      4100Z
REI      2A44R
```

Similarly, the second part of the request can be satisfied with the bottom query in the figure:

List all the products where more than $30,000 of the product has been ordered in a single order.

```
SELECT DISTINCT MFR, PRODUCT
  FROM ORDERS
 WHERE AMOUNT > 30000.00

MFR   PRODUCT
----  --------
IMM   775C
REI   2A44L
REI   2A44R
```

As shown in Figure 6-15, the UNION operation produces a single table of query results that combines the rows of the top query results with the rows of the bottom query results. The SELECT statement that specifies the UNION operation looks like this:

List all the products where the price of the product exceeds $2,000 or where more than $30,000 of the product has been ordered in a single order.

```
SELECT MFR_ID, PRODUCT_ID
  FROM PRODUCTS
 WHERE PRICE > 2000.00
```

```
 UNION
SELECT DISTINCT MFR, PRODUCT
  FROM ORDERS
 WHERE AMOUNT > 30000.00

ACI     4100Y
ACI     4100Z
IMM     775C
REI     2A44L
REI     2A44R
```

There are severe restrictions on the tables that can be combined by a UNION operation:

- The two tables must contain the same number of columns.

- The data type of each column in the first table must be the same as the data type of the corresponding column in the second table.

- Neither of the two tables can be sorted with the ORDER BY clause. However, the combined query results can be sorted, as described in the following section.

Note that the column names of the two queries combined by a UNION do not have to be identical. In the preceding example, the first table of query results has columns named MFR_ID and PRODUCT_ID, while the second table of query results has columns named MFR and PRODUCT. Because the columns in the two tables can have different names, the columns of query results produced by the UNION operation are unnamed.

The ANSI/ISO SQL standard specifies a further restriction on a SELECT statement that participates in a UNION. It permits only column names or an "all columns" specification (SELECT *) in the select list and prohibits expressions in the select list. Most commercial SQL implementations relax this restriction and permit simple expressions in the select list. However, many SQL implementations do not allow the SELECT statements to include the GROUP BY or HAVING clauses, and some do not allow column functions in the select list (prohibiting summary queries as described in Chapter 8). In fact, some SQL implementations (including SQL Server) do not support the UNION operation at all.

Unions and Duplicate Rows *

Because the UNION operation combines the rows from two sets of query results, it would tend to produce query results containing duplicate rows. For example, in the query of Figure 6-15, product REI-2A44L sells for $4,500.00, so it appears in the top set of query results. There is also an order for $31,500.00 worth of this product in the ORDERS table, so it also appears in the bottom set of query results. By default, the

UNION operation *eliminates* duplicate rows as part of its processing. Thus, the combined set of query results contains only *one* row for product REI-2A44L.

If you want to retain duplicate rows in a UNION operation, you can specify the ALL keyword immediately following the word "UNION." This form of the query produces two duplicate rows for product REI-2A44L:

List all the products where the price of the product exceeds $2,000 or where more than $30,000 of the product has been ordered in a single order.

```
SELECT MFR_ID, PRODUCT_ID
  FROM PRODUCTS
 WHERE PRICE > 2000.00
 UNION ALL
SELECT DISTINCT MFR, PRODUCT
  FROM ORDERS
 WHERE AMOUNT > 30000.00

 ACI    4100Y
 REI    2A44L
 ACI    4100Z
 REI    2A44R
 IMM    775C
 REI    2A44L
 REI    2A44R
```

Note that the default duplicate row handling for the UNION operation and for the simple SELECT statement is exactly opposite. For the SELECT statement, SELECT ALL (duplicates retained) is the default. To eliminate duplicate rows, you must explicitly specify SELECT DISTINCT. For the UNION operation, UNION (duplicates eliminated) is the default. To retain duplicate rows, you must explicitly specify UNION ALL.

Database experts have criticized the handling of duplicate rows in SQL and point to this inconsistency as an example of the problems. The reason for the inconsistency is that the SQL defaults were chosen to produce the correct behavior most of the time:

- In practice, most simple SELECT statements do not produce duplicate rows, so the default is no duplicate elimination.

- In practice, most UNION operations would produce unwanted duplicate rows, so the default is duplicate elimination.

Eliminating duplicate rows from query results is a very time-consuming process, especially if the query results contain a large number of rows. If you know, based on the individual queries involved, that a UNION operation cannot produce duplicate rows, you should specifically use the UNION ALL operation because the query will execute much more quickly.

Unions and Sorting *

The ORDER BY clause cannot appear in either of the two SELECT statements combined by a UNION operation. It wouldn't make much sense to sort the two sets of query results anyway, because they are fed directly into the UNION operation and are never visible to the user. However, the *combined* set of query results produced by the UNION operation can be sorted by specifying an ORDER BY clause after the second SELECT statement. Since the columns produced by the UNION operation are not named, the ORDER BY clause must specify the columns by column number.

Here is the same products query as that shown in Figure 6-15, with the query results sorted by manufacturer and product number:

List all the products where the price of the product exceeds $2,000 or where more than $30,000 of the product has been ordered in a single order, sorted by manufacturer and product number.

```
SELECT MFR_ID, PRODUCT_ID
  FROM PRODUCTS
 WHERE PRICE > 2000.00
 UNION
SELECT DISTINCT MFR, PRODUCT
  FROM ORDERS
 WHERE AMOUNT > 30000.00
 ORDER BY 1, 2

 ACI    4100Y
 ACI    4100Z
 IMM    775C
 REI    2A44L
 REI    2A44R
```

Multiple UNIONs *

The UNION operation can be used repeatedly to combine three or more sets of query results, as shown in Figure 6-16. The union of Table B and Table C in the figure produces a single, combined table. This table is then combined with Table A in another UNION operation. The query in the figure is written this way:

```
SELECT *
  FROM A
 UNION (SELECT *
          FROM B
        UNION
       SELECT *
         FROM C)


Bill
Mary
George
Fred
Sue
Julia
Harry
```

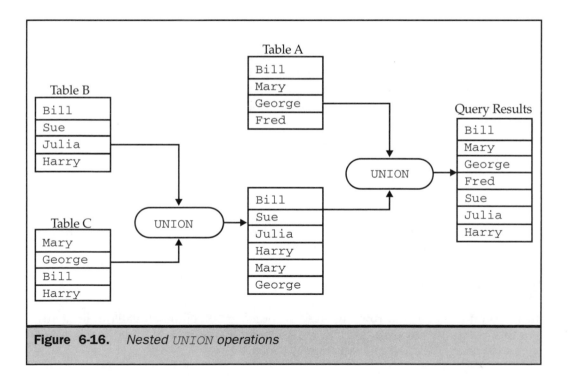

Figure 6-16.   *Nested UNION operations*

The parentheses in the query indicate which UNION should be performed first. In fact, if all of the UNIONs in the statement eliminate duplicate rows, or if all of them retain duplicate rows, the order in which they are performed is unimportant. These three expressions are completely equivalent:

```
A UNION (B UNION C)

(A UNION B) UNION C

(A UNION C) UNION B
```

and produce seven rows of query results. Similarly, the following three expressions are completely equivalent and produce twelve rows of query results, because the duplicates are retained:

```
A UNION ALL (B UNION ALL C)

(A UNION ALL B) UNION ALL C

(A UNION ALL C) UNION ALL B
```

However, if the unions involve a mixture of UNION and UNION ALL, the order of evaluation matters. If this expression:

```
A UNION ALL B UNION C
```

is interpreted as:

```
A UNION ALL (B UNION C)
```

then it produces ten rows of query results (six from the inner UNION, plus four rows from Table A). However, if it is interpreted as:

```
(A UNION ALL B) UNION C
```

then it produces only four rows, because the outer UNION eliminates all duplicate rows. For this reason, it's always a good idea to use parentheses in UNIONs of three or more tables to specify the order of evaluation intended.

Summary

This chapter is the first of four chapters about SQL queries. It described the following query features:

- The SELECT statement is used to express a SQL query. Every SELECT statement produces a table of query results containing one or more columns and zero or more rows.

- The FROM clause specifies the table(s) containing the data to be retrieved by a query.

- The SELECT clause specifies the column(s) of data to be included in the query results, which can be columns of data from the database, or calculated columns.

- The WHERE clause selects the rows to be included in the query results by applying a search condition to rows of the database.

- A search condition can select rows by comparing values, by checking a value against a range or set of values, by matching a string pattern, and by checking for NULL values.

- Simple search conditions can be combined with AND, OR, and NOT to form more complex search conditions.

- The ORDER BY clause specifies that the query results should be sorted in ascending or descending order, based on the values of one or more columns.

- The UNION operation can be used within a SELECT statement to combine two or more sets of query results into a single set.

Chapter 7

Multi-Table Queries (Joins)

M any useful queries request data from two or more tables in a database. For example, these requests for data in the sample database draw data from two, three, or four tables:

- List the salespeople and the offices where they work (SALESREPS and OFFICES tables).

- List each order placed last week, showing the order amount, the name of the customer who placed it, and the name of the product ordered (ORDERS, CUSTOMERS, and SALESREPS tables).

- Show all orders taken by salespeople in the Eastern region, showing the product description and salesperson (ORDERS, SALESREPS, OFFICES, and PRODUCTS tables).

SQL allows you to retrieve data that answers these requests through multi-table queries that *join* data from two or more tables. These queries and the SQL join facility are described in this chapter.

A Two-Table Query Example

The best way to understand the facilities that SQL provides for multi-table queries is to start with a simple request that combines data from two different tables:

"List all orders, showing the order number and amount, and the name and credit limit of the customer who placed it."

The four specific data items requested are clearly stored in two different tables, as shown in Figure 7-1.

- The ORDERS table contains the order number and amount of each order, but doesn't have customer names or credit limits.

- The CUSTOMERS table contains the customer names and balances, but it lacks any information about orders.

There is a link between these two tables, however. In each row of the ORDERS table, the CUST column contains the customer number of the customer who placed the order, which matches the value in the CUST_NUM column in one of the rows in the CUSTOMERS table. Clearly, the SELECT statement that handles the request must somehow use this link between the tables to generate its query results.

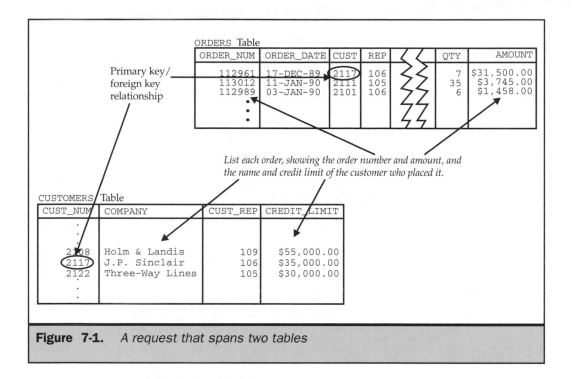

Figure 7-1.   *A request that spans two tables*

Before examining the SELECT statement for the query, it's instructive to think about how you would manually handle the request, using paper and pencil. Figure 7-2 shows what you would probably do:

1. Start by writing down the four column names for the query results. Then move to the ORDERS table, and start with the first order.

2. Look across the row to find the order number (112961) and the order amount ($31,500.00) and copy both values to the first row of query results.

3. Look across the row to find the number of the customer who placed the order (2117), and move to the CUSTOMERS table to find customer number 2117 by searching the CUST_NUM column.

4. Move across the row of the CUSTOMERS table to find the customer's name ("J.P. Sinclair") and credit limit ($35,000.00), and copy them to the query results table.

5. You've generated a row of query results! Move back to the ORDERS table, and go to the next row. Repeat the process, starting with Step 2, until you run out of orders.

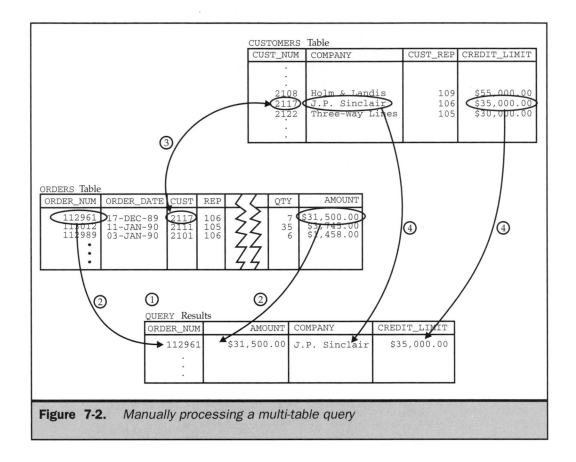

Figure 7-2.   *Manually processing a multi-table query*

Of course this isn't the only way to generate the query results, but regardless of how you do it, two things will be true:

- Each row of query results draws its data from a specific *pair* of rows, one from the ORDERS table and one from the CUSTOMERS table.

- The pair of rows are found by matching the contents of *corresponding columns* from the tables.

Simple Joins (Equi-Joins)

The process of forming pairs of rows by matching the contents of related columns is called *joining* the tables. The resulting table (containing data from both of the original tables) is called a *join* between the two tables. (A join based on an exact match between two columns is more precisely called an *equi-join*. Joins can also be based on other kinds of column comparisons, as described later in this chapter.)

Joins are the foundation of multi-table query processing in SQL. All of the data in a relational database is stored in its columns as explicit data values, so all possible relationships between tables can be formed by matching the contents of related columns. Joins thus provide a powerful facility for *exercising* the data relationships in a database. In fact, because relational databases do not contain pointers or other mechanisms for relating rows to one another, joins are the *only* mechanism for exercising cross-table data relationships.

Because SQL handles multi-table queries by matching columns, it should come as no surprise that the SELECT statement for a multi-table query must contain a search condition that specifies the column match. Here is the SELECT statement for the query that was performed manually in Figure 7-2:

List all orders showing order number, amount, customer name, and the customer's credit limit.

```
SELECT ORDER_NUM, AMOUNT, COMPANY, CREDIT_LIMIT
  FROM ORDERS, CUSTOMERS
 WHERE CUST = CUST_NUM
```

ORDER_NUM	AMOUNT	COMPANY	CREDIT_LIMIT
112989	$1,458.00	Jones Mfg.	$65,000.00
112968	$3,978.00	First Corp.	$65,000.00
112963	$3,276.00	Acme Mfg.	$50,000.00
112987	$27,500.00	Acme Mfg.	$50,000.00
112983	$702.00	Acme Mfg.	$50,000.00
113027	$4,104.00	Acme Mfg.	$50,000.00
112993	$1,896.00	Fred Lewis Corp.	$65,000.00
113065	$2,130.00	Fred Lewis Corp.	$65,000.00
113036	$22,500.00	Ace International	$35,000.00
113034	$632.00	Ace International	$35,000.00
113058	$1,480.00	Holm & Landis	$55,000.00
113055	$150.00	Holm & Landis	$55,000.00
113003	$5,625.00	Holm & Landis	$55,000.00

.
.
.

This looks just like the queries from the previous chapter, with two new features. First, the FROM clause lists two tables instead of just one. Second, the search condition:

```
CUST = CUST_NUM
```

compares columns from two different tables. We call these two columns the *matching* columns for the two tables. Like all search conditions, this one restricts the rows that appear in the query results. Because this is a two-table query, the search condition restricts the *pairs* of rows that generate the query results. In fact, the search condition specifies the same matching columns you used in the paper-and-pencil query processing. It actually captures the spirit of the manual column matching very well, saying:

"Generate query results only for pairs of rows where the customer number (CUST) in the ORDERS table matches the customer number (CUST_NUM) in the CUSTOMERS table."

Notice that the SELECT statement doesn't say anything about *how* SQL should execute the query. There is no mention of "starting with orders" or "starting with customers." Instead, the query tells SQL *what* the query results should look like and leaves it up to SQL to decide how to generate them.

Parent/Child Queries

The most common multi-table queries involve two tables that have a natural parent/child relationship. The query about orders and customers in the preceding section is an example of such a query. Each order (child) has an associated customer (parent), and each customer (parent) can have many associated orders (children). The pairs of rows that generate the query results are parent/child row combinations.

You may recall from Chapter 4 that foreign keys and primary keys create the parent/child relationship in a SQL database. The table containing the foreign key is the child in the relationship; the table with the primary key is the parent. To exercise the parent/child relationship in a query, you must specify a search condition that compares the foreign key and the primary key. Here is another example of a query that exercises a parent/child relationship, shown in Figure 7-3:

List each salesperson and the city and region where they work.

```
SELECT NAME, CITY, REGION
  FROM SALESREPS, OFFICES
 WHERE REP_OFFICE = OFFICE
```

```
NAME            CITY          REGION
--------------  ------------  --------
Mary Jones      New York      Eastern
Sam Clark       New York      Eastern
Bob Smith       Chicago       Eastern
Paul Cruz       Chicago       Eastern
Dan Roberts     Chicago       Eastern
Bill Adams      Atlanta       Eastern
Sue Smith       Los Angeles   Western
Larry Fitch     Los Angeles   Western
Nancy Angelli   Denver        Western
```

The SALESREPS (child) table contains REP_OFFICE, a foreign key for the OFFICES (parent) table. This relationship is used to find the correct OFFICES row for each salesperson, so that the correct city and region can be included in the query results.

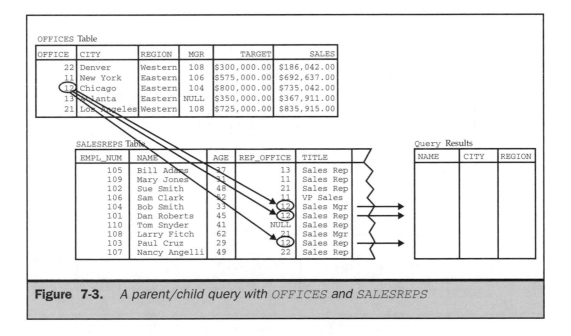

Figure 7-3.   *A parent/child query with* OFFICES *and* SALESREPS

Here's another query involving the same two tables, but with the parent and child roles reversed, as shown in Figure 7-4.

List the offices and the names and titles of their managers.

```
SELECT CITY, NAME, TITLE
  FROM OFFICES, SALESREPS
 WHERE MGR = EMPL_NUM

CITY            NAME            TITLE
------------    ------------    ----------
Chicago         Bob Smith       Sales Mgr
Atlanta         Bill Adams      Sales Rep
New York        Sam Clark       VP Sales
Denver          Larry Fitch     Sales Mgr
Los Angeles     Larry Fitch     Sales Mgr
```

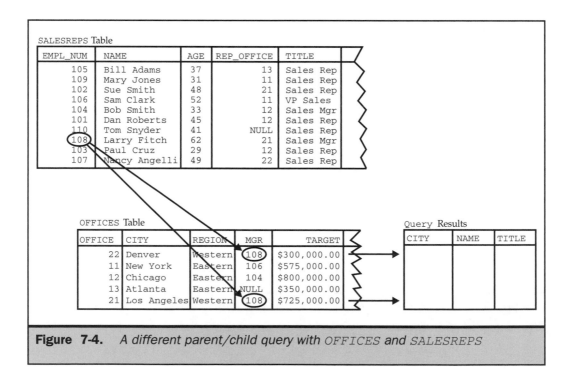

Figure 7-4. *A different parent/child query with* OFFICES *and* SALESREPS

The OFFICES (child) table contains MGR, a foreign key for the SALESREPS (parent) table. This relationship is used to find the correct SALESREPS row for each salesperson, so that the correct name and title of the manager can be included in the query results.

SQL does not require that the matching columns be included in the results of a multi-table query. They are often omitted in practice, as in the two preceding examples. That's because primary keys and foreign keys are often id numbers (such as the office numbers and employee numbers in the examples), which humans find hard to remember, while the associated names (cities, regions, names, titles) are easier to understand. It's quite common for id numbers to be used in the WHERE clause to join two tables, and for more descriptive names to be specified in the SELECT clause to generate columns of query results.

Joins with Row Selection Criteria

The search condition that specifies the matching columns in a multi-table query can be combined with other search conditions to further restrict the contents of the query results. Suppose you want to rerun the preceding query, showing only offices with large sales targets:

List the offices with a target over $600,000.

```
SELECT CITY, NAME, TITLE
  FROM OFFICES, SALESREPS
 WHERE MGR = EMPL_NUM
   AND TARGET > 600000.00

CITY          NAME          TITLE
------------  ------------  ----------
Chicago       Bob Smith     Sales Mgr
Los Angeles   Larry Fitch   Sales Mgr
```

With the additional search condition, the rows that appear in the query results are further restricted. The first test (MGR=EMPL_NUM) selects only pairs of OFFICES and SALESREPS rows that have the proper parent/child relationship; the second test further selects only those pairs of rows where the office is above target.

Multiple Matching Columns

The ORDERS table and the PRODUCTS table in the sample database are related by a composite foreign key/primary key pair. The MFR and PRODUCT columns of the

ORDERS table together form a foreign key for the PRODUCTS table, matching its MFR_ID and PRODUCT_ID columns, respectively. To join the tables based on this parent/child relationship, you must specify *both* pairs of matching columns, as shown in this example:

List all the orders, showing amounts and product descriptions.

```
SELECT ORDER_NUM, AMOUNT, DESCRIPTION
  FROM ORDERS, PRODUCTS
 WHERE MFR = MFR_ID
   AND PRODUCT = PRODUCT_ID

ORDER_NUM     AMOUNT DESCRIPTION
---------- ---------- ----------------
    113027  $4,104.00 Size 2 Widget
    112992    $760.00 Size 2 Widget
    113012  $3,745.00 Size 3 Widget
    112968  $3,978.00 Size 4 Widget
    112963  $3,276.00 Size 4 Widget
    112983    $702.00 Size 4 Widget
    113055    $150.00 Widget Adjuster
    113057    $600.00 Widget Adjuster
       .
       .
       .
```

The search condition in the query tells SQL that the related pairs of rows from the ORDERS and PRODUCTS tables are those where both pairs of matching columns contain the same values. Multi-column joins involving two tables are less common than single-column joins and are usually found in queries involving compound foreign keys such as this one. There is no SQL restriction on the number of columns that are involved in the matching condition, but joins normally mirror the real-world relationships between entities represented in the database tables, and those relationships are usually embodied in one or just a few columns of the tables.

Queries with Three or More Tables

SQL can combine data from three or more tables using the same basic techniques used for two-table queries. Here is a simple example of a three-table join:

List orders over $25,000, including the name of the salesperson who took the order and the name of the customer who placed it.

```
SELECT ORDER_NUM, AMOUNT, COMPANY, NAME
  FROM ORDERS, CUSTOMERS, SALESREPS
 WHERE CUST = CUST_NUM
   AND REP = EMPL_NUM
   AND AMOUNT > 25000.00
```

```
ORDER_NUM        AMOUNT COMPANY             NAME
---------- ----------- ---------------- --------------
    112987 $27,500.00 Acme Mfg.          Bill Adams
    113069 $31,350.00 Chen Associates    Nancy Angelli
    113045 $45,000.00 Zetacorp           Larry Fitch
    112961 $31,500.00 J.P. Sinclair      Sam Clark
```

This query uses two foreign keys in the ORDERS table, as shown in Figure 7-5. The CUST column is a foreign key for the CUSTOMERS table, linking each order to the customer who placed it. The REP column is a foreign key for the SALESREPS table,

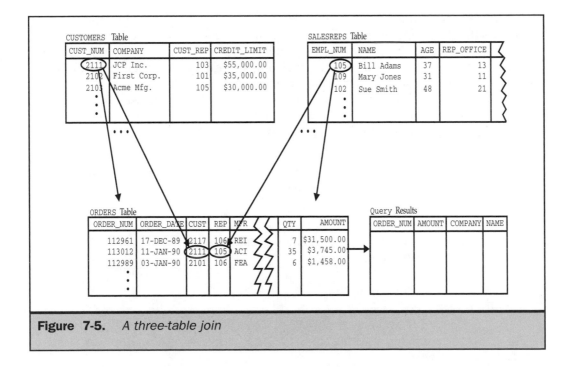

Figure 7-5.   *A three-table join*

linking each order to the salesperson who took it. Informally speaking, the query links each order to its associated customer and salesperson.

Here is another three-table query that uses a different arrangement of parent/child relationships:

List the orders over $25,000, showing the name of the customer who placed the order and the name of the salesperson assigned to that customer.

```
SELECT ORDER_NUM, AMOUNT, COMPANY, NAME
  FROM ORDERS, CUSTOMERS, SALESREPS
 WHERE CUST = CUST_NUM
   AND CUST_REP = EMPL_NUM
   AND AMOUNT > 25000.00
```

ORDER_NUM	AMOUNT	COMPANY	NAME
112987	$27,500.00	Acme Mfg.	Bill Adams
113069	$31,350.00	Chen Associates	Paul Cruz
113045	$45,000.00	Zetacorp	Larry Fitch
112961	$31,500.00	J.P. Sinclair	Sam Clark

Figure 7-6 shows the relationships exercised by this query. The first relationship again uses the CUST column from the ORDERS table as a foreign key to the CUSTOMERS table. The second uses the CUST_REP column from the CUSTOMERS table as a foreign key to the SALESREPS table. Informally speaking, this query links each order to its customer, and each customer to their salesperson.

It's not uncommon to find three-table or even four-table queries used in production SQL applications. Even within the confines of the small, five-table sample database, it's not too hard to find a four-table query that makes sense:

List the orders over $25,000, showing the name of the customer who placed the order, the customer's salesperson, and the office where the salesperson works.

```
SELECT ORDER_NUM, AMOUNT, COMPANY, NAME, CITY
  FROM ORDERS, CUSTOMERS, SALESREPS, OFFICES
 WHERE CUST = CUST_NUM
   AND CUST_REP = EMPL_NUM
   AND REP_OFFICE = OFFICE
   AND AMOUNT > 25000.00
```

```
ORDER_NUM         AMOUNT  COMPANY            NAME         CITY
----------  ------------  ----------------   -----------  -----------
    112987   $27,500.00  Acme Mfg.          Bill Adams   Atlanta
    113069   $31,350.00  Chen Associates    Paul Cruz    Chicago
    113045   $45,000.00  Zetacorp           Larry Fitch  Los Angeles
    112961   $31,500.00  J.P. Sinclair      Sam Clark    New York
```

Figure 7-7 shows the parent/child relationships in this query. Logically, it extends the *join* sequence of the previous example one more step, linking an order to its customer, the customer to their salesperson, and the salesperson to their office.

Other Equi-Joins

The vast majority of multi-table queries are based on parent/child relationships, but SQL does not require that the matching columns be related as a foreign key and primary key. Any pair of columns from two tables can serve as matching columns, provided they have comparable data types. The next example demonstrates a query that uses a pair of dates as matching columns.

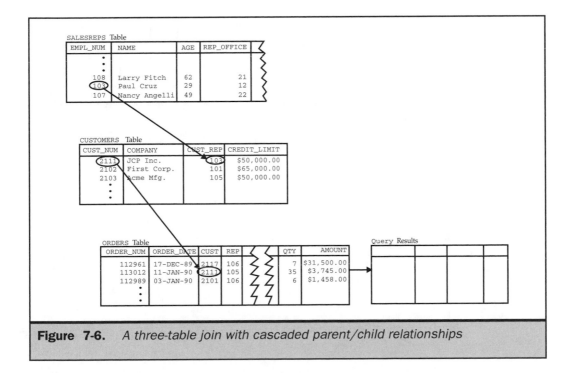

Figure 7-6.   *A three-table join with cascaded parent/child relationships*

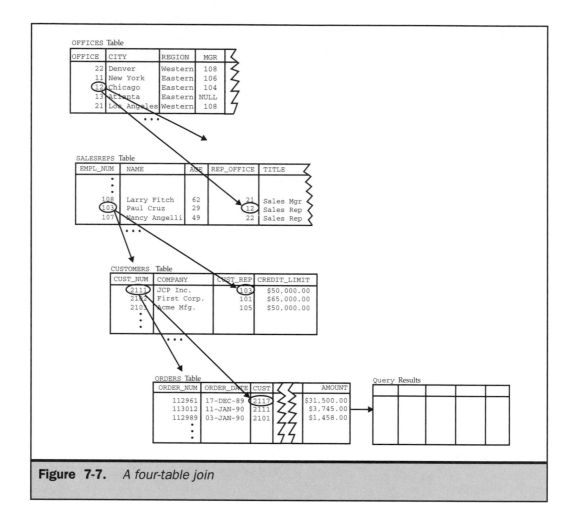

Figure 7-7.   *A four-table join*

Find all orders received on days when a new salesperson was hired.

```
SELECT ORDER_NUM, AMOUNT, ORDER_DATE, NAME
  FROM ORDERS, SALESREPS
 WHERE ORDER_DATE = HIRE_DATE
```

```
ORDER_NUM        AMOUNT ORDER_DATE  NAME
----------   ----------- -----------  ------------
    112968   $3,978.00   12-OCT-89    Mary Jones
    112979  $15,000.00   12-OCT-89    Mary Jones
    112975   $2,100.00   12-OCT-89    Mary Jones
    112968   $3,978.00   12-OCT-89    Larry Fitch
    112979  $15,000.00   12-OCT-89    Larry Fitch
    112975   $2,100.00   12-OCT-89    Larry Fitch
```

The results of this query come from pairs of rows in the ORDERS and SALESREPS tables where the ORDER_DATE happens to match the HIRE_DATE for the salesperson, as shown in Figure 7-8. Neither of these columns is a foreign key or a primary key, and the relationship between the pairs of rows is admittedly a strange one—the only thing the matched orders and salespeople have in common is that they happen to have the same dates. However, SQL happily joins the tables anyway.

Matching columns like the ones in this example generate a many-to-many relationship between the two tables. Many orders can share a single salesperson's hire date, and more than one salesperson may have been hired on a given order's order date. For example, note that three different orders (112968, 112975, and 112979) were received on October 12, 1989, and two different salespeople (Larry Fitch and Mary Jones) were hired that same day. The three orders and two salespeople produce six rows of query results.

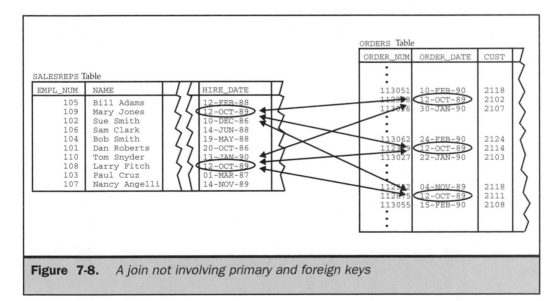

Figure 7-8. *A join not involving primary and foreign keys*

This many-to-many relationship is different from the one-to-many relationship created by primary key/foreign key matching columns. The situation can be summarized as follows:

- Joins that match primary keys to foreign keys always create one-to-many, parent/child relationships.

- Other joins may also generate one-to-many relationships, if the matching column in at least one of the tables has unique values for all rows of the table.

- In general, joins on arbitrary matching columns generate many-to-many relationships.

Note that these three different situations have nothing to do with how you write the SELECT statement that expresses the join. All three types of joins are written the same way—by including a comparison test for the matching column pairs in the WHERE clause. Nonetheless, it's useful to think about joins in this way to understand how to turn an English-language request into the correct SELECT statement.

Non-Equi Joins

The term *join* applies to any query that combines data from two tables by comparing the values in a pair of columns from the tables. Although joins based on equality between matching columns (equi-joins) are by far the most common joins, SQL also allows you to join tables based on other comparison operators. Here's an example where a greater than (>) comparison test is used as the basis for a join:

List all combinations of salespeople and offices where the salesperson's quota is more than the office's target.

```
SELECT NAME, QUOTA, CITY, TARGET
  FROM SALESREPS, OFFICES
 WHERE QUOTA > TARGET

NAME                QUOTA CITY          TARGET
------------ ------------- ------- -------------
Bill Adams    $350,000.00 Denver    $300,000.00
Sue Smith     $350,000.00 Denver    $300,000.00
Larry Fitch   $350,000.00 Denver    $300,000.00
```

As in all two-table queries, each row of the query results comes from a pair of rows, in this case from the SALESREPS and OFFICES tables. The search condition:

```
QUOTA > TARGET
```

selects pairs of rows where the QUOTA column from the SALESREPS row exceeds the TARGET column from the OFFICES row. Note that the pairs of SALESREPS and OFFICES rows selected are related *only* in this way; it is specifically not required that the SALESREPS row represent someone who works in the office represented by the OFFICES row. Admittedly, the example is a bit farfetched, and it illustrates why joins based on inequalities are not very common. However, they can be useful in decision-support applications and other applications that explore more complex interrelationships in the database.

SQL Considerations for Multi-Table Queries

The multi-table queries described thus far have not required any special SQL syntax or language features beyond those described for single-table queries. However, some multi-table queries cannot be expressed without the additional SQL language features described in the following sections. Specifically:

- *Qualified column names* are sometimes needed in multi-table queries to eliminate ambiguous column references.

- *All-column selections* (SELECT *) have a special meaning for multi-table queries.

- *Self-joins* can be used to create a multi-table query that relates a table to itself.

- *Table aliases* can be used in the FROM clause to simplify qualified column names and allow unambiguous column references in self-joins.

Qualified Column Names

The sample database includes several instances where two tables contain columns with the same name. The OFFICES table and the SALESREPS table, for example, both have a column named SALES. The column in the OFFICES table contains year-to-date sales for each office; the one in the SALESREPS table contains year-to-date sales for each salesperson. Normally, there is no confusion between the two columns, because the FROM clause determines which of them is appropriate in any given query, as in these examples:

Show the cities where sales exceed target.

```
SELECT CITY, SALES
  FROM OFFICES
 WHERE SALES > TARGET
```

Show all salespeople with sales over $350,000.

```
SELECT NAME, SALES
  FROM SALESREPS
 WHERE SALES > 350000.00
```

However, here is a query where the duplicate names cause a problem:

Show the name, sales, and office for each salesperson.

```
SELECT NAME, SALES, CITY
  FROM SALESREPS, OFFICES
 WHERE REP_OFFICE = OFFICE

Error: Ambiguous column name "SALES"
```

Although the English description of the query implies that you want the SALES column in the SALESREPS table, the SQL query is ambiguous. The DBMS has no way of knowing whether you want the SALES column from the SALESREPS table or the one from the OFFICES table, since both are contributing data to the query results. To eliminate the ambiguity, you must use a qualified column name to identify the column. Recall from Chapter 5 that a qualified column name specifies the name of a column and the table containing the column. The qualified names of the two SALES columns in the sample database are:

```
OFFICES.SALES and SALESREPS.SALES
```

A qualified column name can be used in a SELECT statement anywhere that a column name is permitted. The table specified in the qualified column name must, of course, match one of the tables specified in the FROM list. Here is a corrected version of the previous query that uses a qualified column name:

Show the name, sales, and office for each salesperson.

```
SELECT NAME, SALESREPS.SALES, CITY
  FROM SALESREPS, OFFICES
 WHERE REP_OFFICE = OFFICE
```

NAME	SALESREPS.SALES	CITY
Mary Jones	$392,725.00	New York
Sam Clark	$299,912.00	New York
Bob Smith	$142,594.00	Chicago
Paul Cruz	$286,775.00	Chicago
Dan Roberts	$305,673.00	Chicago
Bill Adams	$367,911.00	Atlanta
Sue Smith	$474,050.00	Los Angeles
Larry Fitch	$361,865.00	Los Angeles
Nancy Angelli	$186,042.00	Denver

Using qualified column names in a multi-table query is always a good idea. The disadvantage, of course, is that they make the query text longer. When using interactive SQL, you may want to first try a query with unqualified column names and let SQL find any ambiguous columns. If SQL reports an error, you can edit your query to qualify the ambiguous columns.

All-Column Selections

As discussed in Chapter 6, SELECT * can be used to select all columns of the table named in the FROM clause. In a multi-table query, the asterisk selects all columns of *all* tables in the FROM clause. The following query, for example, would produce fifteen columns of query results—the nine columns from the SALESREPS table followed by the six columns from the OFFICES table:

Tell me all about salespeople and the offices where they work.

```
SELECT *
  FROM SALESREPS, OFFICES
 WHERE REP_OFFICE = OFFICE
```

Obviously, the SELECT * form of a query becomes much less practical when there are two, three, or more tables in the FROM clause.

Many SQL dialects treat the asterisk as a special kind of wildcard column name that is expanded into a list of columns. In these dialects, the asterisk can be qualified with a table name, just like a qualified column reference. In the following query, the select item SALESREPS.* is expanded into a list containing only the columns found in the SALESREPS table:

Tell me all about salespeople and the places where they work.

```
SELECT SALESREPS.*, CITY, REGION
  FROM SALESREPS, OFFICES
 WHERE REP_OFFICE = OFFICE
```

The query would produce eleven columns of query results—the nine columns of the SALESREPS table, followed by the two other columns explicitly requested from the OFFICES table. This type of "qualified all-columns" select item is supported in many, but not all brands of SQL-based DBMS. It was not allowed by the SQL1 standard but is part of the ANSI/ISO SQL2 specification.

Self-Joins

Some multi-table queries involve a relationship that a table has with itself. For example, suppose you want to list the names of all salespeople and their managers.

Each salesperson appears as a row in the SALESREPS table, and the MANAGER column contains the employee number of the salesperson's manager. It would appear that the MANAGER column should be a foreign key for the table that holds data about managers. In fact it is—it's a foreign key for the SALESREPS table itself!

If you tried to express this query like any other two-table query involving a foreign key/primary key match, it would look like this:

```
SELECT NAME, NAME
  FROM SALESREPS, SALESREPS
 WHERE MANAGER = EMPL_NUM
```

This SELECT statement is illegal because of the duplicate reference to the SALESREPS table in the FROM clause. You might also try eliminating the second reference to the SALESREPS table:

```
SELECT NAME, NAME
  FROM SALESREPS
 WHERE MANAGER = EMPL_NUM
```

This query is legal, but it won't do what you want it to do! It's a single-table query, so SQL goes through the SALESREPS table one row at a time, applying the search condition:

```
MANAGER = EMPL_NUM
```

The rows that satisfy this condition are those where the two columns have the same value—that is, rows where a salesperson is their own manager. There are no such rows, so the query would produce no results—not exactly the data that the English-language statement of the query requested.

To understand how SQL solves this problem, imagine there were *two identical copies* of the SALESREPS table, one named EMPS, containing employees, and one named MGRS, containing managers, as shown in Figure 7-9. The MANAGER column of the EMPS table would then be a foreign key for the MGRS table, and the following query would work:

List the names of salespeople and their managers.

```
SELECT EMPS.NAME, MGRS.NAME
  FROM EMPS, MGRS
 WHERE EMPS.MANAGER = MGRS.EMPL_NUM
```

Because the columns in the two tables have identical names, all of the column references are qualified. Otherwise, this looks like an ordinary two-table query.

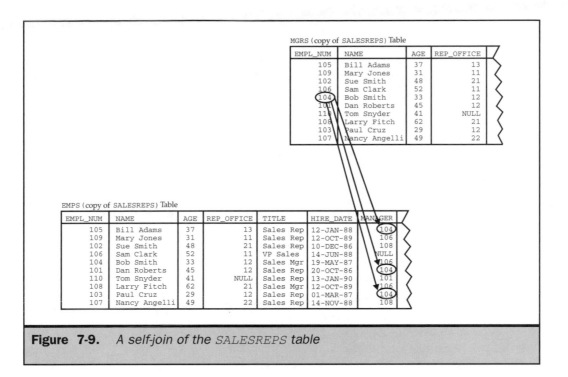

Figure 7-9. *A self-join of the* SALESREPS *table*

SQL uses exactly this "imaginary duplicate table" approach to join a table to itself. Instead of actually duplicating the contents of the table, SQL lets you simply refer to it by a different name, called a *table alias*. Here's the same query, written using the aliases EMPS and MGRS for the SALESREPS table:

List the names of salespeople and their managers.

```
SELECT EMPS.NAME, MGRS.NAME
  FROM SALESREPS EMPS, SALESREPS MGRS
 WHERE EMPS.MANAGER = MGRS.EMPL_NUM

EMPS.NAME        MGRS.NAME
--------------   -----------
Tom Snyder       Dan Roberts
Bill Adams       Bob Smith
Dan Roberts      Bob Smith
Paul Cruz        Bob Smith
Mary Jones       Sam Clark
Bob Smith        Sam Clark
Larry Fitch      Sam Clark
Sue Smith        Larry Fitch
Nancy Angelli    Larry Fitch
```

The FROM clause assigns a different alias to each of the two "copies" of the SALESREPS table that are involved in the query, by specifying the alias name immediately after the actual table name. As the example shows, when a FROM clause contains a table alias, the alias must be used to identify the table in qualified column references. Of course, it's really only necessary to use an alias for one of the two table occurrences in this query. It could just as easily have been written:

```
SELECT SALESREPS.NAME, MGRS.NAME
   FROM SALESREPS, SALESREPS MGRS
  WHERE SALESREPS.MANAGER = MGRS.EMPL_NUM
```

Here the alias MGRS is assigned to one "copy" of the table, while the table's own name is used for the other copy.

Here are some additional examples of self-joins:

List salespeople with a higher quota than their manager.

```
SELECT SALESREPS.NAME, SALESREPS.QUOTA, MGRS.QUOTA
  FROM SALESREPS, SALESREPS MGRS
 WHERE SALESREPS.MANAGER = MGRS.EMPL_NUM
   AND SALESREPS.QUOTA > MGRS.QUOTA
```

SALESREPS.NAME	SALESREPS.QUOTA	MGRS.QUOTA
Bill Adams	$350,000.00	$200,000.00
Dan Roberts	$300,000.00	$200,000.00
Paul Cruz	$275,000.00	$200,000.00
Mary Jones	$300,000.00	$275,000.00
Larry Fitch	$350,000.00	$275,000.00

List salespeople who work in different offices than their manager, showing the name and office where each works.

```
SELECT EMPS.NAME, EMP_OFFICE.CITY, MGRS.NAME, MGR_OFFICE.CITY
  FROM SALESREPS EMPS, SALESREPS MGRS,
       OFFICES EMP_OFFICE, OFFICES MGR_OFFICE
 WHERE EMPS.REP_OFFICE = EMP_OFFICE.OFFICE
   AND MGRS.REP_OFFICE = MGR_OFFICE.OFFICE
   AND EMPS.MANAGER = MGRS.EMPL_NUM
   AND EMPS.REP_OFFICE <> MGRS.REP_OFFICE
```

```
EMPS.NAME        EMP_OFFICE.CITY   MGRS.NAME      MGR_OFFICE.CITY
--------------   ----------------  ------------   ----------------
Bob Smith        Chicago           Sam Clark      New York
Bill Adams       Atlanta           Bob Smith      Chicago
Larry Fitch      Los Angeles       Sam Clark      New York
Nancy Angelli    Denver            Larry Fitch    Los Angeles
```

Table Aliases

As described in the previous section, table aliases are required in queries involving self-joins. However, you can use an alias in any query. For example, if a query refers to another user's table, or if the name of a table is very long, the table name can become tedious to type as a column qualifier. This query, which references the BIRTHDAYS table owned by the user named SAM:

List names, quotas, and birthdays of salespeople.

```
SELECT SALESREPS.NAME, QUOTA, SAM.BIRTHDAYS.BIRTH_DATE
  FROM SALESREPS, BIRTHDAYS
 WHERE SALESREPS.NAME = SAM.BIRTHDAYS.NAME
```

becomes easier to read and type when the aliases S and B are used for the two tables:

List names, quotas, and birthdays of salespeople.

```
SELECT S.NAME, S.QUOTA, B.BIRTH_DATE
  FROM SALESREPS S, SAM.BIRTHDAYS B
 WHERE S.NAME = B.NAME
```

Figure 7-10 shows the basic form of the FROM clause for a multi-table SELECT statement, complete with table aliases. The clause has two important functions:

- The FROM clause identifies all of the tables that contribute data to the query results. Any columns referenced in the SELECT statement must come from one of the tables named in the FROM clause. (There is an exception for *outer* references contained in a subquery, as described in Chapter 9.)

- The FROM clause specifies the *tag* that is used to identify the table in qualified column references within the SELECT statement. If a table alias is specified, it becomes the table tag; otherwise, the table's name, exactly as it appears in the FROM clause, becomes the tag.

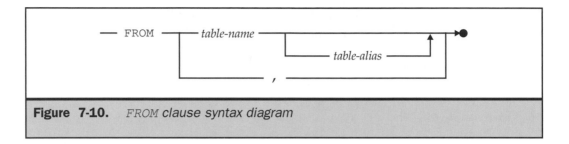

Figure 7-10. *FROM clause syntax diagram*

The only requirement for table tags in the FROM clause is that all of the table tags in a given FROM clause must be distinct from each other. The SQL2 specification optionally allows the keyword AS to appear between a table name and table alias. While this makes the FROM clause easier to read, it may not yet be supported in your specific SQL implementation. (Note that the SQL2 specification uses the term *correlation name* to refer to what we have called a *table alias*. The function and meaning of a correlation name are exactly as described here; many SQL products use the term *alias*, and it is more descriptive of the function that a table alias performs. The SQL2 standard specifies a similar technique for designating alternate *column* names, and in that situation the *column alias* name is actually called an *alias* in the standard.)

Multi-Table Query Performance

As the number of tables in a query grows, the amount of effort required to carry it out increases rapidly. The SQL language itself places no limit on the number of tables joined by a query. Some SQL products do limit the number of tables, with a limit of about eight tables being fairly common. The high processing cost of queries that join many tables imposes an even lower practical limit in many applications.

In online transaction processing (OLTP) applications, it's common for a query to involve only one or two tables. In these applications, response time is critical—the user typically enters one or two items of data and needs a response from the database within a second or two. Here are some typical OLTP queries for the sample database:

- The user enters a customer number into a form, and the DBMS retrieves the customer's credit limit, account balance, and other data (a single-table query).

- A cash register scans a product number from a package and retrieves the product's name and price from the database (a single-table query).

- The user enters a salesperson's name, and the program lists the current orders for that salesperson (a two-table inquiry).

In decision-support applications, by contrast, it's common for a query to involve many different tables and exercise complex relationships in the database. In these applications, the query results are often used to help make expensive decisions, so a query that requires several minutes or even several hours to complete is perfectly acceptable. Here are some typical decision-support queries for the sample database:

- The user enters an office name, and the program lists the 25 largest orders taken by salespeople in that office (a three-table query).

- A report summarizes sales by product type for each salesperson, showing which salespeople are selling which products (a three-table query).

- A manager considers opening a new Seattle sales office and runs a query analyzing the impact on orders, products, customers, and the salespeople who call on them (a four-table query).

The Structure of a Join

For simple joins, it's fairly easy to write the correct SELECT statement based on an English-language request or to look at a SELECT statement and figure out what it does. When many tables are joined or when the search conditions become complex, however, it becomes very difficult just to look at a SELECT statement and figure out what it means. For this reason, it's important to define more carefully and just a bit more formally what a join is, what query results are produced by a given SELECT statement, and just a little bit of the theory of relational database operation that underlies joins.

Table Multiplication

A join is a special case of a more general combination of data from two tables, known as the *Cartesian product* (or just the *product*) of two tables. The product of two tables is another table (the *product table*), which consists of all possible pairs of rows from the two tables. The columns of the product table are all the columns of the first table, followed by all the columns of the second table. Figure 7-11 shows two small sample tables and their product.

   If you specify a two-table query without a WHERE clause, SQL produces the product of the two tables as the query result. For example, this query:

Show all possible combinations of salespeople and cities.

```
SELECT NAME, CITY
   FROM SALESREPS, OFFICES
```

would produce the product of the SALESREPS and OFFICES tables, showing all possible salesperson/city pairs. There would be 50 rows of query results (5 offices * 10 salespeople = 50 combinations). Notice that the SELECT statement is exactly the same

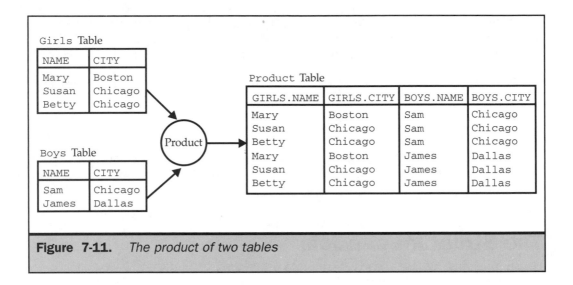

Figure 7-11.   *The product of two tables*

one you would use to join the two tables, without the WHERE clause that compares the matching columns, as follows:

Show all salespeople and the cities where they work.

```
SELECT NAME, CITY
  FROM SALESREPS, OFFICES
 WHERE REP_OFFICE = OFFICE
```

These two queries point out an important relationship between joins and products:

A join between two tables is just the product of the two tables with some of the rows removed. The removed rows are precisely those that do not meet the matching column condition for the join.

Products are important because they are part of the formal definition of how SQL processes a multi-table query, described in the next section.

Rules for Multi-Table Query Processing

The steps following the code below restate the rules for SQL query processing originally introduced in Figure 6-14 and expands them to include multi-table queries. The rules define the meaning of any multi-table SELECT statement by specifying a procedure that always generates the correct set of query results. To see how the procedure works, consider this query:

List the company name and all orders for customer number 2103.

```
SELECT COMPANY, ORDER_NUM, AMOUNT
  FROM CUSTOMERS, ORDERS
 WHERE CUST_NUM = CUST
   AND CUST_NUM = 2103
 ORDER BY ORDER_NUM
```

COMPANY	ORDER_NUM	AMOUNT
Acme Mfg.	112963	$3,276.00
Acme Mfg.	112983	$702.00
Acme Mfg.	112987	$27,500.00
Acme Mfg.	113027	$4,104.00

To generate the query results for a SELECT statement:

1. If the statement is a UNION of SELECT statements, apply steps 2 through 5 to each of the statements to generate their individual query results.

2. Form the product of the tables named in the FROM clause. If the FROM clause names a single table, the product is that table.

3. If there is a WHERE clause, apply its search condition to each row of the product table, retaining those rows for which the search condition is TRUE (and discarding those for which it is FALSE or NULL).

4. For each remaining row, calculate the value of each item in the select list to produce a single row of query results. For each column reference, use the value of the column in the current row.

5. If SELECT DISTINCT is specified, eliminate any duplicate rows of query results that were produced.

6. If the statement is a UNION of SELECT statements, merge the query results for the individual statements into a single table of query results. Eliminate duplicate rows unless UNION ALL is specified.

7. If there is an ORDER BY clause, sort the query results as specified.

The rows generated by this procedure comprise the query results.
Following the previous steps:

1. The FROM clause generates all possible combinations of rows from the CUSTOMERS table (21 rows) and the ORDERS table (30 rows), producing a product table of 630 rows.

2. The WHERE clause selects only those rows of the product table where the customer numbers match (CUST_NUM = CUST) and the customer number is the one specified (CUST_NUM = 2103). Only four rows are selected; the other 626 rows are eliminated.

3. The SELECT clause extracts the three requested columns (COMPANY, ORDER_NUM, and ORD_AMOUNT) from each remaining row of the product table to generate four rows of detailed query results.

4. The ORDER BY clause sorts the four rows on the ORDER_NUM column to generate the final query results.

Obviously no SQL-based DBMS would actually carry out the query this way, but the purpose of the previous definition is not to describe how the query is carried out by a DBMS. Instead, it constitutes a *definition* of how to figure out exactly what a particular multi-table query "means"—that is, the set of query results that it should produce.

Outer Joins *

The SQL join operation combines information from two tables by forming *pairs* of related rows from the two tables. The row pairs that make up the joined table are those where the matching columns in each of the two tables have the same value. If one of the rows of a table is unmatched in this process, the join can produce unexpected results, as illustrated by these queries:

List the salespeople and the offices where they work.

```
SELECT NAME, REP_OFFICE
  FROM SALESREPS

NAME              REP_OFFICE
-------------     ----------
Bill Adams               13
Mary Jones               11
Sue Smith                21
Sam Clark                11
Bob Smith                12
Dan Roberts              12
Tom Snyder             NULL
Larry Fitch              21
Paul Cruz                12
Nancy Angelli            22
```

List the salespeople and the cities where they work.

```
SELECT NAME, CITY
  FROM SALESREPS, OFFICES
 WHERE REP_OFFICE = OFFICE

NAME            CITY
-------------   -----------
Mary Jones      New York
Sam Clark       New York
Bob Smith       Chicago
Paul Cruz       Chicago
Dan Roberts     Chicago
Bill Adams      Atlanta
Sue Smith       Los Angeles
Larry Fitch     Los Angeles
Nancy Angelli   Denver
```

Based on the English-language descriptions of these two queries, you would probably expect them to produce the same number of rows. But the first query includes a row for each of the ten salespeople, while the second query produces only nine. Why? Because Tom Snyder is currently unassigned and has a NULL value in the REP_OFFICE column (which is the matching column for the join). This NULL value doesn't match any of the office numbers in the OFFICES table, so Tom's row in the SALESREPS table is unmatched. As a result, it "vanishes" in the join. The standard SQL join thus has the potential to lose information if the tables being joined contain unmatched rows.

Based on the English-language version of the request, you would probably expect the second query to produce results like these:

List the salespeople and the cities where they work.

```
SELECT NAME, CITY
  FROM SALESREPS, OFFICES
 WHERE REP_OFFICE *= OFFICE

NAME            CITY
-------------   -----------
Tom Snyder      NULL
Mary Jones      New York
Sam Clark       New York
Bob Smith       Chicago
```

```
Paul Cruz      Chicago
Dan Roberts    Chicago
Bill Adams     Atlanta
Sue Smith      Los Angeles
Larry Fitch    Los Angeles
Nancy Angelli  Denver
```

These query results are generated by using a different type of join operation, called an *outer join* (indicated by the "*=" notation in the WHERE clause). The outer join is an extension of the standard join described earlier in this chapter, which is sometimes called an *inner join.* The SQL1 standard specifies only the inner join; it does not include the outer join. The earlier IBM SQL products also support only the inner join. However, the outer join is a well-understood and useful part of the relational database model, and it has been implemented in many non-IBM SQL products, including the flagship database products from Microsoft, Sybase, Oracle, and Informix. The outer join is also the most natural way to express a certain type of query request, as shown in the remainder of this section.

To understand the outer join well, it's useful to move away from the sample database and consider the two simple tables in Figure 7-12. The GIRLS table lists five girls and the cities where they live; the BOYS table lists five boys and the cities where they live. To find the girl/boy pairs who live in the same city, you could use this query, which forms the inner join of the two tables:

List the girls and boys who live in the same city.

```
SELECT *
  FROM GIRLS, BOYS
 WHERE GIRLS.CITY = BOYS.CITY

GIRLS.NAME  GIRLS.CITY  BOYS.NAME  BOYS.CITY
----------  ----------  ---------  ----------
Mary        Boston      John       Boston
Mary        Boston      Henry      Boston
Susan       Chicago     Sam        Chicago
Betty       Chicago     Sam        Chicago
```

The inner join produces four rows of query results. Notice that two of the girls (Anne and Nancy) and two of the boys (James and George) are not represented in the query results. These rows cannot be paired with any row from the other table, and so they are missing from the inner join results. Two of the unmatched rows (Anne and James) have valid values in their CITY columns, but they don't match any cities in the opposite table. The other two unmatched rows (Nancy and George) have NULL values in their CITY columns, and by the rules of SQL NULL handling, the NULL value doesn't match *any* other value (even another NULL value).

Suppose you wanted to list the girl/boy pairs who share the same cities and include the unmatched girls and boys in the list. The outer join of the GIRLS and BOYS tables produces exactly this result. The following list shows the procedure for constructing the outer join, and the outer join is shown graphically in Figure 7-12.

1. Begin with the inner join of the two tables, using matching columns in the normal way.

2. For each row of the first table that is not matched by any row in the second table, add one row to the query results, using the values of the columns in the first table, and assuming a NULL value for all columns of the second table.

3. For each row of the second table that is not matched by any row in the first table, add one row to the query results, using the values of the columns in the second table, and assuming a NULL value for all columns of the first table.

4. The resulting table is the outer join of the two tables.

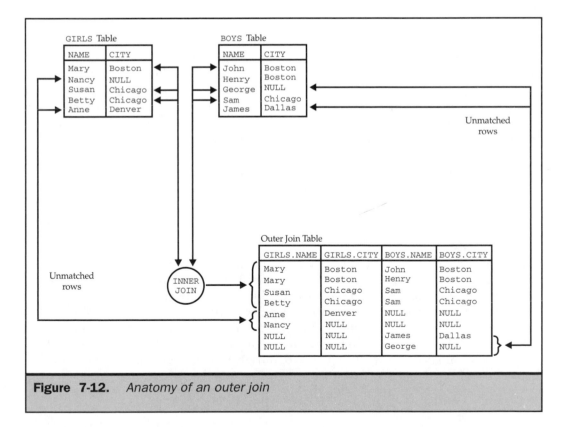

Figure 7-12. *Anatomy of an outer join*

Here is the SQL statement that produces the outer join:

List girls and boys in the same city, including any unmatched girls or boys.

```
SELECT *
  FROM GIRLS, BOYS
 WHERE GIRLS.CITY *=* BOYS.CITY

GIRLS.NAME    GIRLS.CITY    BOYS.NAME    BOYS.CITY
-----------   -----------   ----------   ----------
Mary          Boston        John         Boston
Mary          Boston        Henry        Boston
Susan         Chicago       Sam          Chicago
Betty         Chicago       Sam          Chicago
Anne          Denver        NULL         NULL
Nancy         NULL          NULL         NULL
NULL          NULL          James        Dallas
NULL          NULL          George       NULL
```

The outer join of the two tables contains eight rows. Four of the rows are identical to those of the inner join between the two tables. Two other rows, for Anne and Nancy, come from the unmatched rows of the GIRLS table. These rows have been NULL-*extended* by matching them to an imaginary row of all NULLs in the BOYS table, and added to the query results. The final two rows, for James and George, come from the unmatched rows of the BOYS table. These rows have also been NULL-extended by matching them to an imaginary row of all NULLs in the GIRLS table and added to the query results.

As this example shows, the outer join is an "information-preserving" join. Every row of the BOYS table is represented in the query results (some more than once). Similarly, every row of the GIRLS table is represented in the query results (again, some more than once).

Left and Right Outer Joins *

Technically, the outer join produced by the previous query is called the *full outer join* of the two tables. Both tables are treated symmetrically in the full outer join. Two other well-defined outer joins do not treat the two tables symmetrically.

The *left outer join* between two tables is produced by following Step 1 and Step 2 in the previous numbered list but omitting Step 3. The left outer join thus includes NULL-extended copies of the unmatched rows from the first (left) table but does not include any unmatched rows from the second (right) table. Here is a left outer join between the GIRLS and BOYS tables:

List girls and boys in the same city and any unmatched girls.

```
SELECT *
  FROM GIRLS, BOYS
 WHERE GIRLS.CITY *= BOYS.CITY
```

GIRLS.NAME	GIRLS.CITY	BOYS.NAME	BOYS.CITY
Mary	Boston	John	Boston
Mary	Boston	Henry	Boston
Susan	Chicago	Sam	Chicago
Betty	Chicago	Sam	Chicago
Anne	Denver	NULL	NULL
Nancy	NULL	NULL	NULL

The query produces six rows of query results, showing the matched girl/boy pairs and the unmatched girls. The unmatched boys are missing from the results.

Similarly, the *right outer join* between two tables is produced by following Step 1 and Step 3 in the previous numbered list but omitting Step 2. The right outer join thus includes NULL-extended copies of the unmatched rows from the second (right) table but does not include the unmatched rows of the first (left) table. Here is a right outer join between the GIRLS and BOYS tables:

List girls and boys in the same city and any unmatched boys.

```
SELECT *
  FROM GIRLS, BOYS
 WHERE GIRLS.CITY =* BOYS.CITY
```

GIRLS.NAME	GIRLS.CITY	BOYS.NAME	BOYS.CITY
Mary	Boston	John	Boston
Mary	Boston	Henry	Boston
Susan	Chicago	Sam	Chicago
Betty	Chicago	Sam	Chicago
NULL	NULL	James	Dallas
NULL	NULL	George	NULL

This query also produces six rows of query results, showing the matched girl/boy pairs and the unmatched boys. This time the unmatched girls are missing from the results.

As noted before, the left and right outer joins do not treat the two joined tables symmetrically. It is often useful to think about one of the tables being the "major" table (the one whose rows are all represented in the query results) and the other table being the "minor" table (the one whose columns contain NULL values in the joined query results). In a left outer join, the left (first-mentioned) table is the major table, and the right (later-named) table is the minor table. The roles are reversed in a right outer join (right table is major, left table is minor).

In practice, the left and right outer joins are more useful than the full outer join, especially when joining data from two tables using a parent/child (primary key/ foreign key) relationship. To illustrate, consider once again the sample database. We have already seen one example involving the SALESREPS and OFFICES table. The REP_OFFICE column in the SALESREPS table is a foreign key to the OFFICES table; it tells the office where each salesperson works, and it is allowed to have a NULL value for a new salesperson who has not yet been assigned to an office. Tom Snyder is such a salesperson in the sample database. Any join that exercises this SALESREPS-to-OFFICES relationship and expects to include data for Tom Snyder *must* be an outer join, with the SALESREPS table as the major table. Here is the example used earlier:

List the salespeople and the cities where they work.

```
SELECT NAME, CITY
  FROM SALESREPS, OFFICES
 WHERE REP_OFFICE *= OFFICE

NAME              CITY
--------------    -----------
Tom Snyder        NULL
Mary Jones        New York
Sam Clark         New York
Bob Smith         Chicago
Paul Cruz         Chicago
Dan Roberts       Chicago
Bill Adams        Atlanta
Sue Smith         Los Angeles
Larry Fitch       Los Angeles
Nancy Angelli     Denver
```

Note in this case (a left outer join), the "child" table (SALESREPS, the table with the foreign key) is the major table in the outer join, and the "parent" table (OFFICES) is the minor table. The objective is to retain rows containing NULL foreign key values (like Tom Snyder's) from the child table in the query results, so the child table becomes the major table in the outer join. It doesn't matter whether the query is actually expressed as a left outer join (as it was previously) or as a right outer join like this:

List the salespeople and the cities where they work.

```
SELECT NAME, CITY
  FROM SALESREPS, OFFICES
 WHERE OFFICE =* REP_OFFICE

NAME            CITY
--------------  -----------
Tom Snyder      NULL
Mary Jones      New York
Sam Clark       New York
Bob Smith       Chicago
Paul Cruz       Chicago
Dan Roberts     Chicago
Bill Adams      Atlanta
Sue Smith       Los Angeles
Larry Fitch     Los Angeles
Nancy Angelli   Denver
```

What matters is that the child table is the major table in the outer join.

There are also useful joined queries where the parent is the major table and the child table is the minor table. For example, suppose the company in the sample database opens a new sales office in Dallas, but initially the office has no salespeople assigned to it. If you want to generate a report listing all of the offices and the names of the salespeople who work there, you might want to include a row representing the Dallas office. Here is the outer join query that produces those results:

List the offices and the salespeople who work in each one.

```
SELECT CITY, NAME
  FROM OFFICES, SALESREPS
 WHERE OFFICE *= REP_OFFICE

CITY          NAME
-----------   --------------
New York      Mary Jones
New York      Sam Clark
Chicago       Bob Smith
Chicago       Paul Cruz
Chicago       Dan Roberts
Atlanta       Bill Adams
Los Angeles   Sue Smith
Los Angeles   Larry Fitch
Denver        Nancy Angelli
Dallas        NULL
```

In this case, the parent table (OFFICES) is the major table in the outer join, and the child table (SALESREPS) is the minor table. The objective is to insure that all rows from the OFFICES table are represented in the query results, so it plays the role of major table. The roles of the two tables are precisely reversed from the previous example. Of course, the row for Tom Snyder, which was included in the query results for the earlier example (when SALESREPS was the major table), is missing from this set of query results because SALESREPS is now the minor table.

Outer Join Notation *

Because the outer join was not part of the SQL1 standard and was not implemented in early IBM SQL products, the DBMS vendors who support the outer join have used various notations in their SQL dialects. The "*=*" notation used in the earlier examples of this section is used by SQL Server. This notation indicates an outer join by appending an asterisk (*) to the comparison test in the WHERE clause that defines the join condition. To indicate the full outer join between two tables, TBL1 and TBL2, on columns COL1 and COL2, an asterisk (*) is placed before and after the standard join operator. The resulting full outer join comparison test looks like this:

```
WHERE COL1 *=* COL2
```

To indicate a left outer join of TBL1 to TBL2, only the leading asterisk is specified, giving a comparison test like this:

```
WHERE COL1 *= COL2
```

To indicate a right outer join of TBL1 to TBL2, only the trailing asterisk is specified, giving a comparison test like this:

```
WHERE COL1 =* COL2
```

An outer join can be used with any of the comparison operators using the same notation. For example, a left outer join of TBL1 to TBL2 using a greater than or equal (>=) comparison would produce a comparison test like this:

```
WHERE COL1 *>= COL2
```

Oracle also supports the outer join operation but uses a different notation. This notation indicates the outer join in the WHERE clause by including a parenthesized plus sign following the column *whose table is to have the imaginary* NULL *row added* (that is, the minor table in the outer join). The left outer join of TBL1 to TBL2 produces a search condition that looks like this:

```
WHERE COL1 = COL2 (+)
```

and the right outer join of TBL1 to TBL2 produces a search condition that looks like this:

```
WHERE COL1 (+) = COL2
```

Note that the plus sign appears on the *opposite* side of the comparison from where the asterisk appears in the SQL Server notation. Oracle does not support a full outer join, but as indicated earlier, this does not diminish the practical usefulness of the Oracle outer join capability.

Although both of these outer join notations are relatively convenient, they're also somewhat deceiving. Recall that the rules for multi-table SQL query processing begin by examining the FROM clause of a query and conceptually building the product of the two (or more) tables. Only after the product table is constructed does the DBMS start eliminating rows that do not meet the WHERE clause search condition. But with the SQL Server or Oracle notation, the FROM clause doesn't tell the DBMS whether to build a product table that is only the inner join or one that includes the NULL-extended rows of an outer join. To determine this, the DBMS must "look ahead" to the WHERE clause. A more serious problem is that a join between two tables may involve more than one pair of matching columns, and it's not clear how the notation should be used when there are two or three matching column pairs.

Other problems with the outer join notation arise when it is extended to three or more tables. It's easy to extend the notion of an outer join to three tables:

```
TBL1 OUTER-JOIN TBL2 OUTER-JOIN TBL3
```

This is a perfectly legitimate set of database operations according to the theory of relational databases. But the result depends upon the order in which the outer join operations are performed. The results of:

```
(TBL1 OUTER-JOIN TBL2) OUTER-JOIN TBL3
```

will in general be different from the results of:

```
TBL1 OUTER-JOIN (TBL2 OUTER-JOIN TBL3)
```

Using either the SQL Server or Oracle notations, it's impossible to specify the evaluation order of the outer joins. Because of this, the results produced by the outer join of three or more tables depend upon the specifics of the DBMS implementation.

Joins and the SQL2 Standard

Outer joins posed a problem for the writers of the SQL2 standard. Because outer joins are the only way to represent some extremely useful queries, it was important that the SQL2 standard include support for outer joins. In addition, outer joins were supported in many commercial SQL products and were becoming a more important part of the SQL language. However, the methods used to represent outer joins varied widely among the different SQL products, as shown in the preceding sections. Furthermore, the methods used to denote outer joins in commercial products all had deficiencies and had been chosen more because of their minor impact on the SQL language than because of their clarity or correctness.

Against this background, the SQL2 standard specified a brand new method for supporting outer joins, which was not based on the established notation of a popular SQL product. The SQL2 specification puts the support for outer joins into the FROM clause, with an elaborate syntax that allows the user to specify exactly how the source tables for a query are to be joined together. The outer join support in the SQL2 standard has two distinct advantages. First, the SQL2 standard can express even the most complex of joins. Second, existing database products can support the SQL2 extensions to SQL1 and retain support for their own proprietary outer join syntax without conflict. IBM's DB2 relational database, for example, has added support for most, but not all, of the new SQL2 join syntax at this writing. It's reasonable to expect that most of the major DBMS brands will follow, and that the SQL2-style join features will become a part of the SQL mainstream over the next several years.

The advantages of the SQL2 expanded join support come at the expense of some significant added complexity for what had previously been one of the simpler parts of the SQL language. In fact, the expanded join support is part of a much larger expansion of query capabilities in SQL2 which add even more capability and complexity. The other expanded features include set operations on query results (union, intersection, and differences of tables) and much richer query expressions that manipulate rows and tables and allow them to be used in subqueries. The expanded join-related capabilities are described in this section. The other expanded capabilities are described in the next chapter, after the discussion of basic subqueries.

Inner Joins in SQL2 *

Figure 7-13 shows a simplified form of the extended SQL2 syntax for the FROM clause. It's easiest to understand all of the options provided by considering each type of join, one by one, starting with the basic inner join and then moving to the various forms of outer join. The standard inner join of the GIRLS and BOYS tables can be expressed in SQL1 language:

```
SELECT *
  FROM GIRLS, BOYS
 WHERE GIRLS.CITY = BOYS.CITY
```

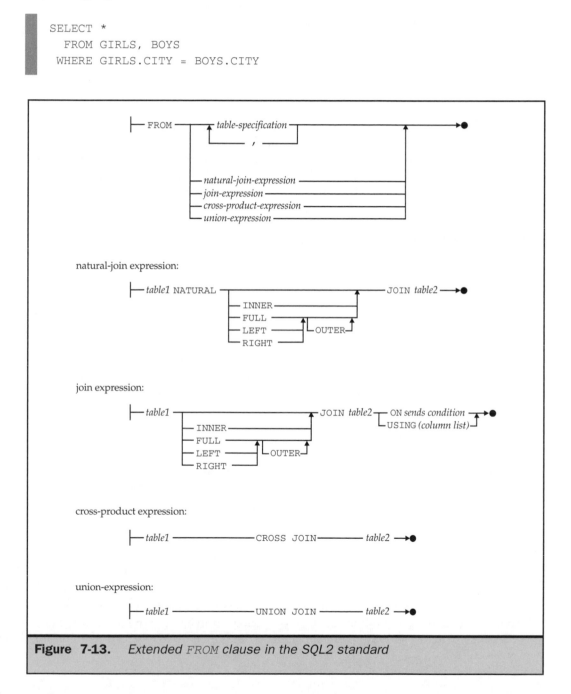

Figure 7-13. *Extended FROM clause in the SQL2 standard*

This is still an acceptable statement in SQL2. The writers of the SQL2 standard really couldn't have made it illegal without "breaking" all of the millions of multi-table SQL queries that had already been written by the early 1990s. But the SQL2 standard specifies an alternative way of expressing the same query:

```
SELECT *
  FROM GIRLS INNER JOIN BOYS
    ON GIRLS.CITY = BOYS.CITY
```

Note that the two tables to be joined are explicitly connected by a JOIN operation, and the search condition that describes the join is now specified in an ON clause within the FROM clause. The search condition following the keyword ON can be any search condition that specifies the criteria used to match rows of the two joined tables. The columns referenced in the search condition must come only from the two joined tables. For example, assume that the BOYS table and the GIRLS table were each extended by adding an AGE column. Here is a join that matches girl/boy pairs in the same city and also requires that the boy and girl in each pair be the same age:

```
SELECT *
  FROM GIRLS INNER JOIN BOYS
    ON (GIRLS.CITY = BOYS.CITY)
   AND (GIRLS.AGE = BOYS.AGE)
```

In these simple two-table joins, the entire contents of the WHERE clause simply moved into the ON clause, and the ON clause doesn't add any functionality to the SQL language. However, recall from earlier in this chapter that in a outer join involving three tables or more, the order in which the joins occur affect the query results. The ON clause provides detailed control over how these multi-table joins are processed, as described later in this chapter.

The SQL2 standard permits another variation on the simple inner join query between the GIRLS and BOYS tables. Because the matching columns in the two tables have the same names and are being compared for equality (which is often the case), an alternative form of the ON clause, specifying a list of matching column names, can be used:

```
SELECT *
  FROM GIRLS INNER JOIN BOYS
 USING (CITY, AGE)
```

The USING clause specifies a comma-separated list of the matching column names, which must be identical in both tables. It is completely equivalent to the ON clause that specifies each matching column pair explicitly, but it's a lot more compact and therefore easier to understand. Of course, if the matching columns have different names in the BOYS table and GIRLS table, then an ON clause or a WHERE clause with an equals test must be used. The ON clause must also be used if the join does not involve equality of the matching columns. For example, if you wanted to select girl/boy pairs where the girl was required to be older than the boy, you must use an ON clause to specify the join:

```
SELECT *
  FROM GIRLS INNER JOIN BOYS
    ON (GIRLS.CITY = BOYS.CITY
   AND GIRLS.AGE > BOYS.AGE)
```

There is one final variation on this simple query that illustrates another feature of the SQL2 FROM clause. A join between two tables where the matching columns are *exactly* those specific columns from the two tables that have identical names is called a *natural join*, because usually this is precisely the most "natural" way to join the two tables. The query selecting girl/boy pairs who live in the same city and have the same age can be expressed as a natural join using this SQL2 query:

```
SELECT *
  FROM GIRLS NATURAL INNER JOIN BOYS
```

If the NATURAL keyword is specified, the ON and USING clauses may not be used in the join specification, because the natural join specifically defines the search condition to be used to join the tables—all of the columns with identical column names in both tables are to be matched.

The SQL2 standard assumes that the "default" join between two tables is an inner join. You can omit the keyword INNER from any of the preceding examples, and the resulting query remains a legal SQL2 statement with the same meaning.

Outer Joins in SQL2 *

The SQL2 standard provides complete support for outer joins using the same clauses described in the preceding section for inner joins and additional keywords. For example, the full outer join of the GIRLS and BOYS tables (without the AGE columns) is generated by this query:

```
SELECT *
  FROM GIRLS FULL OUTER JOIN BOYS
    ON GIRLS.CITY = BOYS.CITY
```

As explained earlier in this chapter, the query results will contain a row for each matched girl/boy pair, as well as one row for each unmatched boy, extended with

NULL values in the columns from the other, unmatched table. SQL2 allows the same variations for outer joins as for inner joins; the query could also have been written:

```
SELECT *
  FROM GIRLS NATURAL FULL OUTER JOIN BOYS
```

or

```
SELECT *
  FROM GIRLS FULL OUTER JOIN BOYS
 USING (CITY)
```

Just as the keyword INNER is optional in the SQL2 language, the SQL2 standard also allows you to omit the keyword OUTER. The preceding query could also have been written:

```
SELECT *
  FROM GIRLS FULL JOIN BOYS
 USING (CITY)
```

The DBMS can infer from the word FULL that an outer join is required.

By specifying LEFT or RIGHT instead of FULL, the SQL2 language extends quite naturally to left or right outer joins. Here is the left outer join version of the same query:

```
SELECT *
  FROM GIRLS LEFT OUTER JOIN BOYS
 USING (CITY)
```

As described earlier in the chapter, the query results will include matched girl/boy pairs and NULL-extended rows for each unmatched row in the GIRLS table (the "left" table in the join), but the results do not include unmatched rows from the BOYS table. Conversely, the right outer join version of the same query, specified like this:

```
SELECT *
  FROM GIRLS RIGHT OUTER JOIN BOYS
 USING (CITY)
```

includes boy/girl pairs and unmatched rows in the BOYS table (the "right" table in the join) but does not include unmatched rows from the GIRLS table.

Cross Joins and Union Joins in SQL2 *

The SQL2 support for extended joins includes two other methods for combining data from two tables. A *cross join* is another name for the Cartesian product of two tables, as described earlier in this chapter. A *union join* is closely related to the full outer join; its query results are a subset of those generated by the full outer join.

Here is a SQL2 query that generates the complete product of the GIRLS and BOYS tables:

```
SELECT *
  FROM GIRLS CROSS JOIN BOYS
```

By definition, the Cartesian product (also sometimes called the *cross product*, hence the name "CROSS JOIN") contains every possible pair of rows from the two tables. It "multiplies" the two tables, turning tables of, for example, three girls and two boys into a table of six (3 x 2 = 6) boy/girl pairs. No "matching columns" or "selection criteria" are associated with the cross products, so the ON clause and the USING clause are not allowed. Note that the cross join really doesn't add any new capabilities to the SQL language. Exactly the same query results can be generated with an inner join that specifies no matching columns. So the preceding query could just as well have been written as:

```
SELECT *
  FROM GIRLS, BOYS
```

The use of the keywords CROSS JOIN in the FROM clause simply makes the cross join more explicit. In most databases, the cross join of two tables by itself is of very little practical use. Its usefulness really comes as a building block for more complex query expressions that start with the cross product of two tables and then use SQL2 summary query capabilities (described in the next chapter) or SQL2 set operations to further manipulate the results.

The union join in SQL2 combines some of the features of the UNION operation (described in the previous chapter) with some of the features of the join operations described in this chapter. Recall that the UNION operation effectively combines the rows of two tables, which must have the same number of columns and the same data types for each corresponding column. This query, which uses a simple UNION operation:

```
SELECT *
  FROM GIRLS
 UNION ALL
SELECT *
  FROM BOYS
```

when applied to a three-row table of girls and a two-row table of boys yields a five-row table of query results. Each row of query results corresponds precisely to either a row of the GIRLS table or a row of the BOYS table from which it was derived. The query results have two columns, NAME and CITY, because the GIRLS and BOYS tables each have these two columns.

The union join of the GIRLS and BOYS tables is specified by this SQL2 query:

```
SELECT *
  FROM GIRLS
 UNION JOIN BOYS
```

The query results again have five rows, and again each row of results is contributed by exactly one of the rows in the GIRLS table or the BOYS table. But unlike the simple union, these query results have four columns—all of the columns of the first table *plus* all of the columns of the second table. In this aspect, the union join is like all of the other joins. For each row of query results contributed by the GIRLS table, the columns that come from the GIRLS table receive the corresponding data values; the other columns (those that come from the BOYS table) have NULL values. Similarly, for each row of query results contributed by the BOYS table, the columns that come from the BOYS table receive the corresponding data values; the other columns (this time, those that come from the GIRLS table) have NULL values.

Another way of looking at the results of the union join is to compare them to the results of a full outer join of the GIRLS and BOYS tables. The union join results include the NULL-extended rows of data from the GIRLS table *and* the NULL-extended rows of data from the BOYS table, but they do *not* include any of the rows generated by matching columns. Referring back to the definition of an outer join in Figure 7-14, the union join is produced by omitting Step 1 and following Step 2 and Step 3.

Finally, it's useful to examine the relationships between the sets of rows produced by the cross join, the various types of outer joins, and the inner join shown in Figure 7-14. When joining two tables, TBL1 with m rows and TBL2 with n rows, the figure shows that:

- The *cross join* will contain m x n rows, consisting of all possible row pairs from the two tables.

- TBL1 INNER JOIN TBL2 will contain some number of rows, r, which is less than m x n. The inner join is strictly a subset of the cross join. It is formed by eliminating those rows from the cross join that do not satisfy the matching condition for the inner join.

- The *left outer join* contains all of the rows from the inner join, plus each unmatched row from TBL1, NULL-extended.

- The *right outer join* also contains all of the rows from the inner join, plus each unmatched row from TBL2, NULL-extended.

- The *full outer join* contains all of the rows from the inner join, plus each unmatched row from TBL1, NULL-extended, plus each unmatched row from TBL2, NULL-extended. Roughly speaking, its query results are equal to the left outer join "plus" the right outer join.

- The *union join* contains all of the rows of TBL1, NULL-extended, plus all of the rows of TBL2, NULL-extended. Roughly speaking, its query results are the full outer join "minus" the inner join.

Multi-Table Joins in SQL2

An important advantage of the SQL2 notation is that it allows very clear specification of three-table or four-table joins. To build these more complex joins, any of the join expressions shown in Figure 7-13 and described in the preceding sections can be enclosed in parentheses. The resulting join expression can itself be used in another join expression, as if it were a simple table. Just as SQL allows you to combine mathematical operations (+, −, *, and /) with parentheses and build more complex expressions, the SQL2 standard allows you to build more complex join expressions in the same way.

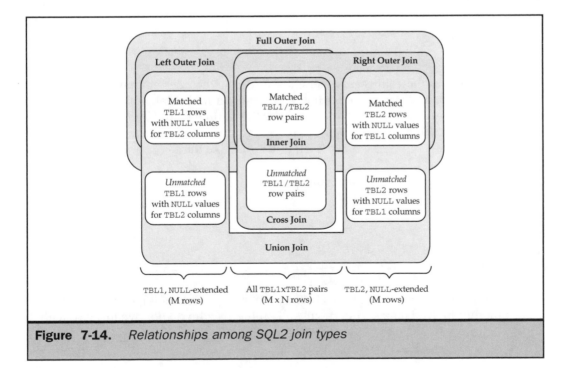

Figure 7-14.   *Relationships among SQL2 join types*

To illustrate multi-table joins, assume that a new PARENTS table has been added to the database containing the GIRLS and BOYS example we have been using. The PARENTS table has three columns:

CHILD	Matches the NAME column in GIRLS or BOYS table
TYPE	Specifies FATHER or MOTHER
PNAME	First name of the parent

A row in the GIRLS or BOYS table can have two matching rows in the PARENTS table, one specifying a MOTHER and one a FATHER, or it can have only one of these rows, or it can have no matching rows if no data on the child's parents is available. The GIRLS, BOYS, and PARENTS tables together provide a rich set of data for some multi-table join examples.

For example, suppose you wanted to make a list of all of the girls, along with the names of their mothers and the names of the boys who live in the same city. Here is one query that produces the list:

```
SELECT GIRLS.NAME, PNAME, BOYS.NAME
  FROM ((GIRLS JOIN PARENTS
    ON PARENT.CHILD = NAME)
  JOIN (BOYS
    ON (GIRLS.CITY = BOYS.CITY))
 WHERE TYPE = "MOTHER"
```

Because both of these joins are inner joins, any girl who does not have a boy living in the same city or any girl who does not have a mother in the database will not show up in the query results. This may or may not be the desired result. To include those girls without a matching mother in the database, you would change the join between the GIRLS and the PARENTS table to a left outer join, like this:

```
SELECT GIRLS.NAME, PNAME, BOYS.NAME
  FROM ((GIRLS LEFT JOIN PARENTS
    ON PARENT.CHILD = NAME)
  JOIN (BOYS
    ON (GIRLS.CITY = BOYS.CITY))
 WHERE (TYPE = "MOTHER") OR (TYPE IS NULL)
```

This query will include all of the girl/boy pairs, regardless of whether the girls have a mother in the database, but it will still omit girls who do not live in a city with any of the boys. To include these girls as well, the second join must also be converted to a left outer join:

```
SELECT GIRLS.NAME, PNAME, BOYS.NAME
  FROM ((GIRLS LEFT JOIN PARENTS
    ON PARENT.CHILD = NAME)
  LEFT JOIN (BOYS
    ON (GIRLS.CITY = BOYS.CITY))
 WHERE (TYPE = "MOTHER") OR (TYPE IS NULL)
```

Note that the NULL-extension of the GIRLS rows by the outer join with their mothers also creates some additional complication in the WHERE clause. The girls without matching mothers will generate rows with not only a NULL mother's name (PNAME) column but also a NULL value in the TYPE column. The simple selection criterion:

```
WHERE (TYPE = "MOTHER")
```

would generate an "unknown" result for these rows, and they will not be included in the query results. But the entire reason for using the left outer join was to make certain they were included! To solve this problem, the WHERE clause is expanded to also test for, and allow, rows where the parent type is NULL.

As one final example, suppose you want to generate a girl/boy listing again, but this time you want to include the name of the boy's father and the girl's mother in the query results. This query requires a four-table join (BOYS, GIRLS, and two copies of the PARENTS table, one for joining to the boys information to get father names and one for joining to the girls information to obtain mother names). Again the potential for unmatched rows in the joins means there are several possible "right" answers to the query. Suppose, as before, that you want to include all girls and boys in the boy/girl pairing, even if the boy or girl does not have a matching row in the PARENTS table. You need to use outer joins for the (BOYS join PARENTS) and (GIRLS join PARENTS) parts of the query, but an inner join for the (BOYS join GIRLS) part of the query. This SQL2 query yields the desired results:

```
SELECT GIRLS.NAME, MOTHERS.PNAME, BOYS.NAME, FATHERS.PNAME
  FROM ((GIRLS LEFT JOIN PARENTS AS MOTHERS
    ON ((CHILD = GIRLS.NAME) AND (TYPE = "MOTHER")))
  JOIN ((BOYS LEFT JOIN PARENTS AS FATHERS
    ON ((CHILD = BOYS.NAME)) AND (TYPE = "FATHER")))
 USING (CITY)
```

This query solves the WHERE-clause test problem in a different way—by moving the test for the TYPE of parent into the ON clause of the join specification. In this position, the test for appropriate TYPE of parent will be performed when the DBMS finds matching columns to construct the join, before the NULL-extended rows are added to the outer join results. Because the PARENTS table is being used twice in the FROM clause, in two different roles, it's necessary to give it two different table aliases so that the correct names can be specified in the select list.

As this example shows, even a four-join query like this one can become quite complex with the SQL2 syntax. However, despite the complexity, the SQL2 query does specify *precisely* the query that the DBMS is to carry out. There is no ambiguity about the order in which the tables are joined, or about which joins are inner or outer joins. Overall, the added capability is well worth the added complexity introduced by the extended SQL2 FROM clause.

Although none of the query examples included in this section had WHERE or ORDER BY clauses, they can be freely used with the extended FROM clause in SQL2. The relationship among the clauses is simple and remains as described earlier in this chapter. The processing specified in the FROM clauses occurs first, including any joins or unions. The join criteria specified in a USING or ON clause are applied as a part of the particular join specification where they appear. When processing of the FROM class is complete, the resulting table is used to apply the selection criteria in the WHERE clause. Thus, the ON clause specifies search criteria that apply to specific joins; the WHERE clause specifies search criteria that apply to the entire table resulting from these joins.

Summary

This chapter described how SQL handles queries that combine data from two or more tables:

- In a multi-table query (a *join*), the tables containing the data are named in the FROM clause.

- Each row of query results is a combination of data from a single row in each of the tables, and it is the *only* row that draws its data from that particular combination.

- The most common multi-table queries use the parent/child relationships created by primary keys and foreign keys.

- In general, joins can be built by comparing *any* pair(s) of columns from the two joined tables, using either a test for equality or any other comparison test.

- A join can be thought of as the product of two tables from which some of the rows have been removed.

- A table can be joined to itself; self-joins require the use of a table alias.

- Outer joins extend the standard (inner) join by retaining unmatched rows of one or both of the joined tables in the query results, and using NULL values for data from the other table.

- The SQL2 standard provides comprehensive support for inner and outer joins, and for combining the results of joins with other multi-table operations such as unions, intersections, and differences.

Chapter 8

Summary Queries

Many requests for information don't require the level of detail provided by the SQL queries described in the last two chapters. For example, each of the following requests asks for a single value or a small number of values that summarize the contents of the database:

- What is the total quota for all salespeople?
- What are the smallest and largest assigned quotas?
- How many salespeople have exceeded their quota?
- What is the size of the average order?
- What is the size of the average order for each sales office?
- How many salespeople are assigned to each sales office?

SQL supports these requests for summary data through column functions and the GROUP BY and HAVING clauses of the SELECT statement, which are described in this chapter.

Column Functions

SQL lets you summarize data from the database through a set of *column functions*. A SQL column function takes an entire column of data as its argument and produces a single data item that summarizes the column. For example, the AVG() column function takes a column of data and computes its average. Here is a query that uses the AVG() column function to compute the average value of two columns from the SALESREPS table:

What are the average quota and average sales of our salespeople?

```
SELECT AVG(QUOTA), AVG(SALES)
  FROM SALESREPS

  AVG(QUOTA)    AVG(SALES)
------------  ------------
 $300,000.00  $289,353.20
```

Figure 8-1 graphically shows how the query results are produced. The first column function in the query takes values in the QUOTA column and computes their average; the second one averages the values in the SALES column. The query produces a single row of query results summarizing the data in the SALESREPS table.

SQL offers six different column functions, as shown in Figure 8-2. The column functions offer different kinds of summary data:

- SUM() computes the total of a column.
- AVG() computes the average value in a column.
- MIN() finds the smallest value in a column.
- MAX() finds the largest value in a column.
- COUNT() counts the number of values in a column.
- COUNT(*) counts rows of query results.

The argument to a column function can be a simple column name, as in the previous example, or it can be a SQL expression, as shown here:

What is the average quota performance of our salespeople?

```
SELECT AVG(100 * (SALES/QUOTA))
  FROM SALESREPS

 AVG(100*(SALES/QUOTA))
----------------------
                102.60
```

Figure 8-1.   *A summary query in operation*

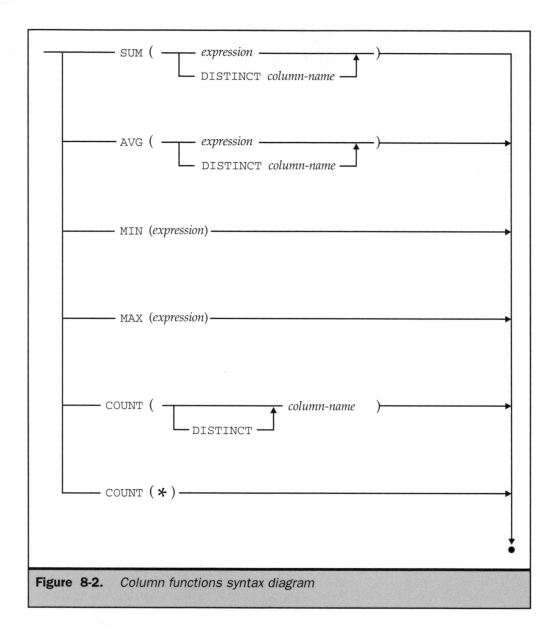

Figure 8-2. *Column functions syntax diagram*

To process this query, SQL constructs a temporary column containing the value of the expression (100 * (SALES/QUOTA)) for each row of the SALESREPS table and then computes the averages of the temporary column.

Computing a Column Total (SUM)

The SUM() column function computes the sum of a column of data values. The data in the column must have a numeric type (integer, decimal, floating point, or money). The result of the SUM() function has the same basic data type as the data in the column, but the result may have a higher precision. For example, if you apply the SUM() function to a column of 16-bit integers, it may produce a 32-bit integer as its result.

Here are some examples that use the SUM() column function:

What are the total quotas and sales for all salespeople?

```
SELECT SUM(QUOTA), SUM(SALES)
  FROM SALESREPS

   SUM(QUOTA)       SUM(SALES)
-------------- --------------
 $2,700,000.00  $2,893,532.00
```

What is the total of the orders taken by Bill Adams?

```
SELECT SUM(AMOUNT)
  FROM ORDERS, SALESREPS
 WHERE NAME = 'Bill Adams'
   AND REP = EMPL_NUM

 SUM(AMOUNT)
------------
  $39,327.00
```

Computing a Column Average (AVG)

The AVG() column function computes the average of a column of data values. As with the SUM() function, the data in the column must have a numeric type. Because the AVG() function adds the values in the column and then divides by the number of values, its result may have a different data type than that of the values in the column. For example, if you apply the AVG() function to a column of integers, the result will be either a decimal or a floating point number, depending on the brand of DBMS you are using.

Here are some examples of the AVG() column function:

Calculate the average price of products from manufacturer ACI.

```
SELECT AVG(PRICE)
  FROM PRODUCTS
 WHERE MFR_ID = 'ACI'

 AVG(PRICE)
 -----------
    $804.29
```

Calculate the average size of an order placed by Acme Mfg. (customer number 2103).

```
SELECT AVG(AMOUNT)
  FROM ORDERS
 WHERE CUST = 2103

 AVG(AMOUNT)
 -----------
   $8,895.50
```

Finding Extreme Values (MIN and MAX)

The MIN() and MAX() column functions find the smallest and largest values in a column, respectively. The data in the column can contain numeric, string, or date/time information. The result of the MIN() or MAX() function has exactly the same data type as the data in the column.

Here are some examples that show the use of these column functions:

What are the smallest and largest assigned quotas?

```
SELECT MIN(QUOTA), MAX(QUOTA)
  FROM SALESREPS

 MIN(QUOTA)    MAX(QUOTA)
 -----------   -----------
 $200,000.00   $350,000.00
```

What is the earliest order date in the database?

```
SELECT MIN(ORDER_DATE)
  FROM ORDERS

MIN(ORDER_DATE)
---------------
04-JAN-89
```

What is the best sales performance of any salesperson?

```
SELECT MAX(100 * (SALES/QUOTA))
  FROM SALESREPS

 MAX(100*(SALES/QUOTA))
----------------------
                135.44
```

When the MIN() and MAX() column functions are applied to numeric data, SQL compares the numbers in algebraic order (large negative numbers are less than small negative numbers, which are less than zero, which is less than all positive numbers). Dates are compared sequentially (earlier dates are smaller than later ones). Durations are compared based on their length (shorter durations are smaller than longer ones).

When using MIN() and MAX() with string data, the comparison of two strings depends upon the character set being used. On a personal computer or minicomputer, both of which use the ASCII character set, digits come before the letters in the sorting sequence, and all of the uppercase characters come before all of the lowercase characters. On IBM mainframes, which use the EBCDIC character set, the lowercase characters precede the uppercase characters, and digits come after the letters. Here is a comparison of the ASCII and EBCDIC collating sequences of a list of strings, from smallest to largest:

ASCII	EBCDIC
1234ABC	acme mfg.
5678ABC	zeta corp.
ACME MFG.	Acme Mfg.
Acme Mfg.	ACME MFG.
ZETA CORP.	Zeta Corp.
Zeta Corp.	ZETA CORP.
acme mfg.	1234ABC
zeta corp.	5678ABC

The difference in the collating sequences means that a query with an ORDER BY clause can produce different results on two different systems.

International characters (for example, accented characters in French, German, Spanish, or Italian or the Cyrillic alphabet letters used in Greek or Russian, or the Kanji symbols used in Japanese) pose additional problems. Some brands of DBMS use special international sorting algorithms to sort these characters into their correct position for each language. Others simply sort them according to the numeric value of the code assigned to the character. To address these issues, the SQL2 standard includes elaborate support for national character sets, user-defined character sets, and alternate collating sequences. Unfortunately, support for these SQL2 features varies widely among popular DBMS products. If your application involves international text, you will want to experiment with your particular DBMS to find out how it handles these characters.

Counting Data Values (COUNT)

The COUNT() column function counts the number of data values in a column. The data in the column can be of any type. The COUNT() function always returns an integer, regardless of the data type of the column. Here are some examples of queries that use the COUNT() column function:

How many customers are there?

```
SELECT COUNT(CUST_NUM)
  FROM CUSTOMERS

COUNT(CUST_NUM)
---------------
             21
```

How many salespeople are over quota?

```
SELECT COUNT(NAME)
  FROM SALESREPS
 WHERE SALES > QUOTA

COUNT(NAME)
-----------
          7
```

How many orders for more than $25,000 are on the books?

```
SELECT COUNT(AMOUNT)
  FROM ORDERS
 WHERE AMOUNT > 25000.00

COUNT(AMOUNT)
-------------
            4
```

Note that the COUNT() function ignores the values of the data items in the column; it simply counts how many data items there are. As a result, it doesn't really matter which column you specify as the argument of the COUNT() function. The last example could just as well have been written this way:

```
SELECT COUNT(ORDER_NUM)
  FROM ORDERS
 WHERE AMOUNT > 25000.00

 COUNT(ORDER_NUM)
 ----------------
                4
```

In fact, it's awkward to think of the query as "counting how many order amounts" or "counting how many order numbers;" it's much easier to think about "counting how many orders." For this reason, SQL supports a special COUNT(*) column function, which counts rows rather than data values. Here is the same query, rewritten once again to use the COUNT(*) function:

```
SELECT COUNT(*)
  FROM ORDERS
 WHERE AMOUNT > 25000.00

 COUNT(*)
 ---------
         4
```

If you think of the COUNT(*) function as a "rowcount" function, it makes the query easier to read. In practice, the COUNT(*) function is almost always used instead of the COUNT() function to count rows.

Column Functions in the Select List

Simple queries with a column function in their select list are fairly easy to understand. However, when the select list includes several column functions, or when the argument to a column function is a complex expression, the query can be harder to read and understand. The following steps show the rules for SQL query processing expanded once more to describe how column functions are handled. As before, the rules are intended to provide a precise definition of what a query means, not a description of how the DBMS actually goes about producing the query results.

To generate the query results for a SELECT statement:

1. If the statement is a UNION of SELECT statements, apply Steps 2 through 5 to each of the statements to generate their individual query results.

2. Form the product of the tables named in the FROM clause. If the FROM clause names a single table, the product is that table.

3. If there is a WHERE clause, apply its search condition to each row of the product table, retaining those rows for which the search condition is TRUE (and discarding those for which it is FALSE or NULL).

4. For each remaining row, calculate the value of each item in the select list to produce a single row of query results. For a simple column reference, use the value of the column in the current row. For a column function, use the entire set of rows as its argument.

5. If SELECT DISTINCT is specified, eliminate any duplicate rows of query results that were produced.

6. If the statement is a UNION of SELECT statements, merge the query results for the individual statements into a single table of query results. Eliminate duplicate rows unless UNION ALL is specified.

7. If there is an ORDER BY clause, sort the query results as specified.

The rows generated by this procedure comprise the query results.

One of the best ways to think about summary queries and column functions is to imagine the query processing broken down into two steps. First, you should imagine how the query would work *without* the column functions, producing many rows of detailed query results. Then you should imagine SQL applying the column functions to the detailed query results, producing a single summary row. For example, consider the following complex query:

Find the average order amount, total order amount, average order amount as a percentage of the customer's credit limit, and average order amount as a percentage of the salesperson's quota.

```
SELECT AVG(AMOUNT), SUM(AMOUNT), (100 * AVG(AMOUNT/CREDIT_LIMIT)),
       (100 * AVG(AMOUNT/QUOTA))
  FROM ORDERS, CUSTOMERS, SALESREPS
 WHERE CUST = CUST_NUM
   AND REP = EMPL_NUM

AVG(AMOUNT)   SUM(AMOUNT)   (100*AVG(AMOUNT/CREDIT_LIMIT))   (100*AVG(AMOUNT/QUOTA))
------------  ------------  ------------------------------   -----------------------
 $8,256.37    $247,691.00                           24.45                      2.51
```

Without the column functions it would look like this:

```
SELECT AMOUNT, AMOUNT, AMOUNT/CREDIT_LIMIT,AMOUNT/QUOTA
  FROM ORDERS, CUSTOMERS, SALESREPS
 WHERE CUST = CUST_NUM AND
   AND REP = EMPL_NUM
```

and would produce one row of detailed query results for each order. The column functions use the columns of this detailed query results table to generate a single-row table of summary query results.

A column function can appear in the select list anywhere that a column name can appear. It can, for example, be part of an expression that adds or subtracts the values of two column functions. However, the argument of a column function cannot contain another column function, because the resulting expression doesn't make sense. This rule is sometimes summarized as "it's illegal to nest column functions."

It's also illegal to mix column functions and ordinary column names in a select list, again because the resulting query doesn't make sense. For example, consider this query:

```
SELECT NAME, SUM(SALES)
  FROM SALESREPS
```

The first select item asks SQL to generate a ten-row table of detailed query results—one row for each salesperson. The second select item asks SQL to generate a one-row column of summary query results containing the total of the SALES column. The two SELECT items contradict one another, producing an error. For this reason, either all column references in the select list must appear within the argument of a column function (producing a summary query), or the select list must not contain any column functions (producing a detailed query). Actually, the rule is slightly more complex when grouped queries and subqueries are considered. The necessary refinements are described later in this chapter.

NULL Values and Column Functions

The SUM(), AVG(), MIN(), MAX(), and COUNT() column functions each take a column of data values as their argument and produce a single data value as a result. What happens if one or more of the data values in the column is a NULL value? The ANSI/ISO SQL standard specifies that NULL values in the column are *ignored* by the column functions.

This query shows how the COUNT() column function ignores any NULL values in a column:

```
SELECT COUNT(*), COUNT(SALES), COUNT(QUOTA)
  FROM SALESREPS

COUNT(*)   COUNT(SALES)   COUNT(QUOTA)
---------  -------------  -------------
       10             10              9
```

The SALESREPS table contains ten rows, so COUNT(*) returns a count of ten. The SALES column contains ten non-NULL values, so the function COUNT(SALES) also returns a count of ten. The QUOTA column is NULL for the newest salesperson. The COUNT(QUOTA) function ignores this NULL value and returns a count of nine. Because of these anomalies, the COUNT(*) function is almost always used instead of the COUNT() function, unless you specifically want to exclude NULL values in a particular column from the total.

Ignoring NULL values has little impact on the MIN() and MAX() column functions. However, it can cause subtle problems for the SUM() and AVG() column functions, as illustrated by this query:

```
SELECT SUM(SALES), SUM(QUOTA), (SUM(SALES) - SUM(QUOTA)), SUM(SALES-QUOTA)
  FROM SALESREPS

    SUM(SALES)      SUM(QUOTA)   (SUM(SALES)-SUM(QUOTA))   SUM(SALES-QUOTA)
--------------  --------------  ------------------------  -----------------
 $2,893,532.00   $2,700,000.00               $193,532.00       $117,547.00
```

You would expect the two expressions:

```
(SUM(SALES) - SUM(QUOTA))    and    SUM(SALES-QUOTA)
```

in the select list to produce identical results, but the example shows that they do not. The salesperson with a NULL value in the QUOTA column is again the reason. The expression:

```
SUM(SALES)
```

totals the sales for all ten salespeople, while the expression:

```
SUM(QUOTA)
```

totals only the nine non-NULL quota values. The expression:

> SUM(SALES) - SUM(QUOTA)

computes the difference of these two amounts. However, the column function:

> SUM(SALES-QUOTA)

has a non-NULL argument value for only nine of the ten salespeople. In the row with a NULL quota value, the subtraction produces a NULL, which is ignored by the SUM() function. Thus, the sales for the salesperson without a quota, which are included in the previous calculation, are excluded from this calculation.

Which is the "correct" answer? Both are! The first expression calculates exactly what it says: "the sum of SALES, less the sum of QUOTA." The second expression also calculates exactly what it says: "the sum of (SALES – QUOTA)." When NULL values occur, however, the two calculations are not quite the same.

The ANSI/ISO standard specifies these precise rules for handling NULL values in column functions:

- If any of the data values in a column are NULL, they are ignored for the purpose of computing the column function's value.

- If every data item in the column is NULL, then the SUM(), AVG(), MIN(), and MAX() column functions return a NULL value; the COUNT() function returns a value of zero.

- If no data items are in the column (that is, the column is empty), then the SUM(), AVG(), MIN(), and MAX() column functions return a NULL value; the COUNT() function returns a value of zero.

- The COUNT(*) counts rows and does not depend on the presence or absence of NULL values in a column. If there are no rows, it returns a value of zero.

Although the standard is very clear in this area, commercial SQL products may produce results different from the standard, especially if all of the data values in a column are NULL or when a column function is applied to an empty table. Before assuming the behavior specified by the standard, you should test your particular DBMS.

Duplicate Row Elimination (DISTINCT)

Recall from Chapter 6 that you can specify the DISTINCT keyword at the beginning of the select list to eliminate duplicate rows of query results. You can also ask SQL to eliminate duplicate values from a column before applying a column function to it. To eliminate duplicate values, the keyword DISTINCT is included before the column function argument, immediately after the opening parenthesis.

Here are two queries that illustrate duplicate row elimination for column functions:

How many different titles are held by salespeople?

```
SELECT COUNT(DISTINCT TITLE)
   FROM SALESREPS

 COUNT(DISTINCT TITLE)
 ---------------------
                     3
```

How many sales offices have salespeople who are over quota?

```
SELECT COUNT(DISTINCT REP_OFFICE)
   FROM SALESREPS
  WHERE SALES > QUOTA

 COUNT(DISTINCT REP_OFFICE)
 --------------------------
                          4
```

The SQL1 standard specified that when the DISTINCT keyword is used, the argument to the column function must be a simple column name; it cannot be an expression. The standard allows the DISTINCT keyword for the SUM() and AVG() column functions. The standard does not permit use of the DISTINCT keyword with the MIN() and MAX() column functions because it has no impact on their results, but many SQL implementations allow it anyway. The standard also *requires* the DISTINCT keyword for the COUNT() column function, but many SQL implementations permit the use of the COUNT() function without it. DISTINCT cannot be specified for the COUNT(*) function, because it doesn't deal with a column of data values at all—it simply counts rows. The SQL2 standard relaxed these restrictions, allowing DISTINCT to be applied for any of the column functions and permitting expressions as arguments for any of the functions as well.

In addition, the DISTINCT keyword can be specified only once in a query. If it appears in the argument of one column function, it can't appear in any others. If it is specified before the select list, it can't appear in any column functions. The only exception is that DISTINCT may be specified a second time inside a subquery (contained within the query). Subqueries are described in Chapter 9.

Grouped Queries (GROUP BY **Clause**)

The summary queries described thus far are like the totals at the bottom of a report. They condense all of the detailed data in the report into a single, summary row of data. Just as subtotals are useful in printed reports, it's often convenient to summarize query results at a "subtotal" level. The GROUP BY clause of the SELECT statement provides this capability.

The function of the GROUP BY clause is most easily understood by example. Consider these two queries:

What is the average order size?

```
SELECT AVG(AMOUNT)
  FROM ORDERS

 AVG(AMOUNT)
------------
   $8,256.37
```

What is the average order size for each salesperson?

```
SELECT REP, AVG(AMOUNT)
  FROM ORDERS
 GROUP BY REP

 REP   AVG(AMOUNT)
----  ------------
 101     $8,876.00
 102     $5,694.00
 103     $1,350.00
 105     $7,865.40
 106    $16,479.00
 107    $11,477.33
 108     $8,376.14
 109     $3,552.50
 110    $11,566.00
```

The first query is a simple summary query like the previous examples in this chapter. The second query produces several summary rows—one row for each group, summarizing the orders taken by a single salesperson. Figure 8-3 shows how the second query works. Conceptually, SQL carries out the query as follows:

1. SQL divides the orders into groups of orders, with one group for each salesperson. Within each group, all of the orders have the same value in the REP column.

2. For each group, SQL computes the average value of the AMOUNT column for all of the rows in the group and generates a single, summary row of query results. The row contains the value of the REP column for the group and the calculated average order size.

A query that includes the GROUP BY clause is called a *grouped query* because it groups the data from its source tables and produces a single summary row for each row group. The columns named in the GROUP BY clause are called the *grouping columns* of the query, because they determine how the rows are divided into groups. Here are some additional examples of grouped queries:

What is the range of assigned quotas in each office?

```
SELECT REP_OFFICE, MIN(QUOTA), MAX(QUOTA)
  FROM SALESREPS
 GROUP BY REP_OFFICE
```

REP_OFFICE	MIN(QUOTA)	MAX(QUOTA)
NULL	NULL	NULL
11	$275,000.00	$300,000.00
12	$200,000.00	$300,000.00
13	$350,000.00	$350,000.00
21	$350,000.00	$350,000.00
22	$300,000.00	$300,000.00

How many salespeople are assigned to each office?

```
SELECT REP_OFFICE, COUNT(*)
  FROM SALESREPS
 GROUP BY REP_OFFICE
```

REP_OFFICE	COUNT(*)
NULL	1
11	2
12	3
13	1
21	2
22	1

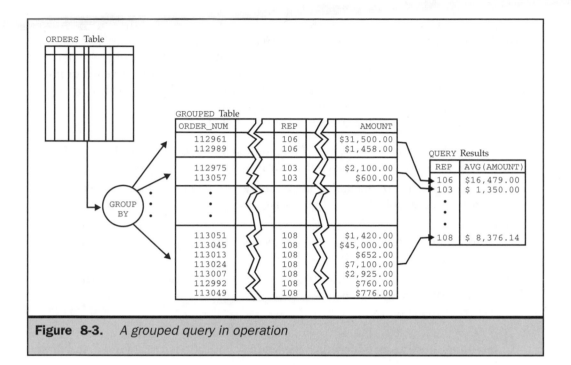

Figure 8-3. *A grouped query in operation*

How many different customers are served by each salesperson?

```
SELECT COUNT(DISTINCT CUST_NUM), 'customers for salesrep', CUST_REP
  FROM CUSTOMERS
 GROUP BY CUST_REP

COUNT(DISTINCT CUST_NUM)   CUSTOMERS FOR SALESREP   CUST_REP
------------------------   ----------------------   ---------
                       3   customers for salesrep        101
                       4   customers for salesrep        102
                       3   customers for salesrep        103
                       1   customers for salesrep        104
                       2   customers for salesrep        105
                       2   customers for salesrep        106
        .
        .
        .
```

There is an intimate link between the SQL column functions and the GROUP BY clause. Remember that the column functions take a column of data values and produce a single result. When the GROUP BY clause is present, it tells SQL to divide the detailed query results into groups and to apply the column function separately to each group, producing a single result for each group. The following steps show the rules for SQL query processing, expanded once again for grouped queries.

To generate the query results for a SELECT statement:

1. If the statement is a UNION of SELECT statements, apply Steps 2 through 7 to each of the statements to generate their individual query results.

2. Form the product of the tables named in the FROM clause. If the FROM clause names a single table, the product is that table.

3. If there is a WHERE clause, apply its search condition to each row of the product table, retaining those rows for which the search condition is TRUE (and discarding those for which it is FALSE or NULL).

4. If there is a GROUP BY clause, arrange the remaining rows of the product table into row groups, so that the rows in each group have identical values in all of the grouping columns.

5. If there is a HAVING clause, apply its search condition to each row group, retaining those groups for which the search condition is TRUE (and discarding those for which it is FALSE or NULL).

6. For each remaining row (or row group), calculate the value of each item in the select list to produce a single row of query results. For a simple column reference, use the value of the column in the current row (or row group). For a column function, use the current row group as its argument if GROUP BY is specified; otherwise, use the entire set of rows.

7. If SELECT DISTINCT is specified, eliminate any duplicate rows of query results that were produced.

8. If the statement is a UNION of SELECT statements, merge the query results for the individual statements into a single table of query results. Eliminate duplicate rows unless UNION ALL is specified.

9. If there is an ORDER BY clause, sort the query results as specified.

The rows generated by this procedure comprise the query results.

Multiple Grouping Columns

SQL can group query results based on the contents of two or more columns. For example, suppose you want to group the orders by salesperson and by customer. This query groups the data based on both criteria:

Calculate the total orders for each customer of each salesperson.

```
SELECT REP, CUST, SUM(AMOUNT)
  FROM ORDERS
 GROUP BY REP, CUST

 REP   CUST   SUM(AMOUNT)
 ----  -----  ------------
 101   2102     $3,978.00
 101   2108       $150.00
 101   2113    $22,500.00
 102   2106     $4,026.00
 102   2114    $15,000.00
 102   2120     $3,750.00
 103   2111     $2,700.00
 105   2103    $35,582.00
 105   2111     $3,745.00
         .
         .
         .
```

Even with multiple grouping columns, SQL provides only a single level of grouping. The query produces a separate summary row for each salesperson/customer pair. It's impossible to create groups and subgroups with two levels of subtotals in SQL. The best you can do is sort the data so that the rows of query results appear in the appropriate order. In many SQL implementations, the GROUP BY clause will automatically have the side effect of sorting the data, but you can override this sort with an ORDER BY clause, as shown here:

Calculate the total orders for each customer of each salesperson, sorted by customer, and within each customer by salesperson.

```
SELECT CUST, REP, SUM(AMOUNT)
  FROM ORDERS
 GROUP BY CUST, REP
 ORDER BY CUST, REP

 CUST   REP   SUM(AMOUNT)
 -----  ----  ------------
 2101   106     $1,458.00
 2102   101     $3,978.00
 2103   105    $35,582.00
```

```
2106  102    $4,026.00
2107  110   $23,132.00
2108  101      $150.00
2108  109    $7,105.00
2109  107   $31,350.00
2111  103    $2,700.00
2111  105    $3,745.00
  .
  .
  .
```

Note that it's also impossible to get both detailed and summary query results from a single query. To get detailed query results with subtotals or to get multilevel subtotals, you must write an application program using programmatic SQL and compute the subtotals within the program logic. SQL Server addresses this limitation of standard SQL by adding an optional COMPUTE clause to the end of the SELECT statement. The COMPUTE clause calculates subtotals and sub-subtotals as shown in this example:

Calculate the total orders for each customer of each salesperson, sorted by salesperson, and within each salesperson by customer.

```
SELECT REP, CUST, AMOUNT
   FROM ORDERS
  ORDER BY REP, CUST
COMPUTE SUM(AMOUNT) BY REP, CUST
COMPUTE SUM(AMOUNT), AVG(AMOUNT) BY REP

REP   CUST         AMOUNT
----  -----  -------------
101   2102       $3,978.00
             sum
                    -------------
                    $3,978.00

REP   CUST         AMOUNT
----  -----  -------------
101   2108         $150.00
             sum
                    -------------
                      $150.00
```

```
REP   CUST        AMOUNT
----  -----  --------------
101   2113      $22,500.00
             sum
             --------------
                $22,500.00
             sum
             --------------
                $26,628.00
             avg
             --------------
                 $8,876.00


REP   CUST        AMOUNT
----  -----  --------------
102   2106       $2,130.00
102   2106       $1,896.00
             sum
             --------------
                 $4,026.00


REP   CUST        AMOUNT
----  -----  --------------
102   2114      $15,000.00
             sum
             --------------
                $15,000.00


REP   CUST        AMOUNT
----  -----  --------------
102   2120       $3,750.00
             sum
             --------------
                 $3,750.00
             sum
             --------------
                $22,776.00
             avg
             --------------
                 $5,694.00
       .
       .
       .
```

The query produces one row of detailed query results for each row of the ORDERS table, sorted by CUST within REP. In addition, it computes the sum of the orders for each customer/salesperson pair (a low-level subtotal) and computes the sum of the orders and average order size for each salesperson (a high-level subtotal). The query results thus contain a mixture of detail rows and summary rows, which include both subtotals and sub-subtotals.

The COMPUTE clause is very nonstandard, and in fact it is unique to the Transact-SQL dialect used by SQL Server. Furthermore, it violates the basic principles of relational queries because the results of the SELECT statement are not a table, but a strange combination of different types of rows. Nonetheless, as the example shows, it can be very useful.

Restrictions on Grouped Queries

Grouped queries are subject to some rather strict limitations. The grouping columns must be actual columns of the tables named in the FROM clause of the query. You cannot group the rows based on the value of a calculated expression.

There are also restrictions on the items that can appear in the select list of a grouped query. All of the items in the select list must have a single value for each group of rows. Basically, this means that a select item in a grouped query can be:

- a constant,
- a column function, which produces a single value summarizing the rows in the group,
- a grouping column, which by definition has the same value in every row of the group, or
- an expression involving combinations of the above.

In practice, a grouped query will always include *both* a grouping column and a column function in its select list. If no column function appears, the query can be expressed more simply using SELECT DISTINCT, without GROUP BY. Conversely, if you don't include a grouping column in the query results, you won't be able to tell which row of query results came from which group!

Another limitation of grouped queries is that SQL ignores information about primary keys and foreign keys when analyzing the validity of a grouped query. Consider this query:

Calculate the total orders for each salesperson.

```
SELECT EMPL_NUM, NAME, SUM(AMOUNT)
  FROM ORDERS, SALESREPS
 WHERE REP = EMPL_NUM
```

```
GROUP BY EMPL_NUM

Error: "NAME" not a GROUP BY expression
```

Given the nature of the data, the query makes perfectly good sense because grouping on the salesperson's employee number is in effect the same as grouping on the salesperson's name. More precisely, EMPL_NUM, the grouping column, is the primary key of the SALESREPS table, so the NAME column must be single-valued for each group. Nonetheless, SQL reports an error because the NAME column is not explicitly specified as a grouping column. To correct the problem, you simply include the NAME column as a second (redundant) grouping column:

Calculate the total orders for each salesperson.

```
SELECT EMPL_NUM, NAME, SUM(AMOUNT)
  FROM ORDERS, SALESREPS
 WHERE REP = EMPL_NUM
 GROUP BY EMPL_NUM, NAME

EMPL_NUM NAME             SUM(AMOUNT)
-------- --------------   -----------
     101 Dan Roberts       $26,628.00
     102 Sue Smith         $22,776.00
     103 Paul Cruz          $2,700.00
     105 Bill Adams        $39,327.00
     106 Sam Clark         $32,958.00
     107 Nancy Angelli     $34,432.00
     108 Larry Fitch       $58,633.00
     109 Mary Jones         $7,105.00
     110 Tom Snyder        $23,132.00
```

Of course, if the salesperson's employee number is not needed in the query results, you can eliminate it entirely from the select list, giving:

Calculate the total orders for each salesperson.

```
SELECT NAME, SUM(AMOUNT)
  FROM ORDERS, SALESREPS
 WHERE REP = EMPL_NUM
 GROUP BY NAME
```

```
NAME            SUM(AMOUNT)
--------------  ------------
Bill Adams        $39,327.00
Dan Roberts       $26,628.00
Larry Fitch       $58,633.00
Mary Jones         $7,105.00
Nancy Angelli     $34,432.00
Paul Cruz          $2,700.00
Sam Clark         $32,958.00
Sue Smith         $22,776.00
Tom Snyder        $23,132.00
```

NULL Values in Grouping Columns

A NULL value poses a special problem when it occurs in a grouping column. If the value of the column is unknown, which group should the row be placed into? In the WHERE clause, when two different NULL values are compared, the result is NULL (not TRUE), that is, the two NULL values are *not* considered to be equal. Applying the same convention to the GROUP BY clause would force SQL to place each row with a NULL grouping column into a separate group by itself.

In practice this rule proves too unwieldy. Instead, the ANSI/ISO SQL standard considers two NULL values to be equal for purposes of the GROUP BY clause. If two rows have NULLs in the same grouping columns and identical values in all of their non-NULL grouping columns, they are grouped together into the same row group. The small sample table in Figure 8-4 illustrates the ANSI/ISO handling of NULL values by the GROUP BY clause, as shown in this query:

```
SELECT HAIR, EYES, COUNT(*)
  FROM PEOPLE
 GROUP BY HAIR, EYES

HAIR    EYES    COUNT(*)
------  ------  ---------
Brown   Blue          1
NULL    Blue          2
NULL    NULL          2
Brown   NULL          3
Brown   Brown         2
Brown   Brown         2
```

Although this behavior of NULLs in grouping columns is clearly specified in the ANSI/ISO standard, it is not implemented in all SQL dialects. It's a good idea to build

NAME	HAIR	EYES
Cindy	Brown	Blue
Louise	NULL	Blue
Harry	NULL	Blue
Samantha	NULL	NULL
Joanne	NULL	NULL
George	Brown	NULL
Mary	Brown	NULL
Paula	Brown	NULL
Kevin	Brown	NULL
Joel	Brown	Brown
Susan	Blonde	Blue
Marie	Blonde	Blue

Figure 8-4. *The PEOPLE table*

a small test table and check the behavior of your DBMS brand before counting on a specific behavior.

Group Search Conditions (HAVING Clause)

Just as the WHERE clause can be used to select and reject the individual rows that participate in a query, the HAVING clause can be used to select and reject row groups. The format of the HAVING clause parallels that of the WHERE clause, consisting of the keyword HAVING followed by a search condition. The HAVING clause thus specifies a search condition for groups.

An example provides the best way to understand the role of the HAVING clause. Consider this query:

What is the average order size for each salesperson whose orders total more than $30,000?

```
SELECT REP, AVG(AMOUNT)
  FROM ORDERS
 GROUP BY REP
HAVING SUM(AMOUNT) > 30000.00
```

```
REP   AVG(AMOUNT)
----  -----------
105      $7,865.40
106     $16,479.00
107     $11,477.33
108      $8,376.14
```

Figure 8-5 shows graphically how SQL carries out the query. The GROUP BY clause first arranges the orders into groups by salesperson. The HAVING clause then eliminates any group where the total of the orders in the group does not exceed $30,000. Finally, the SELECT clause calculates the average order size for each of the remaining groups and generates the query results.

The search conditions you can specify in the HAVING clause are the same ones used in the WHERE clause, as described in Chapters 6 and 9. Here is another example of the use of a group search condition:

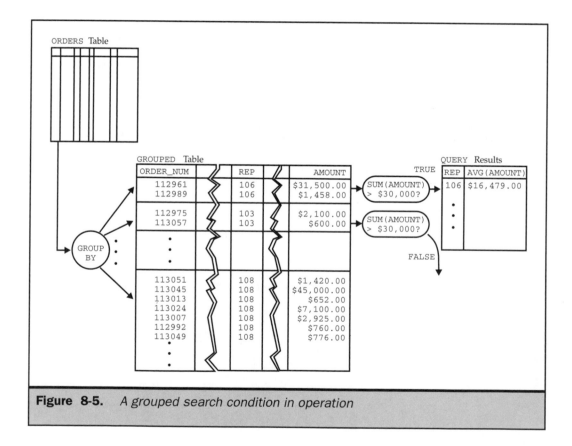

Figure 8-5. *A grouped search condition in operation*

For each office with two or more people, compute the total quota and total sales for all salespeople who work in the office.

```
SELECT CITY, SUM(QUOTA), SUM(SALESREPS.SALES)
  FROM OFFICES, SALESREPS
 WHERE OFFICE = REP_OFFICE
 GROUP BY CITY
HAVING COUNT(*) >= 2
```

CITY	SUM(QUOTA)	SUM(SALESREPS.SALES)
Chicago	$775,000.00	$735,042.00
Los Angeles	$700,000.00	$835,915.00
New York	$575,000.00	$692,637.00

The following steps show the rules for SQL query processing, expanded once again to include group search conditions.

To generate the query results for a SELECT statement:

1. If the statement is a UNION of SELECT statements, apply Steps 2 through 7 to each of the statements to generate their individual query results.

2. Form the product of the tables named in the FROM clause. If the FROM clause names a single table, the product is that table.

3. If there is a WHERE clause, apply its search condition to each row of the product table, retaining those rows for which the search condition is TRUE (and discarding those for which it is FALSE or NULL).

4. If there is a GROUP BY clause, arrange the remaining rows of the product table into row groups, so that the rows in each group have identical values in all of the grouping columns.

5. If there is a HAVING clause, apply its search condition to each row group, retaining those groups for which the search condition is TRUE (and discarding those for which it is FALSE or NULL).

6. For each remaining row (or row group), calculate the value of each item in the select list to produce a single row of query results. For a simple column reference, use the value of the column in the current row (or row group). For a column function, use the current row group as its argument if GROUP BY is specified; otherwise, use the entire set of rows.

7. If SELECT DISTINCT is specified, eliminate any duplicate rows of query results that were produced.

8. If the statement is a UNION of SELECT statements, merge the query results for the individual statements into a single table of query results. Eliminate duplicate rows unless UNION ALL is specified.

9. If there is an ORDER BY clause, sort the query results as specified.

The rows generated by this procedure comprise the query results.

Following the preceding steps, SQL handles this query as follows:

1. Joins the OFFICES and SALESREPS tables to find the city where each salesperson works.

2. Groups the resulting rows by office.

3. Eliminates groups with two or fewer rows—these represent offices that don't meet the HAVING clause criterion.

4. Calculates the total quota and total sales for each group.

Here is one more example, which uses all of the SELECT statement clauses:

Show the price, quantity on hand, and total quantity on order for each product where the total quantity on order is more than 75 percent of the quantity on hand.

```
SELECT DESCRIPTION, PRICE, QTY_ON_HAND, SUM(QTY)
  FROM PRODUCTS, ORDERS
 WHERE MFR = MFR_ID
   AND PRODUCT = PRODUCT_ID
 GROUP BY MFR_ID, PRODUCT_ID, DESCRIPTION, PRICE, QTY_ON_HAND
HAVING SUM(QTY) > (.75 * QTY_ON_HAND)
 ORDER BY QTY_ON_HAND DESC

DESCRIPTION           PRICE   QTY_ON_HAND  SUM(QTY)
----------------    ----------  ------------  ---------
Reducer              $355.00         38          32
Widget Adjuster       $25.00         37          30
Motor Mount          $243.00         15          16
Right Hinge        $4,500.00         12          15
500-lb Brace       $1,425.00          5          22
```

To process this query, SQL conceptually performs the following steps:

1. Joins the ORDERS and PRODUCTS tables to find the description, price, and quantity on hand for each product ordered.

2. Groups the resulting rows by manufacturer and product I.D.

3. Eliminates groups where the quantity ordered (the total of the QTY column for all orders in the group) is less than 75 percent of the quantity on hand.

4. Calculates the total quantity ordered for each group.

5. Generates one summary row of query results for each group.

6. Sorts the query results so that products with the largest quantity on hand appear first.

As described previously, DESCRIPTION, PRICE, and QTY_ON_HAND must be specified as grouping columns in this query solely because they appear in the select list. They actually contribute nothing to the grouping process, because the MFR_ID and PRODUCT_ID completely specify a single row of the PRODUCTS table, automatically making the other three columns single-valued per group.

Restrictions on Group Search Conditions

The HAVING clause is used to include or exclude row groups from the query results, so the search condition it specifies must be one that applies to the group as a whole rather than to individual rows. This means that an item appearing within the search condition in a HAVING clause can be:

- a constant,
- a column function, which produces a single value summarizing the rows in the group,
- a grouping column, which by definition has the same value in every row of the group, or
- an expression involving combinations of the above.

In practice, the search condition in the HAVING clause will always include at least one column function. If it did not, the search condition could be moved to the WHERE clause and applied to individual rows. The easiest way to figure out whether a search condition belongs in the WHERE clause or in the HAVING clause is to remember how the two clauses are applied:

- The WHERE clause is applied to *individual rows,* so the expressions it contains must be computable for individual rows.
- The HAVING clause is applied to *row groups,* so the expressions it contains must be computable for a group of rows.

NULL Values and Group Search Conditions

Like the search condition in the WHERE clause, the HAVING clause search condition can produce one of three results:

- If the search condition is TRUE, the row group is retained, and it contributes a summary row to the query results.
- If the search condition is FALSE, the row group is discarded, and it does not contribute a summary row to the query results.
- If the search condition is NULL, the row group is discarded, and it does not contribute a summary row to the query results.

The anomalies that can occur with NULL values in the search condition are the same as those for the WHERE clause and have been described in Chapter 6.

HAVING **Without** GROUP BY

The HAVING clause is almost always used in conjunction with the GROUP BY clause, but the syntax of the SELECT statement does not require it. If a HAVING clause appears without a GROUP BY clause, SQL considers the entire set of detailed query results to be a single group. In other words, the column functions in the HAVING clause are applied to one and only one group to determine whether the group is included or excluded from the query results, and that group consists of all the rows. The use of a HAVING clause without a corresponding GROUP BY clause is seldom seen in practice.

Summary

This chapter described summary queries, which summarize data from the database:

- Summary queries use SQL column functions to collapse a column of data values into a single value that summarizes the column.
- Column functions can compute the average, sum, minimum, and maximum values of a column, count the number of data values in a column, or count the number of rows of query results.
- A summary query without a GROUP BY clause generates a single row of query results, summarizing all the rows of a table or a joined set of tables.
- A summary query with a GROUP BY clause generates multiple rows of query results, each summarizing the rows in a particular group.
- The HAVING clause acts as a WHERE clause for groups, selecting the row groups that contribute to the summary query results.

Chapter 9

Subqueries and
Query Expressions

The SQL subquery feature lets you use the results of one query as part of another query. The ability to use a query within a query was the original reason for the word "structured" in the name Structured Query Language. The subquery feature is less well known than SQL's join feature, but it plays an important role in SQL for three reasons:

- A SQL statement with a subquery is often the most natural way to express a query, because it most closely parallels the English-language description of the query.

- Subqueries make it easier to write SELECT statements, because they let you "break a query down into pieces" (the query and its subqueries) and then "put the pieces together."

- Some queries cannot be expressed in the SQL language without using a subquery.

The first several sections of this chapter describe subqueries and show how they are used in the WHERE and HAVING clauses of a SQL statement. The later sections of this chapter describe the advanced query expression capabilities that have been added to the SQL2 standard, which substantially expands the power of SQL to perform even the most complex of database operations.

Using Subqueries

A *subquery* is a query-within-a-query. The results of the subquery are used by the DBMS to determine the results of the higher-level query that contains the subquery. In the simplest forms of a subquery, the subquery appears within the WHERE or HAVING clause of another SQL statement. Subqueries provide an efficient, natural way to handle query requests that are themselves expressed in terms of the results of other queries. Here is an example of such a request:

List the offices where the sales target for the office exceeds the sum of the individual salespeople's quotas.

The request asks for a list of offices from the OFFICES table, where the value of the TARGET column meets some condition. It seems reasonable that the SELECT statement that expresses the query should look something like this:

```
SELECT CITY
  FROM OFFICES
 WHERE TARGET > ???
```

The value "???" needs to be filled in and should be equal to "the sum of the quotas of the salespeople assigned to the office in question." How can you specify that value in the query? From Chapter 8, you know that the sum of the quotas for a specific office (say, office number 21) can be obtained with this query:

```
SELECT SUM(QUOTA)
  FROM SALESREPS
 WHERE REP_OFFICE = 21
```

But how can you put the results of this query into the earlier query in place of the question marks? It would seem reasonable to start with the first query and replace the "???" with the second query, as follows:

```
SELECT CITY
  FROM OFFICES
 WHERE TARGET > (SELECT SUM(QUOTA)
                   FROM SALESREPS
                  WHERE REP_OFFICE = OFFICE)
```

In fact, this is a correctly formed SQL query. For each office, the "inner query" (the *subquery*) calculates the sum of the quotas for the salespeople working in that office. The "outer query" (the *main query*) compares the office's target to the calculated total and decides whether to add the office to the main query results. Working together, the main query and the subquery express the original request and retrieve the requested data from the database.

SQL subqueries typically appear as part of the WHERE clause or the HAVING clause. In the WHERE clause, they help to select the individual rows that appear in the query results. In the HAVING clause, they help to select the row groups that appear in the query results.

What Is a Subquery?

Figure 9-1 shows the form of a SQL subquery. The subquery is enclosed in parentheses, but otherwise it has the familiar form of a SELECT statement, with a FROM clause and optional WHERE, GROUP BY, and HAVING clauses. The form of these clauses in a subquery is identical to that in a SELECT statement, and they perform their normal functions when used within a subquery. There are, however, a few differences between a subquery and an actual SELECT statement:

- In the most common uses, a subquery must produce a single column of data as its query results. This means that a subquery almost always has a single select item in its SELECT clause.

■ The ORDER BY clause cannot be specified in a subquery. The subquery results are used internally by the main query and are never visible to the user, so it makes little sense to sort them anyway.

■ Column names appearing in a subquery may refer to columns of tables in the main query. These *outer references* are described in detail later in this chapter.

■ In most implementations, a subquery cannot be the UNION of several different SELECT statements; only a single SELECT is allowed. (The SQL2 standard allows much more powerful query expressions and relaxes this restriction, as described later in the chapter.)

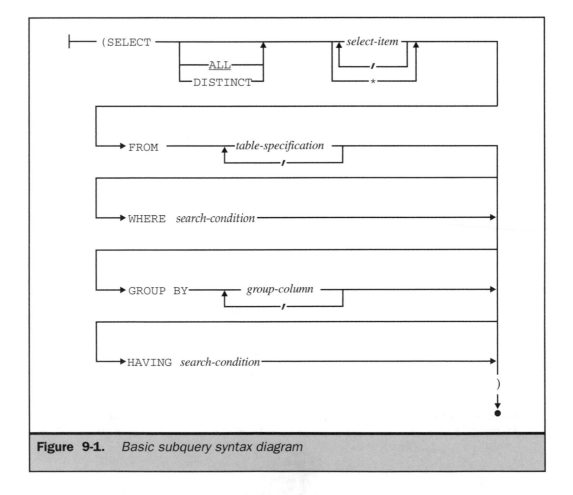

Figure 9-1. *Basic subquery syntax diagram*

Subqueries in the WHERE Clause

Subqueries are most frequently used in the WHERE clause of a SQL statement. When a subquery appears in the WHERE clause, it works as part of the row selection process. The very simplest subqueries appear within a search condition and produce a value that is used to test the search condition. Here is an example of a simple subquery:

List the salespeople whose quota is less than 10% of the company-wide sales target.

```
SELECT NAME
  FROM SALESREPS
 WHERE QUOTA < (.1 * (SELECT SUM(TARGET) FROM OFFICES))

NAME
----------
Bob Smith
```

In this case, the subquery calculates the sum of the sales targets for all of the offices to determine the company-wide target, which is multiplied by 10 percent to determine the "cutoff" sales quota for the query. That value is then used in the search condition to check each row of the SALESREPS table and find the requested names. In this simple case, the subquery produces the same value for every row of the SALESREPS table; the QUOTA value for each salesperson is compared to the same company-wide number. In fact, you could carry out this query by first performing the subquery, to calculate the cutoff quota amount ($275,000 in the sample database), and then carry out the main query using this number in a simple WHERE clause:

```
WHERE QUOTA < 275000
```

It's more convenient to use the subquery, but it's not essential. Usually subqueries are not this simple. For example, consider once again the query from the previous section:

List the offices where the sales target for the office exceeds the sum of the individual salespeople's quotas.

```
SELECT CITY
  FROM OFFICES
 WHERE TARGET > (SELECT SUM(QUOTA)
                   FROM SALESREPS
                  WHERE REP_OFFICE = OFFICE)
```

```
CITY
------------
Chicago
Los Angeles
```

In this (more typical) case, the subquery cannot be calculated once for the entire query. The subquery produces a *different* value for each office, based on the quotas of the salespeople in that particular office. Figure 9-2 shows conceptually how SQL carries out the query. The main query draws its data from the OFFICES table, and the WHERE clause selects which offices will be included in the query results. SQL goes through the rows of the OFFICES table one-by-one, applying the test stated in the WHERE clause. The WHERE clause compares the value of the TARGET column in the current row to the value produced by the subquery. To test the TARGET value, SQL carries out the subquery, finding the sum of the quotas for salespeople in the "current" office. The subquery produces a single number, and the WHERE clause compares the number to the TARGET value, selecting or rejecting the current office based on the comparison. As the figure shows, SQL carries out the subquery repeatedly, once for each row tested by the WHERE clause of the main query.

Outer References

Within the body of a subquery, it's often necessary to refer to the value of a column in the "current" row of the main query. Consider once again the query from the previous sections:

List the offices where the sales target for the office exceeds the sum of the individual salespeople's quotas.

```
SELECT CITY
  FROM OFFICES
 WHERE TARGET > (SELECT SUM(QUOTA)
                   FROM SALESREPS
                  WHERE REP_OFFICE = OFFICE)
```

The role of the subquery in this SELECT statement is to calculate the total quota for those salespeople who work in a particular office—specifically, the office currently being tested by the WHERE clause of the main query. The subquery does this by scanning the SALESREPS table. But notice that the OFFICE column in the WHERE clause of the subquery doesn't refer to a column of the SALESREPS table; it refers to a column of the OFFICES table, which is a part of the main query. As SQL moves through each row of the OFFICES table, it uses the OFFICE value from the current row when it carries out the subquery.

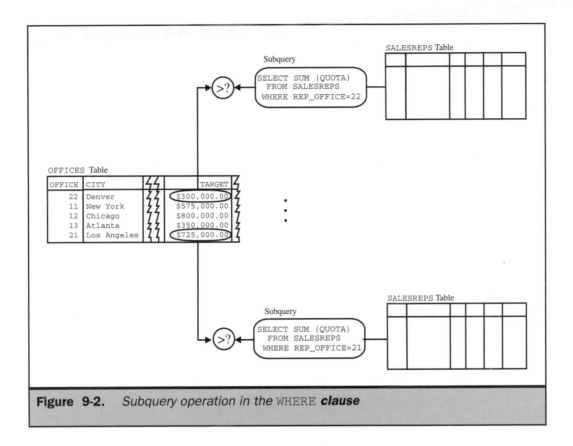

Figure 9-2.   *Subquery operation in the* WHERE ***clause***

The OFFICE column in this subquery is an example of an *outer reference.* An outer reference is a column name that does not refer to any of the tables named in the FROM clause of the subquery in which the column name appears. Instead, the column name refers to a column of a table specified in the FROM clause of the main query. As the previous example shows, when the DBMS examines the search condition in the subquery, the value of the column in an outer reference is taken from the row currently being tested by the main query.

Subquery Search Conditions

A subquery usually appears as part of a search condition in the WHERE or HAVING clause. Chapter 6 described the simple search conditions that can be used in these clauses. In addition, most SQL products offer these *subquery search conditions:*

- *Subquery comparison test.* Compares the value of an expression to a single value produced by a subquery. This test resembles the simple comparison test.

■ *Subquery set membership test.* Checks whether the value of an expression matches one of the set of values produced by a subquery. This test resembles the simple set membership test.

■ *Existence test.* Tests whether a subquery produces any rows of query results.

■ *Quantified comparison test.* Compares the value of an expression to each of the set of values produced by a subquery.

Subquery Comparison Test (=, <>, <, <=, >, >=)

The subquery comparison test is a modified form of the simple comparison test, as shown in Figure 9-3. It compares the value of an expression to the value produced by a subquery and returns a TRUE result if the comparison is true. You use this test to compare a value from the row being tested to a *single* value produced by a subquery, as in this example:

List the salespeople whose quotas are equal to or higher than the target of the Atlanta sales office.

```
SELECT NAME
  FROM SALESREPS
 WHERE QUOTA >= (SELECT TARGET
                   FROM OFFICES
                  WHERE CITY = 'Atlanta')

NAME
------------
Bill Adams
Sue Smith
Larry Fitch
```

The subquery in the example retrieves the sales target of the Atlanta office. The value is then used to select the salespeople whose quotas are higher than the retrieved target.

The subquery comparison test offers the same six comparison operators (=, <>, <, <=, >, >=) available with the simple comparison test. The subquery specified in this test must produce a single value of the appropriate data type—that is, it must produce a *single row* of query results containing exactly one column. If the subquery produces multiple rows, or multiple columns, the comparison does not make sense, and SQL reports an error condition. If the subquery produces no rows or produces a NULL value, the comparison test returns NULL (unknown).

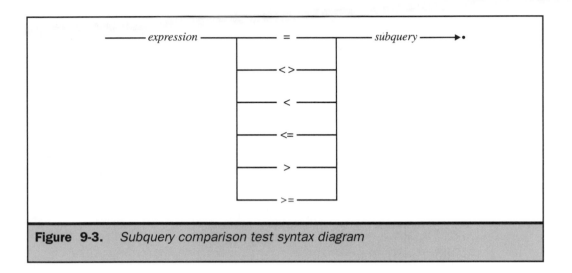

Figure 9-3.   *Subquery comparison test syntax diagram*

Here are some additional examples of subquery comparison tests:

List all customers served by Bill Adams.

```
SELECT COMPANY
  FROM CUSTOMERS
 WHERE CUST_REP = (SELECT EMPL_NUM
                     FROM SALESREPS
                    WHERE NAME = 'Bill Adams')

COMPANY
----------------
Acme Mfg.
Three-Way Lines
```

List all products from manufacturer ACI where the quantity on hand is above the quantity on hand of product ACI-41004.

```
SELECT DESCRIPTION, QTY_ON_HAND
  FROM PRODUCTS
 WHERE MFR_ID = 'ACI'
   AND QTY_ON_HAND > (SELECT QTY_ON_HAND
                        FROM PRODUCTS
                       WHERE MFR_ID = 'ACI'
                         AND PRODUCT_ID = '41004')
```

```
DESCRIPTION      QTY_ON_HAND
-------------    -----------
Size 3 Widget            207
Size 1 Widget            277
Size 2 Widget            167
```

The subquery comparison test specified by the SQL1 standard and supported by all of the leading DBMS products allows a subquery only on the right side of the comparison operator. This comparison:

A < (*subquery*)

is allowed, but this comparison:

(*subquery*) > A

is not permitted. This doesn't limit the power of the comparison test, because the operator in any unequal comparison can always be "turned around" so that the subquery is put on the right side of the inequality. However, it does mean that you must sometimes "turn around" the logic of an English-language request to get a form of the request that corresponds to a legal SQL statement.

The SQL2 standard eliminated this restriction and allows the subquery to appear on either side of the comparison operator. In fact, the SQL2 standard goes considerably further and allows a comparison test to be applied to an *entire row* of values instead of a single value. This and other more advanced "query expression" features of the SQL2 standard are described in the latter sections of this chapter. However, they are not generally supported by the current versions of the major SQL products. Today, it's best to write subqueries that conform to the SQL1 restrictions, as described previously.

Set Membership Test (IN)

The subquery set membership test (IN) is a modified form of the simple set membership test, as shown in Figure 9-4. It compares a single data value to a column of data values produced by a subquery and returns a TRUE result if the data value matches one of the values in the column. You use this test when you need to compare a

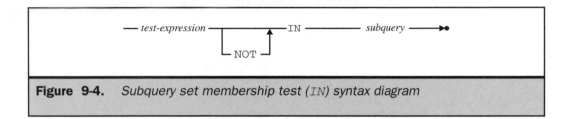

Figure 9-4. *Subquery set membership test (IN) syntax diagram*

value from the row being tested to a *set* of values produced by a subquery. Here is a simple example:

List the salespeople who work in offices that are over target.

```
SELECT NAME
  FROM SALESREPS
 WHERE REP_OFFICE IN (SELECT OFFICE
                        FROM OFFICES
                       WHERE SALES > TARGET)

NAME
-----------
Mary Jones
Sam Clark
Bill Adams
Sue Smith
Larry Fitch
```

The subquery produces a set of office numbers where the sales are above target (in the sample database, there are three such offices, numbered 11, 13, and 21). The main query then checks each row of the SALESREPS table to determine whether that particular salesperson works in an office with one of these numbers. Here are some other examples of subqueries that test set membership:

List the salespeople who do not work in offices managed by Larry Fitch (employee 108).

```
SELECT NAME
  FROM SALESREPS
 WHERE REP_OFFICE NOT IN (SELECT OFFICE
```

```
                                    FROM OFFICES
                              WHERE MGR = 108)


NAME
------------
Bill Adams
Mary Jones
Sam Clark
Bob Smith
Dan Roberts
Paul Cruz
```

List all of the customers who have placed orders for ACI Widgets (manufacturer ACI, product numbers starting with "4100") between January and June 1990.

```
SELECT COMPANY
  FROM CUSTOMERS
 WHERE CUST_NUM IN (SELECT DISTINCT CUST
                      FROM ORDERS
                     WHERE MFR = 'ACI'
                       AND PRODUCT LIKE '4100%'
                       AND ORDER_DATE BETWEEN '01-JAN-90'
                                          AND '30-JUN-90')

COMPANY
------------------
Acme Mfg.
Ace International
Holm & Landis
JCP Inc.
```

In each of these examples, the subquery produces a column of data values, and the WHERE clause of the main query checks to see whether a value from a row of the main query matches one of the values in the column. The subquery form of the IN test thus works exactly like the simple IN test, except that the set of values is produced by a subquery instead of being explicitly listed in the statement.

Existence Test (EXISTS)

The existence test (EXISTS) checks whether a subquery produces any rows of query results, as shown in Figure 9-5. There is no simple comparison test that resembles the existence test; it is used only with subqueries.

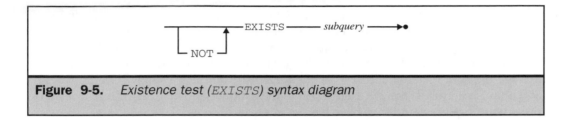

Figure 9-5.   *Existence test (*EXISTS*) syntax diagram*

Here is an example of a request that can be expressed naturally using an existence test:

List the products for which an order of $25,000 or more has been received.

The request could easily be rephrased as:

List the products for which there exists at least one order in the ORDERS *table (a) that is for the product in question and (b) has an amount of at least $25,000.*

The SELECT statement used to retrieve the requested list of products closely resembles the rephrased request:

```
SELECT DISTINCT DESCRIPTION
  FROM PRODUCTS
 WHERE EXISTS (SELECT ORDER_NUM
                 FROM ORDERS
                WHERE PRODUCT = PRODUCT_ID
                  AND MFR = MFR_ID
                  AND AMOUNT >= 25000.00)

DESCRIPTION
---------------
500-lb Brace
Left Hinge
Right Hinge
Widget Remover
```

Conceptually, SQL processes this query by going through the PRODUCTS table and performing the subquery for each product. The subquery produces a column containing the order numbers of any orders for the "current" product that are over $25,000. If there are any such orders (that is, if the column is not empty), the EXISTS test is TRUE. If the subquery produces no rows, the EXISTS test is FALSE. The EXISTS test cannot produce a NULL value.

You can reverse the logic of the EXISTS test using the NOT EXISTS form. In this case, the test is TRUE if the subquery produces no rows, and FALSE otherwise.

Notice that the EXISTS search condition doesn't really *use* the results of the subquery at all. It merely tests to see whether the subquery produces any results. For this reason, SQL relaxes the rule that "subqueries must return a single column of data" and allows you to use the SELECT * form in the subquery of an EXISTS test. The previous subquery could thus have been written:

List the products for which an order of $25,000 or more has been received.

```
SELECT DESCRIPTION
  FROM PRODUCTS
 WHERE EXISTS (SELECT *
                 FROM ORDERS
                WHERE PRODUCT = PRODUCT_ID
                  AND MFR = MFR_ID
                  AND AMOUNT >= 25000.00)
```

In practice, the subquery in an EXISTS test is *always* written using the SELECT * notation.

Here are some additional examples of queries that use EXISTS:

List any customers assigned to Sue Smith who have not placed an order for over $3,000.

```
SELECT COMPANY
  FROM CUSTOMERS
 WHERE CUST_REP = (SELECT EMPL_NUM
                     FROM SALESREPS
                    WHERE NAME = 'Sue Smith')
   AND NOT EXISTS (SELECT *
                     FROM ORDERS
                    WHERE CUST = CUST_NUM
                      AND AMOUNT > 3000.00)

COMPANY
-----------------
Carter & Sons
Fred Lewis Corp.
```

List the offices where there is a salesperson whose quota represents more than 55 percent of the office's target.

```
SELECT CITY
  FROM OFFICES
 WHERE EXISTS (SELECT *
                 FROM SALESREPS
                WHERE REP_OFFICE = OFFICE
                  AND QUOTA > (.55 * TARGET))


CITY
--------
Denver
Atlanta
```

Note that in each of these examples, the subquery includes an outer reference to a column of the table in the main query. In practice, the subquery in an EXISTS test will always contain an outer reference that "links" the subquery to the row currently being tested by the main query.

Quantified Tests (ANY and ALL) *

The subquery version of the IN test checks whether a data value is equal to some value in a column of subquery results. SQL provides two *quantified tests*, ANY and ALL, that extend this notion to other comparison operators, such as greater than (>) and less than (<). Both of these tests compare a data value to the column of data values produced by a subquery, as shown in Figure 9-6.

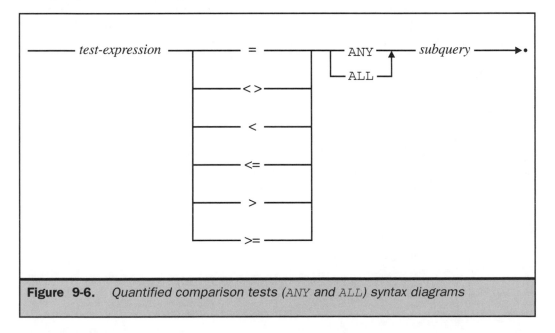

Figure 9-6. *Quantified comparison tests (ANY and ALL) syntax diagrams*

The ANY Test *

The ANY test is used in conjunction with one of the six SQL comparison operators (=, <>, <, <=, >, >=) to compare a single test value to a column of data values produced by a subquery. To perform the test, SQL uses the specified comparison operator to compare the test value to *each* data value in the column, one at a time. If *any* of the individual comparisons yield a TRUE result, the ANY test returns a TRUE result.

Here is an example of a request that can be handled with the ANY test:

List the salespeople who have taken an order that represents more than 10% of their quota.

```
SELECT NAME
  FROM SALESREPS
 WHERE (.1 * QUOTA) < ANY (SELECT AMOUNT
                             FROM ORDERS
                            WHERE REP = EMPL_NUM)

NAME
--------------
Sam Clark
Larry Fitch
Nancy Angelli
```

Conceptually, the main query tests each row of the SALESREPS table, one-by-one. The subquery finds all of the orders taken by the "current" salesperson and returns a column containing the order amounts for those orders. The WHERE clause of the main query then computes 10 percent of the current salesperson's quota and uses it as a test value, comparing it to every order amount produced by the subquery. If there is *any* order amount that exceeds the calculated test value, the "< ANY" test returns TRUE, and the salesperson is included in the query results. If not, the salesperson is not included in the query results. The keyword SOME is an alternative for ANY specified by the ANSI/ISO SQL standard. Either keyword can generally be used, but some DBMS brands do not support SOME.

The ANY test can sometimes be difficult to understand because it involves an entire set of comparisons, not just one. It helps if you read the test in a slightly different way than it appears in the statement. If this ANY test appears:

```
WHERE X < ANY (SELECT Y …)
```

instead of reading the test like this:

```
"where X is less than any select Y…"
```

try reading it like this:

```
"where, for some Y, X is less than Y"
```

When you use this trick, the preceding query becomes:

Select the salespeople where, for some order taken by the salesperson, 10% of the salesperson's quota is less than the order amount.

If the subquery in an ANY test produces no rows of query results, or if the query results include NULL values, the operation of the ANY test may vary from one DBMS to another. The ANSI/ISO SQL standard specifies these detailed rules describing the results of the ANY test when the test value is compared to the column of subquery results:

- If the subquery produces an empty column of query results, the ANY test returns FALSE—there is no value produced by the subquery for which the comparison test holds.

- If the comparison test is TRUE for *at least one* of the data values in the column, then the ANY search condition returns TRUE—there is indeed some value produced by the subquery for which the comparison test holds.

- If the comparison test is FALSE for every data value in the column, then the ANY search condition returns FALSE. In this case, you can conclusively state that there is no value produced by the subquery for which the comparison test holds.

- If the comparison test is not TRUE for any data value in the column, but it is NULL (unknown) for one or more of the data values, then the ANY search condition returns NULL. In this situation, you cannot conclusively state whether there is a value produced by the subquery for which the comparison test holds; there may be or there may not be, depending on the "correct" values for the NULL (unknown) data.

The ANY comparison operator can be very tricky to use in practice, especially in conjunction with the inequality (<>) comparison operator. Here is an example that shows the problem:

List the names and ages of all the people in the sales force who do not manage an office.

It's tempting to express this query as shown on the following page.

```
SELECT NAME, AGE
  FROM SALESREPS
 WHERE EMPL_NUM <> ANY (SELECT MGR
                          FROM OFFICES)
```

The subquery:

```
SELECT MGR
  FROM OFFICES
```

obviously produces the employee numbers of the managers, and therefore the query *seems* to be saying:

Find each salesperson who is not the manager of any office.

But that's *not* what the query says! What it *does* say is this:

Find each salesperson who, for some office, *is not the manager of that office.*

Of course for any given salesperson, it's possible to find *some* office where that salesperson is not the manager. The query results would include *all* the salespeople and therefore fail to answer the question that was posed! The correct query is:

```
SELECT NAME, AGE
  FROM SALESREPS
 WHERE NOT (EMPL_NUM = ANY (SELECT MGR
                              FROM OFFICES))
```

```
NAME            AGE
--------------  ----
Mary Jones       31
Sue Smith        48
Dan Roberts      45
Tom Snyder       41
Paul Cruz        29
Nancy Angelli    49
```

You can always turn a query with an ANY test into a query with an EXISTS test by moving the comparison *inside* the search condition of the subquery. This is usually a very good idea because it eliminates errors like the one just described. Here is an alternative form of the query, using the EXISTS test:

```
SELECT NAME, AGE
  FROM SALESREPS
 WHERE NOT EXISTS (SELECT *
                     FROM OFFICES
                    WHERE EMPL_NUM = MGR)
```

```
NAME              AGE
-------------    ----
Mary Jones         31
Sue Smith          48
Dan Roberts        45
Tom Snyder         41
Paul Cruz          29
Nancy Angelli      49
```

The ALL Test *

Like the ANY test, the ALL test is used in conjunction with one of the six SQL
comparison operators (=, <>, <, <=, >, >=) to compare a single test value to a column of
data values produced by a subquery. To perform the test, SQL uses the specified
comparison operator to compare the test value to *each* data value in the column, one at
a time. If *all* of the individual comparisons yield a TRUE result, the ALL test returns a
TRUE result.

Here is an example of a request that can be handled with the ALL test:

*List the offices and their targets where all of the salespeople have sales that exceed 50% of
the office's target.*

```
SELECT CITY, TARGET
  FROM OFFICES
 WHERE (.50 * TARGET) < ALL (SELECT SALES
                               FROM SALESREPS
                              WHERE REP_OFFICE = OFFICE)
```

```
CITY            TARGET
------------    ------------
Denver          $300,000.00
New York        $575,000.00
Atlanta         $350,000.00
```

Conceptually, the main query tests each row of the OFFICES table, one-by-one. The
subquery finds all of the salespeople who work in the "current" office and returns a
column containing the sales for each salesperson. The WHERE clause of the main query

then computes 50 percent of the office's target and uses it as a test value, comparing it to every sales value produced by the subquery. If *all* of the sales values exceed the calculated test value, the "< ALL" test returns a TRUE, and the office is included in the query results. If not, the office is not included in the query results.

Like the ANY test, the ALL test can be difficult to understand because it involves an entire set of comparisons, not just one. Again, it helps if you read the test in a slightly different way than it appears in the statement. If this ALL test appears:

```
WHERE X < ALL (SELECT Y …)
```

instead of reading like this:

```
"where X is less than all select Y…"
```

try reading the test like this:

```
"where, for all Y, X is less than Y"
```

When you use this trick, the preceding query becomes:

Select the offices where, for all *salespeople who work in the office, 50% of the office's target is less than the salesperson's sales.*

If the subquery in an ALL test produces no rows of query results, or if the query results include NULL values, the operation of the ALL test may vary from one DBMS to another. The ANSI/ISO SQL standard specifies these detailed rules describing the results of the ALL test when the test value is compared to the column of subquery results:

- If the subquery produces an empty column of query results, the ALL test returns TRUE. The comparison test *does* hold for every value produced by the subquery; there just aren't any values.

- If the comparison test is TRUE for every data value in the column, then the ALL search condition returns TRUE. Again, the comparison test holds true for every value produced by the subquery.

- If the comparison test is FALSE for any data value in the column, then the ALL search condition returns FALSE. In this case, you can conclusively state that the comparison test does not hold true for every data value produced by the query.

■ If the comparison test is not `FALSE` for any data value in the column, but it is `NULL` for one or more of the data values, then the `ALL` search condition returns `NULL`. In this situation, you cannot conclusively state whether there is a value produced by the subquery for which the comparison test does not hold true; there may be or there may not be, depending on the "correct" values for the `NULL` (unknown) data.

The subtle errors that can occur when the `ANY` test is combined with the inequality (<>) comparison operator also occur with the `ALL` test. As with the `ANY` test, the `ALL` test can always be converted into an equivalent `EXISTS` test by moving the comparison inside the subquery.

Subqueries and Joins

You may have noticed as you read through this chapter that many of the queries that were written using subqueries could also have been written as multi-table queries, or joins. This is often the case, and SQL allows you to write the query either way. This example illustrates the point:

List the names and ages of salespeople who work in offices in the Western region.

```
SELECT NAME, AGE
  FROM SALESREPS
 WHERE REP_OFFICE IN (SELECT OFFICE
                        FROM OFFICES
                       WHERE REGION = 'Western')

NAME            AGE
-------------- ----
Sue Smith        48
Larry Fitch      62
Nancy Angelli    49
```

This form of the query closely parallels the stated request. The subquery yields a list of offices in the Western region, and the main query finds the salespeople who work in one of the offices in the list. You'll see on the next page an alternative form of the query, using a two-table join.

List the names and ages of salespeople who work in offices in the Western region.

```
SELECT NAME, AGE
  FROM SALESREPS, OFFICES
 WHERE REP_OFFICE = OFFICE
   AND REGION = 'Western'

NAME             AGE
-------------    ----
Sue Smith          48
Larry Fitch        62
Nancy Angelli      49
```

This form of the query joins the SALESREPS table to the OFFICES table to find the region where each salesperson works, and then eliminates those that do not work in the Western region.

Either of the two queries will find the correct salespeople, and neither one is "right" or "wrong." Many people will find the first form (with the subquery) more natural, because the English request doesn't ask for any information about offices, and because it seems a little strange to join the SALESREPS and OFFICES tables to answer the request. Of course if the request is changed to ask for some information from the OFFICES table:

List the names and ages of the salespeople who work in offices in the Western region and the cities where they work.

the subquery form will no longer work, and the two-table query must be used. Conversely, many queries with subqueries *cannot* be translated into an equivalent join. Here is a simple example:

List the names and ages of salespeople who have above average quotas.

```
SELECT NAME, AGE
  FROM SALESREPS
 WHERE QUOTA > (SELECT AVG(QUOTA)
                  FROM SALESREPS)

NAME             AGE
-------------    ----
Bill Adams         37
Sue Smith          48
Larry Fitch        62
```

In this case, the inner query is a summary query and the outer query is not, so there is no way the two queries can be combined into a single join.

Nested Subqueries

All of the queries described thus far in this chapter have been "two-level" queries, involving a main query and a subquery. Just as you can use a subquery "inside" a main query, you can use a subquery inside another subquery. Here is an example of a request that is naturally represented as a three-level query, with a main query, a subquery, and a subsubquery:

List the customers whose salespeople are assigned to offices in the Eastern sales region.

```
SELECT COMPANY
  FROM CUSTOMERS
 WHERE CUST_REP IN (SELECT EMPL_NUM
                      FROM SALESREPS
                     WHERE REP_OFFICE IN (SELECT OFFICE
                                            FROM OFFICES
                                           WHERE REGION = 'Eastern'))

COMPANY
----------------
First Corp.
Smithson Corp.
AAA Investments
JCP Inc.
Chen Associates
QMA Assoc.
Ian & Schmidt
Acme Mfg.
   .
   .
   .
```

In this example, the innermost subquery:

```
SELECT OFFICE
  FROM OFFICES
 WHERE REGION = 'Eastern'
```

produces a column containing the office numbers of the offices in the Eastern region. The next subquery:

```
SELECT EMPL_NUM
   FROM SALESREPS
 WHERE REP_OFFICE IN (subquery)
```

produces a column containing the employee numbers of the salespeople who work in one of the selected offices. Finally, the outermost query:

```
SELECT COMPANY
   FROM CUSTOMERS
  WHERE CUST_REP IN (subquery)
```

finds the customers whose salespeople have one of the selected employee numbers.

The same technique used in this three-level query can be used to build queries with four or more levels. The ANSI/ISO SQL standard does not specify a maximum number of nesting levels, but in practice a query becomes much more time-consuming as the number of levels increases. The query also becomes more difficult to read, understand, and maintain when it involves more than one or two levels of subqueries. Many SQL implementations restrict the number of subquery levels to a relatively small number.

Correlated Subqueries *

In concept, SQL performs a subquery over and over again—once for each row of the main query. For many subqueries, however, the subquery produces the *same* results for every row or row group. Here is an example:

List the sales offices whose sales are below the average target.

```
SELECT CITY
   FROM OFFICES
  WHERE SALES < (SELECT AVG(TARGET)
                    FROM OFFICES)

CITY
--------
Denver
Atlanta
```

In this query, it would be silly to perform the subquery five times (once for each office). The average target doesn't change with each office; it's completely independent of the office currently being tested. As a result, SQL can handle the query by first performing the subquery, yielding the average target ($550,000), and then converting the main query into:

```
SELECT CITY
  FROM OFFICES
 WHERE SALES < 550000.00
```

Commercial SQL implementations automatically detect this situation and use this shortcut whenever possible to reduce the amount of processing required by a subquery. However, the shortcut cannot be used if the subquery contains an outer reference, as in this example:

List all of the offices whose targets exceed the sum of the quotas of the salespeople who work in them:

```
SELECT CITY
  FROM OFFICES
 WHERE TARGET > (SELECT SUM(QUOTA)
                   FROM SALESREPS
                  WHERE REP_OFFICE = OFFICE)

CITY
-----------
Chicago
Los Angeles
```

For each row of the OFFICES table to be tested by the WHERE clause of the main query, the OFFICE column (which appears in the subquery as an outer reference) has a different value. Thus SQL has no choice but to carry out this subquery five times—once for each row in the OFFICES table. A subquery containing an outer reference is called a *correlated subquery* because its results are correlated with each individual row of the main query. For the same reason, an outer reference is sometimes called a *correlated reference.*

A subquery can contain an outer reference to a table in the FROM clause of any query that contains the subquery, no matter how deeply the subqueries are nested. A column name in a fourth-level subquery, for example, may refer to one of the tables named in the FROM clause of the main query, or to a table named in the FROM clause of the second-level subquery or the third-level subquery that contains it. Regardless of the level of nesting, an outer reference always takes on the value of the column in the "current" row of the table being tested.

Because a subquery can contain outer references, there is even more potential for ambiguous column names in a subquery than in a main query. When an unqualified column name appears within a subquery, SQL must determine whether it refers to a table in the subquery's own FROM clause, or to a FROM clause in a query containing the subquery. To minimize the possibility of confusion, SQL always interprets a column reference in a subquery *using the nearest FROM clause possible*. To illustrate this point, in this example the same table is used in the query and in the subquery:

List the salespeople who are over 40 and who manage a salesperson over quota.

```
SELECT NAME
  FROM SALESREPS
 WHERE AGE > 40
   AND EMPL_NUM IN (SELECT MANAGER
                      FROM SALESREPS
                     WHERE SALES > QUOTA)

NAME
------------
Sam Clark
Larry Fitch
```

The MANAGER, QUOTA, and SALES columns in the subquery are references to the SALESREPS table in the subquery's own FROM clause; SQL does *not* interpret them as outer references, and the subquery is not a correlated subquery. As discussed earlier, SQL can perform the subquery first in this case, finding the salespeople who are over quota and generating a list of the employee numbers of their managers. SQL can then turn its attention to the main query, selecting managers whose employee numbers appear in the generated list.

If you want to use an outer reference within a subquery like the one in the previous example, you must use a table alias to force the outer reference. This request, which adds one more qualifying condition to the previous one, shows how:

List the managers who are over 40 and who manage a salesperson who is over quota and who does not work in the same sales office as the manager.

```
SELECT NAME
  FROM SALESREPS MGRS
 WHERE AGE > 40
```

```
AND MGRS.EMPL_NUM IN (SELECT MANAGER
                          FROM SALESREPS EMPS
                         WHERE EMPS.QUOTA > EMPS.SALES
                           AND EMPS.REP_OFFICE <> MGRS.REP_OFFICE)


NAME
------------
Sam Clark
Larry Fitch
```

The copy of the SALESREPS table used in the main query now has the tag MGRS, and the copy in the subquery has the tag EMPS. The subquery contains one additional search condition, requiring that the employee's office number does not match that of the manager. The qualified column name MGRS.OFFICE in the subquery is an outer reference, and this subquery is a correlated subquery.

Subqueries in the HAVING Clause *

Although subqueries are most often found in the WHERE clause, they can also be used in the HAVING clause of a query. When a subquery appears in the HAVING clause, it works as part of the row group selection performed by the HAVING clause. Consider this query with a subquery:

List the salespeople whose average order size for products manufactured by ACI is higher than overall average order size.

```
SELECT NAME, AVG(AMOUNT)
  FROM SALESREPS, ORDERS
 WHERE EMPL_NUM = REP
   AND MFR = 'ACI'
 GROUP BY NAME
HAVING AVG(AMOUNT) > (SELECT AVG(AMOUNT)
                        FROM ORDERS)


NAME           AVG(AMOUNT)
-----------  -------------
Sue Smith      $15,000.00
Tom Snyder     $22,500.00
```

Figure 9-7 shows conceptually how this query works. The subquery calculates the "overall average order size." It is a simple subquery and contains no outer references,

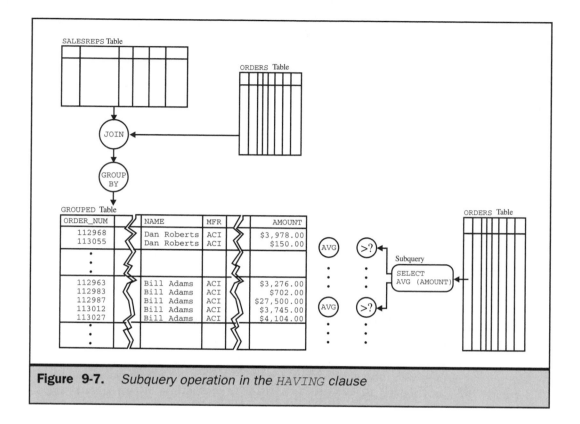

Figure 9-7. *Subquery operation in the HAVING clause*

so SQL can calculate the average once and then use it repeatedly in the HAVING clause. The main query goes through the ORDERS table, finding all orders for ACI products, and groups them by salesperson. The HAVING clause then checks each row group to see whether the average order size in that group is bigger than the average for all orders, calculated earlier. If so, the row group is retained; if not, the row group is discarded. Finally, the SELECT clause produces one summary row for each group, showing the name of the salesperson and the average order size for each.

You can also use a correlated subquery in the HAVING clause. Because the subquery is evaluated once for each row *group*, however, all outer references in the correlated subquery must be single-valued for each row group. Effectively, this means that the outer reference must either be a reference to a grouping column of the outer query or be contained within a column function. In the latter case, the value of the column function for the row group being tested is calculated as part of the subquery processing.

If the previous request is changed slightly, the subquery in the HAVING clause becomes a correlated subquery:

List the salespeople whose average order size for products manufactured by ACI is at least as big as that salesperson's overall average order size.

```
SELECT NAME, AVG(AMOUNT)
  FROM SALESREPS, ORDERS
 WHERE EMPL_NUM = REP
   AND MFR = 'ACI'
 GROUP BY NAME, EMPL_NUM
HAVING AVG(AMOUNT) >= (SELECT AVG(AMOUNT)
                         FROM ORDERS
                        WHERE REP = EMPL_NUM)


NAME           AVG(AMOUNT)
-----------    ------------
Bill Adams       $7,865.40
Sue Smith       $15,000.00
Tom Snyder      $22,500.00
```

In this new example, the subquery must produce "the overall average order size" for the salesperson whose row group is currently being tested by the HAVING clause. The subquery selects orders for that particular salesperson, using the outer reference EMPL_NUM. The outer reference is legal because EMPL_NUM has the same value in all rows of a group produced by the main query.

Subquery Summary

This chapter has described subqueries, which allow you to use the results of one query to help define another query:

- A subquery is a "query within a query." Subqueries appear within one of the subquery search conditions in the WHERE or HAVING clause.

- When a subquery appears in the WHERE clause, the results of the subquery are used to select the individual rows that contribute data to the query results.

- When a subquery appears in the HAVING clause, the results of the subquery are used to select the row groups that contribute data to the query results.

- Subqueries can be nested within other subqueries.

- The subquery form of the comparison test uses one of the simple comparison operators to compare a test value to the single value returned by a subquery.

- The subquery form of the set membership test (IN) matches a test value to the set of values returned by a subquery.

- The existence test (EXISTS) checks whether a subquery returns any values.

- The quantified tests (ANY and ALL) use one of the simple comparison operators to compare a test value to all of the values returned by a subquery, checking to see whether the comparison holds for some or all of the values.

- A subquery may include an *outer reference* to a table in any of the queries that contain it, linking the subquery to the "current" row of that query.

Advanced Queries in SQL2 *

The SQL queries described thus far in Chapters 6–9 are the mainstream capabilities provided by most SQL implementations today. The combination of features they represent—column selection in the SELECT clause, row selection criteria in the WHERE clause, multi-table joins in the FROM clause, summary queries in the GROUP BY and HAVING clauses, and subqueries for more complex requests—give the user a powerful set of data retrieval and data analysis capabilities. However, database experts have pointed out many limitations of these mainstream query capabilities, including these:

- *No decision-making within queries.* Suppose you wanted to generate a two-column report from the sample database showing the name of each sales office and either its annual sales target or its year-to-date sales, whichever is larger. With standard SQL query features, this is hard to do. Or suppose you had a database that kept track of sales by quarter (four columns of data for each office) and wanted to write a program that displayed offices and their sales for a specific (user-supplied) quarter. Again, this program is more difficult to write using standard SQL queries. You must include four separate SQL queries (one for each quarter), and the program logic must select which query to run, based on user input. This simple case isn't too difficult, but in a more general case, the program could become much more complex.

- *Limited use of subqueries.* The simplest example of this limitation is the SQL1 restriction that a subquery can appear only on the right side of a comparison test in a WHERE clause. The database request "list the offices where the sum of the salesperson's quotas is greater than the office target" is most directly expressed as this query:

```
SELECT OFFICE
  FROM OFFICES
 WHERE (SELECT SUM(QUOTA)
          FROM SALESREPS
         WHERE REP_OFFICE = OFFICE) > TARGET)
```

But this isn't a legal SQL1statement. Instead, you must turn the inequality around:

```
SELECT OFFICE
  FROM OFFICES
 WHERE TARGET > (SELECT SUM(QUOTA)
                   FROM SALESREPS
                  WHERE REP_OFFICE = OFFICE)
```

In this simple example, it isn't hard to "turn the logic around," but the restriction is a nuisance at best, and it does prevent you from comparing the results of two subqueries, for example.

■ *Limited row-expressions.* Suppose you wanted to list the suppliers, item numbers, and prices for a set of products that are substitutes for one another. Conceptually, these are a set of products whose "identification" (a manufacturer-id/product-id pair) matches one of a set of values, and it would be natural to write the query using a set-membership test as:

```
SELECT MFR_ID, PRODUCT_ID, PRICE
  FROM PRODUCTS
 WHERE (MFR_ID, PRODUCT_ID) IN (('ACI',41003),('BIC',41089), …)
```

The SQL1 standard doesn't permit this kind of set-membership test. Instead, you must construct the query as a long set of individual comparisons, connected by ANDs and ORs.

■ *Limited table-expressions.* SQL allows you to define a view like this one for large orders:

```
SELECT *
  FROM PRODUCTS
 WHERE AMOUNT > 10000
```

and then use the view as if it were a "real" table in the FROM clause of a query to find out which products, in what quantities, were ordered in these large orders:

```
SELECT MFR, PRODUCT, SUM(QTY)
  FROM BIGORDERS
 GROUP BY MFR, PRODUCT
```

Conceptually, SQL should let you substitute the view definition right into the query, like this:

```
SELECT MFR, PRODUCT, SUM(QTY)
  FROM (SELECT * FROM ORDERS WHERE AMOUNT > 10000)
 GROUP BY MFR, PRODUCT
```

But the SQL1 standard doesn't allow a subquery in this position in the WHERE clause. Yet clearly the DBMS should be able to determine the meaning of this query, since it must basically do the same processing to interpret the BIGORDERS view definition.

As these examples show, the SQL1 standard and mainstream DBMS products today are relatively restrictive in their permitted use of expressions involving individual data items, sets of data items, rows, and tables. The SQL2 standard includes a number of advanced query capabilities that are focused on removing these restrictions, and making the SQL language more general. The spirit of these SQL2 capabilities tends to be "a user should be able to write a query expression that 'makes sense' and have the query expression be a legal SQL query." Because these SQL2 capabilities constitute a major expansion of the language over the SQL1 standard, most of them are required at a Full Compliance level of the standard only.

Scalar-Valued Expressions (SQL2)

The simplest extended query capabilities in SQL2 are those that provide more data manipulation and calculation power involving individual data values (called *scalars* in the SQL2 standard). Within the SQL language, individual data values tend to have three sources:

- The value of an individual column within an individual row of a table
- A literal value, such as 125.7 or "ABC"
- A user-supplied data value, entered into a program

In this SQL query:

```
SELECT NAME, EMPL_NUM, HIRE_DATE, (QUOTA * .9)
  FROM SALESREPS
 WHERE (REP_OFFICE = 13) OR TITLE = 'VP SALES'
```

the column names NAME, EMPL_NUM, HIRE_DATE, and QUOTA generate individual data values for each row of query results, as do the column names REP_OFFICE and TITLE in the WHERE clause. The numbers .9 and 13 and the character string "VP SALES" similarly generate individual data values. If this SQL statement appeared within an embedded SQL program (described in Chapter 17), the program variable office_num might contain an individual data value, and the query might appear as:

```
SELECT NAME, EMPL_NUM, HIRE_DATE, (QUOTA * .9)
  FROM SALESREPS
 WHERE (REP_OFFICE = :office_num) OR TITLE = 'VP SALES'
```

As this query and many previous examples have shown, individual data values can be combined in simple expressions, like the calculated value QUOTA * .9. To these basic SQL1 expressions, SQL2 adds the CAST operator for explicit data type conversion, the CASE operator for decision-making, the NULLIF operation for conditionally creating a NULL value, and the COALESCE operator for conditionally creating non-NULL values.

The CAST Expression (SQL2)

The SQL standard has fairly restrictive rules about combining data of different types in expressions. It specifies that the DBMS shall automatically convert among very similar data types, such as 2-byte integers and 4-byte integers. However, if you try to compare numbers and character data, for example, the standard says that the DBMS should generate an error. The standard considers this an error condition even if the character string contains numeric data. You can, however, *explicitly* ask the DBMS to convert among data types using the CAST expression, whose syntax is shown in Figure 9-8.

The CAST expression tends to be of little importance when you are typing SQL statements directly into an interactive SQL interface. However, it can be critical when using SQL from within a programming language whose data types don't match the data types supported by the SQL standard. For example, the CAST expression in the SELECT clause of this query converts the values for REP_OFFICE (integers in the sample database) and HIRE_DATE (a date in the sample database) into character strings for the returned query results:

```
SELECT NAME, CAST REP_OFFICE AS VARCHAR, HIRE_DATE AS VARCHAR
  FROM SALESREPS
```

The CAST expression can generally appear anywhere that a scalar-valued expression can appear within a SQL statement. In this example, it's used in the WHERE clause to convert a character-string customer number into an integer, so that it can be compared with the data in the database:

```
SELECT PRODUCT, QTY, AMOUNT
  FROM ORDERS
  WHERE CUST = CAST '2107' AS INTEGER
```

Instead of specifying a data type in the CAST expression, you can specify a SQL2 domain. Domains are specific collections of legal data values that can be defined in the

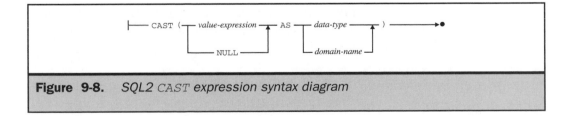

Figure 9-8. *SQL2 CAST expression syntax diagram*

database under the SQL2 standard. They are fully described in Chapter 11 because of the role they play in SQL data integrity. Note that you can also generate a NULL value of the appropriate data type for use in SQL expressions using the CAST expression.

The most common uses for the CAST expression are:

■ To convert data from within a database table where the column is defined with the "wrong" data type. For example, when a column is defined as a character string, but you know it actually contains numbers (that is, strings of digits) or dates (strings that can be interpreted as a month/day/year).

■ To convert data from data types supported by the DBMS which are not supported by a host programming language. For example, most host programming languages do not have explicit date and time data types and require that date/time values be converted into character strings for handling by a program.

■ To eliminate differences between data types in two different tables. For example, if an order date is stored in one table as DATE data, but a product availability date is stored in a different table as a character string, you can still compare the columns from the two tables by CASTing one of the columns into the data type of the other. Similarly, if you want to combine data from two different tables with a UNION operation, their columns must have identical data types. You can achieve this by CASTing the columns of one of the tables.

The CASE Expression (SQL2)

The SQL2 CASE expression provides for limited decision-making within SQL expressions. Its basic structure, shown in Figure 9-9, is similar to the IF...THEN...ELSE statement found in many programming languages. When the DBMS encounters a CASE expression, it evaluates the first *search condition*, and if it is TRUE, then the value of the CASE expression is the value of the first *result expression*. If the result of the first search condition is not TRUE, the DBMS proceeds to the second search condition, and checks whether it is TRUE. If so, the value of the CASE expression is the value of the second result expression, and so on.

Here is a simple example of the use of the CASE expression. Suppose you want to do an "A/B/C analysis" of the customers from the sample database according to their credit limits. The "A" customers are the ones with credit limits over $60,000, the "B" customers are those with limits over $30,000 and the "C" customers are the others. Using SQL1, you would have to retrieve customer names and credit limits from the database and then rely on an application program to look at the credit limit values and assign an "A," "B," or "C" rating. Using a SQL2 CASE expression, you can have the DBMS do the work for you:

```
SELECT COMPANY, CASE WHEN CREDIT_LIMIT > 60000 THEN 'A'
                     WHEN CREDIT_LIMIT > 30000 THEN 'B'
                     ELSE 'C'
  FROM CUSTOMERS
```

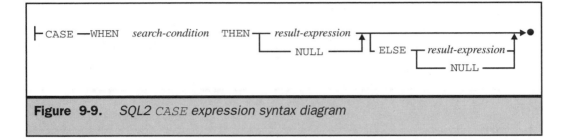

Figure 9-9. *SQL2* CASE *expression syntax diagram*

For each row of query results, the DBMS evaluates the CASE expression by first comparing the credit limit to $60,000, and if the comparison is TRUE, returns an "A" in the second column of query results. If that comparison fails, the comparison to $30,000 is made and returns a "B" if true. Otherwise, the third column of query results will return a "C."

This is a very simple example of a CASE expression. The results of the CASE expression are all literals here, but in general they can be any SQL expression. Similarly, there is no requirement that the tests in each WHEN clause are similar, as they are here. The CASE expression can also appear in other clauses of a query. Here is an example of a query where it's useful in the WHERE clause. Suppose you want to find the total of the salesperson's sales, by office. If a salesperson is not yet assigned to an office, they should be included in the total for their manager's office. Here is a query that generates the appropriate office groupings:

```
SELECT CITY, SUM(SALES)
  FROM OFFICES, SALESREPS
 WHERE OFFICE =
          CASE WHEN (REP_OFFICE IS NOT NULL) THEN REP_OFFICE
               ELSE (SELECT REP_OFFICE
                       FROM SALESREPS AS MGRS
                      WHERE MGRS.EMPL_NUM = MANAGER)
```

The SQL2 standard provides a shorthand version of the CASE expression for the common situation where you want to compare a "test value" of some kind to a sequence of data values (usually literals). This version of the CASE syntax is shown in Figure 9-10. Instead of repeating a search condition of the form:

test_value = value1

in each WHEN clause, it lets you specify the `test_value` calculation once. For example, suppose you wanted to generate a list of all of the offices, showing the names of their managers and the cities and states where they are located. The sample database doesn't

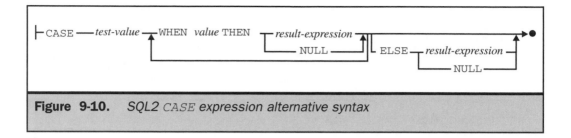

Figure 9-10.   *SQL2 CASE expression alternative syntax*

include state names, so the query must generate this information itself. Here is a query, with a CASE expression in the SELECT list, that does the job:

```
SELECT NAME, CITY, CASE OFFICE WHEN 11 THEN 'New York'
                               WHEN 12 THEN 'Illinois'
                               WHEN 13 THEN 'Georgia'
                               WHEN 21 THEN 'California'
                               WHEN 22 THEN 'Colorado'
  FROM OFFICES, SALESREPS
 WHERE MGR = EMPL_NUM
```

The COALESCE Expression (SQL2)

One of the most common uses for the decision-making capability of the CASE expression is for handling NULL values within the database. For example, it's frequently desirable to have a NULL value from the database represented by some literal value (such as the word "missing") or by some default value when using SQL to generate a report. Here is a report that lists the salespeople and their quotas. If a salesperson has not yet been assigned a quota, assume that the salesperson's actual year-to-date sales should be listed instead. If for some reason the actual year-to-date sales are also NULL (unknown), then a zero amount should be listed. The CASE statement generates the desired IF...THEN...ELSE logic:

```
SELECT NAME, CASE WHEN (QUOTA IS NOT NULL) THEN QUOTA
                  WHEN (SALES IS NOT NULL) THEN SALES
                  ELSE 0.00
  FROM SALESREPS
```

This type of NULL-handling logic is needed frequently so the SQL2 standard includes a specialized form of the CASE expression, the COALESCE expression, to handle it. The syntax for the COALESCE expression is shown in Figure 9-11. The processing rules for the COALESCE expression are very straightforward. The DBMS examines the first value in the list. If its value is not NULL, it becomes the value of the

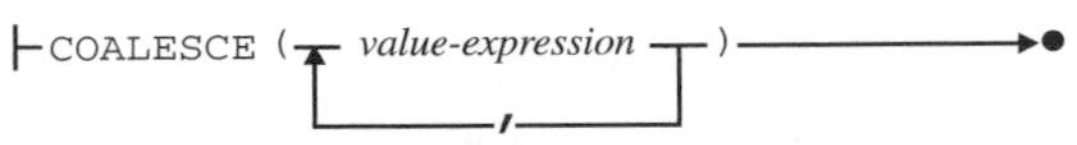

Figure 9-11.   *SQL2 COALESCE expression syntax diagram*

COALESCE expression. If the first value *is* NULL, the DBMS moves to the second value and checks to see whether it is NULL. If not, it becomes the value of the expression. Otherwise, the DBMS moves to the third value, and so on. Here is the same example just given, expressed with the COALESCE expression instead of a CASE expression:

```
SELECT NAME, COALESCE (QUOTA, SALES, 0.00)
  FROM SALESREPS
```

As you can see by comparing the two queries, the simplicity of the COALESCE syntax makes it easier to see, at a glance, the meaning of the query. However, the operation of the two queries is identical. The COALESCE expression adds simplicity, but no new capability, to the SQL2 language.

The NULLIF Expression (SQL2)

Just as the COALESCE expression is used to eliminate NULL values when they are not desired for processing, there are times when you may need to *create* NULL values. In many data processing applications (especially older ones that were developed before relational databases were popular), missing data is not represented by NULL values. Instead, some special "code value" that is otherwise invalid is used to indicate that the data is missing. For example, suppose that in the sample database, the situation where a salesperson had not yet been assigned a manager was indicated by a zero (0) value in the MANAGER column instead of a NULL value. In some situations, you will want to detect this situation within a SQL query and substitute the NULL value for the zero "code." The NULLIF expression, shown in Figure 9-12, is used for this purpose. When the DBMS encounters a NULLIF expression, it examines the first value (usually a column name) and compares it to the second value (usually the "code value" used to indicate missing data). If the two values are equal, the expression generates a NULL value. Otherwise, the expression generates the first value.

Here is a query that handles the case where missing office numbers are represented by a zero:

```
SELECT CITY, SUM(SALES)
  FROM OFFICES, SALESREPS
 WHERE OFFICE = (NULLIF REP_OFFICE, 0)
 GROUP BY CITY
```

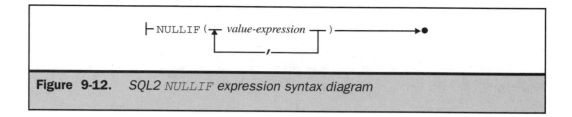

Figure 9-12. *SQL2 NULLIF expression syntax diagram*

Together, the CASE, COALESCE, and NULLIF expressions provide a solid decision-making logic capability for use within SQL statements. They fall far short of the complete logical flow constructs provided by most programming languages (looping, branching, and so on) but do provide for much greater flexibility in query expressions. The net result is that more processing work can be done by the DBMS and reflected in query results, leaving less work to be done by the human user or the application program.

Row Value Expressions (SQL2)

Although columns and the scalar data values they contain are the atomic building blocks of a relational database, the structuring of columns into rows that represent "real-world" entities, such as individual offices or customers or orders, is one of the most important features of the relational model. The SQL1 standard, and most mainstream commercial database products, certainly reflect this row/column structure, but they provide very limited capability to actually manipulate rows and groups of rows. Basically, SQL1 operations allowed you to insert a row into a table, or to retrieve, update or delete groups of rows from a database (using the SELECT, UPDATE or DELETE statements).

The SQL2 standard goes well beyond these capabilities, allowing you to generally use rows in SQL expressions in much the same way that you can use scalar values. It provides a syntax for constructing rows of data. It allows row-valued subqueries. And it defines row-valued meanings for the SQL comparison operators and other SQL structures.

Row Value Constructor (SQL2)

SQL2 allows you to specify a row of data values by using a *row value constructor* expression, whose syntax is shown in Figure 9-13. In its most common form, the row constructor is a comma-separated list of literal values, or expressions. For example, here is a row value constructor for a row of data whose structure matches the OFFICES table in the sample database:

```
(23, 'San Diego', 'Western', NULL, DEFAULT, 0.00)
```

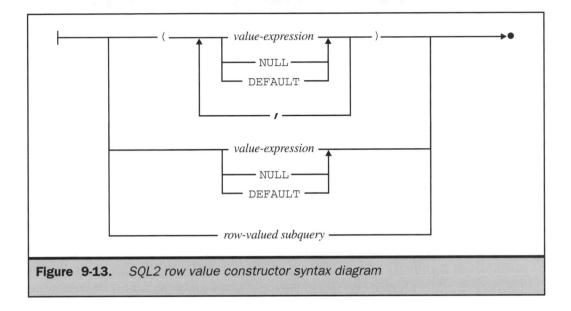

Figure 9-13. *SQL2 row value constructor syntax diagram*

The result of this expression is a single row of data with six columns. The NULL keyword in the fourth column position indicates that the fourth column in the constructed row should contain a NULL (unknown) value. The DEFAULT keyword in the fifth column position indicates that the fifth column in the constructed row should contain the default value for the column. This keyword may appear in a row value constructor only in certain situations—for example, when the row value constructor appears in an INSERT statement to add a new row to a table.

When a row constructor is used in the WHERE clause of a SQL statement, column names can also appear as individual data items within the row constructor, or as part of an expression within the row constructor. For example, consider this query:

List the order number, quantity, and amount of all orders for ACI-41002 widgets.

```
SELECT ORDER_NUM, QTY, AMOUNT
  FROM ORDERS
 WHERE (MFR,PRODUCT) = ('ACI', '41002')
```

Under the normal rules of SQL query processing, the WHERE clause is applied to each row of the ORDERS table, one-by-one. The first row value constructor in the WHERE clause (to the left of the equals sign) generates a two-column row, containing the manufacturer code and the product number for the "current" order being considered. The second row value constructor (to the right of the equals sign) generates a two-column row, containing the (literal) manufacturer code "ACI" and product number "41002." The equals sign now is comparing two *rows* of values, not two scalar values. The SQL2 standard defines this type of row value comparison for equality, which is processed by comparing, pairwise, each of the columns in the two rows. The result of the comparison is TRUE only if all of the pairwise column comparisons are TRUE. Of course, it's possible to write the query without the row value constructors, like this:

List the order number, quantity, and amount of all orders for ACI-41002 widgets.

```
SELECT ORDER_NUM, QTY, AMOUNT
  FROM ORDERS
 WHERE (MFR = 'ACI') AND (PRODUCT = '41002')
```

and in this simple example, the meaning of the query is probably equally clear with either form. However, row value constructors can be very useful in simplifying the appearance of more complex queries, and they become even more useful when combined with row value subqueries.

Row Value Subquery (SQL2)

As described throughout the earlier parts of this chapter, the SQL1 standard provided a subquery capability for expressing more complex database queries. The subquery takes the same form as a SQL query (that is, a SELECT statement), but a SQL1 subquery must be scalar-valued—that is, it must produce a *single data value* as its query results. The value generated by the subquery is then used as part of an expression within the "main" SQL statement that contains the subquery. This use of subqueries is supported by the major enterprise-class relational database systems today.

The SQL2 standard dramatically expands the subquery facility, including support for *row-valued* subqueries. A row-valued subquery returns not just a single data item, but a row of data items, which can be used in SQL2 expressions and compared to other rows. For example, suppose you wanted to show the order numbers and dates for all of the orders placed against the highest-priced product in the sample database. A logical way to start building the appropriate SQL query is to find an expression that will give you the identity (manufacturer code and product number) of the high-priced product in question. Here is a query that finds the right product:

Find the manufacturer-id and product number of the product with the highest unit price.

```
SELECT MFR_ID, PRODUCT_ID
  FROM PRODUCTS
 WHERE PRICE = (SELECT MAX(PRICE)
                  FROM PRODUCTS)
```

Ignoring the possibility of a "tie" for the most expensive product for a moment, this query will generate a single row of query results, consisting of two columns. Using SQL2's row-valued subquery capability, you can embed this entire query as a subquery within a SELECT statement to retrieve the order information:

List the order numbers and dates of all orders placed for the highest-priced product.

```
SELECT ORDER_NUM, ORDER_DATE
  FROM ORDERS
 WHERE (MFR, PRODUCT) = (SELECT MFR_ID, PRODUCT_ID
                           FROM PRODUCTS
                          WHERE PRICE = (SELECT MAX(PRICE)
                                           FROM PRODUCTS))
```

The top-level WHERE clause in this query contains a row value comparison. On the left side of the equals sign is a row value constructor consisting of two column names. Each time the WHERE clause is examined to carry out the top-level query, the value of this row-valued expression is a manufacturer-id/product-number pair from a row of the ORDERS table. On the right side of the equals sign is the subquery that generates the identity of the product with the highest dollar value. The result of this subquery is again a row-value, with two columns, whose data types match those of the row-valued expression on the left side of the equals sign.

It's possible to express this query without the row-valued subquery, but the resulting query will be much less straightforward:

List the order numbers and dates of all orders placed for the highest-priced product.

```
SELECT ORDER_NUM, ORDER_DATE
  FROM ORDERS
 WHERE (MFR = (SELECT MFR_ID
                 FROM PRODUCTS
                WHERE PRICE = (SELECT MAX(PRICE)
                                 FROM PRODUCTS))
   AND (PRODUCT = (SELECT PRODUCT_ID
                     FROM PRODUCTS
                    WHERE PRICE = (SELECT MAX(PRICE)
                                     FROM PRODUCTS)))
```

Instead of a single row-valued comparison in the WHERE clause, the resulting query has two separate scalar-valued comparisons, one for the manufacturer-id and one for the product-id. Because the comparison must be split, the lower-level subquery to find the maximum price must be repeated twice as well. Overall, the form of the query using the row-valued expression is a more direct translation of the English-language request, and it's easier to read and understand.

Row Value Comparisons (SQL2)

The most common use of row value expressions in the WHERE or HAVING clause is within a test for equality, as illustrated by the last few examples. A constructed row (often consisting of column values from a "candidate row" of query results) is compared to another constructed row (perhaps a row of subquery results or a row of literal values), and if the rows are equal, the candidate row is included in the query results. The SQL2 standard also provides for row-valued forms of the inequality comparison tests and the range test. When comparing two rows for inequality, SQL2 uses the same rules that it would use if the columns were being used to sort the rows. It compares the contents of the first column in the two rows, and if they are unequal, uses them to order the rows. If they are equal, the comparison moves to the second column, and then the third, and so on. Here are the resulting comparisons for some three-column constructed rows derived from the ORDERS table:

('ACI','41002',54) < ('REI','2A44R',5)—based on first column
('ACI','41002',54) < ('ACI','41003',35)—based on second column
('ACI','41002',10) < ('ACI','41002',54)—based on third column

Table Value Expressions (SQL2)

In addition to its extended capabilities for expressions involving simple scalar data values and row values, the SQL2 standard dramatically extended the SQL capabilities for table processing. It provides a mechanism for constructing a table of data values"in place" within a SQL statement. It allows table value subqueries and extends the subquery tests described earlier in this chapter to handle them. It also allows subqueries to appear in many more places within a SQL statement—for example, a subquery can appear in the FROM clause of a SELECT statement as of its "source tables." Finally, it provides expanded capabilities for combining tables, including the UNION, INTERSECTION, and DIFFERENCE operations.

Table Value Constructor (SQL2)

SQL2 allows you to specify a table of data values within a SQL statement by using a *table value constructor* expression, whose syntax is shown in Figure 9-14. In its simplest form, the table value constructor is a comma-separated list of row value constructors, each of which contains a comma-separated set of literals that form individual column values. For example, the SQL2 INSERT statement uses a table value constructor as the source of the data to be inserted into a database. While the SQL1 INSERT statement

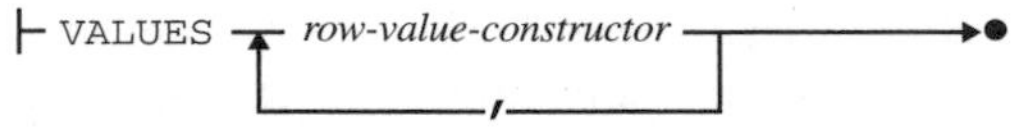

Figure 9-14. *SQL2 table value constructor syntax diagram*

(described in the next chapter) allows you to insert only a single row of data, this SQL2 INSERT statement inserts three rows into the OFFICES table:

Add three offices to the OFFICES table.

```
INSERT INTO OFFICES (OFFICE,CITY,REGION,MGR,SALES)
     VALUES (23, 'San Diego', 'Western', 108, 0.00),
            (24, 'Seattle', 'Western', 104, 0.00),
            (14, 'Boston', 'Eastern, NULL, 0.00)
```

Note that the individual rows in the table value constructor are not restricted to contain only literal values. The source of a data value can be a scalar-valued subquery, or an entire row can be the result of a row-valued subquery. Although it doesn't make much sense in the sample database, this is a legal SQL2 INSERT statement that illustrates these capabilities:

Add three offices to the OFFICES table.

```
INSERT INTO OFFICES (OFFICE,CITY,REGION,MGR,SALES)
     VALUES (23, 'San Diego', 'Western', 108, 0.00),
            (24, 'Seattle', 'Western', (SELECT MANAGER
                                          FROM SALESREPS
                                          WHERE EMPL_NUM = 105), 0.00),
          (SELECT 'BOSTON', 'EASTERN', REGION, MGR, 0.00
             FROM OFFICES
            WHERE OFFICE = 12)
```

Like the preceding example, the VALUES clause in this INSERT statement generates a three-row table to be inserted. The first row is specified with literal values. In the second row, the fourth column is specified as a scalar-valued subquery that retrieves the manager of employee number 105. In the third row, the entire row is generated by a row-valued subquery. In this case, three of the column values in the subquery's SELECT clause are actually literal values, but the third and fourth columns are produced by the subquery, which retrieves the manager and region for the New York office (number 12).

Table-Valued Subqueries (SQL2)

Just as SQL2 expanded the use of scalar subqueries into row-valued subqueries, it also extends the SQL subquery facility to support table-valued subqueries—that is, subqueries that return a full table of results. One useful role for table-valued subqueries is within the WHERE or HAVING clause, where it is combined with extended forms of the subquery tests. For example, suppose you wanted to list the descriptions and prices of all products with orders exceeding $20,000 in the sample database. Perhaps the most straightforward way to express this request is in this SQL2 statement that uses a table-valued subquery:

List the description and price of all products with individual orders over $20,000.

```
SELECT DESCRIPTION, PRICE
  FROM PRODUCTS
 WHERE (MFR_ID, PRODUCT_ID) IN (SELECT MFR, PRODUCT
                                  FROM ORDERS
                                 WHERE AMOUNT > 20000.00)
```

The top-level query is a straightforward statement of the English-language request—it asks for the description and price of those products whose "identification" (as in previous examples, a manufacturer-id/product-id pair) matches some set of products. This is expressed as a subquery set-membership test in the WHERE clause. The subquery generates a two-column table of subquery results, which are the identifications of the products that meet the stated order size criterion.

It's certainly possible to express this query in other ways. From the discussion in Chapter 7, you probably recognize that it can be stated as a join of the PRODUCTS and ORDERS tables with a compound search condition:

List the description and price of all products with individual orders over $20,000.

```
SELECT DESCRIPTION, PRICE
  FROM PRODUCTS, ORDERS
 WHERE (MFR_ID = MFR)
   AND (PRODUCT_ID = PRODUCT)
   AND (AMOUNT > 20000.00)
```

This is an equally valid statement of the query, but it's a lot further removed from the English-language request, and therefore more difficult to understand for most people. As queries become more complex, the ability to use table-valued subqueries becomes even more useful to simplify and clarify SQL requests.

The SQL2 Query Specification

The SQL2 standard formalizes the definition of what we have loosely been calling a "SELECT statement" or a "query" in the last three chapters into a basic building block called a *query specification*. For a complete understanding of the SQL2 table expression capabilities in the next section, it's useful to understand this formal definition. The form of a SQL2 query specification is shown in Figure 9-15. Its components should be familiar from the earlier chapters:

- A *select list* specifies the columns of query results. Each column is specified by an expression that tells the DBMS how to calculate its value. The column can be assigned an optional alias with the AS clause.

- The keywords ALL or UNIQUE control duplicate row elimination in the query results.

- The FROM clause specifies the tables that contribute to the query results.

- The WHERE clause describes how the DBMS should determine which rows are included in the query results and which should be discarded.

- The GROUP BY and HAVING clauses together control the grouping of individual query results rows in a grouped query, and the selection of row groups for inclusion or exclusion in the final results.

The query specification is the basic query building block in the SQL2 standard. Conceptually, it describes the process of combining data from the tables in the FROM clause into a row/column table of query results. The "value" of the query specification is a *table* of data. In the simplest case, a SQL2 query consists of a simple query specification. In a slightly more complex case, a query specification is used to describe a subquery, which appears within another (higher-level) query specification. Finally, query specifications can be combined using table-valued operations to form general-purpose query expressions, as described in the next section.

Query Expressions (SQL2)

The SQL2 standard defines a *query expression* as the full, general-purpose way that you can specify a table of query results in the SQL2 language. The basic building blocks you can use to build a query expression are:

- A query specification, as described in the preceding section (SELECT...FROM...). Its value is a table of query results.

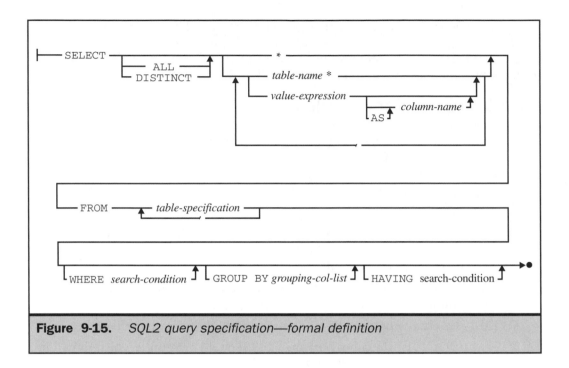

Figure 9-15. *SQL2 query specification—formal definition*

- A table value constructor, as previous described (VALUES ...). Its value is a table of constructed values.

- An explicit table reference (TABLE *tblname*). Its value is the contents of the named table.

Using these building blocks, SQL2 lets you combine their table values using the following operations:

- JOIN. SQL2 provides explicit support for full cross-product (cross-join), natural join, inner joins, and all types of outer joins (left, right, and full), as described in Chapter 6. A join operation takes two tables as its input, and produces a table of combined query results according to the join specification.

- UNION. The SQL2 UNION operation provides explicit support for merging the rows of two compatible tables (that is, two tables having the same number of columns and with corresponding columns having the same data types). The union operation takes two tables as its input and produces a single "merged table" of query results.

- DIFFERENCE. The SQL2 EXCEPT operation takes two tables as its input and produces as its output a table containing the rows that appear in the first table but do not appear in another table—that is, the rows that are "missing" from the second table. Conceptually, the EXCEPT operation is like "table subtraction." The rows of the second table are "taken away" from the rows of the first table, and the answer is the remaining rows of the first table.

■ INTERSECT. The SQL2 INTERSECT operation takes two tables as its input and produces as its output a table containing the rows that appear in both input tables.

SQL2 UNION, INTERSECT, and DIFFERENCE Operations

The SQL2 UNION, INTERSECT, and DIFFERENCE operations provide set operations for combining two input tables to form an output table. All three of the operations require that the two input tables be "union-compatible"—they must have the same number of columns, and the corresponding columns of each table must have identical data types. Here are some simple examples of SQL2 query expressions involving UNION, INTERSECT, and DIFFERENCE operations based on the sample database:

Show all products for which there is an order over $30,000 or more than $30,000 worth of inventory on hand.

```
(SELECT MFR, PRODUCT
   FROM ORDERS
  WHERE AMOUNT > 30000.00)
UNION
(SELECT MFR_ID, PRODUCT_ID)
   FROM PRODUCTS
  WHERE (PRICE * QTY_ON_HAND) > 30000)
```

Show all products for which there is an order over $30,000 and more than $30,000 worth of inventory on hand.

```
(SELECT MFR, PRODUCT
   FROM ORDERS
  WHERE AMOUNT > 30000.00)
INTERSECT
(SELECT MFR_ID, PRODUCT_ID)
   FROM PRODUCTS
  WHERE (PRICE * QTY_ON_HAND) > 30000)
```

Show all products for which there is an order over $30,000 except for those products that sell for under $1000.

```
(SELECT MFR, PRODUCT
   FROM ORDERS
  WHERE AMOUNT > 30000.00)
 EXCEPT
(SELECT MFR_ID, PRODUCT_ID)
   FROM PRODUCTS
  WHERE PRICE < 100.00)
```

By default, the UNION, INTERSECT, and EXCEPT operations eliminate duplicate rows during their processing. This is usually the desired result, as it is in these examples, but there are occasions when you may need to suppress the elimination of duplicate rows. You can do this by specifying the UNION ALL, INTERSECT ALL, or EXCEPT ALL forms of the operations.

Note each of these examples produces a two-column table of query results. The results come from two different source tables within the database—the ORDERS table and the PRODUCTS table. However, the columns selected from these tables have the same corresponding data types, so they can be combined using these operations. In the sample database, the corresponding columns have different names in the two tables (the manufacturer-id column is named MFR in the ORDERS table but named MFR_ID in the PRODUCTS table). However, corresponding columns such as these will often have the *same* name in each of the tables being combined. As a convenience, SQL2 lets you specify the corresponding columns in a CORRESPONDING clause attached to the UNION, INTERSECT, or EXCEPT operation. Here is the preceding UNION example, changed for the situation where the ORDERS and PRODUCTS tables have parallel column names for manufacturer-id and product-id:

Show all products for which there is an order over $30,000 or more than $30,000 worth of inventory on hand.

```
(SELECT *
   FROM ORDERS
  WHERE AMOUNT > 30000.00)
UNION CORRESPONDING BY (MFR, PRODUCT)
(SELECT *
   FROM PRODUCTS
  WHERE (PRICE * QTY_ON_HAND) > 30000)
```

In a case like this one where *all* of the corresponding (that is, identically named) columns from the two tables participate in the UNION operation, SQL2 even allows you to leave off the explicit list of column names:

Show all products for which there is an order over $30,000 or more than $30,000 worth of inventory on hand.

```
(SELECT *
   FROM ORDERS
  WHERE AMOUNT > 30000.00)
UNION CORRESPONDING
(SELECT *
   FROM PRODUCTS
  WHERE (PRICE * QTY_ON_HAND) > 30000)
```

Finally, it's worth noting that the column alias capability of the query specification can be used to rename or assign names to the columns from the individual query results that are being combined with the UNION operation. If we eliminate the assumption that the PRODUCTS and ORDERS tables use the same column names, it's still possible to use the CORRESPONDING form of the UNION operation in this query simply by renaming the columns in one of the tables:

Show all products for which there is an order over $30,000 or more than $30,000 worth of inventory on hand.

```
(SELECT *
   FROM ORDERS
  WHERE AMOUNT > 30000.00)
  UNION CORRESPONDING
(SELECT MFR_ID AS MFR, PRODUCT_ID AS PRODUCT)
   FROM PRODUCTS
  WHERE (PRICE * QTY_ON_HAND) > 30000)
```

In this simple example, there is not much advantage in this construct, but in the more general case where the individual queries involve calculated columns or are grouped queries, the CORRESPONDING clause and column aliases can help to clarify the meaning of the query.

Query Expressions in the FROM Clause

SQL2 query expressions provide a much more powerful and flexible method for generating and combining tables of query results than the simple subquery and UNION operations provided by the SQL1 standard. To make query expressions even more useful and more general-purpose, the SQL2 standard allows them to appear almost anywhere that a table reference could appear in a SQL1 query. In particular, a query expression can appear in place of a table name in the FROM clause. Here is a simple example of a SQL2 query for the sample database that uses this feature:

Show the names and total outstanding orders of all customers with credit limits over $50,000.

```
(SELECT COMPANY, TOT_ORDERS
   FROM CUSTOMER, (SELECT CUST, SUM(AMOUNT) AS TOT_ORDERS
                     FROM ORDERS
                     GROUP BY CUST),
  WHERE (CREDIT_LIMIT > 50000.00)
    AND (CUST_NUM = CUST)
```

The second "table name" in the FROM clause of the main query is not a table name at all, but a full-blown query expression. In fact, the expression could have been much more complex, involving UNION or JOIN operations. When a query expression appears in the FROM clause, as it does here, the DBMS conceptually carries it out *first*, before any other processing of the query, and creates a "temporary table" of the query results generated by the query expression. In this case, this "temporary table" consists of two columns, listing each customer number and the total of orders for that customer number. This temporary table then acts as one of the source tables for the main query. In this example, its contents are joined to the CUSTOMER table to obtain the company name and generate the answer to the main question.

There are many other ways in which this query could be written. The entire query could be written as one top-level grouped query that joins the CUSTOMER and ORDERS table. The join operation could be made explicit with a SQL2 JOIN operator, and then the results of the join could be grouped in the top-level query. As this example shows, one of the benefits of the SQL2 query expression capabilities is that they typically provide several different ways to obtain the same query results. The general philosophy behind the SQL2 capabilities in this area was that the SQL language should provide the flexibility to express a query in the most natural form. The underlying DBMS must be able to take the query, however expressed, break it down into its fundamentals, and then determine the most efficient way to carry out the query. This "internal query execution plan" may be quite different than the apparent plan called for by the actual SQL statement, but so long as it produces the same query results, the net effect is to shift the "optimization" workload from the human user or programmer to the DBMS.

SQL Queries—A Final Summary

This concludes the discussion of the SQL queries and the SELECT statement that began in Chapter 6. As described in the last three chapters, the clauses of the SELECT statement provide a powerful, flexible set of capabilities for retrieving data from the database. Each clause plays a specific role in data retrieval:

- The FROM clause specifies the source tables that contribute data to the query results. Every column name in the body of the SELECT statement must unambiguously identify a column from one of these tables, or it must be an outer reference to a column from a source table of an outer query.

- The WHERE clause, if present, selects individual combinations of rows from the source tables to participate in the query results. Subqueries in the WHERE clause are evaluated for each individual row.

- The GROUP BY clause, if present, groups the individual rows selected by the WHERE clause into row groups.

- The HAVING clause, if present, selects row groups to participate in the query results. Subqueries in the HAVING clause are evaluated for each row group.

- The SELECT clause determines which data values actually appear as columns in the final query results.

- The DISTINCT keyword, if present, eliminates duplicate rows of query results.

- The UNION operator, if present, merges the query results produced by individual SELECT statements into a single set of query results.

- The ORDER BY clause, if present, sorts the final query results based on one or more columns.

- The SQL2 query expression capabilities add row-valued and table-valued expressions and INTERSECT and EXCEPT operations to the SQL1 capabilities. The fundamental flow of query processing is not changed, but the ability to express "queries within queries" is greatly enhanced.

Figure 9-16 shows the final version of the rules for SQL query processing, extended to include subqueries. It provides a complete definition of the query results produced by a SELECT statement.

To generate the query results for a SELECT statement:

1. If the statement is a UNION of SELECT statements, apply Steps 2 through 7 to each of the statements to generate their individual query results.

2. Form the product of the tables named in the FROM clause. If the FROM clause names a single table, the product is that table.

3. If there is a WHERE clause, apply its search condition to each row of the product table, retaining those rows for which the search condition is TRUE (and discarding those for which it is FALSE or NULL). If the HAVING clause contains a subquery, the subquery is performed for each row as it is tested.

4. If there is a GROUP BY clause, arrange the remaining rows of the product table into row groups, so that the rows in each group have identical values in all of the grouping columns.

5. If there is a HAVING clause, apply its search condition to each row group, retaining those groups for which the search condition is TRUE (and discarding those for which it is FALSE or NULL). If the HAVING clause contains a subquery, the subquery is performed for each row group as it is tested.

6. For each remaining row (or row group), calculate the value of each item in the select list to produce a single row of query results. For a simple column reference, use the value of the column in the current row (or row group). For a column function, use the current row group as its argument if GROUP BY is specified; otherwise, use the entire set of rows.

7. If SELECT DISTINCT is specified, eliminate any duplicate rows of query results that were produced.

8. If the statement is a UNION of SELECT statements, merge the query results for the individual statements into a single table of query results. Eliminate duplicate rows unless UNION ALL is specified.

9. If there is an ORDER BY clause, sort the query results as specified.

The rows generated by this procedure comprise the query results.

Figure 9-16. *SQL query processing rules (final version)*

Part III

Updating Data

SQL is not only a query language, it's a complete language for retrieving and modifying data in a database. The next three chapters focus on database updates. Chapter 10 describes SQL statements that add data to a database, remove data from a database, and modify existing database data. Chapter 11 describes how SQL maintains the integrity of stored data when the data is modified. Chapter 12 describes the SQL transaction-processing features that support concurrent database updates by many different users.

Chapter 10

Database Updates

SQL is a complete data manipulation language that is used not only for database queries, but also to modify and update data in the database. Compared to the complexity of the SELECT statement, which supports SQL queries, the SQL statements that modify database contents are extremely simple. However, database updates pose some challenges for a DBMS beyond those presented by database queries. The DBMS must protect the integrity of stored data during changes, ensuring that only valid data is introduced into the database, and that the database remains self-consistent, even in the event of system failures. The DBMS must also coordinate simultaneous updates by multiple users, ensuring that the users and their changes do not interfere with one another.

This chapter describes the three SQL statements that are used to modify the contents of a database:

- INSERT, which adds new rows of data to a table,

- DELETE, which removes rows of data from a table, and

- UPDATE, which modifies existing data in the database.

In Chapter 11, SQL facilities for maintaining data integrity are described. Chapter 12 covers SQL support for multi-user concurrency.

Adding Data to the Database

A new row of data is typically added to a relational database when a new entity represented by the row "appears in the outside world." For example, in the sample database:

- When you hire a new salesperson, a new row must be added to the SALESREPS table to store the salesperson's data.

- When a salesperson signs a new customer, a new row must be added to the CUSTOMERS table, representing the new customer.

- When a customer places an order, a new row must be added to the ORDERS table to contain the order data.

In each case, the new row is added to maintain the database as an accurate model of the real world. The smallest unit of data that can be added to a relational database is a single row. In general, a SQL-based DBMS provides three ways to add new rows of data to a database:

- A *single-row* INSERT statement adds a single new row of data to a table. It is commonly used in daily applications—for example, data entry programs.

■ A *multi-row* INSERT statement extracts rows of data from another part of the database and adds them to a table. It is commonly used in end-of-month or end-of-year processing when "old" rows of a table are moved to an inactive table.

■ A *bulk load* utility adds data to a table from a file that is outside of the database. It is commonly used to initially load the database or to incorporate data downloaded from another computer system or collected from many sites.

The Single-Row INSERT Statement

The single-row INSERT statement, shown in Figure 10-1, adds a new row to a table. The INTO clause specifies the table that receives the new row (the *target* table), and the VALUES clause specifies the data values that the new row will contain. The column list indicates which data value goes into which column of the new row.

Suppose you just hired a new salesperson, Henry Jacobsen, with the following personal data:

Name:	Henry Jacobsen
Age:	36
Employee Number:	111
Title:	Sales Manager
Office:	Atlanta (office number 13)
Hire Date:	July 25, 1990
Quota:	Not yet assigned
Year-to-Date Sales:	$0.00

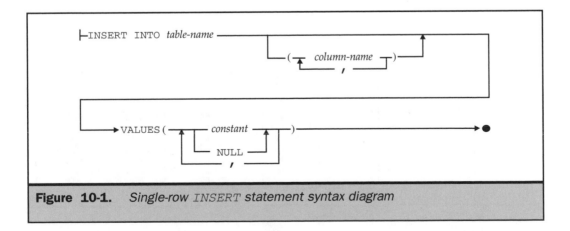

Figure 10-1.   *Single-row INSERT statement syntax diagram*

Here is the INSERT statement that adds Mr. Jacobsen to the sample database:

Add Henry Jacobsen as a new salesperson.

```
INSERT INTO SALESREPS (NAME, AGE, EMPL_NUM, SALES, TITLE,
                       HIRE_DATE, REP_OFFICE)
    VALUES ('Henry Jacobsen', 36, 111, 0.00, 'Sales Mgr',
                       '25-JUL-90', 13)


1 row inserted.
```

Figure 10-2 graphically illustrates how SQL carries out this INSERT statement. Conceptually, the INSERT statement builds a single row of data that matches the column structure of the table, fills it with the data from the VALUES clause, and then adds the new row to the table. The rows of a table are unordered, so there is no notion of inserting the row "at the top" or "at the bottom" or "between two rows" of the table. After the INSERT statement, the new row is simply a part of the table. A subsequent query against the SALESREPS table will include the new row, but it may appear anywhere among the rows of query results.

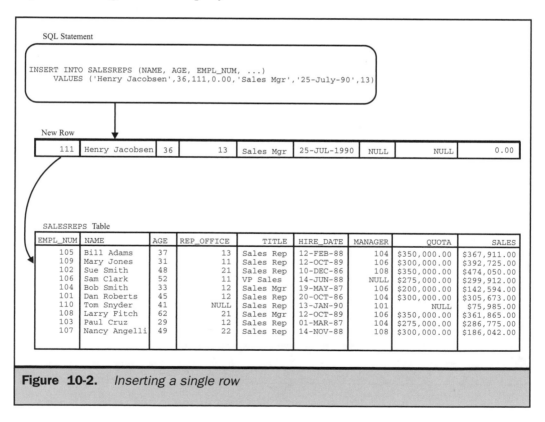

Figure 10-2.   *Inserting a single row*

Suppose that Mr. Jacobsen now receives his first order, from InterCorp, a new customer who is assigned customer number 2126. The order is for 20 ACI-41004 Widgets, for a total price of $2,340, and has been assigned order number 113069. Here are the INSERT statements that add the new customer and the order to the database:

Insert a new customer and order for Mr. Jacobsen.

```
INSERT INTO CUSTOMERS (COMPANY, CUST_NUM, CREDIT_LIMIT, CUST_REP)
     VALUES ('InterCorp', 2126, 15000.00, 111)

1 row inserted.

INSERT INTO ORDERS (AMOUNT, MFR, PRODUCT, QTY, ORDER_DATE,
                    ORDER_NUM, CUST, REP)
     VALUES (2340.00, 'ACI', '41004', 20, CURRENT DATE, 113069,
             2126, 111)

1 row inserted.
```

As this example shows, the INSERT statement can become lengthy if there are many columns of data, but its format is still very straightforward. The second INSERT statement uses the system constant CURRENT DATE in its VALUES clause, causing the current date to be inserted as the order date. This system constant is specified in the SQL2 standard and is supported by many of the popular SQL products. Other brands of DBMS provide other system constants or built-in functions to obtain the current date and time.

You can use the INSERT statement with interactive SQL to add rows to a table that grows very rarely, such as the OFFICES table. In practice, however, data about a new customer, order, or salesperson is almost always added to a database through a forms-oriented data entry program. When the data entry is complete, the application program inserts the new row of data using programmatic SQL. Regardless of whether interactive or programmatic SQL is used, however, the INSERT statement is the same.

The table name specified in the INSERT statement is normally an unqualified table name, specifying a table that you own. To insert data into a table owned by another user, you can specify a qualified table name. Of course you must also have permission to insert data into the table, or the INSERT statement will fail. The SQL security scheme and permissions are described in Chapter 15.

The purpose of the column list in the INSERT statement is to match the data values in the VALUES clause with the columns that are to receive them. The list of values and the list of columns must both contain the same number of items, and the data type of each value must be compatible with the data type of the corresponding column, or an error will occur. The ANSI/ISO standard mandates unqualified column names in the column list, but many implementations allow qualified names. Of course, there can be no ambiguity in the column names anyway, because they must all reference columns of the target table.

Inserting NULL Values

When SQL inserts a new row of data into a table, it automatically assigns a NULL value to any column whose name is missing from the column list in the INSERT statement. In this INSERT statement, which added Mr. Jacobsen to the SALESREPS table, the QUOTA and MANAGER columns were omitted:

```
INSERT INTO SALESREPS (NAME, AGE, EMPL_NUM, SALES, TITLE,
                       HIRE_DATE, REP_OFFICE)
     VALUES ('Henry Jacobsen', 36, 111, 0.00, 'Sales Mgr',
                       '25-JUL-90', 13)
```

As a result, the newly added row has a NULL value in the QUOTA and MANAGER columns, as shown in Figure 10-2. You can make the assignment of a NULL value more explicit by including these columns in the column list and specifying the keyword NULL in the values list. This INSERT statement has exactly the same effect as the previous one:

```
INSERT INTO SALESREPS (NAME, AGE, EMPL_NUM, SALES, QUOTA, TITLE,
                       MANAGER, HIRE_DATE, REP_OFFICE)
     VALUES ('Henry Jacobsen', 36, 111, 0.00, NULL, 'Sales Mgr',
                       NULL, '25-JUL-90', 13)
```

Inserting All Columns

As a convenience, SQL allows you to omit the column list from the INSERT statement. When the column list is omitted, SQL automatically generates a column list consisting of all columns of the table, in left-to-right sequence. This is the same column sequence generated by SQL when you use a SELECT * query. Using this shortcut, the previous INSERT statement could be rewritten equivalently as:

```
INSERT INTO SALESREPS
     VALUES (111, 'Henry Jacobsen', 36, 13, 'Sales Mgr',
                '25-JUL-90', NULL, NULL, 0.00)
```

When you omit the column list, the NULL keyword *must* be used in the values list to explicitly assign NULL values to columns, as shown in the example. In addition, the sequence of data values must correspond *exactly* to the sequence of columns in the table.

Omitting the column list is convenient in interactive SQL because it reduces the length of the INSERT statement you must type. For programmatic SQL, the column list should always be specified because it makes the program easier to read and understand.

The Multi-Row INSERT Statement

The second form of the INSERT statement, shown in Figure 10-3, adds multiple rows of data to its target table. In this form of the INSERT statement, the data values for the new rows are not explicitly specified within the statement text. Instead, the source of new rows is a database query, specified in the statement.

Adding rows whose values come from within the database itself may seem strange at first, but it's very useful in some special situations. For example, suppose that you want to copy the order number, date, and amount of all orders placed before January 1, 1990, from the ORDERS table into another table, called OLDORDERS. The multi-row INSERT statement provides a compact, efficient way to copy the data:

Copy old orders into the OLDORDERS table.

```
INSERT INTO OLDORDERS (ORDER_NUM, ORDER_DATE, AMOUNT)
    SELECT ORDER_NUM, ORDER_DATE, AMOUNT
      FROM ORDERS
     WHERE ORDER_DATE < '01-JAN-90'

9 rows inserted.
```

This INSERT statement looks complicated, but it's really very simple. The statement identifies the table to receive the new rows (OLDORDERS) and the columns to receive the data, just like the single-row INSERT statement. The remainder of the statement is a query that retrieves data from the ORDERS table. Figure 10-4 graphically illustrates the operation of this INSERT statement. Conceptually, SQL first performs the query against the ORDERS table and then inserts the query results, row by row, into the OLDORDERS table.

Here's another situation where you could use the multi-row INSERT statement. Suppose you want to analyze customer-buying patterns by looking at which customers

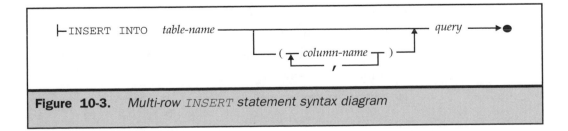

Figure 10-3.   *Multi-row INSERT statement syntax diagram*

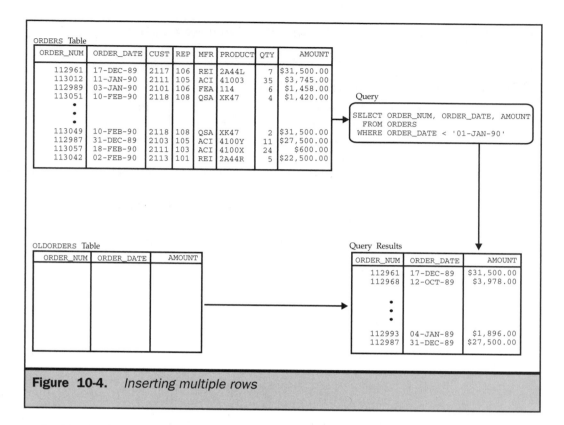

Figure 10-4.   *Inserting multiple rows*

and salespeople are responsible for big orders—those over $15,000. The queries that you will be running will combine data from the CUSTOMERS, SALESREPS, and ORDERS tables. These three-table queries will execute fairly quickly on the small sample database, but in a real corporate database with many thousands of rows, they would take a long time. Rather than running many long, three-table queries, you could create a new table named BIGORDERS to contain the required data, defined as follows:

Column	Information
AMOUNT	Order amount (from ORDERS)
COMPANY	Customer name (from CUSTOMERS)
NAME	Salesperson name (from SALESREPS)
PERF	Amount over/under quota (calculated from SALESREPS)
MFR	Manufacturer id (from ORDERS)
PRODUCT	Product id (from ORDERS)
QTY	Quantity ordered (from ORDERS)

Once you have created the BIGORDERS table, this multi-row INSERT statement can be used to populate it:

Load data into the BIGORDERS table for analysis.

```
INSERT INTO BIGORDERS (AMOUNT, COMPANY, NAME, PERF, PRODUCT, MFR, QTY)
    SELECT AMOUNT, COMPANY, NAME, (SALES - QUOTA), PRODUCT, MFR, QTY
      FROM ORDERS, CUSTOMERS, SALESREPS
     WHERE CUST = CUST_NUM
       AND REP = EMPL_NUM
       AND AMOUNT > 15000.00

6 rows inserted.
```

In a large database, this INSERT statement may take a while to execute because it involves a three-table query. When the statement is complete, the data in the BIGORDERS table will duplicate information in other tables. In addition, the BIGORDERS table won't be automatically kept up to date when new orders are added to the database, so its data may quickly become outdated. Each of these factors seems like a disadvantage. However, the subsequent data analysis queries against the BIGORDERS table can be expressed very simply—they become single-table queries. Furthermore, each of those queries will run much faster than if it were a three-table join. Consequently, this is probably a good strategy for performing the analysis, especially if the three original tables are large.

The SQL1 standard specified several logical restrictions on the query that appears within the multi-row INSERT statement:

- The query cannot contain an ORDER BY clause. It's useless to sort the query results anyway, because they're being inserted into a table that is, like all tables, unordered.

- The query results must contain the same number of columns as the column list in the INSERT statement (or the entire target table, if the column list is omitted), and the data types must be compatible, column by column.

- The query cannot be the UNION of several different SELECT statements. Only a single SELECT statement may be specified.

- The target table of the INSERT statement cannot appear in the FROM clause of the query or any subqueries that it contains. This prohibits inserting part of a table into itself.

The first two restrictions are structural, but the latter two were included in the standard simply to avoid complexity. As a result, these restrictions were relaxed in the SQL2 standard. The standard now allows UNION and join operations and expressions in the query, basically allowing the results of a general database query to be retrieved and then inserted into a table with the INSERT statement. It also allows various forms of "self-insertion," where the source table for the data to be inserted and destination table are the same.

Bulk Load Utilities

Data to be inserted into a database is often downloaded from another computer system or collected from other sites and stored in a sequential file. To load the data into a table, you could write a program with a loop that reads each record of the file and uses the single-row INSERT statement to add the row to the table. However, the overhead of having the DBMS repeatedly execute single-row INSERT statements may be quite high. If inserting a single row takes half of a second under a typical system load, that is probably acceptable performance for an interactive program. But that performance quickly becomes unacceptable when applied to the task of bulk loading 50,000 rows of data. In this case, loading the data would require over six hours.

For this reason, all commercial DBMS products include a bulk load feature that loads data from a file into a table at high speed. The ANSI/ISO SQL standard does not address this function, and it is usually provided as a standalone utility program rather than as part of the SQL language. Each vendor's utility provides a slightly different set of features, functions, and commands.

Deleting Data from the Database

A row of data is typically deleted from a database when the entity represented by the row "disappears from the outside world." For example, in the sample database:

- When a customer cancels an order, the corresponding row of the ORDERS table must be deleted.

- When a salesperson leaves the company, the corresponding row of the SALESREPS table must be deleted.

- When a sales office is closed, the corresponding row of the OFFICES table must be deleted. If the salespeople in the office are terminated, their rows should be deleted from the SALESREPS table as well. If they are reassigned, their REP_OFFICE columns must be updated.

In each case, the row is deleted to maintain the database as an accurate model of the real world. The smallest unit of data that can be deleted from a relational database is a single row.

The DELETE Statement

The DELETE statement, shown in Figure 10-5, removes selected rows of data from a single table. The FROM clause specifies the target table containing the rows. The WHERE clause specifies which rows of the table are to be deleted.

Suppose that Henry Jacobsen, the new salesperson hired earlier in this chapter, has just decided to leave the company. Here is the DELETE statement that removes his row from the SALESREPS table:

Remove Henry Jacobsen from the database.

```
DELETE FROM SALESREPS
  WHERE NAME = 'Henry Jacobsen'

1 row deleted.
```

The WHERE clause in this example identifies a single row of the SALESREPS table, which SQL removes from the table. The WHERE clause should have a familiar appearance—it's exactly the same WHERE clause that you would specify in a SELECT statement to *retrieve* the same row from the table. The search conditions that can be specified in the WHERE clause of the DELETE statement are the same ones available in the WHERE clause of the SELECT statement, as described in Chapters 6 and 9.

Recall that search conditions in the WHERE clause of a SELECT statement can specify a single row or an entire set of rows, depending on the specific search condition. The same is true of the WHERE clause in a DELETE statement. Suppose, for example, that Mr. Jacobsen's customer, InterCorp (customer number 2126), has called to cancel all of their orders. Here is the delete statement that removes the orders from the ORDERS table:

Remove all orders for InterCorp (customer number 2126).

```
DELETE FROM ORDERS
  WHERE CUST = 2126

2 rows deleted.
```

In this case, the WHERE clause selects several rows of the ORDERS table, and SQL removes all of the selected rows from the table. Conceptually, SQL applies the WHERE clause to each row of the ORDERS table, deleting those where the search condition yields a TRUE result and retaining those where the search condition yields a FALSE or

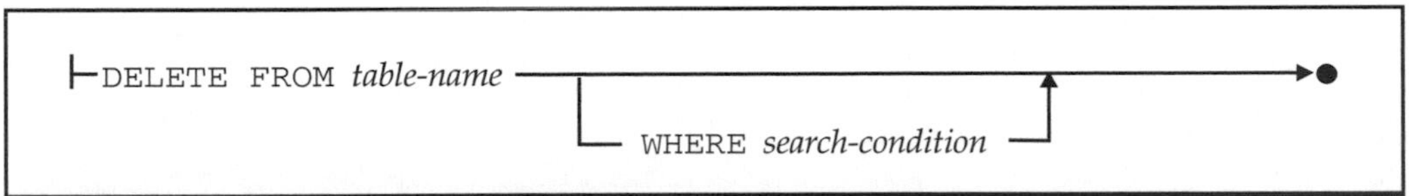

Figure 10-5. *DELETE statement syntax diagram*

NULL result. Because this type of DELETE statement searches through a table for the rows to be deleted, it is sometimes called a *searched* DELETE statement. This term is used to contrast it with another form of the DELETE statement, called the positioned DELETE statement, which always deletes a single row. The positioned DELETE statement applies only to programmatic SQL and is described in Chapter 17.

Here are some additional examples of searched DELETE statements:

Delete all orders placed before November 15, 1989.

```
DELETE FROM ORDERS
 WHERE ORDER_DATE < '15-NOV-89'

5 rows deleted.
```

Delete all rows for customers served by Bill Adams, Mary Jones, or Dan Roberts (employee numbers 105, 109, and 101).

```
DELETE FROM CUSTOMERS
 WHERE CUST_REP IN (105, 109, 101)

7 rows deleted.
```

Delete all salespeople hired before July 1988 who have not yet been assigned a quota.

```
DELETE FROM SALESREPS
 WHERE HIRE_DATE < '01-JUL-88'
   AND QUOTA IS NULL

0 rows deleted.
```

Deleting All Rows

The WHERE clause in a DELETE statement is optional, but it is almost always present. If the WHERE clause is omitted from a DELETE statement, *all* rows of the target table are deleted, as in this example:

Delete all orders.

```
DELETE FROM ORDERS

30 rows deleted.
```

Although this DELETE statement produces an empty table, it does not erase the ORDERS table from the database. The definition of the ORDERS table and its columns is still stored in the database. The table still exists, and new rows can still be inserted into the ORDERS table with the INSERT statement. To erase the definition of the table from the database, the DROP TABLE statement (described in Chapter 13) must be used.

Because of the potential damage from such a DELETE statement, it's important always to specify a search condition and to be careful that it actually selects the rows you want. When using interactive SQL, it's a good idea first to use the WHERE clause in a SELECT statement to display the selected rows, make sure that they are the ones you want to delete, and only then use the WHERE clause in a DELETE statement.

DELETE with Subquery *

DELETE statements with simple search conditions, such as those in the previous examples, select rows for deletion based solely on the contents of the rows themselves. Sometimes the selection of rows must be made based on data from other tables. For example, suppose you want to delete all orders taken by Sue Smith. Without knowing her employee number, you can't find the orders by consulting the ORDERS table alone. To find the orders, you could use a two-table query:

Find the orders taken by Sue Smith.

```
SELECT ORDER_NUM, AMOUNT
  FROM ORDERS, SALESREPS
 WHERE REP = EMPL_NUM
   AND NAME = 'Sue Smith'

ORDER_NUM       AMOUNT
---------- -----------
    112979  $15,000.00
    113065   $2,130.00
    112993   $1,896.00
    113048   $3,750.00
```

But you can't use a join in a DELETE statement. The parallel DELETE statement is illegal:

```
DELETE FROM ORDERS, SALESREPS
  WHERE REP = EMPL_NUM
    AND NAME = 'Sue Smith'

Error: More than one table specified in FROM clause
```

The way to handle the request is with one of the *subquery* search conditions. Here is a valid form of the DELETE statement that handles the request:

Delete the orders taken by Sue Smith.

```
DELETE FROM ORDERS
 WHERE REP = (SELECT EMPL_NUM
                FROM SALESREPS
               WHERE NAME = 'Sue Smith')

4 rows deleted.
```

The subquery finds the employee number for Sue Smith, and the WHERE clause then selects the orders with a matching value. As this example shows, subqueries can play an important role in the DELETE statement because they let you delete rows based on information in other tables. Here are two more examples of DELETE statements that use subquery search conditions:

Delete customers served by salespeople whose sales are less than 80 percent of quota.

```
DELETE FROM CUSTOMERS
 WHERE CUST_REP IN (SELECT EMPL_NUM
                      FROM SALESREPS
                     WHERE SALES < (.8 * QUOTA))

2 rows deleted.
```

Delete any salesperson whose current orders total less than 2 percent of their quota.

```
DELETE FROM SALESREPS
 WHERE (.02 * QUOTA) > (SELECT SUM(AMOUNT)
                          FROM ORDERS
                         WHERE REP = EMPL_NUM)

1 row deleted.
```

Subqueries in the WHERE clause can be nested just as they can be in the WHERE clause of the SELECT statement. They can also contain outer references to the target table of the DELETE statement. In this respect, the FROM clause of the DELETE statement functions like the FROM clause of the SELECT statement. Here is an example of a deletion request that requires a subquery with an outer reference:

Delete customers who have not ordered since November 10, 1989.

```
DELETE FROM CUSTOMERS
 WHERE NOT EXISTS (SELECT *
                     FROM ORDERS
                    WHERE CUST = CUST_NUM
                      AND ORDER_DATE < '10-NOV-89')

16 rows deleted.
```

Conceptually, this DELETE statement operates by going through the CUSTOMERS table, row by row, and checking the search condition. For each customer, the subquery selects any orders placed by that customer before the cutoff date. The reference to the CUST_NUM column in the subquery is an outer reference to the customer number in the row of the CUSTOMERS table currently being checked by the DELETE statement. The subquery in this example is a correlated subquery, as described in Chapter 9.

Outer references will often be found in subqueries of a DELETE statement, because they implement the "join" between the table(s) in the subquery and the target table of the DELETE statement. In the SQL1 standard, a restriction on the use of subqueries in a DELETE statement prevented the target table from appearing in the FROM clause of a subquery or any of its subqueries at any level of nesting. This prevents the subqueries from referencing the target table (some of whose rows may already have been deleted), except for outer references to the row currently being tested by the DELETE statement's search condition. The SQL2 standard eliminated this restriction by specifying that the DELETE statement should treat such a subquery as applying to the entire target table, before any rows have been deleted. This places more overhead on the DBMS (which must handle the subquery processing and row deletion more carefully), but the behavior of the statement is well defined by the standard.

Modifying Data in the Database

Typically, the values of data items stored in a database are modified when corresponding changes occur in the outside world. For example, in the sample database:

- When a customer calls to change the quantity on an order, the QTY column in the appropriate row of the ORDERS table must be modified.

- When a manager moves from one office to another, the MGR column in the OFFICES table and the REP_OFFICE column in the SALESREPS table must be changed to reflect the new assignment.

- When sales quotas are raised by 5 percent in the New York sales office, the QUOTA column of the appropriate rows in the SALESREPS table must be modified.

In each case, data values in the database are updated to maintain the database as an accurate model of the real world. The smallest unit of data that can be modified in a database is a single column of a single row.

The UPDATE Statement

The UPDATE statement, shown in Figure 10-6, modifies the values of one or more columns in selected rows of a single table. The target table to be updated is named in the statement, and you must have the required permission to update the table as well as each of the individual columns that will be modified. The WHERE clause selects the rows of the table to be modified. The SET clause specifies which columns are to be updated and calculates the new values for them.

Here is a simple UPDATE statement that changes the credit limit and salesperson for a customer:

Raise the credit limit for Acme Manufacturing to $60,000 and reassign them to Mary Jones (employee number 109).

```
UPDATE CUSTOMERS
   SET CREDIT_LIMIT = 60000.00, CUST_REP = 109
 WHERE COMPANY = 'Acme Mfg.'

1 row updated.
```

In this example, the WHERE clause identifies a single row of the CUSTOMERS table, and the SET clause assigns new values to two of the columns in that row. The WHERE clause is exactly the same one you would use in a DELETE or SELECT statement to identify the row. In fact, the search conditions that can appear in the WHERE clause of

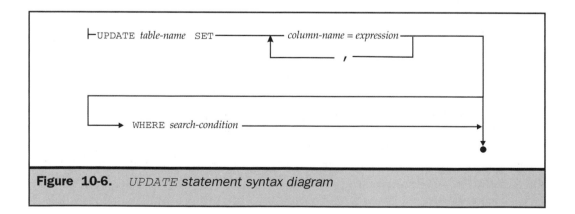

Figure 10-6. *UPDATE statement syntax diagram*

an UPDATE statement are exactly the same as those available in the SELECT and DELETE statements.

Like the DELETE statement, the UPDATE statement can update several rows at once with the proper search condition, as in this example:

Transfer all salespeople from the Chicago office (number 12) to the New York office (number 11), and lower their quotas by 10 percent.

```
UPDATE SALESREPS
   SET REP_OFFICE = 11, QUOTA = .9 * QUOTA
 WHERE REP_OFFICE = 12

3 rows updated.
```

In this case, the WHERE clause selects several rows of the SALESREPS table, and the value of the REP_OFFICE and QUOTA columns are modified in all of them. Conceptually, SQL processes the UPDATE statement by going through the SALESREPS table row by row, updating those rows for which the search condition yields a TRUE result and skipping over those for which the search condition yields a FALSE or NULL result. Because it searches the table, this form of the UPDATE statement is sometimes called a *searched* UPDATE statement. This term distinguishes it from a different form of the UPDATE statement, called a positioned UPDATE statement, which always updates a single row. The positioned UPDATE statement applies only to programmatic SQL and is described in Chapter 17.

Here are some additional examples of searched UPDATE statements:

Reassign all customers served by employee number 105, 106, or 107 to employee number 102.

```
UPDATE CUSTOMERS
   SET CUST_REP = 102
 WHERE CUST_REP IN (105, 106, 107)

5 rows updated.
```

Assign a quota of $100,000 to any salesperson who currently has no quota.

```
UPDATE SALESREPS
   SET QUOTA = 100000.00
 WHERE QUOTA IS NULL

1 row updated.
```

The SET clause in the UPDATE statement is a list of assignments separated by commas. Each assignment identifies a target column to be updated and specifies how to calculate the new value for the target column. Each target column should appear only once in the list; there should not be two assignments for the same target column. The ANSI/ISO specification mandates unqualified names for the target columns, but some SQL implementations allow qualified column names. There can be no ambiguity in the column names anyway, because they must refer to columns of the target table.

The expression in each assignment can be any valid SQL expression that yields a value of the appropriate data type for the target column. The expression must be computable based on the values of the row currently being updated in the target table. In most DBMS implementations, the expression may not include any column functions or subqueries.

If an expression in the assignment list references one of the columns of the target table, the value used to calculate the expression is the value of that column in the current row *before* any updates are applied. The same is true of column references that occur in the WHERE clause. For example, consider this (somewhat contrived) UPDATE statement:

```
UPDATE OFFICES
   SET QUOTA = 400000.00, SALES = QUOTA
 WHERE QUOTA < 400000.00
```

Before the update, Bill Adams had a QUOTA value of $350,000 and a SALES value of $367,911. After the update, his row has a SALES value of $350,000, *not* $400,000. The order of the assignments in the SET clause is thus immaterial; the assignments can be specified in any order.

Updating All Rows

The WHERE clause in the UPDATE statement is optional. If the WHERE clause is omitted, then *all* rows of the target table are updated, as in this example:

Raise all quotas by 5 percent.

```
UPDATE SALESREPS
   SET QUOTA = 1.05 * QUOTA

10 rows updated.
```

Unlike the DELETE statement, in which the WHERE clause is almost never omitted, the UPDATE statement without a WHERE clause performs a useful function. It basically performs a bulk update of the entire table, as demonstrated in the preceding example.

UPDATE with Subquery *

As with the DELETE statement, subqueries can play an important role in the UPDATE statement because they let you select rows to update based on information contained in other tables. Here are several examples of UPDATE statements that use subqueries:

Raise by $5,000 the credit limit of any customer who has placed an order for more than $25,000.

```
UPDATE CUSTOMERS
   SET CREDIT_LIMIT = CREDIT_LIMIT + 5000.00
 WHERE CUST_NUM IN (SELECT DISTINCT CUST
                      FROM ORDERS
                     WHERE AMOUNT > 25000.00)
```

4 rows updated.

Reassign all customers served by salespeople whose sales are less than 80 percent of their quota.

```
UPDATE CUSTOMERS
   SET CUST_REP = 105
 WHERE CUST_REP IN (SELECT EMPL_NUM
                      FROM SALESREPS
                     WHERE SALES < (.8 * QUOTA))
```

2 rows updated.

Have all salespeople who serve over three customers report directly to Sam Clark (employee number 106).

```
UPDATE SALESREPS
   SET MANAGER = 106
 WHERE 3 < (SELECT COUNT(*)
              FROM CUSTOMERS
             WHERE CUST_REP = EMPL_NUM)
```

1 row updated.

As in the DELETE statement, subqueries in the WHERE clause of the UPDATE statement can be nested to any level and can contain outer references to the target table of the UPDATE statement. The column EMPL_NUM in the subquery of the preceding example is such an outer reference; it refers to the EMPL_NUM column in the row of the SALESREPS table currently being checked by the UPDATE statement. The subquery in this example is a correlated subquery, as described in Chapter 9.

Outer references will often be found in subqueries of an UPDATE statement, because they implement the "join" between the table(s) in the subquery and the target table of the UPDATE statement. The same SQL1 restriction applies as for the DELETE statement: the target table cannot appear in the FROM clause of any subquery at any level of nesting. This prevents the subqueries from referencing the target table (some of whose rows may have already been updated). Any references to the target table in the subqueries are thus outer references to the row of the target table currently being tested by the UPDATE statement's WHERE clause. The SQL2 standard again removed this restriction and specifies that a reference to the target table in a subquery is evaluated as if none of the target table had been updated.

Summary

This chapter described the SQL statements that are used to modify the contents of a database:

■ The single-row INSERT statement adds one row of data to a table. The values for the new row are specified in the statement as constants.

■ The multi-row INSERT statement adds zero or more rows to a table. The values for the new rows come from a query, specified as part of the INSERT statement.

■ The DELETE statement deletes zero or more rows of data from a table. The rows to be deleted are specified by a search condition.

■ The UPDATE statement modifies the values of one or more columns in zero or more rows of a table. The rows to be updated are specified by a search condition. The columns to be updated, and the expressions that calculate their new values, are specified in the UPDATE statement.

■ Unlike the SELECT statement, which can operate on multiple tables, the INSERT, DELETE, and UPDATE statements work on only a single table at a time.

■ The search condition used in the DELETE and UPDATE statements has the same form as the search condition for the SELECT statement.

Chapter 11

Data Integrity

The term *data integrity* refers to the correctness and completeness of the data in a database. When the contents of a database are modified with the INSERT, DELETE, or UPDATE statements, the integrity of the stored data can be lost in many different ways. For example:

- Invalid data may be added to the database, such as an order that specifies a nonexistent product.

- Existing data may be modified to an incorrect value, such as reassigning a salesperson to a nonexistent office.

- Changes to the database may be lost due to a system error or power failure.

- Changes may be partially applied, such as adding an order for a product without adjusting the quantity available for sale.

One of the important roles of a relational DBMS is to preserve the integrity of its stored data to the greatest extent possible. This chapter describes the SQL language features that assist the DBMS in this task.

What Is Data Integrity?

To preserve the consistency and correctness of its stored data, a relational DBMS typically imposes one or more *data integrity constraints.* These constraints restrict the data values that can be inserted into the database or created by a database update. Several different types of data integrity constraints are commonly found in relational databases, including:

- *Required data.* Some columns in a database must contain a valid data value in every row; they are not allowed to contain missing or NULL values. In the sample database, every order must have an associated customer who placed the order. Therefore, the CUST column in the ORDERS table is a *required column.* The DBMS can be asked to prevent NULL values in this column.

- *Validity checking.* Every column in a database has a *domain,* a set of data values that are legal for that column. The sample database uses order numbers that begin at 100,001, so the domain of the ORDER_NUM column is positive integers greater than 100,000. Similarly, employee numbers in the EMPL_NUM column must fall within the numeric range of 101 to 999. The DBMS can be asked to prevent other data values in these columns.

- *Entity integrity.* The primary key of a table must contain a unique value in each row, which is different from the values in all other rows. For example, each row of the PRODUCTS table has a unique set of values in its MFR_ID and PRODUCT_ID columns, which uniquely identifies the product represented by that row. Duplicate values are illegal, because they wouldn't allow the database to distinguish one product from another. The DBMS can be asked to enforce this unique values constraint.

- *Referential integrity.* A foreign key in a relational database links each row in the child table containing the foreign key to the row of the parent table containing the matching primary key value. In the sample database, the value in the REP_OFFICE column of each SALESREPS row links the salesperson represented by that row to the office where he or she works. The REP_OFFICE column *must* contain a valid value from the OFFICE column of the OFFICES table, or the salesperson will be assigned to an invalid office. The DBMS can be asked to enforce this foreign key/primary key constraint.

- *Other data relationships.* The real-world situation modeled by a database will often have additional constraints that govern the legal data values that may appear in the database. For example, in the sample database, the sales vice president may want to insure that the quota target for each office does not exceed the total of the quota targets for the salespeople in that office. The DBMS can be asked to check modifications to the office and salesperson quota targets to make sure that their values are constrained in this way.

- *Business rules.* Updates to a database may be constrained by business rules governing the real-world transactions that are represented by the updates. For example, the company using the sample database may have a business rule that forbids accepting an order for which there is an inadequate product inventory. The DBMS can be asked to check each new row added to the ORDERS table to make sure that the value in its QTY column does not violate this business rule.

- *Consistency.* Many real-world transactions cause multiple updates to a database. For example, accepting a customer order may involve adding a row to the ORDERS table, increasing the SALES column in the SALESREPS table for the person who took the order, and increasing the SALES column in the OFFICES table for the office where that salesperson is assigned. The INSERT and both UPDATEs must *all* take place in order for the database to remain in a consistent, correct state. The DBMS can be asked to enforce this type of consistency rule or to support applications that implement such rules.

The ANSI/ISO SQL standard specifies some of the simpler data integrity constraints. For example, the required data constraint is supported by the ANSI/ISO standard and implemented in a uniform way across almost all commercial SQL products. More complex constraints, such as business rules constraints, are not specified by the ANSI/ISO standard, and there is a wide variation in the techniques and SQL syntax used to support them. The SQL features that support the first five integrity constraints are described in this chapter. The SQL transaction mechanism, which supports the consistency constraint, is described in Chapter 12.

Required Data

The simplest data integrity constraint requires that a column contain a non-NULL value. The ANSI/ISO standard and most commercial SQL products support this constraint by allowing you to declare that a column is NOT NULL when the table containing the column is first created. The NOT NULL constraint is specified as part of the CREATE TABLE statement, described in Chapter 13.

When a column is declared NOT NULL, the DBMS enforces the constraint by ensuring the following:

- Every INSERT statement that adds a new row or rows to the table must specify a non-NULL data value for the column. An attempt to insert a row containing a NULL value (either explicitly or implicitly) results in an error.

- Every UPDATE statement that updates the column must assign it a non-NULL data value. Again, an attempt to update the column to a NULL value results in an error.

One disadvantage of the NOT NULL constraint is that it must usually be specified when a table is first created. Typically, you cannot go back to a previously created table and disallow NULL values for a column. Usually this disadvantage is not serious because it's obvious when the table is first created which columns should allow NULLs and which should not.

The inability to add a NOT NULL constraint to an existing table is a result of the way most DBMS brands implement NULL values internally. Usually a DBMS reserves an extra byte in every stored row of data for each column that permits NULL values. The extra byte serves as a "null indicator" for the column and is set to some specified value to indicate a NULL value. When a column is defined as NOT NULL, the indicator byte is not present, saving disk storage space. Dynamically adding and removing NOT NULL constraints would thus require "on the fly" reconfiguration of the stored rows on the disk, which is not practical in a large database.

Simple Validity Checking

The SQL1 standard provides limited support for restricting the legal values that can appear in a column. When a table is created, each column in the table is assigned a data type, and the DBMS ensures that only data of the specified type is introduced into the column. For example, the EMPL_NUM column in the SALESREPS table is defined as an INTEGER, and the DBMS will produce an error if an INSERT or UPDATE statement tries to store a character string or a decimal number in the column.

However, the SQL1 standard and many commercial SQL products do not provide a way to restrict a column to certain specific data values. The DBMS will happily insert a SALESREPS row with an employee number of 12345, even though employee numbers in the sample database have three digits by convention. A hire date of December 25 would also be accepted, even though the company is closed on Christmas day.

Some commercial SQL implementations provide extended features to check for legal data values. In DB2, for example, each table in the database can be assigned a corresponding *validation procedure*, a user-written program to check for valid data values. DB2 invokes the validation procedure each time a SQL statement tries to change or insert a row of the table, and gives the validation procedure the "proposed" column values for the row. The validation procedure checks the data and indicates by its return value whether the data is acceptable. The validation procedure is a conventional program (written in S/370 assembler or PL/I, for example), so it can perform whatever data value checks are required, including range checks and internal consistency checks within the row. However, the validation procedure *cannot* access the database, so it cannot be used to check for unique values or foreign key/primary key relationships.

SQL Server also provides a data validation capability by allowing you to create a *rule* that determines what data can be entered into a particular column. SQL Server checks the rule each time an INSERT or UPDATE statement is attempted for the table that contains the column. Unlike DB2's validation procedures, SQL Server rules are written in the Transact-SQL dialect that is used by SQL Server. For example, here is a Transact-SQL statement that establishes a rule for the QUOTA column in the SALESREPS table:

```
CREATE RULE QUOTA_LIMIT
    AS @VALUE BETWEEN 0.00 AND 500000.00
```

This rule prevents you from inserting or updating a quota to a negative value or to a value greater than $500,000. As shown in the example, SQL Server allows you to assign the rule a name (QUOTA_LIMIT in this example). Like DB2 validation procedures, however, SQL Server rules may not reference columns or other database objects.

The SQL2 standard provides extended support for validity checking through two different features—column check constraints and domains. Both give the database creator a way to tell the DBMS how to determine whether or not a data value is valid. The check-constraint feature specifies the data validity test for a single column. The domain feature lets you specify the validity test once, and then reuse it in the definition of many different columns whose legal data values are the same.

Column Check Constraints (SQL2)

A SQL2 *check constraint* is a search condition, like the search condition in a WHERE clause, that produces a true/false value. When a check constraint is specified for a column, the DBMS automatically checks the value of that column each time a new row is inserted or a row is updated to insure that the search condition is true. If not, the INSERT or UPDATE statement fails. A column check constraint is specified as part of the column definition within the CREATE TABLE statement, described in Chapter 13.

Consider this excerpt from a CREATE TABLE statement, modified from the definition of the demo database to include three check constraints:

```
CREATE TABLE SALESREPS
    (EMPL_NUM INTEGER NOT NULL
            CHECK (EMPL_NUM BETWEEN 101 AND 199),
        AGE INTEGER
            CHECK (AGE >= 21),
        .
        .
        .
     QUOTA MONEY
            CHECK (MONEY >= 0.0)
        .
        .
        .
```

The first constraint (on the EMPL_NUM column) requires that valid employee numbers be three-digit numbers between 101 and 199. The second constraint (on the AGE column) similarly prevents hiring of minors. The third constraint (on the QUOTA column) prevents a salesperson from having a quota target less than $0.00.

All three of these column check constraints are very simple examples of the capability specified by the SQL2 standard. In general, the parentheses following the keyword CHECK can contain any valid search condition that makes sense in the context of a column definition. With this flexibility, a check constraint can compare values from two different columns of the table, or even compare a proposed data value against other values from the database. These capabilities are more fully described later in this chapter.

Domains (SQL2)

A SQL2 *domain* generalizes the check-constraint concept and allows you to easily apply the same check constraint to many different columns within a database. A domain is a collection of legal data values. You specify a domain and assign it a domain name using the SQL2 CREATE DOMAIN statement, described in Chapter 13. As with the check-constraint definition, a search condition is used to define the range of legal data values. For example, here is a SQL2 CREATE DOMAIN statement to create the domain VALID_EMPLOYEE_ID, which includes all legal employee numbers:

```
CREATE DOMAIN VALID_EMPLOYEE_ID INTEGER
  CHECK (VALUE BETWEEN 101 AND 199)
```

After the `VALID_EMPLOYEE_ID` domain has been defined, it may be used to define columns in database tables instead of a data type. Using this capability, the example `CREATE TABLE` statement for the `SALESREPS` table would appear as:

```
CREATE TABLE SALESREPS
    (EMPL_NUM VALID_EMPLOYEE_ID,
        AGE INTEGER
            CHECK (AGE >= 21),
        .
        .
        .
     QUOTA MONEY
            CHECK (MONEY >= 0.0)
        .
        .
        .
```

The advantage of using the domain is that if other columns in other tables also contain employee numbers, the domain name can be used repeatedly, simplifying the table definitions. The `OFFICES` table contains such a column:

```
CREATE TABLE OFFICES
    (OFFICE INTEGER NOT NULL,
       CITY VARCHAR(15) NOT NULL,
     REGION VARCHAR(10) NOT NULL,
        MGR VALID_EMPLOYEE_ID,
     TARGET MONEY,
      SALES MONEY NOT NULL
        .
        .
        .
```

Another advantage of domains is that the definition of "valid data" (such as valid employee numbers in this example) is stored in one, central place within the database. If the definition changes later (for example, if the company grows and employee numbers in the range 200-299 must be allowed), it is much easier to change one domain definition than to change many column constraints scattered throughout the database.

Entity Integrity

A table's primary key must have a unique value for each row of the table, or the database will lose its integrity as a model of the outside world. For example, if two rows of the `SALESREPS` table both had value `106` in their `EMPL_NUM` column, it would be impossible to tell which row really represented the real-world entity associated with that key value—Bill Adams, who is employee number 106. For this reason the requirement that primary keys have unique values is called the *entity integrity* constraint.

Support for primary keys was not found in the first commercial SQL databases but has become much more common. It was added to DB2 in 1988 and was added to the original ANSI/ISO SQL standard in an intermediate update, before the full SQL2 standard appeared. In both DB2 and the ANSI/ISO standard, you specify the primary key as part of the CREATE TABLE statement, described in Chapter 13. The sample database definition in Appendix A includes primary key definitions for all of its tables, following the DB2 and ANSI/ISO standard syntax.

When a primary key is specified for a table, the DBMS automatically checks the uniqueness of the primary key value for every INSERT and UPDATE statement performed on the table. An attempt to insert a row with a duplicate primary key value or to update a row so that its primary key would be a duplicate will fail with an error message.

Other Uniqueness Constraints

It is sometimes appropriate to require a column that is not the primary key of a table to contain a unique value in every row. For example, suppose you wanted to restrict the data in the SALESREPS table so that no two salespeople could have exactly the same name in the table. You could achieve this goal by imposing a *uniqueness* constraint on the NAME column. The DBMS enforces a uniqueness constraint in the same way that it enforces the primary key constraint. Any attempt to insert or update a row in the table that violates the uniqueness constraint will fail.

The ANSI/ISO SQL standard uses the CREATE TABLE statement to specify uniqueness constraints for columns or combinations of columns. However, uniqueness constraints were implemented in DB2 long before the publication of the ANSI/ISO standard, and DB2 made them a part of its CREATE INDEX statement. This statement is one of the SQL database administration statements that deals with physical storage of the database on the disk. Normally the SQL user doesn't have to worry about these statements at all; they are used only by the database administrator.

Many commercial SQL products followed the original DB2 practice rather than the ANSI/ISO standard for uniqueness constraints and required the use of the a CREATE INDEX statement. Subsequent versions of DB2 added a uniqueness constraint to the CREATE TABLE statement. Most of the other commercial vendors already support or will support the ANSI/ISO syntax for the uniqueness constraint as they add support for SQL2 features.

Uniqueness and NULL Values

NULL values pose a problem when they occur in the primary key of a table or in a column that is specified in a uniqueness constraint. Suppose you tried to insert a row with a primary key that was NULL (or partially NULL, if the primary key is composed of more than one column). Because of the NULL value, the DBMS cannot conclusively decide whether the primary key does or does not duplicate one that is already in the table. The answer must be "maybe," depending on the "real" value of the missing (NULL) data.

For this reason, the SQL standard requires that every column that is part of a primary key must be declared NOT NULL. The same restriction applies for every column that is named in a uniqueness constraint. Together, these restrictions ensure that columns that are "supposed to" contain unique data values in each row of a table actually do contain unique values.

Referential Integrity

Chapter 4 discussed primary keys, foreign keys, and the parent/child relationships that they create between tables. Figure 11-1 shows the SALESREPS and OFFICES tables and illustrates once again how foreign keys and primary keys work. The OFFICE column is the primary key for the OFFICES table, and it uniquely identifies each row. The REP_OFFICE column, in the SALESREPS table, is a foreign key for the OFFICES table. It identifies the office where each salesperson is assigned.

The REP_OFFICE and OFFICE columns create a parent/child relationship between the OFFICES and SALESREPS rows. Each OFFICES (parent) row has zero or more SALESREPS (child) rows with matching office numbers. Similarly, each SALESREPS (child) row has exactly one OFFICES (parent) row with a matching office number.

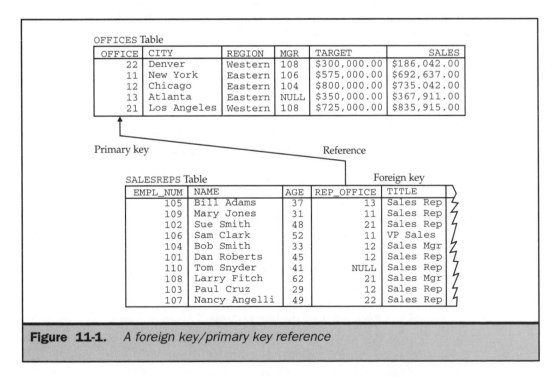

Figure 11-1.   *A foreign key/primary key reference*

Suppose you tried to insert a new row into the SALESREPS table that contained an invalid office number, as in this example:

```
INSERT INTO SALESREPS (EMPL_NUM, NAME, REP_OFFICE, AGE,
                        HIRE_DATE, SALES)
    VALUES (115, 'George Smith', 31, 37, '01-APR-90', 0.00)
```

On the surface, there's nothing wrong with this INSERT statement. In fact, many SQL implementations will successfully add the row. The database will show that George Smith works in office number 31, even though no office number 31 is listed in the OFFICES table. The newly inserted row clearly "breaks" the parent/child relationship between the OFFICES and SALESREPS tables. In fact, the office number in the INSERT statement is probably an error—the user may have intended office number 11, 21, or 13.

It seems clear that every legal value in the REP_OFFICE column should be forced to match some value that appears in the OFFICE column. This rule is known as a *referential integrity* constraint. It ensures the integrity of the parent/child relationships created by foreign keys and primary keys.

Referential integrity has been a key part of the relational model since it was first proposed by Codd. However, referential integrity constraints were not included in IBM's prototype System/R DBMS, nor in early releases of DB2 or SQL/DS. IBM added referential integrity support to DB2 in 1989, and referential integrity was added to the SQL1 standard after its initial release. Most DBMS vendors now have either implemented referential integrity or indicated plans to include referential integrity support in future releases of their products.

Referential Integrity Problems

Four types of database updates can corrupt the referential integrity of the parent/child relationships in a database. Using the OFFICES and SALESREPS tables in Figure 11-1 as illustrations, these four update situations are:

- *Inserting a new child row.* When an INSERT statement adds a new row to the child (SALESREPS) table, its foreign key (REP_OFFICE) value *must* match one of the primary key (OFFICE) values in the parent table (OFFICES). If the foreign key value does not match any primary key, inserting the row will corrupt the database, because there will be a child without a parent (an "orphan"). Note that inserting a row in the parent table never poses a problem; it simply becomes a parent without any children.

- *Updating the foreign key in a child row.* This is a different form of the previous problem. If the foreign key (REP_OFFICE) is modified by an UPDATE statement, the new value must match a primary key (OFFICE) value in the parent (OFFICES) table. Otherwise, the updated row will be an orphan.

- *Deleting a parent row.* If a row of the parent table (OFFICES) that has one or more children (in the SALESREPS table) is deleted, the child rows will become orphans. The foreign key (REP_OFFICE) values in these rows will no longer match any primary key (OFFICE) value in the parent table. Note that deleting a row from the child table never poses a problem; the parent of this row simply has one less child after the deletion.

- *Updating the primary key in a parent row.* This is a different form of the previous problem. If the primary key (OFFICE) of a row in the parent table (OFFICES) is modified, all of the current children of that row become orphans because their foreign keys no longer match a primary key value.

The referential integrity features of DB2 and the ANSI/ISO SQL standard handle each of these four situations. The first problem (INSERT into the child table) is handled by checking the values of the foreign key columns before the INSERT statement is permitted. If they don't match a primary key value, the INSERT statement is rejected with an error message. In Figure 11-1 this means that before a new salesperson can be added to the SALESREPS table, the office to which the salesperson is assigned must already be in the OFFICES table. As you can see, this restriction "makes sense" in the sample database.

The second problem (UPDATE of the child table) is similarly handled by checking the updated foreign key value. If there is no matching primary key value, the UPDATE statement is rejected with an error message. In Figure 11-1 this means that before a salesperson can be reassigned to a different office, that office must already be in the OFFICES table. Again, this restriction makes sense in the sample database.

The third problem (DELETE of a parent row) is more complex. For example, suppose you closed the Los Angeles office and wanted to delete the corresponding row from the OFFICES table in Figure 11-1. What should happen to the two child rows in the SALESREPS table that represent the salespeople assigned to the Los Angeles office? Depending on the situation, you might want to:

- Prevent the office from being deleted until the salespeople are reassigned.

- Automatically delete the two salespeople from the SALESREPS table as well.

- Set the REP_OFFICE column for the two salespeople to NULL, indicating that their office assignment is unknown.

- Set the REP_OFFICE column for the two salespeople to some default value, such as the office number for the headquarters office in New York, indicating that the salespeople are automatically reassigned to that office.

The fourth problem (UPDATE of the primary key in the parent table) has similar complexity. For example, suppose for some reason you wanted to change the office number of the Los Angeles office from 21 to 23. As with the previous example, the question is what should happen to the two child rows in the SALESREPS table that represent salespeople from the Los Angeles office. Again, there are four logical possibilities:

- Prevent the office number from being changed until the salespeople are reassigned. In this case, you should first add a new row to the OFFICES table with the new office number for Los Angeles, then update the SALESREPS table, and finally delete the old OFFICES row for Los Angeles.

- Automatically update the office number for the two salespeople in the SALESREPS table, so that their rows still are linked to the Los Angeles row in the OFFICES table, via its new office number.

- Set the REP_OFFICE column for the two salespeople to NULL, indicating that their office assignment is unknown.

- Set the REP_OFFICE column for the two salespeople to some default value, such as the office number for the headquarters office in New York, indicating that the salespeople are automatically reassigned to that office.

Although some of these alternatives may seem more logical than others in this particular example, it's relatively easy to come up with examples where any one of the four possibilities is the "right" thing to do, if you want the database to accurately model the real-world situation. The SQL1 standard provided only the first possibility for the preceding examples—it prohibited the modification of a primary key value that was "in use" and prohibited the deletion of a row containing such a primary key. DB2, however, permitted other options through its concept of *delete rules*. The SQL2 standard has expanded these delete rules into *delete and update rules* that cover both deleting of parent rows and updating of primary keys.

Delete and Update Rules *

For each parent/child relationship created by a foreign key in a database, the SQL2 standard allows you to specify an associated delete rule and an associated update rule. The delete rule tells the DBMS what to do when a user tries to delete a row of the parent table. These four delete rules can be specified:

- The RESTRICT delete rule prevents you from deleting a row from the parent table if the row has any children. A DELETE statement that attempts to delete such a parent row is rejected with an error message. Deletions from the parent table are thus restricted to rows without any children. Applied to Figure 11-1, this rule can be summarized as "You can't delete an office if any salespeople are assigned to it."

- The CASCADE delete rule tells the DBMS that when a parent row is deleted, all of its child rows should *also* automatically be deleted from the child table. For Figure 11-1, this rule can be summarized as "Deleting an office automatically deletes all the salespeople assigned to that office."

- The SET NULL delete rule tells the DBMS that when a parent row is deleted, the foreign key values in all of its child rows should automatically be set to NULL. Deletions from the parent table thus cause a "set to NULL" update on selected columns of the child table. For the tables in Figure 11-1, this rule can be summarized as "If an office is deleted, indicate that the current office assignment of its salespeople is unknown."

- The SET DEFAULT delete rule tells the DBMS that when a parent row is deleted, the foreign key values in all of its child rows should automatically be set to the default value for that particular column. Deletions from the parent table thus cause a "set to DEFAULT" update on selected columns of the child table. For the tables in Figure 11-1, this rule can be summarized as "If an office is deleted, indicate that the current office assignment of its salespeople is the default office specified in the definition of the SALESREPS table."

There are some slight differences between the SQL2 and DB2 implementations of the delete rules. The current DB2 implementation does not support the SET DEFAULT rule; it is only specified by the SQL2 standard. The SQL2 standard actually calls the previously described RESTRICT rule, NO ACTION. The SQL2 naming is somewhat confusing. It means "if you try to delete a parent row that still has children, the DBMS will take no action on the row." The DBMS will, however, generate an error code. Intuitively, the DB2 name for the rule, "restrict," seems a better description of the situation—the DBMS will restrict the DELETE operation from taking place and generate an error code. The latest release of DB2 supports *both* a RESTRICT and a NO ACTION delete rule. The difference between them is the timing of the enforcement of the rule. The RESTRICT rule is enforced before any other constraints; the NO ACTION rule is enforced after other referential constraints. Under almost all circumstances, the two rules operate identically.

Just as the delete rule tells the DBMS what to do when a user tries to delete a row of the parent table, the update rule tells the DBMS what to do when a user tries to update the value of one of the primary key columns in the parent table. Again, there are four possibilities, paralleling those available for delete rules:

- The RESTRICT update rule prevents you from updating the primary key of a row in the parent table if that row has any children. An UPDATE statement that attempts to modify the primary key of such a parent row is rejected with an error message. Changes to primary keys in the parent table are thus restricted to rows without any children. Applied to Figure 11-1, this rule can be summarized as "You can't change an office number if salespeople are assigned to the office."

- The CASCADE update rule tells the DBMS that when a primary key value is changed in a parent row, the corresponding foreign key value in all of its child rows should *also* automatically be changed in the child table, to match the new primary key. For Figure 11-1, this rule can be summarized as "Changing an office number automatically changes the office number for all the salespeople assigned to that office."

- The SET NULL update rule tells the DBMS that when a primary key value in a parent row is updated, the foreign key values in all of its child rows should automatically be set to NULL. Primary key changes in the parent table thus cause a "set to NULL" update on selected columns of the child table. For the tables in Figure 11-1, this rule can be summarized as "If an office number is changed, indicate that the current office assignment of its salespeople is unknown."

- The SET DEFAULT update rule tells the DBMS that when a primary key value in a parent row is updated, the foreign key values in all of its child rows should automatically be set to the default value for that particular column. Primary key changes in the parent table thus cause a "set to DEFAULT" update on selected columns of the child table. For the tables in Figure 11-1, this rule can be summarized as "If an office number is changed, automatically change the office assignment of its salespeople to the default office specified in the definition of the SALESREPS table."

The same differences between DB2 and the SQL2 standard described for the delete rules apply to the update rules. The SET DEFAULT update rule is present only in the standard, not in the current DB2 implementation. The RESTRICT update rule is a DB2 naming convention; the SQL2 standard again calls this update rule NO ACTION.

You can specify two different rules as the delete rule and the update rule for a parent/child relationship, although in most cases, the two rules will be the same. If you do not specify a rule, the RESTRICT rule is the default, because it has the least potential for accidental destruction or modification of data. Each of the rules is appropriate in different situations. Usually, the real-world behavior modeled by the database will indicate which rule is appropriate. In the sample database, the ORDERS table contains three foreign key/primary key relationships, as shown in Figure 11-2. These three relationships link each order to

1. The product that was ordered
2. The customer who placed the order
3. The salesperson who took the order

For each of these relationships, different rules seem appropriate:

- The relationship between an order and the product that is ordered should probably use the RESTRICT rule for delete and update. It shouldn't be possible to delete product information from the database if there are still current orders for that product, or to change the product number.

- The relationship between an order and the customer who placed it should probably use the CASCADE rule for delete and update. You probably will delete a customer row from the database only if the customer is inactive or ends their relationship with the company. In this case, when you delete the customer, any current orders for that customer should also be deleted. Similarly, changes in a customer number should automatically propagate to orders for that customer.

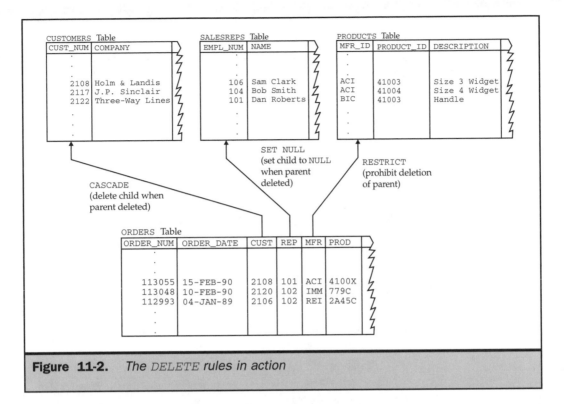

Figure 11-2.   *The* DELETE *rules in action*

■ The relationship between an order and the salesperson who took it should probably use the SET NULL rule. If the salesperson leaves the company, any orders taken by that salesperson become the responsibility of an "unknown salesperson" until they are reassigned. Alternatively, the SET DEFAULT rule could be used to automatically assign these orders to the sales vice president. This relationship should probably use the CASCADE update rule, so that employee number changes automatically propagate to the ORDERS table.

Cascaded Deletes and Updates *

The RESTRICT rule for deletes and updates is a "single-level" rule—it affects only the parent table in a relationship. The CASCADE rule, on the other hand, can be a "multi-level" rule, as shown in Figure 11-3.

Assume for this discussion that the OFFICES/SALESREPS and SALESREPS/ORDERS relationships shown in the figure both have CASCADE rules. What happens when you delete Los Angeles from the OFFICES table? The CASCADE rule for the OFFICES/SALESREPS relationship tells the DBMS to automatically delete all of the SALESREPS rows that refer to the Los Angeles office (office number 21) as well. But deleting the SALESREPS row for Sue Smith brings into play the CASCADE rule for the SALESREPS/ORDERS relationship. This rule

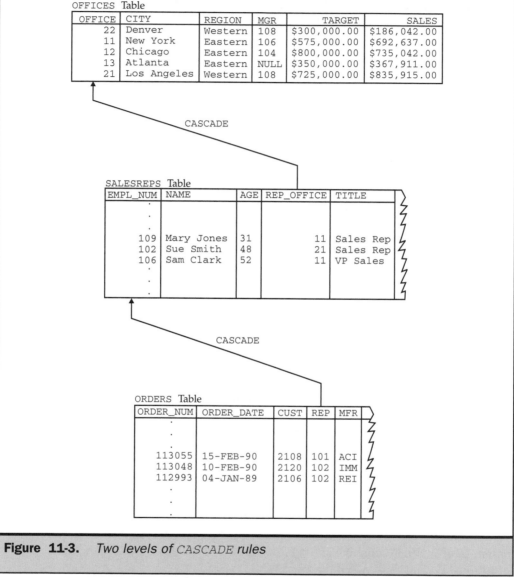

OFFICES Table

OFFICE	CITY	REGION	MGR	TARGET	SALES
22	Denver	Western	108	$300,000.00	$186,042.00
11	New York	Eastern	106	$575,000.00	$692,637.00
12	Chicago	Eastern	104	$800,000.00	$735,042.00
13	Atlanta	Eastern	NULL	$350,000.00	$367,911.00
21	Los Angeles	Western	108	$725,000.00	$835,915.00

CASCADE

SALESREPS Table

EMPL_NUM	NAME	AGE	REP_OFFICE	TITLE
109	Mary Jones	31	11	Sales Rep
102	Sue Smith	48	21	Sales Rep
106	Sam Clark	52	11	VP Sales

CASCADE

ORDERS Table

ORDER_NUM	ORDER_DATE	CUST	REP	MFR
113055	15-FEB-90	2108	101	ACI
113048	10-FEB-90	2120	102	IMM
112993	04-JAN-89	2106	102	REI

Figure 11-3. *Two levels of CASCADE rules*

tells the DBMS to automatically delete all of the ORDERS rows that refer to Sue (employee number 102). Deleting an office thus causes cascaded deletion of salespeople, which causes cascaded deletion of orders. As the example shows, CASCADE delete rules must be specified with care because they can cause widespread automatic deletion of data if they're used incorrectly. Cascaded update rules can cause similar multilevel updates if the foreign key in the child table is also its primary key. In practice, this is not very common, so cascaded updates typically have less far-reaching effects than cascaded deletes.

The SET NULL and SET DEFAULT update and delete rules are both two-level rules; their impact stops with the child table. Figure 11-4 shows the OFFICES, SALESREPS, and ORDERS tables again, with a SET NULL delete rule for the OFFICES/SALESREPS relationship. This time, when the Los Angeles office is deleted,

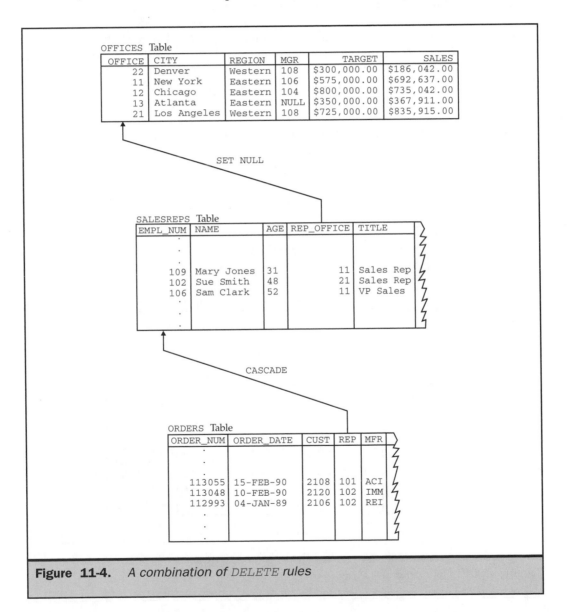

Figure 11-4.   *A combination of DELETE rules*

the SET NULL delete rule tells the DBMS to set the REP_OFFICE column to NULL in the SALESREPS rows that refer to office number 21. The rows remain in the SALESREPS table, however, and the impact of the delete operation extends only to the child table.

Referential Cycles *

In the sample database, the SALESREPS table contains the REP_OFFICE column, a foreign key for the OFFICES table. The OFFICES table contains the MGR column, a foreign key for the SALESREPS table. As shown in Figure 11-5, these two relationships form a *referential cycle*. Any given row of the SALESREPS table refers to a row of the OFFICES table, which refers to a row of the SALESREPS table, and so on. This cycle includes only two tables, but it's also possible to construct cycles of three or more tables.

Regardless of the number of tables that they involve, referential cycles pose special problems for referential integrity constraints. For example, suppose that NULL values were not allowed in the primary or foreign keys of the two tables in Figure 11-5. (This

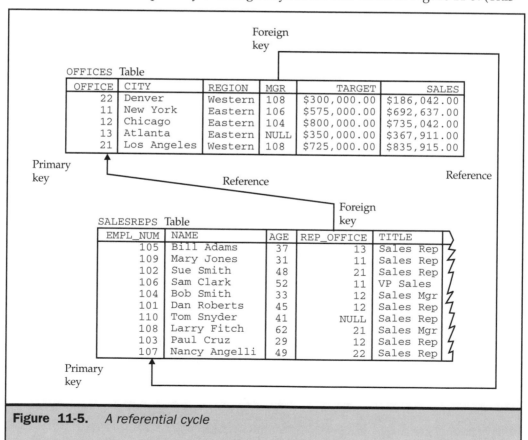

Figure 11-5.   *A referential cycle*

is not, in fact, the way the sample database is actually defined, for reasons that will become obvious in a moment.) Consider this database update request and the INSERT statements that attempt to implement it:

You have just hired a new salesperson, Ben Adams (employee number 115), who is the manager of a new sales office in Detroit (office number 14).

```
INSERT INTO SALESREPS (EMPL_NUM, NAME, REP_OFFICE,
                       HIRE_DATE, SALES)
    VALUES (115,'Ben Adams', 14, '01-APR-90', 0.00)

INSERT INTO OFFICES (OFFICE, CITY, REGION, MGR, TARGET, SALES)
    VALUES (14,'Detroit', 'Eastern', 115, 0.00, 0.00)
```

Unfortunately, the first INSERT statement (for Ben Adams) will fail. Why? Because the new row refers to office number 14, which is not yet in the database! Of course, reversing the order of the INSERT statements doesn't help:

```
INSERT INTO OFFICES (OFFICE, CITY, REGION, MGR, TARGET, SALES)
    VALUES (14,'Detroit', 'Eastern', 115, 0.00, 0.00)

INSERT INTO SALESREPS (EMPL_NUM, NAME, REP_OFFICE,
                       HIRE_DATE, SALES)
    VALUES (115,'Ben Adams', 14, '01-APR-90', 0.00)
```

The first INSERT statement (for Detroit this time) will still fail, because the new row refers to employee number 115 as the office manager, and Ben Adams is not yet in the database! To prevent this "insertion deadlock," at least one of the foreign keys in a referential cycle *must* permit NULL values. In the actual definition of the sample database, the MGR column does not permit NULLs, but the REP_OFFICE does. The two-row insertion can then be accomplished with two INSERTs and an UPDATE, as shown here:

```
INSERT INTO SALESREPS (EMPL_NUM, NAME, REP_OFFICE,
                       HIRE_DATE, SALES)
    VALUES (115,'Ben Adams', NULL, '01-APR-90', 0.00)

INSERT INTO OFFICES (OFFICE, CITY, REGION, MGR, TARGET, SALES)
    VALUES (14,'Detroit', 'Eastern', 115, 0.00, 0.00)

UPDATE SALESREPS
   SET REP_OFFICE = 14
 WHERE EMPL_NUM = 115
```

As the example shows, there are times when it would be convenient if the referential integrity constraint were not checked until after a series of interrelated updates are performed. Unfortunately, this type of complex "deferred checking" is not provided by most current SQL implementations. Some deferred checking capabilities are specified by the SQL2 standard, as described later in this chapter.

Referential cycles also restrict the delete and update rules that can be specified for the relationships that form the cycle. Consider the three tables in the referential cycle shown in Figure 11-6. The PETS table shows three pets and the boys they like, the GIRLS table shows three girls and the pets they like, and the BOYS table shows four boys and the girls they like, forming a referential cycle. All three of the relationships in the cycle specify the

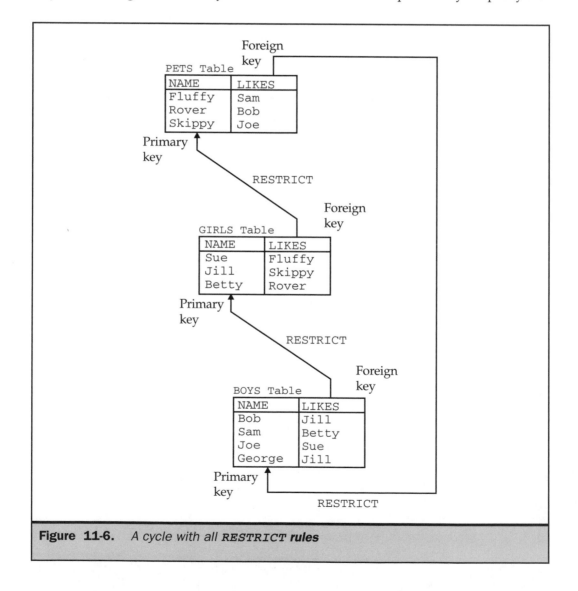

Figure 11-6. *A cycle with all **RESTRICT** rules*

RESTRICT delete rule. Note that George's row is the *only* row you can delete from the three tables. Every other row is the parent in some relationship and is therefore protected from deletion by the RESTRICT rule. Because of this anomaly, you should not specify the RESTRICT rule for all of the relationships in a referential cycle.

The CASCADE rule presents a similar problem, as shown in Figure 11-7. This figure contains exactly the same data as in Figure 11-6, but all three delete rules have been changed to CASCADE. Suppose you try to delete Bob from the BOYS table. The delete rules force the DBMS to delete Rover (who likes Bob) from the PETS table, which forces you to delete Betty (who likes Rover) from the GIRLS table, which forces you to delete Sam (who likes Betty), and so on until all of the rows in all three tables have been

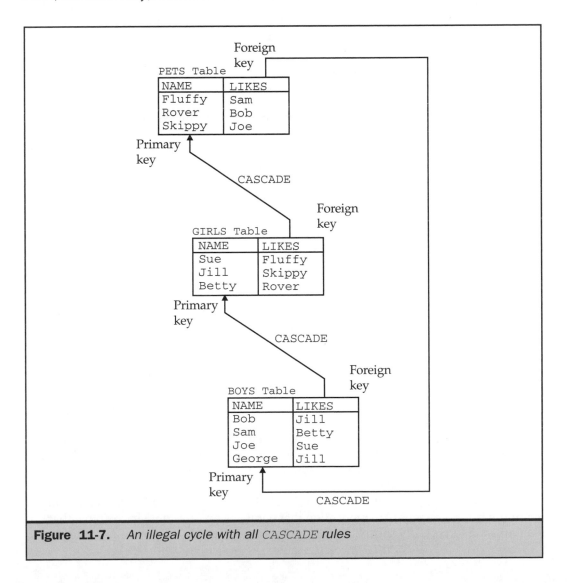

Figure 11-7.   *An illegal cycle with all CASCADE rules*

deleted! For these small tables this might be practical, but for a production database with thousands of rows, it would quickly become impossible to keep track of the cascaded deletions and retain the integrity of the database. For this reason DB2 enforces a rule that prevents referential cycles of two or more tables where all of the delete rules are CASCADE. At least one relationship in the cycle *must* have a RESTRICT or SET NULL delete rule to break the cycle of cascaded deletions.

Foreign Keys and NULL Values *

Unlike primary keys, foreign keys in a relational database are allowed to contain NULL values. In the sample database the foreign key REP_OFFICE, in the SALESREPS table, permits NULL values. In fact, this column does contain a NULL value in Tom Snyder's row, because Tom has not yet been assigned to an office. But the NULL value poses an interesting question about the referential integrity constraint created by the primary key/foreign key relationship. Does the NULL value match one of the primary key values or doesn't it? The answer is "maybe"—it depends on the "real" value of the missing or unknown data.

Both DB2 and the ANSI/ISO SQL1 standard automatically assume that a foreign key that contains a NULL value satisfies the referential integrity constraint. In other words, they give the row "the benefit of the doubt" and allow it to be part of the child table, even though its foreign key value doesn't match any row in the parent table. Interestingly, the referential integrity constraint is assumed to be satisfied if *any part* of the foreign key has a NULL value. This can produce unexpected and unintuitive behavior for compound foreign keys, such as the one that links the ORDERS table to the PRODUCTS table.

Suppose for a moment that the ORDERS table in the sample database permitted NULL values for the PRODUCT column, and that the PRODUCTS/ORDERS relationship had a SET NULL delete rule. (This is not the actual structure of the sample database, for the reasons illustrated by this example.) An order for a product with a manufacturer id (MFR) of ABC and a NULL product id (PRODUCT) can be successfully inserted into the ORDERS table because of the NULL value in the PRODUCT column. DB2 and the ANSI/ISO standard assume that the row meets the referential integrity constraint for ORDERS and PRODUCTS, even though no product in the PRODUCTS table has a manufacturer id of ABC.

The SET NULL delete rule can produce a similar effect. Deleting a row from the PRODUCTS table will cause the foreign key value in all of its child rows in the ORDERS table to be set to NULL. Actually, only those columns of the foreign key that accept NULL values are set to NULL. If there were a single row in the PRODUCTS table for manufacturer DEF, deleting that row would cause its child rows in the ORDERS table to have their PRODUCT column set to NULL, but their MFR column would continue to have the value DEF. As a result, the rows would have a MFR value that did not match any row in the PRODUCTS table.

To avoid creating this situation, you should be very careful with NULL values in compound foreign keys. An application that enters or updates data in the table that contains the foreign key should usually enforce an "all NULLs or no NULLs" rule on the columns of the foreign key. Foreign keys that are partially NULL and partially non-NULL can easily create problems.

The SQL2 standard addresses this problem by giving the database administrator more control over the handling of NULL values in foreign keys for integrity constraints. The integrity constraint in the CREATE TABLE statement provides two options:

- The MATCH FULL option requires that foreign keys in a child table fully match a primary key in the parent table. With this option, no part of the foreign key can contain a NULL value, so the issue of NULL value handling in delete and update rules does not arise.

- The MATCH PARTIAL option allows NULL values in parts of a foreign key, so long as the non-NULL values match the corresponding parts of some primary key in the parent table. With this option, NULL value handling in delete and update rules proceeds as previously described.

Advanced Constraint Capabilities (SQL2)

Primary key and foreign key constraints, uniqueness constraints, and restrictions on missing (NULL) values all provide data integrity checking for very specific structures and situations within a database. The SQL2 standard goes beyond these capabilities to include a much more general capability for specifying and enforcing data integrity constraints. The complete scheme includes four types of constraints:

- *Column constraints* are specified as part of a column definition when a table is created. Conceptually, they restrict the legal values that may appear in the column. Column constraints appear in the individual column definitions within the CREATE TABLE statement.

- *Domains* are a specialized form of column constraints. They provide a limited capability to define new data types within a database. In effect, a domain is one of the predefined database data types plus some additional constraints, which are specified as part of the domain definition. Once a domain is defined and named, the domain name can be used in place of a data type to define new columns. The columns "inherit" the constraints of the domain. Domains are defined outside of the table and column definitions of the database, using the CREATE DOMAIN statement.

- *Table constraints* are specified as part of the table definition when a table is created. Conceptually, they restrict the legal values that may appear in rows of the table. Table constraints are specified in the CREATE TABLE statement that defines a table. Usually they appear as a group after the column definitions, but the SQL2 standard allows them to be interspersed with the column definitions.

- *Assertions* are the most general type of SQL2 constraint. Like domains, they are specified outside of the table and column structure of the database. Conceptually, an assertion specifies a relationship among data values which crosses multiple tables within the database.

Each of the four different types of constraints has its own conceptual purpose, and each appears in a different part of the SQL2 statement syntax. However, the distinctions between them are somewhat arbitrary. Any column constraint that appears for an individual column definition can just as easily be specified as a table constraint. Similarly, any table constraint can be specified as an assertion. In practice, it's probably best to specify each database constraint where it seems to most "naturally" fit, given the real-world situation that the database is trying to model. Constraints that apply globally to the entire situation (business processes, interrelationships among customers and products, and so on) should appear as assertions. Constraints that apply to a specific type of entity (a customer or an order) should appear as table constraints or column constraints within the appropriate table that describes that type of entity. When the same constraint applies to many different columns in the database that all refer to the same type of entity, then a domain is appropriate.

Assertions

Examples of the first three types of constraints have previously appeared in earlier sections of this chapter. An *assertion* is specified using the SQL2 CREATE ASSERTION statement. Here is an assertion that might be useful in the demo database:

Insure that an office's quota target does not exceed the sum of the quotas for its salespeople:

```
CREATE ASSERTION quota_valid
  CHECK ((OFFICES.QUOTA <= SUM(SALESREPS.QUOTA)) AND
         (SALESREPS.REP_OFFICE = OFFICES.OFFICE))
```

Because it is an object in the database (like a table or a column), the assertion must be given a name (in this case, it's "quota_valid"). The name is used in error messages produced by the DBMS when the assertion is violated. The assertion causing an error may be obvious in a small demo database, but in a large database that might contain dozens or hundreds of assertions, it's critical to know which of the assertions was violated.

Here is another example of assertion that might be useful in the sample database:

Insure that the total of the orders for any customer does not exceed their credit limit:

```
CREATE ASSERTION credit_orders
  CHECK (CUSTOMER.CREDIT_LIMIT <=
         SELECT SUM(ORDERS.AMOUNT)
           FROM ORDERS
          WHERE ORDERS.CUST = CUSTOMER.CUST_NUM)
```

As these examples show, a SQL2 assertion is defined by a search condition, which is enclosed in parentheses and follows the keyword CHECK. Every time an attempt is made to modify the contents of the database, through an INSERT or UPDATE or DELETE statement, the search condition is checked against the (proposed) modified database contents. If the search condition remains TRUE, the modification is allowed. If the search condition would become untrue, the DBMS does not carry out the proposed modification, and an error code is returned, indicating an assertion violation.

In theory, assertions could cause a very large amount of database processing overhead as they are checked for each statement that might modify the database. In practice, the DBMS will analyze the assertion and determine which tables and columns it involves. Only changes that involve those particular tables or columns will actually trigger the search condition. Nonetheless, assertions should be defined with great care to insure that they impose a reasonable amount of overhead for the benefit they provide.

SQL2 Constraint Types

The types of constraints that can be specified in SQL2, and the role played by each, can be summarized as follows:

- The NOT NULL constraint can appear only as a column constraint. It prevents the column from being assigned a NULL value.

- A PRIMARY KEY constraint can appear as a column constraint or a table constraint. If the primary key consists of a single column, the column constraint may be more convenient. If it consists of multiple columns, it should be specified as a table constraint.

- A UNIQUE constraint can appear as a column constraint or a table constraint. If the unique values restriction is being enforced for a single column only, the column constraint is the easiest way to specify it. If the unique values restriction applies to a set of two or more columns (that is, the *combination* of values for those columns must be unique for all rows in the table), then the table constraint form should be used.

- A referential (FOREIGN KEY) constraint can appear as a column constraint or a table constraint. If the foreign key consists of a single column, the column constraint may be more convenient. If it consists of multiple columns, it should be specified as a table constraint. If a table has many foreign key relationships to other tables, it may be most convenient to gather *all* of its foreign key constraints together at one place in the table definition, rather than having them scattered throughout the column definitions.

- A CHECK constraint can appear as a column constraint or a table constraint. It is also the *only* kind of constraint that forms part of the definition of a domain or an assertion. The check constraint is specified as a search condition, like the search condition that appears in the WHERE clause of a database query. The constraint is satisfied if the search condition has a TRUE value.

Each individual constraint within a database (no matter what its type) may be assigned a *constraint name* to uniquely identify it from the other constraints. It's probably not necessary to assign constraint names in a simple database where each constraint is clearly associated with a single table, column, or domain, and where there is little potential for confusion. In a more complex database involving multiple constraints on a single table or column, it can be very useful to be able to identify the individual constraints by name (especially when errors start to occur!). Note that the check constraint in an assertion *must* have a constraint name; this name effectively becomes the name of the assertion containing the constraint.

Deferred Constraint Checking

In their simplest form, the various constraints that are specified within a database are checked every time an attempt is made to change the database contents—that is, during the execution of every attempted INSERT, UPDATE, or DELETE statement. For database systems claiming only Intermediate level or Entry level conformance to the SQL2 standard, this is the only mode of operation allowed for database constraints. The Full level SQL2 standard specifies an additional capability for *deferred* constraint checking.

When constraint checking is deferred, the constraints are not checked for each individual SQL statement. Instead, constraint checking is held in abeyance until the end of a SQL transaction. (Transaction processing and the associated SQL statements are described in detail in the next chapter.) When the completion of the transaction is signaled by the SQL COMMIT statement, the DBMS checks the deferred constraints. If all of the constraints are satisfied, then the COMMIT statement can proceed, and the transaction can complete normally. At this point, any changes made to the database during the transaction become permanent. If, however, one or more of the constraints would be violated by the proposed transaction, then the COMMIT statement fails, and the transaction is "rolled back"—that is, all of the proposed changes to the database are reversed, and the database goes back to its state before the transaction began.

Deferred constraint checking can be very important when several updates to a database must all be made "at once" to keep the database in a consistent state. For example, suppose the demo database contained this assertion:

Insure that an office's quota target is exactly equal to the sum of the quotas for its salespeople.

```
CREATE ASSERTION quota_totals
  CHECK ((OFFICES.QUOTA = SUM(SALESREPS.QUOTA)) AND
         (SALESREPS.REP_OFFICE = OFFICES.OFFICE))
```

Without the deferred constraint checking, this constraint would effectively prevent you from ever adding a salesperson to the database. Why? Because to keep the office quota and the salespersons' quotas in the right relationship, you must *both* add a new salesperson row with the appropriate quota (using an INSERT statement) *and* increase the quota for the appropriate office by the same amount (using an UPDATE statement). If you try to perform the INSERT statement on the SALESREPS table first, the OFFICES table will not yet have been updated, the assertion will not be true, and the statement will fail. Similarly, if you try to perform the UPDATE statement on the OFFICES table first, the SALESREPS table will not yet have been updated, the assertion will not be true, and the statement will fail. The only solution to this dilemma is to defer constraint checking until *both* statements have completed, and *then* check to make sure that both operations, taken together, have left the database in a valid state.

The SQL2 deferred constraint mechanism provides for this capability, and much more. Each individual constraint (of all types) within the database can be identified as either DEFERRABLE or NOT DEFERRABLE when it is first created or defined:

- A DEFERRABLE constraint is one whose checking *can be* deferred to the end of a transaction. The assertion in the previous example is one that should be deferrable. When updating quotas or adding new salespeople to the database, you certainly want to be able to defer constraint checking, as the example showed.

- A NOT DEFERRABLE constraint is one whose checking *cannot* be deferred. A primary key constraint, a uniqueness constraint, and many column check constraints would usually fall into this category. These data integrity checks typically don't depend on other database interactions. They can be, and should be, checked after *every* SQL statement that tries to modify the database.

Because it provides the most stringent integrity checking, NOT DEFERRABLE is the default. You must explicitly declare a constraint to be DEFERRABLE if you want to defer its operation. Note also that these constraint attributes only define the *deferrability* of a constraint—that is, whether or not its operation *can be* deferred. The constraint definition may also specify the *initial state* of the constraint:

- An INITIALLY IMMEDIATE constraint is one that "starts out" as an immediate constraint. That is, it will be checked immediately for each SQL statement.

- An INITIALLY DEFERRED constraint is one that "starts out" as a deferred constraint. That is, its checking will be deferred until the end of a transaction. Of course, this option cannot be specified if the constraint is defined as NOT DEFERRABLE.

The constraint is put into the specified initial state when it is first created. It is also reset into this initial state at the beginning of each transaction. Because it provides the most stringent integrity checking, INITIALLY IMMEDIATE is the default. You must explicitly declare a constraint to be INITIALLY DEFERRED if you want it to automatically start out each transaction in a deferred state.

SQL2 adds one more mechanism to control the immediate or deferred processing of constraints. You can dynamically change the processing of a constraint during database operation using the SET CONSTRAINTS statement. For example, suppose the sample database contains this assertion:

```
CREATE ASSERTION quota_totals
 CHECK ((OFFICES.QUOTA = SUM(SALESREPS.QUOTA)) AND
        (SALESREPS.REP_OFFICE = OFFICES.OFFICE))
      DEFERRABLE INITIALLY IMMEDIATE
```

The initially immediate checking causes the constraint to be processed, statement by statement, for all "normal" database processing. For the "special" transaction that adds a new salesperson to the database, however, you will need to temporarily defer constraint processing. This sequence of statements accomplishes the goal:

```
SET CONSTRAINTS quota_totals DEFERRED

    INSERT INTO SALESREPS (EMPL_NUM, NAME, REP_OFFICE, HIRE_DATE,
                QUOTA, SALES)
        VALUES (:num, :name, :office_num, :date, :amount, 0)

    UPDATE OFFICES SET TARGET = TARGET + :amount
     WHERE (OFFICE = :office_num)

    COMMIT
```

After the COMMIT statement ends the transaction, the quota_totals constraint is reset back into IMMEDIATE mode because of the INITIALLY IMMEDIATE specification. If there were more work to be done after the UPDATE statement before the end of the transaction, you could manually set the constraint back into IMMEDIATE mode using this statement:

```
SET CONSTRAINTS quota_totals IMMEDIATE
```

You can set the same mode for several different constraints by including the constraint names in a comma-separated list:

```
SET CONSTRAINTS quota_totals, rep_totals IMMEDIATE
```

Finally, you can set the processing mode for all constraints with a single statement:

```
SET CONSTRAINTS ALL DEFERRED
```

The SQL2 capabilities for deferred constraint checking form a very comprehensive facility for managing the integrity of a database. As with many SQL2 capabilities, individual pieces of the SQL2 capability were taken from existing SQL implementations, and individual pieces have found their way into other implementations since the publication of the standard. IBM's DB2, for example, includes deferred constraint checking capability and supports SQL2-style deferrability options. Its SET CONSTRAINTS statement, however, differs from the SQL2 standard. It operates on individual tables in the database, turning on and off the deferral of constraint checking associated with the table contents.

Business Rules

Many of the data integrity issues in the real world have to do with the rules and procedures of an organization. For example, the company that is modeled by the sample database might have rules like these:

- No customer is allowed to place orders that would exceed the customer's credit limit.

- The sales vice president must be notified whenever any customer is assigned a credit limit higher than $50,000.

- Orders may remain on the books only for six months; orders older than six months must be canceled and reentered.

In addition, there are often "accounting rules" that must be followed to maintain the integrity of totals, counts, and other amounts stored in a database. For the sample database, these rules probably make sense:

- Whenever a new order is taken, the SALES column for the salesperson who took the order and for the office where that salesperson works should be increased by the order amount. Deleting an order or changing the order amount should also cause the SALES columns to be adjusted.

- Whenever a new order is taken, the QTY_ON_HAND column for the product being ordered should be decreased by the quantity of products ordered. Deleting an order, changing the quantity, or changing the product ordered should also cause corresponding adjustments to the QTY_ON_HAND column.

These rules fall outside the realm of the SQL language as defined by the SQL1 standard and as implemented by many SQL-based DBMS products today. The DBMS takes responsibility for storing and organizing data and ensuring its basic integrity, but enforcing the business rules is the responsibility of the application programs that access the database.

Placing the burden of enforcing business rules on the application programs that access the database has several disadvantages:

- *Duplication of effort.* If six different programs deal with various updates to the ORDERS table, each of them must include code that enforces the rules relating to ORDERS updates.

- *Lack of consistency.* If several programs written by different programmers handle updates to a table, they will probably enforce the rules somewhat differently.

- *Maintenance problems.* If the business rules change, the programmers must identify every program that enforces the rules, locate the code, and modify it correctly.

- *Complexity.* There are often many rules to remember. Even in the small sample database, a program that handles order changes must worry about enforcing credit limits, adjusting sales totals for salespeople and offices, and adjusting the quantities on hand. A program that handles simple updates can become complex very quickly.

The requirement that application programs enforce business rules is not unique to SQL. Application programs have had that responsibility since the earliest days of COBOL programs and file systems. However, there has been a steady trend over the years to put more "understanding" of the data and more responsibility for its integrity into the database itself. In 1986 the Sybase DBMS introduced the concept of a *trigger* as a step toward including business rules in a relational database. The concept proved to be very popular, so support for triggers began to appear in many SQL DBMS products in the early 1990s, including those of the mainstream enterprise DBMS vendors.

What Is a Trigger?

The concept of a trigger is relatively straightforward. For any event that causes a change in the contents of a table, a user can specify an associated action that the DBMS should carry out. The three events that can trigger an action are attempts to INSERT, DELETE, or UPDATE rows of the table. The action triggered by an event is specified by a sequence of SQL statements.

To understand how a trigger works, let's examine a concrete example. When a new order is added to the ORDERS table, these two changes to the database should also take place:

- The SALES column for the salesperson who took the order should be increased by the amount of the order.

- The QTY_ON_HAND amount for the product being ordered should be decreased by the quantity ordered.

This Transact-SQL statement defines a SQL Server trigger, named NEWORDER, that causes these database updates to happen automatically:

```
CREATE TRIGGER NEWORDER
    ON ORDERS
   FOR INSERT
   AS UPDATE SALESREPS
         SET SALES = SALES + INSERTED.AMOUNT
        FROM SALESREPS, INSERTED
       WHERE SALESREPS.EMPL_NUM = INSERTED.REP
      UPDATE PRODUCTS
         SET QTY_ON_HAND = QTY_ON_HAND - INSERTED.QTY
        FROM PRODUCTS, INSERTED
       WHERE PRODUCTS.MFR_ID = INSERTED.MFR
         AND PRODUCTS.PRODUCT_ID = INSERTED.PRODUCT
```

The first part of the trigger definition tells SQL Server that the trigger is to be invoked whenever an INSERT statement is attempted on the ORDERS table. The remainder of the definition (after the keyword AS) defines the action of the trigger. In this case, the action is a sequence of two UPDATE statements, one for the SALESREPS table and one for the PRODUCTS table. The row being inserted is referred to using the pseudo-table name inserted within the UPDATE statements. As the example shows, SQL Server extends the SQL language substantially to support triggers. Other extensions not shown here include IF/THEN/ELSE tests, looping, procedure calls, and even PRINT statements that display user messages.

The trigger capability, while popular in many DBMS products, is not a part of the ANSI/ISO SQL2 standard. As with other SQL features whose popularity has preceded standardization, this has led to a considerable divergence in trigger support across various DBMS brands. Some of the differences between brands are merely differences in syntax. Others reflect real differences in the underlying capability.

DB2's trigger support provides an instructive example of the differences. Here is the same trigger definition shown previously for SQL Server, this time using the DB2 syntax:

```
CREATE TRIGGER NEWORDER
        AFTER INSERT ON ORDERS
   REFERENCING NEW AS NEW_ORD
      FOR EACH ROW MODE DB2SQL
          BEGIN ATOMIC
         UPDATE SALESREPS
            SET SALES = SALES + NEW_ORD.AMOUNT
          WHERE SALESREPS.EMPL_NUM = NEW_ORD.REP;
```

```
UPDATE PRODUCTS
    SET QTY_ON_HAND = QTY_ON_HAND - NEW_ORD.QTY
WHERE PRODUCTS.MFR_ID = NEW_ORD.MFR
    AND PRODUCTS.PRODUCT_ID = NEW_ORD.PRODUCT;
    END
```

The beginning of the trigger definition includes the same elements as the SQL Server definition, but rearranges them. It explicitly tells DB2 that the trigger is to be invoked AFTER a new order is inserted into the database. DB2 also allows you to specify that the trigger is to be carried out *before* a triggering action is applied to the database contents. This doesn't make sense in this example, because the triggering event is an INSERT operation, but it does make sense for UPDATE or DELETE operations.

The DB2 REFERENCING clause specifies a *table alias* (NEW_ORD) that will be used to refer to the row being inserted throughout the remainder of the trigger definition. It serves the same function as the INSERTED keyword in the SQL Server trigger. The statement references the "new" values in the inserted row because this is an INSERT operation trigger. For a DELETE operation trigger, the "old" values would be referenced. For an UPDATE operation trigger, DB2 gives you the ability to refer to *both* the "old" (pre-UPDATE) values and "new" (post-UPDATE) values.

The BEGIN ATOMIC and END serve as brackets around the sequence of SQL statements that define the triggered action. The two searched UPDATE statements in the body of the trigger definition are straightforward modifications of their SQL Server counterparts. They follow the standard SQL syntax for searched UPDATE statements, using the table alias specified by the REFERENCING clause to identify the particular row of the SALESREPS table and the PRODUCTS table to be updated. The row being inserted is referred to using the pseudo-table name inserted within the UPDATE statements.

Here is another example of a trigger definition, this time using Informix Universal Server:

```
CREATE TRIGGER NEWORDER
    INSERT ON ORDERS
    AFTER (EXECUTE PROCEDURE NEW_ORDER)
```

This trigger again specifies an action that is to take place AFTER a new order is inserted. In this case, the multiple SQL statements that form the triggered action can't be specified directly in the trigger definition. Instead, the triggered statements are placed into an Informix stored procedure, named NEW_ORDER, and the trigger causes the stored procedure to be executed. As this and the preceding examples show, although the core concepts of a trigger mechanism are very consistent across databases, the specifics vary a great deal. Triggers are certainly among the least portable aspects of SQL databases today.

Triggers and Referential Integrity

Triggers provide an alternative way to implement the referential integrity constraints provided by foreign keys and primary keys. In fact, advocates of the trigger feature point out that the trigger mechanism is more flexible than the strict referential integrity provided by DB2 and the ANSI/ISO standard. For example, here is a trigger that enforces referential integrity for the OFFICES/SALESREPS relationship and displays a message when an attempted update fails:

```
CREATE TRIGGER REP_UPDATE
    ON SALESREPS
  FOR INSERT, UPDATE
   AS IF ((SELECT COUNT(*)
            FROM OFFICES, INSERTED
           WHERE OFFICES.OFFICE = INSERTED.REP_OFFICE) = 0)
      BEGIN
         PRINT "Invalid office number specified."
         ROLLBACK TRANSACTION
      END
```

Triggers can also be used to provide extended forms of referential integrity. For example, DB2 initially provided cascaded deletes through its CASCADE delete rule but did not support "cascaded updates" if a primary key value is changed. This limitation need not apply to triggers, however. The following SQL Server trigger cascades any update of the OFFICE column in the OFFICES table down into the REP_OFFICE column of the SALESREPS table:

```
CREATE TRIGGER CHANGE_REP_OFFICE
    ON OFFICES
  FOR UPDATE
   AS IF UPDATE (OFFICE)
      BEGIN
         UPDATE SALESREPS
            SET SALESREPS.REP_OFFICE = INSERTED.OFFICE
           FROM SALESREPS, INSERTED, DELETED
          WHERE SALESREPS.REP_OFFICE = DELETED.OFFICE
      END
```

As in the previous SQL Server example, the references DELETED.OFFICE and INSERTED.OFFICE in the trigger refer, respectively, to the values of the OFFICE column before and after the UPDATE statement. The trigger definition must be able to differentiate between these "before" and "after" values to perform the appropriate search and update actions specified by the trigger.

Trigger Advantages and Disadvantages

A complete discussion of triggers is beyond the scope of this book, but even these simple examples shows the power of the trigger mechanism. The major advantage of triggers is that business rules can be stored in the database and enforced consistently with each update to the database. This can dramatically reduce the complexity of application programs that access the database. Triggers also have some disadvantages, including these:

- *Database complexity.* When the rules are moved into the database, setting up the database becomes a more complex task. Users who could reasonably be expected to create small, *ad hoc* applications with SQL will find that the programming logic of triggers makes the task much more difficult.

- *Hidden rules.* With the rules hidden away inside the database, programs that appear to perform straightforward database updates may, in fact, generate an enormous amount of database activity. The programmer no longer has total control over what happens to the database. Instead, a program-initiated database action may cause other, hidden actions.

- *Hidden performance implications.* With triggers stored inside the database, the consequences of executing a SQL statement are no longer completely visible to the programmer. In particular, an apparently simple SQL statement could, in concept, trigger a process that involves a sequential scan of a very large database table, which would take a long time to complete. These performance implications of any given SQL statement are invisible to the programmer.

Triggers and the SQL Standard

Triggers were one of the most widely praised and publicized features of Sybase SQL Server when it was first introduced, and they have since found their way into many commercial SQL products. Although the SQL2 standard provided an opportunity to standardize the DBMS implementation of triggers, the standards committee included check constraints instead. As the trigger and check-constraint examples in the preceding sections show, check constraints can be effectively used to limit the data that can be added to a table or modified in a table. However, unlike triggers, they lack the ability to cause an independent action in the database, such as adding a row or changing a data item in another table.

The extra capability provided by triggers has led several industry experts to advocate that they be included in a future SQL3 standard. Other experts have argued that triggers are a pollution of the data management function of a database, and that the functions performed by triggers belong in fourth generation languages (4GLs) and other database tools, rather than in the DBMS itself. While the debate continues, DBMS products have experimented with new trigger capabilities that extend beyond the database itself. These "extended trigger" capabilities allow modifications to data in a database to automatically cause actions such as sending mail, alerting a user, or launching another program to perform a task. This makes triggers even more useful and will add to the debate over including them in future official SQL standards. Regardless of the official stance, it appears that triggers will become a more important part of the SQL language over the next several years.

Summary

The SQL language provides a number of features that help to protect the integrity of data stored in a relational database:

- Required columns can be specified when a table is created, and the DBMS will prevent NULL values in these columns.

- Data validation is limited to data type checking in standard SQL, but many DBMS products offer other data validation features.

- Entity integrity constraints ensure that the primary key uniquely identifies each entity represented in the database.

- Referential integrity constraints ensure that relationships among entities in the database are preserved during database updates.

- The SQL2 standard and newer implementations provide extensive referential integrity support, including delete and update rules that tell the DBMS how to handle the deletion and modification of rows that are referenced by other rows.

- Business rules can be enforced by the DBMS through the trigger mechanism popularized by Sybase and SQL Server. Triggers allow the DBMS to take complex actions in response to events such as attempted INSERT, DELETE, or UPDATE statements. Check constraints provide a more limited way to include business rules in the definition of a database and have the DBMS enforce them.

Chapter 12

Transaction Processing

Database updates are usually triggered by real-world events, such as the receipt of a new order from a customer. In fact, receiving a new order would generate not just one, but this series of *four* updates to the sample database:

- Add the new order to the ORDERS table.
- Update the sales total for the salesperson who took the order.
- Update the sales total for the salesperson's office.
- Update the quantity-on-hand total for the ordered product.

To leave the database in a self-consistent state, all four updates must occur as a unit. If a system failure or another error creates a situation where some of the updates are processed and others are not, the integrity of the database will be lost. Similarly, if another user calculates totals or ratios part way through the sequence of updates, the calculations will be incorrect. The sequence of updates must thus be an "all-or-nothing" proposition in the database. SQL provides precisely this capability through its transaction processing features, which are described in this chapter.

What Is a Transaction?

A *transaction* is a sequence of one or more SQL statements that together form a logical unit of work. The SQL statements that form the transaction are typically closely related and perform interdependent actions. Each statement in the transaction performs some part of a task, but all of them are required to complete the task. Grouping the statements as a single transaction tells the DBMS that the entire statement sequence should be executed *atomically*—all of the statements must be completed for the database to be in a consistent state.

Here are some examples of typical transactions for the sample database, along with the SQL statement sequence that comprises each transaction:

- *Add-an-order*. To accept a customer's order, the order entry program should (a) query the PRODUCTS table to ensure that the product is in stock, (b) insert the order into the ORDERS table, (c) update the PRODUCTS table, subtracting the quantity ordered from the quantity-on-hand of the product, (d) update the SALESREPS table, adding the order amount to the total sales of the salesperson who took the order, and (e) update the OFFICES table, adding the order amount to the total sales of the office where the salesperson works.

- *Cancel-an-order*. To cancel a customer's order, the program should (a) delete the order from the ORDERS table, (b) update the PRODUCTS table, adjusting the quantity-on-hand total for the product, (c) update the SALESREPS table, subtracting the order amount from the salesperson's total sales, and (d) update the OFFICES table, subtracting the order amount from the office's total sales.

■ *Reassign-a-customer.* When a customer is reassigned from one salesperson to another, the program should (a) update the CUSTOMERS table to reflect the change, (b) update the ORDERS table to show the new salesperson for all orders placed by the customer, (c) update the SALESREPS table, reducing the quota for the salesperson losing the customer, and (d) update the SALESREPS table, raising the quota for the salesperson gaining the customer.

In each of these cases a sequence of four or five actions, where each action consists of a separate SQL statement, is required to handle the single "logical" transaction.

The transaction concept is critical for programs that update a database because it ensures the integrity of the database. A SQL-based DBMS makes this commitment about the statements in a transaction:

The statements in a transaction will be executed as an atomic unit of work in the database. Either *all* of the statements will be executed successfully, or *none* of the statements will be executed.

The DBMS is responsible for keeping this commitment even if the application program aborts or a hardware failure occurs in the middle of the transaction, as shown in Figure 12-1. In each case, the DBMS must make sure that when failure recovery is complete, the database never reflects a "partial transaction."

COMMIT **and** ROLLBACK

SQL supports database transactions through two SQL transaction processing statements, shown in Figure 12-2:

■ The COMMIT statement signals the successful end of a transaction. It tells the DBMS that the transaction is now complete; all of the statements that comprise the transaction have been executed, and the database is self-consistent.

■ The ROLLBACK statement signals the unsuccessful end of a transaction. It tells the DBMS that the user does not want to complete the transaction; instead, the DBMS should *back out* any changes made to the database during the transaction. In effect, the DBMS restores the database to its state before the transaction began.

The COMMIT and ROLLBACK statements are executable SQL statements, just like SELECT, INSERT, and UPDATE. Here is an example of a successful update transaction that changes the quantity and amount of an order and adjusts the totals for the product, salesperson, and office associated with the order. A change like this would typically be handled by a forms-based "change order" program, which would use programmatic SQL to execute the statements shown on the next page of text.

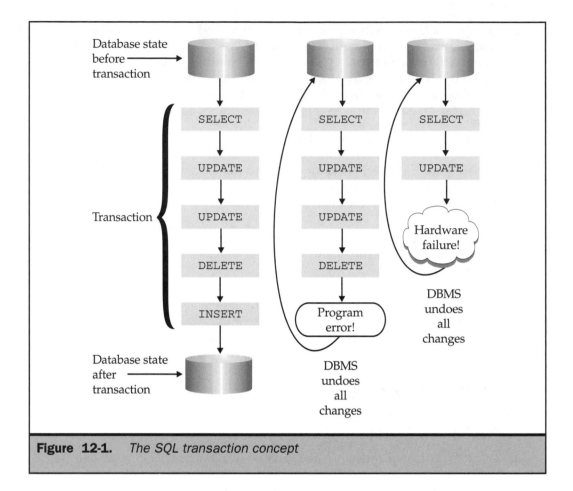

Figure 12-1. *The SQL transaction concept*

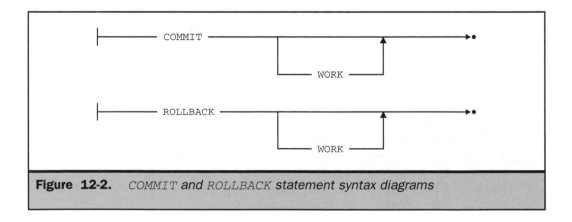

Figure 12-2. *COMMIT and ROLLBACK statement syntax diagrams*

Change the quantity on order number 113051 from 4 to 10, which raises its amount from $1,458 to $3,550. The order is for QSA-XK47 Reducers and was placed with Larry Fitch (employee number 108) who works in Los Angeles (office number 21).

```
UPDATE ORDERS
   SET QTY = 10, AMOUNT = 3550.00
 WHERE ORDER_NR = 113051

UPDATE SALESREPS
   SET SALES = SALES - 1458.00 + 3550.00
 WHERE EMPL_NUM = 108

UPDATE OFFICES
   SET SALES = SALES - 1458.00 + 3550.00
 WHERE OFFICE = 21

UPDATE PRODUCTS
   SET QTY_ON_HAND = QTY_ON_HAND + 4 - 10
 WHERE MFR_ID = 'QSA'
   AND PRODUCT_ID = 'XK47'
```

. . . confirm the change one last time with the customer . . .

```
COMMIT WORK
```

Here is the same transaction, but this time assume that the user makes an error entering the product number. To correct the error, the transaction is rolled back, so that it can be reentered correctly:

Change the quantity on order number 113051 from 4 to 10, which raises its amount from $1,458 to $3,550. The order is for QAS-XK47 Reducers and was placed with Larry Fitch (employee number 108), who works in Los Angeles (office number 21).

```
UPDATE ORDERS
   SET QTY = 10, AMOUNT = 3550.00
 WHERE ORDER_NR = 113051

UPDATE SALESREPS
   SET SALES = SALES - 1458.00 + 3550.00
 WHERE EMPL_NUM = 108
```

```
UPDATE OFFICES
   SET SALES = SALES - 1458.00 + 3550.00
 WHERE OFFICE = 21

UPDATE PRODUCTS
   SET QTY_ON_HAND = QTY_ON_HAND + 4 - 10
 WHERE MFR_ID = 'QAS'
   AND PRODUCT_ID = 'XK47'
```

. . . oops! the manufacturer is "QSA", not "QAS" . . .

```
ROLLBACK WORK
```

The ANSI/ISO Transaction Model

The ANSI/ISO SQL standard defines a SQL *transaction model* and the roles of the COMMIT and ROLLBACK statements. Most, but not all, commercial SQL products use this transaction model, which is based on the transaction support in the early releases of DB2. The standard specifies that a SQL transaction *automatically* begins with the first SQL statement executed by a user or a program. The transaction continues through subsequent SQL statements until it ends in one of four ways:

- A COMMIT statement ends the transaction successfully, making its database changes permanent. A new transaction begins immediately after the COMMIT statement.

- A ROLLBACK statement aborts the transaction, backing out its database changes. A new transaction begins immediately after the ROLLBACK statement.

- Successful program termination (for programmatic SQL) also ends the transaction successfully, just as if a COMMIT statement had been executed. Because the program is finished, there is no new transaction to begin.

- Abnormal program termination (for programmatic SQL) also aborts the transaction, just as if a ROLLBACK statement had been executed. Because the program is finished, there is no new transaction to begin.

Figure 12-3 shows typical transactions that illustrate these four conditions. Note that the user or program is *always* in a transaction under the ANSI/ISO transaction model. No explicit action is required to begin a transaction; it begins automatically with the first SQL statement or immediately after the preceding transaction ends.

Recall that the ANSI/ISO SQL standard is primarily focused on a *programmatic* SQL language for use in application programs. Transactions play an important role in programmatic SQL, because even a simple application program often needs to carry out a sequence of two or three SQL statements to accomplish its task. Because users can

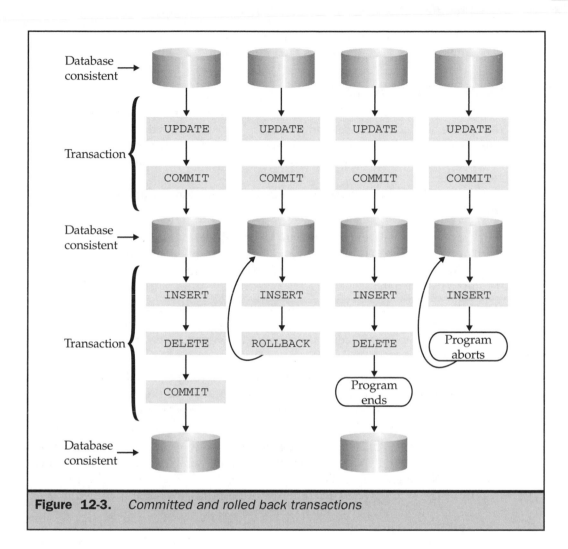

Figure 12-3. *Committed and rolled back transactions*

change their minds and other conditions can occur (such as being out of stock on a product that a customer wants to order), an application program must be able to proceed part way through a transaction and then choose to abort or continue. The COMMIT and ROLLBACK statements provide precisely this capability.

The COMMIT and ROLLBACK statements can also be used in interactive SQL, but in practice they are rarely seen in this context. Interactive SQL is generally used for database queries; updates are less common, and multi-statement updates are almost never performed by typing the statements into an interactive SQL facility. As a result, transactions are typically a minor concern in interactive SQL. In fact, many interactive SQL products default to an "auto-commit" mode, where a COMMIT statement is automatically executed after each SQL statement typed by the user. This effectively makes each interactive SQL statement its own transaction.

Other Transaction Models

A few commercial SQL products depart from the ANSI/ISO and DB2 transaction model to provide additional transaction processing capability for their users. The Sybase DBMS, which is designed for online transaction processing applications, is one example. SQL Server, which was derived from the Sybase product, also uses the Sybase transaction model.

The Transact-SQL dialect used by Sybase includes four transaction processing statements:

- The BEGIN TRANSACTION statement signals the beginning of a transaction. Unlike the ANSI/ISO transaction model, which implicitly begins a new transaction when the previous one ends, Sybase requires an explicit statement to start a transaction.

- The COMMIT TRANSACTION statement signals the successful end of a transaction. As in the ANSI/ISO model, all changes made to the database during the transaction become permanent. However, a new transaction is not automatically started.

- The SAVE TRANSACTION statement establishes a *savepoint* in the middle of a transaction. Sybase saves the state of the database at the current point in the transaction and assigns the saved state a *savepoint name*, specified in the statement.

- The ROLLBACK TRANSACTION statement has two roles. If a savepoint is named in the ROLLBACK statement, Sybase backs out the database changes made since the savepoint, effectively rolling the transaction back to the point where the SAVE TRANSACTION statement was executed. If no savepoint is named, the ROLLBACK statement backs out all database changes made since the BEGIN TRANSACTION statement.

The Sybase savepoint mechanism is especially useful in complex transactions involving many statements, as shown in Figure 12-4. The application program in the figure periodically saves its status as the transaction progresses, establishing two named savepoints. If problems develop later during the transaction, the application program does not have to abort the entire transaction. Instead, it can roll the transaction back to *any* of its savepoints and proceed from there. All of the statements executed before the savepoint remain in effect; those executed since the savepoint are backed out by the rollback operation.

Note that the *entire transaction* is still the logical unit of work for Sybase, as it is for the ANSI/ISO model. If a system or hardware failure occurs in the middle of a transaction, for example, the entire transaction is backed out of the database. Thus,

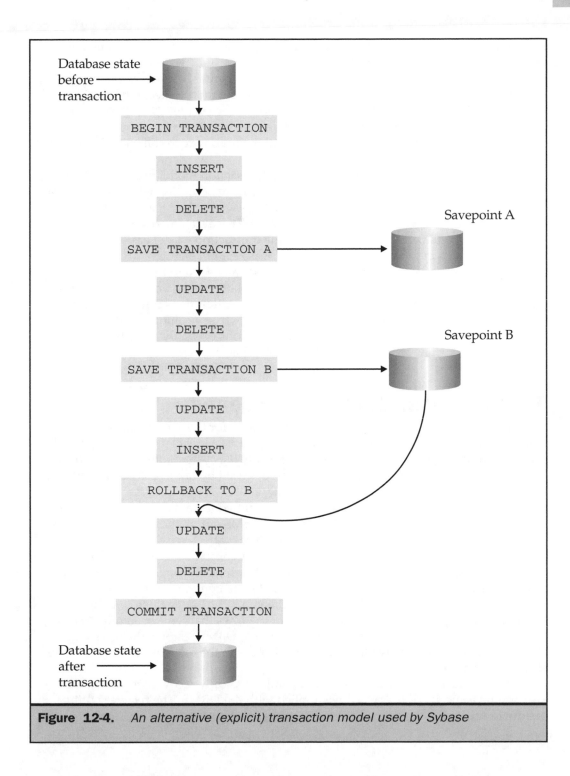

Figure 12-4.   *An alternative (explicit) transaction model used by Sybase*

savepoints are a convenience for the application program, but not a fundamental change to the ANSI/ISO transaction model.

The explicit use of a BEGIN TRANSACTION statement is, however, a significant departure from the ANSI/ISO model. SQL statements that are executed "outside a transaction" (that is, statements that do not appear between a BEGIN/COMMIT or a BEGIN/ROLLBACK statement pair) are effectively handled in "auto-commit" mode. Each statement is committed as it is executed; there is no way to roll back the statement once it has succeeded.

Some DBMS brands that use a Sybase-style transaction model prohibit statements that alter the structure of a database or its security from occurring within a transaction (such as CREATE TABLE, ALTER TABLE, and DROP TABLE, discussed in Chapter 13, and GRANT and REVOKE, discussed in Chapter 15). These statements must be executed outside a transaction. This restriction makes the transaction model easier to implement, because it ensures that the structure of the database cannot change during a transaction. In contrast, the structure of a database can be altered significantly during an ANSI/ISO-style transaction (tables can be dropped, created, and populated, for example), and the DBMS must be able to undo all the alterations if the user later decides to roll back the transaction. In practice, the Sybase prohibitions do not affect the usefulness of the DBMS. Because these prohibitions probably contribute to faster transaction performance, most users gladly make this trade-off.

Transactions: Behind the Scenes *

The "all-or-nothing" commitment that a DBMS makes for the statements in a transaction seems almost like magic to a new SQL user. How can the DBMS possibly back out the changes made to a database, especially if a system failure occurs during the middle of a transaction? The actual techniques used by brands of DBMS vary, but almost all of them are based on a *transaction log*, as shown in Figure 12-5.

Here is how the transaction log works, in simplified form. When a user executes a SQL statement that modifies the database, the DBMS automatically writes a record in the transaction log showing two copies of each row affected by the statement. One copy shows the row *before* the change, and the other copy shows the row *after* the change. Only after the log is written does the DBMS actually modify the row on the disk. If the user subsequently executes a COMMIT statement, the end-of-transaction is noted in the transaction log. If the user executes a ROLLBACK statement, the DBMS examines the log to find the "before" images of the rows that have been modified since the transaction began. Using these images, the DBMS restores the rows to their earlier state, effectively backing out all changes to the database that were made during the transaction.

If a system failure occurs, the system operator typically recovers the database by running a special recovery utility supplied with the DBMS. The recovery utility examines the end of the transaction log, looking for transactions that were not

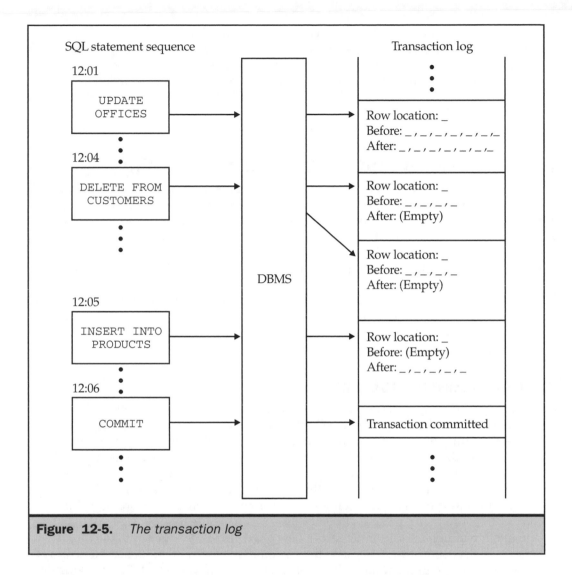

Figure 12-5. *The transaction log*

committed before the failure. The utility rolls back each of these incomplete transactions, so that only committed transactions are reflected in the database; transactions in process at the time of the failure have been rolled back.

The use of a transaction log obviously imposes an overhead on updates to the database. In practice, the mainstream commercial DBMS products use much more sophisticated logging techniques than the simple scheme described here to minimize this overhead. In addition, the transaction log is usually stored on a fast disk drive, different from the one that stores the database, to minimize disk access contention.

Some personal computer DBMS brands allow you to disable transaction logging to increase the performance of the DBMS. This may also be an acceptable alternative in specialized production databases, for example, where the database contents are replicated on a duplicate computer system. In most common production databases, however, a logging scheme and its overhead are an integral part of the database operation.

Transactions and Multi-User Processing

When two or more users concurrently access a database, transaction processing takes on a new dimension. Now the DBMS must not only recover properly from system failures or errors, it must also ensure that the users' actions do not interfere with one another. Ideally, each user should be able to access the database as if he or she had exclusive access to it, without worrying about the actions of other users. The SQL transaction model allows a SQL-based DBMS to insulate users from one another in this way.

The best way to understand how SQL handles concurrent transactions is to look at the problems that result if transactions are not handled properly. Although they can show up in many different ways, four fundamental problems can occur. The next four sections give a simple example of each problem.

The Lost Update Problem

Figure 12-6 shows a simple application where two users accept telephone orders from customers. The order entry program checks the PRODUCTS file for adequate inventory before accepting the customer's order. In the figure, Joe starts entering an order for 100 ACI-41004 Widgets from his customer. At the same time, Mary starts entering her customer's order for 125 ACI-41004 Widgets. Each order entry program does a query on the PRODUCTS file, and each finds that 139 Widgets are in stock—more than enough to cover the customer's request. Joe asks his customer to confirm the order, and his copy of the order entry program updates the PRODUCTS file to show (139 − 100) = 39 Widgets remaining for sale and inserts a new order for 100 Widgets into the ORDERS table. A few seconds later, Mary asks her customer to confirm their order. Her copy of the order entry program updates the PRODUCTS file to show (139 − 125) = 14 Widgets remaining in stock and inserts a new order for 125 Widgets into the ORDERS table.

The handling of the two orders has obviously left the database in an inconsistent state. The first of the two updates to the PRODUCTS file has been lost! Both customers' orders have been accepted, but not enough Widgets are in inventory to satisfy both orders. Further, the database shows that there are still 14 Widgets remaining for sale! This example illustrates the "lost update" problem that can occur whenever two programs read the same data from the database, use the data as the basis for a calculation, and then try to update the data.

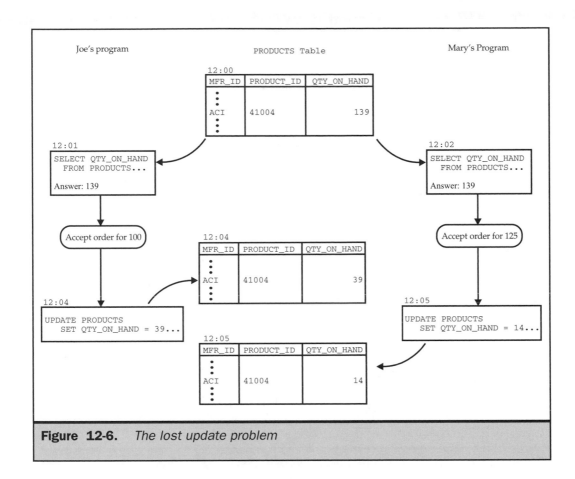

Figure 12-6.   *The lost update problem*

The Uncommitted Data Problem

Figure 12-7 shows the same order-processing application as Figure 12-6. Joe again begins taking an order for 100 ACI-41004 Widgets from his customer. This time, Joe's copy of the order processing program queries the PRODUCTS table, finds 139 Widgets available, and updates the PRODUCTS table to show 39 Widgets remaining after the customer's order. Then Joe begins to discuss with the customer the relative merits of the ACI-41004 and ACI-41005 Widgets. In the meantime, Mary's customer tries to order 125 ACI-41004 Widgets. Mary's copy of the order processing program queries the PRODUCTS table, finds only 39 Widgets available, and refuses the order. It also generates a notice telling the purchasing manager to buy more ACI-41004 Widgets, which are in great demand. Now Joe's customer decides that they don't want the size 4 Widgets after all, and Joe's order entry program does a ROLLBACK to abort its transaction.

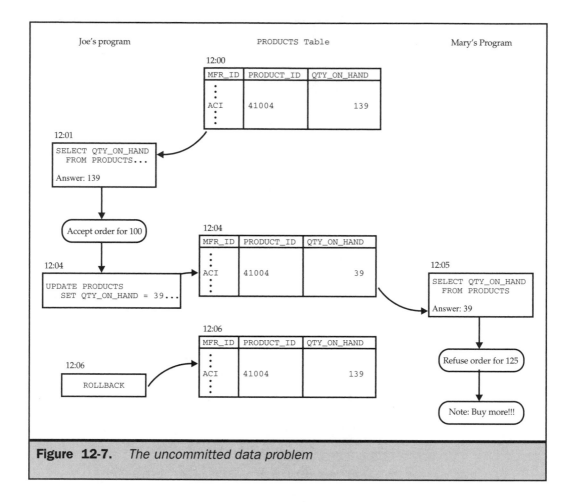

Figure 12-7. *The uncommitted data problem*

Because Mary's order-processing program was allowed to see the uncommitted update of Joe's program, the order from Mary's customer was refused, and the purchasing manager will order more Widgets, even though 139 of them are still in stock. The situation would have been even worse if Mary's customer had decided to settle for the 39 available Widgets. In this case, Mary's program would have updated the PRODUCTS table to show zero units available. But when the ROLLBACK of Joe's transaction occurred, the DBMS would have set the available inventory back to 139 Widgets, even though 39 of them are committed to Mary's customer. The problem in this example is that Mary's program has been allowed to see the uncommitted updates from Joe's program and has acted upon them, producing the erroneous results. The SQL2 standard refers to this as problem "P1," also known as the "dirty read" problem. In the parlance of the standard, the data that Mary's program has seen is "dirty" because it has not been committed by Joe's program.

The Inconsistent Data Problem

Figure 12-8 shows the order-processing application once more. Again, Joe begins taking an order for 100 ACI-41004 Widgets from his customer. A short time later, Mary also begins talking to her customer about the same Widgets, and her program does a single-row query to find out how many are available. This time Mary's customer inquires about the ACI-41005 Widgets as an alternative, and Mary's program does a single-row query on that row. Meanwhile, Joe's customer decides to order the Widgets, so his program updates that row of the database and does a COMMIT to finalize the order in the database. After considering the ACI-41005 Widgets as an alternative, Mary's customer decides to order the ACI-41004 Widgets that Mary originally proposed. Her program does a new single-row query to get the information for the

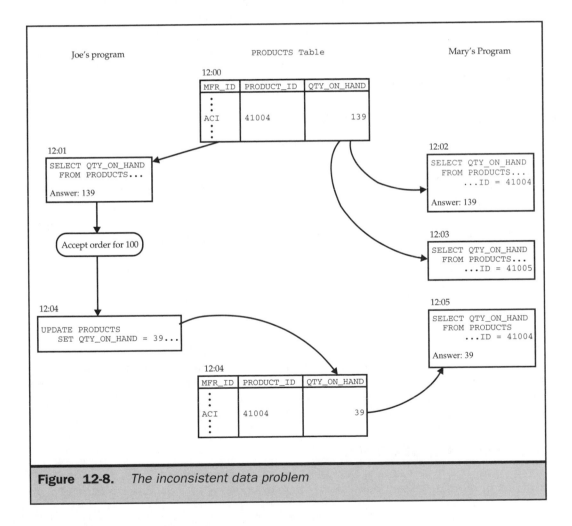

Figure 12-8. *The inconsistent data problem*

ACI-41004 Widgets again. But instead of finding the 139 Widgets that were in stock just a moment ago, the new query shows only 39 in stock.

In this example, unlike the preceding two, the status of the database has remained an accurate model of the real-world situation. There *are* only 39 ACI-41004 Widgets left because Joe's customer has purchased 100 of them. There is no problem with Mary having seen uncommitted data from Joe's program—the order was complete and committed to the database. However, from the point of view of Mary's program, the database did not remain consistent during her transaction. At the beginning of the transaction, a row contained certain data, and later in the same transaction, it contained different data, so "external events" have interfered with her consistent view of the database. This inconsistency can cause problems even if Mary's program never tries to update the database based on the results of the first query. For example, if the program is accumulating totals or calculating statistics, it cannot be sure that the statistics reflect a stable, consistent view of the data. The problem in this case is that Mary's program has been allowed to see committed updates from Joe's program that affect rows that it has already examined. The SQL2 standard refers to this problem as "P2," also known as the "non-repeatable read" problem. The name comes from the fact that Mary's program can't repeat the same read access to the database and obtain the same results.

The Phantom Insert Problem

Figure 12-9 shows an order-processing application once more. This time, the sales manager runs a report program that scans the ORDERS table, printing a list of the orders from customers of Bill Adams and computing their total. In the meantime, a customer calls Bill to place an additional order for $5000. The order is inserted into the database, and the transaction is committed. A short time later, the sales manager's program again scans the ORDERS table, running the very same query. This time, there is an additional order, and the total is $5000 higher than for the first query.

Like the previous example, the problem here is inconsistent data. The database remains an accurate model of the real-world situation, and its integrity is intact, but the same query executed twice during the same transaction yielded two different results. In the previous example, the query was a single-row query, and the inconsistency in the data was caused by a committed UPDATE statement. A committed DELETE statement could cause the same kind of problem. In the example of Figure 12-9, the problem is caused by a committed INSERT statement. The additional row did not participate in the first query, but it shows up as a "phantom row, out of nowhere" in the second query. Like the inconsistent data problem, the consequences of the phantom insert problem can be inconsistent and incorrect calculations. The SQL2 standard refers to this as "P3," and also uses the name "phantom" to describe it.

Concurrent Transactions

As the three multi-user update examples show, when users share access to a database and one or more users is updating data, there is a potential for database corruption.

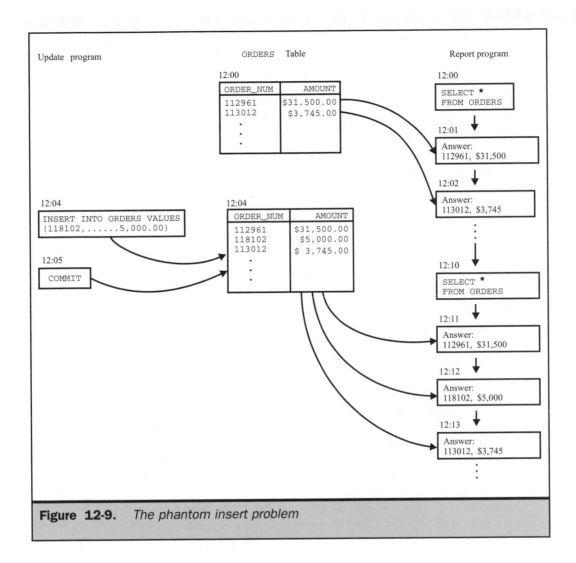

Figure 12-9. *The phantom insert problem*

SQL uses its transaction mechanism to eliminate this source of database corruption. In addition to the "all-or-nothing" commitment for the statements in a transaction, a SQL-based DBMS makes this commitment about transactions:

> During a transaction, the user will see a completely consistent view of the database. The user will never see the uncommitted changes of other users, and even committed changes made by others will not affect data seen by the user in mid-transaction.

Transactions are thus the key to both recovery and concurrency control in a SQL database. The previous commitment can be restated explicitly in terms of concurrent transaction execution:

If two transactions, A and B, are executing concurrently, the DBMS ensures that the results will be the same as they would be if *either* (a) Transaction A were executed first, followed by Transaction B, *or* (b) Transaction B were executed first, followed by Transaction A.

This concept is known as the *serializability* of transactions. Effectively, it means that each database user can access the database as if no other users were concurrently accessing the database.

The fact that SQL insulates you from the actions of other concurrent users doesn't mean, however, that you can forget all about the other users. In fact, the situation is quite the opposite. Because other users want to concurrently update the database, you should keep your transactions as short and simple as possible, to maximize the amount of parallel processing that can occur.

Suppose, for example, that you run a program that performs a sequence of three large queries. Since the program doesn't update the database, it might seem that it doesn't need to worry about transactions. It certainly seems unnecessary to use COMMIT statements. But in fact the program should use a COMMIT statement after each query. Why? Recall that SQL *automatically* begins a transaction with the first SQL statement in a program. Without a COMMIT statement, the transaction continues until the program ends. Further, SQL guarantees that the data retrieved during a transaction will be self-consistent, unaffected by other users' transactions. This means that once your program retrieves a row from the database, *no other user can modify the row until your transaction ends*, because you might try to retrieve the row again later in your transaction, and the DBMS must guarantee that you will see the same data. Thus, as your program performs its three queries, it will prevent other users from updating larger and larger portions of the database.

The moral of this example is simple: you must *always* worry about transactions when writing programs for a production SQL database. Transactions should always be as short as possible. "COMMIT early and COMMIT often" is good advice when one is using programmatic SQL.

In practice, implementing a strict multi-user transaction model can impose a substantial overhead on the operation of a database with dozens, hundreds, or thousands of concurrent users. In addition, the specifics of the application may not require the absolute isolation among the user programs that the SQL transaction model implies. For example, maybe the application designer knows that an order inquiry program has been designed so that it will *never* attempt to read and then reread a row of the database during a single transaction. In this case, the Inconsistent Data problem can't occur, because of the program structure. Alternatively, maybe the application designer knows that all of a program's access to particular tables of a database is read-only. If the programmer can convey information like this to the DBMS, some of the overhead of SQL transactions can be eliminated.

The SQL1 standard did not address this database performance issue, and most of the major DBMS brands implemented proprietary schemes for enhancing the performance of SQL transactions. The SQL2 standard specified a new SET TRANSACTION statement whose function is to specify the level of SQL transaction model support that an application needs. You don't need to use the SET TRANSACTION statement for casual use of SQL or for relatively simple or low-volume SQL transaction processing. To fully understand its operation, it's useful to understand the locking techniques used by commercial DBMS products to implement multi-user SQL transactions. The remainder of this chapter discusses locking and the performance optimizing capabilities of SQL2 and the various DBMS brands that depend on it.

Locking *

Virtually all major DBMS products use sophisticated locking techniques to handle concurrent SQL transactions for many simultaneous users. However, the basic concepts behind locking and transactions are very simple. Figure 12-10 shows a simple locking scheme and how it handles contention between two concurrent transactions.

As Transaction A in the figure accesses the database, the DBMS automatically locks each piece of the database that the transaction retrieves or modifies. Transaction B proceeds in parallel, and the DBMS also locks the pieces of the database that it accesses. If Transaction B tries to access part of the database that has been locked by Transaction A, the DBMS blocks Transaction B, causing it to wait for the data to be unlocked. The DBMS releases the locks held by Transaction A only when it ends in a COMMIT or ROLLBACK operation. The DBMS then "unblocks" Transaction B, allowing it to proceed. Transaction B can now lock that piece of the database on its own behalf, protecting it from the effects of other transactions.

As the figure shows, the locking technique temporarily gives a transaction exclusive access to a piece of a database, preventing other transactions from modifying the locked data. Locking thus solves all of the concurrent transaction problems. It prevents lost updates, uncommitted data, and inconsistent data from corrupting the database. However, locking introduces a new problem—it may cause a transaction to wait for a long time while the pieces of the database that it wants to access are locked by other transactions.

Locking Levels

Locking can be implemented at various levels of the database. In its crudest form, the DBMS could lock the entire database for each transaction. This locking strategy would be simple to implement, but it would allow processing of only one transaction at a time. If the transaction included any "think time" at all (such as time to discuss an order

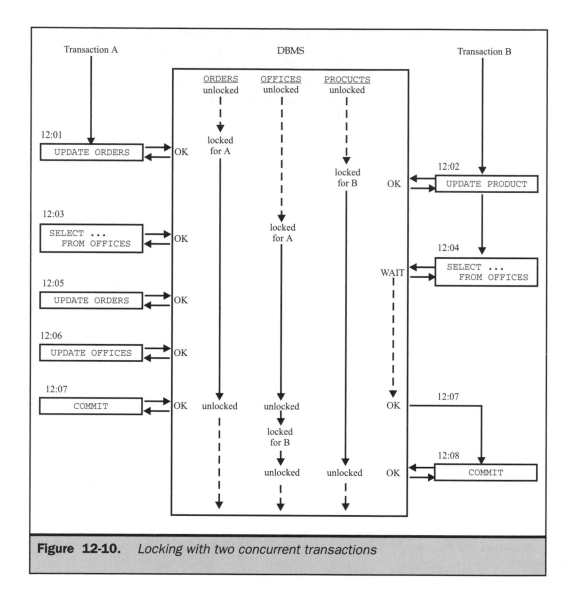

Figure 12-10. *Locking with two concurrent transactions*

with a customer), all other access to the database would be blocked during that time, leading to unacceptably slow performance.

An improved form of locking is *table-level* locking. In this scheme, the DBMS locks only the tables accessed by a transaction. Other transactions can concurrently access other tables. This technique permits more parallel processing, but still leads to unacceptably slow performance in applications such as order entry, where many users must share access to the same table or tables.

Many DBMS products implement locking at the *page level.* In this scheme, the DBMS locks individual blocks of data ("pages") from the disk as they are accessed by a transaction. Other transactions are prevented from accessing the locked pages but may access (and lock for themselves) other pages of data. Page sizes of 2KB, 4KB, and 16KB are commonly used. Since a large table will be spread out over hundreds or thousands of pages, two transactions trying to access two different rows of a table will usually be accessing two different pages, allowing the two transactions to proceed in parallel.

Over the last several years, most of the major commercial DBMS systems have moved beyond page-level locking to *row-level* locks. Row-level locking allows two concurrent transactions that access two different rows of a table to proceed in parallel, even if the two rows fall in the same disk block. While this may seem a remote possibility, it can be a real problem with small tables containing small records, such as the OFFICES table in the sample database.

Row-level locking provides a high degree of parallel transaction execution. Unfortunately, keeping track of locks on variable-length pieces of the database (in other words, rows) rather than fixed-size pages is a much more complex task, so increased parallelism comes at the cost of more sophisticated locking logic and increased overhead. In fact, for certain applications, the overhead of row-level locking might be greater than the performance gains of permitting more parallel operation within the database! The DBMS vendors that stress online transaction processing performance are increasingly supporting row-level locking. It is often provided as an option to a page-level technique.

It's theoretically possible to move beyond row-level locking to locking at the individual data item level. In theory this would provide even more parallelism than row-level locks, because it would allow concurrent access to the same row by two different transactions, provided they were accessing different sets of columns. The overhead in managing item-level locking, however, has thus far outweighed its potential advantages. No commercial SQL DBMS uses item-level locking. In fact, locking is an area of considerable research in database technology, and the locking schemes used in commercial DBMS products are much more sophisticated than the fundamental scheme described here. The most straightforward of these advanced locking schemes, using shared and exclusive locks, is described in the next section.

Shared and Exclusive Locks

To increase concurrent access to a database, most commercial DBMS products use a locking scheme with more than one type of lock. A scheme using shared and exclusive locks is quite common:

- A *shared* lock is used by the DBMS when a transaction wants to read data from the database. Another concurrent transaction can also acquire a shared lock on the same data, allowing the other transaction to also read the data.

■ An *exclusive* lock is used by the DBMS when a transaction wants to update data in the database. When a transaction has an exclusive lock on some data, other transactions cannot acquire any type of lock (shared or exclusive) on the data.

Figure 12-11 shows the rules for this locking scheme and the permitted combinations of locks that can be held by two concurrent transactions. Note that a transaction can acquire an exclusive lock only if no other transaction currently has a shared or an exclusive lock on the data. If a transaction tries to acquire a lock not permitted by the rules in Figure 12-11, it is blocked until other transactions unlock the data that it requires.

Figure 12-12 shows the same transactions shown in Figure 12-10, this time using shared and exclusive locks. If you compare the two figures, you can see how the new locking scheme improves concurrent access to the database. Mature and complex DBMS products, such as DB2, have more than two types of locks and use different locking techniques at different levels of the database. Despite the increased complexity, the goal of the locking scheme remains the same: to prevent unwanted interference between transactions while providing the greatest possible concurrent access to the database, all with minimal locking overhead.

Deadlocks *

Unfortunately, the use of any locking scheme to support concurrent SQL transactions leads to a problem called a *deadlock.* Figure 12-13 illustrates a deadlock situation. Program A updates the ORDERS table, thereby locking part of it. Meanwhile, Program B updates the PRODUCTS table, locking part of it. Now Program A tries to update the PRODUCTS table and Program B tries to update the ORDERS table, in each case trying to update a part of the table that has been previously locked by the other program.

		Transaction B		
		Unlocked	Shared lock	Exclusive lock
Transaction A	Unlocked	OK	OK	OK
	Shared lock	OK	OK	NO
	Exclusive lock	OK	NO	NO

Figure 12-11. *Rules for shared and exclusive locks*

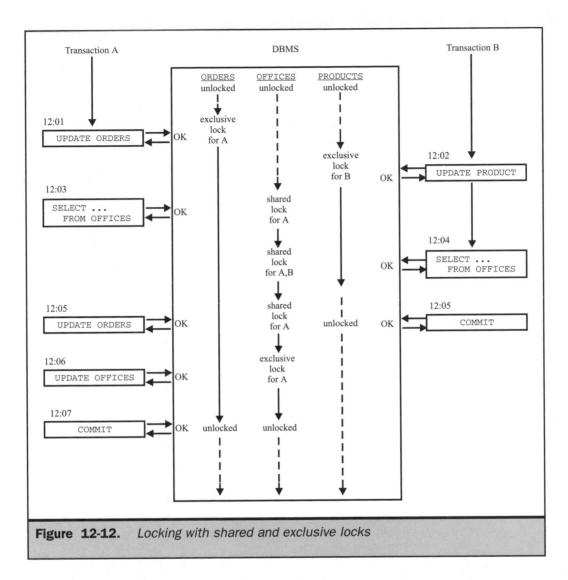

Figure 12-12. *Locking with shared and exclusive locks*

Without outside intervention, each program will wait forever for the other program to commit its transaction and unlock the data. The situation in the figure is a simple deadlock between two programs, but more complex situations can occur where three, four, or more programs are in a "cycle" of locks, each waiting for data that is locked by one of the other programs.

To deal with deadlocks, a DBMS typically includes logic that periodically (say, once every five seconds) checks the locks held by various transactions. When it detects a deadlock, the DBMS arbitrarily chooses one of the transactions as the deadlock "loser"

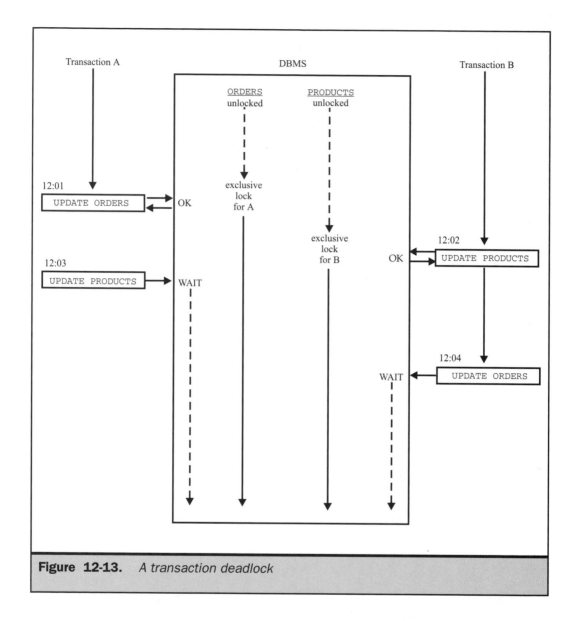

Figure 12-13. *A transaction deadlock*

and rolls back the transaction. This frees the locks held by the losing transaction, allowing the deadlock "winner" to proceed. The losing program receives an error code informing it that it has lost a deadlock and that its current transaction has been rolled back.

This scheme for breaking deadlocks means that *any* SQL statement can potentially return a "deadlock loser" error code, even if nothing is wrong with the statement per se.

Thus, even though COMMIT and ROLLBACK are the SQL "transaction processing" statements, it's possible for other SQL statements—an INSERT statement, for example, or even a SELECT statement—to be a deadlock loser. The transaction attempting the statement is rolled back through no fault of its own, but because of other concurrent activity in the database. This may seem unfair, but in practice it's much better than the other two alternatives—eternal deadlock or database corruption. If a deadlock loser error occurs in interactive SQL, the user can simply retype the SQL statement(s). In programmatic SQL, the application program must be prepared to handle the deadlock loser error code. Typically, the program will respond by either alerting the user or automatically retrying the transaction.

The probability of deadlocks can be dramatically reduced by carefully planning database updates. All programs that update multiple tables during a transaction should, whenever possible, update the tables in the same sequence. This allows the locks to flow smoothly across the tables, minimizing the possibility of deadlocks. In addition, some of the advanced locking features described in later sections of this chapter can be used to further reduce the number of deadlocks that occur.

Advanced Locking Techniques *

Many commercial database products offer advanced locking facilities that go well beyond those provided by standard SQL transactions. These include:

- *Explicit locking*. A program can explicitly lock an entire table or some other part of the database if it will be repeatedly accessed by the program.

- *Isolation levels*. You can tell the DBMS that a specific program will not re-retrieve data during a transaction, allowing the DBMS to release locks before the transaction ends.

- *Locking parameters*. The database administrator can manually adjust the size of the "lockable piece" of the database and other locking parameters to tune locking performance.

These facilities tend to be nonstandard and product specific. However, several of them, particularly those available in DB2, have been implemented in several commercial SQL products and have achieved the status of common, if not standard, features. In fact, the Isolation Level capabilities introduced in DB2 have found their way into the SQL2 standard.

Explicit Locking *

If a transaction repeatedly accesses a table, the overhead of acquiring small locks on many parts of the table can be very substantial. A bulk update program that walks through every row of a table, for example, will lock the entire table, piece by piece, as it proceeds. For this type of transaction, the program should explicitly lock the entire table, process the updates, and then unlock the table. Locking the entire table has three advantages:

■ It eliminates the overhead of row-by-row (or page-by-page) locking.

■ It eliminates the possibility that another transaction will lock part of the table, forcing the bulk update transaction to wait.

■ It eliminates the possibility that another transaction will lock part of the table and deadlock the bulk update transaction, forcing it to be restarted.

Of course, locking the table has the disadvantage that all other transactions attempting to access the table must wait while the update is in process. However, because the bulk update transaction can proceed much more quickly, the overall throughput of the DBMS can be increased by explicitly locking the table.

In the IBM databases, the LOCK TABLE statement, shown in Figure 12-14, is used to explicitly lock an entire table. It offers two locking modes:

■ EXCLUSIVE mode acquires an exclusive lock on the entire table. No other transaction can access any part of the table for any purpose while the lock is held. This is the mode you would request for a bulk update transaction.

■ SHARE mode acquires a shared lock on the entire table. Other transactions can read parts of the table (that is, they can also acquire shared locks), but they cannot update any part of it. Of course if the transaction issuing the LOCK TABLE statement now updates part of the table, it will still incur the overhead of acquiring exclusive locks on the parts of the table that it updates. This is the mode you would request if you wanted a "snapshot" of a table, accurate at a particular point in time.

Oracle also supports a DB2-style LOCK TABLE statement. The same effect can be achieved in Ingres with a different statement. Several other database management systems, including SQL Server and SQLBase, do not support explicit locking at all, choosing instead to optimize their implicit locking techniques.

Isolation Levels *

Under the strict definition of a SQL transaction, no action by a concurrently executing transaction is allowed to impact the data visible during the course of your transaction. If your program performs a database query during a transaction, proceeds with other work, and later performs the same database query a second time, the SQL transaction mechanism guarantees that the data returned by the two queries will be identical (unless *your* transaction acted to change the data). This ability to reliably re-retrieve a row during a transaction is the highest level of isolation that your program can have from other programs and users. The level of isolation is called the *isolation level* of your transaction.

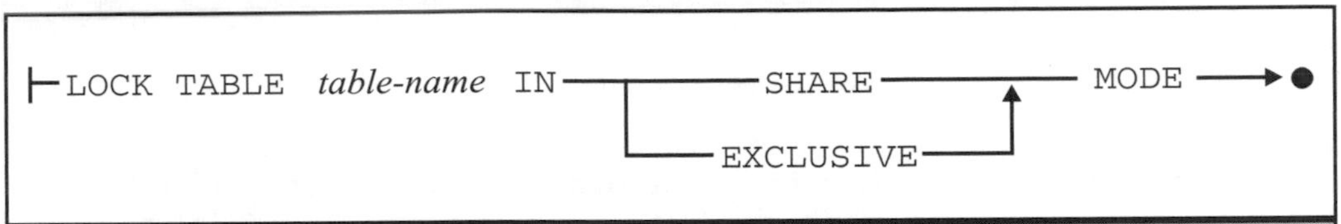

Figure 12-14.   *LOCK TABLE statement syntax diagram*

This absolute isolation of your transaction from all other concurrently executing transactions is very costly in terms of database locking. As your program reads each row of query results, the DBMS must lock the row (with a shared lock) to prevent concurrent transactions from modifying the row. These locks must be held until the end of your transaction, just in case your program performs the query again. In many cases, the DBMS can significantly reduce its locking overhead if it knows in advance how a program will access a database during a transaction. To gain this efficiency, the major IBM mainframe databases added support for the concept of a user-specified *isolation level* that gives the user control over the trade-off between isolation and processing efficiency. The SQL2 specification formalized the IBM isolation level concept and expanded it to include four isolation levels, shown in Figure 12-15. The isolation levels are linked directly to the fundamental multi-user update problems discussed earlier in this chapter. As the level of isolation decreases (moving down the rows of the table), the DBMS insulates the user from fewer of the multi-user update problems.

The SERIALIZABLE isolation level is the highest level provided. At this level, the DBMS guarantees that the effects of concurrently executing transactions are exactly the same as if they executed in sequence. This is the default isolation level, because it is "the way SQL databases are supposed to work." If your program needs to perform the same multi-row query twice during a transaction and be guaranteed that the results will be identical regardless of other activity in the database, then it should use the SERIALIZABLE isolation level.

The REPEATABLE READ isolation level is the second highest level. At this level, your transaction is not allowed to see either committed or uncommitted updates from other transactions, so the lost update, uncommitted data, and modified data problems cannot occur. However, a row inserted into the database by another concurrent transaction may become visible during your transaction. As a result, a multi-row query run early in your transaction may yield different results than the same query run later in the same transaction (the phantom insert problem). If your program does not depend on the ability to repeat a multi-row query during a single transaction, you can safely use the REPEATABLE READ isolation level to improve DBMS performance without sacrificing data integrity. This is one of the isolation levels supported in the IBM mainframe database products.

Multi-User Update Problem				
Isolation Level	Lost Update	Uncommitted Data	Inconsistent Data	Phantom Insert
SERIALIZABLE	Prevented by DBMS	Prevented by DBMS	Prevented by DBMS	Prevented by DBMS
REPEATABLE READ	Prevented by DBMS	Prevented by DBMS	Prevented by DBMS	Can occur
READ COMMITTED	Prevented by DBMS	Prevented by DBMS	Can occur	Can occur
READ UNCOMMITTED	Prevented by DBMS	Can occur	Can occur	Can occur

Figure 12-15.   *Isolation levels and multi-user updates*

The READ COMMITTED isolation level is the third highest level. In this mode, your transaction is not allowed to see uncommitted updates from other transactions, so the Lost Update and the Uncommitted Data problems cannot occur. However, updates that are committed by other concurrently executing transactions may become visible during the course of your transaction. Your program could, for example, perform a single-row SELECT statement twice during the course of a transaction and find that the data in the row had been modified by another user. If your program does not depend on the ability to reread a single row of data during a transaction, and it is not accumulating totals or doing other calculations that rely on a self-consistent set of data, it can safely use the READ COMMITTED isolation level. Note that if your program attempts to update a row that has already been updated by another user, your transaction will automatically be rolled back, to prevent the Lost Update problem from occurring.

The READ UNCOMMITTED isolation level is the lowest level specified in the SQL standard. In this mode, your transaction may be impacted by committed or uncommitted updates from other transaction, so the Uncommitted Data, Modified Data, and Phantom Insert problems can occur. The DBMS still prevents the Lost Update problem. Generally, the READ UNCOMMITTED level is appropriate only for certain ad hoc query applications where the user can tolerate the fact that the query results may contain "dirty" data. If it is important that query results contain only information that has, in fact, been committed to the database, your program should not use this mode.

The SQL2 standard specifies a SET TRANSACTION statement, shown in Figure 12-16, which is used to set the isolation level of the current transaction. The SET TRANSACTION statement also allows you to specify whether the transaction is READ ONLY (that is, it will only query the database) or READ WRITE (it may query or update the database). The DBMS can use this information, along with the isolation level, to optimize its database processing. The default isolation level is SERIALIZABLE. If READ UNCOMMITTED isolation level is specified, then READ ONLY is assumed, and you may not specify a READ WRITE transaction. Otherwise, a READ WRITE transaction is the default. These defaults provide for the maximum "safety" of transactions, at the expense of database performance, but they prevent inexperienced SQL programmers from inadvertently suffering one of the multi-user transaction processing problems.

Note that the SET TRANSACTION statement specified in the SQL2 standard is an executable SQL statement. It's possible, in fact sometimes very desirable, to have one transaction of a program execute in one "mode" and have the next transaction execute in a different mode. However, you can't switch isolation levels or read/write modes in the middle of a transaction. The standard effectively requires that the SET TRANSACTION statement be the first statement of a transaction. This means it must be executed as the first statement after a COMMIT or ROLLBACK, or as the first statement of a program, before any other statements affecting the content or structure of a database.

As noted earlier, many of the commercial DBMS products implemented their own locking and performance enhancement schemes long before the publication of the SQL2 standard, and these locking strategies affect the heart of the internal database architecture and logic. It's not surprising that the adoption of the SQL2 standard in this area has been relatively slow compared to some other areas where implementation was much easier. For example, the IBM mainframe databases (DB2 and SQL/DS) historically offered a choice of two isolation levels—REPEATABLE READ or READ COMMITTED (called *cursor stability mode* in IBM terminology). In the IBM implementations, the choice is made during the program development process, during the BIND step described in Chapter 17. Although the modes are not strictly part of the

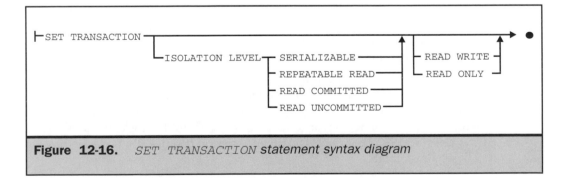

Figure 12-16. *SET TRANSACTION statement syntax diagram*

SQL language, the choice of mode strongly impacts how the application performs and how it can use retrieved data.

The Ingres DBMS offers a capability similar to the isolation modes of the IBM databases but provides it in a different form. Using the SET LOCKMODE statement, an application program can tell Ingres what type of locking to use when handling a database query. The options are:

- *no locking*, which is similar to the IBM cursor stability mode just described,

- *shared locking*, which is similar to the IBM repeatable read mode just described, or

- *exclusive locking*, which provides exclusive access to the table during the query and offers a capability like the IBM LOCK TABLE statement.

The Ingres default is shared locking, which parallels the repeatable read default in the IBM scheme. Note, however, that the Ingres locking modes are set by an executable SQL statement. Unlike the IBM modes, which must be chosen at compile time, the Ingres modes can be chosen when the program executes and can even be changed from one query to the next.

Locking Parameters *

A mature DBMS such as DB2, SQL/DS, Oracle, Informix, Sybase, or SQL Server employs much more complex locking techniques than those described here. The database administrator can improve the performance of these systems by manually setting their locking parameters. Typical parameters that can be tuned include:

- *Lock size*. Some DBMS products offer a choice of table-level, page-level, row-level, and other lock sizes. Depending on the specific application, a different size lock may be appropriate.

- *Number of locks*. A DBMS typically allows each transaction to have some finite number of locks. The database administrator can often set this limit, raising it to permit more complex transactions or lowering it to encourage earlier lock escalation.

- *Lock escalation*. A DBMS will often automatically "escalate" locks, replacing many small locks with a single larger lock (for example, replacing many page-level locks with a table-level lock). The database administrator may have some control over this escalation process.

- *Lock timeout*. Even when a transaction is not deadlocked with another transaction, it may wait a very long time for the other transaction to release its locks. Some DBMS brands implement a *timeout* feature, where a SQL statement fails with a SQL error code if it cannot obtain the locks it needs within a certain period of time. The timeout period can usually be set by the database administrator.

Summary

This chapter described the transaction mechanism provided by the SQL language:

- A transaction is a logical unit of work in a SQL-based database. It consists of a sequence of SQL statements that are effectively executed as a single unit by the DBMS.

- The COMMIT statement signals successful completion of a transaction, making all of its database modifications permanent.

- The ROLLBACK statement asks the DBMS to abort a transaction, backing out all of its database modifications.

- Transactions are the key to recovering a database after a system failure; only transactions that were committed at the time of failure remain in the recovered database.

- Transactions are the key to concurrent access in a multi-user database. A user or program is guaranteed that its transaction will not be interfered with by other concurrent transactions.

- Occasionally a conflict with another concurrently executing transaction may cause the DBMS to roll back a transaction through no fault of its own. An application program that uses SQL must be prepared to deal with this situation if it occurs.

Part IV

Database Structure

An important role of SQL is to define the structure and organization of a database. The next four chapters describe the SQL features that support this role. Chapter 13 describes how to create a database and its tables. Chapter 14 describes views, an important SQL feature that lets users see alternate organizations of database data. The SQL security features that protect stored data are described in Chapter 15. Finally, Chapter 16 discusses the system catalog, a collection of system tables that describe the structure of a database.

Chapter 13

Creating a Database

Many SQL users don't have to worry about creating a database; they use interactive or programmatic SQL to access a database of corporate information or to access some other database that has been created by someone else. In a typical corporate database, for example, the database administrator may give you permission to retrieve and perhaps to update the stored data. However, the administrator will not allow you to create new databases or to modify the structure of the existing tables.

As you grow more comfortable with SQL, you will probably want to start creating your own private tables to store personal data such as engineering test results or sales forecasts. If you are using a multi-user database, you may want to create tables or even entire databases that will be shared with other users. If you are using a personal computer database, you will certainly want to create your own tables and databases to support your personal applications.

This chapter describes the SQL language features that let you create databases and tables and define their structure.

The Data Definition Language

The SELECT, INSERT, DELETE, UPDATE, COMMIT, and ROLLBACK statements described in Parts II and III of this book are all concerned with manipulating the data in a database. These statements collectively are called the SQL *Data Manipulation Language,* or DML. The DML statements can modify the data stored in a database, but they cannot change its structure. None of these statements creates or deletes tables or columns, for example.

Changes to the structure of a database are handled by a different set of SQL statements, usually called the SQL *Data Definition Language,* or DDL. Using DDL statements, you can:

- Define and create a new table
- Remove a table that's no longer needed
- Change the definition of an existing table
- Define a virtual table (or view) of data
- Establish security controls for a database
- Build an index to make table access faster
- Control the physical storage of data by the DBMS

For the most part, the DDL statements insulate you from the low-level details of how data is physically stored in the database. They manipulate abstract database objects, such as tables and columns. However, the DDL cannot avoid physical storage issues entirely, and by necessity, the DDL statements and clauses that control physical storage vary from one DBMS to another.

The core of the Data Definition Language is based on three SQL verbs:

- CREATE, which defines and creates a database object
- DROP, which removes an existing database object
- ALTER, which changes the definition of a database object

In all major SQL-based DBMS products, these three DDL verbs can be used while the DBMS is running. The database structure is thus dynamic. The DBMS can be creating, dropping, or changing the definition of the tables in the database, for example, while it is simultaneously providing access to the database for its users. This is a major advantage of SQL and relational databases over earlier systems, where the DBMS had to be stopped before one could change the structure of the database. It means that a relational database can grow and change easily over time. Production use of a database can continue while new tables and applications are added.

Although the DDL and DML are two distinct parts of the SQL language, in most SQL-based DBMS products the split is a conceptual one only. Usually the DDL and DML statements are submitted to the DBMS in exactly the same way, and they can be freely intermixed in both interactive SQL sessions and programmatic SQL applications. If a program or user needs a table to store its temporary results, it can create the table, populate it, manipulate the data, and then delete the table. Again, this is a major advantage over earlier data models, in which the structure of the database was fixed when the database was created.

Although virtually all commercial SQL products support the DDL as an integral part of the SQL language, the SQL1 standard did not require it. In fact, the SQL1 standard implies a strong separation between the DML and the DDL, allowing vendors to achieve compliance with the DML part of the standard through a SQL layer on top of a non-SQL underlying database. The SQL2 standard still differentiates between different types of SQL statements (it calls the DDL statements "SQL-schema statements" and the DML statements "SQL-data statements" and "SQL-transaction statements"). However, it brings the standard into alignment with the actual implementation of popular SQL products by requiring that DDL statements be executed interactively and by a program.

The SQL2 standard specifies only the parts of the DDL that are relatively independent of physical storage structures, operating system dependencies, and other DBMS brand-specific capabilities. In practice, all DBMS brands include significant extensions to the standard DDL to deal with these issues and other enhanced database capabilities. The differences between the ANSI/ISO standard and the DDL as implemented in popular SQL products are described later in this chapter.

Creating a Database

In a large mainframe or enterprise-level network DBMS installation, the corporate database administrator is solely responsible for creating new databases. On smaller workgroup DBMS installations, individual users may be allowed to create their own personal databases, but it's much more common for databases to be created centrally and then accessed by individual users. If you are using a personal computer DBMS, you are probably both the database administrator and the user, and you will have to create the database(s) that you use personally.

The SQL1 standard specified the SQL language used to describe a database structure, but it did not specify how databases are created, because each DBMS brand had taken a slightly different approach. Those differences persist in present-day mainstream DBMS products. The techniques used by these SQL products illustrate the differences:

- IBM's DB2 has a simple default database structure. A DB2 database is associated with a running copy of the DB2 server software, and users access the database by connecting to the DB2 server. A DB2 "database" is thus effectively defined by an installation of the DB2 software on a particular computer system.

- Oracle by default creates a database as part of the Oracle software installation process, like DB2. For the most part, user tables are always placed in this single, system-wide database, which is named by an Oracle configuration file and associated with this particular copy of the Oracle server software. More recent versions of Oracle have been extended with a CREATE DATABASE statement for defining database names.

- Ingres includes a special utility program, called CREATEDB, which creates a new Ingres database. A companion program, DESTROYDB, erases an unneeded database.

- Microsoft SQL Server and Sybase Adaptive Server include a CREATE DATABASE statement as part of their data definition language. A companion DROP DATABASE statement destroys previously created databases. These statements can be used with interactive or programmatic SQL. The names of these databases are tracked in a special "master" database that is associated with a single installation of SQL Server. Database names must be unique within this SQL Server installation. Options to the CREATE DATABASE statement specify the physical I/O device on which the database is to be located.

- Informix Universal Server supports CREATE DATABASE and DROP DATABASE SQL statements as well. An option to the CREATE DATABASE statement allows the database to be created in a specific *dbspace*, which is a named area of disk storage controlled by the Informix software. Another option controls the type of database logging to be performed for the new database, with trade-offs between performance and data integrity during system failures.

The SQL2 standard specifically avoids a specification of the term "database" because it is so overloaded with contradictory meanings from DBMS products. SQL2 uses the term *catalog* to describe a named collection of tables that is called a "database" by most popular DBMS brands. (Additional information about the database structure specified by the SQL2 standard is provided later in this chapter.) The standard does not specify how a catalog is created or destroyed, and specifically says that creation or destruction is implementation-dependent. It also indicates how many catalogs there are, and whether individual SQL statements that can access data from different catalogs are implementation-defined. In practice, as shown by the preceding examples, many of the major DBMS vendors have moved toward the use of a CREATE DATABASE/DROP DATABASE statement pair.

Table Definitions

The most important structure in a relational database is the table. In a multi-user production database, the major tables are typically created once by the database administrator and then used day after day. As you use the database you will often find it convenient to define your own tables to store personal data or data extracted from other tables. These tables may be temporary, lasting only for a single interactive SQL session, or more permanent, lasting weeks or months. In a personal computer database, the table structure is even more fluid. Because you are both the user and the database administrator, you can create and destroy tables to suit your own needs, without worrying about other users.

Creating a Table (CREATE TABLE)

The CREATE TABLE statement, shown in Figure 13-1, defines a new table in the database and prepares it to accept data. The various clauses of the statement specify the elements of the table definition. The syntax diagram for the statement appears complex because there are so many parts of the definition to be specified and so many options for each element. In addition, some of the options are available in some DBMS brands or in the SQL2 standard, but not in other brands. In practice, creating a new table is relatively straightforward.

When you execute a CREATE TABLE statement, you become the owner of the newly created table, which is given the name specified in the statement. The table name must be a legal SQL name, and it must not conflict with the name of one of your existing tables. The newly created table is empty, but the DBMS prepares it to accept data added with the INSERT statement.

Column Definitions

The columns of the newly created table are defined in the body of the CREATE TABLE statement. The column definitions appear in a comma-separated list enclosed in parentheses. The order of the column definitions determines the left-to-right order of

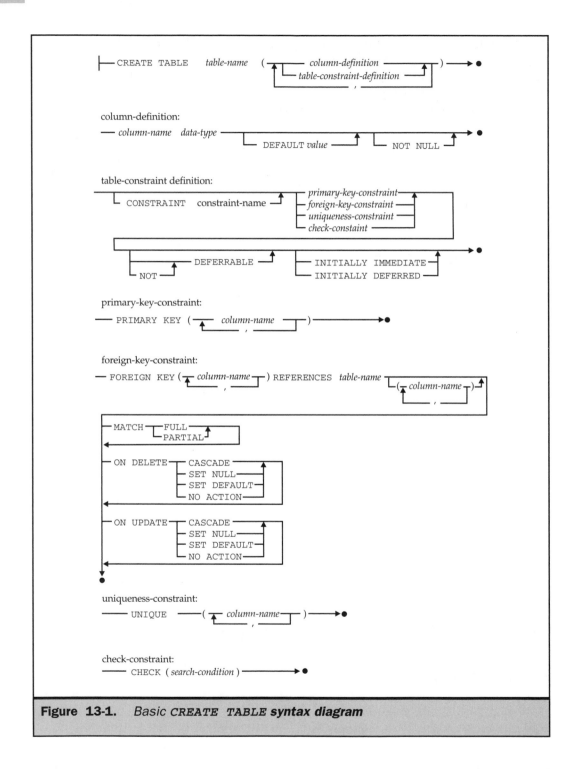

Figure 13-1. *Basic* CREATE TABLE *syntax diagram*

the columns in the table. In the CREATE TABLE statements supported by the major DBMS brands, each column definition specifies:

- The *column name,* which is used to refer to the column in SQL statements. Every column in the table must have a unique name, but the names may duplicate those of columns in other tables.

- The *data type* of the column, identifying the kind of data that the column stores. Data types were discussed in Chapter 5. Some data types, such as VARCHAR and DECIMAL, require additional information, such as the length or number of decimal places in the data. This additional information is enclosed in parentheses following the keyword that specifies the data type.

- Whether the column contains *required data.* The NOT NULL clause prevents NULL values from appearing in the column; otherwise, NULL values are allowed.

- An optional *default value* for the column. The DBMS uses this value when an INSERT statement for the table does not specify a value for the column.

The SQL2 standard allows several additional parts of a column definition, which can be used to require that the column contains unique values, to specify that the column is a primary key or a foreign key or to restrict the data values that the column may contain. These are single-column versions of capabilities provided by other clauses in the CREATE TABLE statement and are described as part of that statement in the following sections.

Here are some simple CREATE TABLE statements for the tables in the sample database:

Define the OFFICES table and its columns.

```
CREATE TABLE OFFICES
    (OFFICE INTEGER NOT NULL,
       CITY VARCHAR(15) NOT NULL,
     REGION VARCHAR(10) NOT NULL,
        MGR INTEGER,
     TARGET MONEY,
      SALES MONEY NOT NULL)
```

Define the ORDERS table and its columns.

```
CREATE TABLE ORDERS
  (ORDER_NUM INTEGER NOT NULL,
  ORDER_DATE DATE NOT NULL,
        CUST INTEGER NOT NULL,
```

```
      REP INTEGER,
      MFR CHAR(3) NOT NULL,
  PRODUCT CHAR(5) NOT NULL,
      QTY INTEGER NOT NULL,
   AMOUNT MONEY NOT NULL)
```

The CREATE TABLE statement for a given table can vary slightly from one DBMS brand to another, because each DBMS supports its own set of data types and uses its own keywords to identify them in the column definitions. In addition, the SQL2 standard allows you to specify a *domain* instead of a data type within a column definition (domains were described in Chapter 11). A domain is a specific collection of valid data values, which is defined within the database and assigned a name. The domain definition is based on one of the DBMS's supported data types but performs additional data value checking that restricts the legal values. For example, if this domain definition appeared in a SQL2-compliant database:

```
CREATE DOMAIN VALID_OFICE_ID INTEGER
 CHECK (VALUE BETWEEN 11 AND 99)
```

then the OFFICES table definition could be modified to:

Define the OFFICES table and its columns.

```
CREATE TABLE OFFICES
    (OFFICE VALID_OFFICE_ID NOT NULL,
       CITY VARCHAR(15) NOT NULL,
     REGION VARCHAR(10) NOT NULL,
        MGR INTEGER,
     TARGET MONEY,
      SALES MONEY NOT NULL)
```

and the DBMS would automatically check any newly inserted rows to insure that their office numbers fall in the designated range. Domains are particularly effective when the same legal data values restrictions apply to many different columns within the database. In the sample database, office numbers appear in the OFFICES and the SALESREPS table, and the VALID_OFFICE_ID domain would be used to define the columns in both of these tables. In a real-world database, there may be dozens or hundreds of such columns whose data is drawn from the same domain.

Missing and Default Values

The definition of each column within a table tells the DBMS whether or not the data for the column is allowed to be "missing"—that is, whether the column is allowed to have a NULL value. In most of the major DBMS brands, and in the SQL standard, the default is to allow missing data for a column. If the column must contain a legal data value for every row of a table, then its definition must include the NOT NULL clause. The Sybase DBMS products and Microsoft SQL Server use the opposite convention, assuming that NULL values are not allowed unless the column is explicitly declared NULL or the default "null mode" defined for the database is set to allow NULLs by default.

The SQL2 standard and many of the major SQL DBMS products support default values for columns. If a column has a default value, it is specified within the column definition. For example, here is a CREATE TABLE statement for the OFFICES table that specifies default values:

Define the OFFICES table with default values (ANSI/ISO syntax).

```
CREATE TABLE OFFICES
    (OFFICE INTEGER NOT NULL,
       CITY VARCHAR(15) NOT NULL,
     REGION VARCHAR(10) NOT NULL DEFAULT 'Eastern',
        MGR INTEGER DEFAULT 106,
     TARGET MONEY DEFAULT NULL,
      SALES MONEY NOT NULL DEFAULT 0.00)
```

With this table definition, only the office number and the city need to be specified when you insert a new office. The region defaults to Eastern, the office manager to Sam Clark (employee number 106), the sales to zero, and the target to NULL. Note that the target would default to NULL even without the DEFAULT NULL specification.

Primary and Foreign Key Definitions

In addition to defining the columns of a table, the CREATE TABLE statement identifies the table's primary key and the table's relationships to other tables in the database. The PRIMARY KEY and FOREIGN KEY clauses handle these functions. These clauses have been supported by the IBM SQL databases for some time and have been added to the ANSI/ISO specification. Most major SQL products have added support for them over the last several years.

The PRIMARY KEY clause specifies the column or columns that form the primary key for the table. Recall from Chapter 4 that this column (or column combination) serves as a unique identifier for each row of the table. The DBMS automatically requires that the primary key value be unique in every row of the table. In addition, the column definition for every column in the primary key must specify that the column is NOT NULL.

The FOREIGN KEY clause specifies a foreign key in the table and the relationship that it creates to another (parent) table in the database. The clause specifies:

- The column or columns that form the foreign key, all of which are columns of the table being created.

- The table that is referenced by the foreign key. This is the parent table in the relationship; the table being defined is the child.

- An optional name for the relationship. The name is not used in any SQL data manipulation statements, but it may appear in error messages and is required if you want to be able to drop the foreign key later.

- How the DBMS should treat a NULL value in one or more columns of the foreign key, when matching it against rows of the parent table.

- An optional delete rule for the relationship (CASCADE, SET NULL, SET DEFAULT, or NO ACTION as described in Chapter 11), which determines the action to take when a parent row is deleted.

- An optional update rule for the relationship as described in Chapter 11, which determines the action to take when part of the primary key in a parent row is updated.

- An optional check constraint, which restricts the data in the table so that its rows meet a specified search condition.

Here is an expanded CREATE TABLE statement for the ORDERS table, which includes a definition of its primary key and the three foreign keys that it contains:

Define the ORDERS table with its primary and foreign keys.

```
CREATE TABLE ORDERS
  (ORDER_NUM INTEGER NOT NULL,
  ORDER_DATE DATE NOT NULL,
        CUST INTEGER NOT NULL,
         REP INTEGER,
         MFR CHAR(3) NOT NULL,
     PRODUCT CHAR(5) NOT NULL,
         QTY INTEGER NOT NULL,
      AMOUNT MONEY NOT NULL,
  PRIMARY KEY (ORDER_NUM),
   CONSTRAINT PLACEDBY
  FOREIGN KEY (CUST)
```

```
   REFERENCES CUSTOMERS
     ON DELETE CASCADE,
   CONSTRAINT TAKENBY
 FOREIGN KEY (REP)
   REFERENCES SALESREPS
     ON DELETE SET NULL,
   CONSTRAINT ISFOR
 FOREIGN KEY (MFR, PRODUCT)
   REFERENCES PRODUCTS
     ON DELETE RESTRICT)
```

Figure 13-2 shows the three relationships created by this statement and the names it assigns to them. In general it's a good idea to assign a relationship name, because it helps to clarify the relationship created by the foreign key. For example, each order was placed by the customer whose number appears in the CUST column of the ORDERS table. The relationship created by this column has been given the name PLACEDBY.

When the DBMS processes the CREATE TABLE statement, it checks each foreign key definition against the definition of the table that it references. The DBMS makes sure that the foreign key and the primary key of the referenced table agree in the number of columns they contain and their data types. The referenced table must already be defined in the database for this checking to succeed.

Note that the FOREIGN KEY clause also specifies the delete and update rules that are to be enforced for the parent/child table relationship that it creates. Delete and update rules, and the actions that can trigger them, are described in Chapter 11. The DBMS enforces the default rules (NO ACTION) if no rule is explicitly specified.

If you want to create two or more tables from a referential cycle (like the OFFICES and SALESREPS tables in the sample database), you cannot include the foreign key definition in the first CREATE TABLE statement because the referenced table does not yet exist. The DBMS will reject the attempted CREATE TABLE statement with an error saying that the table definition refers to an undefined table. Instead, you must create the first table without its foreign key definition and add the foreign key later using the ALTER TABLE statement. (The SQL2 standard and several of the major DBMS products offer a different solution to this problem with the CREATE SCHEMA statement, which creates an entire set of tables at once. This statement and the other database objects that are included within a SQL2 schema are described later in this chapter.)

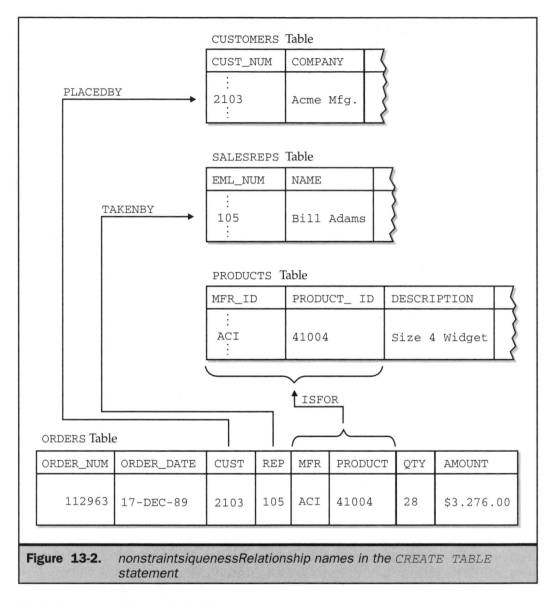

Figure 13-2. *nonstraintsiquenessRelationship names in the* `CREATE TABLE`
statement

Uniqueness Constraints

The SQL2 standard specifies that uniqueness constraints are also defined in the
`CREATE TABLE` statement, using the `UNIQUE` clause shown in Figure 13-1. Here is a
`CREATE TABLE` statement for the `OFFICES` table, modified to require unique
CITY values:

Define the `OFFICES` *table with a uniqueness constraint.*

```
CREATE TABLE OFFICES
     (OFFICE INTEGER NOT NULL,
         CITY VARCHAR(15) NOT NULL,
        REGION VARCHAR(10) NOT NULL,
          MGR INTEGER,
       TARGET MONEY,
        SALES MONEY NOT NULL,
 PRIMARY KEY (OFFICE),
  CONSTRAINT HASMGR
 FOREIGN KEY (MGR)
   REFERENCES SALESREPS
    ON DELETE SET NULL,
        UNIQUE (CITY))
```

If a primary key, foreign key, uniqueness constraint, or check constraint involves a single column, the ANSI/ISO standard permits a "shorthand" form of the definition. The primary key, foreign key, uniqueness constraint, or check constraint is simply added to the end of the column definition, as shown in this example:

Define the `OFFICES` *table with a uniqueness constraint (ANSI/ISO syntax).*

```
CREATE TABLE OFFICES
     (OFFICE INTEGER NOT NULL PRIMARY KEY,
         CITY VARCHAR(15) NOT NULL UNIQUE,
        REGION VARCHAR(10) NOT NULL,
 MGR INTEGER REFERENCES SALESREPS,
        TARGET MONEY,
         SALES MONEY NOT NULL)
```

Several of the major DBMS brands, including SQL Server, Informix, Sybase and DB2, support this shorthand.

Check Constraints

Another SQL2 data integrity feature, the check constraint (described in Chapter 11) is also specified in the `CREATE TABLE` statement. A check constraint specifies a "check condition" (identical in form to a search condition in a SQL query) that is checked every time an attempt is made to modify the contents of the table (with an `INSERT`, `UPDATE`, or `DELETE` statement). If the check condition remains `TRUE` after the modification, it is allowed; otherwise, the DBMS disallows the attempt to modify the data and returns an error. The following is a `CREATE TABLE` statement for the `OFFICES` table, with a very simple check condition to make sure the `TARGET` for the office is greater than $0.00.

Define the OFFICES table with a uniqueness constraint.

```
CREATE TABLE OFFICES
     (OFFICE INTEGER NOT NULL,
         CITY VARCHAR(15) NOT NULL,
       REGION VARCHAR(10) NOT NULL,
          MGR INTEGER,
       TARGET MONEY,
        SALES MONEY NOT NULL,
 PRIMARY KEY (OFFICE),
  CONSTRAINT HASMGR
 FOREIGN KEY (MGR)
  REFERENCES SALESREPS
   ON DELETE SET NULL,
        CHECK (TARGET >= 0.00))
```

You can optionally specify a name for the check constraint, which will be used by the DBMS when it reports an error if the constraint is violated. Here is a slightly more complex check constraint for the SALESREPS table to enforce the rule "salespeople whose hire date is later than January 1, 1988 shall not be assigned quotas higher than $300,000." The CREATE TABLE statement names this constraint QUOTA_CAP:

```
CREATE TABLE SALESREPS
    (EMPL_NUM INTEGER NOT NULL,
        NAME VARCHAR (15) NOT NULL,
         .
         .
         .

  CONSTRAINT WORKSIN
 FOREIGN KEY (REP_OFFICE)
  REFERENCES OFFICES
   ON DELETE SET NULL
  CONSTRAINT QUOTA_CAP CHECK ((HIRE_DATE < "01-JAN-88") OR
                             (QUOTA <= 300000)))
```

This check constraint capability is supported by many of the major DBMS brands.

Physical Storage Definition *

The CREATE TABLE statement typically includes one or more optional clauses that specify physical storage characteristics for a table. Generally these clauses are used only by the database administrator to optimize the performance of a production database. By their nature these clauses are very specific to a particular DBMS.

Although they are of little practical interest to most SQL users, the different physical storage structures provided by various DBMS products illustrate their different intended applications and levels of sophistication.

Most of the personal computer databases provide very simple physical storage mechanisms. Many personal computer database products store an entire database within a single Windows file, or use a separate Windows file for each database table. They may also require that the entire table or database be stored on a single physical disk volume.

Multi-user databases typically provide more sophisticated physical storage schemes to support improved database performance. For example, Ingres allows the database administrator to define multiple named *locations*, which are physical directories where database data can be stored. The locations can be spread across multiple disk volumes to take advantage of parallel disk input/output operations. You can optionally specify one or more locations for a table in the Ingres CREATE TABLE statement:

```
CREATE TABLE OFFICES (table-definition)
  WITH LOCATION = (AREA1, AREA2, AREA3)
```

By specifying multiple locations, you can spread a table's contents across several disk volumes for greater parallel access to the table.

Sybase Adaptive Server offers a similar approach, allowing the database administrator to specify multiple named *logical database devices* that are used to store data. The correspondence between Sybase's logical devices and the actual physical disk drives of the computer system is handled by a Sybase utility program, and not within the SQL language. The Sybase CREATE DATABASE statement can then specify that a database should be stored on one or more database devices:

```
CREATE DATABASE OPDATA
    ON DBFILE1, DBFILE2, DBFILE3
```

Within a given database device, Sybase then allows the database administrator to define logical *segments*, using one of the Sybase system-provided stored procedures. Finally, a Sybase CREATE TABLE statement can specify the segment where a table's data is to be stored:

```
CREATE TABLE OFFICES (table-definition)
    ON SEGMENT SEG1A
```

DB2 offers a similarly comprehensive scheme for managing physical storage, based on the concepts of *tablespaces* and *nodegroups*. A tablespace is a logical-level storage container, while nodegroups are defined more specifically in terms of physical storage. When you create a DB2 table, you can optionally assign it to a specific tablespace:

```
CREATE TABLE OFFICES (table-definition)
    IN ADMINDB.OPSPACE
```

Unlike Sybase, DB2 puts most of the management of these storage entities within the SQL language itself, through the CREATE TABLESPACE and CREATE NODEGROUP statements. A consequence is that these statements include operating system–dependent specifications of filenames and directories, which vary from one supported DB2 operating system to another. Other clauses specify the DB2 buffer pool to be used, the overhead and transfer rate of the storage medium, and other characteristics closely related to the physical storage medium. DB2 uses this information in its performance optimization algorithms.

Removing a Table (DROP TABLE)

Over time the structure of a database grows and changes. New tables are created to represent new entities, and some old tables are no longer needed. You can remove an unneeded table from the database with the DROP TABLE statement, shown in Figure 13-3.

The table name in the statement identifies the table to be dropped. Normally you will be dropping one of your own tables and will use an unqualified table name. With proper permission, you can also drop a table owned by another user by specifying a qualified table name. Here are some examples of the DROP TABLE statement:

The CUSTOMERS table has been replaced by two new tables, CUST_INFO and ACCOUNT_INFO, and is no longer needed.

```
DROP TABLE CUSTOMERS
```

Sam gives you permission to drop his table, named BIRTHDAYS.

```
DROP TABLE SAM.BIRTHDAYS
```

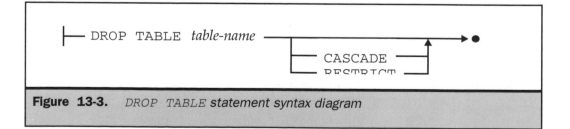

Figure 13-3. *DROP TABLE statement syntax diagram*

When the DROP TABLE statement removes a table from the database, its definition and all of its contents are lost. There is no way to recover the data, and you would have to use a new CREATE TABLE statement to recreate the table definition. Because of its serious consequences, you should use the DROP TABLE statement with care.

The SQL2 standard requires that a DROP TABLE statement include either CASCADE or RESTRICT, which specifies the impact of dropping a table on other database objects (such as views, described in Chapter 14) that depend on the table. If CASCADE is specified, the DROP TABLE statement fails if other database objects reference the table. Most commercial DBMS products accept the DROP TABLE statement with no option specified.

Changing a Table Definition (ALTER TABLE)

After a table has been in use for some time, users often discover that they want to store additional information about the entities represented in the table. In the sample database, for example, you might want to:

- Add the name and phone number of a key contact person to each row of the CUSTOMERS table, as you begin to use it for contacting customers.

- Add a minimum inventory level column to the PRODUCTS table, so the database can automatically alert you when stock of a particular product is low.

- Make the REGION column in the OFFICES table a foreign key for a newly created REGIONS table, whose primary key is the region name.

- Drop the foreign key definition linking the CUST column in the ORDERS table to the CUSTOMERS table, replacing it with two foreign key definitions linking the CUST column to the newly created CUST_INFO and ACCOUNT_INFO tables.

Each of these changes, and some others, can be handled with the ALTER TABLE statement, shown in Figure 13-4. As with the DROP TABLE statement, you will normally use the ALTER TABLE statement on one of your own tables. With proper permission, however, you can specify a qualified table name and alter the definition of another user's table. As shown in the figure, the ALTER TABLE statement can:

- Add a column definition to a table
- Drop a column from a table
- Change the default value for a column
- Add or drop a primary key for a table
- Add or drop a new foreign key for a table
- Add or drop a uniqueness constraint for a table
- Add or drop a check constraint for a table

The clauses in Figure 13-4 are specified in the SQL standard. Many DBMS brands lack support for some of these clauses or offer clauses unique to the DBMS, which alters other table characteristics. The SQL2 standard restricts each ALTER TABLE statement to a single table change. To add a column and define a new foreign key, for example, requires two separate ALTER TABLE statements. Several DBMS brands relax this restriction and allow multiple "action clauses" in a single ALTER TABLE statement.

Adding a Column

The most common use of the ALTER TABLE statement is to add a column to an existing table. The column definition clause in the ALTER TABLE statement is just like the one in the CREATE TABLE statement, and it works the same way. The new column is added to the end of the column definitions for the table, and it appears as the rightmost column in subsequent queries. The DBMS normally assumes a NULL value for a newly added column in all existing rows of the table. If the column is declared to be NOT NULL with a default value, the DBMS instead assumes the default value. Note that you cannot simply declare the new column NOT NULL, because the DBMS would assume NULL values for the column in the existing rows, immediately violating the constraint! (When you add a new column, the DBMS doesn't actually go through all of the existing rows of the table adding a NULL or default value. Instead, it detects the fact that an existing row is "too short" for the new table definition when the row is retrieved, and extends it with a NULL or default value before displaying it or passing it to your program.)

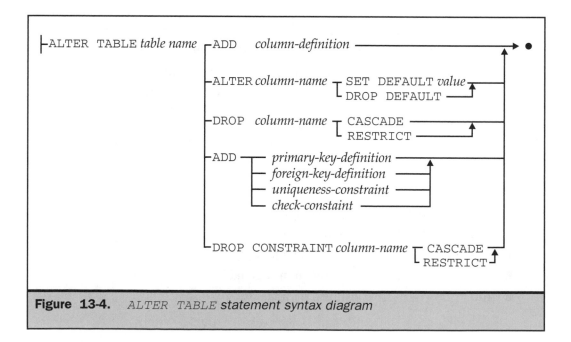

Figure 13-4. *ALTER TABLE statement syntax diagram*

Some sample ALTER TABLE statements that add new columns are:

Add a contact name and phone number to the CUSTOMERS table.

```
ALTER TABLE CUSTOMERS
   ADD CONTACT_NAME VARCHAR(30)

ALTER TABLE CUSTOMERS
   ADD CONTACT_PHONE CHAR(10)
```

Add a minimum inventory level column to the PRODUCTS table.

```
ALTER TABLE PRODUCTS
   ADD MIN_QTY INTEGER NOT NULL WITH DEFAULT 0
```

In the first example, the new columns will have NULL values for existing customers. In the second example, the MIN_QTY column will have the value zero (0) for existing products, which is appropriate.

When the ALTER TABLE statement first appeared in SQL implementations, the only major structure within a table was the column definitions, and it was very clear what the ADD clause meant. Since then, tables have grown to include primary and foreign key definitions and constraints, and the ADD clauses for these types of objects specify what type of object is being added. For consistency with these other ADD/DROP clauses, the SQL2 standard includes the optional keyword COLUMN after the keyword ADD. With this addition, the preceding example becomes:

Add a minimum inventory level column to the PRODUCTS table.

```
ALTER TABLE PRODUCTS
   ADD COLUMN MIN_QTY INTEGER NOT NULL WITH DEFAULT 0
```

Dropping a Column

The ALTER TABLE statement can be used to drop one or more columns from an existing table when they are no longer needed. Here is an example that drops the HIRE_DATE column from the SALESREPS table:

Drop a column from the SALESREPS table.

```
ALTER TABLE SALESREPS
  DROP HIRE_DATE
```

The SQL2 standard forces you to issue a separate ALTER TABLE statement if you want to drop several columns, but several of the major DBMS brands allow you to drop multiple columns with a single statement.

Note that dropping a column can pose the same kinds of data integrity issues that were described in Chapter 11 for database update operations. For example, if you drop a column that is a primary key in some relationship, the foreign key columns that refer to the dropped column become invalid. A similar problem can arise if you drop a column that is referenced in a check constraint—the column that provides the data value for checking the constraint is now gone. A similar problem is created in views that are defined based on the dropped column.

The SQL2 standard deals with these issues in the same way that it handled the potential data integrity problems posed by DELETE and UPDATE statements—with a *drop rule* (actually called a "drop behavior" in the standard) that operates just like the delete rules and update rules. You can specify one of two drop rules:

- RESTRICT. If any other objects in the database (foreign keys, constraints, and so on) depend on the column to be dropped, the ALTER TABLE statement fails with an error and the column is not dropped.

- CASCADE. Any other objects in the database (foreign keys, constraints, and so on) that depend on the column are *also* dropped, as a "cascaded effect" of the ALTER TABLE statement.

The CASCADE effect can cause quite dramatic changes in the database, and therefore it should be used with care. It's usually a better idea to use the RESTRICT mode (explicitly drop the dependent foreign keys and constraints, using the appropriate ALTER or DROP statements) before dropping the column

Changing Primary and Foreign Keys

The other common use for the ALTER TABLE statement is to change or add primary key and foreign key definitions for a table. Since primary key and foreign key support is being provided in new releases of several SQL-based database systems, this form of the ALTER TABLE statement is particularly useful. It can be used to inform the DBMS about inter-table relationships that already exist in a database, but which have not been explicitly specified before.

Unlike column definitions, primary key and foreign key definitions can be added *and* dropped from a table with the ALTER TABLE statement. The clauses that add primary key and foreign key definitions are exactly the same as those in the CREATE TABLE statement, and they work the same way. The clauses that drop a primary key or foreign key are straightforward, as shown in the following examples. Note that you can drop a foreign key only if the relationship that it creates was originally assigned a name. If the relationship was unnamed, there is no way to specify it in the ALTER TABLE statement. In this case, you cannot drop the foreign key unless you drop and recreate the table, using the procedure described for dropping a column.

Here is an example that adds a foreign key definition to an existing table:

Make the REGION column in the OFFICES table a foreign key for the newly created REGIONS table, whose primary key is the region name.

```
    ALTER TABLE OFFICES
ADD CONSTRAINT INREGION
   FOREIGN KEY (REGION)
     REFERENCES REGIONS
```

Here is an example of an ALTER TABLE statement that modifies a primary key. Note that the foreign key corresponding to the original primary key must be dropped because it is no longer a foreign key for the altered table:

Change the primary key of the OFFICES table.

```
ALTER TABLE SALESREPS
      DROP CONSTRAINT WORKSIN
FOREIGN KEY (REP_OFFICE)
 REFERENCES OFFICES

ALTER TABLE OFFICES
      DROP PRIMARY KEY (CITY)
```

Constraint Definitions

The tables in a database define its basic structure, and in most early commercial SQL products, the table definitions were the only specification of database structure. With the advent of primary key/foreign key support in DB2 and in the SQL2 standard, the definition of database structure was expanded to include the *relationships* among the tables in a database. More recently, through the SQL2 standard and the evolution of commercial products, the definition of database structure has expanded to include a new area—database constraints that restrict the data that can be entered into the database. The types of constraints, and the role that they play in maintaining database integrity, are described in Chapter 11.

Four types of database constraints (uniqueness constraints, primary and foreign key constraints, and check constraints) are closely associated with a single database table. They are specified as part of the CREATE TABLE statement and can be modified or dropped using the ALTER TABLE statement. The other two types of database integrity constraints, assertions and domains, are created as independent "objects" within a database, independent of any individual table definition.

Assertions

An *assertion* is a database constraint that restricts the contents of the database as a whole. Like a check constraint, an assertion is specified as a search condition. But unlike a check constraint, the search condition in an assertion can restrict the contents of multiple tables and the data relationships among them. For that reason, an assertion is specified as part of the overall database definition, via a SQL2 CREATE ASSERTION statement. Suppose you wanted to restrict the contents of the sample database so that the total orders for any given customer may not exceed that customer's credit limit. You can implement that restriction with the statement:

```
CREATE ASSERTION CREDLIMIT
        CHECK ((CUSTOMERS.CUST_NUM = ORDERS.CUST) AND
              (SUM (AMOUNT) <= CREDIT_LIMIT))
```

With the assertion named CREDLIMIT as part of the database definition, the DBMS is required to check that the assertion remains true each time a SQL statement attempts to modify the CUSTOMER or ORDERS tables. If you later determine that the assertion is no longer needed, you can drop it using the DROP ASSERTION statement:

```
DROP ASSERTION CREDLIMIT
```

There is no SQL2 ALTER ASSERTION statement. To change an assertion definition, you must drop the old definition and then specify the new one with a new CREATE ASSERTION statement.

Domains

The SQL2 standard implements the formal concept of a domain as a part of a database definition. A domain is a named collection of data values that effectively functions as an additional data type, for use in database definitions. A domain is created with a CREATE DOMAIN statement. Once created, the domain can be referenced as if it were a data type within a column definition. Here is a CREATE DOMAIN statement to define a domain named VALID_EMPL_IDS, which consists of valid employee identification numbers in the sample database. These numbers are three-digit integers in the range 101 to 999, inclusive:

```
CREATE DOMAIN VALID_EMPL_IDS INTEGER
  CHECK (VALUE BETWEEN 101 AND 199)
```

If a domain is no longer needed, you can drop it using one of the forms of the SQL2 DROP DOMAIN statement:

```
DROP DOMAIN VALID_EMPL_IDS CASCADE
```

```
DROP DOMAIN VALID_EMPL_IDS RESTRICT
```

The CASCADE and RESTRICT drop rules operate just as they do for dropped columns. If CASCADE is specified, any column defined in terms of the dropped domain will also be automatically dropped from the database. If RESTRICT is specified, the attempt to drop the domain will fail if there are any column definitions based on it. You must first drop or alter the column definitions so that they no longer depend upon the domain before dropping it. This provides an extra margin of safety against accidentally dropping columns (and more importantly, the data that they contain).

Aliases and Synonyms (CREATE/DROP ALIAS)

Production databases are often organized like the copy of the sample database shown in Figure 13-5, with all of their major tables collected together and owned by the database administrator. The database administrator gives other users permission to access the tables, using the SQL security scheme described in Chapter 15. Recall, however, that you must use qualified table names to refer to another user's tables. In practice, this means that *every* query against the major tables in Figure 13-5 must use qualified table names, which makes queries like the following one long and tedious to type:

List the name, sales, office, and office sales for everyone.

```
SELECT NAME, OP_ADMIN.SALESREPS.SALES, OFFICE, OP_ADMIN.OFFICES.SALES
   FROM OP_ADMIN.SALESREPS, OP_ADMIN.OFFICES
```

To address this problem, many SQL DBMS products provide an *alias* or *synonym* capability. A synonym is a name that you define that stands for the name of some other table. In DB2, you create an alias using the CREATE ALIAS statement. (Older versions of DB2 actually used a CREATE SYNONYM statement, and Oracle still uses this form of the statement, but it has the same effect as the CREATE ALIAS statement.) If you were the user named George in Figure 13-5, for example, you might use this pair of CREATE ALIAS statements:

Create synonyms for two tables owned by another user.

```
CREATE ALIAS REPS
   FOR OP_ADMIN.SALESREPS
```

```
CREATE ALIAS OFFICES
   FOR OP_ADMIN.OFFICES
```

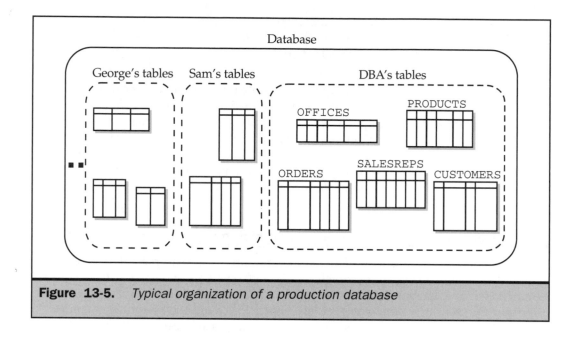

Figure 13-5. *Typical organization of a production database*

Once you have defined a synonym or alias, you can use it just like a table name in SQL queries. The previous query thus becomes:

```
SELECT NAME, REPS.SALES, OFFICE, OFFICES.SALES
  FROM REPS, OFFICES
```

The use of aliases doesn't change the meaning of the query, and you must still have permission to access the other users' tables. Nonetheless, synonyms simplify the SQL statements you use and make it appear as if the tables were your own. If you decide later that you no longer want to use the synonyms, they can be removed with the DROP ALIAS statement:

Drop the synonyms created earlier.

```
DROP ALIAS REPS
```

```
DROP ALIAS OFFICES
```

Synonyms or aliases are supported by DB2, Oracle, and Informix. They are not specified by the ANSI/ISO SQL standard.

Indexes (CREATE/DROP INDEX)

One of the physical storage structures that is provided by most SQL-based database management systems is an *index*. An index is a structure that provides rapid access to the rows of a table based on the values of one or more columns. Figure 13-6 shows the PRODUCTS table and two indexes that have been created for it. One of the indexes provides access based on the DESCRIPTION column. The other provides access based on the primary key of the table, which is a combination of the MFR_ID and PRODUCT_ID columns.

The DBMS uses the index as you might use the index of a book. The index stores data values and pointers to the rows where those data values occur. In the index the data values are arranged in ascending or descending order, so that the DBMS can

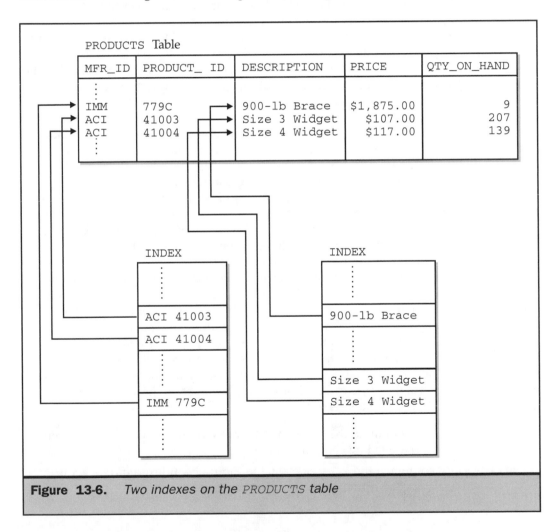

Figure 13-6.   *Two indexes on the PRODUCTS table*

quickly search the index to find a particular value. It can then follow the pointer to locate the row containing the value.

The presence or absence of an index is completely transparent to the SQL user who accesses a table. For example, consider this SELECT statement:

Find the quantity and price for size 4 widgets.

```
SELECT QTY_ON_HAND, PRICE
  FROM PRODUCTS
 WHERE DESCRIPTION = 'Size 4 Widget'
```

The statement doesn't say whether or not there is an index on the DESCRIPTION column, and the DBMS will carry out the query in either case.

If there were no index for the DESCRIPTION column, the DBMS would be forced to process the query by sequentially scanning the PRODUCTS table, row by row, examining the DESCRIPTION column in each row. To make sure it had found all of the rows that satisfied the search condition, it would have to examine *every* row in the table. For a large table with thousands or millions of rows, the scan of the table could take minutes or hours.

With an index for the DESCRIPTION column, the DBMS can locate the requested data with much less effort. It searches the index to find the requested value ("Size 4 Widget") and then follows the pointer to find the requested row(s) of the table. The index search is very rapid because the index is sorted and its rows are very small. Moving from the index to the row(s) is also very rapid because the index tells the DBMS where on the disk the row(s) are located.

As this example shows, the advantage of having an index is that it greatly speeds the execution of SQL statements with search conditions that refer to the indexed column(s). One disadvantage of having an index is that it consumes additional disk space. Another disadvantage is that the index must be updated every time a row is added to the table and every time the indexed column is updated in an existing row. This imposes additional overhead on INSERT and UPDATE statements for the table.

In general it's a good idea to create an index for columns that are used frequently in search conditions. Indexing is also more appropriate when queries against a table are more frequent than inserts and updates. Most DBMS products *always* establish an index for the primary key of a table, because they anticipate that access to the table will most frequently be via the primary key. In the sample database, these columns are good candidates for additional indexes:

- The COMPANY column in the CUSTOMERS table should be indexed if customer data is often retrieved by company name.

- The NAME column in the SALESREPS table should be indexed if data about salespeople is often retrieved by salesperson name.

- The REP column in the ORDERS table should be indexed if orders are frequently retrieved based on the salesperson who took them.
- The CUST column in the ORDERS table should similarly be indexed if orders are frequently retrieved based on the customer who placed them.
- The MFR and PRODUCT columns, together, in the ORDERS table should be indexed if orders are frequently retrieved based on the product ordered.

The SQL2 standard doesn't talk about indexes or how to create them. It treats database indexes as an "implementation detail," which is outside of the core, standardized SQL language. However, the use of indexes is essential to achieve adequate performance in any sizeable enterprise-class database.

In practice, most popular DBMS brands (including Oracle, Microsoft SQL Server, Informix, Sybase, and DB2) support indexes through some form of the CREATE INDEX statement, shown in Figure 13-7. The statement assigns a name to the index and specifies the table for which the index is created. The statement also specifies the column(s) to be indexed and whether they should be indexed in ascending or descending order. The DB2 version of the CREATE INDEX statement, shown in the figure, is the most straightforward. Its only option is the keyword UNIQUE, which is used to specify that the combination of columns being indexed must contain a unique value for every row of the table.

The following is an example of a CREATE INDEX statement that builds an index for the ORDERS table based on the MFR and PRODUCT columns and that requires combinations of columns to have a unique value.

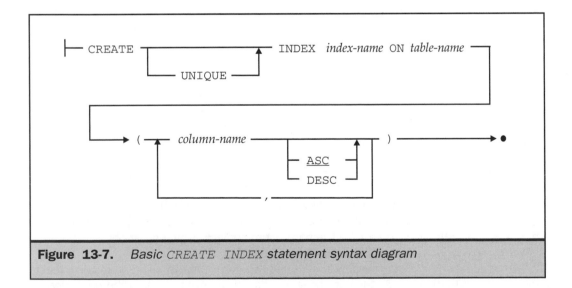

Figure 13-7.   *Basic CREATE INDEX statement syntax diagram*

Create an index for the ORDERS *table.*

```
CREATE UNIQUE INDEX ORD_PROD_IDX
    ON ORDERS (MFR, PRODUCT)
```

In most major DBMS products, the CREATE INDEX statement includes additional DBMS-specific clauses that specify the disk location for the index and for performance-tuning parameters. Typical performance parameters include the size of the index pages, the percentage of free space that the index should allow for new rows, the type of index to be created, whether it should be clustered (an arrangement that places the physical data rows on the disk medium in the same sequence as the index), and so on. These options make the CREATE INDEX statement quite DBMS-specific in actual use.

If you create an index for a table and later decide that it is not needed, the DROP INDEX statement removes the index from the database. The statement removes the index created in the previous example:

Drop the index created earlier.

```
DROP INDEX ORD_PROD_IDX
```

Managing Other Database Objects

The CREATE, DROP, and ALTER verbs form the cornerstone of the SQL Data Definition Language. Statements based on these verbs are used in all SQL implementations to manipulate tables, indexes, and views (described in Chapter 14). Most of the popular SQL-based DBMS products also use these verbs to form additional DDL statements that create, destroy, and modify other database objects unique to that particular brand of DBMS.

The Sybase DBMS, for example, pioneered the use of triggers and stored procedures, which are treated as "objects" within a SQL database, along with its tables, assertions, indexes, and other structures. Sybase added the CREATE TRIGGER and CREATE PROCEDURE statements to its SQL dialect to define these new database structures, and the corresponding DROP statements to delete them when no longer needed. As these features became popular, other DBMS products added the capabilities, along with their own variants of the CREATE TRIGGER and CREATE PROCEDURE statements.

The common conventions across DBMS brands is (a) the use of the CREATE/ DROP/ALTER verbs, (b) the next word in the statement is the type of object being managed, and (c) the third word is the name of the object, which must obey SQL naming conventions. Beyond the first three words, the statements become very DBMS-specific and nonstandard. Nonetheless, this commonality gives a uniform feel to the various SQL dialects. At the very least, it tells you where to look in the reference manual for a description of a new capability. If you encounter a new SQL-based DBMS and know that it supports an object known as a BLOB, the odds are that it uses CREATE BLOB, DROP BLOB, and ALTER BLOB statements. Table 13-1 shows how some of the popular SQL products use the CREATE, DROP, and ALTER verbs in their expanded DDL. The SQL2 standard adopts this same convention to deal with the creation, destruction, and modification of all "objects" in an SQL2 database.

SQL DDL Statements	Managed Object
Supported by almost all DBMS brands	
CREATE/DROP/ALTER TABLE	Table
CREATE/DROP/ALTER VIEW	View
CREATE/DROP/ALTER INDEX	Index
Supported by DB2	
CREATE/DROP ALIAS	Alias for a table or view
CREATE/DROP/ALTER BUFFERPOOL	Collection of I/O buffers used by DB2
CREATE/DROP DISTINCT TYPE	A distinct user-defined data type
CREATE/DROP FUNCTION	User-defined function
CREATE/DROP/ALTER NODEGROUP	Group of database partitions or nodes
DROP PACKAGE	DB2 program access module
CREATE/DROP PROCEDURE	User-defined DB2 stored procedure
CREATE/DROP SCHEMA	Database schema
CREATE/DROP/ALTER TABLESPACE	Tablespace (storage area for DB2 data)
CREATE/DROP TRIGGER	Database trigger
Supported by Informix	
CREATE/DROP CAST	Cast for converting data types
CREATE/DROP DATABASE	Named Informix database
CREATE/DROP DISTINCT TYPE	A distinct user-defined data type
CREATE/DROP FUNCTION	User-defined function
CREATE/DROP OPAQUE TYPE	User-defined opaque data type

Table 13-1.   *DDL Statements in Popular SQL-Based Products*

SQL DDL Statements	Managed Object
CREATE/DROP OPCLASS	User-defined disk storage access method
CREATE/DROP PROCEDURE	User-defined Informix stored procedure
CREATE/DROP ROLE	User role within the database
CREATE/DROP ROUTINE	User-defined Informix stored procedure
CREATE/DROP ROW TYPE	Named row type (object extension)
CREATE SCHEMA	Database schema
CREATE/DROP SYNONYM	Synonym (alias) for table or view
CREATE/DROP TRIGGER	Database trigger
Supported by Microsoft SQL Server	
CREATE/DROP/ALTER DATABASE	Database
CREATE/DROP DEFAULT	Default column value
CREATE/DROP/ALTER PROCEDURE	SQL Server stored procedure
CREATE/DROP RULE	Column integrity rule
CREATE SCHEMA	Database schema
CREATE/DROP/ALTER TRIGGER	Stored trigger
Supported by Oracle	
CREATE/DROP CLUSTER	Cluster of tables for performance tuning
CREATE DATABASE	Named Oracle database
CREATE/DROP DATABASE LINK	Network link for remote table access
CREATE/DROP DIRECTORY	O/S directory for large object storage
CREATE/DROP/ALTER FUNCTION	User-defined function
CREATE/DROP LIBRARY	External functions callable from PL/SQL

Table 13-1. *DDL Statements in Popular SQL-Based Products* (continued)

SQL DDL Statements	Managed Object
CREATE/DROP/ALTER PACKAGE	Group of sharable PL/SQL procedures
CREATE/DROP/ALTER PROCEDURE	User-defined Oracle stored procedure
CREATE/DROP/ALTER PROFILE	Limits on database resource usage
CREATE/DROP/ALTER ROLE	User role within the database
CREATE/DROP/ALTER ROLLBACK SEGMENT	Storage area for database recovery
CREATE SCHEMA	Database schema
CREATE/DROP/ALTER SEQUENCE	User-defined value sequence
CREATE/DROP/ALTER SNAPSHOT	Table of read-only query results
CREATE/DROP SYNONYM	Synonym (alias) for table or view
CREATE/DROP/ALTER TABLESPACE	Tablespace (storage area for Oracle data)
CREATE/DROP/ALTER TRIGGER	Database trigger
CREATE/DROP TYPE	A user-defined abstract data type
CREATE/DROP TYPE BODY	Methods for an abstract data type
CREATE/DROP/ALTER USER	An Oracle user-id
Supported by Sybase Adaptive Server	
CREATE/DROP/ALTER DATABASE	Database
CREATE/DROP DEFAULT	Default column value
CREATE EXISTING TABLE	Local copy of existing remote table
CREATE/DROP PROCEDURE	Sybase stored procedure
CREATE/DROP/ALTER ROLE	User role within the database
CREATE/DROP RULE	Column integrity rule
CREATE SCHEMA	Database schema
CREATE/DROP TRIGGER	Stored trigger

Table 13-1.   *DDL Statements in Popular SQL-Based Products* (continued)

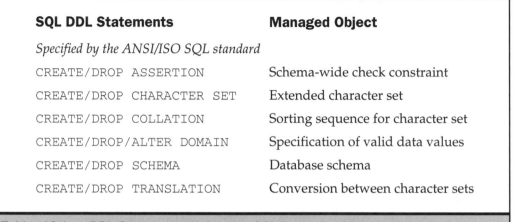

SQL DDL Statements	Managed Object
Specified by the ANSI/ISO SQL standard	
CREATE/DROP ASSERTION	Schema-wide check constraint
CREATE/DROP CHARACTER SET	Extended character set
CREATE/DROP COLLATION	Sorting sequence for character set
CREATE/DROP/ALTER DOMAIN	Specification of valid data values
CREATE/DROP SCHEMA	Database schema
CREATE/DROP TRANSLATION	Conversion between character sets

Table 13-1.   *DDL Statements in Popular SQL-Based Products* (continued)

Database Structure

The SQL1 standard specified a simple structure for the contents of a database, shown in Figure 13-8. Each user of the database has a collection of tables that are owned by that user. Virtually all major DBMS products support this scheme, although some (particularly those focused on special-purpose or embedded applications or personal computer usage) do not support the concept of table ownership. In these systems all of the tables in a database are part of one large collection.

Although different brands of SQL-based database management systems provide the same structure within a single database, there is wide variation in how they organize and structure the various databases on a particular computer system. Some brands assume a single, system-wide database that stores all of the data on that system. Other DBMS brands support multiple databases on a single computer, with each database identified by name. Still other DBMS brands support multiple databases within the context of the computer's directory system.

These variations don't change the way you use SQL to access the data within a database. However, they do affect the way you organize your data—for example do you mix order processing and accounting data in one database or do you divide it into two databases? They also affect the way you initially gain access to the database—for example, if there are multiple databases, you need to tell the DBMS which one you want to use. To illustrate how various DBMS brands deal with these issues, suppose the sample database were expanded to support a payroll and an accounting application, in addition to the order processing tasks it now supports.

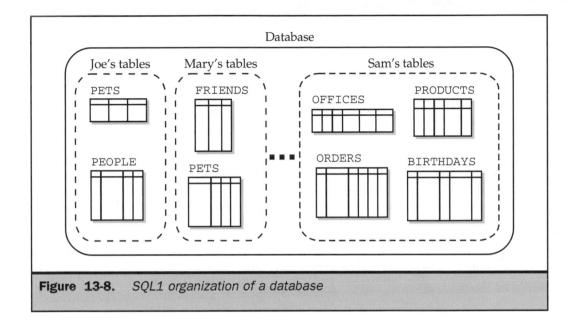

Figure 13-8. *SQL1 organization of a database*

Single-Database Architecture

Figure 13-9 shows a single-database architecture where the DBMS supports one system-wide database. Mainframe and minicomputer databases (such as the mainframe version of DB2 and Oracle) have historically tended to use this approach. Order processing, accounting, and payroll data are all stored in tables within the database. The major tables for each application are gathered together and owned by a single user, who is probably the person in charge of that application on this computer.

An advantage of this architecture is that the tables in the various applications can easily reference one another. The TIMECARDS table of the payroll application, for example, can contain a foreign key that references the OFFICES table, and the applications can use that relationship to calculate commissions. With proper permission, users can run queries that combine data from the various applications.

A disadvantage of this architecture is that the database will grow huge over time as more and more applications are added to it. A DB2 or Oracle database with several hundred tables is not uncommon. The problems of managing a database of that size—performing backups, recovering data, analyzing performance, and so on—usually require a full-time database administrator.

In the single-database architecture, gaining access to the database is very simple—there's only one database, so no choices need to be made. For example, the programmatic SQL statement that connects you to an Oracle database is CONNECT, and users tend to speak in terms of "connecting to Oracle," rather than connecting to a specific database. (In fact, in this architecture, the database is usually associated with a

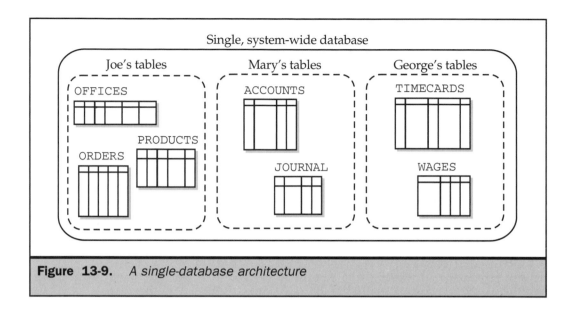

Figure 13-9. *A single-database architecture*

single running copy of the DBMS software, so in a very real sense, the user is "connecting to the DBMS.")

In fact Oracle and DB2 installations frequently do run two separate databases, one for production work and one for testing. Fundamentally, however, all production data is collected into a single database.

Multi-Database Architecture

Figure 13-10 shows a multi-database architecture where each database is assigned a unique name. Sybase Adaptive Server, Microsoft SQL Server, Ingres, and others use this scheme. As shown in the figure, each of the databases in this architecture is usually dedicated to a particular application. When you add a new application, you will probably create a new database.

The main advantage of the multi-database architecture over the single-database architecture is that it divides the data management tasks into smaller, more manageable pieces. Each person responsible for an application can now be the database administrator of their own database, with less worry about overall coordination. When it's time to add a new application, it can be developed in its own database, without disturbing the existing databases. It's also more likely that users and programmers can remember the overall structure of their own databases.

The main disadvantage of the multi-database architecture is that the individual databases may become "islands" of information, unconnected to one another. Typically a table in one database cannot contain a foreign key reference to a table in a different database. Often the DBMS does not support queries across database boundaries,

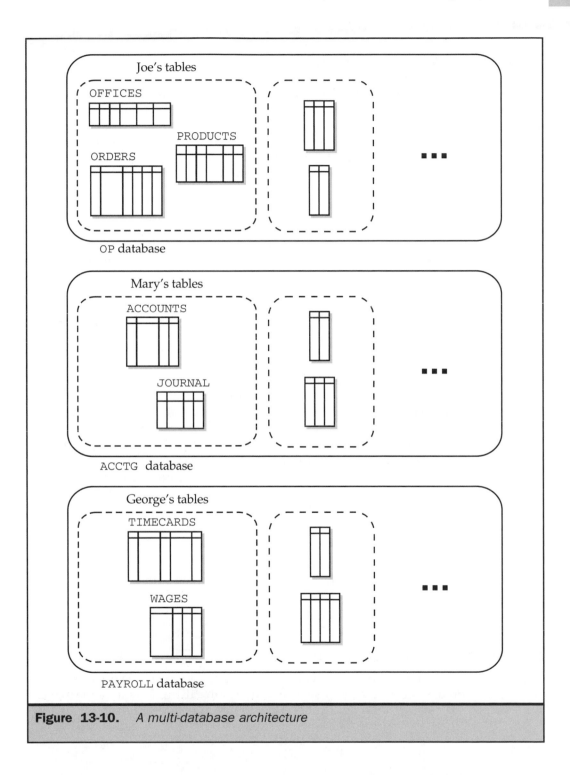

Figure 13-10. *A multi-database architecture*

making it impossible to relate data from two applications. If cross-database queries are supported, they may impose substantial overhead or require the purchase of additional distributed DBMS software from the DBMS vendor.

If a DBMS uses a multi-database architecture and supports queries across databases, it must extend the SQL table and column naming conventions. A qualified table name must specify not only the owner of the table, but also which database contains the table. Typically the DBMS extends the "dot notation" for table names by prefixing the database name to the owner name, separated by a period (.). For example, in a Sybase or SQL Server database, this table reference:

```
OP.JOE.OFFICES
```

refers to the OFFICES table owned by the user JOE in the order processing database named OP, and the following query joins the SALESREPS table in the payroll database with that OFFICES table:

```
SELECT OP.JOE.OFFICES.CITY, PAYROLL.GEORGE.SALESREPS.NAME
  FROM OP.JOE.OFFICES,  PAYROLL.GEORGE.SALESREPS
 WHERE OP.JOE.OFFICES.MGR = PAYROLL.GEORGE.SALESREPS.EMPL_NUM
```

Fortunately, such cross-database queries are the exception rather than the rule, and default database and user names can normally be used.

With a multi-database architecture, gaining access to a database becomes slightly more complex because you must tell the DBMS which database you want to use. The DBMS's interactive SQL program will often display a list of available databases or ask you to enter the database name along with your user name and password to gain access. For programmatic access, the DBMS generally extends the embedded SQL language with a statement that connects the program to a particular database. The Ingres form for connecting to the database named OP is:

```
CONNECT 'OP'
```

For Sybase Adaptive Server and Microsoft SQL Server, the parallel statement is:

```
USE 'OP'
```

Multi-Location Architecture

Figure 13-11 shows a multi-location architecture that supports multiple databases and uses the computer system's directory structure to organize them. Several of the earlier minicomputer databases (including Rdb/VMS and Informix) used this scheme for

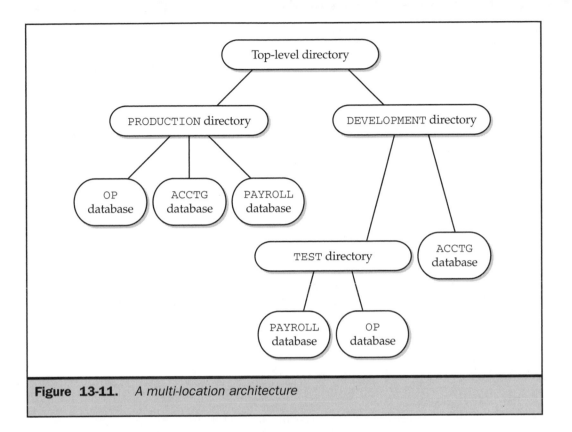

Figure 13-11.   *A multi-location architecture*

supporting multiple databases. As with the multi-database architecture, each application is typically assigned to its own database. As the figure shows, each database has a name, but it's possible for two different databases in two different directories to have the same name.

The major advantage of the multi-location architecture is flexibility. It is especially appropriate in applications such as engineering and design, where many sophisticated users of the computer system may all want to use several databases to structure their own information. The disadvantages of the multi-location architecture are the same as those of the multi-database architecture. In addition, the DBMS typically doesn't know about all of the databases that have been created, which may be spread throughout the system's directory structure. There is no "master database" that keeps track of all the databases, which makes centralized database administration very difficult.

The multi-location architecture makes gaining access to a database more complex once again, because both the name of the database and its location in the directory hierarchy must be specified. The VAX SQL syntax for gaining access to an Rdb/VMS database is the DECLARE DATABASE statement. For example, this DECLARE DATABASE statement establishes a connection to the database named OP in the VAX/VMS directory named SYS$ROOT:[DEVELOPMENT.TEST]:

```
DECLARE DATABASE
        FILENAME 'SYS$ROOT:[DEVELOPMENT.TEST]OP'
```

If the database is in the user's current directory (which is often the case), the statement simplifies to:

```
DECLARE DATABASE
        FILENAME 'OP'
```

Some of the DBMS brands that use this scheme allow you to have access to several databases concurrently, even if they don't support queries across database boundaries. Again, the most common technique used to distinguish among the multiple databases is with a "superqualified" table name. Since two databases in two different directories can have the same name, it's also necessary to introduce a *database alias* to eliminate ambiguity. These VAX SQL statements open two different Rdb/VMS databases that happen to have the same name:

```
DECLARE DATABASE OP1
        FILENAME 'SYS$ROOT:[PRODUCTION\]OP'
DECLARE DATABASE OP2
        FILENAME 'SYS$ROOT:[DEVELOPMENT.TEST]OP'
```

The statements assign the aliases OP1 and OP2 to the two databases, and these aliases are used to qualify table names in subsequent VAX SQL statements.

As this discussion shows, there is tremendous variety in the way that various DBMS brands organize their databases and provide access to them. This area of SQL is one of the most nonstandard, and yet it is often the first one that a user encounters when trying to access a database for the first time. The inconsistencies also make it impossible to transparently move programs developed for one DBMS to another, although the conversion process is usually tedious rather than complex.

Database Structure and the ANSI/ISO Standard

The ANSI/ISO SQL1 standard made a very strong distinction between the SQL Data Manipulation Language and Data Definition Language, defining them effectively as two separate languages. The standard did not require that the DDL statements be accepted by the DBMS during its normal operation. One of the advantages of this separation of the DML and DDL was that the standard permitted a static database structure like that used by older hierarchical and network DBMS products, as shown in Figure 13-12.

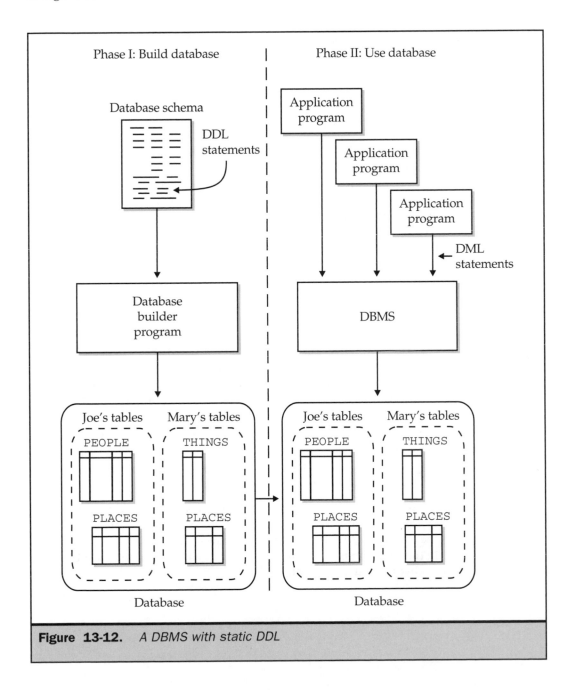

Figure 13-12.   *A DBMS with static DDL*

The database structure specified by the SQL1 standard was fairly straightforward. Collections of tables were defined in a *database schema*, associated with a specific user. In Figure 13-12, the simple database has two schemas. One schema is associated with (the common terminology is "owned by") a user named Joe, and the other is owned by Mary. Joe's schema contains two tables, named PEOPLE and PLACES. Mary's schema also contains two tables, named THINGS and PLACES. Although the database contains two tables named PLACES, it's possible to tell them apart because they have different owners.

The SQL2 standard significantly extended the SQL1 notion of database definition and database schemas. As previously noted, the SQL2 standard requires that data definition statements be executable by an interactive SQL user or by a SQL program. With this capability, changes to the database structure can be made at any time, not just when the database is created. In addition, the SQL1 concepts of schemas and users (officially called "authorization-ids" in the standard) is significantly expanded. Figure 13-13 shows the high-level database structure specified by the SQL2 standard.

The highest-level database structure described by the SQL2 standard is the *SQL-environment*. This is a conceptual collection of the database "entities" associated with a DBMS implementation that conforms to the SQL2 standard. The standard doesn't specify how a SQL-environment is created; that depends on the particular DBMS implementation. The standard defines these components of a SQL-environment:

- *DBMS software* that conforms to the SQL2 standard.

- *Named users* (called "authorization-ids" in the standard) who have the privileges to perform specific actions on the data and structures within the database.

- *Program modules* that are used to access the database. The SQL2 standard specifies the actual execution of SQL statements in terms of a "module language," which in practice is not used by most major commercial SQL products. No matter how the SQL programs are actually created, however, the standard says that, conceptually, the SQL-environment includes the program's database access code.

- *Catalogs* that describe the structure of the database. SQL1-style database schemas are contained within these catalogs.

- *Database data*, which is managed by the DBMS software, accessed by the users through the programs, and whose structure is described in the catalogs. Although the standard conceptually describes the data as "outside" of the catalog structure, it's common to think of data as being contained "in a table" that is "in a schema" that is "in a catalog."

SQL2 Catalogs

Within a SQL-environment, the database structure is defined by one or more named *catalogs*. The word "catalog" in this case is used in the same way that it has historically been used on mainframe systems—to describe a collection of objects (usually files). On minicomputer and personal computer systems, the concept is roughly analogous to a "directory." In the case of a SQL2 database, the catalog is a collection of named database schemas. The catalog also contains a set of system tables (confusingly, often called the "system catalog") that describe the structure of the database. The catalog is

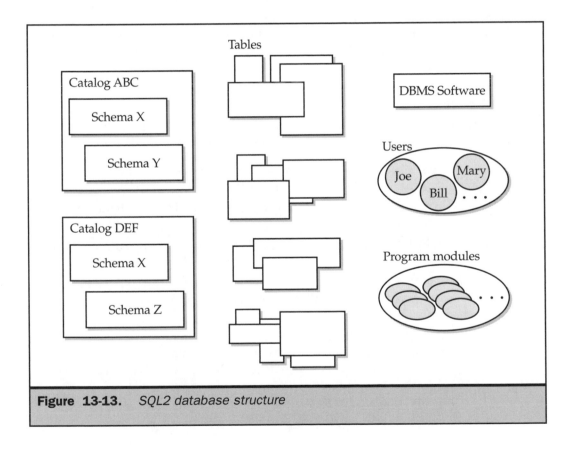

Figure 13-13. *SQL2 database structure*

thus a self-describing entity within the database. This characteristic of SQL2 catalogs (which is provided by all major SQL products) is described in detail in Chapter 16.

The SQL2 standard describes the role of the catalog and specifies that a SQL-environment may contain one or more (actually zero or more) catalogs, each of which must have a distinct name. It explicitly says that the mechanism for creating and destroying catalogs is implementation-defined. The standard also says that the extent to which a DBMS allows access "across catalogs" is implementation-defined. Specifically, whether a single SQL statement can access data from multiple catalogs, whether a single SQL transaction can span multiple catalogs, or even whether a single user session with the DBMS can cross catalog boundaries are all implementation-defined characteristics.

The standard says that when a user or program first establishes contact with a SQL-environment, one of its catalogs is identified as the *default catalog* for the session. (Again, the way in which this catalog is selected is implementation-defined.) During the course of a session, the default catalog can be changed with the SET CATALOG statement.

SQL2 Schemas

The SQL2 *schema* is the key high-level "container" for objects in a SQL2 database structure. A schema is a named entity within the database and includes the definitions for:

- *Tables*, as described earlier in this chapter, along with their associated structures (columns, primary and foreign keys, table constraints, and so on).

- *Views*, which are "virtual tables" derived from the "real tables" in the database, as described in the next chapter.

- *Domains*, which function like extended data types for defining columns within the tables of the schema, as described earlier in this chapter.

- *Assertions*, which are database integrity constraints that restrict the data relationships across tables within the schema, as described earlier in this chapter.

- *Privileges*, which control the capabilities that are given to various users to access and update data in the database and to modify the database structure. The SQL security scheme created by these privileges is described in the next chapter.

- *Character sets*, which are database structures used to support international languages and manage the representation of non-Roman characters in those character sets (for example, the diacritical "accent" marks used by many

European languages or the two-byte representations of the word-symbols used in many Asian languages).

■ *Collations*, which define the sorting sequence for a character set.

■ *Translations*, which control how text data is converted from one character set to another and how comparisons are made of text data from different character sets.

A schema is created with the CREATE SCHEMA statement, shown in Figure 13-14. Here is a simple SQL2 schema definition for the simple two-table schema for the user Joe shown in Figure 13-12:

```
CREATE SCHEMA JSCHEMA AUTHORIZATION JOE
 CREATE TABLE PEOPLE
        (NAME VARCHAR(30),
          AGE INTEGER)
 CREATE TABLE PLACES
        (CITY VARCHAR(30),
        STATE VARCHAR(30))
        GRANT ALL PRIVILEGES
            ON PEOPLE
            TO PUBLIC
        GRANT SELECT
            ON PLACES
            TO MARY
```

The schema defines the two tables and gives certain other users permission to access them. It doesn't define any additional structures, such as views or assertions. Note that the CREATE TABLE statements within the CREATE SCHEMA statement are legitimate SQL statements in their own right, as described earlier in this chapter. If you type them into an interactive SQL program, the DBMS will create the specified tables in the current *default schema* for your interactive SQL session, according to the standard.

Note that in SQL2 the schema structure is related to, but independent of, the user-id structure. A given user can be the owner of several different named schemas. For backward compatibility with the SQL1 standard, however, the SQL2 standard allows you to create a schema with:

■ Both a schema name and a user-id (as in the last example)

■ A schema name only. In this case, the user who executes the CREATE SCHEMA statement automatically becomes the "owner" of the schema.

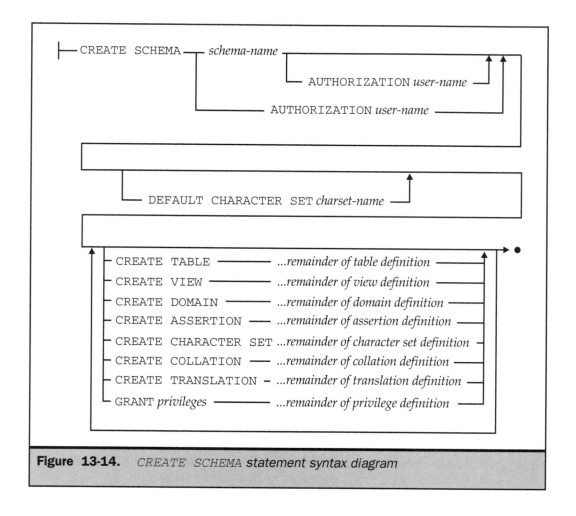

Figure 13-14. *CREATE SCHEMA statement syntax diagram*

- A user-id only. In this case, the schema name becomes the user-id. This conforms to the SQL1 standard, and to the practice of many commercial DBMS products where there was conceptually one schema per user.

A SQL2 schema that is no longer needed can be dropped using the DROP SCHEMA statement, shown in Figure 13-15. The statement requires that you specify one of the drop rules previously described for dropping columns—either CASCADE or RESTRICT. If you specify CASCADE, then all of the structures within the schema definition (tables, views, assertions, and so on) are automatically dropped. If you specify RESTRICT, the statement will not succeed if any of these structures are remaining within the schema. Effectively the RESTRICT rule forces you to first drop the individual tables, views, and other structures within the schema before dropping the schema itself. This is a protection against accidentally dropping a schema that contains data or database definitions of value. No ALTER SCHEMA table is specified by the SQL2 standard. Instead, you can individually alter the definitions of the structures within a schema, using statements like ALTER TABLE.

At any time while a user or program is accessing a SQL2 database, one of its schemas is identified as the *default schema*. Any DDL statements that you execute to create, drop, or alter schema structures implicitly apply to this schema. In addition, all tables named in SQL2 data manipulation statements are assumed to be tables defined within this default schema. The schema name implicitly qualifies the names of all tables used in the SQL statements. As noted in Chapter 5, you can use a qualified table name to refer to tables from other schemas. According to the SQL2 standard, the name used to qualify the table name is the schema name. For example, if the sample database were created as part of a schema named SALES, the qualified table name for the OFFICES table would be:

```
SALES.OFFICES
```

If a SQL2 schema is created with just a user-id as the schema name, then the table qualification scheme becomes exactly the simple one described in Chapter 5. The schema name is the user name, and the qualified table name specifies this name before the dot.

The SQL2 CREATE SCHEMA statement has one other nonobvious advantage. You may recall from the earlier discussion of the CREATE TABLE statement that you could not easily create a referential cycle (two or more tables that refer to one another using foreign key/primary key relationships). Instead, one of the tables had to be created first without its foreign key definition, and then the foreign key definition had to be added (with the ALTER TABLE statement) after the other table(s) had been created. The CREATE SCHEMA statement avoids this problem, since the DBMS does not check the referential integrity constraints specified by the schema until *all* of the tables it defines have been created. In practice, the CREATE SCHEMA statement is generally used to create a "new" set of interrelated tables for the first time. Subsequently, individual tables are added, dropped, or modified using the CREATE/DROP/ALTER TABLE capabilities.

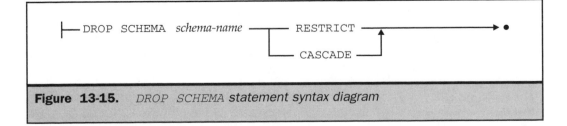

Figure 13-15. *DROP SCHEMA statement syntax diagram*

Many of the major DBMS brands have moved to adopt some form of the CREATE SCHEMA statement, although there are significant variations across the brands. Oracle's CREATE SCHEMA statement allows you to create tables, views, and privileges, but not the other SQL2 structures, and it requires that the schema name and the user name be one and the same. Informix Universal Server follows a similar pattern, requiring a user-id as the schema name and extending the objects within the schema to include indexes, triggers, and synonyms. Sybase Adaptive Server provides similar capabilities. In each case, the offered capabilities conform to the SQL2 Entry Level implementation requirements.

Summary

This chapter described the SQL Data Definition Language features that define and change the structure of a database:

- The CREATE TABLE statement creates a table and defines its columns, primary key, and foreign keys.

- The DROP TABLE statement removes a previously created table from the database.

- The ALTER TABLE statement can be used to add a column to an existing table and to change primary key and foreign key definitions.

- The CREATE INDEX and DROP INDEX statements define indexes, which speed database queries but add overhead to database updates.

- Most DBMS brands support other CREATE, DROP, and ALTER statements used with DBMS-specific objects.

- The SQL2 standard specifies a database schema containing a collection of tables, and the database schema is manipulated with CREATE SCHEMA and DROP SCHEMA statements

- Various DBMS brands use very different approaches to organizing the one or more databases that they manage, and these differences affect the way you design your databases and gain access to them.

The Complete Reference

Chapter 14

Views

The tables of a database define the structure and organization of its data. However, SQL also lets you look at the stored data in other ways by defining alternative views of the data. A *view* is a SQL query that is permanently stored in the database and assigned a name. The results of the stored query are "visible" through the view, and SQL lets you access these query results as if they were, in fact, a "real" table in the database.

Views are an important part of SQL, for several reasons:

■ Views let you tailor the appearance of a database so that different users see it from different perspectives.

■ Views let you restrict access to data, allowing different users to see only certain rows or certain columns of a table.

■ Views simplify database access by presenting the structure of the stored data in the way that is most natural for each user.

This chapter describes how to create views and how to use views to simplify processing and enhance the security of a database.

What Is a View?

A *view* is a "virtual table" in the database whose contents are defined by a query, as shown in Figure 14-1. To the database user, the view appears just like a real table, with a set of named columns and rows of data. But unlike a real table, a view does not exist in the database as a stored set of data values. Instead, the rows and columns of data visible through the view are the query results produced by the query that defines the view. SQL creates the illusion of the view by giving the view a name like a table name and storing the definition of the view in the database.

The view shown in Figure 14-1 is typical. It has been given the name REPDATA and is defined by this two-table query:

```
SELECT NAME, CITY, REGION, QUOTA, SALESREPS.SALES
  FROM SALESREPS, OFFICES
 WHERE REP_OFFICE = OFFICE
```

The data in the view comes from the SALESREPS and OFFICES tables. These tables are called the *source tables* for the view because they are the source of the data that is visible through the view. This view contains one row of information for each salesperson, extended with the name of the city and region where the salesperson works. As shown in the figure, the view appears as a table, and its contents look just like the query results that you would obtain if you actually ran the query.

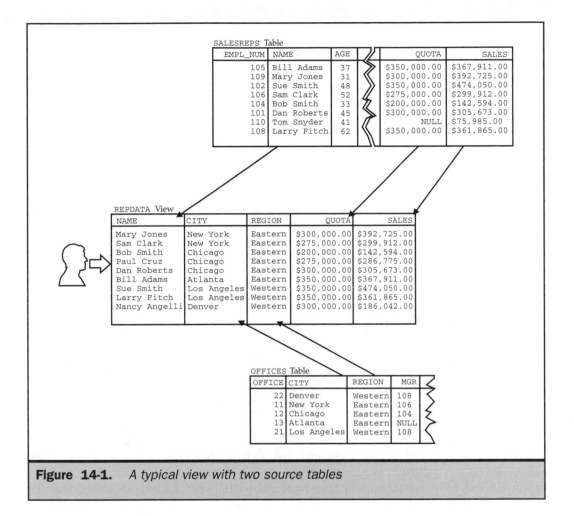

Figure 14-1.   *A typical view with two source tables*

Once a view is defined, you can use it in a SELECT statement, just like a real table, as in this query:

List the salespeople who are over quota, showing the name, city, and region for each salesperson.

```
SELECT NAME, CITY, REGION
  FROM REPDATA
 WHERE SALES > QUOTA
```

```
NAME            CITY           REGION
------------    ------------   --------
Mary Jones      New York       Eastern
Sam Clark       New York       Eastern
Dan Roberts     Chicago        Eastern
Paul Cruz       Chicago        Eastern
Bill Adams      Atlanta        Eastern
Sue Smith       Los Angeles    Western
Larry Fitch     Los Angeles    Western
```

The name of the view, REPDATA, appears in the FROM clause just like a table name, and the columns of the view are referenced in the SELECT statement just like the columns of a real table. For some views you can also use the INSERT, DELETE, and UPDATE statements to modify the data visible through the view, as if it were a real table. Thus, for all practical purposes, the view can be used in SQL statements as if it *were* a real table.

How the DBMS Handles Views

When the DBMS encounters a reference to a view in a SQL statement, it finds the definition of the view stored in the database. Then the DBMS translates the request that references the view into an *equivalent* request against the source tables of the view and carries out the equivalent request. In this way the DBMS maintains the illusion of the view while maintaining the integrity of the source tables.

For simple views, the DBMS may construct each row of the view "on the fly," drawing the data for the row from the source table(s). For more complex views, the DBMS must actually *materialize* the view; that is, the DBMS must actually carry out the query that defines the view and store its results in a temporary table. The DBMS fills your requests for view access from this temporary table and discards the table when it is no longer needed. Regardless of how the DBMS actually handles a particular view, the result is the same for the user—the view can be referenced in SQL statements exactly as if it were a real table in the database.

Advantages of Views

Views provide a variety of benefits and can be useful in many different types of databases. In a personal computer database, views are usually a convenience, defined to simplify database requests. In a production database installation, views play a central role in defining the structure of the database for its users and enforcing its security. Views provide these major benefits:

- *Security*. Each user can be given permission to access the database only through a small set of views that contain the specific data the user is authorized to see, thus restricting the user's access to stored data.

- *Query simplicity*. A view can draw data from several different tables and present it as a single table, turning multi-table queries into single-table queries against the view.

- *Structural simplicity*. Views can give a user a "personalized" view of the database structure, presenting the database as a set of virtual tables that make sense for that user.

- *Insulation from change*. A view can present a consistent, unchanged image of the structure of the database, even if the underlying source tables are split, restructured, or renamed.

- *Data integrity*. If data is accessed and entered through a view, the DBMS can automatically check the data to ensure that it meets specified integrity constraints.

Disadvantages of Views

While views provide substantial advantages, there are also two major disadvantages to using a view instead of a real table:

- *Performance*. Views create the *appearance* of a table, but the DBMS must still translate queries against the view into queries against the underlying source tables. If the view is defined by a complex, multi-table query, then even a simple query against the view becomes a complicated join, and it may take a long time to complete.

- *Update restrictions*. When a user tries to update rows of a view, the DBMS must translate the request into an update on rows of the underlying source tables. This is possible for simple views, but more complex views cannot be updated; they are "read-only."

These disadvantages mean that you cannot indiscriminately define views and use them instead of the source tables. Instead, you must in each case consider the advantages provided by using a view and weigh them against the disadvantages.

Creating a View (CREATE VIEW)

The CREATE VIEW statement, shown in Figure 14-2, is used to create a view. The statement assigns a name to the view and specifies the query that defines the view. To create the view successfully, you must have permission to access all of the tables referenced in the query.

The CREATE VIEW statement can optionally assign a name to each column in the newly created view. If a list of column names is specified, it must have the same number of items as the number of columns produced by the query. Note that only the column names are specified; the data type, length, and other characteristics of each

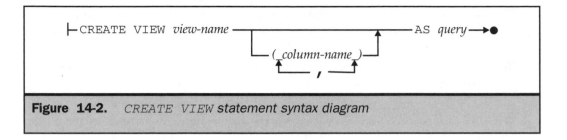

Figure 14-2. *CREATE VIEW statement syntax diagram*

column are derived from the definition of the columns in the source tables. If the list of column names is omitted from the CREATE VIEW statement, each column in the view takes the name of the corresponding column in the query. The list of column names must be specified if the query includes calculated columns or if it produces two columns with identical names.

Although all views are created in the same way, in practice different types of views are typically used for different purposes. The next few sections examine these types of views and give examples of the CREATE VIEW statement.

Horizontal Views

A common use of views is to restrict a user's access to only selected rows of a table. For example, in the sample database, you may want to let a sales manager see only the SALESREPS rows for salespeople in the manager's own region. To accomplish this, you can define two views, as follows:

Create a view showing Eastern region salespeople.

```
CREATE VIEW EASTREPS AS
    SELECT *
      FROM SALESREPS
     WHERE REP_OFFICE IN (11, 12, 13)
```

Create a view showing Western region salespeople.

```
CREATE VIEW WESTREPS AS
    SELECT *
      FROM SALESREPS
     WHERE REP_OFFICE IN (21, 22)
```

Now you can give each sales manager permission to access either the EASTREPS or the WESTREPS view, denying them permission to access the other view and the SALESREPS table itself. This effectively gives the sales manager a customized view of the SALESREPS table, showing only salespeople in the appropriate region.

A view like EASTREPS or WESTREPS is often called a *horizontal view*. As shown in Figure 14-3, a horizontal view "slices" the source table horizontally to create the view. All of the columns of the source table participate in the view, but only some of its rows are visible through the view. Horizontal views are appropriate when the source table contains data that relates to various organizations or users. They provide a "private table" for each user, composed only of the rows needed by that user.

Here are some more examples of horizontal views:

Define a view containing only Eastern region offices.

```
CREATE VIEW EASTOFFICES AS
     SELECT *
        FROM OFFICES
       WHERE REGION = 'Eastern'
```

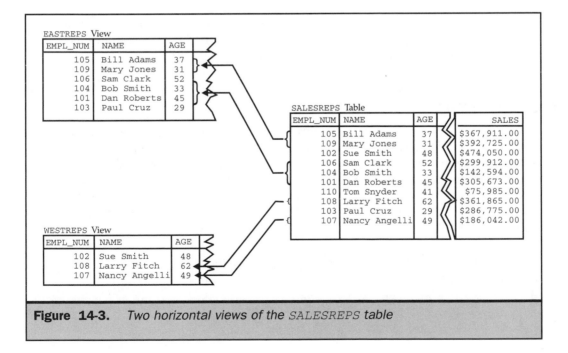

Figure 14-3. *Two horizontal views of the* SALESREPS *table*

Define a view for Sue Smith (employee number 102) containing only orders placed by customers assigned to her.

```
CREATE VIEW SUEORDERS AS
     SELECT *
       FROM ORDERS
      WHERE CUST IN (SELECT CUST_NUM
                       FROM CUSTOMERS
                      WHERE CUST_REP = 102)
```

Define a view showing only those customers who have more than $30,000 worth of orders currently on the books.

```
CREATE VIEW BIGCUSTOMERS AS
     SELECT *
       FROM CUSTOMERS
      WHERE 30000.00 < (SELECT SUM(AMOUNT)
                          FROM ORDERS
                         WHERE CUST = CUST_NUM)
```

In each of these examples, the view is derived from a single source table. The view is defined by a SELECT * query and therefore has exactly the same columns as the source table. The WHERE clause determines which rows of the source table are visible in the view.

Vertical Views

Another common use of views is to restrict a user's access to only certain columns of a table. For example, in the sample database, the order processing department may need access to the employee number, name, and office assignment of each salesperson, because this information may be needed to process an order correctly. However, there is no need for the order processing staff to see the salesperson's year-to-date sales or quota. This selective view of the SALESREPS table can be constructed with the following view:

Create a view showing selected salesperson information.

```
CREATE VIEW REPINFO AS
     SELECT EMPL_NUM, NAME, REP_OFFICE
       FROM SALESREPS
```

By giving the order processing staff access to this view and denying access to the SALESREPS table itself, access to sensitive sales and quota data is effectively restricted.

A view like the REPINFO view is often called a *vertical view*. As shown in Figure 14-4, a vertical view "slices" the source table vertically to create the view. Vertical views are commonly found where the data stored in a table is used by various users or groups of users. They provide a "private table" for each user, composed only of the columns needed by that user.

Here are some more examples of vertical views:

Define a view of the OFFICES *table for the order processing staff that includes the office's city, office number, and region.*

```
CREATE VIEW OFFICEINFO AS
    SELECT OFFICE, CITY, REGION
        FROM OFFICES
```

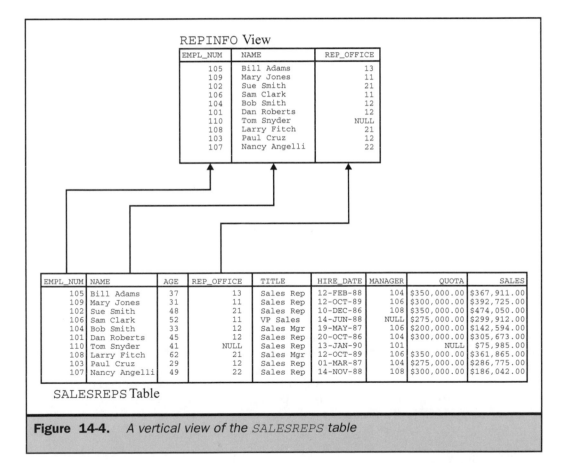

Figure 14-4. *A vertical view of the* SALESREPS *table*

Define a view of the CUSTOMERS *table that includes only customer names and their assignment to salespeople.*

```
CREATE VIEW CUSTINFO AS
    SELECT COMPANY, CUST_REP
      FROM CUSTOMERS
```

In each of these examples, the view is derived from a single source table. The select list in the view definition determines which columns of the source table are visible in the view. Because these are vertical views, every row of the source table is represented in the view, and the view definition does not include a WHERE clause.

Row/Column Subset Views

When you define a view, SQL does not restrict you to purely horizontal or vertical slices of a table. In fact, the SQL language does not include the notion of horizontal and vertical views. These concepts merely help you to visualize how the view presents the information from the source table. It's quite common to define a view that slices a source table in *both* the horizontal and vertical dimensions, as in this example:

Define a view that contains the customer number, company name, and credit limit of all customers assigned to Bill Adams (employee number 105).

```
CREATE VIEW BILLCUST AS
    SELECT CUST_NUM, COMPANY, CREDIT_LIMIT
      FROM CUSTOMERS
     WHERE CUST_REP = 105
```

The data visible through this view is a row/column subset of the CUSTOMERS table. Only the columns explicitly named in the select list of the view and the rows that meet the search condition are visible through the view.

Grouped Views

The query specified in a view definition may include a GROUP BY clause. This type of view is called a *grouped view*, because the data visible through the view is the result of a grouped query. Grouped views perform the same function as grouped queries; they group related rows of data and produce one row of query results for each group, summarizing the data in that group. A grouped view makes these grouped query results into a virtual table, allowing you to perform further queries on them.

Here is an example of a grouped view:

Define a view that contains summary order data for each salesperson.

```
CREATE VIEW ORD_BY_REP (WHO, HOW_MANY, TOTAL, LOW, HIGH, AVERAGE) AS
     SELECT REP, COUNT(*), SUM(AMOUNT), MIN(AMOUNT), MAX(AMOUNT),
             AVG(AMOUNT)
       FROM ORDERS
     GROUP BY REP
```

As this example shows, the definition of a grouped view always includes a column name list. The list assigns names to the columns in the grouped view, which are derived from column functions such as SUM() and MIN(). It may also specify a modified name for a grouping column. In this example, the REP column of the ORDERS table becomes the WHO column in the ORD_BY_REP view.

Once this grouped view is defined, it can be used to simplify queries. For example, this query generates a simple report that summarizes the orders for each salesperson:

Show the name, number of orders, total order amount, and average order size for each salesperson.

```
SELECT NAME, HOW_MANY, TOTAL, AVERAGE
  FROM SALESREPS, ORD_BY_REP
 WHERE WHO = EMPL_NUM
 ORDER BY TOTAL DESC
```

NAME	HOW_MANY	TOTAL	AVERAGE
Larry Fitch	7	$58,633.00	$8,376.14
Bill Adams	5	$39,327.00	$7,865.40
Nancy Angelli	3	$34,432.00	$11,477.33
Sam Clark	2	$32,958.00	$16,479.00
Dan Roberts	3	$26,628.00	$8,876.00
Tom Snyder	2	$23,132.00	$11,566.00
Sue Smith	4	$22,776.00	$5,694.00
Mary Jones	2	$7,105.00	$3,552.50
Paul Cruz	2	$2,700.00	$1,350.00

Unlike a horizontal or vertical view, the rows in a grouped view do not have a one-to-one correspondence with the rows in the source table. A grouped view is not just a filter on its source table that screens out certain rows and columns. It is a summary of the source tables, and therefore a substantial amount of DBMS processing is required to maintain the illusion of a virtual table for grouped views.

Grouped views can be used in queries just like other, simpler views. A grouped view cannot be updated, however. The reason should be obvious from the example.

What would it mean to "update the average order size for salesrep number 105?" Because each row in the grouped view corresponds to a *group* of rows from the source table, and because the columns in the grouped view generally contain calculated data, there is no way to translate the update request into an update against the rows of the source table. Grouped views thus function as "read-only" views, which can participate in queries but not in updates.

Grouped views are also subject to the SQL restrictions on nested column functions. Recall from Chapter 8 that nested column functions, such as:

```
MIN(MIN(A))
```

are not legal in SQL expressions. Although the grouped view "hides" the column functions in its select list from the user, the DBMS still knows about them and enforces the restriction. Consider this example:

For each sales office, show the range of average order sizes for all salespeople who work in the office.

```
SELECT REP_OFFICE, MIN(AVERAGE), MAX(AVERAGE)
  FROM SALESREPS, ORD_BY_REP
 WHERE EMPL_NUM = WHO
 GROUP BY REP_OFFICE

Error: Nested column function reference
```

This query produces an error, even though it appears perfectly reasonable. It's a two-table query that groups the rows of the ORD_BY_REP view based on the office to which the salesperson is assigned. But the column functions MIN() and MAX() in the select list cause a problem. The argument to these column functions, the AVERAGE column, is itself the result of a column function. The "actual" query being requested from SQL is:

```
SELECT REP_OFFICE, MIN(AVG(AMOUNT)), MAX(AVG(AMOUNT))
  FROM SALESREPS, ORDERS
 WHERE EMPL_NUM = REP
 GROUP BY REP
 GROUP BY REP_OFFICE
```

This query is illegal because of the double GROUP BY and the nested column functions. Unfortunately, as this example shows, a perfectly reasonable grouped SELECT statement may, in fact, cause an error if one of its source tables turns out to be a grouped view. There's no way to anticipate this situation; you must just understand the cause of the error when SQL reports it to you.

Joined Views

One of the most frequent reasons for using views is to simplify multi-table queries. By specifying a two-table or three-table query in the view definition, you can create a *joined view* that draws its data from two or three different tables and presents the query results as a single virtual table. Once the view is defined, you can often use a simple, single-table query against the view for requests that would otherwise each require a two-table or three-table join.

For example, suppose that Sam Clark, the vice president of sales, often runs queries against the ORDERS table in the sample database. However, Sam doesn't like to work with customer and employee numbers. Instead, he'd like to be able to use a version of the ORDERS table that has names instead of numbers. Here is a view that meets Sam's needs:

Create a view of the ORDERS table with names instead of numbers.

```
CREATE VIEW ORDER_INFO (ORDER_NUM, COMPANY, REP_NAME, AMOUNT) AS
    SELECT ORDER_NUM, COMPANY, NAME, AMOUNT
      FROM ORDERS, CUSTOMERS, SALESREPS
     WHERE CUST = CUST_NUM
       AND REP = EMPL_NUM
```

This view is defined by a three-table join. As with a grouped view, the processing required to create the illusion of a virtual table for this view is considerable. Each row of the view is derived from a *combination* of one row from the ORDERS table, one row from the CUSTOMERS table, and one row from the SALESREPS table.

Although it has a relatively complex definition, this view can provide some real benefits. Here is a query against the view that generates a report of orders, grouped by salesperson:

Show the total current orders for each company for each salesperson.

```
SELECT REP_NAME, COMPANY, SUM(AMOUNT)
  FROM ORDER_INFO
 GROUP BY REP_NAME, COMPANY
```

REP_NAME	COMPANY	SUM(AMOUNT)
Bill Adams	Acme Mfg.	$35,582.00
Bill Adams	JCP Inc.	$3,745.00
Dan Roberts	First Corp.	$3,978.00
Dan Roberts	Holm & Landis	$150.00
Dan Roberts	Ian & Schmidt	$22,500.00

```
Larry Fitch  Midwest Systems       $3,608.00
Larry Fitch  Orion Corp.           $7,100.00
Larry Fitch  Zetacorp             $47,925.00
    .
    .
    .
```

Note that this query is a single-table SELECT statement, which is considerably simpler than the equivalent three-table SELECT statement for the source tables:

```
SELECT NAME, COMPANY, SUM(AMOUNT)
  FROM SALESREPS, ORDERS, CUSTOMERS
 WHERE REP = EMPL_NUM
   AND CUST = CUST_NUM
 GROUP BY NAME, COMPANY
```

Similarly, it's easy to generate a report of the largest orders, showing who placed them and who received them, with this query against the view:

Show the largest current orders, sorted by amount.

```
SELECT COMPANY, AMOUNT, REP_NAME
  FROM ORDER_INFO
 WHERE AMOUNT > 20000.00
 ORDER BY AMOUNT DESC
```

```
COMPANY                 AMOUNT REP_NAME
------------------  ----------- -------------
Zetacorp            $45,000.00 Larry Fitch
J.P. Sinclair       $31,500.00 Sam Clark
Chen Associates     $31,350.00 Nancy Angelli
Acme Mfg.           $27,500.00 Bill Adams
Ace International   $22,500.00 Tom Snyder
Ian & Schmidt       $22,500.00 Dan Roberts
```

The view makes it much easier to see what's going on in the query than if it were expressed as the equivalent three-table join. Of course the DBMS must work just as hard to generate the query results for the single-table query against the view as it would to generate the query results for the equivalent three-table query. In fact, the

DBMS must perform slightly more work to handle the query against the view. However, for the human user of the database it's much easier to write and understand the single-table query that references the view.

Updating a View

What does it mean to insert a row of data into a view, delete a row from a view, or update a row of a view? For some views these operations can obviously be translated into equivalent operations against the source table(s) of the view. For example, consider once again the EASTREPS view, defined earlier in this chapter:

Create a view showing Eastern region salespeople.

```
CREATE VIEW EASTREPS AS
    SELECT *
      FROM SALESREPS
     WHERE REP_OFFICE IN (11, 12, 13)
```

This is a straightforward horizontal view, derived from a single source table. As shown in Figure 14-5, it makes sense to talk about inserting a row into this view; it means the new row should be inserted into the underlying SALESREPS table from which the view is derived. It also makes sense to delete a row from the EASTREPS view; this would delete the corresponding row from the SALESREPS table. Finally, updating a row of the EASTREPS view makes sense; this would update the corresponding row of the SALESREPS table. In each case the action can be carried out against the corresponding row of the source table, preserving the integrity of both the source table and the view.

However, consider the ORDS_BY_REP grouped view, also defined earlier in this chapter:

Define a view that contains summary order data for each salesperson.

```
CREATE VIEW ORD_BY_REP (WHO, HOW_MANY, TOTAL, LOW, HIGH, AVERAGE) AS
    SELECT REP, COUNT(*), SUM(AMOUNT), MIN(AMOUNT), MAX(AMOUNT),
           AVG(AMOUNT)
      FROM ORDERS
     GROUP BY REP
```

There is no one-to-one correspondence between the rows of this view and the rows of the underlying ORDERS table, so it makes no sense to talk about inserting, deleting,

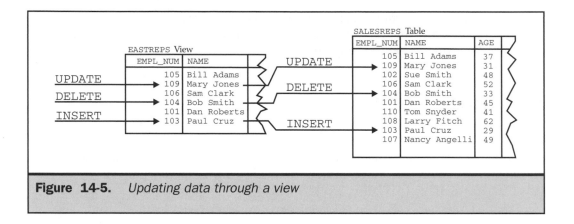

Figure 14-5. *Updating data through a view*

or updating rows of this view. The ORD_BY_REP view is not updateable; it is a read-only view.

The EASTREPS view and the ORD_BY_REP view are two extreme examples in terms of the complexity of their definitions. There are views more complex than EASTREPS where it still makes sense to update the view, and there are views less complex than ORD_BY_REP where updates do not make sense. In fact, which views can be updated and which cannot has been an important relational database research problem over the years.

View Updates and the ANSI/ISO Standard

The ANSI/ISO SQL1 standard specifies the views that must be updateable in a database that claims conformance to the standard. Under the standard, a view can be updated if the query that defines the view meets all of these restrictions:

■ DISTINCT must not be specified; that is, duplicate rows must *not* be eliminated from the query results.

■ The FROM clause must specify only one updateable table; that is, the view must have a single source table for which the user has the required privileges. If the source table is itself a view, then that view must meet these criteria.

■ Each select item must be a simple column reference; the select list cannot contain expressions, calculated columns, or column functions.

■ The WHERE clause must not include a subquery; only simple row-by-row search conditions may appear.

■ The query must not include a GROUP BY or a HAVING clause.

The basic concept behind the restrictions is easier to remember than the rules themselves:

For a view to be updateable, the DBMS must be able to trace any row of the view back to its source row in the source table. Similarly, the DBMS must be able to trace each individual column to be updated back to its source column in the source table.

If the view meets this test, then it's possible to define meaningful INSERT, DELETE, and UPDATE operations for the view in terms of the source table(s).

View Updates in Commercial SQL Products

The SQL1 standard rules on view updates are very restrictive. Many views can be theoretically updated but do not satisfy all of the restrictions. In addition, some views can support some of the update operations but not others, and some views can support updates on certain columns but not others. Most commercial SQL implementations have view update rules that are considerably more permissive than the SQL1 standard. For example, consider this view:

Create a view showing the sales, quota, and the difference between the two for each salesperson.

```
CREATE VIEW SALESPERF (EMPL_NUM, SALES, QUOTA, DIFF) AS
    SELECT EMPL_NUM, SALES, QUOTA, (SALES - QUOTA)
      FROM SALESREPS
```

The SQL1 standard disallows all updates to this view because its fourth column is a calculated column. However, note that each row in the view can be traced back to a single row in the source table (SALESREPS). For this reason DB2 (and several other commercial SQL implementations) allows DELETE operations against this view. Further, DB2 allows UPDATE operations on the EMPL_NUM, SALES, and QUOTA columns because they are directly derived from the source table. Only the DIFF column cannot be updated. DB2 does not allow the INSERT statement for the view because inserting a value for the DIFF column would be meaningless.

The specific rules that determine whether a view can be updated or not vary from one brand of DBMS to another, and they are usually fairly detailed. Some views, such as those based on grouped queries, cannot be updated by any DBMS because the update operations simply do not make sense. Other views may be updateable in one brand of DBMS, partially updateable in another brand, and not updateable in a third brand. The SQL2 standard recognized this and includes a broader definition of updateable views along with considerable latitude for variation among DBMS brands. The best way to find out about updateability of views in your particular DBMS is to consult the user's guide or experiment with different types of views.

Checking View Updates (CHECK OPTION)

If a view is defined by a query that includes a WHERE clause, only rows that meet the search condition are visible in the view. Other rows may be present in the source table(s) from which the view is derived, but they are not visible through the view. For example, the EASTREPS view described earlier in this chapter contains only those rows of the SALESREPS table with specific values in the REP_OFFICE column:

Create a view showing Eastern region salespeople.

```
CREATE VIEW EASTREPS AS
    SELECT *
      FROM SALESREPS
     WHERE REP_OFFICE IN (11, 12, 13)
```

This is an updateable view for most commercial SQL implementations. You can add a new salesperson with this INSERT statement:

```
INSERT INTO EASTREPS (EMPL_NUM, NAME, REP_OFFICE, AGE, SALES)
    VALUES (113, 'Jake Kimball', 11, 43, 0.00)
```

The DBMS will add the new row to the underlying SALESREPS table, and the row will be visible through the EASTREPS view. But consider what happens when you add a new salesperson with this INSERT statement:

```
INSERT INTO EASTREPS (EMPL_NUM, NAME, REP_OFFICE, AGE, SALES)
    VALUES (114, 'Fred Roberts', 21, 47, 0.00)
```

This is a perfectly legal SQL statement, and the DBMS will insert a new row with the specified column values into the SALESREPS table. However, the newly inserted row doesn't meet the search condition for the view. Its REP_OFFICE value (21) specifies the Los Angeles office, which is in the Western region. As a result, if you run this query immediately after the INSERT statement:

```
SELECT EMPL_NUM, NAME, REP_OFFICE
  FROM EASTREPS
```

```
EMPL_NUM NAME          REP_OFFICE
-------- ------------- -----------
     105 Bill Adams            13
     109 Mary Jones            11
     106 Sam Clark             11
     104 Bob Smith             12
     101 Dan Roberts           12
     103 Paul Cruz             12
```

the newly added row doesn't show up in the view. The same thing happens if you change the office assignment for one of the salespeople currently in the view. This UPDATE statement:

```
UPDATE EASTREPS
   SET REP_OFFICE = 21
 WHERE EMPL_NUM = 104
```

modifies one of the columns for Bob Smith's row and immediately causes it to disappear from the view. Of course, both of the "vanishing" rows show up in a query against the underlying table:

```
SELECT EMPL_NUM, NAME, REP_OFFICE
  FROM SALESREPS

EMPL_NUM NAME           REP_OFFICE
-------- -------------- -----------
     105 Bill Adams             13
     109 Mary Jones             11
     102 Sue Smith              21
     106 Sam Clark              11
     104 Bob Smith              21
     101 Dan Roberts            12
     110 Tom Snyder           NULL
     108 Larry Fitch            21
     103 Paul Cruz              12
     107 Nancy Angelli          22
     114 Fred Roberts           21
```

The fact that the rows vanish from the view as a result of an INSERT or UPDATE statement is disconcerting, at best. You probably want the DBMS to detect and prevent this type of INSERT or UPDATE from taking place through the view. SQL allows you to specify this kind of integrity checking for views by creating the view with a *check option*. The check option is specified in the CREATE VIEW statement, as shown in this redefinition of the EASTREPS view:

```
CREATE VIEW EASTREPS AS
     SELECT *
       FROM SALESREPS
      WHERE REP_OFFICE IN (11, 12, 13)
 WITH CHECK OPTION
```

When the check option is requested for a view, SQL *automatically* checks each INSERT and each UPDATE operation for the view to make sure that the resulting row(s) meet the search criteria in the view definition. If an inserted or modified row would not meet the condition, the INSERT or UPDATE statement fails, and the operation is not carried out.

The SQL2 standard specifies one additional refinement to the check option: the choice of CASCADED or LOCAL application of the check option. This choice applies when a view is created, and its definition is based, not on an underlying table, but on one or more other views. The definitions of these "underlying" views might, in turn, be based on still other views, and so on. Each of the underlying views might or might not have the check option specified. If the new view is created WITH CASCADED CHECK OPTION, any attempt to update the view causes the DBMS go down through the entire hierarchy of view definitions on which it is based, processing the check option for each view where it is specified. If the new view is created WITH LOCAL CHECK OPTION, then the DBMS checks only that view; the underlying views are not checked. The SQL2 standard specifies CASCADED as the default, if the WITH CHECK OPTION clause is used without specifying LOCAL or CASCADED.

It's probably clear from the discussion that the check option can add significant overhead to the INSERT and UPDATE operations, especially if you are updating a view which is defined based on a few layers of underlying view definitions. However, the check option plays an important role to ensure the integrity of the database. After all, if the update was intended to apply to data not visible through the view or to effectively "switch" a row of data from one view to another, then logically the update "should" be made through an underlying view or base table. When you create an updateable view as part of a security scheme, it's almost always a good idea to specify the check option. It prevents modifications made through the view from affecting data that isn't accessible to the user in the first place.

Dropping a View (DROP VIEW)

Recall that the SQL1 standard treated the SQL Data Definition Language (DDL) as a static specification of the structure of a database, including its tables and views. For this reason, the SQL1 standard did not provide the ability to drop a view when it was no longer needed. However, all major DBMS brands have provided this capability for some time. Because views behave like tables and a view cannot have the same name as a table, some DBMS brands used the DROP TABLE statement to drop views as well. Other SQL implementations provided a separate DROP VIEW statement.

The SQL2 standard formalized support for dropping views through a DROP VIEW statement. It also provides for detailed control over what happens when a user attempts to drop a view when the definition of another view depends on it. For example, suppose two views on the SALESREPS table have been created by these two CREATE VIEW statements:

```
CREATE VIEW EASTREPS AS
     SELECT *
       FROM SALESREPS
      WHERE REP_OFFICE IN (11, 12, 13)

CREATE VIEW NYREPS AS
     SELECT *
       FROM EASTREPS
      WHERE REP_OFFICE = 11
```

For purposes of illustration, the NYREPS view is defined in terms of the EASTREPS view, although it could just as easily have been defined in terms of the underlying table. Under the SQL2 standard, the following DROP VIEW statement removes *both* of the views from the database:

```
DROP VIEW EASTREPS CASCADE
```

The CASCADE option tells the DBMS to delete not only the named view, but also any views that depend on its definition. In contrast this DROP VIEW statement:

```
DROP VIEW EASTREPS RESTRICT
```

fails with an error, because the RESTRICT option tells the DBMS to remove the view only if no other views depend on it. This provides an added precaution against unintentional side-effects of a DROP VIEW statement. The SQL2 standard requires that either RESTRICT or CASCADE be specified, but many commercial SQL products support a version of the DROP VIEW statement without an explicitly specified option for backward compatibility with earlier versions of their products released before the publication of the SQL2 standard The specific behavior of dependent views in this case depends on the particular DBMS brand.

Summary

Views allow you to redefine the structure of a database, giving each user a personalized view of the database structure and contents:

- A view is a virtual table defined by a query. The view appears to contain rows and columns of data, just like a "real" table, but the data visible through the view is, in fact, the results of the query.

- A view can be a simple row/column subset of a single table, it can summarize a table (a grouped view), or it can draw its data from two or more tables (a joined view).

- A view can be referenced like a real table in a SELECT, INSERT, DELETE, or UPDATE statement. However, more complex views cannot be updated; they are read-only views.

- Views are commonly used to simplify the apparent structure of a database, to simplify queries, and to protect certain rows and/or columns from unauthorized access.

Chapter 15

SQL Security

W hen you entrust your data to a database management system, the security of the stored data is a major concern. Security is especially important in a SQL-based DBMS because interactive SQL makes database access very easy. The security requirements of a typical production database are many and varied:

- The data in any given table should be accessible to some users, but access by other users should be prevented.

- Some users should be allowed to update data in a particular table; others should only be allowed to retrieve data.

- For some tables, access should be restricted on a column-by-column basis.

- Some users should be denied interactive SQL access to a table but should be allowed to use applications programs that update the table.

The SQL security scheme, described in this chapter, provides these types of protection for data in a relational database.

SQL Security Concepts

Implementing a security scheme and enforcing security restrictions are the responsibility of the DBMS software. The SQL language defines an overall framework for database security, and SQL statements are used to specify security restrictions. The SQL security scheme is based on three central concepts:

- *Users* are the actors in the database. Each time the DBMS retrieves, inserts, deletes, or updates data, it does so on behalf of some user. The DBMS permits or prohibits the action depending on which user is making the request.

- *Database objects* are the items to which SQL security protection can be applied. Security is usually applied to tables and views, but other objects such as forms, application programs, and entire databases can also be protected. Most users will have permission to use certain database objects but will be prohibited from using others.

- *Privileges* are the actions that a user is permitted to carry out for a given database object. A user may have permission to SELECT and INSERT rows in a certain table, for example, but may lack permission to DELETE or UPDATE rows of the table. A different user may have a different set of privileges.

Figure 15-1 shows how these security concepts might be used in a security scheme for the sample database.

To establish a security scheme for a database, you use the SQL GRANT statement to specify which users have which privileges on which database objects. For example,

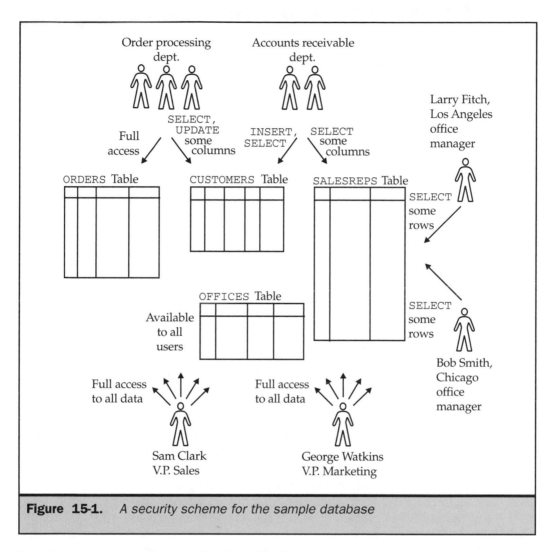

Figure 15-1.   *A security scheme for the sample database*

here is a GRANT statement that lets Sam Clark retrieve and insert data in the OFFICES table of the sample database:

Let Sam Clark retrieve and insert data in the OFFICES table.

```
GRANT SELECT, INSERT
   ON OFFICES
   TO SAM
```

The GRANT statement specifies a combination of a user-id (SAM), an object (the OFFICES table), and privileges (SELECT and INSERT). Once granted, the privileges can be rescinded later with this REVOKE statement:

Take away the privileges granted earlier to Sam Clark.

```
REVOKE SELECT, INSERT
   ON OFFICES
 FROM SAM
```

The GRANT and REVOKE statements are described in detail later in this chapter.

User-Ids

Each user of a SQL-based database is typically assigned a *user-id*, a short name that identifies the user to the DBMS software. The user-id is at the heart of SQL security. Every SQL statement executed by the DBMS is carried out on behalf of a specific user-id. The user-id determines whether the statement will be permitted or pro-hibited by the DBMS. In a production database, user-ids are assigned by the database administrator. A personal computer database may have only a single user-id, identifying the user who created and who owns the database. In special purpose databases (for example, those designed to be embedded within an appli-cation or a special purpose system), there may be no need for the additional overhead associated with SQL security. These databases typically operate as if there were a single user-id.

In practice, the restrictions on the names that can be chosen as user-ids vary from implementation to implementation. The SQL1 standard permitted user-ids of up to 18 characters and required them to be valid SQL names. In some mainframe DBMS systems, user-ids may have no more than eight characters. In Sybase and SQL Server, user-ids may have up to 30 characters. If portability is a concern, it's best to limit user-ids to eight or fewer characters. Figure 15-2 shows various users who need access to the sample database and typical user-ids assigned to them. Note that all of the users in the order processing department can be assigned the same user-id because they are to have identical privileges in the database.

The ANSI/ISO SQL standard uses the term *authorization-id* instead of user-id, and you will occasionally find this term used in other SQL documentation. Technically, "authorization-id" is a more accurate term because the role of the id is to determine authorization or privileges in the database. There are situations, as in Figure 15-2, where it makes sense to assign the same user-id to different users. In other situations, a single person may use two or three different user-ids. In a production database, authorization-ids may be associated with programs and groups of programs, rather than with human users. In each of these situations, "authorization-id" is a more precise and less confusing term than "user-id." However, the most common practice is to

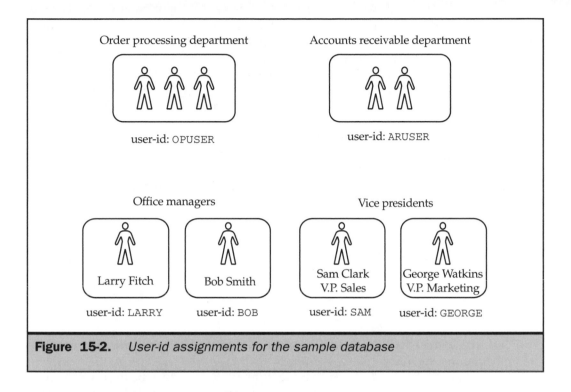

Figure 15-2. *User-id assignments for the sample database*

assign a different user-id to each person, and most SQL-based DBMS use the term "user-id" in their documentation.

User Authentication

The SQL standard specified that user-ids provide database security, but the specific mechanism for associating a user-id with a SQL statement is outside the scope of the standard because a database can be accessed in many different ways. For example, when you type SQL statements into an interactive SQL utility, how does the DBMS determine what user-id is associated with the statements? If you use a forms-based data entry or query program, how does the DBMS determine your user-id? On a database server, a report-generating program might be scheduled to run at a preset time every evening; what is the user-id in this situation, where there is no human "user"? Finally, how are user-ids handled when you access a database across a network, where your user identity on the system where you are actively working might be different than the user-id established on the system where the database resides?

Most commercial SQL implementations establish a user-id for each database *session*. In interactive SQL, the session begins when you start the interactive SQL program, and it lasts until you exit the program. In an application program using programmatic SQL, the session begins when the application program connects to the DBMS, and it ends when the application program terminates. All of the SQL statements used during the session are associated with the user-id specified for the session.

Usually you must supply both a user-id and an associated password at the beginning of a session. The DBMS checks the password to verify that you are, in fact, authorized to use the user-id that you supply. Although user-ids and passwords are common across most SQL products, the specific techniques used to specify the user-id and password vary from one product to another.

Some DBMS brands, especially those that are available on many different operating system platforms, implement their own user-id/password security. For example, when you use Oracle's interactive SQL program, called SQLPLUS, you specify a user name and associated password in the command that starts the program, like this:

```
SQLPLUS SCOTT/TIGER
```

The Sybase interactive SQL program, called ISQL, also accepts a user name and password, using this command format:

```
ISQL /USER=SCOTT /PASSWORD=TIGER
```

In each case, the DBMS validates the user-id (SCOTT) and the password (TIGER) before beginning the interactive SQL session.

Many other DBMS brands, including Ingres and Informix, use the user names of the host computer's operating system as database user-ids. For example, when you log in to a VAX/VMS computer system, you must supply a valid VMS user name and password to gain access. To start the Ingres interactive SQL utility, you simply give the command:

```
ISQL SALESDB
```

where SALESDB is the name of the Ingres database you want to use. Ingres automatically obtains your VMS user name and makes it your Ingres user-id for the session. Thus you don't have to specify a separate database user-id and password. DB2's interactive SQL, running under MVS/TSO, uses a similar technique. Your TSO login name automatically becomes your DB2 user-id for the interactive SQL session.

SQL security also applies to programmatic access to a database, so the DBMS must determine and authenticate the user-id for every application program that tries to access the database. Again, the techniques and rules for establishing the user-id vary from one brand of DBMS to another. For widely used utility programs, such as a data entry or an inquiry program, it is common for the program to ask the user for a user-id and password at the beginning of the session, via a screen dialog. For more specialized or custom-written programs, the appropriate user-id may be obvious from the application to be performed and "hard-wired" into the program. The SQL2 standard also allows a program to use an authorization-id associated with a specific set of SQL statements (called a *module*), rather than the user-id of the particular person running the program. With this mechanism, a program may be given the ability to perform very specific operations on a database on behalf of many different users, even if those users are not otherwise authorized to access the target data. This is a convenient capability that is finding its way into mainstream SQL implementations. The specifics of SQL security for database access programs are described in Chapter 17, which covers programmatic SQL.

User Groups

A large production database often has groups of users with similar needs. In the sample database, for example, the three people in the order processing department form a natural user group, and the two people in the accounts receivable department form another natural group. Within each group, all of the users have identical needs for data access and should have identical privileges.

Under the ANSI/ISO SQL security scheme, you can handle groups of users with similar needs in one of two ways:

- You can assign the same user-id to every person in the group, as shown in Figure 15-2. This scheme simplifies security administration because it allows you to specify data access privileges once for the single user-id. However, under this scheme the people sharing the user-id cannot be distinguished from one another in system operator displays and DBMS reports.

- You can assign a different user-id to every person in the group. This scheme lets you differentiate between the users in reports produced by the DBMS, and it lets you establish different privileges for the individual users later. However, you must specify privileges for each user individually, making security administration tedious and error-prone.

The scheme you choose will depend upon the trade-offs in your particular database and application.

Several DBMS brands, including Sybase and SQL Server, offer a third alternative for dealing with groups of similar users. They support group-ids, which identify groups of related user-ids. Privileges can be granted both to individual user-ids and to group-ids, and a user may carry out a database action if it is permitted by either the user-id or group-id privileges. Group-ids thus simplify the administration of privileges given to groups of users. However, they are nonstandard and a database design using them may not be portable to another DBMS brand.

DB2 also supports groups of users but takes a different approach. The DB2 database administrator can configure DB2 so that when you first connect to DB2 and supply your user-id (known as your *primary authorization-id*), DB2 automatically looks up a set of additional user-ids (known as *secondary authorization-ids*) that you may use. When DB2 later checks your privileges, it checks the privileges for all of your authorization-ids, primary and secondary. The DB2 database administrator normally sets up the secondary authorization-ids so that they are the same as the user group names used by RACF, the IBM mainframe security facility. Thus the DB2 approach effectively provides group-ids but does so without adding to the user-id mechanism.

Security Objects

SQL security protections apply to specific *objects* contained in a database. The SQL1 standard specified two types of security objects—tables and views. Thus each table and view can be individually protected. Access to a table or view can be permitted for certain user-ids and prohibited for other user-ids. The SQL2 standard expanded security protections to include other objects, including domains and user-defined character sets, and added a new type of protection for table or view access.

Most commercial SQL products support additional security objects. In a SQL Server database, for example, a stored procedure is an important database object. The SQL security scheme determines which users can create and drop stored procedures and which users are allowed to execute them. In IBM's DB2, the physical tablespaces where tables are stored are treated as security objects. The database administrator can give some user-ids permission to create new tables in a particular tablespace and deny that permission to other user-ids. Other SQL implementations support other security objects. However, the underlying SQL security scheme—of specific privileges applied to specific objects, granted or revoked through the same SQL statements—is almost universally applied.

Privileges

The set of actions that a user can carry out against a database object are called the *privileges* for the object. The SQL1 standard specified four basic privileges for tables and views:

- The SELECT privilege allows you to retrieve data from a table or view. With this privilege, you can specify the table or view in the FROM clause of a SELECT statement or subquery.

- The INSERT privilege allows you to insert new rows into a table or view. With this privilege, you can specify the table or view in the INTO clause of an INSERT statement.

- The DELETE privilege allows you to delete rows of data from a table or view. With this privilege, you can specify the table or view in the FROM clause of a DELETE statement.

- The UPDATE privilege allows you to modify rows of data in a table or view. With this privilege, you can specify the table or view as the target table in an UPDATE statement. The UPDATE privilege can be restricted to specific columns of the table or view, allowing updates to these columns but disallowing updates to any other columns.

These four privileges are supported by virtually all commercial SQL products.

SQL2 Extended Privileges

The SQL2 standard expanded the basic SQL1 privileges in several dimensions. It added new capabilities to the SQL1 INSERT and UPDATE privileges. It added a new REFERENCES privilege that restricts a user's ability to create a reference to a table from a foreign key in another table. It also added a new USAGE privilege that controls access to the new SQL2 database structures of domains, character sets, collation sequences, and translations.

The SQL2 extensions to the INSERT and UPDATE privileges are straightforward. These privileges may now be granted for a specific column or columns within a table, instead of applying to the entire table. The sample database provides a simple example of how this capability can be useful. Suppose you wanted to give your human resources manager the responsibility to insert new employees into the SALESREPS table, once their hiring paperwork is complete. The HR manager should supply the employee number, name, and similar information. But it should be the responsibility of the sales VP to set the QUOTA column for the new employee. Adjustments to the SALES column for existing employees would be similarly restricted. Using the new SQL2 capabilities, you could implement this scheme by giving the HR manager INSERT privileges on the appropriate columns. The other columns (such as SALES and QUOTA) for any newly inserted employees would initially have the NULL value. With the UPDATE privilege on the other columns, the sales VP can then set the appropriate quota. Without the ability to specify these privileges on specific columns, you would have to either relax the restrictions on column access or define extraneous views on the table simply to restrict access.

The SQL2 standard does not allow the SELECT privilege to be applied to specific columns like the new INSERT and UPDATE capabilities; it must still be specified for an entire table. Theoretically, this capability isn't really needed, since you can achieve the same effect by defining a view on the table, limiting the view to specific columns, and then defining the appropriate privileges on the view. However, a column-specific SELECT privilege can be a much more straightforward approach. It keeps the structure of the database simpler (fewer view definitions) and concentrates the security scheme more tightly in one place (the GRANT statements). Several major DBMS brands, including Sybase and SQL Server, allow you to specify column-specific SELECT privileges, using the same syntax as for the column-specific UPDATE and INSERT. The SQL2 standard includes a note that this capability is also intended to be considered for future updates of the standard.

The new SQL2 REFERENCES privilege deals with a more subtle SQL security issue posed by the SQL2 capabilities of foreign keys and check constraints. Using the sample database as an example, suppose an employee has the ability to create a new table in the database (for example, a table containing new product information) but does not have any access to the employee information in the SALESREPS table. You might assume, given this security scheme, that there is no way for him to determine the employee numbers being used or whether a new employee has been hired. However, this isn't strictly true. The employee could create a new table, with a column that is defined as a foreign key to the SALESREPS table (recall that this means the only legal values for this column are primary key values for the SALESREPS table—that is, valid employee numbers). With this new table, the employee can simply try to insert new rows with different values in the foreign key column. The INSERT statements that succeed tell the employee that that he has discovered a valid employee number; those that fail represent invalid employee numbers.

Even more serious problems can be created by a new table defined with a check constraint on a column. For example, suppose the employee tries to execute this CREATE TABLE statement:

```
CREATE TABLE XYZ (TRYIT MONEY,
      CHECK ((SELECT QUOTA
                 FROM SALESREPS
                 WHERE TITLE = 'VP Sales')
   BETWEEN 400000 AND 500000))
```

Because of the column constraint linked to a value from the SALESREPS table, if this statement succeeds, it means the VP sales has a quota in the specified range! If it doesn't, the employee can keep trying similar CREATE TABLE statements until she has determined the appropriate quota.

To eliminate this "backdoor" access to data, the SQL2 standard specifies a new REFERENCES privilege. Like the INSERT and UPDATE privileges, the REFERENCES privilege is granted for specific columns of a table. Only if a user has the REFERENCES privilege for a column is he or she allowed to create a new table that refers to that existing column in any way (for example, as the target of a foreign key reference, or in a check constraint, as in the previous examples). In databases that don't yet implement the REFERENCES privilege but do support foreign keys or check constraints, the SELECT privilege is sometimes used in this role.

Finally, the SQL2 standard specifies the USAGE privilege to control access to domains (sets of legal column values), user-defined character sets, collating sequences, and translations. The USAGE privilege is a simple on/off switch that either allows or disallows the use of these SQL2 database objects, by name, for individual user-ids. For example, with the USAGE privilege on a domain, you can define a new table with a column whose data type is defined as that domain. Without the privilege, you cannot create such a column definition. These privileges are directed mostly toward simplifying administration of large corporate databases that are used and modified by many different development teams. They typically do not present the same kinds of security issues as the table and column access privileges.

Ownership Privileges

When you create a table with the CREATE TABLE statement, you become its owner and receive full privileges for the table (SELECT, INSERT, DELETE, UPDATE, and any other privileges supported by the DBMS). Other users initially have no privileges on the newly created table. If they are to be given access to the table, you must explicitly grant privileges to them, using the GRANT statement.

When you create a view with the CREATE VIEW statement, you become the owner of the view, but you do not necessarily receive full privileges on it. In order to create the view successfully, you must already have the SELECT privilege on each of the source tables for the view; therefore, the DBMS gives you the SELECT privilege for the view automatically. For each of the other privileges (INSERT, DELETE, and UPDATE), the DBMS gives you the privilege on the view only if you hold that same privilege on *every* source table for the view.

Other Privileges

Many commercial DBMS products offer additional table and view privileges beyond the basic SELECT, INSERT, DELETE, and UPDATE privileges. For example, Oracle and the IBM mainframe databases support an ALTER and an INDEX privilege for tables. A user with the ALTER privilege on a particular table can use the ALTER TABLE statement to modify the definition of the table; a user with the INDEX privilege can create an index for the table with the CREATE INDEX statement. In DBMS brands that do not support the ALTER and INDEX privileges, only the owner may use the ALTER TABLE and CREATE INDEX statements.

Additional privileges are frequently supported for DBMS security objects other than tables and views. For example, Sybase and SQL Server support an EXECUTE privilege for stored procedures, which determines whether a user is allowed to execute a stored procedure. DB2 supports a USE privilege for tablespaces, which determines whether a user can create tables in a specific tablespace.

Views and SQL Security

In addition to the restrictions on table access provided by the SQL privileges, views also play a key role in SQL security. By carefully defining a view and giving a user permission to access the view but not its source tables, you can effectively restrict the user's access to only selected columns and rows. Views thus offer a way to exercise very precise control over what data is made visible to which users.

For example, suppose you wanted to enforce this security rule in the sample database:

Accounts receivable personnel should be able to retrieve employee numbers, names, and office numbers from the SALESREPS table, but data about sales and quotas should not be available to them.

You can implement this security rule by defining a view as follows:

```
CREATE VIEW REPINFO AS
    SELECT EMPL_NUM, NAME, REP_OFFICE
        FROM SALESREPS
```

and giving the SELECT privilege for the view to the ARUSER user-id, as shown in Figure 15-3. This example uses a vertical view to restrict access to specific columns.

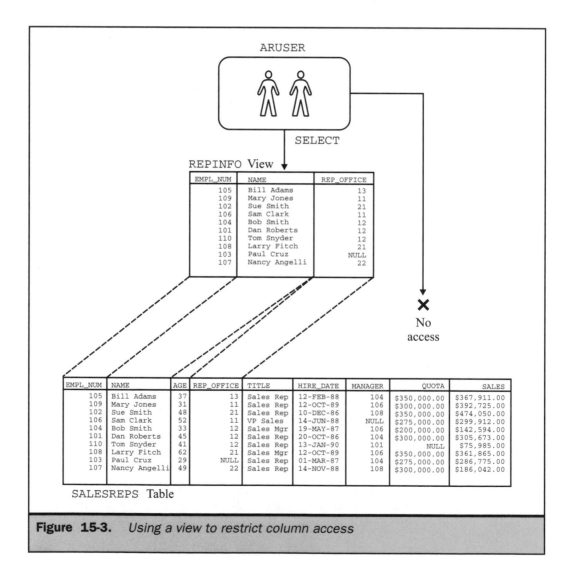

Figure 15-3. *Using a view to restrict column access*

Horizontal views are also effective for enforcing security rules such as this one:

The sales managers in each region should have full access to SALESREPS data for the salespeople assigned to that region.

As shown in Figure 15-4, you can define two views, EASTVIEWS and WESTVIEWS, containing SALESREPS data for each of the two regions, and then grant each office manager access to the appropriate view.

Of course, views can be much more complex than the simple row and column subsets of a single table shown in these examples. By defining a view with a grouped query, you can give a user access to summary data but not to the detailed rows in the underlying table. A view can also combine data from two or more tables, providing precisely the data needed by a particular user and denying access to all other data. The usefulness of views for implementing SQL security is limited by the two fundamental restrictions described earlier in Chapter 14:

- *Update restrictions*. The SELECT privilege can be used with read-only views to limit data retrieval, but the INSERT, DELETE, and UPDATE privileges are meaningless for these views. If a user must update the data visible in a

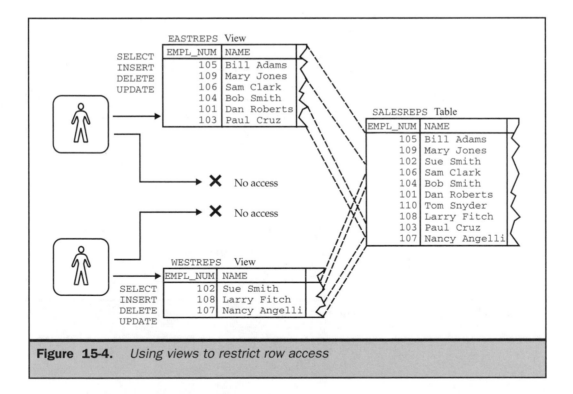

Figure 15-4.   *Using views to restrict row access*

read-only view, the user must be given permission to update the underlying tables and must use INSERT, DELETE, and UPDATE statements that reference those tables.

■ *Performance.* Because the DBMS translates every access to a view into a corresponding access to its source tables, views can add significant overhead to database operations. Views cannot be used indiscriminately to restrict database access without causing overall database performance to suffer.

Granting Privileges (GRANT)

The basic GRANT statement, shown in Figure 15-5, is used to grant security privileges on database objects to specific users. Normally the GRANT statement is used by the owner of a table or view to give other users access to the data. As shown in the figure, the GRANT statement includes a specific list of the privileges to be granted, the name of the table to which the privileges apply, and the user-id to which the privileges are granted.

The GRANT statement shown in the syntax diagram conforms to the ANSI/ISO SQL standard. Many DBMS brands follow the DB2 GRANT statement syntax, which is more

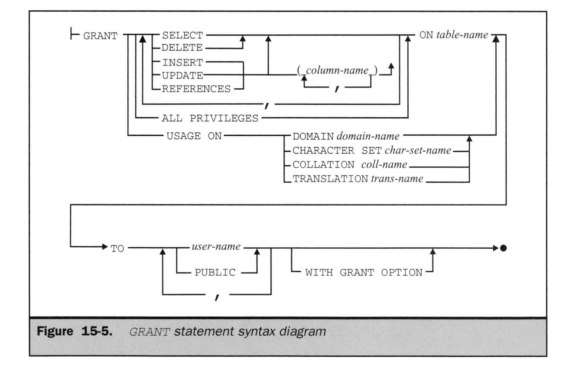

Figure 15-5. *GRANT statement syntax diagram*

flexible. The DB2 syntax allows you to specify a list of user-ids and a list of tables, making it simpler to grant many privileges at once. Here are some examples of simple GRANT statements for the sample database:

Give order processing users full access to the ORDERS table.

```
GRANT SELECT, INSERT, DELETE, UPDATE
   ON ORDERS
   TO OPUSER
```

Let accounts receivable users retrieve customer data and add new customers to the CUSTOMERS table, but give order processing users read-only access.

```
GRANT SELECT, INSERT
   ON CUSTOMERS
   TO ARUSER
```

```
GRANT SELECT
   ON CUSTOMERS
   TO OPUSER
```

Allow Sam Clark to insert or delete an office.

```
GRANT INSERT, DELETE
   ON OFFICES
   TO SAM
```

For convenience, the GRANT statement provides two shortcuts that you can use when granting many privileges or when granting them to many users. Instead of specifically listing all of the privileges available for a particular object, you can use the keywords ALL PRIVILEGES. This GRANT statement gives Sam Clark, the vice president of sales, full access to the SALESREPS table:

Give all privileges on the SALESREPS table to Sam Clark.

```
GRANT ALL PRIVILEGES
   ON SALESREPS
   TO SAM
```

Instead of giving privileges to every user of the database one-by-one, you can use the keyword PUBLIC to grant a privilege to every authorized database user. This GRANT statement lets anyone retrieve data from the OFFICES table:

Give all users SELECT access to the OFFICES table.

```
GRANT SELECT
   ON OFFICES
   TO PUBLIC
```

Note that this GRANT statement grants access to all present and future authorized users, not just to the user-ids currently known to the DBMS. This eliminates the need for you to explicitly grant privileges to new users as they are authorized.

Column Privileges

The SQL1 standard allowed you to grant the UPDATE privilege for individual columns of a table or view, and the SQL2 standard allows a column list for INSERT and REFERENCES privileges as well. The columns are listed after the UPDATE, INSERT, or REFERENCES keyword and enclosed in parentheses. Here is a GRANT statement that allows the order processing department to update only the company name and assigned salesperson columns of the CUSTOMERS table:

Let order processing users change company names and salesperson assignments.

```
GRANT UPDATE (COMPANY, CUST_REP)
   ON CUSTOMERS
   TO OPUSER
```

If the column list is omitted, the privilege applies to all columns of the table or view, as in this example:

Let accounts receivable users change any customer information.

```
GRANT UPDATE
   ON CUSTOMERS
   TO ARUSER
```

The ANSI/ISO standard does not permit a column list for the SELECT privilege; it requires that the SELECT privilege apply to all of the columns of a table or view. In practice, this isn't a serious restriction. To grant access to specific columns, you first define a view on the table that includes only those columns and then grant the SELECT privilege for the view only, as described earlier in this chapter. However, views defined solely for security purposes can clog the structure of an otherwise simple database. For this reason, some DBMS brands allow a column list for the SELECT privilege. For example, the following GRANT statement is legal for the Sybase, SQL Server, and Informix DBMS brands:

Give accounts receivable users read-only access to the employee number, name, and sales office columns of the SALESREPS table.

```
GRANT SELECT (EMPL_NUM, NAME, REP_OFFICE)
   ON SALESREPS
   TO ARUSER
```

This GRANT statement eliminates the need for the REPINFO view defined in Figure 15-3, and in practice it can eliminate the need for many views in a production database. However, the use of a column list for the SELECT privilege is unique to certain SQL dialects, and it is not permitted by the ANSI/ISO standard or by the IBM SQL products.

Passing Privileges (GRANT OPTION)

When you create a database object and become its owner, you are the only person who can grant privileges to use the object. When you grant privileges to other users, they are allowed to use the object, but they cannot pass those privileges on to other users. In this way, the owner of an object maintains very tight control both over who has permission to use the object and over what forms of access are allowed.

Occasionally you may want to allow other users to grant privileges on an object that you own. For example, consider again the EASTREPS and WESTREPS views in the sample database. Sam Clark, the vice president of sales, created these views and owns them. He can give the Los Angeles office manager, Larry Fitch, permission to use the WESTREPS view with this GRANT statement:

```
GRANT SELECT
   ON WESTREPS
   TO LARRY
```

What happens if Larry wants to give Sue Smith (user-id SUE) permission to access the WESTREPS data because she is doing some sales forecasting for the Los Angeles office? With the preceding GRANT statement, he cannot give her the required privilege. Only Sam Clark can grant the privilege, because he owns the view.

If Sam wants to give Larry discretion over who may use the WESTREPS view, he can use this variation of the previous GRANT statement:

```
GRANT SELECT
   ON WESTREPS
   TO LARRY
 WITH GRANT OPTION
```

Because of the WITH GRANT OPTION clause, this GRANT statement conveys, along with the specified privileges, the right to grant those privileges to other users.

Larry can now issue this GRANT statement:

```
GRANT SELECT
   ON WESTREPS
   TO SUE
```

which allows Sue Smith to retrieve data from the WESTREPS view. Figure 15-6 graphically illustrates the flow of privileges, first from Sam to Larry, and then from Larry to Sue. Because the GRANT statement issued by Larry did not include the WITH GRANT OPTION clause, the chain of permissions ends with Sue; she can retrieve the WESTREPS data but cannot grant access to another user. However, if Larry's grant of privileges to Sue had included the GRANT OPTION, the chain could continue to another level, allowing Sue to grant access to other users.

Alternatively, Larry might construct a view for Sue including only the salespeople in the Los Angeles office and give her access to that view:

```
CREATE VIEW LAREPS AS
     SELECT *
       FROM WESTREPS
      WHERE OFFICE = 21

GRANT ALL PRIVILEGES
   ON LAREPS
   TO SUE
```

Larry is the owner of the LAREPS view, but he does not own the WESTREPS view from which this new view is derived. To maintain effective security, the DBMS requires that Larry not only have SELECT privilege on WESTREPS, but also requires that he have the GRANT OPTION for that privilege before allowing him to grant the SELECT privilege on LAREPS to Sue.

Once a user has been granted certain privileges with the GRANT OPTION, that user may grant those privileges *and the GRANT OPTION* to other users. Those other users can,

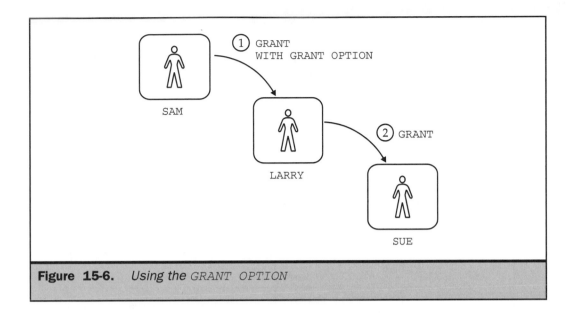

Figure 15-6. *Using the* GRANT OPTION

in turn, continue to grant both the privileges and the GRANT OPTION. For this reason you should use great care when giving other users the GRANT OPTION. Note that the GRANT OPTION applies only to the specific privileges named in the GRANT statement. If you want to grant certain privileges with the GRANT OPTION and grant other privileges without it, you must use two separate GRANT statements, as in this example:

Let Larry Fitch retrieve, insert, update, and delete data from the WESTREPS *table, and let him grant retrieval permission to other users.*

```
GRANT SELECT
    ON WESTREPS
    TO LARRY
 WITH GRANT OPTION

GRANT INSERT, DELETE, UPDATE
    ON WESTREPS
    TO LARRY
```

Revoking Privileges (REVOKE)

In most SQL-based databases, the privileges that you have granted with the GRANT statement can be taken away with the REVOKE statement, shown in Figure 15-7.

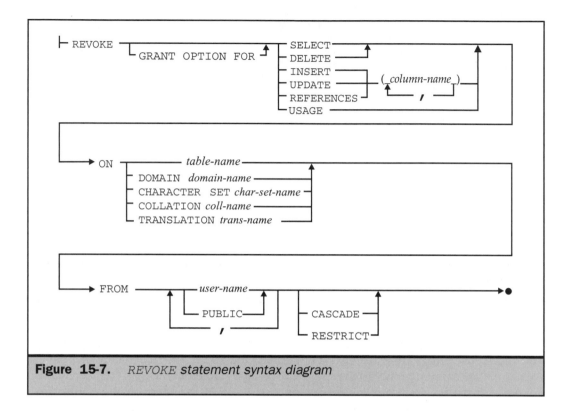

Figure 15-7. *REVOKE statement syntax diagram*

The REVOKE statement has a structure that closely parallels the GRANT statement, specifying a specific set of privileges to be taken away, for a specific database object, from one or more user-ids.

A REVOKE statement may take away all or some of the privileges that you previously granted to a user-id. For example, consider this statement sequence:

Grant and then revoke some SALESREPS table privileges.

```
GRANT SELECT, INSERT, UPDATE
   ON SALESREPS
   TO ARUSER, OPUSER

REVOKE INSERT, UPDATE
   ON SALESREPS
 FROM OPUSER
```

The INSERT and UPDATE privileges on the SALESREPS table are first given to the two users and then revoked from one of them. However, the SELECT privilege remains for both user-ids. Here are some other examples of the REVOKE statement:

Take away all privileges granted earlier on the OFFICES table.

```
REVOKE ALL PRIVILEGES
    ON OFFICES
  FROM ARUSER
```

Take away UPDATE and DELETE privileges for two user-ids.

```
REVOKE UPDATE, DELETE
    ON OFFICES
  FROM ARUSER, OPUSER
```

Take away all privileges on the OFFICES that were formerly granted to all users.

```
REVOKE ALL PRIVILEGES
    ON OFFICES
  FROM PUBLIC
```

When you issue a REVOKE statement, you can take away only those privileges that *you* previously granted to another user. That user may also have privileges that were granted by other users; those privileges are not affected by your REVOKE statement. Note specifically that if two different users grant the same privilege on the same object to a user and one of them later revokes the privilege, the second user's grant will still allow the user to access the object. This handling of "overlapping grants" of privileges is illustrated in the following example sequence.

Suppose that Sam Clark, the sales vice president, gives Larry Fitch SELECT privileges for the SALESREPS table and SELECT and UPDATE privileges for the ORDERS table, using the following statements:

```
GRANT SELECT
    ON SALESREPS
    TO LARRY

GRANT SELECT, UPDATE
    ON ORDERS
    TO LARRY
```

A few days later George Watkins, the marketing vice president, gives Larry the SELECT and DELETE privileges for the ORDERS table and the SELECT privilege for the CUSTOMERS table, using these statements:

```
GRANT SELECT, DELETE
   ON ORDERS
   TO LARRY

GRANT SELECT
   ON CUSTOMERS
   TO LARRY
```

Note that Larry has received privileges on the ORDERS table from two different sources. In fact, the SELECT privilege on the ORDERS table has been granted by both sources. A few days later, Sam revokes the privileges he previously granted to Larry for the ORDERS table:

```
REVOKE SELECT, UPDATE
   ON ORDERS
 FROM LARRY
```

After the DBMS processes the REVOKE statement, Larry still retains the SELECT privilege on the SALESREPS table, the SELECT and DELETE privileges on the ORDERS table, and the SELECT privilege on the CUSTOMERS table, but he has lost the UPDATE privilege on the ORDERS table.

REVOKE and the GRANT OPTION

When you grant privileges with the GRANT OPTION and later revoke these privileges, most DBMS brands will *automatically* revoke all privileges derived from the original grant. Consider again the chain of privileges in Figure 15-6, from Sam Clark, the sales vice president, to Larry Fitch, the Los Angeles office manager, and then to Sue Smith. If Sam now revokes Larry's privileges for the WESTREPS view, Sue's privilege is automatically revoked as well.

The situation gets more complicated if two or more users have granted privileges and one of them later revokes the privileges. Consider Figure 15-8, a slight variation on the last example. Here Larry receives the SELECT privilege with the GRANT OPTION from both Sam (the sales vice president) and George (the marketing vice president) and then grants privileges to Sue. This time when Sam revokes Larry's privileges, the grant of privileges from George remains. Furthermore, Sue's privileges also remain because they can be derived from George's grant.

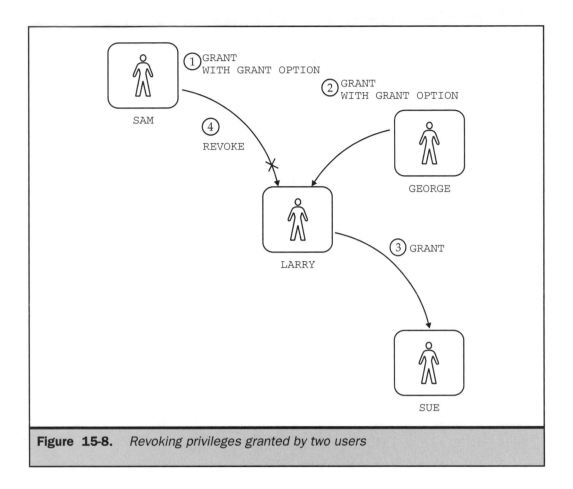

Figure 15-8. *Revoking privileges granted by two users*

However, consider another variation on the chain of privileges, with the events slightly rearranged, as shown in Figure 15-9. Here Larry receives the privilege with the GRANT OPTION from Sam, grants the privilege to Sue, and *then* receives the grant, with the GRANT OPTION, from George. This time when Sam revokes Larry's privileges, the results are slightly different, and they may vary from one DBMS to another. As in Figure 15-8, Larry retains the SELECT privilege on the WESTREPS view because the grant from George is still intact. But in a DB2 or SQL/DS database, Sue automatically loses her SELECT privilege on the table. Why? Because the grant from Larry to Sue was clearly derived from the grant from Sam to Larry, which has just been revoked. It could not have been derived from George's grant to Larry because that grant had not yet taken place when the grant from Larry to Sue was made.

In a different brand of DBMS, Sue's privileges might remain intact because the grant from George to Larry remains intact. Thus the time sequence of GRANT and

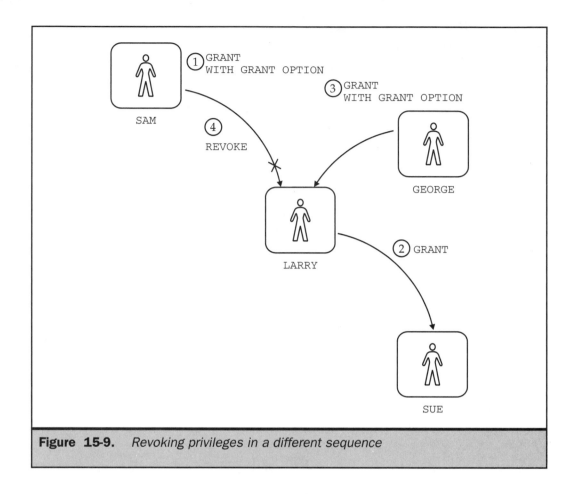

Figure 15-9. *Revoking privileges in a different sequence*

REVOKE statements, rather than just the privileges themselves, can determine how far the effects of a REVOKE statement will cascade. Granting and revoking privileges with the GRANT OPTION must be handled very carefully, to ensure that the results are those you intend.

REVOKE **and the ANSI/ISO Standard**

The SQL1 standard specified the GRANT statement as part of the SQL Data Definition Language (DDL). Recall from Chapter 13 that the SQL1 standard treated the DDL as a separate, static definition of a database and did not require that the DBMS permit dynamic changes to database structure. This approach applies to database security as well. Under the SQL1 standard, accessibility to tables and views in the database is determined by a series of GRANT statements included in the database schema. There is no mechanism for changing the security scheme once the database structure is defined. The REVOKE statement is therefore absent from the SQL1 standard, just as the DROP TABLE statement is missing from the standard.

Despite its absence from the SQL1 standard, the REVOKE statement was provided by virtually all commercial SQL-based DBMS products since their earliest versions. As with the DROP and ALTER statements, the DB2 dialect of SQL has effectively set the standard for the REVOKE statement. The SQL2 standard includes a specification for the REVOKE statement based on the DB2 statement with some extensions. One of the extensions gives the user more explicit control over how privileges are revoked when the privileges have, in turn, been granted to others. The other provides a way to revoke the GRANT OPTION without revoking the privileges themselves.

To specify how the DBMS should handle the revoking of privileges that have been in turn granted to others, the SQL2 standard requires that a CASCADE or RESTRICT option be specified in a REVOKE statement. (A similar requirement applies to many of the DROP statements in the SQL2 standard, as described in Chapter 13.) Suppose that SELECT and UPDATE privileges have previously been granted to Larry on the ORDERS table, with the GRANT OPTION, and that Larry has further granted these options to Bill. Then this REVOKE statement:

```
REVOKE SELECT, UPDATE
    ON ORDERS
  FROM LARRY CASCADE
```

revokes not only Larry's privileges, but Bill's as well. The effect of the REVOKE statement thus "cascades" to all other users whose privileges have flowed from the original GRANT.

Now, assume the same circumstances and this REVOKE statement:

```
REVOKE SELECT, UPDATE
    ON ORDERS
  FROM LARRY RESTRICT
```

In this case, the REVOKE fails. The RESTRICT option tells the DBMS not to execute the statement if it will affect any other privileges in the database. The resulting error calls the user's attention to the fact that there are (possibly unintentional) side-effects of the REVOKE statement and allows the user to reconsider the action. If the user wants to go ahead and revoke the privileges, the CASCADE option can be specified.

The SQL2 version of the REVOKE statement also gives a user more explicit, separate control over privileges and the GRANT OPTION for those privileges. Suppose again that Larry has been granted privileges on the ORDERS table, with the GRANT OPTION for those privileges. The usual REVOKE statement for those privileges:

```
REVOKE SELECT, UPDATE
    ON ORDERS
  FROM LARRY
```

takes away both the privileges and the ability to grant those privileges to others. The SQL2 standard permits this version of the REVOKE statement:

```
REVOKE GRANT OPTION FOR SELECT, UPDATE
    ON ORDERS
  FROM LARRY CASCADE
```

If the statement is successful, Larry will lose the ability to grant these privileges to other users, but he will not lose the privileges themselves. As before, the SQL2 standard requires the CASCADE or the RESTRICT option to specify how the DBMS should handle the statement if Larry has, in turn, granted the GRANT OPTION to other users.

Summary

The SQL language is used to specify the security restrictions for a SQL-based database:

- The SQL security scheme is built around privileges (permitted actions) that can be granted on specific database objects (such as tables and views) to specific user-ids (users or groups of users).

- Views also play a key role in SQL security because they can be used to restrict access to specific rows or specific columns of a table.

- The GRANT statement is used to grant privileges; privileges that you grant to a user with the GRANT OPTION can in turn be granted by that user to others.

- The REVOKE statement is used to revoke privileges previously granted with the GRANT statement.

Chapter 16

The System Catalog

A database management system must keep track of a great deal of information about the structure of a database in order to perform its data management functions. In a relational database, this information is typically stored in the *system catalog*, a collection of system tables that the DBMS maintains for its own use. The information in the system catalog describes the tables, views, columns, privileges, and other structural features of the database.

Although the DBMS maintains the system catalog primarily for its own internal purposes, the system tables or views based on them are usually accessible to database users, as well, through standard SQL queries. A relational database is thus self-describing; using queries against the system tables, you can ask the database to describe its own structure. General-purpose database "front-ends," such as query tools and report writers, use this self-describing feature to generate lists of tables and columns for user selection, simplifying database access.

This chapter describes the system catalogs provided by several popular SQL-based DBMS products and the information that the catalogs contain. It also describes the system catalog capabilities specified by the ANSI/ISO SQL2 standard.

What Is the System Catalog?

The system catalog is a collection of special tables in a database that are owned, created, and maintained by the DBMS itself. These *system tables* contain data that describes the structure of the database. The tables in the system catalog are automatically created when the database is created. They are usually gathered under a special "system user-id" with a name like SYSTEM, SYSIBM, MASTER, or DBA.

The DBMS constantly refers to the data in the system catalog while processing SQL statements. For example, to process a two-table SELECT statement, the DBMS must:

- Verify that the two named tables actually exist.
- Ensure that the user has permission to access them.
- Check whether the columns referenced in the query exist.
- Resolve any unqualified column names to one of the tables.
- Determine the data type of each column.

By storing structural information in system tables, the DBMS can use its own access methods and logic to rapidly and efficiently retrieve the information it needs to perform these tasks.

If the system tables were only used internally to the DBMS, they would be of little interest to database users. However, the DBMS generally makes the system tables available for user access as well. If the system tables themselves are not made available, the DBMS generally provides views based on the system tables that offer a set of user-retrievable catalog information. User queries against the system catalogs or views are almost always permitted by personal computer and minicomputer databases.

These queries are also supported by mainframe DBMS products, but the database administrator may restrict system catalog access to provide an additional measure of database security. By querying the system catalogs, you can discover information about the structure of a database, even if you have never used it before.

User access to the system catalog is read-only. The DBMS prevents users from directly updating or modifying the system tables because such modifications would destroy the integrity of the database. Instead, the DBMS itself takes care of inserting, deleting, and updating rows of the system tables as it modifies the structure of a database. DDL statements such as CREATE, ALTER, DROP, GRANT, and REVOKE produce changes in the system tables as a by-product of their actions. In some DBMS products, even DML statements that modify the database, such as INSERT and DELETE, may produce changes in the system tables, which keep track of how many rows are in each table.

The Catalog and Query Tools

One of the most important benefits of the system catalog is that it makes possible user-friendly query tools, as shown in Figure 16-1. The objective of such a tool is to let users simply and transparently access the database without learning the SQL language. Typically, the tool leads the user through a series of steps like this one:

1. The user gives a name and password for database access.

2. The query tool displays a list of available tables.

3. The user chooses a table, causing the query tool to display a list of the columns it contains.

4. The user chooses columns of interest, perhaps by clicking on their names as they appear on a PC screen.

5. The user chooses columns from other tables or restricts the data to be retrieved with a search condition.

6. The query tool retrieves the requested data and displays it on the user's screen.

A general-purpose query tool like the one in Figure 16-1 will be used by many different users, and it will be used to access many different databases. The tool cannot possibly know in advance the structure of the database that it will access during any given session. Thus, it must be able to dynamically learn about the tables and columns of a database. The tool uses system catalog queries for this purpose.

The Catalog and the ANSI/ISO Standard

The ANSI/ISO SQL1 standard did not specify the structure and contents of the system catalog. In fact, the SQL1 standard does not require a system catalog at all. However, all of the major SQL-based DBMS products provide a system catalog in one form or another. The structure of the catalog and the tables it contains vary considerably from one brand of DBMS to another.

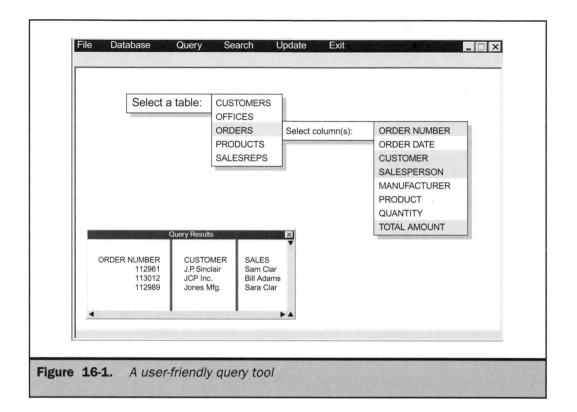

Figure 16-1. *A user-friendly query tool*

Because of the growing importance of general-purpose database tools that must access the system catalog, the SQL2 standard includes a specification of a set of views that provide standardized access to information typically found in the system catalog. A DBMS that conforms to the SQL2 standard must support these views, which are collectively called the INFORMATION_SCHEMA. Because this schema is more complex than the actual system catalogs used by commercial DBMS products, and is only slowly being supported, it is described in a separate section near the end of this chapter.

Catalog Contents

Each table in the system catalog contains information about a single kind of structural element in the database. Although the details vary, almost all commercial SQL products include system tables that describe each of these five entities:

- *Tables.* The catalog describes each table in the database, identifying its table name, its owner, the number of columns it contains, its size, and so on.

- *Columns.* The catalog describes each column in the database, giving the column's name, the table to which it belongs, its data type, its size, whether NULLs are allowed, and so on.

- *Users.* The catalog describes each authorized database user, including the user's name, an encrypted form of the user's password, and other data.

- *Views.* The catalog describes each view defined in the database, including its name, the name of its owner, the query that defines the view, and so on.

- *Privileges.* The catalog describes each set of privileges granted in the database, including the names of the grantor and grantee, the privileges granted, the object on which the privileges have been granted, and so on.

Table 16-1 shows the names of the system tables that provide this information in each of the major SQL-based DBMS products. The remainder of this chapter describes some typical system tables in more detail and gives examples of system catalog access. Because of the wide variations among the system catalogs among DBMS brands, a complete description of the system catalogs and complete examples for all of the major DBMS brands is beyond the scope of this book. With the information provided here, you should be able to consult the system documentation for your DBMS brand and construct the appropriate system catalog queries.

Table Information

Each of the major SQL products has a system table or view that keeps track of the tables in the database. In DB2, for example, this information is provided by a system catalog view named SYSCAT.TABLES. (All of the DB2 system catalog views are part of a schema named SYSCAT, so they all have qualified table/view names of the form SYSCAT.*xxx*.)

Table 16-2 shows some of the columns of the SYSCAT.TABLES view. It contains one row for each table, view, or alias defined in the database. The information in this view is typical of that provided by the corresponding views in other major DBMS products.

You can use queries like the following examples to find out information about the tables in a DB2 database. Similar queries, using different table and column names, can be used to obtain the same information from other DBMS brands.

List the names and owners of all tables in the database.

```
SELECT DEFINER, TABNAME
  FROM SYSCAT.TABLES
 WHERE TYPE = 'T'
```

DBMS	Tables	Columns	Users	Views	Privileges
DB2[1]	SCHEMATA TABLES REFERENCES KEYCOLUSE	COLUMNS	DBAUTH	VIEWS VIEWDEP	SCHEMAAUTH TABAUTH COLAUTH

Oracle	USER_
	  CATALOG
	USER_TABLES
	ALL_TABLES
	USER_
	  SYNONYMS
		USER_TAB_
		  COLUMNS
		ALL_TAB_
		  COLUMNS
			ALL_USERS	USER_VIEWS
				ALL_VIEWS
					USER_TAB_
					  PRIVS
					USER_COL_
					  PRIVS
					USER_SYS_
					  PRIVS

Informix	SYSTABLES SYSREFER- ENCES SYSSYNONYMS	SYSCOLUMNS	SYSUSERS	SYSVIEWS SYSDEPEND	SYSTABAUTH SYSCOLAUTH
Sybase	SYSDATA- BASES SYSOBJECTS SYSKEYS	SYSCOLUMNS	SYSUSERS	SYSOBJECTS SYSCOMMENTS	

SQL Server	SYSDATA-
	  BASES
	SYSOBJECTS
	SYSFOREIGN-
	  KEYS
	SYSREFER-
	  ENCES
		SYSCOLUMNS	SYSUSERS
			SYSLOGINS
			SYSMEMBERS
				SYSOBJECTS
				SYSDEPENDS
				SYSCOMMENTS
					SYSPROTECTS

[1]DB2 tables have the qualifier SYSCAT (e.g. SYSCAT.TABLES)

Table 16-1. *Selected System Tables in Popular SQL-Based Products*

Column Name	Data Type	Information
TABSCHEMA	CHAR(8)	Schema containing the table, view or alias
TABNAME	VARCHAR(18)	Name of the table, view or alias
DEFINER	CHAR(8)	User-id of table/view/alias creator
TYPE	CHAR(1)	T=table / V=view / A=alias
STATUS	CHAR(1)	Status of object (system use)
BASE_TABSCHEMA	CHAR(8)	Schema of "base" table for an alias
BASE_TABNAME	VARCHAR(18)	Name of "base" table for an alias
CREATE_TIME	TIMESTAMP	Time of object creation
STATS_TIME	TIMESTAMP	Time when last statistics computed
COLCOUNT	SMALLINT	Number of columns in table
TABLEID	SMALLINT	Internal table-id number
TBSPACEID	SMALLINT	id of primary table space for this table
CARD	INTEGER	Number of rows in table ("cardinality")
NPAGES	INTEGER	Number of disk pages containing table data
FPAGES	INTEGER	Total number of disk pages for table
OVERFLOW	INTEGER	Number of overflow records for table
TBSPACE	VARCHAR(18)	Primary tablespace for storing table data
INDEX_TBSPACE	VARCHAR(18)	Tablespace for storing table indexes
LONG_TBSPACE	VARCHAR(18)	Tablespace for storing large-object data
PARENTS	SMALLINT	Number of parent tables for this table
CHILDREN	SMALLINT	Number of child tables for this table
SELFREFS	SMALLINT	Number of self-references for this table
KEYCOLUMNS	SMALLINT	Number of columns in table's primary key
KEYINDEXID	SMALLINT	Internal id for primary key index
KEYUNIQUE	SMALLINT	Number of unique constraints for table

Table 16-2. *The SYSCAT.TABLES view (DB2)*

Column Name	Data Type	Information
CHECKCOUNT	SMALLINT	Number of check constraints for table
DATACAPTURE	CHAR(1)	Indicates replicated table
CONST_CHECKED	CHAR(32)	Constraint-checking flags
PMAP_ID	SMALLINT	Internal id for table's partitioning map
PARTITION_MODE	CHAR(1)	Mode for partitioned database tables
LOG_ATTRIBUTE	CHAR(1)	Whether logging is initially enabled for table
PCTFREE	SMALLINT	Percentage of page to reserve for future data
REMARKS	VARCHAR(254)	User-provided comments for table

Table 16-2. *The SYSCAT.TABLES view (DB2) (continued)*

List the names of all tables, views, and aliases in the database.

```
SELECT TABNAME
  FROM SYSCAT.TABLES
```

List the names and creation times of my tables only.

```
SELECT TABNAME, CREATE_TIME
  FROM SYSCAT.TABLES
 WHERE TYPE = 'T'
   AND DEFINER = USER
```

In an Oracle database, a pair of system views named USER_TABLES and ALL_TABLES perform a similar function to the DB2 SYSCAT.TABLES view. The USER_TABLES view contains one row for each database table that is owned by the current user. The ALL_TABLES view contains one row for each table to which the current user has access. The ALL_TABLES view thus will include all of the rows from USER_TABLES, plus additional rows representing tables owned by other users to which the current user has been granted at least one of the access privileges. Here is a typical query against these Oracle system catalog views:

List the names and owners of all tables to which I have access.

```
SELECT TABLE_NAME, OWNER
  FROM ALL_TABLES
```

The SQL Server equivalent of the DB2 `SYSCAT.TABLES` view is a system table named `SYSOBJECTS`, described in Table 16-3. The `SYSOBJECTS` table stores information about SQL Server tables and views and other SQL Server objects such as stored procedures, rules, and triggers. Note also how the `SYSOBJECTS` table uses an internal id number instead of a name to identify the table owner.

The Informix Universal Server "table information" system table is named `SYSTABLES`. Like the DB2 catalog, it contains information only about tables, views and aliases; other database objects are described in other system tables. Here is a typical query against this Informix system table:

List the name, owner, and creation date of all tables in the database.

```
SELECT TABNAME, OWNER, CREATED
  FROM SYSTABLES
 WHERE TABTYPE = 'T'
```

Column Name	Data Type	Information
name	SYSNAME	Name of the object
id	INT	Internal object id number
uid	SMALLINT	User-id of object owner
type	CHAR(2)	Object type code*
crdate	DATETIME	Date/time object was created
deltrig	INT	Procedure id of DELETE trigger
instrig	INT	Procedure id of INSERT trigger
updtrig	INT	Procedure id of UPDATE trigger

* S = system table, U = user table, V = view, L = log, P = stored procedure,
   TR = trigger, etc.

Table 16-3. *Selected Columns of the SYSOBJECTS table (SQL Server)*

As these examples show, the queries to obtain table information have a similar structure across DBMS brands. However, the specific names of the system table(s) or view(s) containing the information, and the relevant columns, vary considerably across brands.

Column Information

All of the major SQL products have a system table that keeps track of the columns in the database. There is one row in this table for each column in each table or view in the database. Most DBMS brands restrict access to this base system table, but provide user column information through a view that shows only columns in tables owned by, or accessible to, the current user. In an Oracle8 database, two system catalog views provide this information—USER_TAB_COLUMNS, which includes one row for each column in each table owned by the current user, and ALL_TAB_COLUMNS, which contains one row for each column in each table accessible to the current user.

Most of the information in the "system columns" table or view stores the definition of a column—its name, its data type, its length, whether it can take NULL values, and so on. In addition, the table sometimes includes information about the distribution of data values found in each column. This statistical information helps the DBMS decide how to carry out a query in the optimal way.

Here is a typical query you could use to find out about the columns in an Oracle8 database:

List the names and data types of the columns in my OFFICES *table.*

```
SELECT COLUMN_NAME, DATA_TYPE
  FROM USER_TAB_COLUMNS
 WHERE TABLE_NAME = 'OFFICES'
```

Like the table information in the system catalog, the column information varies across DBMS brands. Table 16-4 shows the contents of the SYSCAT.COLUMNS system table, which contains column information in the DB2 catalog. Here are some queries that apply to this DBMS brand:

Find all columns in the database with a DATE *data type.*

```
SELECT TABSCHEMA, TABNAME, COLNAME
  FROM SYSCAT.COLUMNS
 WHERE TYPESCHEMA = 'SYSIBMD' AND TYPENAME = 'DATE'
```

List the owner, view name, column name, data type, and length for all text columns longer than ten characters defined in views.

```
SELECT DEFINER, COLS.TABNAME, COLNAME, TYPENAME, LENGTH
  FROM SYSCAT.COLUMNS COLS, SYSCAT.TABLES TBLS
 WHERE TBLS.TABSCHEMA = COLS.TABSCHEMA
   AND TBLS.TBLNAME = COLS.TBLNAME
   AND (TYPENAME = 'VARCHAR' OR TYPENAME = 'CHARACTER')
   AND LENGTH > 10
   AND TYPE = 'V'
```

Column Name	Data Type	Information
TABSCHEMA	CHAR(8)	Schema of table containing the column
TABNAME	VARCHAR(18)	Name of table containing the column
COLNAME	VARCHAR(18)	Name of the column
COLNO	SMALLINT	Position of column in table (first column = 0)
TYPESCHEMA	CHAR(8)	Schema of column's domain (or SYSIBM)
TYPENAME	VARCHAR(18)	Name of data type or domain for column
LENGTH	INTEGER	Max. data length for variable-length types
SCALE	SMALLINT	Scale for DECIMAL data types
DEFAULT	VARCHAR(254)	Default value for column
NULLS	CHAR(1)	NULLs allowed? (Y/N)
CODEPAGE	SMALLINT	Code page for extended character types
LOGGED	CHAR(1)	Logging enabled (Y/N) for large object columns
COMPACT	CHAR(1)	Is large object column compacted (Y/N)
COLCARD	INTEGER	Number of distinct data values (cardinality)
HIGH2KEY	VARCHAR(33)	Second-highest column value in table
LOW2KEY	VARCHAR(33)	Second-lowest column value in table

Table 16-4.   *The SYSCAT.COLUMNS view (DB2)*

Column Name	Data Type	Information
AVGCOLLEN	INTEGER	Avg. data length for variable-length types
KEYSEQ	SMALLINT	Column position within primary key (or 0)
PARTKEYSEQ	SMALLINT	Column position within partitioning key (or 0)
NQUANTILES	SMALLINT	Number of quantiles in column statistics
NMOSTFREQ	SMALLINT	Number of frequent values in column statistics
REMARKS	VARCHAR(254)	User-supplied comments for column

Table 16-4. *The SYSCAT.COLUMNS view (DB2) (continued)*

There is considerable variation in the way that the column definition is provided by the system catalogs of various DBMS brands. For comparison, Table 16-5 shows the definition of the Informix Universal Server SYSCOLUMNS table. Some of the differences between the column information tables are simply matters of style:

- The names of the columns in the two tables are completely different, even when they contain similar data.

- The DB2 catalog uses a combination of the schema name and table name to identify the table containing a given column; the Informix catalog uses an internal table id number, which is a foreign key to its SYSTABLES table.

- The DB2 specifies data types in text form (for example, CHARACTER); the Informix catalog uses integer data type codes.

Other differences reflect the different capabilities provided by the two DBMS brands:

- DB2 allows you to specify up to 254 characters of remarks about each column; Informix does not provide this feature.

- The Informix system table keeps track of the minimum and maximum length of actual data values stored in a variable-length column; this information is not available directly from the DB2 system catalog.

View Information

The definitions of the views in a database are usually stored by the DBMS in the system catalog. The DB2 catalog contains two system tables that keep track of views. The SYSCAT.VIEWS table, described in Table 16-6, contains the SQL text definition of each

Column Name	Data Type	Information
COLNAME	CHAR(18)	Name of the column
TABID	INTEGER	Internal table-id of table containing column
COLNO	SMALLINT	Position of column in table
COLTYPE	SMALLINT	Data type of column and if NULLs allowed
COLLENGTH	SMALLINT	Column length
COLMIN	INTEGER	Second-smallest column data value
COLMAX	INTEGER	Second-largest column data value
MINLEN	INTEGER	Minimum actual data length
MAXLEN	INTEGER	Maximum actual data length
EXTENDED_ID	INTEGER	Internal id of extended data type

Table 16-5.   *The SYSCOLUMNS table (Informix)*

view. If the definition exceeds 3,600 characters, it is stored in multiple rows, with sequence numbers 1, 2, 3, and so on.

The DB2 SYSCAT.VIEWDEP table, described in Table 16-7, describes how each view depends on other tables or views. There is one row in the table for each dependency, so a view with three source tables will be represented by three rows.

Using these two tables, you can see the definitions of the views in the database and quickly determine which tables in the database serve as the source tables for a view. As with many mainstream DBMS products, information about views is tightly linked to information about tables in the DB2 catalog. This means there is often more than one way to find the answer to a catalog inquiry. For example, here is a direct query against the DB2 VIEWS system table to obtain the names and creators of all views defined in the database:

List the views defined in the database.

```
SELECT DISTINCT VIEWSCHAME, VIEWNAME, DEFINER
  FROM SYSCAT.VIEWS
```

Column Name	Data Type	Information
VIEWSCHEMA	CHAR(8)	Schema containing the view
VIEWNAME	VARCHAR(18)	Name of the view
DEFINER	CHAR(8)	User-id who created the view
SEQNO	SMALLINT	Sequence number for this row of SQL text
VIEWCHECK	CHAR(1)	Type of view checking
READONLY	CHAR(1)	Is view read-only? (Y/N)
VALID	CHAR(1)	Is view definition valid? (Y/N)
FUNC_PATH	VARCHAR(254)	Path for resolving function calls in view
TEXT	VARCHAR(3600)	SQL text of view definition ("SELECT...")

Table 16-6. *The SYSCAT.VIEWS view (DB2)*

Column Name	Data Type	Information
VIEWSCHEMA	CHAR(8)	Schema containing the view
VIEWNAME	VARCHAR(18)	Name of the view
DEFINER	CHAR(8)	User-id who created the view
BTYPE	CHAR(1)	Type of object on which view depends (T=table, V=view, A=alias, etc.)
BSCHEMA	CHAR(8)	Schema containing the object on which view depends
TABAUTH	SMALLINT	Flags indicating privileges on the object on which this view depends.

Table 16-7. *The SYSCAT.VIEWDEP view (DB2)*

Note the use of DISTINCT to eliminate duplicate rows that would be present for views with long text definitions. Perhaps an easier way to obtain the same information is to query the DB2 TABLES system table directly, selecting only rows with a "view" type:

List the views defined in the database.

```
SELECT TABSCHEMA, TABNAME, DEFINER
  FROM SYSCAT.TABLES
 WHERE TYPE = 'V'
```

Most of the major DBMS products treat views in this same way within their system catalog structure. Informix Universal Server, for example, has a system table named SYSVIEWS that contains view definitions. Each of its rows holds a 64-character "chunk" of the SQL SELECT statement that defines a view. View definitions that span multiple rows are handled by sequence numbers, as with DB2. The Informix SYSVIEWS table includes only one other column—the table-id which links the SYSVIEWS table to the corresponding row in the SYSTABLES table. Thus, Informix duplicates less information between the SYSTABLES and SYSVIEWS tables, but you must explicitly join the tables for the most common view information requests.

Oracle8 takes a similar approach by making the SQL text that defines a view available via system views. As with table and column information, there are two system views of interest—USER_VIEWS, which contains information about all views created and owned by the current user, and ALL_VIEWS, which also includes information about views accessible to the current user but created by other users. Unlike the DB2 and Informix approaches, which split the SQL text defining the view into multiple rows with sequence numbers if it is lengthy, Oracle's system views contain only one row per view. The SQL text defining the view is held in a LONG (large object) column and can conceivably run to thousands of characters. A "length" column tells the length of the stored SQL text definition of the view. Here is a query to obtain Oracle view information:

List the current user's views and their definitions.

```
SELECT VIEW_NAME, TEXT_LENGTH, TEXT
  FROM USER_VIEWS
```

Note that most interactive SQL products (including Oracle's SQLPlus) truncate the text containing the view definition if it is too long to be displayed effectively. The actual text stored in the database is complete.

Remarks

IBM's DB2 products allow you to associate up to 254 characters of *remarks* with each table, view, and column defined in the database. The remarks allow you to store a brief description of the table or data item in the system catalog. The remarks are stored in the SYSCAT.TABLES and SYSCAT.COLUMNS system tables of the system catalog. Unlike the other elements of table and column definitions, the remarks and labels are not specified by the CREATE TABLE statement. Instead, the COMMENT statement is used. Its syntax is shown in Figure 16-2. Here are some examples:

Define remarks for the OFFICES table.

```
COMMENT ON TABLE OFFICES
     IS 'This table stores data about our sales offices'
```

Associate some remarks with the TARGET and SALES columns of the OFFICES table.

```
COMMENT ON OFFICES
(TARGET IS 'This is the annual sales target for the office',
  SALES IS 'This is the year-to-date sales for the office')
```

Because this is a capability carried forward from some of the earliest IBM SQL products, Oracle also supports the COMMENT ON statement for attaching comments to tables and columns. The comments are not stored "inline" with other table and column information, however. They are accessible via the Oracle system views USER_TAB_COMMENTS and USER_COL_COMMENTS. The DB2 COMMENT capability has been expanded over the years to allow comments on constraints, stored procedures, schemas, tablespaces, triggers, and other DB2 database "objects". This capability is not a part of the SQL standard and has generally not been adopted by other major DBMS products.

Relationship Information

With the introduction of referential integrity into the major enterprise DBMS products during the mid-1990s, system catalogs were expanded to describe primary keys, foreign keys, and the parent/child relationships that they create. In DB2, which was among the first to support referential integrity, the description is provided by the SYSCAT.REFERENCES system catalog table, described in Table 16-8. Every parent/child

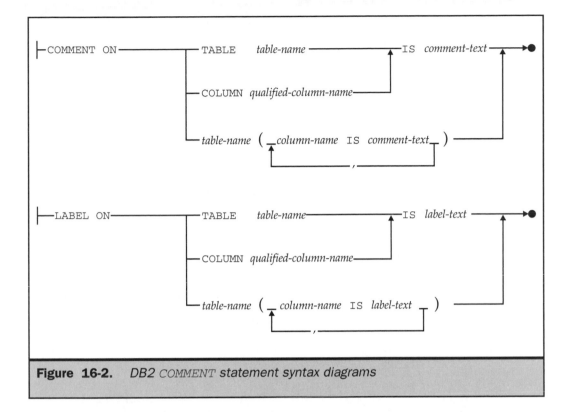

Figure 16-2. *DB2 COMMENT statement syntax diagrams*

relationship between two tables in the database is represented by a single row in the SYSCAT.REFERENCES table. The row identifies the names of the parent and child tables, the name of the relationship, and the delete and update rules for the relationship. You can query it to find out about the relationships in the database:

List all of the parent/child relationships among my tables, showing the name of the relationship, the name of the parent table, the name of the child table, and the delete rule for each one.

```
SELECT CONSTNAME, REFTABNAME, TABNAME, DELETERULE
  FROM SYSCAT.REFERENCES
 WHERE DEFINER = USER
```

List all of the tables related to the SALESREPS table as either a parent or a child.

```
SELECT REFTABNAME
  FROM SYSCAT.REFERENCES
 WHERE TABNAME = 'SALESREPS'
 UNION
SELECT TABNAME
  FROM SYSCAT.REFERENCES
 WHERE REFTABNAME = 'SALESREPS'
```

The names of the foreign key columns and the corresponding primary key columns are listed (as text) in the FK_COLNAMES and PK_COLNAMES columns of the REFERENCES system table. A second system table, SYSCAT.KEYCOLUSE, shown in Table 16-9, provides a somewhat more useful form of the information. There is one row in this system table for each column in each foreign key, primary key, or uniqueness

Column Name	Data Type	Information
CONSTNAME	VARCHAR(18)	Name of constraint described by this row
TABSCHEMA	CHAR(8)	Schema containing the constraint
TABNAME	VARCHAR(18)	Table to which constraint applies
DEFINER	CHAR(8)	Creator of table to which constraint applies
REFKEYNAME	VARCHAR(18)	Name of parent key
REFTABSCHEMA	CHAR(8)	Schema containing parent table
REFTABNAME	VARCHAR(18)	Name of parent table
COLCOUNT	SMALLINT	Number of columns in the foreign key
DELETERULE	CHAR(1)	Delete rule for foreign key constraint (A=no action, C=cascade, R=restrict, etc.)
UPDATERULE	CHAR(1)	Update rule for foreign key constraint (A=no action, R=restrict)
CREATE_TIME	TIMESTAMP	Creation time of constraint
FK_COLNAMES	VARCHAR(320)	Names of foreign key columns
PK_COLNAMES	VARCHAR(320)	Names of primary key columns

Table 16-8. *The SYSCAT.REFERENCES view (DB2)*

Column Name	Data Type	Information
CONSTNAME	VARCHAR(18)	Name of constraint (unique, primary key or foreign key) described by this row
TABSCHEMA	CHAR(8)	Schema containing the constraint
TABNAME	VARCHAR(18)	Table to which constraint applies
COLNAME	VARCHAR(18)	Name of column in the constraint
COLSEQ	SMALLINT	Position of column within the constraint

Table 16-9. *The* SYSCAT.KEYCOLUSE *view (DB2)*

constraint defined in the database. A sequence number defines the order of the columns in a compound key. You can use this system table to find out the names of the columns that link a table to its parent, using a query like this one:

List the columns that link ORDERS *to* PRODUCTS *in the relationship named* ISFOR.

```
SELECT COLNAME, COLSEQ
  FROM SYSCAT.KEYCOLUSE
 WHERE CONSTNAME = 'ISFOR'
 ORDER BY COLSEQ
```

The primary key of a table and the parent/child relationships in which it participates are also summarized in the SYSCAT.TABLES and SYSCAT.COLUMNS system tables, shown previously in Tables 16-2 and 16-4. If a table has a primary key, the KEYCOLUMNS column in its row of the SYSCAT.TABLES system table is nonzero and tells how many columns make up the primary key (1 for a simple key, 2 or more for a composite key). In the SYSCAT.COLUMNS system table, the rows for the columns that make up the primary key have a nonzero value in their KEYSEQ column. The value in this column indicates the position (1, 2, and so on) of the primary key column within the primary key.

You can query the SYSCAT.COLUMNS table to find a table's primary key:

List the columns that form the primary key of the PRODUCTS *table.*

```
SELECT COLNAME, KEYSEQ, TYPENAME, REMARKS
  FROM SYSCAT.COLUMNS
 WHERE TABNAME = 'PRODUCTS'
```

```
AND KEYSEQ > 0
ORDER BY KEYSEQ
```

The DB2 catalog support for primary and foreign keys is typical of that found in other major SQL products. The Oracle system view USER_CONSTRAINTS, for example, provides the same information as the DB2 SYSCAT.REFERENCES system table. Information about the specific columns that make up a foreign key or primary key appears in the Oracle USER_CONS_COLUMNS system view, which is analogous to the DB2 SYSCAT.KEYCOLUSE system table. Microsoft SQL Server has a similar system catalog structure, with foreign key information divided between the SYSFOREIGNKEYS and SYSREFERENCES system tables.

Informix Universal Server takes a similar approach to the DB2 catalog, but with the same types of differences previously illustrated in its table information and column information support. Each constraint defined within the database generates one row in the Informix SYSCONSTRAINTS system table, which defines the name of the constraint and its type (check-constraint, primary key, referential, and so on). This system table also assigns an internal "constraint-id" number to identify the constraint within the catalog. The table to which the constraint applies is also identified by table-id (which serves as a foreign key to the SYSTABLES system table). Further information about referential constraints (foreign keys) is contained in a SYSREFERENCES system table. Again in this table, the constraint, the primary key, and the parent table are identified by internal "ids" that link the foreign key information to the SYSCONSTRAINTS and SYSTABLES system tables. The SYSREFERENCES table contains information about the delete rule and update rule that apply to the foreign key relationship and similar information.

User Information

The system catalog generally contains a table that identifies the users who are authorized to access the database. The DBMS may use this system table to validate the user name and password when a user first attempts to connect to the database. The table may also store other data about the user.

SQL Server stores user information in its SYSUSERS system table, shown in Table 16-10. Each row of this table describes a single user or user group in the SQL Server security scheme. Informix takes a similar approach, with a system table that is also called SYSUSERS. The corresponding Oracle table is called ALL_USERS. Following are two equivalent queries that list the authorized users for SQL Server and Oracle.

Column Name	Data Type	Information
uid	SMALLINT	Internal user-id number in this database
gid	SMALLINT	Internal user group-id number in this database
name	SYSNAME	User or group name

Table 16-10. *Selected Columns of the SYSUSERS table (SQL Server)*

List all the user-ids known to SQL Server.

```
SELECT NAME
  FROM SYSUSERS
 WHERE UID <> GID
```

List all the user-ids known to Oracle.

```
SELECT USERNAME
  FROM ALL_USERS
```

The DB2 system catalog table that contains user names also contains the information about their roles and privileges within the database (that is, whether they are a database administrator, whether or not they can create tables, whether they can create programs that access the database). Here is the equivalent query to those preceding for retrieving user names from the DB2 catalog:

List all the user-ids known to DB2.

```
SELECT DISTINCT GRANTEE
  FROM SYSCAT.DBAUTH
 WHERE GRANTEETYPE = 'U'
```

Privileges Information

In addition to storing database structure information, the system catalog generally stores the information required by the DBMS to enforce database security. As described in Chapter 15, various DBMS products offer different variations on the basic SQL privileges scheme. These variations are reflected in the structure of the system catalogs for the various DBMS brands.

DB2 has one of the most comprehensive schemes for user privileges, extending down to the individual columns of a table. Table 16-11 shows the DB2 system catalogs that store information about privileges and briefly describes the role of each one.

The authorization scheme used by SQL Server is more fundamental and streamlined than that of DB2. It treats databases, tables, stored procedures, triggers, and other entities uniformly as objects to which privileges apply. This streamlined structure is reflected in the system table, SYSPROTECTS, shown in Table 16-12, which implements the entire privileges scheme for SQL Server. Each row in the table represents a single GRANT or REVOKE statement that has been issued.

System Table	Role
TABAUTH	Implements table-level privileges by telling which users have permissions to access which tables, for which operations (SELECT, INSERT, DELETE, UPDATE, ALTER, and INDEX).
COLAUTH	Implements column-level privileges by telling which users have permission to update or to reference which columns of which tables.
DBAUTH	Determines which users have permission to connect to the database, to create tables and to perform various database administration functions.
SCHEMAAUTH	Implements schema-level privileges by telling which users have permission to create, drop or alter objects (tables, views, domains, etc.) within a schema.
INDEXAUTH	Implements index-level privileges by telling which users have control privileges over various indexes.
PACKAGEAUTH	Implements programmatic access privileges by telling which users have the ability to control, bind (create) and execute various database access programs ("packages").

Table 16-11. *DB2 System Catalog Views that Implement Permissions*

Column Name	Data Type	Information
id	INT	Internal id of protected object
uid	SMALLINT	Internal id of user or group with privilege
action	TINYINT	Numerical privilege code
protecttype	TINYINT	Numerical code for grant or revoke
columns	VARBINARY(32)	Bit map for column-level update privileges

Table 16-12. *Selected Columns of the SYSPROTECTS table (SQL Server)*

The SQL2 Information Schema

The SQL2 standard does not directly specify the structure of a system catalog that must be supported by DBMS implementations. In practice, given the widely differing features supported by different DBMS brands and the major differences in the system catalogs that were already being used by commercial SQL products when the SQL2 standard was adopted, it would have been impossible to reach an agreement on a standard catalog definition. Instead, the writers of the SQL2 standard defined an "idealized" system catalog that a DBMS vendor might design if they were building a DBMS to support the SQL2 standard "from scratch." The tables in this idealized system catalog (called the *definition schema* in the standard) are summarized in Table 16-13.

System Table	Contents
USERS	One row for each user ("authorization-id") in the catalog cluster
SCHEMATA	On row for each schema in the catalog cluster
DATA_TYPE_DESCRIPTOR	One row for each domain or column defined with a data type
DOMAINS	One row for each domain
DOMAIN_CONSTRAINTS	One row for each domain constraint
TABLES	One row for each table or view

Table 16-13. *Idealized System Catalog Used by the SQL2 Standard*

System Table	Contents
VIEWS	One row for each table or view
COLUMNS	One row for each column in each table or view definition
VIEW_TABLE_USAGE	One row for each table referenced in each view definition (if a view is defined by a query on multiple tables, there will be a row for each table)
VIEW_COLUMN_USAGE	One row for each column referenced by a view
TABLE_CONSTRAINTS	One row for each table constraint specified in a table definition
KEY_COLUMN_USAGE	One row for each column specified in each primary key, each foreign key, and each uniqueness constraint (if multiple columns are specified in a key definition or uniqueness constraint, there will be multiple rows representing that constraint)
REFERENTIAL_CONSTRAINTS	One row for each foreign key definition specified in a table definition
CHECK_CONSTRAINTS	One row for each check constraint specified in a table definition
CHECK_TABLE_USAGE	One row for each table referenced in each check constraint, domain constraint, or assertion
CHECK_COLUMN_USAGE	One row for each column referenced in each check constraint, domain constraint, or assertion
ASSERTIONS	One row for each assertion defined
TABLE_PRIVILEGES	One row for each privilege granted on each table
COLUMN_PRIVILEGES	One row for each privilege granted on each column
CHARACTER_SETS	One row for each character set defined
COLLATIONS	One row for each collation defined
TRANSLATIONS	One row for each translation defined
SQL_LANGUAGES	One row for each language (e.g., COBOL, C, etc.) supported by this DBMS brand

Table 16-13.   *Idealized System Catalog Used by the SQL2 Standard (continued)*

The SQL2 standard does not require a DBMS to actually support the system catalog tables in Table 16-13, or any system catalog at all. Instead, it defines a series of views on these catalog tables that identify database objects that are accessible to the current user. (These "catalog views" are called an *information schema* in the standard.) Any DBMS that claims Intermediate-Level or Full-Level conformance to the SQL2 standard must support these views. This effectively gives a user a standardized way to find out about the objects in the database that are available to him or her by issuing standard SQL queries against the catalog views. It's worth noting that support for the catalog views is not required for Entry-Level conformance to the SQL2 standard, and support for this area of the standard has been slow to appear in commercial DBMS products.

Commercial DBMS products that support the SQL2 standard catalog views typically do so by defining corresponding views on the tables in their own system catalogs. In most cases, the information in the DBMS's own system catalogs is similar enough to that required by the standard that the "first 90 percent" of the conformance to the SQL2 standard is relatively easy. The "last 10 percent" has proven to be difficult, given the variations among DBMS brands and the degree to which even the SQL2 catalog views expose the specific features and capabilities of the underlying DBMS.

The catalog views required by the SQL2 standard are summarized in Table 16-14, along with a brief description of the information contained in each view. The standard

System Catalog View	Contents
INFORMATION_SCHEMA_ CATALOG_NAME	A single row specifying the name of the database for each user ("catalog in the language of the SQL2 standard) described by this information_schema
SCHEMATA	One row for each schema in the database that is owned by the current user specifying the schema name, default character set, etc.
DOMAINS	One row for each domain accessible by the current user specifying the name of the domain, the underlying data type, character set, maximum length, scale, precision, etc.
DOMAIN_CONSTRAINTS	One row for each domain constraint specifying the name of the constraint and its deferability characteristics
TABLES	One row for each table or view accessible to the current user specifying its name and type (table or view)

Table 16-14. *Catalog Views Mandated by the SQL2 Standard*

System Catalog View	Contents
VIEWS	One row for each view accessible to the current user specifying its name, check option, and updatability
COLUMNS	One row for each column accessible to the current user specifying its name, the table or view that contains it, its data type, precision, scale, character set, etc.
TABLE_PRIVILEGES	One row for each privilege on a table granted to or by the current user specifying the table type, the type of privilege, the grantor and grantee, and whether the privilege is grantable by the current user
COLUMN_PRIVILEGES	One row for each privilege on a column granted to or by the current user specifying the table and the column, the type of privilege, the grantor and grantee, and whether the privilege is grantable by the current user
USAGE_PRIVILEGES	One row for each usage granted to or by the current user
TABLE_CONSTRAINTS	One row for each table constraint (primary key, foreign key, uniqueness constraint, or check constraint) specified on a table owned by the current user, specifying the name of the constraint, the table, the type of constraint, and its deferability
REFERENTIAL_ CONSTRAINTS	One row for each referential constraint (foreign key definition) for a table owned by the current user specifying the names of the constraint and the child and parent tables
CHECK_CONSTRAINTS	One row for each check constraint for a table owned by the current user
KEY_COLUMN_USAGE	One row for each column specified in each primary key, each foreign key, and each uniqueness constraint in a table owned by the current user, specifying the column and table names, and the position of the column in the key

Table 16-14. *Catalog Views Mandated by the SQL2 Standard (continued)*

System Catalog View	Contents
ASSERTIONS	One row for each assertion owned by the current user, specifying its name and its deferability
CHARACTER_SETS	One row for each character set definition accessible to the current user
COLLATIONS	One row for each collation definition accessible to the current user
TRANSLATIONS	One row for each translation definition accessible to the current user
VIEW_TABLE_USAGE	One row for each table referenced in each view definition owned by the current user, specifying the name of the table
VIEW_COLUMN_USAGE	One row for each column referenced by a view owned by the current user, specifying its name and the table containing it
CONSTRAINT_TABLE_ USAGE	One row for each table referenced in each check constraint, uniqueness constraint, foreign key definition, and assertion owned by the current user
CONSTRAINT_COLUMN_ USAGE	One row for each column referenced in each check constraint, uniqueness constraint, foreign key definition, and assertion owned by the current user
SQL_LANGUAGES	One row for each language (i.e., COBOL, C, etc.) supported by this DBMS brand, specifying its level of conformance to the SQL2 standard, the type of SQL supported, etc.

Table 16-14. *Catalog Views Mandated by the SQL2 Standard (continued)*

also defines three domains that are used by the catalog views and are also available to users. These domains are summarized in Table 16-15. Appendix E contains a complete summary of the major SQL2 catalog views and their contents. Following are some sample queries that can be used to extract information about database structure from the SQL2-defined system catalog views.

System Domain	Values
SQL_INDENTIFIER	The domain of all variable-length character strings that are legal SQL identifiers under the SQL2 standard. A value drawn from this domain is a legal table name, column name, etc.
CHARACTER_DATA	The domain of all variable-length character strings with a length between zero and the maximum length supported by this DBMS. A value drawn from this domain is a legal character string.
CARDINAL_NUMBER	The domain of all non-negative numbers, from zero up to the maximum number represented by an INTEGER for this DBMS. A value drawn from this is zero or a legal positive number.

Table 16-15. *Domains Defined by the SQL2 Standard*

List the names of all tables and views owned by the current user.

```
SELECT TABLE_NAME
  FROM TABLES
```

List the name, position, and data type of all columns in all views.

```
SELECT TABLE_NAME, C.COLUMN_NAME, ORDINAL_POSITION, DATA_TYPE
  FROM COLUMNS
 WHERE (COLUMNS.TABLE_NAME IN (SELECT TABLE_NAME FROM VIEWS))
```

Determine how many columns are in the table named OFFICES.

```
SELECT COUNT(*)
  FROM COLUMNS
 WHERE (TABLE_NAME = 'OFFICES')
```

At this writing, none of the major enterprise-class SQL DBMS products support the full-blown SQL2 Information Schema views. Informix Universal Server does provide a set of Information Schema views, but they are based on the X/Open Common

Application Environment standard and do not conform to the ANSI/ISO SQL standard in their details.

Other Catalog Information

The system catalog is a reflection of the capabilities and features of the DBMS that uses it. Because of the many SQL extensions and additional features offered by popular DBMS products, their system catalogs always contain several tables unique to the DBMS. Here are just a few examples:

- DB2 and Oracle support aliases and synonyms (alternate names for tables). DB2 stores alias information with other table information in the SYSCAT.TABLES system table. Oracle makes synonym information available through its USER_SYNONYMNS system view.

- SQL Server supports multiple named databases. It has a system table called SYSDATABASES that identifies the databases managed by a single server.

- Many DBMS brands now support stored procedures, and the catalog contains one or more tables that describes them. Sybase stores information about stored procedures in its SYSPROCEDURES system table.

- Ingres supports tables that are distributed across several disk volumes. Its IIMULTI_LOCATIONS system table keeps track of the locations of multi-volume tables.

Summary

The system catalog is a collection of system tables that describe the structure of a relational database:

- The DBMS maintains the data in the system tables, updating it as the structure of the database changes.

- A user can query the system tables to find out information about tables, columns, and privileges in the database.

- Front-end query tools use the system tables to help users navigate their way through the database in a user-friendly way.

- The names and organization of the system tables differ widely from one brand of DBMS to another; and there are even differences among different DBMS products from the same vendor, reflecting the different internal structures and capabilities of the products.

- The SQL2 standard does not require that a DBMS actually have a set of system catalog tables, but it does define a set of standard catalog views for products that claim higher levels of SQL2 conformance.

Part V

Programming with SQL

In addition to its role as an interactive data access language, SQL supports database access by application programs. The next three chapters describe the special SQL features and techniques that apply to programmatic SQL. Chapter 17 describes embedded SQL, the programmatic SQL technique used by most SQL products. Dynamic SQL, an advanced form of embedded SQL that is used to build general-purpose database tools, is described in Chapter 18. Chapter 19 describes an alternative to embedded SQL—the function call interface provided by several popular DBMS products.

Chapter 17

Embedded SQL

S QL is a *dual-mode language*. It is both an interactive database language used for *ad hoc* queries and updates and a programmatic database language used by application programs for database access. For the most part, the SQL language is identical in both modes. The dual-mode nature of SQL has several advantages:

- It is relatively easy for programmers to learn how to write programs that access the database.

- Capabilities available through the interactive query language are also automatically available to application programs.

- The SQL statements to be used in a program can be tried out first using interactive SQL and then coded into the program.

- Programs can work with tables of data and query results instead of navigating their way through the database.

This chapter summarizes the types of programmatic SQL offered by the leading SQL-based products and then describes the programmatic SQL used by the IBM SQL products, which is called *embedded SQL*.

Programmatic SQL Techniques

SQL is a language and can be used programmatically, but it would be incorrect to call SQL a programming language. SQL lacks even the most primitive features of "real" programming languages. It has no provision for declaring variables, no GOTO statement, no IF statement for testing conditions, no FOR, DO, or WHILE statements to construct loops, no block structure, and so on. SQL is a database *sublanguage* that handles special purpose database management tasks. To write a program that accesses a database, you must start with a conventional programming language, such as COBOL, PL/I, FORTRAN, Pascal, or C and then "add SQL to the program."

The initial ANSI/ISO SQL standard was concerned exclusively with this programmatic use of SQL. In fact, the standard did not even include the interactive SELECT statement described in Chapters 6 through 9. It only specified the programmatic SELECT statement described later in this chapter. The SQL2 standard, published in 1992, expanded its focus to include interactive SQL (called "direct invocation of SQL" in the standard) and more advanced forms of programmatic SQL (the *dynamic SQL* capabilities described in Chapter 20).

Commercial SQL database vendors offer two basic techniques for using SQL within an application program:

- *Embedded SQL*. In this approach, SQL statements are embedded directly into the program's source code, intermixed with the other programming language statements. Special embedded SQL statements are used to retrieve data into the program. A special SQL precompiler accepts the combined source code and, along with other programming tools, converts it into an executable program.

■ *Application program interface.* In this approach, the program communicates with the DBMS through a set of function calls called an *application program interface*, or API. The program passes SQL statements to the DBMS through the API calls and uses API calls to retrieve query results. This approach does not require a special precompiler.

The initial IBM SQL products used an embedded SQL approach, and it was adopted by most commercial SQL products in the 1980s. The original ANSI/ISO SQL standard specified only an awkward "module language" for programmatic SQL, but commercial SQL products continued to follow the IBM *de facto* standard. In 1989, the ANSI/ISO standard was extended to include a definition of how to embed SQL statements within the Ada, C, COBOL, FORTRAN, Pascal, and PL/I programming languages, this time following the IBM approach. The SQL2 standard continued this specification.

In parallel with this evolution of embedded SQL, several DBMS vendors who were focused on minicomputer systems introduced callable database APIs in the 1980s. When the Sybase DBMS was introduced, it offered *only* a callable API. Microsoft's SQL Server, derived from the Sybase DBMS, also used the API approach exclusively. Soon after the debut of SQL Server, Microsoft introduced Open Database Connectivity (ODBC), another callable API. ODBC is roughly based on the SQL Server API, but with the additional goals of being database independent and permitting concurrent access to two or more different DBMS brands through a common API. More recently, Java Database Connectivity (JDBC) has emerged as an important API for accessing a relational database from within programs written in Java. With the growing popularity of callable APIs, the callable and embedded approaches are both in active use today. The following table summarizes the programmatic interfaces offered by some of the leading SQL-based DBMS products.

DBMS	Callable API	Embedded SQL Language Support
DB2	ODBC, JDBC	APL, Assembler, BASIC, COBOL, FORTRAN, Java, PL/I
Informix	ODBC, JDBC	C, Cobol
Microsoft SQL Server	DB Library (dblib), ODBC	C
Oracle	Oracle Call Interface (OCI), ODBC, JDBC	C, COBOL, FORTRAN, Pascal, PL/I
Sybase	DB Library (dblib), ODBC, JDBC	C, COBOL

The basic techniques of embedded SQL, called *static* SQL, are described in this chapter. Some advanced features of embedded SQL, called *dynamic* SQL, are discussed in Chapter 20. Callable SQL APIs, including the Sybase/SQL Server API, ODBC, and JDBC, are discussed in Chapter 21.

DBMS Statement Processing

To understand any of the programmatic SQL techniques, it helps to understand a little bit more about how the DBMS processes SQL statements. To process a SQL statement, the DBMS goes through a series of five steps, shown in Figure 17-1:

1. The DBMS begins by *parsing* the SQL statement. It breaks the statement up into individual words, makes sure that the statement has a valid verb, legal clauses, and so on. Syntax errors and misspellings can be detected in this step.

2. The DBMS *validates* the statement. It checks the statement against the system catalog. Do all the tables named in the statement exist in the database? Do all of the columns exist, and are the column names unambiguous? Does the user have the required privileges to execute the statement? Semantic errors are detected in this step.

3. The DBMS *optimizes* the statement. It explores various ways to carry out the statement. Can an index be used to speed a search? Should the DBMS first apply a search condition to Table A and then join it to Table B, or should it begin with the join and use the search condition afterward? Can a sequential search through a table be avoided or reduced to a subset of the table? After exploring alternatives, the DBMS chooses one of them.

4. The DBMS then generates an *application plan* for the statement. The application plan is a binary representation of the steps that are required to carry out the statement; it is the DBMS equivalent of "executable code."

5. Finally, the DBMS carries out the statement by executing the application plan.

Note that the steps in Figure 17-1 vary in the amount of database access they require and the amount of CPU time they take. Parsing a SQL statement does not require access to the database and typically can be done very quickly. Optimization, on the other hand, is a very CPU-intensive process and requires access to the database's system catalog. For a complex, multi-table query, the optimizer may explore more than a dozen different ways of carrying out the query. However, the cost in computer processing time of doing the query the "wrong" way is usually so high compared to the cost of doing it the "right" way (or at least a "better" way) that the time spent in optimization is more than gained back in increased query execution speed.

When you type a SQL statement to interactive SQL, the DBMS goes through all five steps while you wait for its response. The DBMS has little choice in the matter—it doesn't know what statement you are going to type until you type it, and so none of the processing can be done ahead of time. In programmatic SQL, however, the

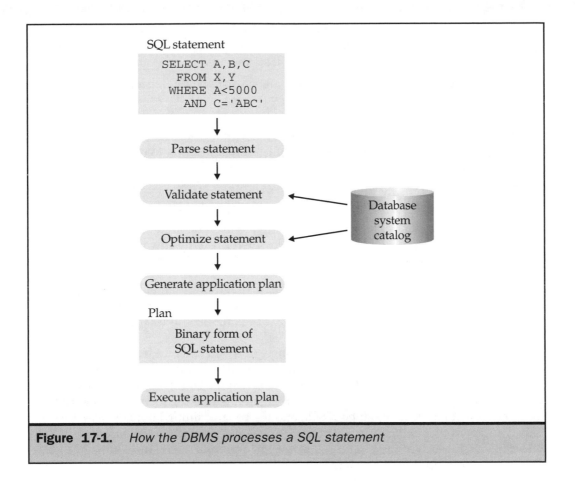

SQL statement

```
SELECT A,B,C
  FROM X,Y
 WHERE A<5000
   AND C='ABC'
```

Parse statement

Validate statement ← Database system catalog

Optimize statement ←

Generate application plan

Plan

Binary form of SQL statement

Execute application plan

Figure 17-1. *How the DBMS processes a SQL statement*

situation is quite different. Some of the early steps can be done at *compile time*, when the programmer is developing the program. This leaves only the later steps to be done at *run-time*, when the program is executed by a user. When you use programmatic SQL, all DBMS products try to move as much processing as possible to compile time, because once the final version of the program is developed, it may be executed thousands of times by users in a production application. In particular, the goal is to move optimization to compile time if at all possible.

Embedded SQL Concepts

The central idea of embedded SQL is to blend SQL language statements directly into a program written in a "host" programming language, such as C, Pascal, COBOL, FORTRAN, PL/I, or Assembler. Embedded SQL uses the following techniques to embed the SQL statements:

- SQL statements are intermixed with statements of the host language in the source program. This "embedded SQL source program" is submitted to a SQL precompiler, which processes the SQL statements.

- Variables of the host programming language can be referenced in the embedded SQL statements, allowing values calculated by the program to be used by the SQL statements.

- Program language variables also are used by the embedded SQL statements to receive the results of SQL queries, allowing the program to use and process the retrieved values.

- Special program variables are used to assign NULL values to database columns and to support the retrieval of NULL values from the database.

- Several new SQL statements that are unique to embedded SQL are added to the interactive SQL language, to provide for row-by-row processing of query results.

Figure 17-2 shows a simple embedded SQL program, written in C. The program illustrates many, but not all, of the embedded SQL techniques. The program prompts the user for an office number, retrieves the city, region, sales, and target for the office, and displays them on the screen.

Don't worry if the program appears strange, or if you can't understand all of the statements that it contains before reading the rest of this chapter. One of the disadvantages of the embedded SQL approach is that the source code for a program becomes an impure "blend" of two different languages, making the program hard to understand without training in both SQL and the programming language. Another disadvantage is that embedded SQL uses SQL language constructs not used in interactive SQL, such as the WHENEVER statement and the INTO clause of the SELECT statement—both used in this program.

Developing an Embedded SQL Program

An embedded SQL program contains a mix of SQL and programming language statements, so it can't be submitted directly to a compiler for the programming language. Instead, it moves through a multi-step development process, shown in Figure 17-3. The steps in the figure are actually those used by the IBM mainframe databases (DB2, SQL/DS), but all products that support embedded SQL use a similar process:

1. The embedded SQL source program is submitted to the SQL precompiler, a programming tool. The precompiler scans the program, finds the embedded SQL statements, and processes them. A different precompiler is required for each programming language supported by the DBMS. Commercial SQL products typically offer precompilers for one or more languages, including C, Pascal, COBOL, FORTRAN, Ada, PL/I, RPG, and various assembly languages.

```
main()
{
   exec sql include sqlca;
   exec sql begin declare section;
      int    officenum;              /* office number (from user) */
      char   cityname[16];           /* retrieved city name */
      char   regionname[11];         /* retrieved region name */
      float  targetval;              /* retrieved target and sales */
      float  salesval;               /* retrieved target and sales */
   exec sql end declare section;

   /* Set up error processing */
   exec sql whenever sqlerror goto query_error;
   exec sql whenever not found goto bad_number;

   /* Prompt the user for the employee number */
   printf("Enter office number:");
   scanf("%d", &officenum);

   /* Execute the SQL query */
   exec sql select city, region, target, sales
            from offices
            where office = :officenum
            into :cityname, :regionname, :targetval, :salesval;

   /* Display the results */
   printf("City:   %s\n",  cityname);
   printf("Region: %s\n", regionname);
   printf("Target: %f\n", targetval);
   printf("Sales:  %f\n", salesval);
   exit();

query_error:
   printf("SQL error: %ld\n", sqlca.sqlcode);
   exit();

bad_number:
   printf("Invalid office number.\n");
   exit();
}
```

Figure 17-2.   *A typical embedded SQL program*

2. The precompiler produces two files as its output. The first file is the source program, stripped of its embedded SQL statements. In their place, the precompiler substitutes calls to the "private" DBMS routines that provide the run-time link between the program and the DBMS. Typically, the names and calling sequences of these routines are known only to the precompiler and the DBMS; they are not a public interface to the DBMS. The second file is a copy of all the embedded SQL statements used in the program. This file is sometimes called a *database request module*, or DBRM.

3. The source file output from the precompiler is submitted to the standard compiler for the host programming language (such as a C or COBOL compiler). The compiler processes the source code and produces object code as its output. Note that this step has nothing in particular to do with the DBMS or with SQL.

4. The *linker* accepts the object modules generated by the compiler, links them with various library routines, and produces an executable program. The library routines linked into the executable program include the "private" DBMS routines described in Step 2.

5. The database request module generated by the precompiler is submitted to a special BIND program. This program examines the SQL statements, parses, validates, and optimizes them, and produces an application plan for each statement. The result is a combined application plan for the entire program, representing a DBMS-executable version of its embedded SQL statements. The BIND program stores the plan in the database, usually assigning it the name of the application program that created it.

The program development steps in Figure 17-3 correlate with the DBMS statement processing steps in Figure 17-1. In particular, the precompiler usually handles statement parsing (the first step), and the BIND utility handles verification, optimization, and plan generation (the second, third, and fourth steps). Thus the first four steps of Figure 17-1 all take place at compile time when you use embedded SQL. Only the fifth step, the actual execution of the application plan, remains to be done at run-time.

The embedded SQL development process turns the original embedded SQL source program into two executable parts:

- An *executable program*, stored in a file on the computer in the same format as any executable program
- An *executable application plan*, stored within the database in the format expected by the DBMS

The embedded SQL development cycle may seem cumbersome, and it is more awkward than developing a standard C or COBOL program. In most cases, all of the steps in Figure 17-3 are automated by a single command procedure, so the individual steps are made invisible to the application programmer. The process does have several major advantages from a DBMS point of view:

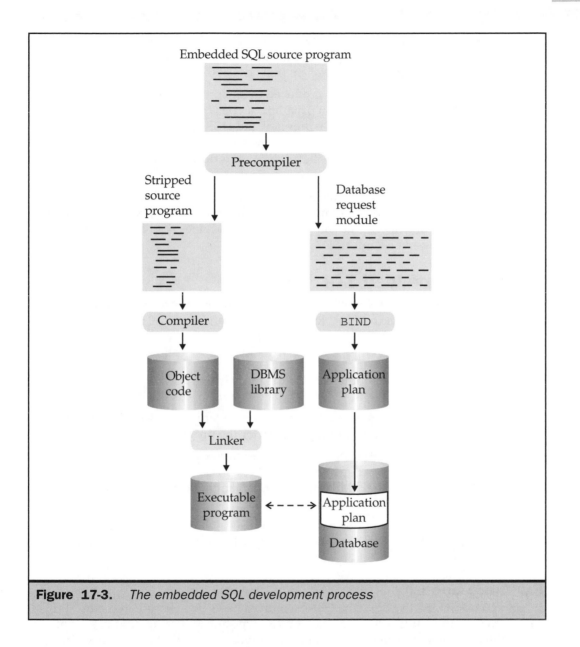

Figure 17-3. *The embedded SQL development process*

■ The blending of SQL and programming language statements in the embedded SQL source program is an effective way to merge the two languages. The host programming language provides flow of control, variables, block structure, and input/output functions; SQL handles database access and does not have to provide these other constructs.

- The use of a precompiler means that the compute-intensive work of parsing and optimization can take place *during the development cycle*. The resulting executable program is very efficient in its use of CPU resources.

- The database request module produced by the precompiler provides portability of applications. An application program can be written and tested on one system, and then its executable program and DBRM can be moved to another system. After the BIND program on the new system creates the application plan and installs it in the database, the application program can use it without being recompiled itself.

- The program's actual run-time interface to the private DBMS routines is completely hidden from the application programmer. The programmer works with embedded SQL at the source code level and does not have to worry about other, more complex interfaces.

Running an Embedded SQL Program

Recall from Figure 17-3 that the embedded SQL development process produces two executable components, the executable program itself and the program's application plan, stored in the database. When you run an embedded SQL program, these two components are brought together to do the work of the application:

1. When you ask the computer system to run the program, the computer loads the executable program in the usual way and begins to execute its instructions.

2. One of the first calls generated by the precompiler is a call to a DBMS routine that finds and loads the application plan for the program.

3. For each embedded SQL statement, the program calls one or more private DBMS routines, requesting execution of the corresponding statement in the application plan. The DBMS finds the statement, executes that part of the plan, and then returns control to the program.

4. Execution continues in this way, with the executable program and the DBMS cooperating to carry out the task defined by the original embedded SQL source program.

Run-time Security

When you use interactive SQL, the DBMS enforces its security based on the user-id you supply to the interactive SQL program. You can type any SQL statement you want, but the privileges granted to your user-id determine whether the DBMS will or will not execute the statement you type. When you run a program that uses embedded SQL, there are *two* user-ids to consider:

- The user-id of the person who *developed* the program, or more specifically, the person who ran the BIND program to create the application plan

- The user-id of the person who is now *executing* the program and the corresponding application plan

It may seem strange to consider the user-id of the person who ran the BIND program (or more generally, the person who developed the application program or installed it on the computer system), but in fact DB2 and several other commercial SQL products use both user-ids in their security scheme. To understand how the security scheme works, suppose that user JOE runs the ORDMAINT order maintenance program, which updates the ORDERS, SALES, and OFFICES tables. The application plan for the ORDMAINT program was originally bound by user-id OPADMIN, which belongs to the order-processing administrator.

In the DB2 scheme, each application plan is a database object, protected by DB2 security. To execute a plan, JOE must have the EXECUTE privilege for it. If he does not, execution fails immediately. As the ORDMAINT program executes, its embedded INSERT, UPDATE, and DELETE statements update the database. The privileges of the OPADMIN user determine whether the plan will be allowed to perform these updates. Note that the plan may update the tables even if JOE does not have the required privileges. However, the updates that can be performed are *only* those that have been explicitly coded into the embedded SQL statements of the program. Thus DB2 provides very fine control over database security. The privileges of users to access tables can be very limited, without diminishing their ability to use "canned" programs.

Not all DBMS products provide security protection for application plans. For those that do not, the privileges of the user executing an embedded SQL program determine the privileges of the program's application plan. Under this scheme, the user must have privileges to perform all of the actions performed by the plan, or the program will fail. If the user is not to have these same permissions in an interactive SQL environment, access to the interactive SQL program itself must be restricted, which is a disadvantage of this approach.

Automatic Rebinding

Note that an application plan is optimized for the database structure as it exists at the time the plan is placed in the database by the BIND program. If the structure changes later (for example, if an index is dropped or a column is deleted from a table), any application plan that references the changed structures may become invalid. To handle this situation, the DBMS usually stores, along with the application plan, a copy of the original SQL statements that produced it. The DBMS also keeps track of all the database objects upon which each application plan depends. If any of these objects are modified by a DDL statement, the DBMS can find the plans that depend on it and automatically marks those plans as "invalid." The next time the program tries to use the plan, the DBMS can detect the situation, and in most cases it will *automatically rebind* the statements to produce a new bind image. Because the DBMS has maintained a great deal of information about the application plan, it can make this automatic rebinding completely transparent to the application program. However, a SQL statement may take much longer to execute when its plan is rebound than when the plan is simply executed.

Although the DBMS can automatically rebind a plan when one of the structures upon which it depends is changed, the DBMS cannot automatically detect changes in the database that may make a better plan possible. For example, suppose a plan uses a sequential scan of a table to locate particular rows because no appropriate index existed when it was bound. It's possible that a subsequent CREATE INDEX statement will create an appropriate index. To take advantage of the new structure, you must explicitly run the BIND program to rebind the plan.

Simple Embedded SQL Statements

The simplest SQL statements to embed in a program are those that are self-contained and do not produce any query results. For example, consider this interactive SQL statement:

Delete all salespeople with sales under $150,000.

```
DELETE FROM SALESREPS
  WHERE SALES < 150000.00
```

Figures 17-4, 17-5, and 17-6 show three programs that perform the same task as this interactive SQL statement, using embedded SQL. The program in Figure 17-4 is written in C, the program in Figure 17-5 is written in COBOL, and the program in Figure 17-6 is written in FORTRAN. Although the programs are extremely simple, they illustrate the most basic features of embedded SQL:

- The embedded SQL statements appear in the midst of host programming language statements. It usually doesn't matter whether the SQL statement is written in uppercase or lowercase; the most common practice is to follow the style of the host language.

- Every embedded SQL statement begins with an *introducer* that flags it as a SQL statement. The IBM SQL products use the introducer EXEC SQL for most host languages, and the ANSI/ISO SQL2 standard specifies it as well. Some embedded SQL products still support other introducers, for backward compatibility with their earlier versions.

■ If an embedded SQL statement extends over multiple lines, the host language strategy for statement continuation is used. For COBOL, PL/I, and C programs, no special continuation character is required. For FORTRAN programs, the second and subsequent lines of the statement must have a continuation character in column 6.

■ Every embedded SQL statement ends with a *terminator* that signals the end of the SQL statement. The terminator varies with the style of the host language. In COBOL, the terminator is the string END-EXEC., which ends in a period like other COBOL statements. For PL/I and C, the terminator is a semicolon (;), which also is the statement termination character in those languages. In FORTRAN, the embedded SQL statement ends when no more continuation lines are indicated.

```
main()
{
   exec sql include sqlca;
   exec sql declare salesreps table
                     (empl_num integer not null,
                          name varchar(15) not null,
                           age integer
                    rep_office integer,
                         title varchar(10),
                     hire_date date not null,
                       manager integer,
                         quota money,
                         sales money not null);

   /* Display a message for the user */
   printf("Deleting salesreps with low quota.\n");

   /*Execute the SQL statement */
   exec sql delete from salesreps
           where sales < 150000.00;

   /* Display another message */
   printf("Finished deleting.\n");
   exit();
}
```

Figure 17-4.   *An embedded SQL program written in C*

```
        IDENTIFICATION DIVISION.
        PROGRAM-ID. SAMPLE.
        ENVIRONMENT DIVISION.
        DATA DIVISION.
        FILE SECTION.
        WORKING-STORAGE SECTION.
                EXEC SQL INCLUDE SQLCA.
                EXEC SQL DECLARE SALESREPS TABLE
                              (EMPL_NUM INTEGER NOT NULL,
                                  NAME VARCHAR(15) NOT NULL,
                                   AGE INTEGER,
                            REP_OFFICE INTEGER,
                                 TITLE VARCHAR(10),
                             HIRE_DATE DATE NOT NULL,
                               MANAGER INTEGER,
                                 QUOTA MONEY,
                                 SALES MONEY NOT NULL)
                END-EXEC.
        PROCEDURE DIVISION.
        *
        *       DISPLAY A MESSAGE FOR THE USER
                DISPLAY "Deleting salesreps with low quota.".
        *
        *       EXECUTE THE SQL STATEMENT
                EXEC SQL DELETE FROM SALESREPS
                        WHERE QUOTA < 150000
                END EXEC.
        *
        *       DISPLAY ANOTHER MESSAGE
                DISPLAY "Finished deleting.".
```

Figure 17-5.   *An embedded SQL program written in COBOL*

The embedding technique shown in the three figures works for any SQL statement that (a) does not depend on the values of host language variables for its execution and (b) does not retrieve data from the database. For example, the C program in Figure 17-7 creates a new REGIONS table and inserts two rows into it, using exactly the same embedded SQL features as the program in Figure 17-4. For consistency, all of the remaining program examples in the book will use the C programming language, except when a particular host language feature is being illustrated.

```
      PROGRAM SAMPLE
100 FORMAT (' ',A35)
      EXEC SQL INCLUDE SQLCA
      EXEC SQL DECLARE SALESREPS TABLE
    C                     (EMPL_NUM INTEGER NOT NULL,
    C                         NAME VARCHAR(15) NOT NULL,
    C                          AGE INTEGER,
    C                   REP_OFFICE INTEGER,
    C                        TITLE VARCHAR(10),
    C                    HIRE_DATE DATE NOT NULL,
    C                      MANAGER INTEGER,
    C                        QUOTA MONEY,
    C                        SALES MONEY NOT NULL)
  *
  *   DISPLAY A MESSAGE FOR THE USER
      WRITE (6,100) 'Deleting salesreps with low quota.'
  *
  *   EXECUTE THE SQL STATEMENT
      EXEC SQL DELETE FROM REPS
    C            WHERE QUOTA < 150000
  *
  *   DISPLAY ANOTHER MESSAGE
      WRITE (6,100) 'Finished deleting.'
      RETURN
      END
```

Figure 17-6.   *An embedded SQL program written in FORTRAN*

Declaring Tables

In the IBM SQL products, the embedded DECLARE TABLE statement, shown in Figure 17-8, declares a table that will be referenced by one or more embedded SQL statements in your program. This is an optional statement that aids the precompiler in its task of parsing and validating the embedded SQL statements. By using the DECLARE TABLE statement, your program explicitly specifies its assumptions about the columns in the table and their data types and sizes. The precompiler checks the table and column references in your program to make sure they conform to your table declaration.

The programs in Figures 17-4, 17-5, and 17-6 all use the DECLARE TABLE statement. It's important to note that the statement appears purely for documentation purposes and for the use of the precompiler. It is not an executable statement, and you

```
main()
{
  exec sql include sqlca;

  /* Create a new REGIONS table */
  exec sql create table regions
                  (name char(15),
              hq_city char(15),
              manager integer,
               target money,
                sales money,
          primary key name,
          foreign key manager
            references salesreps);
  printf("Table created.\n");

  /* Insert two rows; one for each region */
  exec sql insert into regions
              values ('Eastern', 'New York', 106, 0.00, 0.00);
  exec sql insert into regions
              values ('Western', 'Los Angeles', 108, 0.00, 0.00);
  printf("Table populated.\n");

  exit();
}
```

Figure 17-7. *Using embedded SQL to create a table*

do not need to explicitly declare tables before referring to them in embedded DML or DDL statements. However, using the DECLARE TABLE statement does make your program more self-documenting and simpler to maintain. The IBM SQL products all support the DECLARE TABLE statement, but most other SQL products do not support it, and their precompilers will generate an error message if you use it.

Error Handling

When you type an interactive SQL statement that causes an error, the interactive SQL program displays an error message, aborts the statement, and prompts you to type a new statement. In embedded SQL, error handling becomes the responsibility of the application program. Actually, embedded SQL statements can produce two distinct types of errors:

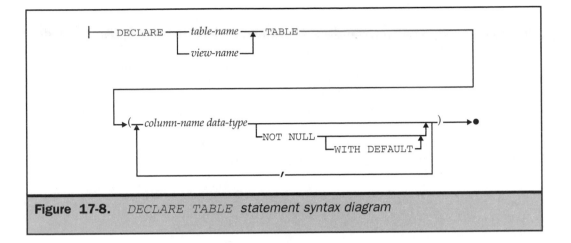

Figure 17-8.   *DECLARE TABLE statement syntax diagram*

- *Compile time errors.* Misplaced commas, misspelled SQL keywords, and similar errors in embedded SQL statements are detected by the SQL precompiler and reported to the programmer. The programmer can fix the errors and recompile the application program.

- *Run-time errors.* An attempt to insert an invalid data value or lack of permission to update a table can be detected only at run-time. Errors such as these must be detected and handled by the application program.

In embedded SQL programs, the DBMS reports run-time errors to the application program through a returned error code. If an error is detected, a further description of the error, and other information about the statement just executed is available through additional diagnostic information. The earliest IBM embedded SQL implementations defined an error-reporting mechanism that was adopted, with variations, by most of the major DBMS vendors. The central part of this scheme—an error status variable named SQLCODE—was also defined in the original ANSI/ISO SQL standard. The SQL2 standard, published in 1992, defined an entirely new, parallel error-reporting mechanism, built around an error status variable named SQLSTATE. These mechanisms are described in the next two sections.

Error Handling with SQLCODE

Under this scheme, pioneered by the earliest IBM products, the DBMS communicates status information to the embedded SQL program through an area of program storage called the *SQL Communications Area*, or SQLCA. The SQLCA is a data structure that contains error variables and status indicators. By examining the SQLCA, the application program can determine the success or failure of its embedded SQL statements and act accordingly.

Notice in Figures 17-4, 17-5, 17-6, and 17-7 that the first embedded SQL statement in the program is INCLUDE SQLCA. This statement tells the SQL precompiler to include a SQL Communications Area in this program. The specific contents of the SQLCA vary slightly from one brand of DBMS to another, but the SQLCA always provides the same type of information. Figure 17-9 shows the definition of the SQLCA used by the IBM databases. The most important part of the SQLCA, the SQLCODE variable, is supported by all of the major embedded SQL products and was specified by the ANSI/ISO SQL1 standard.

As the DBMS executes each embedded SQL statement, it sets the value of the variable SQLCODE in the SQLCA to indicate the completion status of the statement:

```
struct sqlca {
    unsigned char sqlcaid[8];       /* the string "SQLCA  " */
    long           sqlcabc;         /* length of SQLCA, in bytes */
    long           sqlcode;         /* SQL status code */
    short          sqlerrml;        /* length of sqlerrmc array data */
    unsigned char sqlerrmc[70];     /* name(s) of object(s) causing error */
    unsigned char sqlerrp[8];       /* diagnostic information */
    long           sqlerrd[6];      /* various counts and error code */
    unsigned char sqlwarn[8];       /* warning flag array */
    unsigned char sqlext[8];        /* extension to sqlwarn array */
}

#define SQLCODE  sqlca.sqlcode     /* SQL status code */

/* A 'W' in any of the SQLWARN fields signals a warning condition;
   otherwise these fields each contain a blank */

#define SQLWARN0 sqlca.sqlwarn[0]  /* master warning flag */
#define SQLWARN1 sqlca.sqlwarn[1]  /* string truncated */
#define SQLWARN2 sqlca.sqlwarn[2]  /* NULLs eliminated from column function */
#define SQLWARN3 sqlca.sqlwarn[3]  /* too few/too many host variables */
#define SQLWARN4 sqlca.sqlwarn[4]  /* prepared UPDATE/DELETE without WHERE */
#define SQLWARN5 sqlca.sqlwarn[5]  /* SQL/DS vs DB2 incompatibility */
#define SQLWARN6 sqlca.sqlwarn[6]  /* invalid date in arithmetic expr */
#define SQLWARN7 sqlca.sqlwarn[7]  /* reserved */
```

Figure 17-9.   *The SQL Communications Area (SQLCA) for IBM databases*

- A SQLCODE of zero indicates successful completion of the statement, without any errors or warnings.

- A negative SQLCODE value indicates a serious error that prevented the statement from executing correctly. For example, an attempt to update a read-only view would produce a negative SQLCODE value. A separate negative value is assigned to each run-time error that can occur.

- A positive SQLCODE value indicates a warning condition. For example, truncation or rounding of a data item retrieved by the program would produce a warning. A separate positive value is assigned to each run-time warning that can occur. The most common warning, with a value of +100 in most implementations and in the SQL1 standard, is the "out-of-data" warning returned when a program tries to retrieve the next row of query results and no more rows are left to retrieve.

Because every executable embedded SQL statement can potentially generate an error, a well-written program will check the SQLCODE value after *every* executable embedded SQL statement. Figure 17-10 shows a C program excerpt that checks the SQLCODE value. Figure 17-11 shows a similar excerpt from a COBOL program.

```
          .
          .
          .
      exec sql delete from salesreps
              where quota < 150000;
      if (sqlca.sqlcode < 0)
         goto error_routine;
          .
          .
          .


      error_routine:
         printf("SQL error: %ld\n, sqlca.sqlcode);
         exit();
          .
          .
          .
```

Figure 17-10. *A C program excerpt with SQLCODE error checking*

```
          .
          .
          .
     01    PRINT_MESSAGE.
           02    FILLER     PIC X(11) VALUE 'SQL error:'.
           02    PRINT-CODE PIC SZ(9).
          .
          .
          .


              EXEC SQL DELETE FROM SALESREPS
                      WHERE QUOTA < 150000
              END EXEC.
              IF SQLCODE NOT = ZERO GOTO ERROR-ROUTINE.
          .
          .
          .

     ERROR-ROUTINE.
              MOVE SQLCODE TO PRINT-CODE.
              DISPLAY PRINT_MESSAGE.
          .
          .
          .
```

Figure 17-11. *A COBOL program excerpt with SQLCODE error checking*

Error Handling with SQLSTATE

By the time the SQL2 standard was being written, virtually all commercial SQL products were using the SQLCODE variable to report error conditions in an embedded SQL program. However, there was no standardization of the error numbers used by the different products to report the same or similar error conditions. Further, because of the significant differences among SQL implementations permitted by the SQL1 standard, considerable differences in the errors could occur from one implementation to another. Finally, the definition of the SQLCA varied in significant ways from one DBMS brand to another, and all of the major brands had a large installed base of applications that would be "broken" by any change to their SQLCA structure.

Instead of tackling the impossible task of getting all of the DBMS vendors to agree to change their SQLCODE values to some standard, the writers of the SQL2 standard took a different approach. They included the SQLCODE error value, but identified it as a "deprecated feature," meaning that it was considered obsolete and would be removed from the standard at some future time. To take its place, they introduced a new error variable, called SQLSTATE. The standard also specifies, in detail, the error conditions that can be reported through the SQLSTATE variable, and the error code assigned to each error. To conform to the SQL2 standard, a SQL product must report errors using *both* the SQLCODE and SQLSTATE error variables. In this way, existing programs that use SQLCODE will still function, but new programs can be written to use the standardized SQLSTATE error codes.

The SQLSTATE variable consists of two parts:

- A two-character *error class* that identifies the general classification of the error (such as a "connection error," an "invalid data error," or a "warning")

- A three-character *error subclass* that identifies a specific type of error within a general error class. For example, within the "invalid data" class, the error subclass might identify a "divide by zero" error, an "invalid numeric value" error, or "invalid datetime data"

Errors specified in the SQL2 standard have an error class code that begins with a digit from zero to four (inclusive) or a letter between A and H (inclusive). For example, data errors are indicated by error class 22. A violation of an integrity constraint (such as a foreign key definition) is indicated by error class 23. A transaction rollback is indicated by error class 40. Within each error class, the standard subclass codes also follow the same initial number/letter restrictions. For example, within error class 40 (transaction rollback), the subclass codes are 001 for serialization failure (that is, your program was chosen as the loser in a deadlock), 002 for an integrity constraint violation, and 003 for errors where the completion status of the SQL statement is unknown (for example, when a network connection breaks or a server crashes before the statement completes). Figure 17-12 shows the same C program as Figure 17-10, but uses the SQLSTATE variable for error checking instead of SQLCODE.

The standard specifically reserves error class codes that begin with digits from five to nine (inclusive) and letters between I and Z (inclusive) as implementation-specific errors that are not standardized. While this allows differences among DBMS brands to continue, all of the most common errors caused by SQL statements are included in the standardized error class codes. As commercial DBMS implementations move to support the SQLSTATE variable, one of the most troublesome incompatibilities between different SQL products is gradually being eliminated.

The SQL2 standard provides additional error and diagnostics information through a new GET DIAGNOSTICS statement, shown in Figure 17-13. The statement allows an embedded SQL program to retrieve one or more items of information about the SQL statement just executed, or about an error condition that was just raised. Support for the GET DIAGNOSTICS statement is required for Intermediate SQL or Full SQL conformance to the standard but is not required or allowed in Entry SQL. Figure 17-14 shows a C program excerpt like that in Figure 17-12, extended to include the GET DIAGNOSTICS statement.

```
          .
          .
          .
       exec sql delete from salesreps
                  where quota < 150000;
       if (strcmp(sqlca.sqlstate,"00000"))
          goto error_routine;
          .
          .
          .
       error_routine:
          printf("SQL error: %s\n",sqlca.sqlstate);
          exit();
          .
          .
          .
```

Figure 17-12. *A C program excerpt with* SQLSTATE *error checking*

The WHENEVER Statement

It quickly becomes tedious for a programmer to write programs that explicitly check the SQLCODE value after each embedded SQL statement. To simplify error handling, embedded SQL supports the WHENEVER statement, shown in Figure 17-15. The WHENEVER statement is a directive to the SQL precompiler, not an executable statement. It tells the precompiler to *automatically* generate error-handling code following every executable embedded SQL statement and specifies what the generated code should do.

You can use the WHENEVER statement to tell the precompiler how to handle three different exception conditions:

■ WHENEVER SQLERROR tells the precompiler to generate code to handle errors (negative SQLCODEs).

■ WHENEVER SQLWARNING tells the precompiler to generate code to handle warnings (positive SQLCODEs).

■ WHENEVER NOT FOUND tells the precompiler to generate code that handles a particular warning—the warning generated by the DBMS when your program tries to retrieve query results when no more are remaining. This use of the WHENEVER statement is specific to the singleton SELECT and the FETCH statements and is described later in this chapter.

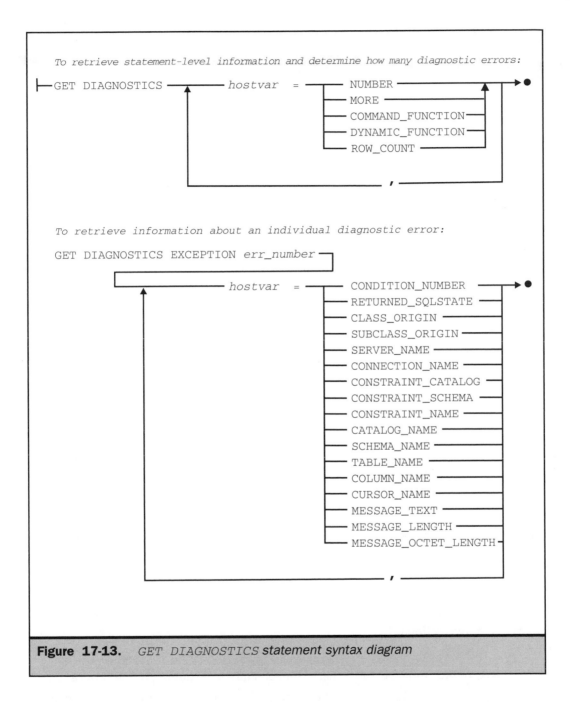

Figure 17-13. *GET DIAGNOSTICS statement syntax diagram*

Note that the SQL2 standard does not specify the SQLWARNING form of the WHENEVER statement, but most commercial SQL products support it.

```
           .
           .
           .
      /* execute the DELETE statement & check for errors */
      exec sql delete from salesreps
              where quota < 150000;
      if (strcmp(sqlca.sqlstate,"00000"))
         goto error_routine;

      /* DELETE successful; check how many rows deleted */
      exec sql get diagnostics :numrows = ROW_COUNT;
      printf("%ld rows deleted\n",numrows);
           .
           .
           .
   error_routine:
      /* Determine how many errors reported */
      exec sql get diagnostics :count = NUMBER;
      for (i=1; i<count; i++) {
         exec sql get diagnostics EXCEPTION :I
                       :err = RETURNED_SQLSTATE,
                       :msg = MESSAGE_TEXT;
         printf("SQL error # %d: code: %s message: %s\n",
                 i, err, msg);
      }
      exit();
           .
           .
           .
```

Figure 17-14. *A C program excerpt with* GET DIAGNOSTICS *error checking*

For any of these three conditions, you can tell the precompiler to generate code that takes one of two actions:

■ WHENEVER/GOTO tells the precompiler to generate a branch to the specified *label*, which must be a statement label or statement number in the program.

■ WHENEVER/CONTINUE tells the precompiler to let the program's flow of control proceed to the next host language statement.

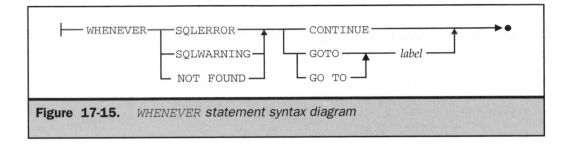

Figure 17-15.   *WHENEVER statement syntax diagram*

The WHENEVER statement is a directive to the precompiler, and its effect can be super-seded by another WHENEVER statement appearing later in the program text. Figure 17-16 shows a program excerpt with three WHENEVER statements and four executable SQL statements. In this program, an error in either of the two DELETE statements results in a branch to error1 because of the first WHENEVER statement. An error in the embedded UPDATE statement flows directly into the following statements of the program. An error in the embedded INSERT statement results in a branch to error2. As this example shows, the main use of the WHENEVER/CONTINUE form of the statement is to cancel the effect of a previous WHENEVER statement.

The WHENEVER statement makes embedded SQL error handling much simpler, and it is more common for an application program to use it than to check SQLCODE or SQLSTATE directly. Remember, however, that after a WHENEVER/GOTO statement appears, the precompiler will generate a test and a branch to the specified label for *every* embedded SQL statement that follows it. You must arrange your program so that the specified label is a valid target for branching from these embedded SQL statements, or use another WHENEVER statement to specify a different destination or cancel the effects of the WHENEVER/GOTO.

Using Host Variables

The embedded SQL programs in the previous figures don't provide any real interaction between the programming statements and the embedded SQL statements. In most applications, you will want to use the value of one or more program variables in the embedded SQL statements. For example, suppose you wanted to write a program to adjust all sales quotas up or down by some dollar amount. The program should prompt the user for the amount and then use an embedded UPDATE statement to change the QUOTA column in the SALESREPS table.

Embedded SQL supports this capability through the use of *host variables*. A host variable is a program variable declared in the host language (for example, a COBOL or C variable) that is referenced in an embedded SQL statement. To identify the host variable, the variable name is prefixed by a colon (:) when it appears in an embedded SQL statement. The colon allows the precompiler to distinguish easily between host variables and database objects (such as tables or columns) that may have the same name.

```
              .
              .
              .
          exec sql whenever sqlerror goto error1;

          exec sql delete from salesreps
                    where quota < 150000;

          exec sql delete from customers
                    where credit_limit < 20000;

          exec sql whenever sqlerror continue;

          exec sql update salesreps
                    set quota = quota * 1.05;

          exec sql whenever sqlerror goto error2;

          exec sql insert into salesreps (empl_num, name, quota)
                    values (116, 'Jan Hamilton', 100000.00);
              .
              .
              .
      error1:
         printf("SQL DELETE error: %dl\n", sqlca.sqlcode);
         exit();

      error2:
         printf("SQL INSERT error: %ld\n", sqlca.sqlcode);
         exit();
              .
              .
              .
```

Figure 17-16. *Using the WHENEVER statement*

Figure 17-17 shows a C program that implements the quota adjustment application using a host variable. The program prompts the user for the adjustment amount and stores the entered value in the variable named amount. This host variable is referenced in the embedded UPDATE statement. Conceptually, when the UPDATE statement is executed, the value of the amount variable is obtained, and that value is substituted for the host variable in the SQL statement. For example, if you enter the amount 500 in response to the prompt, the DBMS effectively executes this UPDATE statement:

```
exec sql update salesreps
          set quota = quota + 500;
```

A host variable can appear in an embedded SQL statement wherever a constant can appear. In particular, a host variable can be used in an assignment expression:

```
exec sql update salesreps
          set quota = quota + :amount;
```

A host variable can appear in a search condition:

```
exec sql delete from salesreps
          where quota < :amount;
```

A host variable can also be used in the VALUES clause of an insert statement:

```
exec sql insert into salesreps (empl_num, name, quota)
          values (116, 'Bill Roberts', :amount);
```

In each case, note that the host variable is part of the program's *input* to the DBMS; it forms part of the SQL statement submitted to the DBMS for execution. Later in this chapter, you will see how host variables are also used to receive *output* from the DBMS; they receive query results returned from the DBMS to the program.

Note that a host variable *cannot* be used instead of a SQL identifier. This attempted use of the host variable colname is illegal:

```
char *colname = "quota";

exec sql insert into salesreps (empl_num, name, :colname)
          values (116, 'Bill Roberts', 0.00);
```

Declaring Host Variables

When you use a host variable in an embedded SQL statement, you must declare the variable using the normal method for declaring variables in the host programming language. For example, in Figure 17-17, the host variable amount is declared using the

```
main()
{
    exec sql include sqlca;
    exec sql begin declare section;
        float amount;                   /* amount (from user) */
    exec sql end declare section;

    /* Prompt the user for the amount of quota increase/decrease */
    printf("Raise/lower quotas by how much:");
    scanf("%f", &amount);

    /* Update the QUOTA column in the SALESREPS table */
    exec sql update salesreps
               set quota = quota + :amount;

    /* Check results of statement execution */
    if (sqlqa.sqlcode != 0)
        printf("Error during update.\n");
    else
        printf("Update successful.\n");

    exit();
}
```

Figure 17-17. *Using host variables*

normal C language syntax (`float amount;`). When the precompiler processes the source code for the program, it notes the name of each variable it encounters, along with its data type and size. The precompiler uses this information to generate correct code later when it encounters a use of the variable as a host variable in a SQL statement.

The two embedded SQL statements BEGIN DECLARE SECTION and END DECLARE SECTION bracket the host variable declarations, as shown in Figure 17-17. These two statements are unique to embedded SQL, and they are not executable. They are directives to the precompiler, telling it when it must "pay attention" to variable declarations and when it can ignore them.

In a simple embedded SQL program, it may be possible to gather together all of the host variable declarations in one "declare section." Usually, however, the host variables must be declared at various points within the program, especially in block-structured languages such as C, Pascal, and PL/I. In this case each declaration of host variables must be bracketed with a BEGIN DECLARE SECTION/END DECLARE SECTION statement pair.

The BEGIN DECLARE SECTION and END DECLARE SECTION statements are relatively new to the embedded SQL language. They are specified in the ANSI/ISO SQL standard, and DB2 requires them in embedded SQL for C, which was introduced in DB2 Version 2. However, DB2 and many other DBMS brands did not historically require declare sections, and some SQL precompilers do not yet support the BEGIN DECLARE SECTION and END DECLARE SECTION statements. In this case the precompiler scans and processes all variable declarations in the host program.

When you use a host variable, the precompiler may limit your flexibility in declaring the variable in the host programming language. For example, consider the following C language source code:

```
#define BIGBUFSIZE 256
     .
     .
     .
exec sql begin declare section;
    char bigbuffer[BIGBUFSIZE+1];
exec sql end declare section;
```

This is a valid C declaration of the variable bigbuffer. However, if you try to use bigbuffer as a host variable in an embedded SQL statement like this:

```
exec sql update salesreps
          set quota = 300000
        where name = :bigbuffer;
```

many precompilers will generate an error message, complaining about an illegal declaration of bigbuffer. The problem is that some precompilers don't recognize symbolic constants like BIGBUFSIZE. This is just one example of the special considerations that apply when using embedded SQL and a precompiler. Fortunately, the precompilers offered by the major DBMS vendors are being improved steadily, and the number of special case problems like this one is decreasing.

Host Variables and Data Types

The data types supported by a SQL-based DBMS and the data types supported by a programming language such as C or FORTRAN are often quite different. These differences impact host variables because they play a dual role. On the one hand, a host variable is a program variable, declared using the data types of the programming language and manipulated by programming language statements. On the other hand, a host variable is used in embedded SQL statements to contain database data.

Consider the four embedded UPDATE statements in Figure 17-18. In the first UPDATE statement, the MANAGER column has an INTEGER data type, so hostvar1 should be declared as a C integer variable. In the second statement, the NAME column has a VARCHAR data type, so hostvar2 should contain string data. The program should declare hostvar2 as an array of C character data, and most DBMS products will expect the data in the array to be terminated by a null character (0). In the third UPDATE statement, the QUOTA column has a MONEY data type. There is no corresponding data type in C, and C does not support a packed decimal data type. For most DBMS brands, you can declare hostvar3 as a C floating point variable, and the DBMS will automatically translate the floating point value into the DBMS MONEY format. Finally, in the fourth UPDATE statement, the HIRE_DATE column has a DATE data type in the database. For most DBMS brands, you should declare hostvar4 as an array of C character data and fill the array with a text form of the date acceptable to the DBMS. As Figure 17-18 shows, the data types of host variables must be chosen carefully to match their intended usage in embedded SQL statements. Table 17-1 shows the SQL data types specified in the ANSI/ISO SQL2 standard and the corresponding data types used in four of the most popular embedded SQL programming languages, as specified in the standard. The standard specifies data type correspondences and embedded SQL rules for the Ada, C, COBOL, Fortran, MUMPS, Pascal, and PL/I languages. Note, however, that in many cases there is not a one-to-one correspondence between data types. In addition, each brand of DBMS has its own data type idiosyncrasies and its own rules for data type conversion when using host variables. Before counting on a specific data conversion behavior, consult the documentation for your particular DBMS brand and carefully read the description for the particular programming language you are using.

Host Variables and NULL Values

Most programming languages do not provide SQL-style support for unknown or missing values. A C, COBOL, or FORTRAN variable, for example, always has a value. There is no concept of the value being NULL or missing. This causes a problem when you want to store NULL values in the database or retrieve NULL values from the database using programmatic SQL. Embedded SQL solves this problem by allowing each host variable to have a companion *host indicator variable*. In an embedded SQL statement, the host variable and the indicator variable *together* specify a single SQL-style value, as follows:

- An indicator value of zero means that the host variable contains a valid value and that this value is to be used.

- A negative indicator value means that the host variable should be assumed to have a NULL value; the actual value of the host variable is irrelevant and should be disregarded.

SQL Type	C Type	COBOL Type	FORTRAN Type	PL/I Type
SMALLINT	short	PIC S9 (4) COMP	INTEGER*2	FIXED BIN(15)
INTEGER	long	PIC S9 (9) COMP	INTEGER*4	FIXED BIN(31)
REAL	float	COMP-1	REAL*4	BIN FLOAT(21)
DOUBLE PRECISION	double	COMP-2	REAL*8	BIN FLOAT(53)
NUMERIC(p,s) DECIMAL(p,s)	double[1]	PIC S9 ($p-s$) V9(s) COMP-3	REAL*8[1]	FIXED DEC(p,s)
CHAR(n)	char x[$n+1$][2]	PIC X (n)	CHARACTER*n	CHAR(n)
VARCHAR(n)	char x[$n+1$][2]	Req. conv.[4]	Req. conv.[4]	CHAR(n) VAR
BIT(n)	char x[1][3]	PIC X (1)	CHARACTER*L[3]	BIT(n)
BIT VARYING(n)	char x[1][3]	Req. conv.[4]	Req. conv.[4]	BIT(n) VAR
DATE	Req. conv.[5]	Req. conv.[5]	Req. conv.[5]	Req. conv.[5]
TIME	Req. conv.[5]	Req. conv.[5]	Req. conv.[5]	Req. conv.[5]
TIMESTAMP	Req. conv.[5]	Req. conv.[5]	Req. conv.[5]	Req. conv.[5]
INTERVAL	Req. conv.[5]	Req. conv.[5]	Req. conv.[5]	Req. conv.[5]

Notes:

[1]Host language does not support packed decimal data; conversion to or from floating-point data may cause truncation or round off errors.

[2]The SQL standard specifies a C string with a null-terminator; older DBMS implementations returned a separate length value in a data structure.

[3]The length of the host character string (l) is the number of bits (n), divided by the bits-per-character for the host language (typically 8), rounded up.

[4]Host language does not support variable-length strings; most DBMS brands will convert to fixed-length strings.

[5]Host languages do not support native date/time data types; requires conversion to/from host language character string data types with text date, time & interval representations.

Table 17-1. *SQL Data Types*

- A positive indicator value means that the host variable contains a valid value, which may have been rounded off or truncated. This situation only occurs when data is retrieved from the database and is described later in this chapter.

```
                                    .
                                    .
                                    .
                    exec sql begin declare section;
                        int     hostvar1  = 106;
                        char    *hostvar2 = "Joe Smith";
                        float   hostvar3  = 150000.00;
                        char    *hostvar4 = "01-JUN-1990";
                    exec sql end declare section;

                    exec sql update salesreps
                            set manager = :hostvar1
                            where empl_num = 102;

                    exec sql update salesreps
                            set name = :hostvar2
                            where empl_num = 102:

                    exec sql update salesreps
                            set quota = :hostvar3
                            where empl_num = 102;

                    exec sql update salesreps
                            set hire_date = :hostvar4
                            where empl_num = 102;
                                    .
                                    .
                                    .
```

Figure 17-18. *Host variables and data types*

When you specify a host variable in an embedded SQL statement, you can follow it immediately with the name of the corresponding indicator variable. Both variable names are preceded by a colon. Here is an embedded UPDATE statement that uses the host variable amount with the companion indicator variable amount_ind:

```
exec sql update salesreps
        set quota = :amount :amount_ind, sales = :amount2
        where quota < 20000.00;
```

If `amount_ind` has a nonnegative value when the UPDATE statement is executed, the DBMS treats the statement as if it read:

```
exec sql update salesreps
         set quota = :amount, sales = :amount2
      where quota < 20000.00;
```

If `amount_ind` has a negative value when the UPDATE statement is executed, the DBMS treats the statement as if it read:

```
exec sql update salesreps
         set quota = NULL, sales = :amount2
      where quota < 20000.00;
```

A host variable/indicator variable pair can appear in the assignment clause of an embedded UPDATE statement (as shown here) or in the values clause of an embedded INSERT statement. You cannot use an indicator variable in a search condition, so this embedded SQL statement is illegal:

```
exec sql delete from salesreps
      where quota = :amount :amount_ind;
```

This prohibition exists for the same reason that the NULL keyword is not allowed in the search condition—it makes no sense to test whether QUOTA and NULL are equal, because the answer will always be NULL (unknown). Instead of using the indicator variable, you must use an explicit IS NULL test. This pair of embedded SQL statements accomplishes the intended task of the preceding illegal statement:

```
if (amount_ind < 0) {
   exec sql delete from salesreps
            where quota is null;
}
else {
   exec sql delete from salesreps
            where quota = :amount;
}
```

Indicator variables are especially useful when you are retrieving data from the database into your program and the retrieved data values may be NULL. This use of indicator variables is described later in this chapter.

Data Retrieval in Embedded SQL

Using the embedded SQL features described thus far, you can embed any interactive SQL statement *except* the SELECT statement in an application program. Retrieving data with an embedded SQL program requires some special extensions to the SELECT statement. The reason for these extensions is that there is a fundamental mismatch between the SQL language and programming languages such as C and COBOL: a SQL query produces an entire table of query results, but most programming languages can only manipulate individual data items or individual records (rows) of data.

Embedded SQL must build a "bridge" between the table-level logic of the SQL SELECT statement and the row-by-row processing of C, COBOL, and other host programming languages. For this reason, embedded SQL divides SQL queries into two groups:

- *Single-row queries*, where you expect the query results to contain a single row of data. Looking up a customer's credit limit or retrieving the sales and quota for a particular salesperson are examples of this type of query.

- *Multi-row queries*, where you expect that the query results may contain zero, one, or many rows of data. Listing the orders with amounts over $20,000 or retrieving the names of all salespeople who are over quota are examples of this type of query.

Interactive SQL does not distinguish between these two types of queries; the same interactive SELECT statement handles them both. In embedded SQL, however, the two types of queries are handled very differently. Single-row queries are simpler to handle and are discussed in the next section. Multi-row queries are discussed later in this chapter.

Single-Row Queries

Many useful SQL queries return a single row of query results. Single-row queries are especially common in transaction processing programs, where a user enters a customer number or an order number and the program retrieves relevant data about the customer or order. In embedded SQL, single-row queries are handled by the *singleton* SELECT statement, shown in Figure 17-19. The singleton SELECT statement has a syntax much like that of the interactive SELECT statement. It has a SELECT clause, a FROM clause, and an optional WHERE clause. Because the singleton SELECT statement returns a single row of data, there is no need for a GROUP BY, HAVING or ORDER BY clause. The INTO clause specifies the host variables that are to receive the data retrieved by the statement.

Figure 17-20 shows a simple program with a singleton SELECT statement. The program prompts the user for an employee number and then retrieves the name, quota, and sales of the corresponding salesperson. The DBMS places the three retrieved data items into the host variables repname, repquota, and repsales, respectively.

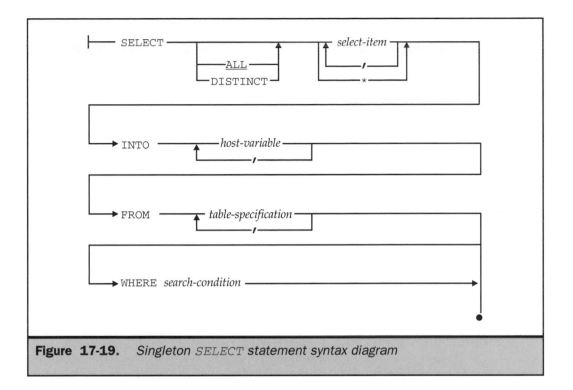

Figure 17-19. *Singleton* `SELECT` *statement syntax diagram*

Recall that the host variables used in the `INSERT`, `DELETE`, and `UPDATE` statements in the previous examples were input host variables. In contrast, the host variables specified in the `INTO` clause of the singleton `SELECT` statement are *output* host variables. Each host variable named in the `INTO` clause receives a single column from the row of query results. The select list items and the corresponding host variables are paired in sequence, as they appear in their respective clauses, and the number of query results columns must be the same as the number of host variables. In addition, the data type of each host variable must be compatible with the data type of the corresponding column of query results.

As discussed earlier, most DBMS brands will automatically handle "reasonable" conversions between DBMS data types and the data types supported by the programming language. For example, most DBMS products will convert `MONEY` data retrieved from the database into packed decimal (`COMP-3`) data before storing it in a COBOL variable, or into floating-point data before storing it in a C variable. The precompiler uses its knowledge of the host variable's data type to handle the conversion correctly.

Variable-length text data must also be converted before being stored in a host variable. Typically, a DBMS converts `VARCHAR` data into a null-terminated string for C programs and into a variable-length string (with a leading character count) for Pascal

```
main()
{
   exec sql    begin declare section;
      int       repnum;               /* employee number (from user) */
      char      repname[16];          /* retrieved salesperson name */
      float     repquota;             /* retrieved quota */
      float     repsales;             /* retrieved sales */
   exec sql    end declare section;

   /* Prompt the user for the employee number */
   printf("Enter salesrep number: ");
   scanf("%d", &repnum);

   /* Execute the SQL query */
   exec sql select name, quota, sales
             from salesreps
            where empl_num = :repnum
             into :repname, :repquota, :repsales;

   /* Display the retrieved data */
   if (sqlca.sqlcode = = 0) {
      printf("Name:  %s\n", repname);
      printf("Quota: %f\n", repquota);
      printf("Sales: %f\n", repsales);
   }
   else if (sqlca.sqlcode = = 100)
      printf("No salesperson with that employee number.\n");
   else
      printf("SQL error: %ld\n", sqlca.sqlcode);

   exit();
}
```

Figure 17-20.   *Using the singleton SELECT statement*

programs. For COBOL and FORTRAN programs, the host variable must generally be declared as a data structure with an integer "count" field and a character array. The DBMS returns the actual characters of data in the character array, and it returns the length of the data in the count field of the data structure.

If a DBMS supports date/time data or other data types, other conversions are necessary. Some DBMS products return their internal date/time representations into an integer host variable. Others convert the date/time data to text format and return it into a string host variable. Table 17-1 summarized the data type conversions typically provided by DBMS products, but you must consult the embedded SQL documentation for your particular DBMS brand for specific information.

The NOT FOUND Condition

Like all embedded SQL statements, the singleton SELECT statement sets the values of the SQLCODE and SQLSTATE variables to indicate its completion status:

- If a *single row* of query results is successfully retrieved, SQLCODE is set to zero and SQLSTATE is set to 00000; the host variables named in the INTO clause contain the retrieved values.

- If the query produced an *error*, SQLCODE is set to a negative value and SQLSTATE is set to a nonzero error class (first two characters of the five-digit SQLSTATE string); the host variables do not contain retrieved values.

- If the query produced *no rows* of query results, a special NOT FOUND warning value is returned in SQLCODE, and SQLSTATE returns a NO DATA error class .

- If the query produced *more than one row* of query results, it is treated as an error, and a negative SQLCODE is returned.

The SQL1 standard specifies the NOT FOUND warning condition, but it does not specify a particular value to be returned. DB2 uses the value +100, and most other SQL products follow this convention, including the other IBM SQL products, Ingres, and SQLBase. This value is also specified in the SQL2 standard, but as noted previously, SQL2 strongly encourages the use of the new SQLSTATE error variable instead of the older SQLCODE values.

Retrieving NULL Values

If the data to be retrieved from a database may contain NULL values, the singleton SELECT statement must provide a way for the DBMS to communicate the NULL values to the application program. To handle NULL values, embedded SQL uses indicator variables in the INTO clause, just as they are used in the VALUES clause of the INSERT statement and the SET clause of the UPDATE statement.

When you specify a host variable in the INTO clause, you can follow it immediately with the name of a companion host indicator variable. Figure 17-21 shows a revised version of the program in Figure 17-20 that uses the indicator variable repquota_ind with the host variable repquota. Because the NAME and SALES columns are declared NOT NULL in the definition of the SALESREPS table, they cannot produce NULL output values, and no indicator variable is needed for those columns.

```
main()
{
   exec sql include sqlca;
   exec sql begin declare section;
      int   repnum;                    /* employee number (from user) */
      char  repname[16];               /* retrieved salesperson name */
      float repquota;                  /* retrieved quota */
      float repsales;                  /* retrieved sales */
      short repquota_ind;              /* null quota indicator */
   exec sql end declare section;

   /* Prompt the user for the employee number */
   printf("Enter salesrep number: ");
   scanf("%d", &repnum);

   /* Execute the SQL query */
   exec sql select name, quota, sales
            from salesreps
            where empl_num = :repnum
              into :repname, :repquota, :repquota_ind, :repsales;

   /* Display the retrieved data */
   if (sqlca.sqlcode = = 0) {
      printf("Name:  %s\n", repname);
      if (repquota_ind < 0)
         printf("quota is NULL\n");
      else
         printf("Quota: %f\n", repquota);
      printf("Sales: %f\n", repsales);
   }
   else if (sqlca.sqlcode = = 100)
      printf("No salesperson with that employee number.\n");
   else
      printf("SQL error: %ld\n", sqlca.sqlcode);

   exit();
}
```

Figure 17-21.   *Using singleton* SELECT *with indicator variables*

After the SELECT statement has been executed, the value of the indicator variable tells the program how to interpret the returned data:

■ An indicator value of zero means the host variable has been assigned a retrieved value by the DBMS. The application program can use the value of the host variable in its processing.

■ A negative indicator value means the retrieved value was NULL. The value of the host variable is irrelevant and should not be used by the application program.

■ A positive indicator value indicates a warning condition of some kind, such as a rounding error or string truncation.

Because you cannot tell in advance when a NULL value will be retrieved, you should *always* specify an indicator variable in the INTO clause for any column of query results that may contain a NULL value. If the SELECT statement produces a column containing a NULL value and you have not specified an indicator variable for the column, the DBMS will treat the statement as an error and return a negative SQLCODE. Thus indicator variables *must* be used to successfully retrieve rows containing NULL data.

Although the major use of indicator variables is for handling NULL values, the DBMS also uses indicator variables to signal warning conditions. For example, if an arithmetic overflow or division by zero makes one of the query results columns invalid, DB2 returns a warning SQLCODE of +802 and sets the indicator variable for the affected column to −2. The application program can respond to the SQLCODE and examine the indicator variables to determine which column contains invalid data.

DB2 also uses indicator variables to signal string truncation. If the query results contain a column of character data that is too large for the corresponding host variable, DB2 copies the first part of the character string into the host variable and sets the corresponding indicator variable to the full length of the string. The application program can examine the indicator variable and may want to retry the SELECT statement with a different host variable that can hold a larger string.

These additional uses of indicator variables are fairly common in commercial SQL products, but the specific warning code values vary from one product to another. They are not specified by the ANSI/ISO SQL standard. Instead, the SQL2 standard specifies error classes and subclasses to indicate these and similar conditions, and the program must use the GET DIAGNOSTICS statement to determine more specific information about the host variable causing the error.

Retrieval Using Data Structures

Some programming languages support *data structures*, which are named collections of variables. For these languages, a SQL precompiler may allow you to treat the entire data structure as a single, composite host variable in the INTO clause. Instead of specifying a separate host variable as the destination for each column of query results, you can specify a data structure as the destination for the entire row. Figure 17-22 shows the program from Figure 17-21, rewritten to use a C data structure.

```
main()
{
   exec sql include sqlca;
   exec sql begin declare section;
      int repnum;                         /* employee number (from user) */
      struct {
         char  name[16];                  /* retrieved salesperson name */
         float quota;                     /* retrieved quota */
         float sales;                     /* retrieved sales */
      } repinfo;
      short rep_ind[3];                    /* null indicator array */
   exec sql end declare section;

   /* Prompt the user for the employee number */
   printf("Enter salesrep number: ");
   scanf("%d", &repnum);

   /* Execute the SQL query */
   exec sql select name, quota, sales
            from salesreps
            where empl_num = :repnum
            into :repinfo :rep_ind;

   /* Display the retrieved data */
   if (sqlca.sqlcode = = 0) {
      printf("Name:  %s\n", repinfo.name);
      if (rep_ind[1] < 0)
         printf("quota is NULL\n");
      else
         printf("Quota: %f\n", repinfo.quota);
      printf("Sales: %f\n", repinfo.sales);
   }
   else if (sqlca.sqlcode = = 100)
      printf("No salesperson with that employee number.\n");
   else
      printf("SQL error: %ld\n", sqlca.sqlcode);

   exit();
}
```

Figure 17-22.   *Using a data structure as a host variable*

When the precompiler encounters a data structure reference in the INTO clause, it replaces the structure reference with a list of the individual variables in the structure, in the order they are declared within the structure. Thus the number of items in the structure and their data types must correspond to the columns of query results. The use of data structures in the INTO clause is, in effect, a "shortcut." It does not fundamentally change the way the INTO clause works.

Support for the use of data structures as host variables varies widely among DBMS brands. It is also restricted to certain programming languages. DB2 supports C and PL/I structures but does not support COBOL or assembly language structures, for example.

Input and Output Host Variables

Host variables provide two-way communication between the program and the DBMS. In the program shown in Figure 17-21, the host variables repnum and repname illustrate the two different roles played by host variables:

- The repnum host variable is an *input* host variable, used to pass data from the program to the DBMS. The program assigns a value to the variable before executing the embedded statement, and that value becomes part of the SELECT statement to be executed by the DBMS. The DBMS does nothing to alter the value of the variable.

- The repname host variable is an output host variable, used to pass data back from the DBMS to the program. The DBMS assigns a value to this variable as it executes the embedded SELECT statement. After the statement has been executed, the program can use the resulting value.

Input and output host variables are declared the same way and are specified using the same colon notation within an embedded SQL statement. However, it's often useful to think in terms of input and output host variables when you're actually coding an embedded SQL program. Input host variables can be used in any SQL statement where a constant can appear. Output host variables are used only with the singleton SELECT statement and with the FETCH statement, described later in this chapter.

Multi-Row Queries

When a query produces an entire table of query results, embedded SQL must provide a way for the application program to process the query results one row at a time. Embedded SQL supports this capability by defining a new SQL concept, called a *cursor*, and adding several statements to the interactive SQL language. Here is an overview of embedded SQL technique for multi-row query processing and the new statements it requires:

1. The DECLARE CURSOR statement specifies the query to be performed and associates a *cursor* name with the query.

2. The OPEN statement asks the DBMS to start executing the query and generating query results. It positions the cursor before the first row of query results.

3. The FETCH statement advances the cursor to the first row of query results and retrieves its data into host variables for use by the application program. Subsequent FETCH statements move through the query results row by row, advancing the cursor to the next row of query results and retrieving its data into the host variables.

4. The CLOSE statement ends access to the query results and breaks the association between the cursor and the query results.

Figure 17-23 shows a program that uses embedded SQL to perform a simple multi-row query. The numbered callouts in the figure correspond to the numbers in the preceding steps. The program retrieves and displays, in alphabetical order, the name, quota, and year-to-date sales of each salesperson whose sales exceed quota. The interactive SQL query that prints this information is:

```
SELECT NAME, QUOTA, SALES
  FROM SALESREPS
 WHERE SALES > QUOTA
 ORDER BY NAME
```

Notice that this query appears, word for word, in the embedded DECLARE CURSOR statement in Figure 17-23. The statement also associates the cursor name repcurs with the query. This cursor name is used later in the OPEN CURSOR statement to start the query and position the cursor before the first row of query results.

The FETCH statement inside the for loop fetches the next row of query results each time the loop is executed. The INTO clause of the FETCH statement works just like the INTO clause of the singleton SELECT statement. It specifies the host variables that are to receive the fetched data items—one host variable for each column of query results. As in previous examples, a host indicator variable (repquota_ind) is used when a fetched data item may contain NULL values.

When no more rows of query results are to be fetched, the DBMS returns the NOT FOUND warning in response to the FETCH statement. This is exactly the same warning code that is returned when the singleton SELECT statement does not retrieve a row of data. In this program, the WHENEVER NOT FOUND statement causes the precompiler to generate code that checks the SQLCODE value after the FETCH statement. This generated code branches to the label done when the NOT FOUND condition arises, and to the label error if an error occurs. At the end of the program, the CLOSE statement ends the query and terminates the program's access to the query results.

Cursors

As the program in Figure 17-23 illustrates, an embedded SQL cursor behaves much like a filename or "file handle" in a programming language such as C or COBOL. Just as a program opens a file to access the file's contents, it opens a cursor to gain access to the

```
main()
{
    exec sql include sqlca;
    exec sql begin declare section;
        char   repname[16];                /* retrieved salesperson name */
        float repquota;                    /* retrieved quota */
        float repsales;                    /* retrieved sales */
        short repquota_ind;                /* null quota indicator */
    exec sql end declare section;

    /* Declare the cursor for the query */
    exec sql declare repcurs cursor for   ◄──────────────────── ①
                select name, quota, sales
                    from salesreps
                  where sales > quota
                  order by name;

    /* Set up error processing */
    whenever sqlerror goto error;
    whenever not found goto done;

    /* Open the cursor to start the query */
    exec sql open repcurs;   ◄──────────────────────────────── ②

    /* Loop through each row of query results */
    for (;;) {

        /* Fetch the next row of query results */
        exec sql fetch repcurs   ◄──────────────────────────── ③
                    into :repname, :repquota, :repquota_ind, repsales;

    /* Display the retrieved data */
    printf("Name: %s\n", repname);
    if (repquota_ind < 0)
        printf("Quota is NULL\n");
    else
        printf("Quota: %f\n", repquota);
    printf("Sales: %f\n", repsales);
    }

error:
   printf("SQL error: %ld\n", sqlca.sqlcode);
   exit();

done:
   /* Query complete; close the cursor */
   exec sql close repcurs;   ◄──────────────────────────────── ④
   exit();
}
```

Figure 17-23. *Multi-row query processing*

query results. Similarly, the program closes a file to end its access and closes a cursor to end access to the query results. Finally, just as a file handle keeps track of the program's current position within an open file, a cursor keeps track of the program's current position within the query results. These parallels between file input/output and SQL cursors make the cursor concept relatively easy for application programmers to understand.

Despite the parallels between files and cursors, there are also some differences. Opening a SQL cursor usually involves much more overhead than opening a file, because opening the cursor actually causes the DBMS to begin carrying out the associated query. In addition, SQL cursors support only sequential motion through the query results, like sequential file processing. In most current SQL implementations, there is no cursor analog to the random access provided to the individual records of a file.

Cursors provide a great deal of flexibility for processing queries in an embedded SQL program. By declaring and opening multiple cursors, the program can process several sets of query results in parallel. For example, the program might retrieve some rows of query results, display them on the screen for its user, and then respond to a user's request for more detailed data by launching a second query. The following sections describe in detail the four embedded SQL statements that define and manipulate cursors.

The DECLARE CURSOR Statement

The DECLARE CURSOR statement, shown in Figure 17-24, defines a query to be performed. The statement also associates a cursor name with the query. The cursor name must be a valid SQL identifier. It is used to identify the query and its results in other embedded SQL statements. The cursor name is specifically *not* a host language variable; it is declared by the DECLARE CURSOR statement, not in a host language declaration.

The SELECT statement in the DECLARE CURSOR statement defines the query associated with the cursor. The select statement can be any valid interactive SQL SELECT statement, as described in Chapters 6 through 9. In particular, the SELECT statement must include a FROM clause and may optionally include WHERE, GROUP BY, HAVING, and ORDER BY clauses. The SELECT statement may also include the UNION

|———— DECLARE *cursor-name* CURSOR FOR *select-statement* ————————►●

Figure 17-24. *DECLARE CURSOR* statement syntax diagram

operator, as described in Chapter 6. Thus an embedded SQL query can use any of the query capabilities that are available in the interactive SQL language.

The query specified in the DECLARE CURSOR statement may also include input host variables. These host variables perform exactly the same function as in the embedded INSERT, DELETE, UPDATE, and singleton SELECT statements. An input host variable can appear within the query anywhere that a constant can appear. Note that output host variables *cannot* appear in the query. Unlike the singleton SELECT statement, the SELECT statement within the DECLARE CURSOR statement has no INTO clause and does not retrieve any data. The INTO clause appears as part of the FETCH statement, described later in this chapter.

As its name implies, the DECLARE CURSOR statement is a declaration of the cursor. In most SQL implementations, including the IBM SQL products, this statement is a directive for the SQL precompiler; it is not an executable statement, and the precompiler does not produce any code for it. Like all declarations, the DECLARE CURSOR statement must physically appear in the program before any statements that reference the cursor that it declares. Most SQL implementations treat the cursor name as a global name that can be referenced inside any procedures, functions, or subroutines that appear after the DECLARE CURSOR statement.

It's worth noting that not all SQL implementations treat the DECLARE CURSOR statement strictly as a declarative statement, and this can lead to subtle problems. Some SQL precompilers actually generate code for the DECLARE CURSOR statement (either host language declarations or calls to the DBMS, or both), giving it some of the qualities of an executable statement. For these precompilers, the DECLARE CURSOR statement must not only physically precede the OPEN, FETCH, and CLOSE statements that reference its cursor, it must sometimes precede these statements in the flow of execution or be placed in the same block as the other statements.

In general you can avoid problems with the DECLARE CURSOR statement by following these guidelines:

■ Place the DECLARE CURSOR statement right before the OPEN statement for the cursor. This placement ensures the correct physical statement sequence, it puts the DECLARE CURSOR and the OPEN statements in the same block, and it ensures that the flow of control passes through the DECLARE CURSOR statement, if necessary. It also helps to document just what query is being requested by the OPEN statement.

■ Make sure that the FETCH and CLOSE statements for the cursor follow the OPEN statement physically as well as in the flow of control.

The OPEN Statement

The OPEN statement, shown in Figure 17-25, conceptually "opens" the table of query results for access by the application program. In practice, the OPEN statement actually causes the DBMS to process the query, or at least to begin processing it. The OPEN statement thus causes the DBMS to perform the same work as an interactive

SELECT statement, stopping just short of the point where it produces the first row of query results.

The single parameter of the OPEN statement is the name of the cursor to be opened. This cursor must have been previously declared by a DECLARE CURSOR statement. If the query associated with the cursor contains an error, the OPEN statement will produce a negative SQLCODE value. Most query processing errors, such as a reference to an unknown table, an ambiguous column name, or an attempt to retrieve data from a table without the proper permission, will be reported as a result of the OPEN statement. In practice, very few errors occur during the subsequent FETCH statements.

Once opened, a cursor remains in the open state until it is closed with the CLOSE statement. The DBMS also closes all open cursors automatically at the end of a transaction (that is, when the DBMS executes a COMMIT or ROLLBACK statement). After the cursor has been closed, it can be reopened by executing the OPEN statement a second time. Note that the DBMS restarts the query "from scratch" each time it executes the OPEN statement.

The FETCH Statement

The FETCH statement, shown in Figure 17-26, retrieves the *next* row of query results for use by the application program. The cursor named in the FETCH statement specifies which row of query results is to be fetched. It must identify a cursor previously opened by the OPEN statement.

The FETCH statement fetches the row of data items into a list of host variables, which are specified in the INTO clause of the statement. An indicator variable can be associated with each host variable to handle retrieval of NULL data. The behavior of the indicator variable and the values that it can assume are identical to those described earlier in this chapter for the singleton SELECT statement. The number of host variables in the list must be the same as the number of columns in the query results, and the data types of the host variables must be compatible, column by column, with the columns of query results.

As shown in Figure 17-27, the FETCH statement moves the cursor through the query results, row by row, according to these rules:

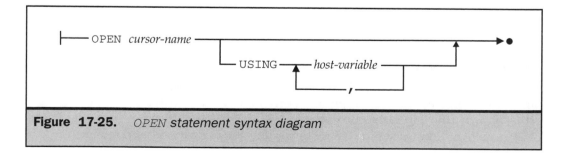

Figure 17-25. *OPEN statement syntax diagram*

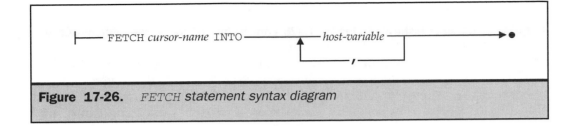

Figure 17-26. *FETCH statement syntax diagram*

- The OPEN statement positions the cursor *before* the first row of query results. In this state, the cursor has no current row.

- The FETCH statement advances the cursor to the next available row of query results, if there is one. This row becomes the current row of the cursor.

- If a FETCH statement advances the cursor past the last row of query results, the FETCH statement returns a NOT FOUND warning. In this state, the cursor again has no current row.

- The CLOSE statement ends access to the query results and places the cursor in a closed state.

If there are no rows of query results, the OPEN statement still positions the cursor *before* the (empty) query results and returns successfully. The program cannot detect that the OPEN statement has produced an empty set of query results. However, the very first FETCH statement produces the NOT FOUND warning and positions the cursor after the end of the (empty) query results.

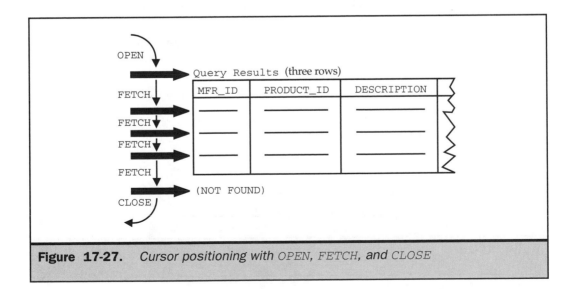

Figure 17-27. *Cursor positioning with OPEN, FETCH, and CLOSE*

The CLOSE Statement

The CLOSE statement, shown in Figure 17-28, conceptually "closes" the table of query results created by the OPEN statement, ending access by the application program. Its single parameter is the name of the cursor associated with the query results, which must be a cursor previously opened by an OPEN statement. The CLOSE statement can be executed at any time after the cursor has been opened. In particular, it is not necessary to FETCH all rows of query results before closing the cursor, although this will usually be the case. All cursors are automatically closed at the end of a transaction. Once a cursor is closed, its query results are no longer available to the application program.

Scroll Cursors

The SQL1 standard specifies that a cursor can only move forward through the query results. Until the last few years, most commercial SQL products also supported only this form of forward, sequential cursor motion. If a program wants to re-retrieve a row once the cursor has moved past it, the program must CLOSE the cursor and re-OPEN it (causing the DBMS to perform the query again), and then FETCH through the rows until the desired row is reached.

In the early 1990s a few commercial SQL products extended the cursor concept with the concept of a *scroll cursor*. Unlike standard cursors, a scroll cursor provides random access to the rows of query results. The program specifies which row it wants to retrieve through an extension of the FETCH statement, shown in Figure 19-28:

- ■ FETCH FIRST retrieves the first row of query results.
- ■ FETCH LAST retrieves the last row of query results.
- ■ FETCH PRIOR retrieves the row of query results that immediately precedes the current row of the cursor.
- ■ FETCH NEXT retrieves the row of query results that immediately follows the current row of the cursor. This is the default behavior if no motion is specified and corresponds to the standard cursor motion.
- ■ FETCH ABSOLUTE retrieves a specific row by its row number.
- ■ FETCH RELATIVE moves the cursor forward or backward a specific number of rows relative to its current position.

```
          |—— CLOSE cursor-name ————————▶●
```

Figure 17-28.   *CLOSE statement syntax diagram*

Scroll cursors can be especially useful in programs that allow a user to browse database contents. In response to the user's request to move forward or backward through the data a row or a screenful at a time, the program can simply fetch the required rows of the query results. However, scroll cursors are also a great deal harder for the DBMS to implement than a normal, unidirectional cursor. To support a scroll cursor, the DBMS must keep track of the previous query results that it provided for a program, and the order in which it supplied those rows of results. The DBMS must also insure that no other concurrently executing transaction modifies any data that has become visible to a program through a scroll cursor, because the program can use the extended FETCH statement to re-retrieve the row, even after the cursor has moved past the row.

If you use a scroll cursor, you should be aware that certain FETCH statements on a scroll cursor may have a very high overhead for some DBMS brands. If the DBMS brand normally carries out a query step by step as your program FETCH-es its way down through the query results, your program may wait a much longer time than normal if you request a FETCH NEXT operation when the cursor is positioned at the first row of query results. It's best to understand the performance characteristics of your particular DBMS brand before writing programs that depend on scroll cursor functionality for production applications.

Because of the usefulness of scroll cursors, and because a few DBMS vendors had begun to ship scroll cursor implementations that were slightly different from one another, the SQL2 standard was expanded to include support for scroll cursors. The Entry SQL level of the standard only requires the older-style, sequential forward cursor, but conformance at the Intermediate SQL or Full SQL levels requires full support for the scroll cursor syntax shown in Figure 17-29. The standard also specifies that if any motion other than FETCH NEXT (the default) is used on a cursor, its DECLARE CURSOR statement must explicitly identify it as a scroll cursor. Using the SQL2 syntax, the cursor declaration in Figure 17-22 would appear as:

```
exec sql declare repcurs scroll cursor for
        select name, quota, sales
          from salesreps
         where sales > quota
         order by name;
```

Cursor-Based Deletes and Updates

Application programs often use cursors to allow the user to browse through a table of data row by row. For example, the user may ask to see all of the orders placed by a particular customer. The program declares a cursor for a query of the ORDERS table and displays each order on the screen, possibly in a computer-generated form, waiting for a signal from the user to advance to the next row. Browsing continues in this fashion until the user reaches the end of the query results. The cursor serves as a

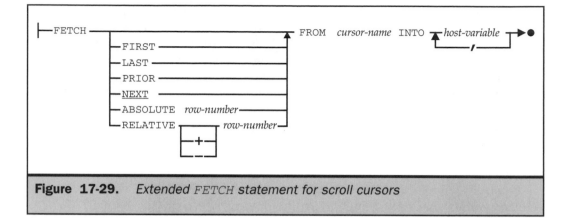

Figure 17-29. *Extended FETCH statement for scroll cursors*

pointer to the current row of query results. If the query draws its data from a single table, and it is not a summary query, as in this example, the cursor implicitly points to a row of a database table, because each row of query results is drawn from a single row of the table.

While browsing the data, the user may spot data that should be changed. For example, the order quantity in one of the orders may be incorrect, or the customer may want to delete one of the orders. In this situation, the user wants to update or delete "this" order. The row is not identified by the usual SQL search condition; rather, the program uses the cursor as a pointer to indicate which particular row is to be updated or deleted.

Embedded SQL supports this capability through special versions of the DELETE and UPDATE statements, called the *positioned* DELETE and *positioned* UPDATE statements, respectively.

The positioned DELETE statement, shown in Figure 17-30, deletes a single row from a table. The deleted row is the current row of a cursor that references the table. To process the statement, the DBMS locates the row of the base table that corresponds to the current row of the cursor and deletes that row from the base table. After the row is deleted, the cursor has no current row. Instead, the cursor is effectively positioned in the "empty space" left by the deleted row, waiting to be advanced to the next row by a subsequent FETCH statement.

The positioned UPDATE statement, shown in Figure 17-31, updates a single row of a table. The updated row is the current row of a cursor that references the table. To process the statement, the DBMS locates the row of the base table that corresponds to the current row of the cursor and updates that row as specified in the SET clause. After the row is updated, it remains the current row of the cursor. Figure 17-32 shows an order browsing program that uses the positioned UPDATE and DELETE statements:

1. The program first prompts the user for a customer number and then queries the ORDERS table to locate all of the orders placed by that customer.

├─── DELETE FROM *cursor-name* WHERE CURRENT OF *cursor-name* ────▶●

Figure 17-30. *Positioned DELETE statement syntax diagram*

---

2. As it retrieves each row of query results, it displays the order information on the screen and asks the user what to do next.

3. If the user types an "N", the program does not modify the current order, but moves directly to the next order.

4. If the user types a "D", the program deletes the current order using a positioned DELETE statement.

5. If the user types a "U", the program prompts the user for a new quantity and amount, and then updates these two columns of the current order using a positioned UPDATE statement.

6. If the user types an "X", the program halts the query and terminates.

Although it is primitive compared to a real application program, the example in Figure 17-32 shows all of the logic and embedded SQL statements required to implement a browsing application with cursor-based database updates.

The SQL1 standard specified that the positioned DELETE and UPDATE statements can be used only with cursors that meet these very strict criteria:

■ The query associated with the cursor must draw its data from a single source table; that is, there must be only one table named in the FROM clause of the query specified in the DECLARE CURSOR statement.

■ The query cannot specify an ORDER BY clause; the cursor must not identify a sorted set of query results.

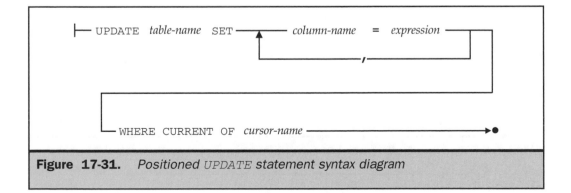

Figure 17-31. *Positioned UPDATE statement syntax diagram*

```
main()
{
    exec sql include sqlca;
    exec sql begin declare section;
        int    custnum;                 /* customer number entered by user*/
        int    ordnum;                  /* retrieved order number */
        char   orddate[12];             /* retrieved order date */
        char   ordmfr[4];               /* retrieved manufacturer-id */
        char   ordproduct[6];           /* retrieved product-id */
        int    ordqty;                  /* retrieved order quantity */
        float  ordamount;               /* retrieved order amount */
    exec sql end declare section;
    char inbuf[101]                     /* character entered by user */

    /* Declare the cursor for the query */
    exec sql declare ordcurs cursor for
            select order_num, ord_date, mfr, product, qty, amount
              from orders
             where cust = cust_num
             order by order_num
               for update of qty, amount;

    /* Prompt the user for a customer number */
    printf("Enter customer number: ");                          1
    scanf("%d", &custnum);

    /* Set up error processing */
    whenever sqlerror goto error;
    whenever not found goto done;

    /* Open the cursor to start the query */
    exec sql open ordcurs;

    /* Loop through each row of query results */
    for (;;) {

        /* Fetch the next row of query results */
        exec sql fetch ordcurs                                  2
                into :ordnum, :orddate, :ordmfr, :ordproduct,
                        :ordqty, :ordamount;

    /* Display the retrieved data */
    printf("Order Number: %d\n", ordnum);
    printf("Order Date:   %s\n", orddate);
    printf("Manufacturer: %s\n", ordmfr);
```

Figure 17-32.   *Using the positioned* DELETE *and* UPDATE *statements*

■ The query cannot specify the DISTINCT keyword.

■ The query must not include a GROUP BY or a HAVING clause.

■ The user must have the UPDATE or DELETE privilege (as appropriate) on the base table.

The IBM databases (DB2, SQL/DS) extended the SQL1 restrictions a step further. They require that the cursor be explicitly declared as an updateable cursor in the DECLARE CURSOR statement. The extended IBM form of the DECLARE CURSOR statement is shown in Figure 17-33. In addition to declaring an updateable cursor, the FOR UPDATE clause can optionally specify particular columns that may be updated through the cursor. If the column list is specified in the cursor declarations, positioned UPDATE statements for the cursor may update only those columns.

In practice, all commercial SQL implementations that support positioned DELETE and UPDATE statements follow the IBM SQL approach. It is a great advantage for the DBMS to know, in advance, whether a cursor will be used for updates or whether its data will be read-only, because read-only processing is simpler. The FOR UPDATE clause provides this advance notice and can be considered a *de facto* standard of the embedded SQL language.

Because of its widespread use, the SQL2 standard included the IBM-style FOR UPDATE clause as an option in its DECLARE CURSOR statement. However, unlike the IBM products, the SQL2 standard automatically assumes that a cursor is opened for update unless it is a scroll cursor or it is explicitly declared FOR READ ONLY. The FOR READ ONLY specification in the SQL2 DECLARE CURSOR statement appears in exactly the same position as the FOR UPDATE clause and explicitly tells the DBMS that the program will not attempt a positioned DELETE or UPDATE operation using the cursor. Because they can significantly affect database overhead and performance, it can be very important to understand the specific assumptions that your particular DBMS brand makes about the updateability of cursors and the clauses or sUPDATtatements that can

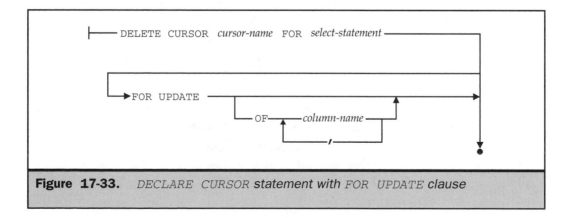

Figure 17-33.   *DECLARE CURSOR* statement with *FOR UPDATE clause*

be used to override them. In addition, programs that explicitly declare whether their intention is to allow updates via an opened cursor are more maintainable.

Cursors and Transaction Processing

The way that your program handles its cursors can have a major impact on database performance. Recall from Chapter 12 that the SQL transaction model guarantees the consistency of data during a transaction. In cursor terms, this means that your program can declare a cursor, open it, fetch the query results, close it, reopen it, and fetch the query results again—and be guaranteed that the query results will be identical both times. The program can also fetch the same row through two different cursors and be guaranteed that the results will be identical. In fact, the data is guaranteed to remain consistent until your program issues a COMMIT or ROLLBACK to end the transaction. Because the consistency is not guaranteed across transactions, both the COMMIT and ROLLBACK statements automatically close all open cursors.

Behind the scenes, the DBMS provides this consistency guarantee by locking all of the rows of query results, preventing other users from modifying them. If the query produces many rows of data, a major portion of a table may be locked by the cursor. Furthermore, if your program waits for user input after fetching each row (for example, to let the user verify data displayed on the screen), parts of the database may be locked for a very long time. In an extreme case, the user might leave for lunch in mid-transaction, locking out other users for an hour or more!

To minimize the amount of locking required, you should follow these guidelines when writing interactive query programs:

- Keep transactions as short as possible.

- Issue a COMMIT statement immediately after every query and as soon as possible after your program has completed an update.

- Avoid programs that require a great deal of user interaction or that browse through many rows of data.

- If you know that the program will not try to refetch a row of data after the cursor has moved past it, use one of the less restrictive isolation modes described in Chapter 12. This allows the DBMS to unlock a row as soon as the next FETCH statement is issued.

- Avoid the use of scroll cursors unless you have taken other actions to eliminate or minimize the extra database locking they will cause.

- Explicitly specify a READ ONLY cursor, if possible.

Summary

In addition to its role as an interactive database language, SQL is used for programmatic access to relational databases:

- The most common technique for programmatic use of SQL is embedded SQL, where SQL statements are embedded into the application program, intermixed with the statements of a host programming language such as C or COBOL.

- Embedded SQL statements are processed by a special SQL precompiler. They begin with a special introducer (usually EXEC SQL) and end with a terminator, which varies from one host language to another.

- Variables from the application program, called host variables, can be used in embedded SQL statements wherever a constant can appear. These input host variables tailor the embedded SQL statement to the particular situation.

- Host variables are also used to receive the results of database queries. The values of these output host variables can then be processed by the application program.

- Queries that produce a single row of data are handled with the singleton SELECT statement of embedded SQL, which specifies both the query and the host variables to receive the retrieved data.

- Queries that produce multiple rows of query results are handled with cursors in embedded SQL. The DECLARE CURSOR statement defines the query, the OPEN statement begins query processing, the FETCH statement retrieves successive rows of query results, and the CLOSE statement ends query processing.

- The positioned UPDATE and DELETE statements can be used to update or delete the row currently selected by a cursor.

The Complete Reference

Chapter 18

Dynamic SQL *

The embedded SQL programming features described in the preceding chapter are collectively known as *static SQL*. Static SQL is adequate for writing all of the programs typically required in a data processing application. For example, in the order processing application of the sample database, you can use static SQL to write programs that handle order entry, order updates, order inquiries, customer inquiries, customer file maintenance, and programs that produce all types of reports. In every one of these programs, the pattern of database access is decided by the programmer and "hard-coded" into the program as a series of embedded SQL statements.

There is an important class of applications, however, where the pattern of database access cannot be determined in advance. A graphic query tool or a report writer, for example, must be able to decide at run-time which SQL statements it will use to access the database. A personal computer spreadsheet that supports host database access must also be able to send a query to the host DBMS for execution "on the fly." These programs and other general-purpose database front-ends cannot be written using static SQL techniques. They require an advanced form of embedded SQL, called *dynamic SQL*, described in this chapter.

Limitations of Static SQL

As the name "static SQL" implies, a program built using the embedded SQL features described in Chapter 17 (host variables, cursors, and the DECLARE CURSOR, OPEN, FETCH, and CLOSE statements) has a predetermined, fixed pattern of database access. For each embedded SQL statement in the program, the tables and columns referenced by that statement are determined in advance by the programmer and hard-coded into the embedded SQL statement. Input host variables provide some flexibility in static SQL, but they don't fundamentally alter its static nature. Recall that a host variable can appear anywhere a constant is allowed in a SQL statement. You can use a host variable to alter a search condition:

```
exec sql select name, quota, sales
        from salesreps
        where quota > :cutoff_amount;
```

You can also use a host variable to change the data inserted or updated in a database:

```
exec sql update salesreps
         set quota = quota + :increase
         where quota >:cutoff_amount;
```

However, you cannot use a host variable in place of a table name or a column reference. The attempted use of the host variables `which_table` and `which_column` in these statements is illegal:

```
exec sql update :which_table
            set :which_column = 0;

exec sql declare cursor cursor7 for
        select *
            from :which_table;
```

Even if you could use a host variable in this way (and you cannot), another problem would immediately arise. The number of columns produced by the query in the second statement would vary, depending on which table was specified by the host variable. For the OFFICES table, the query results would have six columns; for the SALESREPS table, they would have nine columns. Furthermore, the data types of the columns would be different for the two tables. But to write a FETCH statement for the query, you must know in advance how many columns of query results there will be and their data types, because you must specify a host variable to receive each column:

```
exec sql fetch cursor7
            into :var1, :var2, :var3;
```

As this discussion illustrates, if a program must be able to determine at run-time which SQL statements it will use, or which tables and columns it will reference, static SQL is inadequate for the task. Dynamic SQL overcomes these limitations.

Dynamic SQL has been supported by the IBM SQL products since their introduction, and it has been supported for many years by the minicomputer-based and UNIX-based commercial RDBMS products. However, dynamic SQL was not specified by the original ANSI/ISO SQL1 standard; the standard defined only static SQL. The absence of dynamic SQL from the SQL1 standard was ironic, given the popular notion that the standard allowed you to build front-end database tools that are portable across many different DBMS brands. In fact, such front-end tools must almost always be built using dynamic SQL.

In the absence of an ANSI/ISO standard, DB2 set the *de facto* standard for dynamic SQL. The other IBM databases of the day (SQL/DS and OS/2 Extended Edition) were nearly identical to DB2 in their dynamic SQL support, and most other SQL products also followed the DB2 standard. In 1992, the SQL2 standard added "official" support for dynamic SQL, mostly following the path set by IBM. The SQL2 standard does not require dynamic SQL support at the lowest level of compliance (Entry SQL), but dynamic SQL support is required for products claiming Intermediate- or Full-level compliance to the SQL standard.

Dynamic SQL Concepts

The central concept of dynamic SQL is simple: don't hard-code an embedded SQL statement into the program's source code. Instead, let the program build the text of a SQL statement in one of its data areas at runtime. The program then passes the statement text to the DBMS for execution "on the fly." Although the details get quite complex, all of dynamic SQL is built on this simple concept, and it's a good idea to keep it in mind.

To understand dynamic SQL and how it compares with static SQL, it's useful to consider once again the process the DBMS goes through to execute a SQL statement, originally shown in Figure 17-1 and repeated here in Figure 18-1. Recall from Chapter 17 that a static SQL statement goes through the first four steps of the process at compile-time. The BIND utility (or the equivalent part of the DBMS run-time system) analyzes the SQL statement, determines the best way to carry it out, and stores the application plan for the statement in the database as part of the program development process. When the static SQL statement is executed at run-time, the DBMS simply executes the stored application plan.

In dynamic SQL, the situation is quite different. The SQL statement to be executed isn't known until run-time, so the DBMS cannot prepare for the statement in advance. When the program is actually executed, the DBMS receives the text of the statement to be dynamically executed (called the *statement string*) and goes through all five of the steps shown in Figure 18-1 at run-time.

As you might expect, dynamic SQL is less efficient than static SQL. For this reason, static SQL is used whenever possible, and many application programmers never need to learn about dynamic SQL. However, dynamic SQL has grown in importance as more and more database access has moved to a client/server, front-end/back-end architecture over the last ten years. Database access from within personal computer applications such as spreadsheets and word processors has grown dramatically, and an entire set of PC-based front-end data entry and data access tools has emerged. All of these applications require the features of dynamic SQL.

More recently, the emergence of Internet-based "three-tier" architectures, with applications logic executing on one ("mid-tier") system and the database logic executing on another ("back-end" system), have added new importance to capabilities that have grown out of dynamic SQL. In most of these three-tier environments, the applications logic running in the middle tier is quite dynamic. It must be changed frequently to respond to new business conditions and to implement new business rules. This frequently changing environment is at odds with the very tight coupling of applications programs and database contents implied by static SQL. As a result, most three-tier architectures use a callable SQL API (described in the next chapter) to link the

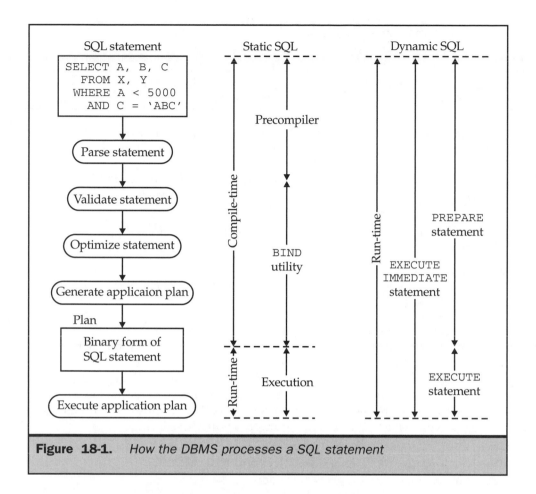

Figure 18-1. *How the DBMS processes a SQL statement*

middle tier to back-end databases. These APIs explicitly borrow the key concepts of dynamic SQL (for example, separate PREPARE and EXECUTE steps and the EXECUTE IMMEDIATE capability) to provide their database access. A solid understanding of dynamic SQL concepts is thus important to help a programmer understand what's going on "behind the scenes" of the SQL API. In performance-sensitive applications, this understanding can make all the difference between an application design that provides good performance and response times and one that does not.

Dynamic Statement Execution (EXECUTE IMMEDIATE)

The simplest form of dynamic SQL is provided by the EXECUTE IMMEDIATE statement, shown in Figure 18-2. This statement passes the text of a dynamic SQL

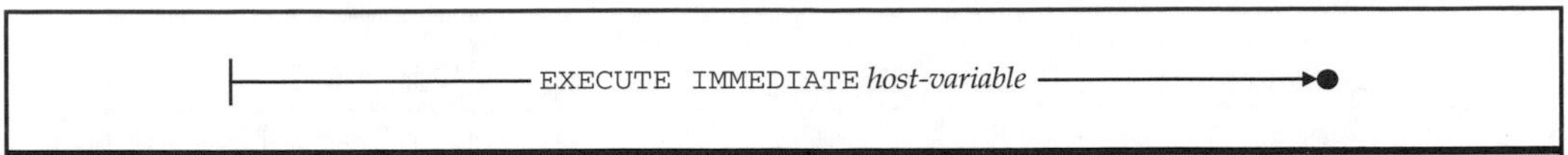

Figure 18-2. *EXECUTE IMMEDIATE* statement syntax diagram

statement to the DBMS and asks the DBMS to execute the dynamic statement immediately. To use this statement, your program goes through the following steps:

1. The program constructs a SQL statement as a string of text in one of its data areas (usually called a *buffer*). The statement can be almost any SQL statement that does not retrieve data.

2. The program passes the SQL statement to the DBMS with the EXECUTE IMMEDIATE statement.

3. The DBMS executes the statement and sets the SQLCODE / SQLSTATE values to indicate the completion status, exactly as if the statement had been hard-coded using static SQL.

Figure 18-3 shows a simple C program that follows these steps. The program prompts the user for a table name and a SQL search condition, and builds the text of a DELETE statement based upon the user's responses. The program then uses the EXECUTE IMMEDIATE statement to execute the DELETE statement. This program cannot use a static SQL embedded DELETE statement, because neither the table name nor the search condition are known until the user enters them at run-time. It must use dynamic SQL. If you run the program in Figure 18-3 with these inputs:

```
Enter table name:       staff
Enter search condition: quota < 20000
Delete from staff successful.
```

the program passes this statement text to the DBMS:

```
delete from staff
 where quota < 20000
```

If you run the program with these inputs:

```
Enter table name:       orders
Enter search condition: cust = 2105
Delete from orders successful
```

```
main()
{
   /* This program deletes rows from a user-specified table
      according to a user-specified search condition.
   */

   exec sql include sqlca;
   exec sql begin declare section;
      char stmtbuf[301];              /* SQL text to be executed */
   exec sql end declare section;

   char tblname[101];                 /* table name entered by user */
   char search_cond[101];             /* search condition entered by user */

   /* Start building the DELETE statement in stmtbuf */
   strcpy(stmtbuf,"delete from ");

   /* Prompt user for table name; add it to the DELETE statement text */
   printf("Enter table name:      ");
   gets(tblname);
   strcat(stmtbuf, tblname);

   /* Prompt user for search condition; add it to the text */
   printf("Enter search condition:");
   gets(search_cond);
   if (strlen(search_cond) > 0) {
      strcat(stmtbuf, " where ");
      strcat(stmtbuf, search_cond);
   }

   /* Now ask the DBMS to execute the statement */
   exec sql execute immediate :stmtbuf;
   if (sqlca.sqlcode < 0)
      printf("SQL error: %ld\n", sqlca.sqlcode);
   else
      printf("Delete from %s successful.\n", tblname);

   exit();
}
```

Figure 18-3.   *Using the EXECUTE IMMEDIATE statement*

the program passes this statement text to the DBMS:

```
delete from orders
 where cust = 2105
```

The EXECUTE IMMEDIATE statement thus gives the program great flexibility in the type of DELETE statement that it executes.

The EXECUTE IMMEDIATE statement uses exactly one host variable—the variable containing the entire SQL statement string. The statement string itself cannot include host variable references, but there's no need for them. Instead of using a static SQL statement with a host variable like this:

```
exec sql delete from orders
          where cust = :cust_num;
```

a dynamic SQL program achieves the same effect by building the *entire* statement in a buffer and executing it:

```
sprintf(buffer, "delete from orders where cust = %d", cust_num)
exec sql execute immediate :buffer;
```

The EXECUTE IMMEDIATE statement is the simplest form of dynamic SQL, but it is very versatile. You can use it to dynamically execute most DML statements, including INSERT, DELETE, UPDATE, COMMIT, and ROLLBACK. You can also use EXECUTE IMMEDIATE to dynamically execute most DDL statements, including the CREATE, DROP, GRANT, and REVOKE statements.

The EXECUTE IMMEDIATE statement does have one significant limitation, however. You cannot use it to dynamically execute a SELECT statement, because it does not provide a mechanism to process the query results. Just as static SQL requires cursors and special-purpose statements (DECLARE CURSOR, OPEN, FETCH, and CLOSE) for programmatic queries, dynamic SQL uses cursors and some new special-purpose statements to handle dynamic queries. The dynamic SQL features that support dynamic queries are discussed later in this chapter.

Two-Step Dynamic Execution

The EXECUTE IMMEDIATE statement provides one-step support for dynamic statement execution. As described previously, the DBMS goes through all five steps of Figure 18-1 for the dynamically executed statement. The overhead of this process can be very significant if your program executes many dynamic statements, and it's wasteful if the statements to be executed are identical or very similar. In practice, the EXECUTE IMMEDIATE statement should only be used for "one-time" statements that will be executed once by a program and then never executed again.

To deal with the large overhead of the one-step approach, dynamic SQL offers an alternative, two-step method for executing SQL statements dynamically. In practice, this two-step approach is used for *all* SQL statements in a program that are executed more than once, and especially for those that are executed repeatedly, hundreds or thousands of times, in response to user interaction. Here is an overview of the two-step technique:

1. The program constructs a SQL statement string in a buffer, just as it does for the EXECUTE IMMEDIATE statement. A question mark (?) can be substituted for a constant anywhere in the statement text to indicate that a value for the constant will be supplied later. The question mark is called a *parameter marker*.

2. The PREPARE statement asks the DBMS to parse, validate, and optimize the statement and to generate an application plan for it. The DBMS sets the SQLCODE/SQLSTATE values to indicate any errors found in the statement and retains the application plan for later execution. Note that the DBMS does *not* execute the plan in response to the PREPARE statement.

3. When the program wants to execute the previously prepared statement, it uses the EXECUTE statement and passes a value for each parameter marker to the DBMS. The DBMS substitutes the parameter values, executes the previously generated application plan, and sets the SQLCODE/SQLSTATE values to indicate its completion status.

4. The program can use the EXECUTE statement repeatedly, supplying different parameter values each time the dynamic statement is executed.

Figure 18-4 shows a C program that uses these steps, which are labeled by the callouts in the figure. The program is a general-purpose table update program. It prompts the user for a table name and two column names, and constructs an UPDATE statement for the table that looks like this:

```
update table-name
   set second-column-name = ?
 where first-column-name = ?
```

The user's input thus determines the table to be updated, the column to be updated, and the search condition to be used. The search comparison value and the updated data value are specified as parameters, to be supplied later when the UPDATE statement is actually executed.

```
main()
{
    /* This is a general-purpose update program. It can be used
       for any update where a numeric column is to be updated in
       all rows where a second numeric column has a specified
       value. For example, you can use it to update quotas for
       selected salespeople or to update credit limits for
       selected customers.
    /*

    exec sql include sqlca;
    exec sql begin declare section;
        char  stmtbuf[301]              /* SQL text to be executed */
        float search_value;            /* parameter value for searching */
        float new_value;               /* parameter value for update */
    exec sql end declare section;

    char tblname[31];                  /* table to be updated */
    char searchcol[31];                /* name of search column */
    char updatecol[31];                /* name of update column */
    char yes_no[31];                   /* yes/no response from user */

    /* Prompt user for tablename and column name * /
    printf("Enter name of table to be updated:   ");
    gets(tblname);
    printf("Enter name of column to be searched: ");
    gets(searchcol);
    printf("Enter name of column to be updated:  ");
    gets(updatecol);

    /* Build SQL statement in buffer; ask DBMS to compile it */
    sprintf(stmtbuf, "update %s set %s = ? where %s = ?",  ◄────────── ①
                     tblname, searchcol, updatecol);
    exec sql prepare mystmt from :stmtbuf;  ◄────────────────────────── ②
    if (sqlca.sqlcode) {
        printf("PREPARE error: %ld\n", sqlca.sqlcode);
        exit();
    }
```

Figure 18-4.   *Using the PREPARE and EXECUTE statements*

```
    /* Loop prompting user for parameters and performing updates */
    for ( ; ; ) {
       printf("\nEnter search value for %s: ", searchcol);
       scanf("%f", &search_value);
       printf("Enter new value for %s: ", updatecol);
       scanf("%f", &new_value);

       /* Ask the DBMS to execute the UPDATE statement */
       execute mystmt using :search_value, :new_value;          3

       if (sqlca.sqlcode) {
          printf("EXECUTE error: %ld\n", sqlca.sqlcode);
          exit();
       }

       /*Ask user if there is another update */
       printf("Another (y/n)? ");          4
       gets(yes_no);
       if (yes_no[0] == 'n')
          break;
    }

    printf("\nUpdates complete.\n");

    exit();
}
```

Figure 18-4.   *Using the* PREPARE *and* EXECUTE *statements* (continued)

After building the UPDATE statement text in its buffer, the program asks the DBMS to compile it with the PREPARE statement. The program then enters a loop, prompting the user to enter pairs of parameter values to perform a sequence of table updates. This user dialog shows how you could use the program in Figure 18-4 to update the quotas for selected salespeople:

```
Enter name of table to be updated:    staff
Enter name of column to be searched:  empl_num
Enter name of column to be updated:   quota

Enter search value for empl_num: 106
Enter new value for quota: 150000.00
```

```
Another (y/n)? y

Enter search value for empl_num: 102
Enter new value for quota: 225000.00
Another (y/n)? y

Enter search value for empl_num: 107
Enter new value for quota: 215000.00
Another (y/n)? n

Updates complete.
```

This program is a good example of a situation where two-step dynamic execution is appropriate. The DBMS compiles the dynamic UPDATE statement only once but executes it three times, once for each set of parameter values entered by the user. If the program had been written using EXECUTE IMMEDIATE instead, the dynamic UPDATE statement would have been compiled three times and executed three times. Thus the two-step dynamic execution of PREPARE and EXECUTE helps to eliminate some of the performance disadvantage of dynamic SQL. As mentioned earlier, this same two-step approach is used by all of the callable SQL APIs described in the next chapter.

The PREPARE Statement

The PREPARE statement, shown in Figure 18-5, is unique to dynamic SQL. It accepts a host variable containing a SQL statement string and passes the statement to the DBMS. The DBMS compiles the statement text and prepares it for execution by generating an application plan. The DBMS sets the SQLCODE/SQLSTATE variables to indicate any errors detected in the statement text. As described previously, the statement string can contain a parameter marker, indicated by a question mark, anywhere that a constant can appear. The parameter marker signals the DBMS that a value for the parameter will be supplied later, when the statement is actually executed.

As a result of the PREPARE statement, the DBMS assigns the specified *statement name* to the prepared statement. The statement name is a SQL identifier, like a cursor name. You specify the statement name in subsequent EXECUTE statements when you want to execute the statement. DBMS brands differ in how long they retain the prepared statement and the associated statement name. For some brands, the prepared statement can only be reexecuted until the end of the current transaction (that is, until the next COMMIT or ROLLBACK statement). If you want to execute the same dynamic statement later during another transaction, you must prepare it again. Other brands relax this restriction and retain the prepared statement throughout the current session with the DBMS. The ANSI/ISO SQL2 standard acknowledges these differences and

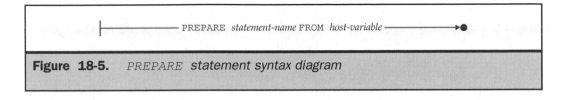

Figure 18-5. *PREPARE* statement syntax diagram

explicitly says that the validity of a prepared statement outside of the current transaction is implementation dependent.

The PREPARE statement can be used to prepare almost any executable DML or DDL statement, including the SELECT statement. Embedded SQL statements that are actually precompiler directives (such as the WHENEVER or DECLARE CURSOR statements) cannot be prepared, of course, because they are not executable.

The EXECUTE Statement

The EXECUTE statement, shown in Figure 18-6, is unique to dynamic SQL. It asks the DBMS to execute a statement previously prepared with the PREPARE statement. You can execute any statement that can be prepared, with one exception. Like the EXECUTE IMMEDIATE statement, the EXECUTE statement cannot be used to execute a SELECT statement, because it lacks a mechanism for handling query results.

If the dynamic statement to be executed contains one or more parameter markers, the EXECUTE statement must provide a value for each of the parameters. The values can be provided in two different ways, described in the next two sections. The ANSI/ISO SQL2 standard includes both of these methods.

EXECUTE with Host Variables

The easiest way to pass parameter values to the EXECUTE statement is by specifying a list of host variables in the USING clause. The EXECUTE statement substitutes the values of the host variables, in sequence, for the parameter markers in the prepared statement text. The host variables thus serve as input host variables for the dynamically

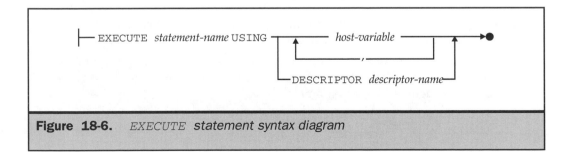

Figure 18-6. *EXECUTE* statement syntax diagram

executed statement. This technique was used in the program shown in Figure 18-4. It is supported by all of the popular DBMS brands that support dynamic SQL and is included in the ANSI/ISO SQL2 standard for dynamic SQL.

The number of host variables in the USING clause must match the number of parameter markers in the dynamic statement, and the data type of each host variable must be compatible with the data type required for the corresponding parameter. Each host variable in the list may also have a companion host indicator variable. If the indicator variable contains a negative value when the EXECUTE statement is processed, the corresponding parameter marker is assigned the NULL value.

EXECUTE with SQLDA

The second way to pass parameters to the EXECUTE statement is with a special dynamic SQL data structure called a *SQL Data Area*, or SQLDA. You must use a SQLDA to pass parameters when you don't know the number of parameters to be passed and their data types at the time that you write the program. For example, suppose you wanted to modify the general-purpose update program in Figure 18-4 so that the user could select more than one column to be updated. You could easily modify the program to generate an UPDATE statement with a variable number of assignments, but the list of host variables in the EXECUTE statement poses a problem; it must be replaced with a variable-length list. The SQLDA provides a way to specify such a variable-length parameter list.

Figure 18-7 shows the layout of the SQLDA used by the IBM databases, including DB2 that set the *de facto* standard for dynamic SQL. Most other DBMS products also use this IBM SQLDA format or one very similar to it. The ANSI/ISO SQL2 standard provides a similar structure, called a *SQL Descriptor Area*. The types of information contained in the ANSI/ISO SQL descriptor area and the DB2-style SQLDA are the same, and both structures play the same role in dynamic SQL processing. However, the details of use—how program locations are associated with SQL statement parameters, how information is placed into the descriptor area and retrieved from it, and so on—are quite different. In practice, the DB2-style SQLDA is the more important, because dynamic SQL support appeared in most major DBMS brands, modeled on the DB2 implementation, long before the SQL2 standard was written.

The SQLDA is a variable-size data structure with two distinct parts:

- The *fixed part* is located at the beginning of the SQLDA. Its fields identify the data structure as a SQLDA and specify the size of this particular SQLDA.

- The *variable part* is an array of one or more SQLVAR data structures. When you use a SQLDA to pass parameters to an EXECUTE statement, there must be one SQLVAR structure for each parameter.

```
struct sqlda {
   unsigned char sqldaid[8];
   long          sqldabc;
   short         sqln;
   short         sqld;
   struct sqlvar {
      short          sqltype;
      short          sqllen;
      unsigned char *sqldata;
      short          *sqlind;
      struct sqlname {
         short          length;
         unsigned char data[30];
      } sqlname;
   } sqlvar[1];
} ;
```

Figure 18-7.   *The SQL Data Area (SQLDA) for IBM databases*

The fields in the SQLVAR structure describe the data being passed to the EXECUTE statement as a parameter value:

- The SQLTYPE field contains an integer *data type code* that specifies the data type of the parameter being passed. For example, the DB2 data type code is 500 for a two-byte integer, 496 for a four-byte integer, and 448 for a variable-length character string.

- The SQLLEN field specifies the *length* of the data being passed. It will contain a 2 for a two-byte integer and a 4 for a four-byte integer. When you pass a character string as a parameter, SQLLEN contains the number of characters in the string.

- The SQLDATA field is a pointer to the *data area* within your program that contains the parameter value. The DBMS uses this pointer to find the data value as it executes the dynamic SQL statement. The SQLTYPE and SQLLEN fields tell the DBMS what type of data is being pointed to and its length.

■ The SQLIND field is a pointer to a two-byte integer that is used as an *indicator variable* for the parameter. The DBMS checks the indicator variable to determine whether you are passing a NULL value. If you are not using an indicator variable for a particular parameter, the SQLIND field must be set to zero.

The other fields in the SQLVAR and SQLDA structures are not used to pass parameter values to the EXECUTE statement. They are used when you use a SQLDA to retrieve data from the database, as described later in this chapter.

Figure 18-8 shows a dynamic SQL program that uses a SQLDA to specify input parameters. The program updates the SALESREPS table, but it allows the user to select the columns that are to be updated at the beginning of the program. Then it enters a loop, prompting the user for an employee number and then prompting for a new value for each column to be updated. If the user types an asterisk (*) in response to the "new value" prompt, the program assigns the corresponding column a NULL value.

```
main()
{
   /* This program updates user-specified columns of the
      SALESREPS table. It first asks the user to select the
      columns to be updated, and then prompts repeatedly for the
      employee number of a salesperson and new values for the
      selected columns.
   */

   #define COLCNT 6                    /* six columns in SALESREPS table */

   exec sql include sqlca;
   exec sql include sqlda;
   exec sql begin declare section;
      char stmtbuf[2001];             /* SQL text to be executed */
   exec sql end declare section;

   char *malloc()
   struct {
      char  prompt[31];               /* prompt for this column */
      char  name[31];                 /* name for this column */
      short typecode;                 /* its data type code */
      short buflen;                   /* length of its buffer */
      char  selected;                 /* "selected" flag (y/n) */
   } columns[] = { "Name",     "NAME",        449, 16, 'n',
                   "Office",   "REP_OFFICE",  497,  4, 'n',
```

Figure 18-8.   *Using EXECUTE with a SQLDA*

```
                    "Manager",  "MANAGER",    497, 4, 'n',
                    "Hire Date","HIRE_DATE",  449, 12, 'n',
                    "Quota",    "QUOTA",      481, 8, 'n',
                    "Sales",    "SALES",      481, 8, 'n'};

struct sqlda  *parmda;              /* SQLDA for parameter values */
struct sqlvar *parmvar;             /* SQLVAR for current parm value */
int           parmcnt;              /* running parameter count */
int           empl_num;             /* employee number entered by user */
int           i;                    /* index for columns[] array */
int           j;                    /* index for sqlvar array in sqlda */
char          inbuf[101];           /* input entered by user */

/* Prompt the user to select the columns to be updated */
printf("*** Salesperson Update Program ***\n\n");
parmcnt = 1;
for (i = 0; i < COLCNT; i++) {

   /* Ask about this column */
   printf("Update %s column (y/n)? ");
   gets(inbuf);
   if (inbuf[0] == 'y') {
       columns[i].selected = 'y';
       parmcnt += 1;
   }
}

/* Allocate a SQLDA structure to pass parameter values */
parmda = malloc(16 = (44 * parmcnt));                               ①
strcpy(parmda -> sqldaid, "SQLDA  ");
parmda->sqldabc = (16 = (44 * parmcnt));
parmda->sqln = parmcnt;

/* Start building the UPDATE statement in statement buffer */
strcpy(stmtbuf, "update orders set ");

/* Loop through columns, processing the selected ones */
for (i = 0; j = 0; i++; i < COLCNT) {                               ②

   /* Skip over non-selected columns */
   if (columns[i].selected == 'n')
      continue;

   /* Add an assignment to the dynamic UPDATE statement */
```

Figure 18-8.   *Using EXECUTE with a SQLDA* (continued)

```
      if (parmcnt > 0) strcat(stmtbuf, ", ");
      strcat(stmtbuf, columns[i].name);
      strcat(stmtbuf, " = ?");

      /* Allocate space for data and indicator variable, and */
      /* fill in the SQLVAR with information for this column */
      parmvar = parmda -> sqlvar + j;
      parmvar -> sqltype = columns[i].typecode;        ◄──────────── ③
      parmvar -> sqllen  = columns[i].buflen;          ◄──────────── ④
      parmvar -> sqldata = malloc(columns[i].buflen);  ◄──────────── ⑤
      parmvar -> sqlind  = malloc920;                  ◄──────────── ⑥
      strcpy(parmvar -> sqlname.data, columns[i].prompt);
      j += 1;
}
/* Fill in the last SQLVAR for parameter in the WHERE clause */
strcat(stmbuf, " where empl_num = ?");
parmvar = parmda + parmcnt;
parmvar->sqltype = 496;
parmvar->sqllen  = 4;
parmvar->sqldata = &empl_num;
parmvar->sqlind  = 0;
parmda->sqld = parmcnt;>   ◄──────────────────────────────────────── ⑦

/* Ask the DBMS to compile the complete dynamic UPDATE statement */
exec sql prepare updatestmt from :stmtbuf;
if (sqlca.sqlcode < 0) {
   printf("PREPARE error: %ld\n", sqlca.sqlcode);
   exit();
}

/* Now loop, prompting for parameters and doing UPDATEs */
for ( ; ; ) {

   /* Prompt user for order number of order to be updated */
   printf("\nEnter Salesperson's Employee Number: ");
   scanf("%ld", &empl_num);
   if (empl_num == 0) break;

   /* Get new values for the updated columns */
   for (j = 0; j < (parmcnt-1); j++) {
      parmvar = parmda + j;
      printf("Enter new value for %s: ", parmvar->sqlname.data);
      gets(inbuf);   ◄──────────────────────────────────────────── ⑧
      if (inbuf[0] == '*') {
          /* If user enters '*', set column to a NULL value */
```

Figure 18-8. *Using EXECUTE with a SQLDA (continued)*

```
                 *(parmvar -> sqlind) = -1;
                 continue;
            }
            else {
                 /* Otherwise, set indicator for non-NULL value */
                 *(parmvar -> sqlind) = 0;

                 switch(parmvar -> sqltype) {

                 case 481:
                     /* Convert entered data to 8-byte floating point */
                     sscanf(inbuf, "%lf", parmvar -> sqldata);       8
                     break;

                 case 449:
                     /* Pass entered data as variable-length string */
                     stccpy(parmvar -> sqldata, inbuf, strlen(inbuf));
                     parmvar -> sqllen = strlen(inbuf);
                     break;

                 case 501:
                     /* Convert entered data to 4-byte integer */
                     sscanf(inbuf, "%ld", parmvar->sqldata);
                     break;
                 }
            }
        }


        /* Execute the statement */
        exec sql execute updatestmt using :parmda;       9
        if (sqlca.sqlcode < 0)    {
            printf("EXECUTE error: %ld\n", sqlca.sqlcode);
            exit();
        }
    }

    /* All finished with updates */
    exec sql execute immediate "commit work";
    if (sqlca.sqlcode)
        printf("COMMIT error: %ld\n", sqlca.sqlcode);
    else
        printf("\nAll updates committed.\n");

    exit();
}
```

Figure 18-8. *Using EXECUTE with a SQLDA* (continued)

Because the user can select different columns each time the program is run, this program must use a SQLDA to pass the parameter values to the EXECUTE statement. The program illustrates the general technique for using a SQLDA, indicated by callouts in Figure 18-8:

1. The program allocates a SQLDA large enough to hold a SQLVAR structure for each parameter to be passed. It sets the SQLN field to indicate how many SQLVARs can be accommodated.

2. For each parameter to be passed, the program fills in one of the SQLVAR structures with information describing the parameter.

3. The program determines the data type of a parameter and places the correct data type code in the SQLTYPE field.

4. The program determines the length of the parameter and places it in the SQLLEN field.

5. The program allocates memory to hold the parameter value and puts the address of the allocated memory in the SQLDATA field.

6. The program allocates memory to hold an indicator variable for the parameter and puts the address of the indicator variable in the SQLIND field.

7. Now, the program sets the SQLD field in the SQLDA header to indicate how many parameters are being passed. This tells the DBMS how many SQLVAR structures within the SQLDA contain valid data.

8. The program prompts the user for data values and places them into the data areas allocated in Steps 5 and 6.

9. The program uses an EXECUTE statement with the USING DESCRIPTOR clause to pass parameter values via the SQLDA.

Note that this particular program copies the "prompt string" for each parameter value into the SQLNAME structure. The program does this solely for its own convenience; the DBMS ignores the SQLNAME structure when you use the SQLDA to pass parameters. Here is a sample user dialog with the program in Figure 18-8:

```
*** Salesperson Update Program ***

Update Name column (y/n)? y
Update Office column (y/n)? y
Update Manager column (y/n)? n
Update Hire Date column (y/n)? n
Update Quota column (y/n)? y
Update Sales column (y/n)? n
```

```
Enter Salesperson's Employee Number: 106
Enter new value for Name: Sue Jackson
Enter new value for Office: 22
Enter new value for Quota: 175000.00

Enter Salesperson's Employee Number: 104
Enter new value for Name: Joe Smith
Enter new value for Office: *
Enter new value for Quota: 275000.00

Enter Salesperson's Employee Number: 0

All updates committed.
```

Based on the user's response to the initial questions, the program generates this dynamic UPDATE statement and prepares it:

```
update salesreps
   set name = ?, office = ?, quota = ?
 where empl_num = ?
```

The statement specifies four parameters, and the program allocates a SQLDA big enough to handle four SQLVAR structures. When the user supplies the first set of parameter values, the dynamic UPDATE statement becomes:

```
update salesreps
   set name = 'Sue Jackson', office = 22, quota = 175000.00
 where empl_num = 106
```

and with the second set of parameter values, it becomes:

```
update salesreps
   set name = 'Joe Smith', office = NULL, quota = 275000.00
 where empl_num = 104
```

This program is somewhat complex, but it's simple compared to a real general-purpose database update utility. It also illustrates all of the dynamic SQL features required to dynamically execute statements with a variable number of parameters.

Dynamic Queries

The EXECUTE IMMEDIATE, PREPARE, and EXECUTE statements as described thus far support dynamic execution of most SQL statements. However, they can't support dynamic queries because they lack a mechanism for retrieving the query results. To support dynamic queries, SQL *combines* the dynamic SQL features of the PREPARE and EXECUTE statements with extensions to the static SQL query processing statements, and adds a new statement. Here is an overview of how a program performs a dynamic query:

1. A dynamic version of the DECLARE CURSOR statement declares a cursor for the query. Unlike the static DECLARE CURSOR statement, which includes a hard-coded SELECT statement, the dynamic form of the DECLARE CURSOR statement specifies the statement name that will be associated with the dynamic SELECT statement.

2. The program constructs a valid SELECT statement in a buffer, just as it would construct a dynamic UPDATE or DELETE statement. The SELECT statement may contain parameter markers like those used in other dynamic SQL statements.

3. The program uses the PREPARE statement to pass the statement string to the DBMS, which parses, validates, and optimizes the statement and generates an application plan. This is identical to the PREPARE processing used for other dynamic SQL statements.

4. The program uses the DESCRIBE statement to request a description of the query results that will be produced by the query. The DBMS returns a column-by-column description of the query results in a SQL Data Area (SQLDA) supplied by the program, telling the program how many columns of query results there are, and the name, data type, and length of each column. The DESCRIBE statement is used exclusively for dynamic queries.

5. The program uses the column descriptions in the SQLDA to allocate a block of memory to receive each column of query results. The program may also allocate space for an indicator variable for the column. The program places the address of the data area and the address of the indicator variable into the SQLDA to tell the DBMS where to return the query results.

6. A dynamic version of the OPEN statement asks the DBMS to start executing the query and passes values for the parameters specified in the dynamic SELECT statement. The OPEN statement positions the cursor before the first row of query results.

7. A dynamic version of the FETCH statement advances the cursor to the first row of query results and retrieves the data into the program's data areas and indicator variables. Unlike the static FETCH statement, which specifies a list of host variables to receive the data, the dynamic FETCH statement uses the SQLDA to tell the DBMS where to return the data. Subsequent FETCH statements move

through the query results row by row, advancing the cursor to the next row of query results and retrieving its data into the program's data areas.

8. The CLOSE statement ends access to the query results and breaks the association between the cursor and the query results. This CLOSE statement is identical to the static SQL CLOSE statement; no extensions are required for dynamic queries.

The programming required to perform a dynamic query is more extensive than the programming for any other embedded SQL statement. However, the programming is typically more tedious than complex. Figure 18-9 shows a small query program that uses dynamic SQL to retrieve and display selected columns from a user-specified table. The callouts in the figure identify the eight steps in the preceding list.

```
main()
{
    /* This is a simple general-purpose query program. It prompts
       the user for a table name, and then asks the user which
       columns of the table are to be included in the query.
       After the user's selections are complete, the program runs
       the requested query and displays the results.
    */

    exec sql include sqlca;
    exec sql include sqlda;
    exec sql begin declare section;
        char stmtbuf[2001];                /* SQL text to be executed */
        char querytbl[32];                 /* user-specified table */
        char querycol[32];                 /* user-specified column */
    exec sql end declare section;

    /* Cursor for system catalog query that retrieves column names */
    exec sql declare tblcurs cursor for
            select colname from system.syscolumns
                where tblname = :querytbl and owner = user;

    exec sql declare qrycurs cursor for querystmt;  ◄─────────────── ①

    /* Data structures for the program */
    int            colcount = 0;           /* number of columns chosen */
    struct sqlda  *qry_da;                 /* allocated SQLDA for query */
    struct sqlvar *qry_var;                /* SQLVAR for current column */
```

Figure 18-9.   *Data retrieval with dynamic SQL*

```
      int             i;                         /* index for SQLVAR array in SQLDA */
      char            inbuf[101];                /* input entered by user */

   /* Prompt the user for which table to query */
   printf("*** Mini-Query Program ***\n\n")
   printf("Enter name of table for query: ");
   gets(querytbl);

   /* Start the SELECT statement in the buffer */
   strcpy(stmtbuf, "select ");                                           ②

   /* Set up error processing */
   exec sql whenever sqlerror goto handle_error;
   exec sql whenever not found goto no_more_columns;

   /* Query the system catalog to get column names for the table */
   exec sql open tblcurs;
   for ( ; ; ) {

      /* Get name of next column and prompt the user */
      exec sql feth tblcurs into :querycol;
      printf("Include column %s (y/n)? ", querycol);
      gets(inbuf);
      if (inbuf[0] == 'y') {
         /* User wants the column; add it to the select list */
         if (colcount++ > 0)
            strcat(stmtbuf, ", ");
         strcat(stmtbuf, querycol);                                      ②
      }
   }

no_more_columns:
   exec sql close tblcurs;

   /* Finish the SELECT statement with a FROM clause */
   strcat(stmtbuf, "from ");
   strcat(stmtbuf, querytbl);

   /* Allocate SQLDA for the dynamic query */
   query_da = (SQLDA *)malloc(sizeof(SQLDA) + colcount * sizeof(SQLVAR));
   query_da->sqln = colcount;

   /* Prepare the query and ask the DBMS to describe it */
   exec sql prepare querystmt from :stmtbuf;                             ③
```

Figure 18-9. *Data retrieval with dynamic SQL* (continued)

```
   exec sql describe querystmt into qry_da;  ◄──────────────── ④

/* Loop through SQLVARs, allocating memory for each column */
for (i = 0; i < colcount; i++) {
  qry_var = qry_da->sqlvar + i;
  qry_var->sqldat = malloc(qry_var->sqllen);  ◄──────────── ⑤
  qry_var->sqlind = malloc(sizeof(short));
}

/* SQLDA is all set; do the query and retrieve the results! */
exec sql open qrycurs;  ◄─────────────────────────── ⑥
exec sql whenever not found goto no_more_data;
for ( ; ; ) {

   /* Fetch the row of data into our buffers */
   exec sql fetch sqlcurs using descriptor qry_da;  ◄──────── ⑦
   printf("\n");

   /* Loop printing data for each column of the row */
   for (i = 0; i < colcount; i++) {

      /* Find the SQLVAR for this column; print column label */
      qry_var = qry_da->sqlvar + i;
      printf(" Column # %d (%s): ", i+1, qry_var->sqlname);

      /* Check indicator variable for NULL indication */
      if (*(qry_var -> sqlind)) != 0) {
         puts("is NULL!\n");
         continue;
      }

      /* Actual data returned; handle each type separately */
      switch (qry_var -> sqltype) {

      case 448:
      case 449:
         /* VARCHAR data -- just display it */
         puts(qry_var -> sqldata);
         break;

      case 496:
      case 497:
         /* Four-byte integer data -- convert & display it */
         printf("%ld", *((int *) (qry_var->sqldata)));
         break;
```

Figure 18-9.   *Data retrieval with dynamic SQL* (continued)

```
              case 500:
              case 501:
                  /* Two-byte integer data -- convert & dispay it */
                  printf("%d", *((short *)(qry_var->sqldata)));
                  break;

              case 480:
              case 481:
                  /* Floating-point data -- convert & display it */
                  printf("%lf", *((double *)(qry_var->sqldat)));
                  break;
          }
      }
  }

no_more_data:
   printf("\nEnd of data.\n");

   /* Clean up allocated storage */
   for (i = 0; i < colcount; i++) {
      qry_var = qry_da->sqlvar + i;
      free(qry_var->sqldata);
      free(qry_var->sqlind);
   }
   free(qry_da);
   close qrycurs; ◄─────────────────────────────── ⑧

   exit();
}
```

Figure 18-9.   *Data retrieval with dynamic SQL* (continued)

The program in the figure begins by prompting the user for the table name and then queries the system catalog to discover the names of the columns in that table. It asks the user to select the column(s) to be retrieved and constructs a dynamic SELECT statement based on the user's responses. The step-by-step mechanical construction of a select list in this example is very typical of database front-end programs that generate dynamic SQL. In real applications, the generated select list might include expressions or aggregate functions, and there might be additional program logic to generate GROUP BY, HAVING, and ORDER BY clauses. A graphical user interface would also be used instead of the primitive user prompting in the sample program. However, the programming steps and concepts remain the same. Notice that the generated SELECT statement is identical to the interactive SELECT statement that you would use to perform the requested query.

The handling of the PREPARE and DESCRIBE statements and the method of allocating storage for the retrieved data in this program are also typical of dynamic query programs. Note how the program uses the column descriptions placed in the SQLVAR array to allocate a data storage block of the proper size for each column. This program also allocates space for an indicator variable for each column. The program places the address of the data block and indicator variable back into the SQLVAR structure.

The OPEN, FETCH, and CLOSE statements play the same role for dynamic queries as they do for static queries, as illustrated by this program. Note that the FETCH statement specifies the SQLDA instead of a list of host variables. Because the program has previously filled in the SQLDATA and SQLIND fields of the SQLVAR array, the DBMS knows where to place each retrieved column of data.

As this example shows, much of the programming required for a dynamic query is concerned with setting up the SQLDA and allocating storage for the SQLDA and the retrieved data. The program must also sort out the various types of data that can be returned by the query and handle each one correctly, taking into account the possibility that the returned data will be NULL. These characteristics of the sample program are typical of production applications that use dynamic queries. Despite the complexity, the programming is not too difficult in languages like C, C++, Pascal, PL/I, or Java. Languages such as COBOL and FORTRAN, which lack the ability to dynamically allocate storage and work with variable-length data structures, cannot be used for dynamic query processing.

The following sections discuss the DESCRIBE statement and the dynamic versions of the DECLARE CURSOR, OPEN, and FETCH statements.

The DESCRIBE Statement

The DESCRIBE statement, shown in Figure 18-10, is unique to dynamic queries. It is used to request a description of a dynamic query from the DBMS. The DESCRIBE statement is used after the dynamic query has been compiled with the PREPARE statement but before it is executed with the OPEN statement. The query to be described is identified by its statement name. The DBMS returns the query description in a SQLDA supplied by the program.

The SQLDA is a variable-length structure with an array of one or more SQLVAR structures, as described earlier in this chapter and shown in Figure 18-7. Before passing the SQLDA to the DESCRIBE statement, your program must fill in the SQLN field in the SQLDA header, telling the DBMS how large the SQLVAR array is in this particular SQLDA. As the first step of its DESCRIBE processing, the DBMS fills in the SQLD field in the SQLDA header with the number of columns of query results. If the size of the

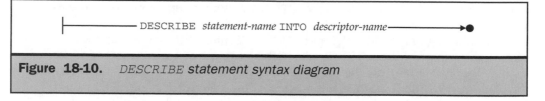

Figure 18-10.   *DESCRIBE statement syntax diagram*

SQLVAR array (as specified by the SQLN field) is too small to hold all of the column descriptions, the DBMS does not fill in the remainder of the SQLDA. Otherwise, the DBMS fills in one SQLVAR structure for each column of query results, in left-to-right order. The fields of each SQLVAR describe the corresponding column:

- The SQLNAME structure specifies the name of the column (with the name in the DATA field and the length of the name in the LENGTH field). If the column is derived from an expression, the SQLNAME field is not used.

- The SQLTYPE field specifies an integer data type code for the column. The data type codes used by different brands of DBMS vary. For the IBM SQL products, the data type code indicates both the data type and whether NULL values are allowed, as shown in Table 18-1.

Data Type	NULL Allowed	NOT NULL
CHAR	452	453
VARCHAR	448	449
LONG VARCHAR	456	457
SMALLINT	500	501
INTEGER	496	497
FLOAT	480	481
DECIMAL	484	485
DATE	384	385
TIME	388	389
TIMESTAMP	392	393
GRAPHIC	468	469
VARGRAPHIC	464	465

Table 18-1.   *SQLDA Data Type Codes for DB2*

■ The SQLLEN field specifies the length of the column. For variable-length data types (such as VARCHAR), the reported length is the maximum length of the data; the length of the columns in individual rows of query results will not exceed this length. For DB2 (and many other SQL products), the length returned for a DECIMAL data type specifies both the size of the decimal number (in the upper byte) and the scale of the number (in the lower byte).

■ The SQLDATA and SQLIND fields are not filled in by the DBMS. Your application program fills in these fields with the addresses of the data buffer and indicator variable for the column before using the SQLDA later in a FETCH statement.

A complication of using the DESCRIBE statement is that your program may not know in advance how many columns of query results there will be, and therefore it may not know how large a SQLDA must be allocated to receive the description. One of three strategies is typically used to ensure that the SQLDA has enough space for the returned descriptions.

■ If the program has generated the select list of the query, it can keep a running count of the select items as it generates them. In this case, the program can allocate a SQLDA with exactly the right number of SQLVAR structures to receive the column descriptions. This approach was used in the program shown in Figure 18-9.

■ If it is inconvenient for the program to count the number of select list items, it can initially DESCRIBE the dynamic query into a minimal SQLDA with a one-element SQLVAR array. When the DESCRIBE statement returns, the SQLD value tells the program how large the SQLDA must be. The program can then allocate a SQLDA of the correct size and reexecute the DESCRIBE statement, specifying the new SQLDA. There is no limit to the number of times that a prepared statement can be described.

■ Alternatively, the program can allocate a SQLDA with a SQLVAR array large enough to accommodate a typical query. A DESCRIBE statement using this SQLDA will succeed most of the time. If the SQLDA turns out to be too small for the query, the SQLD value tells the program how large the SQLDA must be, and it can allocate a larger one and DESCRIBE the statement again into that SQLDA.

The DESCRIBE statement is normally used for dynamic queries, but you can ask the DBMS to DESCRIBE any previously prepared statement. This feature is useful, for example, if a program needs to process an unknown SQL statement typed by a user. The program can PREPARE and DESCRIBE the statement and examine the SQLD field in the SQLDA. If the SQLD field is zero, the statement text was not a query, and the EXECUTE statement can be used to execute it. If the SQLD field is positive, the statement text was a query, and the OPEN/FETCH/CLOSE statement sequence must be used to execute it.

The DECLARE CURSOR Statement

The dynamic DECLARE CURSOR statement, shown in Figure 18-11, is a variation of the static DECLARE CURSOR statement. Recall from Chapter 17 that the static DECLARE CURSOR statement literally specifies a query by including the SELECT statement as one of its clauses. By contrast, the dynamic DECLARE CURSOR statement specifies the query indirectly, by specifying the statement name associated with the query by the PREPARE statement.

Like the static DECLARE CURSOR statement, the dynamic DECLARE CURSOR statement is a directive to the SQL precompiler rather than an executable statement. It must appear before any other references to the cursor that it declares. The cursor name declared by this statement is used in subsequent OPEN, FETCH, and CLOSE statements to process the results of the dynamic query.

The Dynamic OPEN Statement

The dynamic OPEN statement, shown in Figure 18-12, is a variation of the static OPEN statement. It causes the DBMS to begin executing a query and positions the associated cursor just before the first row of query results. When the OPEN statement completes successfully, the cursor is in an open state and is ready to be used in a FETCH statement.

The role of the OPEN statement for dynamic queries parallels the role of the EXECUTE statement for other dynamic SQL statements. Both the EXECUTE and the OPEN statements cause the DBMS to execute a statement previously compiled by the PREPARE statement. If the dynamic query text includes one or more parameter markers, then the OPEN statement, like the EXECUTE statement, must supply values for these parameters. The USING clause is used to specify parameter values, and it has an identical format in both the EXECUTE and OPEN statements.

If the number of parameters that will appear in a dynamic query is known in advance, the program can pass the parameter values to the DBMS through a list of host variables in the USING clause of the OPEN statement. As in the EXECUTE statement, the number of host variables must match the number of parameters, the data type of each host variable must be compatible with the type required by the corresponding parameter, and an indicator variable can be specified for each host variable, if

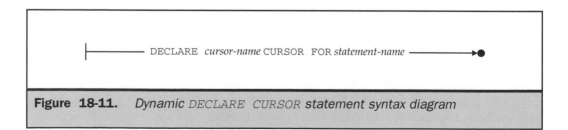

Figure 18-11.   *Dynamic DECLARE CURSOR statement syntax diagram*

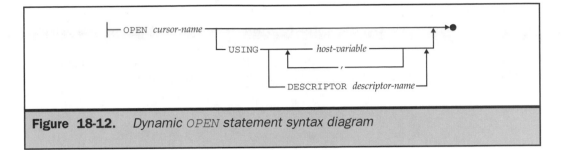

Figure 18-12. *Dynamic OPEN statement syntax diagram*

necessary. Figure 18-13 shows a program excerpt where the dynamic query has three parameters whose values are specified by host variables.

```
        .
        .
        .
    /* Program has previously generated and prepared a SELECT
       statement like this one:

           SELECT A, B, C ...
             FROM SALESREPS
             WHERE SALES BETWEEN ? AND ?

       with two parameters to be specified
    */


    /* Prompt the user for low & high values and do the query */
    printf("Enter low end of sales range: ");
    scanf("%f", &low_end);
    printf("Enter high end of sales range: ");
    scanf("%f", &high_end);

    /* Open the cursor to start the query, passing parameters */
    exec sql open qrycursor using :low_end, :high_end;
        .
        .
        .
```

Figure 18-13. *OPEN statement with host variable parameter passing*

If the number of parameters is not known until run-time, the program must pass the parameter values using a SQLDA structure. This technique for passing parameter values was described for the EXECUTE statement earlier in this chapter. The same technique is used for the OPEN statement. Figure 18-14 shows a program excerpt like the one in Figure 18-13, except that it uses a SQLDA to pass parameters.

```
            .
            .
            .
    /* Program has previously generated and prepared a SELECT
       statement like this one:

            SELECT A, B, C ...
              FROM SALESREPS
              WHERE EMPL_NUM IN (?, ?, ... ?)

       with a variable number of parameters to be specified. The
       number of parameters for this execution is stored in the
       variable parmcnt.
    */

    char    *malloc()
    SQLDA   *parmda;
    SQLVAR  *parmvar;
    long    parm_value[101];

    /* Allocate a SQLDA to pass parameter values */
    parmda = (SQLDA *)malloc(sizeof(SQLDA) + parmcnt * sizeof(SQLVAR));
    parmda->sqln = parmcnt;

    /*Prompt the user for parameter values */
    for (i = 0; i < parmcnt; i++) {
       printf("Enter employee number: ");
       scanf("%ld", &(parm_value[i]));
       parmvar = parmda -> sqlvar + i;
       parmvar->sqltype = 496;
       parmvar->sqllen  = 4;
       parmvar->sqldata = &(parm_value[i]);
       parmvar->sqlind  = 0;
    }

    /* Open the cursor to start the query, passing parameters */
    exec sql open qrycursor using descriptor :parmda;
            .
            .
            .
```

Figure 18-14. *OPEN statement with SQLDA parameter passing*

Note carefully that the SQLDA used in the OPEN statement has *absolutely nothing* to do with the SQLDA used in the DESCRIBE and FETCH statements:

■ The SQLDA in the OPEN statement is used to pass parameter values *to* the DBMS for dynamic query execution. The elements of its SQLVAR array correspond to the *parameter markers* in the dynamic statement text.

■ The SQLDA in the DESCRIBE and FETCH statements receives descriptions of the query results columns *from* the DBMS and tells the DBMS where to place the retrieved query results. The elements of its SQLVAR array correspond to the *columns of query results* produced by the dynamic query.

The Dynamic FETCH Statement

The dynamic FETCH statement, shown in Figure 18-15, is a variation of the static FETCH statement. It advances the cursor to the next available row of query results and retrieves the values of its columns into the program's data areas. Recall from Chapter 17 that the static FETCH statement includes an INTO clause with a list of host variables that receive the retrieved column values. In the dynamic FETCH statement, the list of host variables is replaced by a SQLDA.

Before using the dynamic FETCH statement, it is the application program's responsibility to provide data areas to receive the retrieved data and indicator variable for each column. The application program must also fill in the SQLDATA, SQLIND, and SQLLEN fields in the SQLVAR structure for each column, as follows:

■ The SQLDATA field must point to the data area for the retrieved data.

■ The SQLLEN field must specify the length of the data area pointed to by the SQLDATA field. This value must be correctly specified to make sure the DBMS does not copy retrieved data beyond the end of the data area.

■ The SQLIND field must point to an indicator variable for the column (a two-byte integer). If no indicator variable is used for a particular column, the SQLIND field for the corresponding SQLVAR structure should be set to zero.

Normally, the application program allocates a SQLDA, uses the DESCRIBE statement to get a description of the query results, allocates storage for each column of query results, and sets the SQLDATA and SQLIND values, all before opening the cursor.

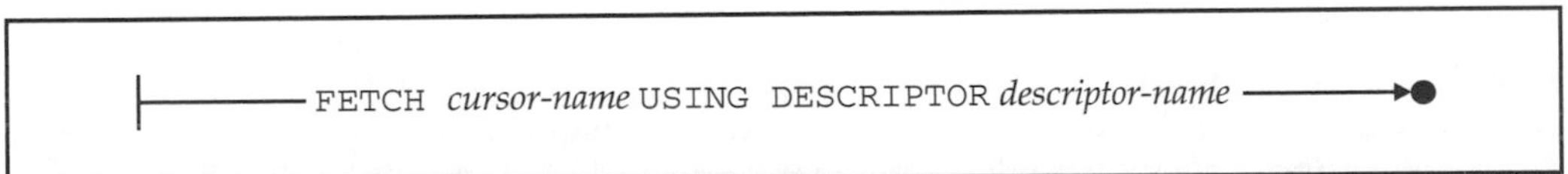

FETCH *cursor-name* USING DESCRIPTOR *descriptor-name*

Figure 18-15. *Dynamic FETCH statement syntax diagram*

This same SQLDA is then passed to the FETCH statement. However, there is no requirement that the same SQLDA be used or that the SQLDA specify the same data areas for each FETCH statement. It is perfectly acceptable for the application program to change the SQLDATA and SQLIND pointers between FETCH statements, retrieving two successive rows into different locations.

The Dynamic CLOSE Statement

The dynamic form of the CLOSE statement is identical in syntax and function to the static CLOSE statement shown in Figure 17-25. In both cases, the CLOSE statement ends access to the query results. When a program closes a cursor for a dynamic query, the program normally should also deallocate the resources associated with the dynamic query, including:

- The SQLDA allocated for the dynamic query and used in the DESCRIBE and FETCH statements

- A possible second SQLDA, used to pass parameter values to the OPEN statement

- The data areas allocated to receive each column of query results retrieved by a FETCH statement

- The data areas allocated as indicator variables for the columns of query results

It may not be necessary to deallocate these data areas if the program will terminate immediately after the CLOSE statement.

Dynamic SQL Dialects

Like the other parts of the SQL language, dynamic SQL varies from one brand of DBMS to another. In fact, the differences in dynamic SQL support are more serious than for static SQL, because dynamic SQL exposes more of the "nuts and bolts" of the underlying DBMS—data types, data formats, and so on. As a practical matter, these differences make it impossible to write a single, general-purpose database front-end that is portable across different DBMS brands using dynamic SQL. Instead, database front-end programs must include a "translation layer," often called a *driver*, for each brand of DBMS that they support to accommodate the differences.

The early front-end products usually shipped with a separate driver for each of the popular DBMS brands. The introduction of ODBC as a uniform SQL API layer made this job simpler, since an ODBC driver could be written once for each DBMS brand, and the front-end program could be written to solely use the ODBC interface. In practice, however, ODBC's "least common denominator" approach meant that the front-end programs couldn't take advantage of the unique capabilities of the various supported DBMS systems, and it limited the performance of the application. As a result, most modern front-end programs and tools still include a separate, explicit driver for each of the popular DBMS brands. An ODBC driver is usually included to provide access to the others.

A detailed description of the dynamic SQL features supported by all of the major DBMS brands is beyond the scope of this book. However, it is instructive to examine the dynamic SQL support provided by SQL/DS and by Oracle as examples of the kinds of differences and extensions to dynamic SQL that you may find in your particular DBMS.

Dynamic SQL in SQL/DS

SQL/DS, for many years IBM's flagship relational database for IBM's mainframe VM operating system, provides the same basic dynamic SQL support as DB2. It also supports a feature called *extended dynamic SQL*. With extended dynamic SQL, you can write a program that prepares a statement string and permanently stores the compiled statement in the database. The compiled statement can then be executed very efficiently, either by the same program or by a different program, without having to be prepared again. Thus extended dynamic SQL provides some of the performance advantages of static SQL in a dynamic SQL context.

The prepared statements in a SQL/DS database are stored in an *access module,* which is a named collection of compiled statements. SQL/DS users may have their own sets of access modules, protected by SQL/DS privileges. To create an empty access module, you use the SQL/DS CREATE PROGRAM statement, specifying a name of up to eight characters:

```
CREATE PROGRAM OPSTMTS
```

You can later remove the access module from the database with the DROP PROGRAM statement:

```
DROP PROGRAM OPSTMTS
```

Note that although the statements are called CREATE PROGRAM and DROP PROGRAM, they actually operate on access modules. Often, however, the set of compiled statements stored in an access module are, in fact, the set of statements used by a single program.

Once an access module has been created, a program can store compiled statements in it and execute those compiled statements. Special extended versions of the dynamic SQL PREPARE, DROP, DESCRIBE, EXECUTE, DECLARE CURSOR, OPEN, FETCH, and CLOSE statements, shown in Figure 18-16, are used for this purpose. These statements are supported by the SQL/DS precompiler for use in host programs written in IBM S/370 assembly language.

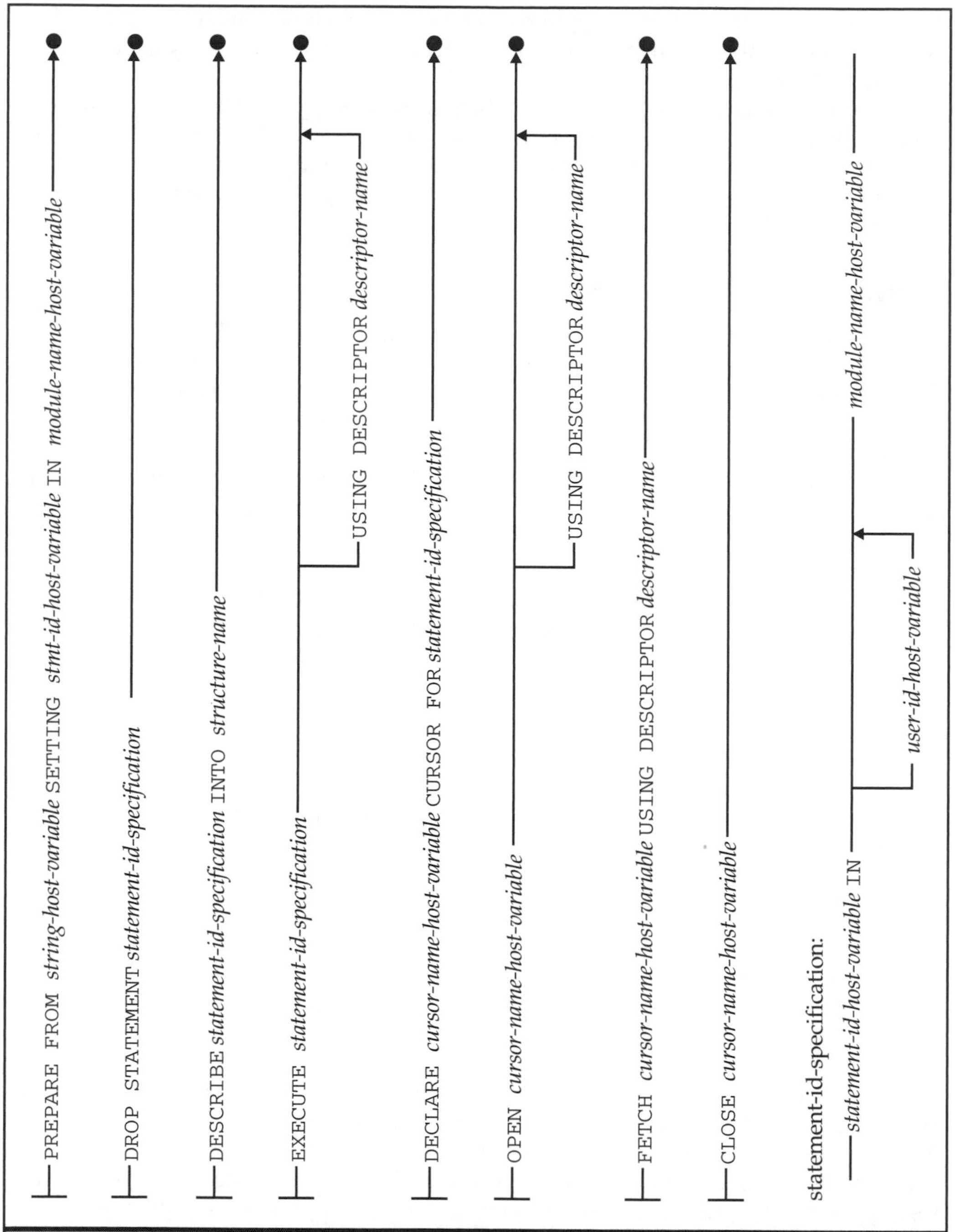

Figure 18-16. Extended dynamic SQL statements in SQL/DS

To compile a SQL statement string and store the compiled statement in an access module, your program must use the extended PREPARE statement. SQL/DS assigns the compiled statement a unique *statement-id* (a 32-bit number) and returns the statement-id into a host variable in your program. This statement-id is used by all of the other extended dynamic SQL statements to identify the compiled statement. An individual statement can be removed from the access module with the DROP STATEMENT statement.

To execute a stored statement, your program uses an extended EXECUTE statement like this one:

```
EXECUTE :STMT_ID IN :MODULE_NAME USING DESCRIPTOR :PARM_DA
```

The program passes the name of the access module and the statement-id for the statement to be executed in a pair of host variables (:MODULENAME and :STMT_ID). It also passes any parameters for the dynamic statement through a SQLDA (:PARM_DA), as described earlier in this chapter. Like the "standard" EXECUTE statement, the extended dynamic EXECUTE statement cannot be used to execute queries.

To execute a stored query, your program uses an extended DECLARE CURSOR statement like this one to associate a cursor name with the query:

```
DECLARE :CURS_NAME CURSOR FOR :STMT_ID IN :MODULE_NAME
```

Note that the cursor name is not hard-coded into the DECLARE CURSOR statement but is passed as a character string in a host variable (:CURS_NAME). Similarly, the query associated with the cursor is neither hard-coded into the DECLARE CURSOR statement (as in static SQL) nor specified by a statement name (as in dynamic SQL). Instead, the statement is specified by using host variables to pass the name of the access module (:MODULE_NAME) and the statement-id for the statement (:STMT_ID). Thus the extended DECLARE CURSOR statement provides a dynamic association between a cursor name and a query.

The extended DESCRIBE statement also uses host variables to specify the access module name and the statement-id of the statement to be described into a SQLDA:

```
DESCRIBE :STMT_ID IN :MODULE_NAME INTO :QUERY_DA
```

The extended OPEN, FETCH, and CLOSE statements are similar to their dynamic SQL counterparts. In each case, however, the name of the cursor is not hard-coded into the statement. Instead, the name of the cursor to be opened, fetched, or closed is passed in a host variable, as shown here:

```
OPEN :CURS_NAME USING :PARM_DA
```

```
FETCH :CURS_NAME USING DESCRIPTOR :QUERY_DA

CLOSE :CURS_NAME
```

This allows a single set of OPEN, FETCH, and CLOSE statements to be used with different queries at different times, increasing the flexibility of a program that uses extended dynamic SQL.

Extended dynamic SQL provides significantly more flexibility than dynamic SQL, and it can be used to gain performance advantages over dynamic SQL as well. However, it is a feature of SQL/DS only, and not a part of IBM's mainstream DB2 offering. The capabilities of extended dynamic SQL are typical of the useful, performance-enhancing functions that DBMS vendors are constantly adding to their products. In this case, the SQL/DS feature foreshadowed the more formal development of named stored database procedures, which first appeared in Sybase and SQL Server. Today, most of the major DBMS brands provide some type of stored procedure capability, including the newer versions of DB2 that IBM has released as successors to SQL/DS.

Dynamic SQL in Oracle *

The Oracle DBMS preceded DB2 into the market and based its dynamic SQL support upon IBM's System/R prototype. For this reason, the Oracle support for dynamic SQL differs somewhat from the IBM SQL standard. Although Oracle and DB2 are broadly compatible, they differ substantially at the detail level. These differences include Oracle's use of parameter markers, its use of the SQLDA, the format of its SQLDA, and its support for data type conversion. The Oracle differences from DB2 are similar to those you may encounter in other DBMS brands. For that reason it is instructive to briefly examine Oracle's dynamic SQL support and its points of difference from DB2.

Named Parameters

Recall that DB2 does not allow host variable references in a dynamically prepared statement. Instead, parameters in the statement are identified by question marks (parameter markers), and values for the parameters are specified in the EXECUTE or OPEN statement. Oracle allows you to specify parameters in a dynamically prepared statement using the syntax for host variables. For example, this sequence of embedded SQL statements is legal for Oracle:

```
exec sql begin declare section;
    char    stmtbuf[1001];
    int     employee_number;
exec sql end declare section;
```

```
          .
          .
          .
strcpy(stmtbuf, "delete from salesreps
                where empl_num = :rep_number;");
exec sql prepare delstmt from :stmtbuf;
exec sql execute delstmt using :employee_number;
```

Although `rep_number` appears to be a host variable in the dynamic DELETE statement, it is in fact a *named parameter*. As shown in the example, the named parameter behaves exactly like the parameter markers in DB2. A value for the parameter is supplied from a "real" host variable in the EXECUTE statement. Named parameters are a real convenience when you use dynamic statements with a variable number of parameters.

The DESCRIBE Statement

The Oracle DESCRIBE statement is used, like the DB2 DESCRIBE statement, to describe the query results of a dynamic query. Like DB2, Oracle returns the descriptions in a SQLDA. The Oracle DESCRIBE statement can also be used to request a description of the named parameters in a dynamically prepared statement. Oracle also returns these parameter descriptions in a SQLDA.

This Oracle DESCRIBE statement requests a description of the columns of query results from a previously prepared dynamic query:

```
exec sql describe select list for qrystmt into qry_sqlda;
```

It corresponds to the DB2 statement:

```
exec sql describe qrystmt into qry_sqlda;
```

This Oracle DESCRIBE statement requests a description of the named parameters in a previously prepared dynamic statement. The statement might be a query or some other SQL statement:

```
exec sql describe bind list for thestmt into the_sqlda;
```

This Oracle statement has no DB2 equivalent. Following this DESCRIBE statement, your program would typically examine the information in the SQLDA, fill in the pointers in the SQLDA to point to the parameter values the program wants to supply, and then execute the statement using the SQLDA form of the OPEN or EXECUTE statement:

```
exec sql execute thestmt using descriptor the_sqlda;
exec sql open qrycursor using descriptor the_sqlda;
```

The information returned by both forms of the Oracle DESCRIBE statement is the same and is described in the next section.

The Oracle SQLDA

The Oracle SQLDA performs the same functions as the DB2 SQLDA, but its format, shown in Figure 18-17, differs substantially from that of DB2. The two important fields in the DB2 SQLDA header both have counterparts in the Oracle SQLDA:

■ The N field in the Oracle SQLDA specifies the size of the arrays used to hold column definitions. It corresponds to the SQLN field in the DB2 SQLDA.

■ The F field in the Oracle SQLDA indicates how many columns are currently described in the arrays of the SQLDA. It corresponds to the SQLD field in the DB2 SQLDA.

```
struct sqlda {
    int      N;   /* number of entries in the SQLDA arrays */
    char   **V;   /* pointer to array of pointers to data areas */
    int     *L;   /* pointer to array of buffer lengths */
    short   *T;   /* pointer to array of data type codes */
    short  **I;   /* pointer to array of pointers to indicator variables */
    int      F;   /* number of active entries in the SQLDA arrays */
    char   **S;   /* pointer to array of pointers to column/parameter names */
    short   *M;   /* pointer to array of name buffer lengths */
    short   *C;   /* pointer to array of current lengths of names */
    char   **X;   /* pointer to array of pointers to indicator parameter names */
    short   *Y;   /* pointer to array of indicator name buffer lengths */
    short   *Z;   /* pointer to array of current lengths of indicator names */
} ;
```

Figure 18-17. *The Oracle SQLDA*

Instead of DB2's single array of SQLVAR structures that contain column descriptions, the Oracle SQLDA contains pointers to a series of arrays, each of which describes one aspect of a column:

- The T field points to an array of integers that specify the data type for each query results column or named parameter. The integers in this array correspond to the SQLTYPE field in each DB2 SQLVAR structure.

- The V field points to an array of pointers that specify the buffer for each column of query results or each passed parameter value. The pointers in this array correspond to the SQLDATA field in each DB2 SQLVAR structure.

- The L field points to an array of integers that specify the length of each buffer pointed to by the V array. The integers in this array correspond to the SQLLEN field in each DB2 SQLVAR structure.

- The I field points to an array of data pointers that specify the indicator variable for each query results column or named parameter. The pointers in this array correspond to the SQLIND field in each DB2 SQLVAR structure.

- The S field points to an array of string pointers that specify the buffers where Oracle is to return the name of each query results column or named parameter. The buffers pointed to by this array correspond to the SQLNAME structure in each DB2 SQLVAR structure.

- The M field points to an array of integers that specify the size of each buffer pointed to by the S array. For DB2, the SQLNAME structure has a fixed-length buffer, so there is no equivalent to the M field.

- The C field points to an array of integers that specify the actual lengths of the names pointed to by the S array. When Oracle returns the column or parameter names, it sets the integers in this array to indicate their actual lengths. For DB2, the SQLNAME structure has a fixed-length buffer, so there is no equivalent to the C field.

- The X field points to an array of string pointers that specify the buffers where Oracle is to return the name of each named indicator parameter. These buffers are used only by the Oracle DESCRIBE BLIND LIST statement; they have no DB2 equivalent.

- The Y field points to an array of integers specifying the size of each buffer pointed to by the X array. There is no DB2 equivalent.

- The Z field points to an array of integers specifying actual lengths of the indicator parameter names pointed to by the X array. When Oracle returns the indicator parameter names, it sets the integers in this array to indicate their actual lengths. There is no DB2 equivalent.

Data Type Conversions

The data type formats that DB2 uses to receive parameter values and return query results are those supported by the IBM S/370 architecture mainframes that run DB2. Because it was designed as a portable DBMS, Oracle uses its own internal data type formats. Oracle automatically converts between its internal data formats and those of the computer system on which it is running when it receives parameter values from your program and when it returns query results to your program.

Your program can use the Oracle SQLDA to control the data type conversion performed by Oracle. For example, suppose that your program uses the DESCRIBE statement to describe the results of a dynamic query and discovers (from the data type code in the SQLDA) that the first column contains numeric data. Your program can request conversion of the numeric data by changing the data type code in the SQLDA before it fetches the data. If the program places the data type code for a character string into the SQLDA, for example, Oracle will convert the first column of query results and return it to your program as a string of digits.

The data type conversion feature of the Oracle SQLDA provides excellent portability, both across different computer systems and across different programming languages. A similar feature is supported by several other DBMS brands, but not by the IBM SQL products.

Dynamic SQL and the SQL2 Standard

The SQL1 standard did not address dynamic SQL, so the *de facto* standard for dynamic SQL, as described in the preceding sections, was set by IBM's implementation in DB2. The SQL2 standard explicitly included a standard for dynamic SQL, specified in a separate chapter of the standard that is nearly 50 pages long. In the simplest areas of dynamic SQL, the new SQL2 standard closely follows the dynamic SQL currently used by commercial DBMS products. But in other areas, including even the most basic dynamic SQL queries, the new standard introduces incompatibilities with existing DBMS products, which will require the rewriting of applications. The next several sections describe the SQL2 standard for dynamic SQL in detail, with an emphasis on the differences from the DB2-style dynamic SQL described in the preceding sections.

In practice, support for SQL2-style dynamic SQL is appearing slowly in commercial DBMS products, and most dynamic SQL programming still requires the use of the "old," DB2-style dynamic SQL. Even when a new version of a DBMS product supports the new SQL2 statements, the DBMS vendor always provides a precompiler option that accepts the "old" dynamic SQL structure used by the particular DBMS. Often, this is the default option for the precompiler, because with thousands and thousands of SQL programs already in existence, the DBMS vendor has an absolute requirement that new DBMS versions do not "break" old programs. Thus, the migration to portions of SQL2 that represent incompatibilities with current practice will be a slow and evolutionary one.

Basic Dynamic SQL2 Statements

The SQL2 statements that implement basic dynamic SQL statement execution (that is, dynamic SQL that does not involve database queries) are shown in Figure 18-18. These statements closely follow the DB2 structure and language. This includes the single-step and two-step methods of executing dynamic SQL statements.

The SQL2 EXECUTE IMMEDIATE statement has an identical syntax and operation to that of its DB2 counterpart. It immediately executes the SQL statement passed to the DBMS as a character string. Thus, the EXECUTE IMMEDIATE statement in Figure 18-3 conforms to the SQL2 standard.

The SQL2 PREPARE and EXECUTE statements also operate identically to their DB2-style counterparts. The PREPARE statement passes a text string containing a SQL statement to the DBMS and causes the DBMS to analyze the statement, optimize it, and build an application plan for it. The EXECUTE statement causes the DBMS to actually

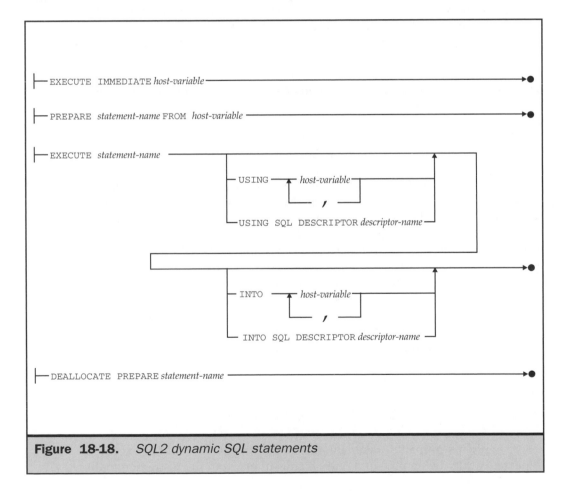

Figure 18-18. *SQL2 dynamic SQL statements*

execute a previously prepared statement. Like the DB2 version, the SQL2 EXECUTE statement optionally accepts host variables that pass the specific values to be used when executing the SQL statement. The PREPARE and EXECUTE statements in Figure 18-4 (called out as item 2) thus conform to the SQL2 standard.

Two useful extensions to the PREPARE/EXECUTE structure are a part of the Full-Level SQL2 standard specification (neither is part of the Entry-Level or Intermediate-Level specification). The first is a useful companion to the PREPARE statement that "unprepares" a previously compiled dynamic SQL statement. The DEALLOCATE PREPARE statement provides this capability. When the DBMS processes this statement, it can free the resources associated with the compiled statement, which will usually include some internal representation of the application plan for the statement. The statement named in the DEALLOCATE PREPARE statement must match the name specified in a previously-executed PREPARE statement.

In the absence of a capability like that provided by DEALLOCATE PREPARE, the DBMS has no way of knowing whether a previously prepared statement will be executed again or not, and so must retain all of the information associated with the statement. In practice, some DBMS brands maintain the compiled version of the statement only until the end of a transaction; in these systems, a statement must be re-prepared for each subsequent transaction where it is used. Because of the overhead involved in this process, other DBMS brands maintain the compiled statement information indefinitely. The DEALLOCATE PREPARE can play a more important role in these systems, where a database session might last for hours. Note, however, that the SQL2 standard explicitly says that whether a prepared statement is valid outside of the transaction in which it is prepared is "implementation dependent."

The SQL2 extension to the DB2-style EXECUTE statement may be even more useful in practice. It allows the EXECUTE statement to be used to process simple "singleton SELECT" statements that return a single row of query results. Like the DB2 EXECUTE statement, the SQL2 statement includes a USING clause that names the host variables that supply the values for parameters in the statement being executed. But the SQL2 statement also permits an optional INTO clause that names the host variables that *receive* the values *returned* by a single-row query. Suppose you have written a program that dynamically generates a query statement that retrieves the name and quota of a salesperson, with the salesperson's employee number as an input parameter. Using DB2-style dynamic SQL, even this simple query involves the use of a SQLDA, cursors, a FETCH statement loop, and so on. Using SQL2 dynamic SQL, the statement can be executed using the simple two-statement sequence:

```
PREPARE qrystmt FROM :statement_buffer;

EXECUTE qrystmt USING :emplnum INTO :name, :quota;
```

As with any prepared statement, this single-row query could be executed repeatedly after being prepared once. It still suffers from the restriction that the number of returned columns, and their data types, must know when the program is written, since they must match exactly the number and data types of the host variables in the INTO clause. This restriction is removed by allowing the use of a SQLDA-style descriptor area instead of a list of host variables, as described in the next section.

SQL2 and the SQLDA

Although its support for PREPARE/EXECUTE processing closely parallels that of DB2 dynamic SQL, the SQL2 standard diverges substantially from DB2 style in the area of dynamic query processing. In particular, the SQL2 standard includes major changes to the DB2 SQL Data Area (SQLDA), which is at the heart of dynamic multi-row queries. Recall from the previous description in this chapter that a SQL Data Area (SQLDA) provides two important functions:

■ A flexible way to pass parameters to be used in the execution of a dynamic SQL statement (passing data from the host program *to* the DBMS)

■ The way that the query results are returned to the program in the execution of a dynamic SQL query (passing data from the DBMS back to the host program)

The DB2-style SQLDA handles these functions with flexibility, but it has some serious disadvantages. It is a very low-level data structure, which tends to be very specific to a particular programming language. For example, the variable-length structure of a DB2-style SQLDA makes it very difficult to represent in the FORTRAN language. The SQLDA structure also implicitly makes assumptions about the memory of the computer system on which the dynamic SQL program is running, how data items in a structure are aligned on such a system, and so on. For the writers of the SQL2 standard, these low-level dependencies were unacceptable barriers to portability. Therefore, they replaced the DB2 SQLDA structure with a set of statements for manipulating a more abstract structure called a dynamic SQL *descriptor*.

The structure of a SQL2 descriptor is shown in Figure 18-19. Conceptually, the SQL2 descriptor is parallel to, and plays exactly the same role as, the DB2-style SQLDA shown in Figure 18-7. The fixed part of the SQL2 descriptor specifies a count of the number of items in the variable part of the descriptor. Each item in the variable part contains information about a single parameter being passed, such as its data type, its length, an indicator telling whether or not a NULL value is being passed, and so on. But unlike the DB2 SQLDA, the SQL2 descriptor is not an actual data structure within the host program. Instead it is a collection of data items "owned" by the DBMS software. The host program manipulates SQL2 descriptors—creating them, destroying them, placing data items into them, extracting data from them—via a new set of dynamic SQL statements specially designed for that purpose. Figure 18-20 summarizes these SQL2 descriptor management statements.

To understand how the SQL2 descriptor management statements work, it's instructive to reexamine the dynamic SQL update program in Figure 18-8. This program illustrates the use of a DB2-style SQLDA in an EXECUTE statement. The flow of

Fixed part	
COUNT	number of items described

Variable part—one occurrence per item (parameter or query results column):

TYPE	data type of item
LENGTH	length of item
OCTET_LENGTH	length of item (in 8-bit octets)
RETURNED_LENGTH	length of returned data item
RETURNED_OCTET_LENGTH	length of returned data (in 8-bit octets)
PRECISION	precision of data item
SCALE	scale of data item
DATETIME_INTERVAL_CODE	type of date/time interval data
DATETIME_INTERVAL_PRECISION	precision of date/time interval data
NULLABLE	can item be NULL?
INDICATOR	is data item NULL? (indicator value)
DATA	data item itself
NAME	name of data item
UNNAMED	is data item unnamed?

Figure 18-19.   *SQL2 descriptor structure*

the program remains identical if a SQL2 descriptor is used instead, but the specifics change quite a lot.

Before using the descriptor, the program must create it, using the statement:

```
ALLOCATE DESCRIPTOR parmdesc WITH MAX :parmcnt;
```

This statement replaces the allocation of storage for the parmda data structure at callout 1 in Figure 18-8. The descriptor (named parmdesc) will perform the same functions as the parmda. Note that the program in Figure 18-8 had to calculate how much storage would be required for the parmda structure before allocating it. With the

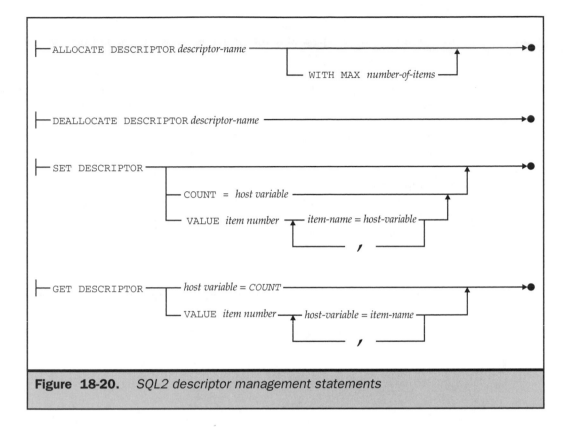

Figure 18-20. *SQL2 descriptor management statements*

SQL2 descriptor, that calculation is eliminated, and the host program simply tells the DBMS how many items the variable part of the descriptor must be able to hold.

The next step in the program is to set up the descriptor so that it describes the parameters to be passed—their data types, lengths, and so on. The loop at callout 2 of the program remains intact, but again the details of how the descriptor is initialized differ from those for the SQLDA. At callout 3 and callout 4, the data type and length for the parameter are specified with a form of the SET DESCRIPTOR statement, with this code excerpt:

```
typecode = columns[i].typecode;
length = columns[i].buflen;
SET DESCRIPTOR parmdesc VALUE (:i + 1) TYPE = :typecode
SET DESCRIPTOR parmdesc VALUE (:i + 1) LENGTH = :length;
```

The differences from Figure 18-8 are instructive. Because the descriptor is maintained by the DBMS, the data type and length must be passed to the DBMS, through the SET DESCRIPTOR statement, using host variables. In this particular example, the simple variables typecode and length are used. Additionally, the data type codes in Figure 18-8 were specific to DB2. The fact that each DBMS vendor used different codes to represent different SQL data types was a major source of portability problems in dynamic SQL. The SQL2 standard specifies integer data type codes for all of the data types specified in the standard, eliminating this issue. The SQL2 data type codes are summarized in Table 18-2. So, in addition to the other changes, the data type codes in the columns structure of Figure 18-8 would need to be modified to use these SQL2 standard data type codes.

The statements at callouts 5 and 6 in Figure 18-8 were used to "bind" the SQLDA structure to the program buffers used to contain the parameter data and the corresponding indicator variable. Effectively, they put pointers to these program

Data Type	Code
Data Type Codes (TYPE)	
INTEGER	4
SMALLINT	5
NUMERIC	2
DECIMAL	3
FLOAT	6
REAL	7
DOUBLE PRECISION	8
CHARACTER	1
CHARACTER VARYING	12
BIT	14
BIT VARYING	15
DATE/TIME/TIMESTAMP	9
INTERVAL	10

Table 18-2.   *SQL2 Data Type Codes*

Data Type	Code
Date/Time Subcodes (`Interval_Code`)	
DATE	1
TIME	2
TIME WITH TIME ZONE	4
TIMESTAMP	3
TIMESTAMP WITH TIME ZONE	5
Date/Time Subcodes (`Interval_Precision`)	
YEAR	1
MONTH	2
DAY	3
HOUR	4
MINUTE	5
SECOND	6
YEAR – MONTH	7
DAY – HOUR	8
DAY – MINUTE	9
DAY – SECOND	10
HOUR – MINUTE	11
HOUR – SECOND	12
MINUTE – SECOND	13

Table 18-2. *SQL2 Data Type Codes* (continued)

buffers into the SQLDA for the use of the DBMS. With SQL2 descriptors, this type of binding is not possible. Instead, the data value and indicator value are specifically passed as host variables, later in the program. Thus, the statements at callouts 5 and 6 would be eliminated in the conversion to SQL2.

The statement at callout 7 in Figure 18-8 sets the SQLDA to indicate how many parameter values are actually being passed to the DBMS. The SQL2 descriptor must similarly be set to indicate the number of passed parameters. This is done with a form of the SET DESCRIPTOR statement:

```
SET DESCRIPTOR parmdesc COUNT = :parmcnt;
```

Strictly speaking, this SET DESCRIPTOR statement should probably be placed earlier in the program and should be executed before those for the individual items. The SQL2 standard specifies a complete set of rules that describe how setting values in some parts of the descriptor causes values in other parts of the descriptor to be reset. For the most part, these rules simply specify the natural hierarchy of information. For example, if you set the data type for a particular item to indicate an integer, the standard says that the corresponding information in the descriptor that tells the length of the same item will be reset to some implementation-dependent value. Normally this doesn't impact your programming, but it does mean that you can't assume that just because you set some value within the descriptor previously that it still retains the same value. It's best to fill the descriptor "hierarchically," starting with "higher-level" information (for example, the number of items and their data types) and then proceeding to "lower-level" information (data type lengths, subtypes, whether NULL values are allowed, and so on).The flow of the program in Figure 18-8 can now continue unmodified. The PREPARE statement compiles the dynamic UPDATE statement, and its form does not change for SQL2. The program then enters the for loop, prompting the user for parameters. Here again, the concepts are the same, but the details of manipulating the SQLDA structure and the SQL2 descriptor differ.

If the user indicates a NULL value is to be assigned (by typing an asterisk in response to the prompt), the program in Figure 18-8 sets the parameter indicator buffer appropriately with the statement:

```
*(parmvar->sqlind) = -1;
```

and if the value is not NULL, the program again sets the indicator buffer with the statement:

```
*(parmvar->sqlind) = 0;
```

For the SQL2 descriptor, these statements would again be converted to a pair of SET DESCRIPTOR statements:

```
SET DESCRIPTOR parmdesc VALUE(:j + 1) INDICATOR = -1;
SET DESCRIPTOR parmdesc VALUE (:j + 1) INDICATOR = 0;
```

Note again the use of the loop control variable to specify which item in the descriptor is being set, and the direct passing of data (in this case, constants) rather than the use of pointers to buffers in the SQLDA structure.

Finally the program in Figure 18-8 passes the actual parameter value typed by the user to the DBMS, via the SQLDA. The statements at callout 8 accomplish this for data of different types, by first converting the typed characters into binary representations of the data and placing the binary data into the data buffers pointed to by the SQLDA. Again, the conversion to SQL2 involves replacing these pointers and direct SQLDA manipulation with a SET DESCRIPTOR statement. For example, these statements pass the data and its length for a variable-length character string:

```
length = strlen(inbuf);
SET DESCRIPTOR parmdesc VALUE (:j + 1) DATA = :inbuf;
SET DESCRIPTOR parmdesc VALUE (:j + 1) LENGTH = :length;
```

For data items that do not require a length specification, passing the data is even easier, since only the DATA form of the SET DESCRIPTOR statement is required. It's also useful to note that SQL2 specifies implicit data type conversions between host variables (such as inbuf) and SQL data types. Following the SQL standard, it would be necessary for the program in Figure 18-8 to perform all of the data type conversion in the sscanf() functions. Instead, the data could be passed to the DBMS as character data, for automatic conversion and error detection.

With the SQLDA finally set up as required, the program in Figure 18-8 executes the dynamic UPDATE statement with the passed parameters at callout 9, using an EXECUTE statement that specifies a SQLDA. The conversion of this statement to a SQL2 descriptor is straightforward; it becomes

```
EXECUTE updatestmt USING SQL DESCRIPTOR parmdesc;
```

The keywords in the EXECUTE statement change slightly, and the name of the descriptor is specified instead of the name of the SQLDA.

Finally, the program in Figure 18-8 should be modified like this to tell the DBMS to deallocate the SQL2 descriptor. The statement that does this is:

```
DEALLOCATE DESCRIPTOR parmdesc;
```

In a simple program like this one, the DEALLOCATE is not very necessary, but in a more complex real-world program with multiple descriptors, it's a very good idea to deallocate them when the program no longer requires them.

SQL2 and Dynamic SQL Queries

In the dynamic SQL statements of the preceding sections, the SQL2 descriptor, like the SQLDA it replaces, is used to pass parameter information from the host program to the DBMS, for use in dynamic statement execution. The SQL2 standard also uses the SQL descriptor in dynamic query statements where, like the SQLDA it replaces, it controls the passing of query result from the DBMS back to the host program. Figure 18-9 lists a DB2-style dynamic SQL query program. It's useful to examine how the program in Figure 18-9 would change to conform to the SQL2 standard. Again the flow of the program remains identical under SQL2, but the specifics change quite a lot. The SQL2 forms of the dynamic SQL query-processing statements are shown in Figure 18-21.

The declaration of the cursor for the dynamic query, in callout 1 of Figure 18-9, remains unchanged under SQL2. The construction of the dynamic SELECT statement in callout 2 is also unchanged, as is the PREPARE statement of callout 3. The changes to the program begin at callout 4, where the program uses the DESCRIBE statement to obtain a description of the query results, which is returned in a SQLDA named qry_da. For SQL2, this DESCRIBE statement must be modified to refer to a SQL2 descriptor, which must have been previously allocated. Assuming the descriptor is named qrydesc, the statements would be:

```
ALLOCATE DESCRIPTOR qrydesc WITH MAX :colcount;
DESCRIBE querystmt USING SQL DESCRIPTOR qrydesc;
```

The SQL2 form of the DESCRIBE statement has a parallel effect on the one it replaces. Descriptions of the query result columns are returned, column by column, into the SQL2 descriptor, instead of into the SQLDA. Because the descriptor is a DBMS structure, rather than an actual data structure in the program, the host program must retrieve the information from the descriptor, piece by piece, as required. The GET DESCRIPTOR statement performs this function, just as the SET DESCRIPTOR function performs the opposite function of putting information into the SQL2 descriptor. In the program of Figure 18-9, the statements at callout 5, which obtains the length of a particular column of query results from a SQLDA, would be replaced with this statement:

```
GET DESCRIPTOR qrydesc VALUE (:i + 1) :length = LENGTH;
qry_var -> sqldat = malloc(length);
```

The statement at callout 5 that allocates buffers for each item of query results is still needed, but the method for telling the DBMS where to put the results changes for SQL2. Instead of placing the address of the program destination for each item into the SQLDA, the program must place these addresses into the SQL2 descriptor, using the

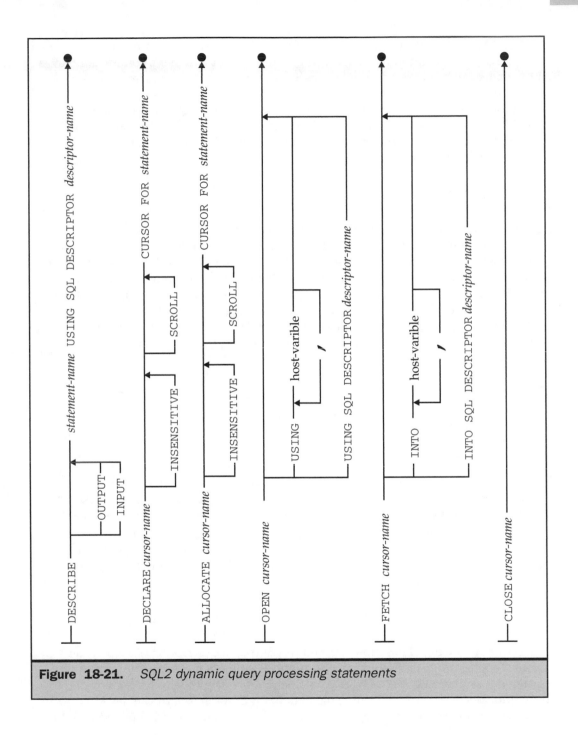

Figure 18-21.   *SQL2 dynamic query processing statements*

SET DESCRIPTOR statement. The buffers for the indicator variables are not needed with the SQL2 descriptor. Instead, the information about whether a column contains a NULL value can be obtained from the descriptor for each row as it is fetched, as seen later in the program example.

In this particular example, the number of columns in the query results are calculated by the program as it builds the query. The program could also obtain the number of columns from the SQL2 descriptor with this form of the GET DESCRIPTOR statement:

```
GET DESCRIPTOR qrydesc :colcount = COUNT;
```

Having obtained the description of the query results, the program performs the query by opening the cursor at callout 6. The simple form of the OPEN statement, without any input parameters, conforms to the SQL2 standard. If the dynamic query specified parameters, they could be passed to the DBMS either as a series of host variables or via a SQL2 descriptor. The SQL2 OPEN statement using host variables is identical to the DB2 style, shown in the program in Figure 18-13. The SQL2 OPEN statement using a descriptor is parallel to the SQL2 EXECUTE statement using a descriptor, and differs from the DB2 style. For example, the OPEN statement of Figure 18-14:

```
OPEN qrycursor USING DESCRIPTOR :parmda;
```

is changed for SQL2 into this OPEN statement:

```
OPEN qrycursor USING SQL DESCRIPTOR parmdesc;
```

The technique for passing input parameters to the OPEN statement via the SQL2 descriptor is exactly the same as that described earlier for the EXECUTE statement.

Like the Oracle implementation of dynamic SQL, the SQL2 standard provides a way for the host program to obtain a description of the parameters in a dynamic query as well as a description of the query results. For the program fragment in Figure 18-14, this DESCRIBE statement:

```
DESCRIBE INPUT querystmt USING SQL DESCRIPTOR parmdesc;
```

will return, in the SQL2 descriptor named parmdesc, a description of each of the parameters that appears in the dynamic query. The number of parameters can be obtained with the GET DESCRIPTOR statement, retrieving the COUNT item from the descriptor. As with the Oracle implementation, the SQL2 standard can have two descriptors associated with a dynamic query. The input descriptor, obtained with the

DESCRIBE INPUT statement, contains descriptions of the parameters. The output descriptor contains descriptions of the query results columns. The standard allows you to explicitly ask for the output description:

```
DESCRIBE OUTPUT querystmt USING SQL DESCRIPTOR qrydesc;
```

but the DESCRIBE OUTPUT form of the statement is the default, and the most common practice is to omit the keyword OUTPUT.

Returning to the dynamic query example of Figure 18-9, the cursor has been opened at callout 7, and it's time to fetch rows of query results at callout 8. Again, the SQL2 form of the FETCH statement is slightly modified to use the SQL2-style descriptor:

```
FETCH sqlcurs USING SQL DESCRIPTOR qrydesc;
```

The FETCH statement advances the cursor to the next row of query results and brings the values for that row into the program buffers, as specified within the descriptor structure. The program must still use the descriptor to determine information about each column of returned results, such as its length or whether it contains a NULL value. For example, to determine the returned length of a column of character data, the program might use the statement:

```
GET DESCRIPTOR qrydesc VALUE(:i + 1) :length = RETURNED_LENGTH;
```

To determine whether the value in the column was NULL, the program can use the statement:

```
GET DESCRIPTOR qrydesc VALUE(:i + 1) :indbuf = INDICATOR;
```

and similarly to determine the data type of the column, the program can use the statement:

```
GET DESCRIPTOR qrydesc VALUE(:i + 1) :type = TYPE;
```

As you can see, the details of row-by-row query processing within the for loop of the program will differ dramatically from those in Figure 18-9.

Having processed all rows of query results, the program closes the cursor at callout 8. The CLOSE statement remains unchanged under SQL2. Following the closing of the cursor, it would be good practice to deallocate the SQL2 descriptor(s), which would have been allocated at the very beginning of the program.

The changes required to the dynamic SQL programs in Figures 18-8, 18-9, and 18-14 to make them conform to the SQL2 standard illustrate, in detail, the new features specified by the standard and the degree to which they differ from common dynamic SQL usage today. In summary, the changes from DB2-style dynamic SQL are:

- The SQLDA structure is replaced with a named SQL2 descriptor.

- The ALLOCATE DESCRIPTOR and DEALLOCATE DESCRIPTOR statements are used to create and destroy descriptors, replacing allocation and deallocation of host program SQLDA data structures.

- Instead of directly manipulating elements of the SQLDA, the program specifies parameter values and information through the SET DESCRIPTOR statement.

- Instead of directly manipulating elements of the SQLDA, the program obtains information about query results and obtains the query result data itself through the GET DESCRIPTOR statement.

- The DESCRIBE statement is used both to obtain descriptions of query results (DESCRIBE OUTPUT) and to obtain descriptions of parameters (DESCRIBE INPUT).

- The EXECUTE, OPEN, and FETCH statements are slightly modified to specify the SQL2 descriptor by name instead of the SQLDA.

Summary

This chapter described dynamic SQL, an advanced form of embedded SQL. Dynamic SQL is rarely needed to write simple data processing applications, but it is crucial for building general-purpose database front-ends. Static SQL and dynamic SQL present a classic trade-off between efficiency and flexibility, which can be summarized as follows:

- *Simplicity.* Static SQL is relatively simple; even its most complex feature, cursors, can be easily understood in terms of familiar file input/output concepts. Dynamic SQL is complex, requiring dynamic statement generation, variable-length data structures, and memory management, with memory allocation/deallocation, data type alignment, pointer management, and associated issues.

- *Performance.* Static SQL is compiled into an application plan at compile-time; dynamic SQL must be compiled at run-time. As a result, static SQL performance is generally much better than that of dynamic SQL. The performance of dynamic SQL is dramatically impacted by the quality of the application design; a design that minimizes the amount of compilation overhead can approach static SQL performance.

- *Flexibility.* Dynamic SQL allows a program to decide at run-time what specific SQL statements it will execute. Static SQL requires that all SQL statements be coded in advance, when the program is written, limiting the flexibility of the program.

Dynamic SQL uses a set of extended embedded SQL statements to support its dynamic features:

- The EXECUTE IMMEDIATE statement passes the text of a dynamic SQL statement to the DBMS, which executes it immediately.

- The PREPARE statement passes the text of a dynamic SQL statement to the DBMS, which compiles it into an application plan but does not execute it. The dynamic statement may include parameter markers whose values are specified when the statement is executed.

- The EXECUTE statement asks the DBMS to execute a dynamic statement previously compiled by a PREPARE statement. It also supplies parameter values for the statement that is to be executed.

- The DESCRIBE statement returns a description of a previously prepared dynamic statement into a SQLDA. If the dynamic statement is a query, the description includes a description of each column of query results.

- The DECLARE CURSOR statement for a dynamic query specifies the query by the statement name assigned to it when it was compiled by the PREPARE statement.

- The OPEN statement for a dynamic query passes parameter values for the dynamic SELECT statement and requests query execution.

- The FETCH statement for a dynamic query fetches a row of query results into program data areas specified by a SQLDA structure.

- The CLOSE statement for a dynamic query ends access to the query results.

Chapter 19

SQL APIs

The embedded SQL technique for programmatic access to SQL-based databases was pioneered by the early IBM relational database prototypes and was widely adopted by mainstream SQL products. However, several major DBMS products, led by Sybase's first SQL Server implementation, took a very different approach. Instead of trying to blend SQL with another programming language, these products provide a library of function calls as an application programming interface (API) for the DBMS. To pass SQL statements to the DBMS, an application program calls functions in the API, and it calls other functions to retrieve query results and status information from the DBMS.

For many programmers, a SQL API is a very straightforward way to use SQL. Most programmers have some experience in using function libraries for other purposes, such as string manipulation, mathematical functions, file input/output, and screen forms management. Modern operating systems, such as Unix and Windows, extensively use API suites to extend the core capabilities provided by the OS itself. The SQL API thus becomes "just another library" for the programmer to learn.

Over the last several years, SQL APIs have become very popular, equaling if not surpassing the popularity of the embedded SQL approach for new applications development. This chapter describes the general concepts used by all SQL API interfaces. It also describes specific features of some of the APIs used by popular SQL-based DBMS systems, and Microsoft's ODBC API that has become a *de facto* SQL API standard. Finally, it covers the ANSI/ISO SQL Call Level Interface standard, which is based on the core of the ODBC interface.

API Concepts

When a DBMS supports a function call interface, an application program communicates with the DBMS exclusively through a set of calls that are collectively known as an *application program interface,* or API. The basic operation of a typical DBMS API is illustrated in Figure 19-1:

- The program begins its database access with one or more API calls that connect the program to the DBMS and often to a specific database.

- To send a SQL statement to the DBMS, the program builds the statement as a text string in a buffer and then makes an API call to pass the buffer contents to the DBMS.

- The program makes API calls to check the status of its DBMS request and to handle errors.

- If the request is a query, the program uses API calls to retrieve the query results into the program's buffers. Typically, the calls return data a row at a time or a column at a time.

- The program ends its database access with an API call that disconnects it from the DBMS.

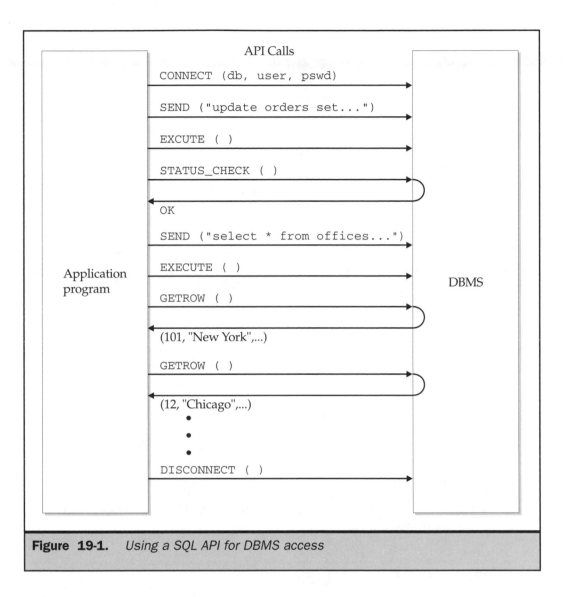

Figure 19-1.   *Using a SQL API for DBMS access*

A SQL API is often used when the application program and the database are on two different systems in a client/server architecture, as shown in Figure 19-2. In this configuration, the code for the API functions is located on the client system, where the application program executes. The DBMS software is located on the server system, where the database resides. Calls from the application program to the API take place locally within the client system, and the API code translates the calls into messages that

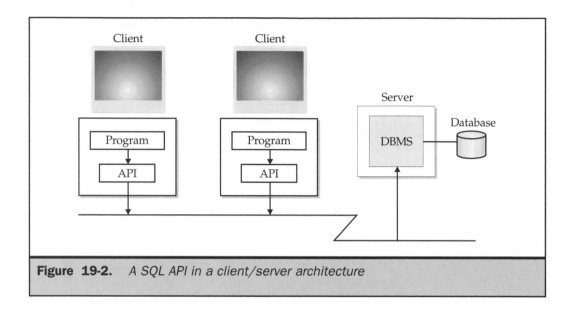

Figure 19-2. *A SQL API in a client/server architecture*

it sends to and receives from the DBMS over a network. As explained later in this chapter, a SQL API offers particular advantages for a client/server architecture because it can minimize the amount of network traffic between the API and the DBMS.

The early APIs offered by various DBMS products differed substantially from one another. Like many parts of the SQL language, proprietary SQL APIs proliferated long before there was an attempt to standardize them. In addition, SQL APIs tend to expose the underlying capabilities of the DBMS more than the embedded SQL approach, leading to even more differences. Nonetheless, all of the SQL APIs available in commercial SQL products are based on the same fundamental concepts illustrated in Figures 19-1 and 19-2. These concepts also apply to the ODBC API and more recent ANSI/ISO standards based on it.

The `dblib` API (SQL Server)

The first major DBMS product to emphasize its callable API was Sybase's and Microsoft's SQL Server. For many years, the SQL Server callable API was the *only* interface offered by these products. Both Microsoft and Sybase now offer embedded SQL capabilities and have added newer or higher-level callable APIs, but the original SQL Server API remains a very popular way to access these DBMS brands. The SQL Server API also provided the model for much of Microsoft's ODBC API. SQL Server and its API are also an excellent example of a DBMS designed from the ground up around a client/server architecture. For all of these reasons, it's useful to begin our exploration of SQL APIs by examining the basic SQL Server API.

The original SQL Server API, which is called the *database library* or *dblib*, consists of about 100 functions available to an application program. The API is very comprehensive, but a typical program uses only about a dozen of the function calls, which are summarized in Table 19-1. The other calls provide advanced features, alternative methods of interacting with the DBMS, or single-call versions of features that otherwise would require multiple calls.

Function	Description
Database connection/disconnection	
dblogin()	Provides a data structure for login information
dbopen()	Opens a connection to SQL Server
dbuse()	Establishes the default database
dbexit()	Closes a connection to SQL Server
Basic statement processing	
dbcmd()	Passes SQL statement text to dblib
dbsqlexec()	Requests execution of a statement batch
dbresults()	Obtains results of next SQL statement in a batch
dbcancel()	Cancels the remainder of a statement batch
Error handling	
dbmsghandle()	Establishes a user-written message handler procedure
dberrhandle()	Establishes a user-written error handler procedure
Query results processing	
dbbind()	Binds a query results column to a program variable
dbnextrow()	Fetches the next row of query results
dbnumcols()	Obtains the number of columns of query results

Table 19-1. *Basic dblib API Functions*

Function	Description
dbcolname()	Obtains the name of a query results column
dbcoltype()	Obtains the data type of a query results column
dbcollen()	Obtains the maximum length of a query results column
dbdata()	Obtains a pointer to a retrieved data value
dbdatlen()	Obtains the actual length of a retrieved data value
dbcanquery()	Cancels a query before all rows are fetched

Table 19-1. *Basic* dblib *API Functions* (continued)

Basic SQL Server Techniques

A simple SQL Server program that updates a database can use a very small set of dblib calls to do its work. The program in Figure 19-3 implements a simple quota update application for the SALESREPS table in the sample database. It is identical to the program in Figure 17-17, but uses the SQL Server API instead of embedded SQL. The figure illustrates the basic interaction between a program and SQL Server:

1. The program prepares a "login record," filling in the user name, password, and any other information required to connect to the DBMS.

2. The program calls dbopen() to establish a connection to the DBMS. A connection must exist before the program can send SQL statements to SQL Server.

3. The program builds a SQL statement in a buffer and calls dbcmd() to pass the SQL text to dblib. Successive calls to dbcmd() add to the previously passed text; there is no requirement that a complete SQL statement be sent in a single dbcmd() call.

4. The program calls dbsqlexec(), instructing SQL Server to execute the statement previously passed with dbcmd().

5. The program calls dbresults() to determine the success or failure of the statement.

6. The program calls dbexit() to close down the connection to SQL Server.

```
main()
{
    LOGINREC  *loginrec;        /* data structure for login information */
    DBPROCESS *dbproc;          /* data structure for connection */
    char       amount_str[31];  /* amount entered by user (as a string) */
    int        status;          /* dblib call return status */

    /* Get a login structure and set user name & password */
    loginrec = dblogin();                                              ①
    DBSETLUSER(loginrec, "scott");
    DBSETLPWD (loginrec, "tiger");

    /* Connect to SQL Server */
    dbproc = dbopen(loginrec, "");                                     ②

    /* Prompt the user for the amount of quota increase/decrease */
    printf("Raise/lower by how much: ");
    gets(amount_str);

    /* Pass SQL statement to dblib */
    dbcmd(dbproc, "update salesreps set quota = quota +");             ③
    dbcmd(dbproc, amount_str);

    /* Ask SQL Server to execute the statement */
    dbsqlexec(dbproc);                                                 ④

    /* Get results of statement execution */
    status = dbresults(dbproc);                                        ⑤
    if (status ! = SUCCEED)
        printf("Error during update.\n");
    else
        printf("Update successful.\n");

    /* Break connection to SQL Server */
    dbexit(dbproc);                                                    ⑥
    exit();
}
```

Figure 19-3. *A simple program using* dblib

It's instructive to compare the programs in Figure 19-3 and Figure 17-17 to see the differences between the embedded SQL and the dblib approach:

- The embedded SQL program either implicitly connects to the only available database (as in DB2), or it includes an embedded SQL statement for connection (such as the CONNECT statement specified by the SQL2 standard). The dblib program connects to a particular SQL Server with the dbopen() call.

- The actual SQL UPDATE statement processed by the DBMS is identical in both programs. With embedded SQL, the statement is part of the program's source code. With dblib, the statement is passed to the API as a sequence of one or more character strings. In fact, the dblib approach more closely resembles the dynamic SQL EXECUTE IMMEDIATE statement than static SQL.

- In the embedded SQL program, host variables provide the link between the SQL statements and the values of program variables. With dblib, the program passes variable values to the DBMS in the same way that it passes program text—as part of a SQL statement string.

- With embedded SQL, errors are returned in the SQLCODE or SQLSTATE field of the SQLCA structure. With dblib, the dbresults() call retrieves the status of each SQL statement.

Overall, the embedded SQL program in Figure 17-17 is shorter and probably easier to read. However, the program is neither purely C nor purely SQL, and a programmer must be trained in the use of embedded SQL to understand it. The use of host variables means that the interactive and embedded forms of the SQL statement are different. In addition, the embedded SQL program must be processed both by the SQL precompiler and by the C compiler, lengthening the compilation cycle. In contrast, the SQL Server program is a "plain vanilla" C program, directly acceptable to the C compiler, and does not require special coding techniques.

Statement Batches

The program in Figure 19-3 sends a single SQL statement to SQL Server and checks its status. If an application program must execute several SQL statements, it can repeat the dbcmd() / dbsqlexec() / dbresults() cycle for each statement. Alternatively, the program can send several statements as a single *statement batch* to be executed by SQL Server.

Figure 19-4 shows a program that uses a batch of three SQL statements. As in Figure 19-3, the program calls dbcmd() to pass SQL text to dblib. The API simply concatenates the text from each call. Note that it's the program's responsibility to include any required spaces or punctuation in the passed text. SQL Server does not begin executing the statements until the program calls dbsqlexec(). In this example, three statements have been sent to SQL Server, so the program calls dbresults() three times in succession. Each call to dbresults() "advances" the API to the results

```
main()
{
    LOGINREC    *loginrec;        /* data structure for login information */
    DBPROCESS   *dbproc;          /* data structure for connection */
        •
        •
        •
    /* Delete salespeople with low sales */
    dbcmd(dbproc, "delete from salesreps where sales < 10000.00");

    /* Increase quota for salespeople with moderate sales */
    dbcmd(dbproc, "update salesreps set quota = quota + 10000.00");
    dbcmd(dbproc, "where sales <= 150000.00");

    /* Increase quota for salespeople with high sales */
    dbcmd(dbproc, "update salesreps set quota = quota + 20000.00");
    dbcmd(dbproc, "where sales > 150000.00");

    /* Ask SQL Server to execute the statement batch */
    dbsqlexec(dbproc);

    /* Check results of each of the three statements */
    if (dbresults(dbproc) != SUCCEED) goto do_error;
    if (dbresults(dbproc) != SUCCEED goto do_error;
    if (dbresults(dbproc) != SUCCEED goto do_error;
        •
        •
        •
}
```

Figure 19-4.   *Using a* dblib *statement batch*

of the next statement in the batch and tells the program whether the statement succeeded or failed.

In the program shown in Figure 19-4, the programmer knows in advance that three statements are in the batch, and the programmer can code three corresponding calls to dbresults(). If the number of statements in the batch is not known in advance, the program can call dbresults() repeatedly until it receives the error code NO_MORE_RESULTS. The program excerpt in Figure 19-5 illustrates this technique.

```
        •
        •
        •
    /* Execute statements previously with dbcmd() calls */
    dbsqlexec(dbproc);

    /* Loop checking results of each statement in the batch */
    while (status = dbresults(dbproc) != NO_MORE_RESULTS {
        if (status == FAIL)
            goto handle_error;
        else
            printf("Statement succeeded.\n");
    }

    /* Done with loop; batch completed successfully */
    printf("Batch complete.\n");
    exit();
        •
        •
        •
```

Figure 19-5. *Processing the results of a* `dblib` *statement batch*

Error Handling

The value returned by the `dbresults()` function tells the program whether the corresponding statement in the statement batch succeeded or failed. To get more detailed information about a failure, your program must provide its own *message-handling function*. The `dblib` software automatically calls the message-handling function when SQL Server encounters an error while executing SQL statements. Note that `dblib` calls the message-handling function during its processing of the `dbsqlexec()` or `dbresults()` function calls, before it returns to your program. This allows the message-handling function to do its own error processing.

Figure 19-6 shows an excerpt from a SQL Server program which includes a message-handling function called `msg_rtn()`. When the program begins, it activates the message-handling function by calling `msghandle()`. Suppose that an error occurs later, while SQL Server is processing the `DELETE` statement. When the program calls `dbsqlexec()` or `dbresults()` and `dblib` receives the error message from SQL Server, it "up-calls" the `msg_rtn()` routine in the program, passing it five parameters:

- *dbproc.* The connection on which the error occurred
- *msgno.* The SQL Server error number identifying the error

- *msgstate.* Providing information about the error context
- *severity.* A number indicating the seriousness of the error
- *msgtext.* An error message corresponding to msgno

```
            •
            •
            •
/* External variables to hold error information */
int   errcode;                          /* saved error code */
char errmsg[256];                       /* saved error message */

/* Define our own message-handling function */
int msg_rtn(dbproc, msgno, msgstate, severity, msgtext)
   DBPROCESS    *dbproc;
   DBINT         msgno;
   int           msgstate;
   int           severity;
   char         *msgtext;
   extern int    errcode;
   extern char *errmsg;
   {
      /* Print out the error number and message */
      printf("*** Error: %d Message: %s\n", msgno, msgtext);

      /* Save the error information for the application program */
      errcode = msgno;
      strcpy(errmsg, msgtext);

      /* Return to dlib to complete the API call */
      return(0);
   }

main()
{
   DBPROCESS *dbproc;            /* data structure for connection */
      •
      •
      •
```

Figure 19-6.   *Error handling in a dblib program*

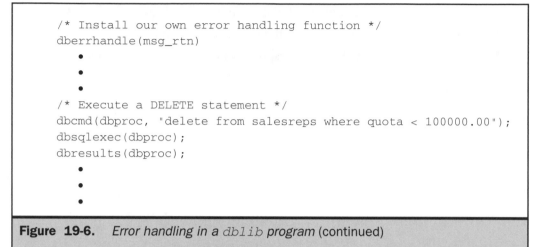

```
        /* Install our own error handling function */
        dberrhandle(msg_rtn)
            •
            •
            •

        /* Execute a DELETE statement */
        dbcmd(dbproc, "delete from salesreps where quota < 100000.00");
        dbsqlexec(dbproc);
        dbresults(dbproc);
            •
            •
            •
```

Figure 19-6. *Error handling in a* `dblib` *program* (continued)

The `msg_rtn()` function in this program handles the message by printing it and saving the error number in a program variable for use later in the program. When the message-handling function returns to `dblib` (which called it), `dblib` completes its own processing and then returns to the program with a `FAIL` status. The program can detect this return value and perform further error processing, if appropriate.

The program excerpt in the figure actually presents a simplified view of SQL Server error handling. In addition to SQL statement errors detected by SQL Server, errors can also occur within the `dblib` API itself. For example, if the network connection to the SQL Server is lost, a `dblib` call may time out waiting for a response from SQL Server, resulting in an error. The API handles these errors by up-calling a separate *error-handling function*, which operates much like the message-handling function described here.

A comparison of Figure 19-6 with Figures 17-10 and 17-13 illustrates the differences in error-handling techniques between `dblib` and embedded SQL:

- In embedded SQL, the `SQLCA` structure is used to signal errors and warnings to the program. SQL Server communicates errors and warnings by up-calling special functions within the application program and returning a failure status for the API function that encountered the error.

- In embedded SQL, error processing is synchronous. The embedded SQL statement fails, control returns to the program, and the `SQLCODE` or `SQLSTATE` value is tested. SQL Server error processing is asynchronous. When an API call fails, SQL Server calls the application program's error-handling or message-handling function *during* the API call. It returns to the application program with an error status later.

■ Embedded SQL has only a single type of error and a single mechanism for reporting it. The SQL Server scheme has two types of errors and two parallel mechanisms.

In summary, error handling in embedded SQL is simple and straightforward, but there are a limited number of responses that the application program can make when an error occurs. A SQL Server program has more flexibility in handling errors. However, the "up-call" scheme used by dblib is more sophisticated, and while it is familiar to systems programmers, it may be unfamiliar to application programmers.

SQL Server Queries

The SQL Server technique for handling programmatic queries is very similar to its technique for handling other SQL statements. To perform a query, a program sends a SELECT statement to SQL Server and uses dblib to retrieve the query results row by row. The program in Figure 19-7 illustrates the SQL Server query-processing technique:

1. The program uses the dbcmd() and dbsqlexec() calls to pass a SELECT statement to SQL Server and request its execution.

2. When the program calls dbresults() for the SELECT statement, dblib returns the completion status for the query and also makes the query results available for processing.

3. The program calls dbbind() once for each column of query results, telling dblib where it should return the data for that particular column. The arguments to dbbind() indicate the column number, the buffer to receive its data, the size of the buffer, and the expected data type.

4. The program loops, calling dbnextrow() repeatedly to obtain the rows of query results. The API places the returned data into the data areas indicated in the previous dbbind() calls.

5. When no more rows of query results are available, the dbnextrow() call returns the value NO_MORE_ROWS. If more statements were in the statement batch following the SELECT statement, the program could call dbresults() to advance to the next statement.

```
main()
{
   LOGINREC   *loginrec;           /* data structure for login information */
   DBPROCESS *dbproc;              /* data structure for connection */
   char       repname[16];         /* retrieved city for the office */
   short      repquota;            /* retrieved employee number of mgr */
   float      repsales;            /* retrieved sales for office */

   /* Open a connection to SQL Server */
   loginrec = dblogin();
   DBSETLUSER(loginrec, "scott");
   DBSETLPWD (loginrec, "tiger");
   dbproc = dbopen(loginrec, "");

   /* Pass query to dblib and ask SQL Server to execute it */
   dbcmd(dbproc, "select name, quota, sales from salesreps ");
   dbcmd(dbproc, "where sales > quota order by name ");    ◄────────────① 
   dbsqlexec(dbproc);    ◄

   /* Get first statement in the batch */
   dbresults(dbproc);    ◄────────────────────────────────────②

   /* Bind each column to a variable in this program */
   dbbind(dbproc, 1, NTBSTRINGBIND, 16, &repname);  ◄
   dbbind(dbproc, 2, FLT4BIND,        0, &repquota); ◄──────③
   dbbind(dbproc, 3, FLT4BIND,        0, &repsales); ◄

   /* Loop retrieving rows of query results */
   while (status = dbnextrow(dbproc) == SUCCEED) {   ◄──────────④

      /* Print data for this salesperson */
      printf("Name:  %s\n",   repname);
      printf("Quota: %f\n\n", repquota);
      printf("Sales: %f\n",   repsales);
   }

   /* Check for errors and close connection */  ◄──────────────⑤
   if (status == FAIL) {
      printf("SQL error.\n");
   dbexit(dbproc);
   exit();
}
```

Figure 19-7. *Retrieving query results using* `dblib`

Two of the `dblib` calls in Figure 19-7, `dbbind()` and `dbnextrow()`, support processing of the SQL Server query results. The `dbbind()` call sets up a one-to-one correspondence between each column of query results and the program variable that is to receive the retrieved data. This process is called *binding* the column. In the figure, the first column `(NAME)` is bound to a 16-byte character array and will be returned as a null-terminated string. The second and third columns, `QUOTA` and `SALES`, are both bound to floating-point numbers. It is the programmer's responsibility to make sure that the data type of each column of query results is compatible with the data type of the program variable to which it is bound.

Once again, it is useful to compare the SQL Server query processing in Figure 19-7 with the embedded SQL queries in Figure 17-20 and Figure 17-23:

- Embedded SQL has two different query-processing techniques—one for single-row queries (singleton `SELECT`) and one for multi-row queries (cursors). The `dblib` API uses a single technique, regardless of the number of rows of query results.

- To specify the query, embedded SQL replaces the interactive `SELECT` statement with the singleton `SELECT` statement or the `DECLARE CURSOR` statement. With SQL Server, the `SELECT` statement sent by the program is *identical* to the interactive `SELECT` statement for the query.

- With embedded SQL, the host variables that receive the query results are named in the `INTO` clause of the singleton `SELECT` or the `FETCH` statement. With SQL Server, the variables to receive query results are specified in the `dbbind()` calls.

- With embedded SQL, row-by-row access to query results is provided by special-purpose embedded SQL statements (`OPEN`, `FETCH`, and `CLOSE`). With SQL Server, access to query results is through `dblib` function calls (`dbresults()` and `dbnextrow()`), which keep the SQL language itself more streamlined.

Because of its relative simplicity and its similarity to the interactive SQL interface, many programmers find the SQL Server interface easier to use for query processing than the embedded SQL interface.

Retrieving `NULL` Values

The `dbnextrow()` and `dbbind()` calls shown in Figure 19-7 provide a simple way to retrieve query results, but they do not support `NULL` values. When a row retrieved by `dbnextrow()` includes a column with a `NULL` value, SQL Server replaces the `NULL` with a *null substitution value*. By default, SQL Server uses zero as a substitution value for numeric data types, a string of blanks for fixed-length strings, and an empty string for variable-length strings. The application program can change the default value for any data type by calling the API function `dbsetnull()`.

In the program shown in Figure 19-7, if one of the offices had a `NULL` value in its `QUOTA` column, the `dbnextrow()` call for that office would retrieve a zero into the quota_value variable. Note that the program cannot tell from the retrieved data whether the QUOTA column for the row really has a zero value, or whether it is NULL. In some applications the use of substitution values is acceptable, but in others it is important to be able to detect NULL values. These latter applications must use an alternative scheme for retrieving query results, described in the next section.

Retrieval Using Pointers

With the basic SQL Server data retrieval technique, the dbnextrow() call copies the data value for each column into one of your program's variables. If there are many rows of query results or many long columns of text data, copying the data into your program's data areas can create a significant overhead. In addition, the dbnextrow() call lacks a mechanism for returning NULL values to your program.

To solve these two problems, dblib offers an alternate method of retrieving query results. Figure 19-8 shows the program excerpt from Figure 19-7, rewritten to use this alternate method:

1. The program sends the query to SQL Server and uses dbresults() to access the results, as it does for any SQL statement. However, the program does *not* call dbbind() to bind the columns of query results to program variables.

2. The program calls dbnextrow() to advance, row by row, through the query results.

3. For each column of each row, the program calls dbdata() to obtain a *pointer* to the data value for the column. The pointer points to a location within dblib's internal buffers.

4. If a column contains variable-length data, such as a VARCHAR data item, the program calls dbdatlen() to find out the length of the data item.

5. If a column has a NULL value, the dbdata() function returns a null pointer (0), and dbdatlen() returns 0 as the length of the item. These return values give the program a way to detect and respond to NULL values in the query results.

The program in Figure 19-8 is more cumbersome than the one in Figure 19-7. In general, it's easier to use the dbbind() function than the dbdata() approach, unless your program needs to handle NULL values or will be handling a large volume of query results.

Random Row Retrieval

A program normally processes SQL Server query results by moving through them sequentially using the dbnextrow() call. For browsing applications, dblib also provides limited random access to the rows of query results. Your program must explicitly enable random row access by turning on a dblib option. The dbgetrow() call can then be used to retrieve a row by its row number.

```
main()
{
   LOGINREC  *loginrec;         /* data structure for login information */
   DBPROCESS *dbproc;           /* data structure for connection */
   char      *namep;            /* pointer to NAME column data */
   int        citylen;          /* length of NAME column data */
   float     *quotap;           /* pointer to QUOTA column data */
   float     *salesp;           /* pointer to SALES column data */

   /* Open a connection to SQL Server */
   loginrec = dblogin();
   DBSETLUSER(loginrec, "scott");
   DBSETLPWD (loginrec, "tiger");
   dbproc = dbopen(loginrec, "");

   /* Pass query to dblib and ask SQL Server to execute it */
   dbcmd(dbproc, "select name, quota, sales from salesreps ");
   dbcmd(dbproc, "where sales > quota order by name ");
   dbsqlexec(dbproc);

   /* Get to first statement in the batch */          ◄─────────────── ①
   dbresults(dbproc);
   /* Retrieve the single row of query results */
   while (status = dbnextrow(dbproc) == SUCCEED) {     ◄─────────────── ②

      /* Get the address of each data item in this row */
      namep   = dbdata(dbproc, 1);   ◄─┐
      quotap  = dbdata(dbproc, 2);   ◄─┼──────────────────────────── ③
      salesp  = dbdata(dbproc, 3);   ◄─┘
      namelen = dbdatlen(dbproc, 1); ◄─────────────────────────────── ④

      /* Copy NAME value into our own buffer & null-terminate it */
      strncpy(namebuf, namep, namelen);
      *(namebuf + namelen) = (char) 0;
```

Figure 19-8.   *Retrieval using the* dbdata() *function*

```
        /* Print data for this salesperson */
        printf("Name:  %s\n", namebuf);
        if (quotap == 0)     ⟵──────────────────────────⑤
            printf("Quota is NULL.\n");
        else
            printf("Quota: %f\n", *quotap);
        printf("Sales: %f\n", *salesp);
    }


    /* Check for successful completion */
    if (status == FAIL)
        printf("SQL error.\n");
    dbexit(dbproc);
    exit();
}
```

Figure 19-8.   *Retrieval using the* `dbdata()` *function* (continued)

To support random row retrieval, `dblib` stores the rows of query results in an internal buffer. If the query results fit entirely within the `dblib` buffer, `dbgetrow()` supports random retrieval of any row. If the query results exceed the size of the buffer, only the initial rows of query results are stored. The program can randomly retrieve these rows, but a `dbnextrow()` call that attempts to retrieve a row past the end of the buffer returns the special `BUF_FULL` error condition. The program must then discard some of the saved rows from the buffer, using the `dbclrbuf()` call, to make room for the new row. Once the rows are discarded, they cannot be re-retrieved with the `dbgetrow()` function. Thus `dblib` supports random retrieval of query results within a limited "window," dictated by the size of the row buffer, as shown in Figure 19-9. Your program can specify the size of the `dblib` row buffer by calling the `dblib` routine `dbsetopt()`.

The random access provided by `dbgetrow()` is similar to the scroll cursors supported by several DBMS products and specified by the SQL2 standard. In both cases, random retrieval by row number is supported. However, a scroll cursor is a true pointer into the entire set of query results; it can range from the first to the last row, even if the query results contain thousands of rows. By contrast, the `dbgetrow()` function provides random access only within a limited window. This is adequate for limited browsing applications but cannot easily be extended to large queries.

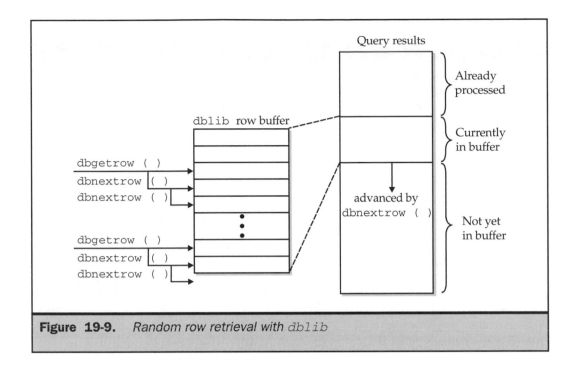

Figure 19-9.   *Random row retrieval with* `dblib`

Positioned Updates

In an embedded SQL program, a cursor provides a direct, intimate link between the program and the DBMS query processing. The program communicates with the DBMS row by row as it uses the FETCH statement to retrieve query results. If the query is a simple, single-table query, the DBMS can maintain a direct correspondence between the current row of query results and the corresponding row within the database. Using this correspondence, the program can use the positioned update statements (UPDATE... WHERE CURRENT OF and DELETE... WHERE CURRENT OF) to modify or delete the current row of query results.

SQL Server query processing uses a much more detached, asynchronous connection between the program and the DBMS. In response to a statement batch containing one or more SELECT statements, SQL Server sends the query results back to the dblib software, which manages them. Row-by-row retrieval is handled by the dblib API calls, not by SQL language statements. As a result, early versions of SQL Server could not support positioned updates because its notion of a "current" row applied to query results within the dblib API, not to rows of the actual database tables.

Later versions of SQL Server (and Sybase Adaptive Server) added complete support for standard SQL cursors, with their associated DECLARE/OPEN/FETCH/CLOSE SQL statements. Cursors actually operate within Transact-SQL stored procedures, and the action of the FETCH statement is to fetch data from the database into the stored procedure for processing—not to actually retrieve it into the application program which called the stored procedure. Stored procedures and their operation within various popular SQL DBMS products are discussed in Chapter 20.

Dynamic Queries

In the program examples thus far in this chapter, the queries to be performed were known in advance. The columns of query results could be bound to program variables by explicit dbbind() calls hard-coded in the program. Most programs that use SQL Server can be written using this technique. (This static column binding corresponds to the fixed list of host variables used in the static SQL FETCH statement in standard embedded SQL, described in Chapter 17.)

If the query to be carried out by a program is not known at the time the program is written, the program cannot include hard-coded dbbind() calls. Instead, the program must ask dblib for a description of each column of query results, using special API functions. The program can then bind the columns "on the fly" to data areas that it allocates at run-time. (This dynamic column binding corresponds to the use of the dynamic SQL DBNUMCOLS() statement and SQLDA, in dynamic embedded SQL, as described in Chapter 18.)

Figure 19-10 shows an interactive query program that illustrates the dblib technique for handling dynamic queries. The program accepts a table name entered by the user and then prompts the user to choose which columns are to be retrieved from the table. As the user selects the columns, the program constructs a SELECT statement and then uses these steps to execute the SELECT statement and display the data from the selected columns:

1. The program passes the generated SELECT statement to SQL Server using the dbcmd() call, requests its execution with the dbsqlexec() call, and calls dbresults() to advance the API to the query results, as it does for all queries.

2. The program calls dbnumcols() to find out how many columns of query results were produced by the SELECT statement.

3. For *each* column, the program calls dbcolname() to find out the name of the column, calls dbcoltype() to find out its data type, and calls dbcollen() to find out its maximum length.

4. The program allocates a buffer to receive each column of query results and calls dbbind() to bind each column to its buffer.

5. When all columns have been bound, the program calls dbnextrow() repeatedly to retrieve each row of query results.

```
main()
{
    /* This is a simple general-purpose query program. It prompts
       the user for a table name and then asks the user which columns
       of the table are to be included in the query. After the user's
       selections are complete, the program runs the requested query and
       displays the results.
    */

    LOGINREC   *loginrec;          /* data structure for login information */
    DBPROCESS  *dbproc;            /* data structure for connection */
    char       stmbuf[2001];       /* SQL text to be executed */
    char       querytbl[32];       /* user-specified table */
    char       querycol[32];       /* user-specified column */
    int        status;             /* dblib return status */
    int        first_col = 0;      /* is this the first column chosen? */
    int        colcount;           /* number of columns of query results */
    int        i;                  /* index for columns */
    char       inbuf[101];         /* input entered by user */
    char       *item_name[100];    /* array to track column names */
    char       *item_data[100];    /* array to track column buffers */
    int        item_type[100];     /* array to track column data types */
    char       *address;           /* address of buffer for current column */
    int        length;             /* length of buffer for current column */

    /* Open a connection to SQL Server */
    loginrec = dblogin();
    DBSETLUSER(loginrec, "scott");
    DBSETLPWD (loginrec, "tiger");
    dbproc = dbopen(loginrec, "");

    /* Prompt the user for which table to query */
    printf("*** Mini-Query Program ***\n");
    printf("Enter name of table for query: ");
    gets(querytbl);

    /* Start the SELECT statement in the buffer */
    strcpy(stmbuf, "select ");
```

Figure 19-10.   *Using dblib for a dynamic query*

```
    /* Query the SQL Server system catalog to get column names */
    dbcmd(dbproc, "select name from syscolumns ");
    dbcmd(dbproc, "where id = (select id from sysobjects ");
    dbcmd(dbproc, "where type = 'U' and name = ");
    dbcmd(dbproc, querytbl);
    dbcmd(dbproc, ")");
    dbsqlexec(dbproc);

    /* Process the results of the query */
    dbresults(dbproc);
    dbbind(dbproc, querycol);
    while (status = dbnextrow(dbproc) == SUCCEED) {
        printf("Include column %s (y/n)? ", querycol);
        gets(inbuf);
        if (inbuf[0] == 'y') {
            /* User wants the column; add it to the select list */
            if (first_col++ > 0)  strcat(stmbuf, ", ");
            strcat(stmbuf, querycol);
        }
    }

    /* Finish the SELECT statement with a FROM clause */
    strcat(stmbuf, "from ");
    strcat(stmbuf, querytbl);

    /* Execute the query and advance to the query results */
    dbcmd(dbproc, stmbuf);          ◄
    dbsqlexec(dbproc);            ◄                                    ①
    dbresults(dbproc);           ◄

    /* Ask dblib to describe each column, allocate memory & bind it */
    colcount = dbnumcols(dbproc);        ◄                             ②
    for (i = 0; i < colcount; i++) {
        item_name[i] = dbcolname(dbproc, i);    ◄                      ③
        type = dbcoltype(dbproc, i);     ◄
        switch(type) {

        case SQLCHAR:
        case SQLTEXT:
```

Figure 19-10. *Using dblib for a dynamic query* (continued)

```
        case SQLDATETIME:
           length = dbcollen(dbproc, i) + 1;
           item_data[i] = address = malloc(length);         ◄─────────────④
           item_type[i] = NTBSTRINGBIND;
           dbind(dbproc, i, NTBSTRINGBIND, length, address);
           break;

        case SQLINT1:
        case SQLINT2:
        case SQLINT4:
           item_data[i] = address = malloc(sizeof(long)):
           item_type[i] = INTBIND;
           dbbind(dbproc, i, INTBIND, sizeof(long), address);
           break;
        case SQLFLT8:
        case SQLMONEY:
           item_data[i] = address = malloc(sizeof(double));
           item_type[i] = FLT8BIND;
           dbbind(dbproc, i, FLT8BIND, sizeof(double), address);
           break;
        }
    }

/* Fetch and display the rows of query results */
while (status = dbnextrow(dbproc) == SUCCEED) {          ◄─────────────⑤

    /* Loop, printing data for each column of the row */
    printf("\n");
    for (i = 0; i < colcount; i++) {

        /* Find the SQLVAR for this column; print column label */
        printf("Column # %d (%s): ", i+1, item_name[i];

        /* Handle each data type separately */
        switch(item_type[i]) {

        case NTBSTRINGBIND:
           /* Text data -- just dispay it */
           puts(item_data[i]);
           break;
```

Figure 19-10.   *Using* `dblib` *for a dynamic query* (continued)

```
          case INTBIND:
             /* Four-byte integer data -- convert & display it */
             printf("%lf", *((double *) (item_data[i])));
             break;

          case FLT8BIND:
             /* Floating-point data -- convert & display it */
             printf("%lf", *((double *) (item_data[i])));
             break;
          }
       }
    }

    printf("\nEnd of data.\n");

    /* Clean up allocated storage */
    for (i = 0; i < colcount; i++) {
       free(item_data[i]);
    }
    dbexit(dbproc);
    exit();
}
```

Figure 19-10. *Using dblib for a dynamic query* (continued)

The dblib-based program in Figure 19-10 performs exactly the same function as the dynamic embedded SQL program in Figure 18-9. It's instructive to compare the two programs and the techniques they use:

■ For both embedded SQL and dblib, the program builds a SELECT statement in its buffers and submits it to the DBMS for processing. With dynamic SQL, the special PREPARE statement handles this task; with the SQL Server API, the standard dbcmd() and dbsqlexec() functions are used.

■ For both interfaces, the program must request a description of the columns of query results from the DBMS. With dynamic SQL, the special DBNUMCOLS() statement handles this task, and the description is returned in a SQLDA data structure. With dblib, the description is obtained by calling API functions. Note that the program in Figure 19-10 maintains its *own* arrays to keep track of the column information.

■ For both interfaces, the program must allocate buffers to receive the query results and must bind individual columns to those buffer locations. With dynamic SQL, the program binds columns by placing the buffer addresses into the `SQLVAR` structures in the `SQLDA`. With SQL Server, the program uses the `dbbind()` function to bind the columns.

■ For both interfaces, the query results are returned into the program's buffers, row by row. With dynamic SQL, the program retrieves a row of query results using a special version of the `FETCH` statement that specifies the `SQLDA`. With SQL Server, the program calls `dbnextrow()` to retrieve a row.

Overall, the strategy used to handle dynamic queries is very similar for both interfaces. The dynamic SQL technique uses special statements and data structures that are unique to dynamic SQL; they are quite different from the techniques used for static SQL queries. In contrast, the `dblib` techniques for dynamic queries are basically the same as those used for all other queries. The only added features are the `dblib` functions that return information about the columns of query results. This tends to make the callable API approach easier to understand for the less experienced SQL programmer.

ODBC and the SQL/CLI Standard

Open Database Connectivity (ODBC) is a database-independent callable API suite originally developed by Microsoft. Although Microsoft plays an important role as a database software vendor, its development of ODBC was motivated even more by its role as a major operating system developer. Microsoft wanted to make it easier for developers of Windows applications to incorporate database access. But the large differences between the various database systems and their APIs made this very difficult. If an application developer wanted a program to work with several different DBMS brands, it had to provide a separate, specially written database interface module (usually called a "driver") for each one. Each application program that wanted to provide access to multiple databases had to provide a set of drivers.

Microsoft's solution to this problem was to create ODBC as a uniform, standardized database access interface, and incorporate it into the Windows operating system. For application developers, ODBC eliminated the need to write custom database drivers. For database vendors, ODBC provided a way to gain support from a broader range of application programs.

Call-Level Interface Standardization

ODBC would have been important even as a Microsoft-only standard. However, Microsoft worked to make it a vendor-independent standard as well. A database vendor association called the SQL Access Group was working on standardizing client/server protocols for remote database access at about the same time as Microsoft's original development of ODBC. Microsoft persuaded the SQL Access Group to expand their focus and adopt ODBC as their standard for vendor-independent database access. Management of the SQL Access Group standard was eventually turned over to the

European X/Open consortium, another standards organization, as part of its overall standards for a Common Application Environment (CAE).

With the growing popularity of call-level APIs for database access, the official SQL standards groups eventually turned their attention to standardization of this aspect of SQL. The X/Open standard (based on Microsoft's earlier ODBC work) was taken as a starting point and slightly modified to create an official ANSI/ISO standard. The resulting SQL/Call Level Interface (SQL/CLI) standard was published in 1995 as ANSI/ISO/IEC 9075-3-1995. It is officially Part 3 of a contemplated multi-part standard that will be an evolution of the SQL2 standard published in 1992.

Microsoft has since evolved ODBC to conform to the official SQL/CLI standard. The CLI standard roughly forms the core level of Microsoft's ODBC 3 revision. Other, higher-level capabilities of ODBC 3 go beyond the CLI specification to provide more API functionality and to deal with the specific problems of managing ODBC as part of the Windows operating system. In practice, the core-level ODBC capabilities and the SQL/CLI specification form the effective "callable API standard."

Because of its substantial advantages for both application developers and database vendors, ODBC/CLI has become a very widely supported standard. Virtually all SQL-based database systems provide an ODBC/CLI interface as one of their supported interfaces. Some DBMS brands have even adopted ODBC/CLI as their standard database API. Thousands of application programs support ODBC/CLI, including all of the leading programming tools packages, query- and forms-processing tools and report writers, and popular productivity software such as spreadsheets and graphics programs.

The SQL/CLI standard includes about forty different API calls, summarized in Table 19-2. The calls provide a comprehensive facility for establishing connections to a database server, executing SQL statements, retrieving and processing query results, and handling errors in database processing. They provide all of the capabilities available through the standard's embedded SQL interface, including both static SQL and dynamic SQL capabilities.

The simple CLI program in Figure 19-11 repeats the program in Figure 19-3 and 17-14, but it uses the CLI functions. It follows the sequence of steps used by most CLI-based applications:

1. The program connects to the CLI and allocates data structures for its use.

2. It connects to a specific database server.

3. The program builds SQL statements in its memory buffers.

4. It makes CLI calls to request statement execution and check status.

5. On successful completion, it makes a CLI call to commit the database transaction.

6. It disconnects from the database and releases its data structures.

Function	Description
Resource and connection management	
SQLAllocHandle()	Allocates resources for environment, connection, descriptor, or statement
SQLFreeHandle()	Frees previously allocated resources
SQLAllocEnv()	Allocates resources for a SQL environment
SQLFreeEnv()	Frees resources for a SQL environment
SQLAllocConnect()	Allocates resources for a database connection
SQLFreeConnect()	Frees resources for a database connection
SQLAllocStmt()	Allocates resources for a SQL statement
SQLFreeStmt()	Frees resources for a SQL statement
SQLConnect()	Establishes a database connection
SQLDisconnect()	Ends an established database connection
Statement execution	
SQLExecDirect()	Directly executes a SQL statement
SQLPrepare()	Prepares a SQL statement for subsequent execution
SQLExecute()	Executes a previously-prepared SQL statement
SQLRowCount()	Gets number of rows affected by last SQL statement
Transaction management	
SQLEndTran()	Ends a SQL transaction
SQLCancel()	Cancels execution of a SQL statement
Parameter handling	
SQLBindParam()	Binds program location to a parameter value

Table 19-2.   *SQL/CLI API Functions*

Function	Description
SQLParamData()	Processes deferred parameter values
SQLPutData()	Provides deferred parameter value or a portion of a character string value
Query results processing	
SQLSetCursorName()	Sets the name of a cursor
SQLGetCursorName()	Obtains the name of a cursor
SQLFetch()	Fetches a row of query results
SQLFetchScroll()	Fetches a row of query results with scrolling
SQLCloseCursor()	Closes an open cursor
SQLGetData()	Obtains the value of a query results column
Query results description	
SQLNumResultCols()	Determines the number of query results columns
SQLDescribeCol()	Describes result column of a query
SQLColAttribute()	Gets attribute of a query results column
SQLGetDescField()	Gets value of a descriptor field
SQLSetDescField()	Sets value of a descriptor field
SQLGetDescRec()	Gets values from a descriptor record
SQLSetDescRec()	Sets values in a descriptor record
SQLCopyDesc()	Copies descriptor area values
Error handling	
SQLError()	Obtains error information
SQLGetDiagField()	Gets value of a diagnostic record field
SQLGetDiagRec()	Gets value of the diagnostic record

Table 19-2. *SQL/CLI API Functions* (continued)

Function	Description
Attribute management	
SQLSetEnvAttr()	Sets attribute value for a SQL environment
SQLGetEnvAttr()	Retrieves attribute value for a SQL environment
SQLSetStmtAttr()	Sets descriptor area to be used for a SQL statement
SQLGetStmtAttr()	Gets descriptor area for a SQL statement
Driver management	
SQLDataSources()	Gets a list of available SQL servers
SQLGetFunctions()	Gets information about supported features of a SQL implementation
SQLGetInfo()	Gets information about supported features of a SQL implementation

Table 19-2.   *SQL/CLI API Functions* (continued)

```
/* Program to raise all quotas by a user-specified amount */
#include <sqlcli.h>                    /* header file with CLI definitions */
main()
{
   SQLHENV    env_hdl;                 /* SQL-environment handle */
   SQLHDBC    conn_hdl;                /* connection handle */
   SQLHSTMT   stmt_hdl;               /* statement handle */
   SQLRETURN  status;                 /* CLI routine return status */
   char       *svr_name  = "demo";    /* server name */
   char       *user_name = "joe";     /* user name for connection */
   char       *user_pswd = "xyz";     /* user password for connection */
   char       amount_str[31];         /* amount entered by user */
   char       stmt_buf[128];          /* buffer for SQL statement */
```

Figure 19-11.   *A simple program using AWL/CLI*

```
/* Allocate handles for SQL environment, connection, statement */
SQLAllocHandle(SQL_HANDLE_ENV, SQL_NULL_HANDLE, &env_hdl);
SQLAllocHandle(SQL_HANDLE_DBC, env_hdl, &conn_hdl);
SQLAllocHandle(SQL_HANDLE_STMT, conn_hdl, &stmt_hdl);

/* Connect to the database, passing server name, user, password */
/* SQL_NTS says NULL-terminated string instead of passing length */
SQLConnect(conn_hdl, svr_name, SQL_NTS,
                     user_name, SQL_NTS,
                     user_pswd, SQL_NTS);

/* Prompt the user for the amount of quota increase/decrease */
printf("Raise/lower quotas by how much: ");
gets(amount_str);

/* Assemble UPDATE statement and ask DBMS to execute it */
strcpy(stmt_buf, "update salesreps set quota = quota + ");
strcat(stmt_buf, amount_str);
status = SQLExecDirect(stmt_hdl, stmt_buf, SQL_NTS);
if (status)
    printf("Error during update\n");
else
    printf("Update successful.\n");

/* Commit updates and disconnect from database server */
SQLEndTran(SQL_HANDLE_ENV, env_hdl, SQL_COMMIT);
SQLDisconnect(conn_hdl);

/* Deallocate handles and exit */
SQLFreeHandle(SQL_HANDLE_STMT, stmt_hdl);
SQLFreeHandle(SQL_HANDLE_DBC, conn_hdl);
SQLFreeHandle(SQL_HANDLE_ENV, env_hdl);
exit();
}
```

Figure 19-11. *A simple program using AWL/CLI* (continued)

All of the CLI routines return a status code indicating either successful completion of the routine or some type of error or warning about its execution. The values for the CLI return status codes are summarized in Table 19-3. Some of the program examples in this book omit the checking of return status codes to shorten the example and focus on the specific features being illustrated. However, production programs that call CLI

CLI Return Value	Meaning
0	Statement completed successfully
1	Successful completion with warning
100	No data found (when retrieving query results)
99	Data needed (required dynamic parameter missing)
-1	Error during SQL statement execution
-2	Error—invalid handle supplied in call

Table 19-3. *CLI Return Status Codes*

functions should always check the return value to insure that the function was completed successfully. Symbolic constant names for the return status codes as well as many other values, such as data type codes and statement-id codes, are typically defined in a header file that is included at the beginning of a program that uses the CLI.

CLI Structures

The CLI manages interactions between an application program and a supported database through a hierarchy of concepts, reflected in a hierarchy of CLI data structures:

- *SQL-environment.* The highest-level "environment" within which database access takes place. The CLI uses the data structure associated with a SQL-environment to keep track of the various application programs that are using it.

- *SQL-connection.* A logical "connection" to a specific database server. Conceptually, the CLI allows a single application program to connect to several different database servers concurrently. Each connection has its own data structure, which the CLI uses to track connection status.

- *SQL-statement.* An individual SQL statement to be processed by a database server. A statement may move through several stages of processing, as the DBMS prepares (compiles) it, executes it, processes any errors, and in the case of queries, returns the results to the application program. Conceptually, an application program may have multiple SQL statements moving through these processing stages in parallel. Each statement has its own data structure, which the CLI uses to track its progress.

The CLI uses a technique commonly used by modern operating systems and library packages to manage these conceptual entities. A symbolic pointer called a *handle* is associated with the overall SQL environment, with a SQL connection to a specific database server, and with the execution of a SQL statement. The handle identifies an area of storage managed by the CLI itself. Some type of handle is passed as one of the parameters in every CLI call. The CLI routines that manage handles are shown in Figure 19-12.

A handle is created ("allocated") using the CLI SQLAllocHandle() routine. One of the parameters of the routine tells the CLI what type of handle is to be allocated. Another parameter returns the handle value to the application program. Once allocated, a handle is passed to subsequent CLI routines to maintain a context for the CLI calls. In this way, different threads of execution within a program or different concurrently running programs (processes) can each establish their own connection to the CLI and can maintain their own contexts, independent of one another. Handles also allow a single program to have multiple CLI connections to different database servers, and to process more than one SQL statement in parallel. When a handle is no longer needed, the application calls SQLFreeHandle() to tell the CLI.

In addition to the general-purpose handle management routines, SQLAllocHandle() and SQLFreeHandle(), the CLI specification includes separate routines to create and free an environment, connection, or statement handle. These routines (SQLAllocEnv(), SQLAllocStmt(), and so on) were a part of the original ODBC API and are still supported in current ODBC implementations for backward compatibility. However, Microsoft has indicated that the general handle-management routines are now the preferred ODBC functions, and the specific routines may be dropped in future ODBC releases. For maximum cross-platform portability, it's best to use the general-purpose routines.

SQL Environment

The SQL-environment is the highest-level context used by an application program in its calls to the CLI. In a single-threaded application, there will typically be one SQL-environment for the entire program. In a multi-threaded application, there may be one SQL-environment per thread or one overall SQL-environment, depending on the architecture of the program. The CLI conceptually permits multiple connections, possibly to several different database servers, from within one SQL-environment. A specific CLI implementation for a specific DBMS may or may not actually support multiple connections.

SQL Connections

Within a SQL-environment, an application program may establish one or more SQL-connections. A SQL-connection is a linkage between the program and a specific SQL server (database server) over which SQL statements are processed. In practice, a SQL-connection often is actually a virtual network connection to a database server

```
/* Allocate a handle for use in subsequent CLI calls */
short SQLAllocHandle (
   short  HdlType,                /* IN:  integer handle type code */
   long   inHdl,                  /* IN:  environment or conn handle */
   long   *rtnHdl)                /* OUT: returned handle */

/* Free a handle previously allocated by SQLAllocHandle() */
short SQLFreeHandle (
   short  HdlType,                /* IN:  integer handle type code */
   long   inHdl)                  /* IN:  handle to be freed */

/* Allocate a handle for a new SQL-environment */
short SQLAllocEnv (
   long   *envHdl)                /* OUT: returned environment handle */

/* Free an environment handle previously allocated by SQLAllocEnv() */
short SQLFreeEnv (
   long   envHdl)                 /* IN:  environment handle */

/* Allocate a handle for a new SQL-connection */
short SQLAllocConnect (
   long   envHdl,                 /* IN:  environment handle */
   long   *connHdl)               /* OUT: returned handle */

/* Free a connection handle previously allocated */
short SQLFreeConnect (
   long   connHdl)                /* IN:  connection handle */

short SQLAllocStmt (
   long   envHdl,                 /* IN:  environment handle */
   long   *stmtHdl)               /* OUT: statement handle */

/* Free a connection handle previously allocated */
short SQLFreeStmt (
   long   stmtHdl,                /* IN:  statement handle */
   long   option)                 /* IN:  cursor and unbind options */
```

Figure 19-12.   *CLI handle management routines*

located on another computer system. However, a SQL-connection may also be a logical connection between a program and a DBMS located on the same computer system.

Figure 19-13 shows the CLI routines that are used to manage SQL-connections. To establish a connection, an application program first allocates a connection handle by calling SQLAllocHandle() with the appropriate handle type. It then attempts to connect to the target SQL server with a SQLConnect() call. SQL statements can subsequently be processed over the connection. The connection handle is passed as a parameter to all of the statement-processing calls to indicate which connection is being used. When the connection is no longer needed, a call to SQLDisconnect() terminates it, and a call to SQLFreeHandle() releases the associated connection handle in the CLI.

Normally an application program knows the name of the specific database server (in terms of the standard, the "SQL server") that it wants to access. In certain

```
/* Initiate a connection to a SQL-server */
short SQLConnect(
   long    connHdl,          /* IN:  connection handle */
   char   *svrName,          /* IN:  name of target SQL-server */
   short   svrnamlen,        /* IN:  length of SQL-server name */
   char   *userName,         /* IN:  user name for connection */
   short   usrnamlen,        /* IN:  length of user name */
   char   *passwd,           /* IN:  connection password */
   short   pswlen)           /* IN:  password length */

/* Disconnect from a SQL-server */
short SQLDisconnect(
   long    connHdl)          /* IN:  connection handle */

/* Get the name(s) of accessible SQL-servers for connection */
short SQLDataSources (
   long    envHdl,           /* IN:  environment handle */
   short   direction,        /* IN:  indicates first/next request */
   char   *svrname,          /* OUT: buffer for server name */
   short   buflen,           /* IN:  length of server name buffer */
   short  *namlen,           /* OUT: actual length of server name */
   char   *descrip,          /* OUT: buffer for description */
   short   buf2len,          /* IN:  length of description buffer */
   short  *dsclen)           /* OUT: actual length of description */
```

Figure 19-13.   *CLI connection management routines*

applications (such as general-purpose query or data entry tools), it may be desirable to let the user choose which database server is to be used. The CLI SQLDataSources() call returns the names of the SQL servers which are "known" to the CLI—that is, the data sources that can be legally specified as server names in SQLConnect() calls. To obtain the list of server names, the application repeatedly calls SQLDataSources(). Each call returns a single server description, until the call returns an error indicating no more data. A parameter to the call can be optionally used to alter this sequential retrieval of server names.

CLI Statement Processing

The CLI processes SQL statements using a technique very similar to that described for dynamic embedded SQL in the previous chapter. The SQL statement is passed to the CLI in text form, as a character string. It can be executed in a one-step or two-step process.

Figure 19-14 shows the basic SQL statement-processing calls. The application program must first call SQLAllocHandle() to obtain a statement handle, which identifies the statement to the program and the CLI. All subsequent SQLExecDirect(), SQLPrepare(), and SQLExecute() calls reference this statement handle. When the handle is no longer needed, it is freed with a SQLFreeHandle() call.

For one-step execution, the application program calls SQL SQLExecDirect(), passing the SQL statement text as one of the parameters to the call. The DBMS processes the statement as a result of the call and returns the completion status of the statement. This one-step process was used in the simple example program in Figure 19-11. It corresponds to the one-step EXECUTE IMMEDIATE statement in embedded dynamic SQL, described in the previous chapter.

For two-step execution, the application program calls SQLPrepare(), passing the SQL statement text as one of the parameters to the call. The DBMS analyzes the statement, determines how to carry it out, and retains this information. It does not immediately carry out the statement. Instead, subsequent calls to the SQLExecute() routine cause the statement to actually be executed. This two-step process corresponds exactly to the PREPARE and EXECUTE embedded dynamic SQL statements described in the previous chapter. You should always use it for any SQL operations that will be carried out repeatedly, because it causes the DBMS to go through the overhead of statement analysis and optimization only once, in response to the SQLPrepare() call. Parameters can be passed through the CLI to tailor the operation of the multiple SQLExecute() calls that follow.

Statement Execution with Parameters

In many cases, a SQL statement must be repeatedly executed with only changes in some of the values that it specifies. For example, an INSERT statement to add an order to the sample database is identical for every order except for the specific information

```
/* Directly execute a SQL statement */
short SQLExecDirect (
   long   stmtHdl,          /* IN:  statement handle */
   char  *stmttext,         /* IN:  SQL statement text */
   short  textlen)          /* IN:  statement text length */

/* Prepare a SQL statement */
short SQLPrepare (
   long   stmtHdl,          /* IN:  statement handle */
   char  *stmttext,         /* IN:  SQL statement text */
   short  textlen)          /* IN:  statement text length */

/* Execute a previously-prepared SQL statement */
short SQLExecute (
   long   stmtHdl)          /* IN:  statement handle */

/* Bind a SQL statement parameter to a program data area */
short SQLBindParam (
   long   stmtHdl,          /* IN:  statement handle */
   short  parmnr,           /* IN:  parameter number (1,2,3...) */
   short  valtype,          /* IN:  data type of value supplied */
   short  parmtype,         /* IN:  data type of parameter */
   short  colsize,          /* IN:  column size */
   short  decdigits,        /* IN:  number of decimal digits */
   void  *value,            /* IN:  pointer to parameter value buf */
   long  *lenind)           /* IN:  pointer to length/indicator buf */

/* Get parameter-tag for next required dynamic parameter */
short SQLParamData (
   long   stmtHdl,          /* IN:  stmt handle w/dynamic parms */
   void  *prmtag)           /* OUT: returned parameter-tag value */

/* Obtain detailed info about an item described by a CLI descriptor */
short SQLPutData (
   long   stmtHdl,          /* IN:  stmt handle w/dynamic parms */
   void  *prmdata,          /* IN:  buffer with data for parameter */
   short  prmlenind)        /* IN:  parameter length or NULL ind */
```

Figure 19-14. *CLI statement-processing routines*

about the customer number, product and manufacturer, and quantity ordered. As described in the previous chapter for dynamic embedded SQL, such statements can be processed efficiently by specifying the variable parts of the statement as input parameters. The statement text passed to the SQLPrepare() call has a parameter marker—a question mark (?)—in its text at each position where a parameter value is to be inserted. When the statement is later executed, values must be supplied for each of its input parameters.

The most straightforward way to supply input parameter values is with the SQLBindParam() call. Each call to SQLBindParam() establishes a linkage between one of the parameter markers in the SQL statement (identified by number) and a variable in the application program (identified by its memory address). In addition, an association is optionally established with a second application program variable (an integer) that provides the length of variable-length input parameters. If the parameter is a null-terminated string like those used in C programs, a special negative code value, defined in the header file as the symbolic constant SQL_NTS, can be passed, indicating that the string length can be obtained from the data itself by the CLI routines. Similarly, a negative code is used to indicate a NULL value for an input parameter. If there are three input parameter markers in the statement, there will be three calls to SQLBindParam(), one for each input parameter.

Once the association between application program variables (more accurately, program storage locations) and the statement parameters is established, the statement can be executed with a call to SQLExecute(). To change the parameter values for subsequent statements, it is only necessary to place new values in the application program buffer areas before the next call to SQLExecute(). Alternatively, the parameters can be rebound to different data areas within the application program by subsequent calls to SQLBindParam(). Figure 19-15 shows a program that includes a SQL statement with two input parameters. The program repeatedly prompts the user for a customer number and a new credit limit for the customer. The values provided by the user become the input parameters to an UPDATE statement for the CUSTOMERS table.

The SQLParamData() and SQLPutData() calls in Figure 19-15 provide an alternative method of passing parameter data at run-time, called *deferred parameter passing*. The selection of this technique for a particular statement parameter is indicated in the corresponding call to SQLBindParam(). Instead of actually supplying a program data location to which the parameter is bound, the SQLBindParam() call indicates that deferred parameter passing will be used and provides a value that will later be used to identify the particular parameter being processed in this way.

After statement execution is requested (by a SQLExecute() or SQLExecDirect() call), the program calls SQLParamData() to determine whether deferred parameter data is required by the statement. If so, the CLI returns a status code (SQL_NEED_DATA) along with an indicator of which parameter needs a value. The program then calls SQLPutData() to actually provide the value for the parameter. Typically the program then calls SQLParamData() again to determine if

```
/* Program to raise selected user-specified customer credit limits */
#include <sqlcli.h>                       /* header file with CLI defs */
main()
{
    SQLHENV     env_hdl;                   /* SQL-environment handle */
    SQLHDBC     conn_hdl;                  /* connection handle */
    SQLHSTMT    stmt_hdl;                  /* statement handle */
    SQLRETURN   status;                   /* CLI routine return status */
    char        *svr_name = "demo";       /* server name */
    char        *user_name = "joe";       /* user name for connection */
    char        *user_pswd = "xyz";       /* user password for connection */
    char        amt_buf[31];              /* amount entered by user */
    int         amt_ind = SQL_NTS;        /* amount ind (NULL-term string) */
    char        cust_buf[31];             /* cust # entered by user */
    int         cust_ind = SQL_NTS;       /* cust # ind (NULL-term string) */
    char        stmt_buf[128];            /* buffer for SQL statement */

    /* Allocate handles for SQL environment, connection, statement */
    SQLAllocHandle(SQL_HANDLE_ENV, SQL_NULL_HANDLE, &env_hdl);
    SQLAllocHandle(SQL_HANDLE_DBC, env_hdl, &conn_hdl);
    SQLAllocHandle(SQL_HANDLE_STMT, conn_hdl, &stmt_hdl);

    /* Connect to the database, passing server name, user, password */
    /* SQL_NTS says NULL-terminated string instead of passing length */
    SQLConnect(conn_hdl, svr_name, SQL_NTS,
                         user_name, SQL_NTS,
                         user_pswd, SQL_NTS);

    /* Prepare an UPDATE statement with parameter markers */
    strcpy(stmt_buf, "update customers set credit_limit = ? ");
    strcat(stmt_buf, "where cust_num = ?");
    SQLPrepare(stmt_hdl, stmt_buf, SQL_NTS);

    / * Bind parameters to the program's buffers */
    SQLBindParam(stmt_hdl,1,SQL_C_CHAR,SQL_DECIMAL,9,2,&amt_buf,&amt_ind);
    SQLBindParam(stmt_hdl,2,SQL_C_CHAR,SQL_INTEGER,0,0,&cust_buf,&cust_ind);

    / * Loop to process each credit limit change */
    for ( ; ; ) {
```

Figure 19-15. *CLI program using input parameters*

```
      /* Prompt the user for the customer and new credit limit */
      printf("Enter customer number: ");
      gets(cust_buf);
      if (strlen(cust_buf) == 0)
         break;
      printf("Enter new credit limit: ");
      gets(amt_buf);

      / * Execute the statement with the parameters */
      status = SQLExecute(stmt_hdl);
      if (status)
         printf("Error during update\n");
      else
         printf("Credit limit change successful.\n");

      /* Commit the update */
      SQLEndTran(SQL_HANDLE_ENV, env_hdl, SQL_COMMIT);
   }

   / * Disconnect, deallocate handles and exit */
   SQLDisconnect(conn_hdl);
   SQLFreeHandle(SQL_HANDLE_STMT, stmt_hdl);
   SQLFreeHandle(SQL_HANDLE_DBC, conn_hdl);
   SQLFreeHandle(SQL_HANDLE_ENV, env_hdl);
   exit();
```

Figure 19-15.   *CLI program using input parameters* (continued)

another parameter requires dynamic data. The cycle repeats until all required dynamic data has been supplied, and SQL statement execution then continues normally.

This alternative parameter passing method is considerably more complex than the straightforward process of binding parameters to application program locations. It has two advantages. The first is that the actual passing of data values (and the allocation of storage to contain those values) can be delayed until the last possible moment when the data is actually needed. The second advantage is that the technique can be used to pass very long parameter values piece by piece. For selected long data types, the CLI allows repeated calls to SQLPutData() for the same parameter, with each call passing the next part of the data. For example, the text of a document that is supplied as a parameter for the VALUES clause of an INSERT statement might be passed in

1,000-character pieces through repeated SQLPutData() calls until all of the document has been passed. This avoids the need to allocate a single very large memory buffer within the application program to hold the entire parameter value.

CLI Transaction Management

The COMMIT and ROLLBACK functions for SQL transaction processing also apply to SQL operation via the CLI. However, because the CLI itself must be aware that a transaction is being completed, the COMMIT and ROLLBACK SQL statements are replaced by the CLI SQLEndTran() call, shown in Figure 19-16. This call was used to commit the transactions in the program examples of Figures 19-11 and 19-15. The same CLI routine is used to execute either a COMMIT or a ROLLBACK operation; the particular operation to be performed is specified by the completion type parameter to the call.

The CLI SQLCancel() call, also shown in Figure 19-16, does not actually provide a transaction management function, but in practice it is almost always used in conjunction with a ROLLBACK operation. It is used to cancel the execution of a SQL statement that was previously initiated by a SQLExecDirect() or SQLExecute() call. This would be appropriate in a program that is using deferred parameter processing, as described in the previous section. If the program determines that it should cancel the statement execution instead of supplying a value for a deferred parameter, the program can call SQLCancel() to achieve this result. The SQLCancel() call can also be used in a multi-threaded application to cancel the effect of a SQLExecute() or SQLExecDirect() call that has not yet completed. In this situation, the thread making the original "execute" call will still be waiting for the call to complete, but another concurrently executing thread may call SQLCancel() using the same statement handle. The specifics of this technique, and how "interruptible" a CLI call is, tend to be very implementation dependent.

```
/* COMMIT or ROLLBACK a SQL transaction */
short SQLEndTran (
   short   hdltype,          /* IN:  type of handle */
   long    txnHdl,           /* IN:  env, conn or stmt handle */
   short   compltype)        /* IN:  txn typ (COMMIT/ROLLBACK) */

/* Cancel a currently-executing SQL statement */
short SQLCancel (
   short   stmtHdl)          /* IN:  statement handle */
```

Figure 19-16. *CLI transaction management routines*

Processing Query Results with CLI

The CLI routines described thus far can be used to process SQL data definition statements or SQL data manipulation statements other than queries (that is, UPDATE, DELETE, and INSERT statements). For query processing, some additional CLI calls, shown in Figure 19-17, are required. The simplest way to process query results is with the SQLBindCol() and SQLFetch() calls. To carry out a query using these calls, the application program goes through the following steps (assuming a connection has already been established):

1. The program allocates a statement handle using SQLAllocHandle().

2. The program calls SQLPrepare(), passing the text of the SQL SELECT statement for the query.

3. The program calls SQLExecute() to carry out the query.

4. The program calls SQLBindCol() once for each column of query results that will be returned. Each call associates a program buffer area with a returned data column.

```
/* Bind a query results column to a program data area */
short SQLBindCol (
    long    stmtHdl,            /* IN:  statement handle */
    short   colnr,              /* IN:  column number to be bound */
    short   tgttype,            /* IN:  data type of program data area */
    void    value,              /* IN:  ptr to program data area */
    long    buflen,             /* IN:  length of program buffer */
    long    lenind)             /* IN:  ptr to length/indicator buffer */

/* Advance the cursor to the next row of query results */
short SQLFetch (
    long    stmtHdl)            /* IN:  statement handle */

/* Scroll the cursor up or down through the query results */
short SQLFetchScroll (
    long    stmtHdl,            /* IN:  statement handle */
    short   fetchdir,           /* IN:  direction (first/next/prev) */
    long    offset)             /* IN:  offset (number of rows) */
```

Figure 19-17.   *CLI query results-processing routines*

```
/* Get the data for a single column of query results */
short SQLGetData (
    long    stmtHdl,            /* IN:  statement handle */
    short   colnr,              /* IN:  column number to be retrieved */
    short   tgttype,            /* IN:  data type to return to program */
    void    *value,             /* IN:  ptr to buffer for column data */
    long    buflen,             /* IN:  length of program buffer */
    long    *lenind)            /* OUT: actual length and/or NULL ind */

/* Close a cursor to end access to query results */
short SQLCloseCursor (
    long    stmtHdl)            /* IN:  statement handle */

/* Establish a cursor name for an open cursor */
short SQLSetCursorName (
    long    stmtHdl,            /* IN:  statement handle */
    char    cursname,           /* IN:  name for cursor */
    short   namelen)            /* IN:  length of cursor name */

/* Retrieve the name of an open cursor */
short SQLGetCursorName (
    long    stmtHdl,            /* IN:  statement handle */
    char    cursname,           /* OUT: buffer for returned name */
    short   buflen,             /* IN:  length of buffer */
    short   *namlen)            /* OUT: actual length of returned name */
```

Figure 19-17. *CLI query results-processing routines* (continued)

5. The program calls SQLFetch() to fetch a row of query results. The data value for each row in the newly fetched row is placed into the appropriate program buffer as indicated in the previous SQLBindCol() calls.

6. If the query produces multiple rows, the program repeats Step 5 until the SQLFetch() call returns a value indicating that there are no more rows.

7. When all query results have been processed, the program calls SQLCloseCursor() to end access to the query results.

The program excerpt in Figure 19-18 shows a simple query carried out using this technique. The program is identical in function to the dblib-based program example in Figure 19-7. It's instructive to compare the two programs. The specifics of the calls and their parameters are quite different, but the flow of the programs and the logical sequence of calls that they make are the same. Each call to SQLBindCol() establishes an association between one column of query results (identified by column number) and an application program buffer (identified by its address). With each call to SQLFetch(), the CLI uses this binding to copy the appropriate data value for the column into the program's buffer area. When appropriate, a second program data area is specified as the indicator-variable buffer for the column. Each call to SQLFetch() sets this program variable to indicate the actual length of the returned data value (for variable-length data) and to indicate when a NULL value is returned. When the program has finished processing all of the query results, it calls SQLCloseCursor().

The CLI routines in Figure 19-17 can also be used to implement an alternative method of processing query results. In this technique, the columns of query results are not bound to locations in the application program in advance. Instead, each call to SQLFetch() only advances the cursor to the next row of query results. It does not actually cause retrieval of data into host program data areas. Instead, a call to SQLGetData() is made to actually retrieve the data. One of the parameters of SQLGetData() specifies which column of query results is to be retrieved. The other parameters specify the data type to be returned and the location of the buffer to receive the data and an associated indicator variable value.

At the basic level, the SQLGetData() call is simply an alternative to the host-variable binding approach provided by SQLBindCol(), but SQLGetData() provides an important advantage when processing very large data items. Some databases support long binary or character-valued columns that can contain thousands or millions of bytes of data. It's usually impractical to allocate a program buffer to hold all of the data in such a column. Using SQLGetData(), the program can allocate a buffer of "reasonable" size and work its way through the data a few thousand bytes at a time.

It's possible to intermix the SQLBindCol() and SQLGetData() styles to process the query results of a single statement. In this case, the SQLFetch() call actually retrieves the data values for the bound columns (those for which a SQLBindCol() call has been made), but the program must explicitly call SQLGetData() to process the other columns. This technique may be especially appropriate if a query retrieves several columns of typical SQL data (names, dates, money amounts) and a column or two of long data, such as the text of a contract. Note that some CLI implementations severely restrict the ability to intermix the two styles of processing. In particular, some implementations require that all of the bound columns appear first in the left-to-right order of query results, before any columns retrieved using SQLGetData().

```
/* Program to display a report of sales reps over quota */
#include <sqlcli.h>              /* header file with CLI definitions */
main()
{
    SQLHENV    env_hdl;          /* SQL-environment handle */
    SQLHDBC    conn_hdl;         /* connection handle */
    SQLHSTMT   stmt_hdl;         /* statement handle */
    SQLRETURN  status;           /* CLI routine return status */
    char       *svr_name = "demo";  /* server name */
    char       *user_name = "joe";  /* user name for connection */
    char       *user_pswd = "xyz";  /* user password for connection */
    char       repname[16];      /* retrieved salesperson's name */
    float      repquota;         /* retrieved quota */
    float      repsales;         /* retrieved sales */
    short      repquota_ind;     /* NULL quota indicator */
    char       stmt_buf[128];    /* buffer for SQL statement */

    /* Allocate handles and connect to the database */
    SQLAllocHandle(SQL_HANDLE_ENV, SQL_NULL_HANDLE, &env_hdl);
    SQLAllocHandle(SQL_HANDLE_DBC, env_hdl, &conn_hdl);
    SQLAllocHandle(SQL_HANDLE_STMT, conn_hdl, &stmt_hdl);
    SQLConnect(conn_hdl, svr_name, SQL_NTS,
                         user_name, SQL_NTS,
                         user_pswd, SQL_NTS);

    /* Request execution of the query */
    strcpy(stmt_buf, "select name, quota, sales from salesreps ");
    strcat(stmt_buf, "where sales > quota order by name");
    SQLExecDirect(stmt_hdl, stmt_buf, SQL_NTS);

    / * Bind retrieved columns to the program's buffers */
    SQLBindCol(stmt_hdl,1,SQL_C_CHAR,repname,15,NULL);
    SQLBindCol(stmt_hdl,2,SQL_C_FLOAT,&repquota,0,&quota_ind);
    SQLBindCol(stmt_hdl,3,SQL_C_FLOAT,&repsales,0,NULL);

    / * Loop through each row of query results */
    for ( ; ; ) {

        /* Fetch the next row of query results */
        if (SQLFetch(stmt_hdl) != SQL_SUCCESS)
            break;
```

Figure 19-18. *Retrieving CLI query results*

```
      /* Display the retrieved data */
      printf("Name: %s\n", repname);
      if (repquota_ind < 0)
         printf("Quota is NULL\n");
      else
         printf("Quota: %f\n", repquota);
      printf("Sales: %f\n", repsales);
   }

   / * Disconnect, deallocate handles and exit */
   SQLDisconnect(conn_hdl);
   SQLFreeHandle(SQL_HANDLE_STMT, stmt_hdl);
   SQLFreeHandle(SQL_HANDLE_DBC, conn_hdl);
   SQLFreeHandle(SQL_HANDLE_ENV, env_hdl);
   exit();
```

Figure 19-18. *Retrieving CLI query results* (continued)

Scrolling Cursors

The SQL/CLI standard specifies CLI support for scrolling cursors that parallels the scrolling cursor support originally included in the SQL2 standard for embedded SQL. The SQLFetchScroll() call, shown in Figure 19-17 provides the extended FETCH functions needed for forward/backward and random retrieval of query results. One of its parameters specifies the statement handle for the query, just as for the simple SQLFetch() call. The other two parameters specify the direction of fetch motion (PREVIOUS, NEXT, and so on) and the offset for fetch motions that require it (absolute and relative random row retrieval). The operation of SQLBindCol() and SQLGetData() for processing returned values is identical to that described for the SQLFetch() call.

Named Cursors

Note that the CLI doesn't include an explicit "cursor declaration" call to parallel the embedded SQL DECLARE CURSOR statement. Instead, SQL query text (that is, a SELECT statement) is passed to the CLI for execution in the same manner as any other SQL statement, using either a SQLExecDirect() call or SQLPrepare() / SQLExecute() call sequence. The results of the query are identified by the statement handle in subsequent SQLFetch(), SQLBindCol(), and similar calls. For these purposes, the statement handle takes the place of the cursor name used in embedded SQL.

A problem with this scheme arises in the case of positioned (cursor-based) updates and positioned deletes. As described in Chapter 17, a positioned database update or delete statement (UPDATE... WHERE CURRENT OF or DELETE... WHERE CURRENT OF) can be used to modify or delete the current (that is, just fetched) row of query results. These embedded SQL statements use the cursor name to identify the particular row to be processed, since an application program may have more than one cursor open at a time to process more than one set of query results.

To support positioned updates, the CLI provides the SQLSetCursorName() call shown in Figure 19-17. The call is used to assign a cursor name, specified as one of its parameters, to a set of query results, identified by the statement handle that produced them. Once the call has been made, the cursor name can be used in subsequent positioned update or delete statements, which can be passed to the CLI for execution. A companion call, SQLGetCursorName(), can be used to obtain a previously assigned cursor name, given its statement handle.

Dynamic Query Processing With CLI

If the columns to be retrieved by a SQL query are not known in advance when a program is developed, the program can use the query-processing calls in Figure 19-19 to determine the characteristics of the query results at run-time. These calls implement the same type of dynamic SQL query-processing capability that was described for dynamic embedded SQL in Chapter 18. Here are the steps for dynamic query processing using CLI:

1. The program allocates a statement handle using SQLAllocHandle().

2. The program calls Prepare(), passing the text of the SQL SELECT statement for the query.

3. The program calls SQLExecute() to carry out the query.

4. The program calls SQLNumResultCols() to determine the number of columns of query results.

5. The program calls SQLDescribeCol() once for each column of returned query results to determine its data type, size, whether it may contain NULL values, and so on.

6. The program allocates memory to receive the returned query results and binds these memory locations to the columns by calling SQLBindCol() once for each column.

7. The program calls SQLFetch() to fetch a row of query results. The SQLFetch() call advances the cursor to the next row of query results and returns each column of results into the appropriate area in the application program, as specified in the SQLBindCol() calls.

8. If the query produces multiple rows, the program repeats Step 7 until the SQLFetch() call returns a value indicating that there are no more rows.

9. When all query results have been processed, the program calls SQLCloseCursor() to end access to the query results.

```
/* Determine the number of result columns in a query */
short SQLNumResultCols (
   long    stmtHdl,               /* IN:  statement handle */
   short *colcount)               /* OUT: returned number of columns */


/* Determine the characteristics of a column of query results */
short SQLDescribeCol (
   long    stmtHdl,               /* IN:  statement handle */
   short   colnr,                 /* IN:  number of column to describe */
   char  *colname,                /* OUT: name of query results column */
   short   buflen,                /* IN:  length of column name buffer */
   short *namlen,                 /* OUT: actual column name length */
   short *coltype,                /* OUT: returned column data type code */
   short *colsize,                /* OUT: returned column data length */
   short *decdigits,              /* OUT: returned # of digits in column */
   short *nullable)               /* OUT: can column have NULL values */


/* Obtain detailed info about a column of query results */
short SQLColAttribute (
   long    stmtHdl,               /* IN:  statement handle */
   short   colnr,                 /* IN:  number of column to describe */
   short   attrcode,              /* IN:  code of attribute to retrieve */
   char  *attrinfo,               /* OUT: buffer for string attr. info */
   short   buflen,                /* IN:  length of col attribute buffer */
   short *actlen,                 /* OUT: actual attribute info length */
   int   *numattr)                /* OUT: returned integer attr. info */


/* Retrieve frequently used info from a CLI descriptor */
short SQLGetDescRec (
   long    descHdl,               /* IN:  descriptor handle */
   short   recnr,                 /* IN:  descriptor record number */
   char  *name,                   /* OUT: name of item being described */
   short   buflen,                /* IN:  length of name buffer */
   short *namlen,                 /* OUT: actual length of returned name */
   short *datatype,               /* OUT: data type code for item */
   short *subtype,                /* OUT: data type subcode for item */
   short *length,                 /* OUT: length of item */
   short *precis,                 /* OUT: precision of item, if numeric */
   short *scale,                  /* OUT: scale of item, if numeric */
   short *nullable)               /* OUT: can item have NULL values */
```

Figure 19-19.   *CLI dynamic query-processing calls*

```
/* Set frequently used info in a CLI descriptor */
short SQLSetDescRec (
    long    descHdl,            /* IN:  descriptor handle */
    short   recnr,              /* IN:  descriptor record number */
    short   datatype,           /* IN:  data type code for item */
    short   subtype,            /* IN:  data type subcode for item */
    short   length,             /* IN:  length of item */
    short   precis,             /* IN:  precision of item, if numeric */
    short   scale,              /* IN:  scale of item, if numeric */
    void   *databuf,            /* IN:  data buffer address for item */
    short   buflen,             /* IN:  data buffer length */
    short  *indbuf)             /* IN:  indicator buffer addr for item */

/* Get detailed info about an item described by a CLI descriptor */
short SQLGetDescField (
    long    descHdl,            /* IN:  descriptor handle */
    short   recnr,              /* IN:  descriptor record number */
    short   attrcode,           /* IN:  code of attribute to describe */
    void   *attrinfo,           /* IN:  buffer for attribute info */
    short   buflen,             /* IN:  length of attribute info */
    short  *actlen)             /* OUT: actual length of returned info */

/* Set value of an item described by a CLI descriptor */
short SQLSetDescField (
    long    descHdl,            /* IN:  descriptor handle */
    short   recnr,              /* IN:  descriptor record number */
    short   attrcode,           /* IN:  code of attribute to describe */
    void   *attrinfo,           /* IN:  buffer with attribute value */
    short   buflen)             /* IN:  length of attribute info */

/* Copy a CLI descriptor contents into another descriptor */
short SQLCopyDesc (
    long    indscHdl,           /* IN:  source descriptor handle */
    long    outdscHdl)          /* IN:  destination descriptor handle */
```

Figure 19-19. *CLI dynamic query-processing calls* (continued)

Figure 19-20 shows a program that uses these techniques to process a dynamic query. The program is identical in its concept and purpose to the embedded dynamic SQL query program shown in Figure 18-9 and the dblib-based dynamic SQL query program shown in Figure 19-10. Once again, it's instructive to compare the program examples to enhance your understanding of dynamic query processing. The API calls have quite different names, but the sequence of functions calls for the dblib program

```
main()
{
   /* This is a simple general-purpose query program.  It prompts
      the user for a table name, and then asks the user which
      columns of the table are to be included in the query.  After
      the user's selections are complete, the program runs the
      requested query and displays the results.
   */

   SQLHENV      env_hdl;             /* SQL-environment handle */
   SQLHDBC      conn_hdl;            /* connection handle */
   SQLHSTMT     stmt1_hdl;           /* statement handle for main query */
   SQLHSTMT     stmt2_hdl;           /* statement handle for col name query */
   SQLRETURN    status;              /* CLI routine return status */
   char         *svr_name = "demo";  /* server name */
   char         *user_name = "joe";  /* user name for connection */
   char         *user_pswd = "xyz";  /* user password for connection */
   char         stmtbuf[2001];       /* main SQL query text to be executed */
   char         stmt2buf[2001];      /* SQL text for column name query */
   char         querytbl[32];        /* user-specified query table */
   char         querycol[32];        /* user-specified column */
   int          first_col = 0;       /* is this the first column chosen? */
   short        colcount;            /* number of columns of query results */
   char         *nameptr;            /* address for CLI to return column name */
   short        namelen;             /* returned CLI column name length */
   short        type;                /* CLI data type code for column */
   short        size;                /* returned CLI column size */
   short        digits;              /* returned CLI column # digits */
   short        nullable;            /* returned CLI nullability */
   short        i;                   /* index for columns */
   char         inbuf[101];          /* inp ut entered by user */
   char         *item_name[100];     /* array to track column names */
   char         *item_data[100];     /* array to track column buffers */
   int          item_ind[100];       /* array of indicator variables */
   short        item_type[100];      /* array to track column data types */
   char         *dataptr;            /* address of buffer for current column */
```

Figure 19-20. *Using CLI for a dynamic query*

```
/* Open a connection to the demo database via CLI */
SQLAllocHandle(SQL_HANDLE_ENV, SQL_NULL_HANDLE, &env_hdl);
SQLAllocHandle(SQL_HANDLE_DBC, env_hdl, &conn_hdl);
SQLAllocHandle(SQL_HANDLE_STMT, conn_hdl, &stmt1_hdl);
SQLAllocHandle(SQL_HANDLE_STMT, conn_hdl, &stmt2_hdl);
SQLConnect(conn_hdl, svr_name, SQL_NTS,
                         user_name, SQL_NTS,
                         user_pswd, SQL_NTS);

/* Prompt the user for which table to query * /
printf("*** Mini-Query Program ***\n");
printf("Enter name of table for query: ");
gets(querytbl);

/* Start the SELECT statement in the buffer */
strcpy(stmtbuf, "select ");

/* Query the Information Schema to get column names */
strcpy(stmt2buf, "select column_name from columns where table_name = ");
strcat(stmt2buf, querytbl);
SQLExecDirect(stmt2_hdl, stmt2buf, SQL_NTS);

/* Process the results of the query */
SQLBindCol(stmt2_hdl, 1, SQL_C_CHAR, querycol, 31, (int *)0);
while (status = SQLFetch(stmt2_hdl) == SQL_SUCCESS) {
   printf("Include column %s (y/n)? ", querycol);
   gets(inbuf);
   if (inbuf[0] == 'y') {
      /* User wants the column, add it to the select list */
      if (first_col++ > 0) strcat(stmtbuf,", ");
      strcat(stmtbuf, querycol);
   }
}

/* Finish the SELECT statement with a FROM clause */
strcat(stmtbuf, "from ");
strcat(stmtbuf, querytbl);

/* Execute the query and get ready to fetch query results */
SQLExecDirect(stmt1_hdl, stmtbuf, SQL_NTS);

/* Ask CLI to describe each column, allocate memory & bind it */
SQLNumResultCols(stmt1_hdl, &colcount);
for (i =0; i < colcount; i++) {
   item_name[i] = nameptr = malloc(32);
   indptr = &item_ind[i];
```

Figure 19-20. *Using CLI for a dynamic query* (continued)

```
    SQLDescribeCol(stmt1_hdl, i, nameptr, 32, &namelen, &type, &size,
                                               &digits, &nullable);
    switch(type) {

    case SQL_CHAR:
    case SQL_VARCHAR:
       /* Allocate buffer for string & bind the column to it */
       item_data[i] = dataptr = malloc(size+1);
       item_type[i] = SQL_C_CHAR;
       SQLBindCol(stmt1_hdl, i, SQL_C_CHAR, dataptr, size+1, indptr);
       break;

    case SQL_TYPE_DATE:
    case SQL_TYPE_TIME:
    case SQL_TYPE_TIME_WITH_TIMEZONE:
    case SQL_TYPE_TIMESTAMP:
    case SQL_TYPE TIMESTAMP_WITH_TIMEZONE:
    case SQL_INTERVAL_DAY:
    case SQL_INTERVAL_DAY_TO_HOUR:
    case SQL_INTERVAL_DAY_TO_MINUTE:
    case SQL_INTERVAL_DAY_TO_SECOND:
    case SQL_INTERVAL_HOUR:
    case SQL_INTERVAL_HOUR_TO_MINUTE:
    case SQL_INTERVAL_HOUR_TO_SECOND:
    case SQL_INTERVAL_MINUTE:
    case SQL_INTERVAL_MINUTE_TO_SECOND:
    case SQL_INTERVAL_MONTH:
    case SQL_INTERVAL_SECOND:
    case SQL_INTERVAL_YEAR:
    case SQL_INTERVAL_YEAR_TO_MONTH:
       /* Request ODBC/CLI conversion of these types to C-strings */
       item_data[i] = dataptr = malloc(31);
       item_type[i] = SQL_C_CHAR;
       SQLBindCol(stmt1_hdl, i, SQL_C_CHAR, dataptr, 31, indptr);
       break;

    case SQL_INTEGER:
    case SQL_SMALLINT:
       /* Convert these types to C long integers */
       item_data[i] = dataptr = malloc(sizeof(integer));
       item_type[i] = SQL_C_SLONG;
       SQLBindCol(stmt1_hdl, i, SQL_C_SLONG, dataptr, sizeof(integer), indptr);
       break;
```

Figure 19-20. *Using CLI for a dynamic query* (continued)

```
        case SQL_NUMERIC:
        case SQL_DECIMAL:
        case SQL_FLOAT:
        case SQL_REAL:

        case SQL_DOUBLE:
            /* For illustration, convert these types to C double floats */
            item_data[i] = dataptr = malloc(sizeof(long));
            item_type[i] = SQL_C_DOUBLE;
            SQLBindCol(stmt1_hdl, i, SQL_C_DOUBLE, dataptr, sizeof(double), indptr);
            break;


        default:
            /* For simplicity, we don't handle bit strings, etc. */
            printf("Cannot handle data type %d\n", (integer)type);
            exit();
        }
    }


/* Fetch and display the rows of query results */
while (status = SQLFetch(stmt1_hdl) == SQL_SUCCESS) {

    /* Loop, printing data for each column of the row /
    printf("\n");
    for(i = 0; i < colcount; i++) {

        /* Print column label */
        printf("Column # %d (%s): ", i+1, item_name[i]);

        /* Check indicator variable for NULL indication */
        if (item_ind[i] == SQL_NULL_DATA){
            puts("is NULL!\n");
            continue;
        }

        /* Handle each returned (maybe converted) data type separately /
        switch(item_type[i]) {
```

Figure 19-20. *Using CLI for a dynamic query* (continued)

```
      case SQL_C_CHAR:
          /* Returned as text data -- just display it */
          puts(item_data[i]);
          break;

      case SQL_C_SLONG:
          /* Four-byte integer data -- convert & display it */
          printf("%ld", *((int *)(item_data[i])));
          break;

      case SQL_C_DOUBLE:
          /* Floating-point data - convert & display it */
          printf("%lf", *((double *)(item_data[i])));
          break;


      }
    }
  }

  printf("\nEnd of data.\n"):

  /* Clean up allocated storage */
  for (i = 0; i < colcount; i++) {
    free(item_data[i]);
    free(item_name[i]);
  }
  SQLDisconnect(conn_hdl);
  SQLFreeHandle(SQL_HANDLE_STMT, stmt1_hdl);
  SQLFreeHandle(SQL_HANDLE_STMT, stmt2_hdl);
  SQLFreeHandle(SQL_HANDLE_DBC, conn_hdl);
  SQLFreeHandle(SQL_HANDLE_ENV, env_hdl);

  exit();
}
```

Figure 19-20. *Using CLI for a dynamic query* (continued)

(Figure 19-10) and the CLI program (Figure 19-20) are nearly identical. The dbcmd() / dbsqlexec() / dbresults() call sequence is replaced by SQLExecDirect() (in this case, the query will be executed only once, so there's no advantage to using SQLPrepare() and SQLExecute() separately). The dbnumcols() call becomes

SQLNumResultCols(). The calls to obtain column information (dbcolname(), dbcoltype(), dbcollen()) become a single call to SQLDescribeCol(). The dbnextrow() call becomes SQLFetch(). All of the other changes in the program are made to support these changes in the API functions.

If you compare the program in Figure 19-20 with the corresponding embedded dynamic embedded SQL program in Figure 18-9, one of the major differences is embedded SQL's use of the special SQL Data Area (SQLDA) for column binding and column description. The CLI splits these functions between the SQLNumResultCols(), SQLDescribeCol(), and SQLBindCol() functions, and most programmers find the CLI structure easier to use and understand. However, the CLI provides an alternative, lower-level method that offers capabilities like those provided by the embedded SQLDA.

The alternative CLI method for dynamic query processing involves CLI *descriptors*. A CLI descriptor contains low-level information about a statement parameter (a parameter descriptor) or a column of query results (a row descriptor). The information in the descriptor is like that contained in the variable area of the SQLDA—the column or parameter's name, data type and subtype, length, data buffer location, null indicator location, and so on. The parameter descriptors and row descriptors thus correspond to the "input" and "output" SQLDAs provided by some DBMS brands in their embedded dynamic SQL implementations. CLI descriptors are identified by descriptor handles. The CLI provides a default set of descriptors for parameters and query results columns when a statement is prepared. Alternatively, the program can allocate its own descriptors and use them. The handles of the descriptors for a statement are considered statement attributes, and they are associated with a particular statement handle. The descriptor handle values can be retrieved and set by the application program using the attribute management routines, described in a later section.

Two calls are used to retrieve information from a descriptor, given its handle. The SQLGetDescField() call retrieves a particular field of a descriptor, which is identified by a code value. It typically is used to obtain the data type or length of a query results column, for example. The SQLGetDescRec() call retrieves many pieces of information in one call, including the column or parameter name, data type and subtype, length, precision and scale, and whether it may contain NULL values. A corresponding set of calls is used to place information into a descriptor. The SQLSetDescField() call sets the value of a single piece of information within a descriptor. The SQLSetDescRec() sets multiple values in a single call, including the data type and subtype, length, precision and scale, and nullability. For convenience, the CLI provides a SQLCopyDesc() call that copies all of the values from one descriptor to another.

CLI Errors and Diagnostic Information

Each CLI function returns a short integer value that indicates its completion status. If the completion status indicates an error, the error-handling CLI calls shown in Figure 19-21 can be used to obtain more information about the error and diagnose it. The

```
/* Retrieve error information associated with a previous CLI call */
short SQLError (
    long    envHdl,              /* IN:  environment handle */
    long    connHdl,             /* IN:  connection handle */
    long    stmtHdl,             /* IN:  statement handle */
    char    *sqlstate,           /* OUT: five-character SQLSTATE value */
    long    *nativeerr,          /* OUT: returned native error code */
    char    *msgbuf,             /* OUT: buffer for err message text */
    short   buflen,              /* IN:  length of err msg text buffer */
    short   *msglen)             /* OUT: returned actual msg length */

/* Determine number of rows affected by previous SQL statement */
short SQLRowCount (
    long    stmtHdl,             /* IN:  statement handle */
    long    *rowcnt)             /* OUT: number of rows */

/* Retrieve info from one of the CLI diagnostic error records */
short SQLGetDiagRec (
    short   hdltype,             /* IN:  handle type code */
    long    inHdl,               /* IN:  CLI handle */
    short   recnr,               /* IN:  requested err record number */
    char    *sqlstate,           /* OUT: returned 5-char SQLSTATE code */
    long    *nativeerr,          /* OUT: returned native error code */
    char    *msgbuf,             /* OUT: buffer for err message text */
    short   buflen,              /* IN:  length of err msg text buffer */
    short   *msglen)             /* OUT: returned actual msg length */

/* Retrieve a field from one of the CLI diagnostic error records */
short SQLGetDiagField (
    short   hdltype,             /* IN:  handle type code */
    long    inHdl,               /* IN:  CLI handle */
    short   recnr,               /* IN:  requested err record number */
    short   diagid,              /* IN:  diagnostic field id */
    void    *diaginfo,           /* OUT: returned diagnostic info */
    short   buflen,              /* IN:  length of diagonal info buffer */
    short   *actlen)             /* OUT: returned actual info length */
```

Figure 19-21.   *CLI error-handling routines*

most basic error-handling call is SQLError(). The application program passes the
environment, connection, and statement handles and is returned the SQL2 SQLSTATE
result code, the native error code of the subsystem producing the error, and an error
message in text form.

The SQLError() routine actually retrieves specific, frequently used information
from the CLI diagnostics area. The other error-handling routines provide more

complete information through direct access to the diagnostic records created and maintained by the CLI. In general, a CLI call can produce multiple errors, which result in multiple diagnostic records. The SQLGetDiagRec() call retrieves an individual diagnostic record, by record number. Through repeated calls, the application program can retrieve complete information about all error records produced by a CLI call. Even more complete information can be obtained by interrogating individual diagnostic fields within the record. This capability is provided by the SQLGetDiagField() call.

Although not strictly an error-processing function, the SQLRowCount() function, like the error-handling functions, is called *after* a previous CLI SQLExecute() call. It is used to determine the impact of the previous statement when it was successful. A returned value indicates the number of rows of data affected by the previously executed statement (for example, the value 4 would be returned for a searched UPDATE statement that updates four rows).

CLI Attributes

The CLI provides a number of options that control some of the details of its processing. Some of these control relatively minor but critical details, such as whether or not the CLI should automatically assume that parameters passed as string values are null-terminated. Others control broader aspects of CLI operation, such as the scrollability of cursors.

The CLI gives application programs the ability to control these processing options through a set of CLI *attributes*. The attributes are structured in a hierarchy, paralleling the environment / connection / statement hierarchy of the CLI handle structure. Environment attributes control overall operational options. Connection options apply to a particular connection created by the SQLConnect() call but may vary from one connection to another. Statement attributes apply to the processing of an individual statement, identified by a CLI statement handle.

A set of CLI calls, shown in Figure 19-22, are used by an application program to control attributes. The "get" calls (SQLGetEnvAttr(), SQLGetConnectAttr(), and SQLGetStmtAttr()) obtain current attribute values. The "set" calls (SQLSetEnvAttr(), SQLSetConnectAttr(), and SQLSetStmtAttr()) modify the current attribute values. In all of the calls, the particular attribute being processed is indicated by a code value.

Although the CLI standard provides this elaborate attribute structure, it actually specifies relatively few attributes. The single environment attribute specified is NULL TERMINATION; it controls null-terminated strings. The single connection attribute specified controls whether the CLI automatically populates a parameter descriptor when a statement is prepared or executed. Statement-level attributes control the scrollability and sensitivity of cursors. Perhaps the most important of the CLI-specified attributes are the handles of the four CLI descriptors that may be associated with a statement (two parameter descriptors and two row descriptors). The calls in Figure 19-22 are used to obtain and set these descriptor handles when using descriptor-based statement processing.

```
/* Obtain the value of a SQL-environment attribute */
short SQLGetEnvAttr(
    long    envHdl,             /* IN:  environment handle */
    long    attrCode,           /* IN:  integer attribute code */
    void   *rtnVal,             /* OUT: return value */
    long    bufLen,             /* IN:  length of rtnVal buffer */
    long   *strLen)             /* OUT: length of actual data */

/* Set the value of a SQL-environment attribute */
short SQLSetEnvAttr(
    long    envHdl,             /* IN:  environment handle */
    long    attrCode,           /* IN:  integer attribute code */
    void   *attrVal,            /* IN:  new attribute value */
    long   *strLen)             /* IN:  length of data */

/* Obtain the value of a SQL-connection attribute */
short SQLGetConnectAttr(
    long    connHdl,            /* IN:  connection handle */
    long    attrCode,           /* IN:  integer attribute code */
    void   *rtnVal,             /* OUT: return value */
    long    bufLen,             /* IN:  length of rtnVal buffer */
    long   *strLen)             /* OUT: length of actual data */

/* Set the value of a SQL-connection attribute */
short SQLSetConnectAttr(
    long    connHdl,            /* IN:  connection handle */
    long    attrCode,           /* IN:  integer attribute code */
    void   *attrVal,            /* IN:  new attribute value */
    long   *strLen)             /* IN:  length of data */

/* Obtain the value of a SQL-statement attribute */
short SQLGetStmtAttr(
    long    stmtHdl,            /* IN:  statement handle */
    long    attrCode,           /* IN:  integer attribute code */
    void   *rtnVal,             /* OUT: return value */
    long    bufLen,             /* IN:  length of rtnVal buffer */
    long   *strLen)             /* OUT: length of actual data */

/* Set the value of a SQL-statement attribute */
short SQLSetStmtAttr(
    long    stmtHdl,            /* IN:  statement handle */
    long    attrCode,           /* IN:  integer attribute code */
    void   *attrVal,            /* IN:  new attribute value */
    long   *strLen)             /* IN:  length of data */
```

Figure 19-22. *CLI attribute management calls*

The ODBC API, on which the SQL/CLI standard was originally based, includes many more attributes. For example, ODBC connection attributes can be used to specify a read-only connection, to enable asynchronous statement processing, to specify the timeout for a connection request, and so on. An ODBC environment attributes control automatic translation of ODBC calls from earlier versions of the ODBC standard. ODBC statement attributes control transaction isolation levels, specify whether or not a cursor is scrollable, and limit the number of rows of query results that might be generated by a runaway query.

CLI Information Calls

The CLI includes three specific calls that can be used to obtain information about the particular CLI implementation. In general, these calls will not be used by an application program written for a specific purpose. They are needed by general-purpose programs (such as a query or report writing program) that need to determine the specific characteristics of the CLI they are using. The calls are shown in Figure 19-23.

The SQLGetFunctions() call is used to determine whether a specific implementation supports a particular CLI function call. It is called with a function code value corresponding to one of the CLI functions, and returns a parameter indicating whether or not the function is supported. The SQLGetInfo() call is used to obtain much more detailed information about a CLI implementation, such as the maximum

```
/* Retrieve detailed info about capabilities of a CLI implementation */
short SQLGetInfo (
    long    connHdl,        /* IN:  connection handle */
    short   infotype,       /* IN:  type of info requested */
    void    *infoval,       /* OUT: buffer for retrieved info */
    short   buflen,         /* IN:  length of info buffer */
    short   *infolen)       /* OUT: returned info actual length */

/* Determine number of rows affected by previous SQL statement */
short SQLGetFunctions (
    long    connHdl,        /* IN:  connection handle */
    short   functid,        /* IN:  function id code */
    short   *supported)     /* OUT: whether function supported */

/* Determine information about supported data types */
short SQLGetTypeInfo (
    long    stmtHdl,        /* IN:  statement handle */
    short   datatype)       /* IN:  ALL TYPES or type requested */
```

Figure 19-23. *CLI implementation information routines*

lengths of table and user names, whether the DBMS supports outer joins or transactions, and whether or not SQL identifiers are case-sensitive.

The SQLGetTypeInfo() call is used to obtain information about a particular supported data type or about all types supported via the CLI interface. The call actually behaves as if it were a query against a system catalog of data type information. It produces a set of query results rows, each row containing information about one specific supported type. The supplied information indicates the name of the type, its size, whether it is nullable, whether it is searchable, and so on.

The ODBC API

As described earlier in this chapter, Microsoft originally developed the Open Database Connectivity (ODBC) API to provide a database-brand-independent API for database access on its Windows operating systems. The early ODBC API became the foundation for the SQL/CLI standard, which is now the official ANSI/ISO standard for a SQL call-level interface. The original ODBC API was extended and modified during the standardization process to create the SQL/CLI specification. With the introduction of ODBC release 3.0, Microsoft brought ODBC into conformance with the SQL/CLI standard. With this revision, ODBC becomes a superset of the SQL/CLI specification.

ODBC goes beyond the SQL/CLI capabilities in several areas, in part because Microsoft's goals for ODBC were broader than simply creating a standardized database access API. Microsoft also wanted to allow a single Windows application program to be able to concurrently access several different databases using the ODBC API. It also wanted to provide a structure where database vendors could support ODBC without giving up their proprietary APIs, and where the software that provided ODBC support for a particular brand of DBMS could be distributed by the database vendor and installed on Windows-based client systems as needed. The layered structure of ODBC and special ODBC management calls provide these capabilities.

The Structure of ODBC

The structure of ODBC as it is provided on Windows-based or other operating systems as shown in Figure 19-24. There are three basic layers to the ODBC software:

- *Callable API.* At the top layer, ODBC provides a single, callable database access API that can be used by all application programs. The API is packaged as a dynamic-linked library (DLL), which is an integral part of the various Windows operating systems.

- *ODBC drivers.* At the bottom layer of the ODBC structure is a collection of ODBC drivers. There is a separate driver for each of the DBMS brands. The purpose of the driver is to translate the standardized ODBC calls into the appropriate call or calls for the specific DBMS that it supports. Each driver can be independently installed on a particular computer system. This allows the DBMS vendors to provide an ODBC driver for their particular brand of DBMS and distribute the driver independent of the Windows operating system software. If the database resides on the same system as the ODBC driver, the driver is usually linked directly to the database's native API code. If the database is to be accessed over a network, the driver may call a native DBMS client to handle the client/server connection, or the driver might handle the network connection itself.

■ *Driver manager.* In the middle layer of the ODBC structure is the ODBC driver manager. Its role is to load and unload the various ODBC drivers, on request from application programs. The driver manager is also responsible for routing the API calls made by application programs to the appropriate driver for execution.

When an application program wants to access a database via ODBC, it goes through the same initiation sequence specified by the SQL/CLI standard. The program allocates an environment handle, and then a connection handle, and then calls

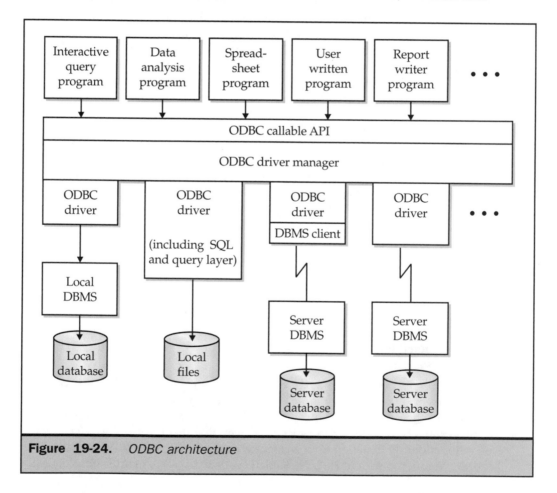

Figure 19-24.   *ODBC architecture*

SQLConnect(), specifying the particular data source to be accessed. When it receives the SQLConnect() call, the ODBC driver manager examines the connection information provided and determines the appropriate ODBC driver that is needed. The driver manager loads the driver into memory if it's not already being used by another application program. Subsequent calls by the application program on this particular CLI/ODBC connection are routed to this driver. The application program can, if appropriate, make other SQLConnect() calls for other data sources that will cause the driver manager to concurrently load other drivers for other DBMS brands. The application program can then use ODBC to communicate with two or more different databases, of different brands, using a uniform API.

ODBC and DBMS Independence

By providing a uniform API and its driver manager architecture, ODBC goes a long way toward providing a cross-vendor API for database access, but it's impossible to provide fully transparent access. The ODBC drivers for the various database systems can easily mask cosmetic differences in their SQL dialects and API suites, but more fundamental differences are difficult or impossible to mask. ODBC provides a partial solution to this problem by providing several different "levels" of ODBC capability, and by making each ODBC driver "self-describing" through the ODBC/CLI calls that return information about general functionality, supported functions, and supported data types. However, the existence of different capability levels and profiles effectively pushes the DBMS differences right back into the application program, which must deal with this nonuniformity of ODBC drivers. In practice, the vast majority of application programs rely on only the basic, core set of ODBC functionality and don't bother with more advanced features or profiles.

ODBC Catalog Functions

One of the areas where ODBC offers capability beyond the SQL/CLI standard is the retrieval of information about the structure of a database from its system catalog. As a part of the ANSI/ISO SQL standard, the CLI assumes that this information (about tables, columns, privileges, and so forth) is available through the SQL2 Information Schema, as described in Chapter 16. ODBC doesn't assume the presence of an Information Schema. Instead, it provides a set of specialized functions, shown in Table 19-4, that provide information about the structure of a data source. By calling these functions and processing their results, an application program can determine, at run-time, information about the tables, columns, privileges, primary keys, foreign keys, and stored procedures that form the structure of a data source.

The ODBC catalog functions typically aren't needed by an application program that is written for a specific purpose. However, they are essential for a general-purpose program, such as a query program, report generator, or data analysis tool. The catalog

Function	Description
SQLTables()	Returns a list of tables within specified catalog(s) and schema(s)
SQLTablePrivileges()	Returns a list of privileges for a table or tables
SQLColumns()	Returns a list of the column names in a specified table or tables
SQLColumnPrivileges()	Returns a list of columns and their privileges for a particular table
SQLPrimaryKeys()	Returns a list of the column names that make up the primary key for a table
SQLForeignKeys()	Returns a list of foreign keys in a specified table and a list of foreign keys in other tables that refer to the specified table
SQLSpecialColumns()	Returns a list of the columns that uniquely identify rows in a table or columns that are automatically updated when a row is updated
SQLStatistics()	Returns a list of statistics about a table and its indexes
SQLProcedures()	Returns a list of the stored procedures available within a data source
SQLProcedureColumns()	Returns a list of the input and output parameters and the names of the returned columns for a specified stored procedure or procedures

Table 19-4. *ODBC Catalog Functions*

functions can be called any time after a connection to a data source has been made. For example, a report writing program might call SQLConnect() and then immediately call SQLTables() to determine what tables are available in the target data source. The tables could then be presented in a list on the screen, allowing the user to select which table should be used to generate a report.

All of the catalog functions return their information as if they were a set of query results. The application program uses the techniques already described for CLI query processing to bind the columns of returned information to program variable areas. The program then calls SQLFetch() to work its way through the returned information. For example, in the results returned by the SQLTables() call, each SQLFetch() retrieves information about one table in the data source.

Extended ODBC Capabilities

ODBC provides a set of extended capabilities beyond those specified in the SQL/CLI standard. Many of the capabilities are designed to improve the performance of ODBC-based applications by minimizing the number of ODBC function calls an application program must make and/or the amount of network traffic generated by the ODBC calls. Other capabilities provide useful features for maintaining database independence or aid an application program in the database connection process. Some of the capabilities are provided through the additional set of ODBC function calls shown in Table 19-5. Others are provided through statement or connection attributes. Many of these additional capabilities were introduced in the 3.0 revision of ODBC and are not yet supported by most ODBC drivers or ODBC-based applications.

Extended Connection Capabilities

Two of the extended ODBC features are focused on the connection process. *Connection browsing* is designed to simplify the data source connection process and make it more database independent. SQLBrowseConnect() supports an iterative style of connection for access to ODBC data sources. An application program first calls the function with basic information about the target data source, and the function returns additional connection attributes needed (such as a user name or password). The application program can obtain this information (for example, by prompting the user) and then recalls SQLBrowseConnect() with the additional information. The cycle continues until the application has determined all of the information required for a successful SQLConnect() call.

The *connection pooling* capability is designed to improve the efficiency of ODBC connect/disconnect processing in a client/server environment. When connection pooling is activated, ODBC does not actually terminate network connections upon receiving a SQLDisconnect() call. Instead, the connections are held open in an idle state for some period of time and reused if a SQLConnect() call is made for the same data source. This reuse of connections can significantly cut down the network and login/logout overhead in client/server applications that involve short transactions and high transaction rates.

Function	Description
SQLBrowseConnect()	Supplies information about available ODBC data sources and the attributes required to connect to each
SQLDrivers()	Returns a list of the available drivers and driver attribute names
SQLDriverConnect()	Extended form of the SQLConnect() call for passing additional connection information
SQLNumParams()	Returns the number of parameters in a previously prepared SQL statement
SQLBindParameter()	Provides extended functionality beyond the SQL/CLI SQLBindParam() call
SQLDescribeParam()	Returns information about a parameter
SQLBulkOperations()	Performs bulk insertion and bookmark operations
SQLMoreResults()	Determines whether more results are available for a statement
SQLSetPos()	Sets the cursor position within a retrieved rowset for positioned operations
SQLNativeSQL()	Returns the native SQL translation of a supplied ODBC-compliant SQL statement text

Table 19-5. *Additional ODBC Functions*

SQL Dialect Translation

ODBC specifies not just a set of API calls but also a standard SQL language dialect that is a subset of the SQL2 standard. It is the responsibility of ODBC drivers to translate the ODBC dialect into statements appropriate for the target data source (for example, modifying date/time literals, quote conventions, keywords, and so on). The SQLNativeSQL() call allows the application program to see the effect of this translation. ODBC also supports "escape sequences" that allow an application program to more explicitly direct the translation of SQL features that tend to be less consistent across SQL dialects, such as outer joins and pattern-matching search conditions.

Asynchronous Execution

An ODBC driver may support asynchronous execution of ODBC functions. When an application program makes an asynchronous mode ODBC call, ODBC initiates the required processing (usually statement preparation or execution) and then immediately returns control to the application program. The application program can proceed with other work and later resynchronize with the ODBC function to determine its completion status. Asynchronous execution can be requested on a per-connection or a per-statement basis. In some cases, asynchronously executing functions can be terminated with a SQLCancel() call, giving the application program a method for aborting long running ODBC operations.

Statement Processing Efficiency

Each ODBC call to execute a SQL statement can involve a significant amount of overhead, especially if the data source involves a client/server network connection. To reduce this overhead, an ODBC driver may support *statement batches*. With this capability, an application program can pass a sequence of two or more SQL statements as a "batch" to be executed in a single SQLExecDirect() or SQLExecute() call. For example, a series of a dozen INSERT or UPDATE statements could be executed as a batch in this way. It can significantly reduce network traffic in a client/server environment, but it complicates error detection and recovery, which tend to become driver-specific when statement batches are used.

Many DBMS products address the efficiency of multi-statement transactions in a different way. They support stored procedures within the database itself, which can collect a sequence of SQL operations, together with the associated flow-control logic, and allow the statements to be invoked with a single "call" to the procedure. ODBC provides a set of capabilities that allow an application program to directly call a stored procedure in the target data source. For databases that allow stored procedure parameters to be passed by name, ODBC allows parameters to be bound by name instead of by position. For data sources that provide metadata information about stored procedure parameters, the SQLDescribeParam() call allows the application program to determine, at run-time, the required parameter data type. Output parameters of a stored procedure are supported either through SQLBindParam() (in which case the application program's data buffer is modified upon return from the SQLExecute() or SQLExecDirect() call) or through SQLGetData(), which allows retrieval of long returned data.

Two other extended ODBC capabilities provide efficiency when a single SQL statement (such as an INSERT or UPDATE statement) is to be executed repeatedly. Both address the binding of parameters for this situation. With the *binding offset* feature, once a statement parameter has been bound and the statement has been executed, ODBC allows the application program to change its binding for the next statement execution by specifying a new memory location as an offset from the original location. This is an effective way of binding a parameter to individual items in an array for repeated statement execution. In general, modifying an offset value is much more efficient than rebinding the parameter with repeated calls to SQLBindParam().

ODBC *parameter arrays* provide an alternative mechanism for an application program to pass multiple sets of parameter values in a single call. For example, if an application program needs to insert multiple rows into a table, it can request execution of a parameterized INSERT statement and bind the parameters to arrays of data values. The effective result is as if multiple INSERT statements are performed—one for each set of parameter values. ODBC supports both row-wise parameter arrays (each array element holds one "set" of parameter values) or column-wise parameter arrays (each parameter value is bound to its own individual array, which holds its values).

Query-Processing Efficiency

In a client/server environment, the network overhead involved in fetching many rows of query results can be very substantial. To cut this overhead, an ODBC driver may support "multi-row fetches" through the ODBC *block cursor* capability. With a block cursor, each SQLFetch() or SQLFetchScroll() call retrieves multiple rows (termed the "current rowset" of the cursor) from the data source. The application must bind the returned columns to arrays to hold the multiple rows of fetched data. Either row-wise or column-wise binding of the rowset data is supported, using the same techniques as those used for parameter arrays. In addition, the SQLSetPos() function may be used to establish one of the rows of the rowset as the "current" row for positioned update and delete operations.

ODBC *bookmarks* provide a different efficiency boost for an application program that needs to operate on retrieved rows of data. An ODBC bookmark is a database-independent "unique row-id" for SQL operations. (A driver may actually use primary keys or DBMS-specific row-ids or other methods to support bookmarks, but it is transparent to the application program.) When bookmarks are enabled, the bookmark (row-id) is returned for each row of query results. The bookmark can be used with scrolling cursors to return to a particular row. It can be used to perform a positioned update or delete based on a bookmark. Bookmarks can also be used to determine if a particular row retrieved by two different queries is, in fact, the same row or two different rows with the same data values. Bookmarks can make some operations much more efficient (for example, performing positioned updates via a bookmark rather than respecifying a complex search condition to identify the row). However, there can be substantial overhead for some DBMS brands and ODBC drivers in maintaining the bookmark information, so this trade-off must be considered carefully.

ODBC bookmarks form the basis for ODBC bulk operations, another efficiency-related feature. The SQLBulkOperations() call allows an application program to efficiently update, insert, delete or refetch multiple rows based on their bookmarks. It operates in conjunction with block cursors and works on the rows in the current rowset. The application program places the bookmarks for the rows to be affected into an array, and places into other arrays the values to be inserted or deleted. It then calls SQLBulkOperations() with a function code indicating whether the identified rows are to be updated, deleted, or refetched, or whether a set of new rows is to be added. This call completely bypasses the normal SQL statement syntax for these operations, and because it can operate on multiple rows in a single call, can be a very efficient mechanism for bulk insertion, deletion, or update of data.

The Oracle Call Interface (OCI)

The most popular programmatic interface to Oracle is embedded SQL. However, Oracle also provides an alternative callable API, known as the *Oracle Call Interface*, or OCI. OCI has been available for many years and remained fairly stable through a number of major Oracle upgrade cycles, including all of the Oracle7 versions. With the introduction of Oracle8, OCI underwent a major revision, and many of the original OCI calls were replaced by new, improved versions. However, the original OCI calls are still supported, and tens of thousands of applications depend on them and thousands of programmers are familiar with them.

Legacy OCI

The original OCI API includes about twenty calls, summarized in Table 19-6. The OCI functions use the term "cursor" to refer to a connection to the Oracle database. A program uses the olon() call to logon to the Oracle database, but it must use the

Function	Description
Database connection/disconnection	
olon()	Logs on to an Oracle database
oopen()	Opens a cursor (connection) for SQL statement processing
oclose()	Closes an open cursor (connection)
ologof()	Logs off from an Oracle database
Basic statement processing	
osql3()	Prepares (compiles) a SQL statement string
oexec()	Executes a previously compiled statement

Table 19-6. *Oracle Call Interface Functions*

Function	Description
oexn()	Executes with an array of bind variables
obreak()	Aborts the current Oracle call interface function
oermsg()	Obtains error message text
Statement parameters	
obndrv()	Binds a parameter to a program variable (by name)
obndrn()	Binds a parameter to a program variable (by number)
Transaction processing	
ocom()	Commits the current transaction
orol()	Rolls back the current transaction
ocon()	Turns on auto-commit mode
ocof()	Turns off auto-commit mode
Query results processing	
odsc()	Obtains a description of a query results column
oname()	Obtains the name of a query results column
odefin()	Binds a query results column to a program variable
ofetch()	Fetches the next row of query results
ofen()	Fetches multiple rows of query results into an array

Table 19-6. *Oracle Call Interface Functions* (continued)

oopen() call to open a cursor through which SQL statements can be executed. By issuing multiple oopen() calls, the application program can establish multiple cursors (connections) and execute statements in parallel. For example, a program might be retrieving query results on one of its connections and use a different connection to issue UPDATE statements.

The most remarkable feature of the Oracle Call Interface is that it very closely parallels the embedded dynamic SQL interface. Figure 19-25 shows excerpts from two programs that access an Oracle database, one using embedded SQL and one using OCI. Note the one-to-one correspondence between the embedded SQL CONNECT, PREPARE, EXECUTE, COMMIT, and ROLLBACK statements and the equivalent calls. In the case of the EXECUTE statement, the host variables that supply parameter values are listed in the embedded EXECUTE statement and specified by obndrv() calls in the call interface. Note also that the embedded UPDATE statement in the figure has no direct

```
Embedded SQL Interface                      Oracle Call Interface

EXEC SQL BEGIN DECLARE SECTION
char    text1[255];    /* stmt text */     char    text1[255];    /* stmt text */
char    text[255];     /* stmt text */     char    text2[255];    /* stmt text */
int     parm1;         /* parameter */     int     parm1;         /* parameter */
float   parm2;         /* parameter */     float   parm2;         /* parameter */
char    city[31];      /* retrieved */     char    city[31];      /* retrieved */
float   sales;         /* retrieved */     float   sales;         /* retrieved */
EXEC SQL END DECLARE SECTION               LDA     *lda;          /* logon area */
                                           CDA     *crs;          /* cursor area */

EXEC SQL CONNECT USING SCOTT/TIGER;        olon(lda, "SCOTT/TIGER",. . .);

EXEC SQL UPDATE OFFICES                    oopen(crs, lda, . . .);
         SET QUOTA = 0;                    osql3(crs, "UPDATE OFFICES SET QUOTA = 0");
                                           oexec(crs);

EXEC SQL ROLLBACK WORK;                    orol(lda);

EXEC SQL PREPARE stmt2 USING :text2;       osql3(crs, text2);

EXEC SQL EXECUTE stmt2                     obndrn(crs, 1, &parm1, sizeof(int));
         USING :parm1, parm2;              obndrn(crs, 2, &parm2, sizeof(float), 4);

EXEC SQL COMMIT WORK;                      ocom(lda);

EXEC SQL DECLARE C1 CURSOR FOR             osql3(crs, "SELECT CITY, SALES FROM OFFICES");
         SELECT CITY, SALES                odefin(crs, 1, city, 30, 5);
            FROM OFFICES;                  odefin(crs, 2, &sales, sizeof(float), 40;
EXEC SQL OPEN C1;                          oexec(crs);

EXEC SQL FETCH C1                          ofetch(crs);
         INTO :city, :sales;

EXEC SQL CLOSE C1;                         ocan(crs);

EXEC SQL COMMIT WORK RELEASE;              oclose(crs);
                                           ologof(lda);
```

Figure 19-25.   *Comparing Oracle's programmatic SQL interfaces*

counterpart in the call interface; it must be prepared and executed with calls to `osql3()` and `oexec()`.

The dynamic query-processing features of the two Oracle interfaces are also very parallel:

- The embedded `DBNUMCOLS()` statement becomes a series of calls to `oname()` and `odsc()` to retrieve the column names and data type information for query results. Each call returns data for a single column.

- Instead of having the program set `SQLDA` fields to bind query results columns to host variables, the OCI program uses calls to `odefin()` to bind columns.

- The embedded `FETCH` statement becomes a call to `ofetch()` instead.

- The embedded `CLOSE` statement becomes a call to `ocan()`, which ends access to query results.

One unique and useful feature of the Oracle Call Interface is its ability to interrupt a long-running query. In embedded SQL and most SQL call interfaces, a program passes control to the DBMS when it issues an embedded `OPEN` statement or an "execute" call to start a query. The program does not regain control until the query processing is complete. Thus there is no mechanism for the program to interrupt the query. The Oracle Call Interface provides an `obreak()` function that can be called asynchronously, while the Oracle DBMS has control, to interrupt Oracle processing. Thus, if the program can regain control during a query (typically by setting a timer and receiving an interrupt when the time expires), the program can call `obreak()` to asynchronously terminate the query.

OCI and Oracle8

With the introduction of Oracle8, the Oracle Call Interface was effectively replaced with a newer, more modern, and far more complex OCI. The "new" OCI uses many of the same concepts as the SQL/CLI standard and ODBC, including the use of handles to identify interface "objects." Several hundred routines are defined in the API, and a complete description of them is beyond the scope of this book. The following sections identify the major routines that will be used by most application programs and their functions.

OCI Handles

The new OCI uses a hierarchy of handles to manage interaction with an Oracle database, like the handle hierarchy of the SQL/CLI described earlier in this chapter. The handles are:

- *Environment handle*. The top-level handle associated with an OCI interaction
- *Service context handle*. Identifies an Oracle server connection for statement processing

■ *Server handle*. Identifies an Oracle database server (for multi-session applications)

■ *Session handle*. Identifies an active user session (for multi-session applications)

■ *Statement handle*. Identifies an Oracle-SQL statement being processed

■ *Bind handle*. Identifies an Oracle statement input parameter

■ *Define handle*. Identifies an Oracle query results column

■ *Transaction handle*. Identifies a SQL transaction in progress

■ *Complex object handle*. Used to retrieve data from an Oracle object

■ *Error handle*. Used to report and process OCI errors

An application program manages OCI handles using the routines shown in Table 19-7. The allocate and free routines function like their SQL/CLI counterparts. The get-attribute and set-attribute functions operate like the similarly named SQL/CLI routines that get and set environment, connection, and statement attributes.

An error handle is used to pass information back from OCI to the application. The error handle to be used for error reporting is typically passed as a parameter to OCI calls. If the return status indicates an error, information about the error can be retrieved from the error handle using OCIErrorGet().

Oracle Server Connection

The initialization and connection sequence for OCI parallels those already illustrated for CLI/ODBC and dblib. The OCI routines associated with connection management are shown in Table 19-8. An application program first calls OCIInitialize() to initialize the Oracle Call Interface. This call also indicates whether OCI will be used in multi-threaded mode, whether the application program will use OCI object-mode functions, and other options. After initialization, the application program calls OCIEnvInit() to initialize an environment handle. As with CLI/ODBC, all OCI interactions take place within the context of the environment defined by this handle.

Routine	Function
OCIHandleAlloc()	Allocates a handle for use
OCIHandleFree()	Frees a handle previously allocated
OCIAttrGet()	Retrieves a particular attribute of a handle
OCIAttrSet()	Sets the value of a particular handle attribute

Table 19-7. *OCI Handle Management Routines*

Routine	Function
OCIInitialize()	Initializes the Oracle Call Interface for use
OCIEnvInit()	Establishes an environment handle for OCI interaction
OCILogon()	Connects to an Oracle database server for an OCI session
OCILogoff()	Terminates a previous logon connection
OCIServerAttach()	Attaches to an Oracle server for multi-session operations
OCIServerDetach()	Detaches from an Oracle server
OCIServerVersion()	Returns server version information
OCISessionBegin()	Begins a user session on a previously attached server
OCIPasswordChange()	Changes a user's password on the server
OCISessionEnd()	Ends a previously begun user session

Table 19-8. *OCI Initialization and Connection Management Routines*

After these initial steps, most applications call OCILogon() to establish a session with an Oracle database server. Subsequent OCI calls take place within the context of this session and use the supplied user-id to determine their privileges within the Oracle database. A call to OCILogoff() terminates the session. The other calls provide more advanced session management for multi-threaded and multi-connection applications. The OCIServerVersion() call can be used to determine the version of the Oracle server software. The OCIChangePassword() call can be used to change an expired password.

Statement Execution

The OCI functions shown in Table 19-9 implement SQL statement execution. OCIStmtPrepare() and OCIStmtExecute() support the two-step prepare/execute process. The OCIStmtExecute() function can also be used to describe query results (similar to the embedded SQL DESCRIBE statement) without actually executing the query by passing a specific flag. OCI automatically provides a description of query results when OCIStmtExecute() is called in the normal statement execution mode. The description is available as an attribute of the statement handle for the executed query.

Routine	Function
OCIStmtPrepare()	Prepares a statement for execution
OCIStmtExecute()	Executes a previously prepared statement
OCIBreak()	Aborts current OCI operation on a server
OCIBindbyPos()	Binds a parameter based on its position
OCIBindbyName()	Binds a parameter based on its name
OCIStmtGetBindInfo()	Obtains the names of bind and indicator variables
OCIBindArrayOfStruct()	Sets up array binding for passing multiple parameter values
OCIBindDynamic()	Registers callback routine for a previously bound parameter that will use run-time binding
OCIBindObject()	Provides additional information for a previously bound parameter with a complex object data type
OCIStmtGetPieceInfo()	Obtains information about a dynamic piece-wise parameter value needed at execute-time by OCI (or a dynamic piece-wise query results column being returned)
OCIStmtSetPieceInfo()	Sets information (buffer, length, indicator, etc.) for a dynamic piece-wise parameter value being supplied at execute-time to OCI (or a dynamic piece-wise query results column being accepted at run-time)

Table 19-9.   *OCI Statement Processing and Parameter Handling Routines*

The OCIBindbyPos() and OCIBindbyName() functions are used to bind application program locations to statement parameters, using either parameter positions or parameter names. These calls automatically allocate bind handles for the parameters when they are called, or they may be called with explicitly allocated bind handles. The other calls implement more advanced binding techniques, including binding of multiple parameter values (arrays) and binding of complex object data types. They also provide execute-time parameter (and query results) processing, corresponding to the deferred parameter mode supported by CLI/ODBC and described in an earlier section of this chapter. The "piece info" calls support this mode of operation.

Query Results Processing

The OCI functions shown in Table 19-10 are used to process query results. The `OCIDefineByPos()` function is used to bind a query results column (identified by column number) to an application program storage location. (The OCI terminology refers to this as the "define" process; the term "binding" is reserved for input parameters.) The other "define" calls support dynamic (execute-time) binding, array binding (for multi-row fetch operations), and binding of complex object data types. The `OCIStmtFetch()` call retrieves a row of query results, and provides the SQL FETCH statement functionality.

Descriptor Handling

OCI uses *descriptors* to provide information about parameters, Oracle database objects (tables, views, stored procedures, and so on), large objects, complex objects, row-ids, and other OCI objects. A descriptor provides information to the application program and is used in some cases to manage the details of the processing of these objects. The routines shown in Table 19-11 are used to manage descriptors. They allocate and free the descriptors and retrieve and set individual data values within the descriptors.

Routine	Function
OCIStmtFetch()	Fetches a row or rows of query results
OCIDefineByPos()	Binds a query results column
OCIDefineArrayofStruct()	Sets up array binding for multi-row results retrieval
OCIDefineDynamic()	Registers a callback routine for dynamic processing of query results column
OCIDefineObject()	Provides additional information for a previously bound query results column with a complex object type

Table 19-10. *OCI Query Results Processing Routines*

Routine	Function
OCIDescriptorAlloc()	Allocates a descriptor or LOB locator
OCIDescriptorFree()	Frees a previously allocated descriptor
OCIParamGet()	Gets a descriptor for a parameter
OCIParamSet()	Sets parameter descriptor in a complex object retrieval handle

Table 19-11. *OCI Descriptor Management Routines*

Transaction Management

Application programs use the functions shown in Table 19-12 to implement SQL transaction management. The OCITransCommit() and OCITransRollback() calls provide the basic ability to commit and roll back transactions, and correspond to the usual SQL COMMIT and ROLLBACK statements. The other functions provide a very rich and complex transaction scheme, including the specification of read-only, serializable, and loosely or tightly coupled transactions, and control over distributed transactions. The transaction management routines take a service context handle that identifies a current connection as an input parameter.

Routine	Function
OCITransCommit()	Commits a transaction
OCITransRollback()	Rolls back a transaction
OCITransStart()	Initiates or reattaches a special transaction
OCITransPrepare()	Prepares-to-commit for a distributed transaction
OCITransForget()	Forgets a previously prepared transaction
OCITransDetach()	Detaches a distributed transaction

Table 19-12. *OCI Transaction Management Routines*

Error Handling

The OCI functions return a status code indicating whether they completed successfully. In addition, most OCI functions accept an error handle as an input parameter. If an error occurs during processing, error information is associated with this handle. Upon return from the function, the application program can call `OCIErrorGet()` on the error handle to obtain further information about the error, including the error number and error message.

Catalog Information

The `OCIDescribeAny()` call provides access to Oracle system catalog information. An application program calls this routine with the name of a table, view, synonym, stored procedure, data type, or other Oracle schema object. The routine populates a descriptor (identified by a descriptor handle) with information about the attributes of the object. Subsequent calls to `OCIAttrGet()` on the descriptor handle can be used to obtain complete data about the object at run-time.

Large Object Manipulation

OCI includes a large group of routines, shown in Table 19-13, for processing Oracle large object (LOB) data types and large objects stored in files referenced in Oracle columns. Because large objects may be tens of thousands to millions of bytes in length,

Routine	Function
OCILobRead()	Reads a piece of a LOB into application program data area
OCILobWrite()	Writes data from an application program data area into a LOB
OCILobAppend()	Appends data to the end of a LOB
OCILobErase()	Erases data within a LOB
OCILobTrim()	Truncates data from the end of a LOB
OCILobGetLength()	Obtains the length of a LOB
OCILobLocatorIsInit()	Checks whether a LOB locator is valid
OCILobCopy()	Copies data from one LOB to another
OCILobAssign()	Assigns one LOB locator to another

Table 19-13.   *OCI Large Object Processing Routines*

Routine	Function
OCILobIsEqual()	Compares two LOB locators
OCILobFileOpen()	Opens a file containing large object data
OCILobFileClose()	Closes a previously opened LOB file
OCILobFileCloseAll()	Closes all previously opened LOB files
OCILobFileIsOpen()	Checks whether a LOB file is open
OCILobFileGetName()	Obtains the name of a LOB file, given a LOB locator
OCILobFileSetName()	Sets the name of a LOB file in a LOB locator
OCILobFileExists()	Checks if a LOB file exists
OCILobLoadFromFile()	Loads a LOB from a LOB file

Table 19-13.   *OCI Large Object Processing Routines* (continued)

they typically cannot be bound directly to application program buffers in their entirety. Instead, OCI uses a LOB *locator*, which functions like a "handle" for the LOB data item. The locator is returned for LOB data in query results and used as an input parameter for LOB data being inserted or updated. The LOB handling routines support piece-by-piece processing of LOB data, allowing it to be transferred between an Oracle database and an application program. The routines accept one or more LOB locators as parameters.

Summary

Many SQL-based DBMS products provide a callable API for programmatic database access:

- Depending on the particular DBMS brand and its history, the callable API may be an alternative to an embedded SQL approach, or it may be the primary method by which an application program accesses the database.

- A callable interface puts query processing, parameter passing, statement compilation, statement execution, and similar tasks into the call interface, keeping the programmatic SQL language identical to interactive SQL. With embedded SQL, these tasks are handled by special SQL statements (OPEN, FETCH, CLOSE, PREPARE, EXECUTE, and so on) that are unique to programmatic SQL.

- Microsoft's ODBC is a widely supported, callable API that provides an effective way for an application program to achieve independence from a particular DBMS. However, differences between DBMS brands are reflected in varying support for ODBC functions and capabilities.

- The SQL/Call Level Interface (SQL/CLI) standard is based on ODBC and is compatible with it at the core level. SQL/CLI provides a callable API to complement the embedded SQL interface specified in SQL2. Despite its relatively recent publication (in 1995), many DBMS vendors already support the SQL/CLI because of their historical support for ODBC.

- The callable APIs of the different DBMS brands all offer the same basic features, but they vary dramatically in the extended features that they offer and in the details of the calls and data structures that they use.

Part VI

SQL Today and Tomorrow

The influence of SQL continues to expand as new SQL capabilities address new types of data management requirements. Chapters 20 through 22 describe three of these newer areas—stored procedures and expanded SQL processing capabilities, SQL's role in data warehousing, and SQL networking and the Internet. Chapter 23 discusses the interplay between SQL and object-oriented technologies and the new generation of object/relational databases. Finally, Chapter 24 describes the key trends that will drive the evolution of SQL for the coming decade.

Chapter 20

Database Processing and
Stored Procedures

The long-term trend in the database market is for databases to take on a progressively larger role in the overall data processing architecture. The pre-relational database systems basically handled data storage and retrieval only; applications programs were responsible for navigating their way through the database, sorting and selecting data, and all processing of the data. With the advent of relational databases and SQL, the DBMS took on expanded responsibilities. Database searching and sorting were embodied in SQL language clauses and provided by the DBMS, along with the ability to summarize data. Explicit navigation through the database became unnecessary. Subsequent SQL enhancements such as primary and foreign keys and check constraints continued the trend, taking over data-checking and data integrity functions that had remained the responsibility of application programs with earlier SQL implementations. At each step, having the DBMS take on more responsibility provided more centralized control and reduced the possibility of data corruption due to application programming errors.

Two important features of modern enterprise-scale relational databases—stored procedures and triggers—continue this trend. *Stored procedures* provide the capability to perform database-related application processing *within the database itself*. For example, a stored procedure might implement the application's logic to accept a customer order or to transfer money from one bank account to another. *Triggers* are used to automatically invoke the processing capability of a stored procedure based on conditions that arise within the database. For example, a trigger might automatically transfer funds from a savings account to a checking account if the checking account becomes overdrawn. This chapter describes these capabilities, their implementation in several popular DBMS brands, and their standardization. Stored procedures and triggers basically extend SQL into a more complete programming language, and this chapter assumes that you are familiar with basic programming concepts.

Stored Procedure Concepts

In its original form, SQL was not envisioned as a complete programming language. It was designed and implemented as a language for expressing database operations—creating database structures, entering data into the database, updating database data—and especially for expressing database queries and retrieving the answers. SQL could be used interactively by typing SQL statements at a keyboard, one by one. In this case, the sequence of database operations was determined by the human user. SQL could also be embedded within another programming language, such as COBOL or C. In this case, the sequence of database operations was determined by the flow of control within the COBOL or C program.

With stored procedures, several capabilities normally associated with programming languages are "grafted onto" the SQL language. Sequences of "extended SQL" statements are grouped together to form SQL programs or procedures. The specifics vary from one implementation to another, but generally these capabilities are provided:

- *Conditional execution.* An IF...THEN...ELSE structure allows a SQL procedure to test a condition and carry out different operations depending on the result.

- *Looping.* A WHILE or FOR loop or similar structure allows a sequence of SQL operations to be performed repeatedly, until some terminating condition is met. Some implementations provide a special cursor-based looping structure to process each row of query results.

- *Block structure.* A sequence of SQL statements can be grouped into a single block and used in other flow-of-control constructs as if the statement block were a single statement.

- *Named variables.* A SQL procedure may store a value that it has calculated, retrieved from the database, or derived in some other way into a program variable, and later retrieve the stored value for use in subsequent calculations.

- *Named procedures.* A sequence of SQL statements may be grouped together, given a name, and assigned formal input and output parameters, like a subroutine or function in a conventional programming language. Once defined in this way, the procedure may be called by name, passing it appropriate values for its input parameters. If the procedure is a function returning a value, it may be used in SQL value expressions.

Collectively, the structures that implement these capabilities form a stored procedure language (SPL). Stored procedures were first introduced by Sybase in the original Sybase SQL Server product. Since then, they have been added to many DBMS products. Some of these products have modeled their SPL structures on C or Pascal language constructs. Others have tried to match the style of the SQL DML and DDL statements. As a result, while stored procedure concepts are very similar from one SQL dialect to another, the specific syntax varies considerably.

A Basic Example

It's easiest to explain the basics of stored procedures through an example. Consider the process of adding a customer to the sample database. Here are the steps that may be involved:

1. Obtain the customer number, name, credit limit, and target sales amount for the customer, as well as the assigned salesperson and office.

2. Add a row to the customer table containing the customer's data.

3. Update the row for the assigned salesperson, raising the quota target by the specified amount.

4. Update the row for the office, raising the sales target by the specified amount.

5. Commit the changes to the database, if all were successful.

Without a stored procedure capability, here is a SQL statement sequence that does this work for XYZ Corporation, new customer number 2137, with a credit limit of $30,000 and first-year target sales of $50,000 to be assigned to Paul Cruz (employee #103) of the Chicago office:

```
INSERT INTO CUSTOMERS (CUST_NUM, COMPANY, CUST_REP, CREDIT_LIMIT)
    VALUES (2137, 'XYZ Corporation', 30000.00);
    UPDATE SALESREPS
       SET QUOTA = QUOTA + 50000.00
     WHERE EMPL_NUM = 103;
    UPDATE OFFICES
       SET TARGET = TARGET + 50000.00
     WHERE CITY = 'Chicago';
    COMMIT;
```

With a stored procedure, all of this work can be embedded into a single defined SQL routine. Figure 20-1 shows a stored procedure for this task, expressed in Oracle's PL/SQL stored procedure dialect. The procedure is named ADD_CUST, and it accepts six parameters—the customer name, number, credit limit, and target sales, the employee number of the assigned salesperson, and the city where the assigned sales office is located.

Once this procedure has been created in the database, a statement like this one:

```
ADD_CUST('XYZ Corporation',2137,30000.00,50000.00, 103,'Chicago')
```

calls the stored procedure and passes it the six specified values as its parameters. The DBMS executes the stored procedure, carrying out each SQL statement in the procedure definition one by one. If the ADD_CUST procedure completes its execution successfully, a committed transaction has been carried out within the DBMS. If not, the returned error code and message indicates what went wrong.

Using Stored Procedures

The procedure defined in Figure 20-1 illustrates several of the basic structures common to all SPL dialects. Nearly all dialects use a CREATE PROCEDURE statement to initially define a stored procedure. A corresponding DROP PROCEDURE statement is used to discard procedures that are no longer needed. The CREATE PROCEDURE statement defines the following.

```
/* Add a customer procedure */
create procedure add_cust (
    c_name   in varchar(20),              /* input customer name */
    c_num    in integer,                  /* input customer number */
    cred_lim in number(16,2),             /* input credit limit */
    tgt_sls  in number(16,2),             /* input target sales */
    c_rep    in integer,                  /* input salesrep emp # */
    c_offc   in varchar(15))              /* input office city */
as
begin
    /* Insert new row of CUSTOMERS table */
    insert into customers (cust_num, company, cust_rep, credit_limit)
        values (c_num, c_name, c_rep, cred_lim);

    /* Update row of SALESREPS table */
    update salesreps
       set quota = quota + quota + tgt_sls
     where empl_num = c_rep;

    /* Update row of OFFICES table */
    update offices
       set target = target + tgt_sls
     where city = c_offc;

    /* Commit transaction and we are done */
    commit;
end;
```

Figure 20-1. *A basic stored procedure in PL/SQL*

- The name of the stored procedure
- The number and data types of its parameters
- The names and data types of any local variables used by the procedure
- The sequence of statements that are executed when the procedure is called

The following sections describe these elements and the special SQL statements that are used to control the flow of execution within the body of a stored procedure.

Creating a Stored Procedure

In many common SPL dialects, the CREATE PROCEDURE statement is used to create a stored procedure and specify how it operates. The CREATE PROCEDURE statement assigns the newly defined procedure a name, which is used to call it. The name must typically follow the rules for SQL identifiers (the procedure in Figure 20-1 is named ADD_CUST). A stored procedure accepts zero or more parameters as its arguments (this one has six parameters, C_NAME, C_NUM, CRED_LIMI, TGT_SLS, C_REP, and C_OFFC). In all of the common SPL dialects, the values for the parameters appear in a comma-separated list, enclosed in parentheses, following the procedure name when the procedure is called. The header of the stored procedure definition specifies the names of the parameters and their data types. The same SQL data types supported by the DBMS for columns within the database can be used as parameter data types.

In Figure 20-1, all of the parameters are *input* parameters (signified by the IN keyword in the procedure header in the Oracle PL/SQL dialect). When the procedure is called, the parameters are assigned the values specified in the procedure call, and the statements in the procedure body begin to execute. The parameter names may appear within the procedure body (and particularly within standard SQL statements in the procedure body) anywhere that a constant may appear. When a parameter name appears, the DBMS uses its current value. In Figure 20-1, the parameters are used in the INSERT statement and the UPDATE statement, both as data values to be used in column calculations and search conditions.

In addition to input parameters, some SPL dialects also support *output* parameters. These allow a stored procedure to "pass back" values that it calculates during its execution. Output parameters aren't useful for stored procedures invoked from interactive SQL, but they provide an important capability for passing back information from one stored procedure to another stored procedure that calls it. Some SPL dialects support parameters that operate as *both* input and output parameters. In this case, the parameter passes a value to the stored procedure, and any changes to the value during the procedure execution are reflected in the calling procedure.

Figure 20-2 shows the same ADD_CUST procedure definition, expressed in the Sybase Transact-SQL dialect. (The Transact-SQL dialect is also used by Microsoft SQL Server; its basics are largely unchanged since the original Sybase SQL Server version, which was the foundation for both the Microsoft and Sybase product lines.) Note the differences from the Oracle dialect:

- The keyword PROCEDURE can be abbreviated to PROC.

- No parenthesized list of parameters follow the procedure name. Instead, the parameter declarations immediately follow the name of the stored procedure.

- The parameter names all begin with an at sign (@), both when they are declared at the beginning of the procedure and when they appear within SQL statements in the procedure body.

```
/* Add a customer procedure */
create proc add_cust
   @c_name    varchar(20),              /* input customer name */
   @c_num     integer,                  /* input customer number */
   @cred_lim money,                     /* input credit limit */
   @tgt_sls  money,                     /* input target sales */
   @c_rep     integer,                  /* input salesrep emp # */
   @c_offc   varchar(15)                /* input office city */
as
begin
   /* Insert new row of CUSTOMERS table */
   insert into customers (cust_num, company, cust_rep, credit_limit)
       values (@c_num, @c_name, @c_rep, @cred_lim)

   /* Update row of SALESREPS table */
   update salesreps
      set quota = quota + quota + @tgt_sls
    where empl_num = @c_rep

   /* Update row of OFFICES table */
   update offices
      set target = target + @tgt_sls
    where city = @c_offc

   /* Commit transaction and we are done */
   commit trans
end
```

Figure 20-2.   *The* ADD_CUST *procedure in Transact-SQL*

- There is no formal "end of procedure body" marker. Instead, the procedure body is a single Transact-SQL statement. If more than one statement is needed, the Transact-SQL block structure is used to group the statements.

Figure 20-3 shows the ADD_CUST procedure again, this time expressed in the Informix stored procedure dialect. The declaration of the procedure head itself and the parameters more closely follows the Oracle dialect. Unlike the Transact-SQL example,

```
/* Add a customer procedure */
create procedure add_cust (
    c_name    varchar(20),              /* input customer name */
    c_num     integer,                  /* input customer number */
    cred_lim  money(16,2),              /* input credit limit */
    tgt_sls   money(16,2),              /* input target sales */
    c_rep     integer,                  /* input salesrep emp # */
    c_offc    varchar(15))              /* input office city */

    /* Insert new row of CUSTOMERS table */
    insert into customers (cust_num, company, cust_rep, credit_limit)
        values (c_num, c_name, c_rep, cred_lim);

    /* Update row of SALESREPS table */
    update salesreps
       set quota = quota + quota + tgt_sls
     where empl_num = c_rep;

    /* Update row of OFFICES table */
    update offices
       set target = target + tgt_sls
     where city = c_offc;

    /* Commit transaction and we are done */
    commit transaction;
end procedure;
```

Figure 20-3.   *The* ADD_CUST *procedure in Informix SPL*

the local variables and parameters use ordinary SQL identifiers as their names, without any special identifying symbols. The procedure definition is formally ended with an END PROCEDURE clause, which makes the syntax less error-prone.

In all dialects that use the CREATE PROCEDURE statement, the procedure can be dropped when no longer needed by a corresponding DROP PROCEDURE statement:

```
DROP PROCEDURE ADD_CUST
```

Calling a Stored Procedure

Once defined by the CREATE PROCEDURE statement, a stored procedure can be used. An application program may request execution of the stored procedure, using the appropriate SQL statement. Another stored procedure may call it to perform a specific function. The stored procedure may also be invoked through an interactive SQL interface.

The various SQL dialects differ in the specific syntax used to call a stored procedure. Here is a call to the ADD_CUST procedure in the PL/SQL dialect:

```
EXECUTE ADD_CUST('XYZ Corporation',2137,30000.00,50000.00,103,'Chicago')
```

The values to be used for the procedure's parameters are specified, in order, in a list that is enclosed by parentheses. When called from within another procedure or a trigger, the EXECUTE statement may be omitted, and the call becomes simply:

```
ADD_CUST('XYZ Corporation',2137,30000.00,50000.00,103,'Chicago')
```

In the Transact-SQL dialect, the call to the stored procedure becomes:

```
EXECUTE ADD_CUST 'XYZ Corporation',2137,30000.00,50000.00,103,'Chicago'
```

The parentheses aren't required, and the values to be used for parameters again form a comma-separated list. The keyword EXECUTE can be abbreviated to EXEC, and the parameter names can be explicitly specified in the call, allowing you to specify the parameter values in any order you wish. Here is an alternative, equivalent Transact-SQL call to the ADD_CUST stored procedure:

```
EXEC ADD_CUST @C_NAME = 'XYZ Corporation',
              @C_NUM = 2137,
            @CRED_LIM = 30000.00,
             @C_OFFC = 'Chicago',
              @C_REP = 103,
            @TGT_SLS = 50000.00
```

The Informix SPL form of the same EXECUTE command is:

```
EXECUTE PROCEDURE ADD_CUST('XYZ Corporation',2137,30000.00,
                           50000.00,103,'Chicago')
```

Again the parameters are enclosed in a comma-separated, parenthesized list. This form of the execute statement may be used in any context. For example, it may be used by an embedded SQL application program to invoke a stored procedure. Within a stored procedure itself, another stored procedure can be called using this equivalent statement:

```
CALL ADD_CUST('XYZ Corporation',2137,30000.00,50000.00,103,'Chicago')
```

Stored Procedure Variables

In addition to the parameters passed into a stored procedure, it's often convenient or necessary to define other variables to hold intermediate values during the procedure's execution. All stored procedure dialects provide this capability. Usually the variables are declared at the beginning of the procedure body, just after the procedure header and before the list of SQL statements. The data types of the variables can be any of the SQL data types supported as column data types by the DBMS.

Figure 20-4 shows a simple Transact-SQL stored procedure fragment that computes the total outstanding order amount for a specific customer number, and sets up one of two messages depending on whether the total order amount is over or under $30,000. Note that Transact-SQL local variable names, like parameter names, begin with an at sign (@). The DECLARE statement declares the local variables for this procedure. In this case, there are two variables, one with the MONEY data type and one VARCHAR.

In Transact-SQL, the SELECT statement assumes the additional function of assigning values to variables. A simple form of this use of SELECT is the assignment of the message text:

```
SELECT @MSG_TEXT = "high order total"
```

The assignment of the total order amount at the beginning of the procedure body is a more complex example, where the SELECT is used both to assign a value and as the introducer of the query that generates the value to be assigned.

Figure 20-5 shows the Informix SPL version of the same stored procedure. There are several differences from the Transact-SQL version:

- Local variables are declared using the DEFINE statement. This example shows only a very limited subset of the options that are available.

- Variable names are ordinary SQL identifiers; there is no special first character.

- A specialized SELECT INTO statement is used within SPL to assign the results of a singleton SELECT statement into a local variable.

- The LET statement provides simple assignment of variable values.

```
/* Check order total for a customer */
create proc chk_tot
   @c_num integer       /* one input parameter */
as

   /* Declare two local variables */
   declare @tot_ord money, @msg_text varchar(30)

   begin
      /* Calculate total orders for customer */
      select @tot_ord = sum(amount)
        from orders
       where cust = @c_num

      /* Load appropriate message, based on total */
      if tot_ord < 30000.00
         select @msg_text = "high order total"
      else
         select @msg_text = "low order total"

      /* Do other processing for message text */
      . . .

   end
```

Figure 20-4.   *Using local variables in Transact-SQL*

Figure 20-6 shows the Oracle PL/SQL version of the same stored procedure. Again, there are several differences to note from the Transact-SQL and Informix SPL examples:

- Local variable declarations occur in a separate DECLARE section. This section is actually an integral part of the Oracle BEGIN...END block structure; it declares local variables for use within the block.

- The SELECT INTO statement has the same form as the Informix procedure; it is used to select values from a single-row query directly into local variables.

- The assignment statements use Pascal-style (: =) notation instead of a separate LET statement.

```
/* Check order total for a customer */
create procedure chk_tot (c_num integer)

   /* Declare two local variables */
   define tot_ord money(16,2);
   define msg_text varchar(30);

   /* Calculate total orders for requested customer */
   select sum(amount) into tot_ord
     from orders
    where cust = c_num;

   /* Load appropriate message, based on total */
   if tot_ord < 30000.00
      let msg_text = "high order total"
   else
      let msg_text = "low order total"

   /* Do other processing for message text */
   . . .


end procedure;
```

Figure 20-5.   *Using local variables in Informix SPL*

Local variables within a stored procedure can be used as a source of data within SQL expressions anywhere that a constant may appear. The current value of the variable is used in the execution of the statement. In addition, local variables may be destinations for data derived from SQL expressions or queries, as shown in the preceding examples.

Statement Blocks

In all but the very simplest stored procedures, it is often necessary to group a sequence of SQL statements together so that they will be treated as if they were a single statement. For example, in the IF...THEN...ELSE structure typically used to control the flow of execution within a stored procedure, most stored procedure dialects expect a single statement following the THEN keyword. If a procedure needs to perform a

```
/* Check order total for a customer */
create procedure chk_tot (c_num in integer)
as
declare
   /* Declare two local variables */
   tot_ord number(16,2);
   msg_text varchar(30);

begin
   /* Calculate total orders for requested customer */
   select sum(amount) into tot_ord
     from orders
    where cust = c_num;

   /* Load appropriate message, based on total */
   if tot_ord < 30000.00
      msg_text := 'high order total';
   else
      msg_text := 'low order total';

   /* Do other processing for message text */
   . . .

end;
```

Figure 20-6.   *Using local variables in Oracle PL/SQL*

sequence of several SQL statements when the tested condition is true, it must group the statements together as a statement block, and this block will appear after THEN.

In Transact-SQL, a statement block has this simple structure:

```
/* Transact-SQL block of statements */
begin
   /* Sequence of SQL statements appears here */
   . . .

end
```

The sole function of the BEGIN...END pair is to create a statement block; they do not impact the scope of local variables or other database objects. The Transact-SQL procedure definition, conditional execution and looping constructs, and others, are all designed to operate with single SQL statements, so statement blocks are frequently used in each of these contexts to group statements together as a single unit.

In Informix SPL, a statement block includes not only a statement sequence but may optionally declare local variables for use within the block and exception handlers to handle errors that may occur within the block. Here is the structure of an Informix SQL statement block:

```
/* Informix SPL block of statements */
/* Declaration of any local variables */
define . . .

/* Declare handling for exceptions */
on exception . . .

/* Define the sequence of SQL statements */
begin. . .

end
```

The variable declaration section is optional; we have already seen an example of it in the Informix stored procedure body in Figure 20-5. The exception handling section is also optional; its role is described later in this chapter. The BEGIN... END sequence performs the same function as it does for Transact-SQL. Informix also allows a single statement to appear in this position, if the block consists of just the other two components and a single SQL or SPL statement.

The Informix SQL language structures don't require the use of statement blocks as often as the Transact-SQL structures. In the Informix dialect, the looping conditional execution statements each include an explicit termination (IF... END IF, WHILE...END WHILE, FOR... END FOR). Within the structure, a single SQL statement or a sequence of statements (each ending with a semicolon) may appear. As a result, an explicit block structure is not always needed simply to group together a sequence of SQL statements.

The Oracle PL/SQL block structure has the same capabilities as the Informix structure. It offers the ability to declare variables and exception conditions, using this format:

```
/* Oracle PL/SQL statement block */
/* Declaration of any local variables */
declare . . .
```

```
/* Specify the sequence of statements */
begin . . .

/* Declare handling for exceptions */
exception . . .

end;
```

All three sections of the block structure are optional. It's common to see the structure used with only the BEGIN...END sequence to define a statement sequence, or with a DECLARE...BEGIN...END sequence to declare variables and a sequence of statements. As with Informix, the Oracle structures that specify conditional execution and looping have a self-defining end-of-statement marker, so sequences of statements within these structures do not necessarily need an explicit BEGIN...END statement block structure.

Returning a Value

In addition to stored procedures, most SPL dialects support a stored *function* capability. The distinction is that a stored function returns a value while a stored procedure does not. Here's a simple example of a stored function. Assume you want to define a stored procedure that, given a customer number, calculates the total current order amount for that customer. If you define the procedure as a function, the total amount can be returned as its value.

Figure 20-7 shows an Oracle stored function that calculates the total amount of current orders for a customer, given the customer number. Note the RETURNS clause in the procedure definition, which tells the DBMS the data type of the value being returned. In most DBMS products, if you enter a function call via the interactive SQL capability, the function value is displayed in response. Within a stored procedure, you can call a stored function and use its return value in calculations or store it in a variable.

Many SPL dialects also allow you to use a stored function as a user-defined function within SQL value expressions. This is true of the Oracle PL/SQL dialect, so this use of the function defined in Figure 20-7 within a search condition is legal:

```
SELECT COMPANY, NAME
  FROM CUSTOMERS, SALESREPS
 WHERE CUST_REP = EMPL_NUM
   AND GET_TOT_ORDS(CUST_NUM) > 10000.00
```

As the DBMS evaluates the search condition for each row of prospective query results, it uses the customer number of the current "candidate" row as an argument to the GET_TOT_ORDERS function and checks to see if it exceeds the $10,000 threshold. This same query could be expressed as a grouped query, with the ORDERS table also

```
/* Return total order amount for a customer */
create function get_tot_ords(c_num in integer)
        return number(16,2)
as

/* Declare one local variable to hold the total */
declare tot_ord number(16,2);

begin
   /* Simple single-row query to get total */
   select sum(amount) into tot_ord
     from orders
    where cust = c_num;

   /* return the retrieved value as fcn value */
   return tot_ord;
end;
```

Figure 20-7. *An Oracle PL/SQL stored function*

included in the FROM clause, and the results grouped by customer and salesperson. In many implementations, the DBMS carries out the grouped query more efficiently than the preceding one, which probably forces the DBMS to process the orders table once for each customer.

Figure 20-8 shows the Informix SPL definition for the same stored function shown in Figure 20-7. Except for stylistic variations, it differs very little from the Oracle version.

Transact-SQL does not have a stored function capability like the one illustrated in Figures 20-7 and 20-8. Transact-SQL stored procedures can explicitly return a status code, and they use a RETURN statement for this purpose. However, the returned value is always an integer status value. A zero return value indicates successful completion of the stored procedure; negative return values are used to indicate various types of errors. The system-defined stored procedures in Sybase Adaptive Server and Microsoft SQL Server all use this return status value convention. The return status of a called procedure can be stored into a local variable by using this "assignment form" of the EXECUTE statement:

```
declare sts_val int
execute sts_val = add_cust 'XYZ Corporation',2137,30000.00,
                          50000.00,103,'Chicago'
```

```
/* Return total order amount for a customer */
create function get_tot_ords(c_num in integer)
      returning money(16,2)

/* Declare one local variable to hold the total */
define tot_ord money(16,2);

begin
   /* Simple single-row query to get total */
   select sum(amount) into tot_ord
     from orders
    where cust = c_num;

   /* Return the retrieved value as fcn value */
   return tot_ord;
end function;
```

Figure 20-8. *An Informix SPL stored function*

Returning Values via Parameters

The stored function capability provides only the ability to return a single value from a stored routine. Several stored procedure dialects provide a method for returning more than one value, by passing the values back to the calling routine through *output parameters*. The output parameters are listed in the stored procedure's parameter list, just like the input parameters seen in the previous examples. However, instead of being used to pass data values *into* the stored procedure when it is called, the output parameters are used to pass data *back out of* the stored procedure to the calling procedure.

Figure 20-9 shows a PL/SQL stored procedure to retrieve the name of a customer, their salesperson, and the sales office to which the customer is assigned, given a supplied customer number. The procedure has four parameters. The first one, CNUM, is an input parameter and supplies the requested customer number. The other three parameters are output parameters, used to pass the retrieved data values back to the calling procedure. In this simple example, the SELECT INTO form of the query places the returned variables directly into the output parameters. In a more complex stored procedure, the returned values might be calculated and placed into the output parameters with a PL/SQL assignment statement.

When a stored procedure with output parameters is called, the "value" passed for each output parameter must be an acceptable *target* that can receive a returned data value. The "target" may be a local variable, for example, or a parameter of a higher-level

```
/* Get customer name, sales rep and office */
create procedure get_cust_info(c_num   in   integer,
                                  c_name out varchar(20),
                                  r_name out varchar(15),
                                  c_offc out varchar(15))
as
begin
   /* Simple single-row query to get info */
   select company, name, city
     into c_name, r_name, c_offc
     from customers, salesreps, offices
    where cust_num = c_num
      and empl_num = cust_rep
      and office = rep_office;
end;
```

Figure 20-9. *PL/SQL stored procedure with output parameters*

procedure that is calling a lower-level procedure to do some work for it. Here is a fragment of an Oracle PL/SQL procedure that makes an appropriate call to the GET_CUST_INFO procedure in Figure 20-9:

```
/* Get the customer info for customer 2111 */
declare the_name varchar(20),
        the_rep  varchar(15),
        the_city varchar(15);
execute get_cust_info(2111,the_name,the_rep,the_city);
```

Of course, it would be unusual to call this procedure with a literal customer number, but it's perfectly legal since that is an input parameter. The remaining three parameters have acceptable data assignment targets (in this case, they are PL/SQL variables) passed to them so that they can receive the returned values. Here is an *illegal* call to the same procedure:

```
/* Get the customer info for customer 2111 */
execute get_cust_info(2111,"XYZ Co",the_rep,the_city)
```

because the second parameter is an output parameter and cannot receive a literal value. In addition to input and output parameters, Oracle allows you to specify procedure parameters that are *both* input and output (INOUT) parameters. They must obey the same previously cited restrictions for output parameters, but in addition, their values are used as input by the procedure.

Figure 20-10 shows a version of the GET_CUST_INFO procedure defined in the Transact-SQL dialect. The way in which the output parameters are identified in the procedure header differs slightly from the Oracle version, and the single-row select statement has a different form. Otherwise, the structure of the procedure and its operation are identical to the Oracle example

When this procedure is called from another Transact-SQL procedure, the fact that the second, third, and fourth parameters are output parameters must be indicated in the *call* to the procedure, as well as in its definition. Here is the Transact-SQL syntax for calling the procedure in Figure 20-10:

```
/* Get the customer info for customer 2111 */
declare the_name varchar(20);
declare the_rep  varchar(15);
declare the_city varchar(15);
exec get_cust_info @c_num = 2111,
                   @c_name = the_name output,
                   @r_name = the_rep output,
                   @c_offc = the_city output
```

```
/* Get customer name, sales rep and office */
create procedure get_cust_info(c_num  in  integer,
                               c_name out varchar(20),
                               r_name out varchar(15),
                               c_offc out varchar(15))
as
begin
   /* Simple single-row query to get info */
   select company, name, city
     into c_name, r_name, c_offc
     from customers, salesreps, offices
    where cust_num = c_num
      and empl_num = cust_rep
      and office = rep_office;
end;
```

Figure 20-10.   *Transact-SQL stored procedure with output parameters*

Figure 20-11 shows the Informix SPL version of the same stored procedure example. Informix takes a different approach to handling multiple return values. Instead of output parameters, Informix extends the definition of a stored function to allow multiple return values. Thus, the GET_CUST_INFO procedure becomes a function for the Informix dialect. The multiple return values are specified in the RETURNING clause of the procedure header, and they are actually returned by the RETURN statement.

The Informix CALL statement that invokes the stored function uses a special RETURNING clause to receive the returned values:

```
/* Get the customer info for customer 2111 */
define the_name varchar(20);
define the_rep  varchar(15);
define the_city varchar(15);
call get_cust_info (2111)
        returning the_name, the_rep, the_city;
```

```
/* Get customer name, sales rep and office */
create function get_cust_info(c_num integer)
     returning varchar(20), varchar(15), varchar(15)

  define c_name varchar(20);
  define r_name varchar(15);
  define c_offc varchar(15);

  /* Simple single-row query to get info */
  select company, name, city
    into cname, r_name, c_offc
    from customers, salesreps, offices
   where cust_num = c_num
     and empl_num = cust_rep
     and office = rep_office;

  /* Return the three values */
  return cname, r_name, c_offc;
end procedure;
```

Figure 20-11. *Informix stored function with multiple return values*

As in the Transact-SQL dialect, Informix also allows a version of the CALL statement that passes the parameters by name:

```
call get_cust_info (c_num = 2111)
        returning the_name, the_rep, the_city;
```

Conditional Execution

One of the most basic features of stored procedures is an IF...THEN...ELSE construct for decision-making within the procedure. Look back at the original ADD_CUST procedure defined in Figure 20-1 for adding a new customer. Suppose that the rules for adding new customers are modified so that there is a cap on the amount by which a salesperson's quota should be increased for a new customer. If the customer's anticipated first year orders are $20,000 or less, that amount should be added to the quota, but if they are more than $20,000, the quota should be increased only by $20,000. Figure 20-12 shows a modified procedure that implements this new policy. The IF...THEN...ELSE logic operates exactly as it does in any conventional programming language.

All of the stored procedure dialects allow nested IF statements for more complex decision making. Several provide extended conditional logic to streamline multi-way branching. For example, suppose you wanted to do three different things within the ADD_CUST stored procedure, depending on whether the customer's anticipated first year orders are under $20,000, between $20,000 and $50,000, or over $50,000. In Oracle's PL/SQL, you could express the three-way decision this way:

```
/* Process sales target by range */
if tgt_sls < 20000.00
   then
   /* Handle low-target customers here */
   . . .
elsif tgt_sls < 50000.00
   then
   /* Handle mid-target customers here */
   . . .
else
   /* Handle high-target customers here */
   . . .
end if;
```

In the Informix dialect, the same multi-way branch structure is allowed. The keyword ELSIF becomes ELIF, but all other aspects remain the same.

```
/* Add a customer procedure */
create procedure add_cust (
   c_name    in varchar(20),         /* input customer name */
   c_num     in integer,             /* input customer number */
   cred_lim  in number(16,2),        /* input credit limit */
   tgt_sls   in number(16,2),        /* input target sales */
   c_rep     in integer,             /* input salesrep empl # */
   c_offc    in varchar(15))         /* input office city */
as
begin
   /* Insert new row of CUSTOMERS table */
   insert into customers (cust_num, company, cust_rep, credit_limit)
       values (c_num, c_name, c_rep, cred_lim);

   if tgt_sales <= 20000.00
   then
      /* Update row of SALESREPS table */
      update salesreps
         set quota = quota + quota + tgt_sls
       where empl_num = c_rep;
   else
      /* Update row of SALESREPS table */
      update salesreps
         set quota = quota + quota + 20000.00
       where empl_num = c_rep;
   end if

   /* Update row of OFFICES table */
   update offices
      set target = target + tgt_sls
    where city = c_offc;

   /* Commit transaction and we are done */
   commit;
end;
```

Figure 20-12.   *Conditional logic in a stored procedure*

Repeated Execution

Another feature common to almost all stored procedure dialects is a construct for repeated execution of a group of statements (looping). Depending on the dialect, there may be support for Basic-style FOR loops (where an integer loop control value is counted up or counted down) or C-style WHILE loops with a test condition executed at the beginning or end of the loop.

In the sample database, it's hard to come up with an uncontrived example of simple loop processing. Assume you want to process some group of statements repeatedly, while the value of a loop-control variable, named ITEM_NUM, ranges from 1 to 10. Here is an Oracle PL/SQL loop that handles this situation:

```
/* Process each of ten items */
for item_num in 1..10 loop
   /* Process this particular item */
   . . .

   /* Test whether to end the loop early */
   exit when (item_num = special_item);
end loop;
```

The statements in the body of the loop are normally executed ten times, each time with a larger integer value of the ITEM_NUM variable. The EXIT statement provides the ability to exit an Oracle PL/SQL loop early. It can be unconditional, or it can be used with a built-in test condition, as in this example.

Here is the same loop structure expressed in Informix SPL, showing some of its additional capabilities and the dialectic differences from PL/SQL:

```
/* Process each of ten items */
for item_num = 1 to 10 step 1
   /* Process this particular item */
   . . .

   /* Test whether to end the loop early */
   if (item_num = special_item)
      then exit for;
end for;
```

The other common form of looping is when a sequence of statements is executed repeatedly while a certain condition exists or until a specified condition exists. Here is an Oracle PL/SQL loop construct that repeats indefinitely. Such a loop must, of course, provide a test within the body of the loop that detects a loop-terminating condition (in this case, a match of two variable values) and explicitly exits the loop:

```
/* Repeatedly process some data */
loop
   /* Do some kind of processing each time */
   . . .

   /* Test whether to end the loop early */
   exit when (test_value = exit_value);
end loop;
```

A more common looping construct is one that builds the test into the loop structure itself. The loop is repeatedly executed so long as the test is true. For example, suppose you want to reduce targets for the offices in the sample database until the total of the targets is less than $2,400,000. Each office's target is to be reduced by the same amount, which should be a multiple of $10,000. Here is a (not very efficient) Transact-SQL stored procedure loop that gradually lowers office targets until the total is below the threshold:

```
/* Lower targets until total below $2,400,000 */
while (select sum(target) from offices) < 2400000.00
   begin
      update offices
         set target = target - 10000.00
   end
```

The BEGIN...END block in this WHILE loop isn't strictly necessary, but most Transact-SQL WHILE loops include one. Transact-SQL repeats the single SQL statement following the test condition as the "body" of the while loop. If the body of the loop consists of more than one statement, you must use a BEGIN...END block to group the statements.

Here is the Oracle PL/SQL version of the same loop:

```
/* Lower targets until total below $2,400,000 */
select sum(target) into total_tgt from offices;
while (total_tgt < 2400000.00)
loop
   update offices
      set target = target - 10000.00;
   select sum(target) into total_tgt from offices;
end loop;
```

The subquery-style version of the SELECT statement from Transact-SQL has been replaced by the PL/SQL SELECT INTO form of the statement, with a local variable used to hold the total of the office targets. Each time the loop is executed, the OFFICES table is updated, and then the total of the targets is recalculated.

Here is the same loop once more, expressed using Informix SPL's WHILE statement:

```
/* Lower targets until total below $2,400,000 */
select sum(target) into total_tgt from offices;
while (total_tgt < 2400000.00)
   update offices
      set target = target - 10000.00;
   select sum(target) into total_tgt from offices;
end while;
```

Other variants of these loop-processing constructs are provided by the various dialects, but the capabilities and syntax are similar to these examples.

Other Flow-of-Control Constructs

Some stored procedure dialects provide statements to control looping and alter the flow of control. In Informix, for example, the EXIT statement interrupts the normal flow within a loop and causes execution to resume with the next statement *following* the loop itself. The CONTINUE statement interrupts the normal flow within the loop but causes execution to resume *with the next loop iteration*. Both of these statements have three forms, depending on the type of loop being interrupted:

```
exit for;
continue for;
exit while;
continue while;
exit foreach;
continue foreach;
```

In Transact-SQL, a single statement, BREAK, provides the equivalent of the Informix EXIT statement variants, and there is a single form of the CONTINUE statement as well. In Oracle, the EXIT statement performs the same function as for Informix, and there is no CONTINUE statement.

Additional control over the flow of execution within a stored procedure is provided by statement labels and the GOTO statement. In most dialects, the statement label is an identifier, followed by a colon. The GOTO statement names the label to which control should be transferred. There is typically a restriction that you cannot transfer control out of a loop or a conditional testing statement, and always a prohibition against transferring control into the middle of such a statement. As in structured programming languages, the use of GOTO statements is discouraged because it makes stored procedure code harder to understand and debug.

Cursor-Based Repetition

One common need for repetition of statements within a stored procedure is when the procedure executes a query and needs to process the query results, row by row. All of the major dialects provide a structure for this type of processing. Conceptually, the structures parallel the DECLARE CURSOR, OPEN CURSOR, FETCH, and CLOSE CURSOR statements in embedded SQL or the corresponding SQL API calls. However, instead of fetching the query results into the application program, in this case they are being fetched into the stored procedure, which is executing within the DBMS itself. Instead of retrieving the query results into application program variables (host variables), the stored procedure retrieves them into local stored procedure variables.

To illustrate this capability, assume that you want to populate two tables with data from the ORDERS table. One table, named BIGORDERS, should contain customer name and order size for any orders over $10,000. The other, SMALLORDERS, should contain the salesperson's name and order size for any orders under $1000. The best and most efficient way to do this would actually be with two separate SQL INSERT statements with subqueries, but for purposes of illustration, consider this method instead:

1. Execute a query to retrieve the order amount, customer name, and salesperson name for each order.

2. For each row of query results, check the order amount to see whether it falls into the proper range for including in the BIGORDERS or SMALLORDERS tables.

3. Depending on the amount, INSERT the appropriate row into the BIGORDERS or SMALLORDERS table.

4. Repeat Steps 2 and 3 until all rows of query results are exhausted.

5. Commit the updates to the database.

Figure 20-13 shows an Oracle stored procedure that carries out this method. The cursor that defines the query is defined in the declare section of the procedure and assigned the name O_CURSOR. The variable CURS_ROW, defined in the same section, is defined as an Oracle "row type." It is a structured Oracle "row variable" with individual components (like a C-language structure). By declaring it as having the same ROWTYPE as the cursor, the individual components of CURS_ROW have the same data types and names as the cursor's query results columns.

The query described by the cursor is actually carried out by the cursor-based FOR loop. It basically tells the DBMS to carry out the query described by the cursor (equivalent to the OPEN statement in embedded SQL) before starting the loop processing. The DBMS then executes the FOR loop repeatedly, by fetching a row of query results at the top of the loop, placing the column values into the CURS_ROW

```
create procedure sort_orders()
declare
   /* Cursor for the query */
   cursor o_cursor is
   select amount, company, name
     from orders, customers, salesreps
    where cust = cust_num
      and rep = empl_num;

   /* Row variable to receive query results values */
   curs_row o_cursor%rowtype;

begin

   /* Loop through each row of query results */
   for curs_row in o_cursor
   loop

      /* Check for small orders and handle */
      if (curs_row.amount < 1000.00)
      then insert into smallorders
              values (curs_row.name, curs_row.amount);

      /* Check for big orders and handle */
      elsif (curs_row.amount > 10000.00)
      then insert into bigorders
              values (curs_row.company, curs_row.amount);
      end if;
   end loop;
```

Figure 20-13.   *A cursor-based* FOR *loop in Oracle PL/SQL*

variable and then executing the statements in the loop body. When there are no more rows of query results to be fetched, the cursor is closed, and processing continues after the loop.

Figure 20-14 shows an equivalent stored procedure with the specialized FOR loop structure of Informix SPL. In this case, the query results are retrieved into ordinary local variables; there is no special "row" data type used. The FOREACH statement incorporates several different functions. It defines the query to be carried out, through the SELECT expression that it contains. It marks the beginning of the loop that is to be

```
create procedure sort_orders()

    /* Local variables to hold query results */
    define ord_amt money(16,2);                /* order amount */
    define c_name varchar(20);                 /* customer name */
    define r_name varchar(15);                 /* salesrep name */

    /* Execute query and process each results row */
    foreach select amount, company, name
            into ord_amt, c_name, r_name
            from orders, customers, salesreps
          where cust = cust_num
            and rep = empl_num;
       begin

          /* Check for small orders and handle */
          if (ord_amt < 1000.00)
          then insert into smallorders
                   values (r_name, ord_amt);

          /* Check for big orders and handle */
          elif (ord_amt > 10000.00)
          then insert into bigorders
                   values (c_name, ord_amt);
          end if;
       end;
    end foreach;
end procedure;
```

Figure 20-14.   *A cursor-based* FOREACH *loop in Informix SPL*

executed for each row of query results (the end of the loop is marked by the END
FOREACH statement). When the FOREACH statement is executed, it carries out the query
and then fetches rows of query results repeatedly, putting their column values into the
local variables as specified in the statement. After each row is fetched, the body of the
loop is executed. When there are no more rows of query results, the cursor is
automatically closed, and execution continues with the next statement following the
FOREACH. Note that in this example, the cursor isn't even assigned a specific name
because all cursor processing is tightly specified within the single FOREACH statement.

The Transact-SQL dialect doesn't have a specialized FOR loop structure for cursor-based query results processing. Instead, the DECLARE CURSOR, OPEN, FETCH, and CLOSE statements of embedded SQL have direct counterparts within the Transact-SQL language. Figure 20-15 shows a Transact-SQL version of the sort_orders procedure. Note the separate DECLARE, OPEN, FETCH, and CLOSE statements for the

```
create proc sort_orders()
as
/* Local variables to hold query results */
declare @ord_amt money(16,2);                /* order amount */
declare @c_name varchar(20);                 /* customer name */
declare @r_name varchar(15);                 /* salesrep name */

/* Declare cursor for the query */
declare o_curs cursor for
        select amount, company, name
          from orders, customers, salesreps
         where cust = cust_num
           and rep = empl_num

begin

   /* Open cursor and fetch first row of results */
   open o_curs
   fetch o_curs into @ord_amt, @c_name, @r_name

   /* If no rows, return immediately */
   if (@@sqlstatus = 2)
   begin
      close o_curs
      return
   end

   /* Loop through each row of query results */
   while (@@sqlstatus = 0)
   begin
```

Figure 20-15.   *A cursor-based* WHILE *loop in Transact-SQL*

```
        /* Check for small orders and handle */
        if (@ord_amt < 1000.00)
            insert into smallorders
                values (@r_name, @ord_amt)

        /* Check for big orders and handle */
        else if (curs_row.amount > 10000.00)
            insert into bigorders
                values (@c_name, @ord_amt)
    end

    /* Done with results; close cursor and return */
    close o_curs
end
```

Figure 20-15. *A cursor-based* WHILE *loop in Transact-SQL* (continued)

cursor. Loop control is provided by testing the system variable @@SQLSTATUS, which is the Transact-SQL equivalent of the SQLSTATE code. It receives a value of zero when a fetch is successful, and a nonzero value when there are no more rows to fetch.

Handling Error Conditions

When an application program uses Embedded SQL or a SQL API for database processing, the application program is responsible for handling errors that arise. Error status codes are returned to the application program, and more error information is typically available through additional API calls or access to an extended diagnostics area. When database processing takes place within a stored procedure, the procedure itself must handle errors.

Transact-SQL provides error handling through a set of global system variables. The specific error-handling variables are only a few of well over one hundred system variables that provide information on the state of the server, transaction state, open connections, and other database configuration and status information. The two most useful global variables for error handling are:

■ *@@ERROR*. Contains error status of the most recently executed statement batch.

■ *@@SQLSTATUS*. Contains status of the last fetch operation.

The "normal completion" values for both variables are zero; other values indicate various errors and warnings. The global variables can be used in the same way as local variables within a Transact-SQL procedure. Specifically, their values can be checked for branching and loop control.

Oracle's PL/SQL provides a different style of error handling. The Oracle DBMS provides a set of system-defined "exceptions," which are errors or warning conditions that can arise during SQL statement processing. Within an Oracle stored procedure (actually, any Oracle statement block), the EXCEPTION section tells the DBMS how it should handle any exception conditions that occur during the execution of the procedure. There are over a dozen different predefined Oracle-detected exception conditions. In addition, you can define your own exception conditions.

Most of the previous examples in this chapter don't provide any real error-handling capability. Figure 20-16 shows a revised version of the Oracle stored function in Figure 20-7. This improved version detects the specific situation where the supplied customer number does not have any associated orders (that is, where the query to

```
/* Return total order amount for a customer */
create function get_tot_ords(c_num in integer)
        return number(16,2)
as

/* Declare one local variable to hold the total */
declare tot_ord number(16,2);

begin
   /* Simple single-row query to get total */
   select sum(amount) into tot_ord
     from orders
    where cust = c_num;

   /* return the retrieved value as fcn value */
   return tot_ord;

exception
   /* Handle the situation where no orders found */
   when no_data_found
   then raise_application_error (-20123, 'Bad cust#');

   /* Handle any other exceptions */
   when others
   then raise_application_error (-20199,'Unknown error');
end;
```

Figure 20-16. *PL/SQL stored function with error handling*

calculate total orders returns a NO_DATA_FOUND exception). It responds to this situation by signaling back to the application program an application-level error and associated message. Any other exception conditions that arise are caught by the WHEN OTHERS exception handler.

The Informix SPL takes a similar approach to exception handling. Figure 20-17 shows the Informix version of the stored function, with Informix-style exception handling. The ON EXCEPTION statement is a declarative statement and specifies the sequence of SQL statements to be executed when a specific exception arises. A comma-separated list of exception numbers may be specified.

```
/* Return total order amount for a customer */
create function get_tot_ords(c_num in integer)
      returning money(16,2)

/* Declare one local variable to hold the total */
define tot_ord money(16,2);

/* Define exception handler for error #-123 and -121 */
on exception in (-121, -123)
    /* Do whatever is appropriate here */
    . . .
end exception;
on exception
    /* Handle any other exceptions in here */
    . . .
end exception;

begin
    /* Simple single-row query to get total */
    select sum(amount)
      into tot_ord
      from orders
     where cust = c_num;

    /* Return the retrieved value as fcn value */
    return tot_ord;

end function;
```

Figure 20-17. *Informix SPL stored function with condition handling*

Advantages of Stored Procedures

Stored procedures offer several advantages, both for database users and database administrators, including:

- *Run-time performance*. Many DBMS brands compile stored procedures (either automatically or at the user's request) into an internal representation that can be executed very efficiently by the DBMS at run-time. Executing a precompiled stored procedure can be much faster than running the equivalent SQL statements through the PREPARE/EXECUTE process.

- *Reusability*. Once a stored procedure has been defined for a specific function, that procedure may be called from many different application programs that need to perform the function, permitting very easy reuse of application logic and reducing the risk of application programmer error.

- *Reduced network traffic*. In a client/server configuration, sending a stored procedure call across the network and receiving the results in a reply message generates much less network traffic than using a network round-trip for each individual SQL statement. This can improve overall system performance considerably in a network with heavy traffic or one that has lower speed connections.

- *Security*. In most DBMS brands, the stored procedure is treated as a "trusted" entity within the database and executes with its own privileges. The user executing the stored procedure needs to have only permission to execute it, not permission on the underlying tables that the stored procedure may access or modify. Thus, the stored procedure allows the database administrator to maintain tighter security on the underlying data, while still giving individual users the specific data update or data access capabilities they require.

- *Encapsulation*. Stored procedures are a way to achieve one of the core objectives of object-oriented programming—the "encapsulation" of data values, structures, and access within a set of very limited, well-defined external interfaces. In object terminology, stored procedures can be the "methods" through which the objects in the underlying RDBMS are exclusively manipulated. To fully attain the object-oriented approach, all direct access to the underlying data via SQL must be disallowed through the RDBMS security system, leaving *only* the stored procedures for database access. In practice, few if any production relational databases operate in this restricted way.

Stored Procedure Performance

Different DBMS brands vary in the way they actually implement stored procedures. In several brands, the stored procedure text is stored within the database and is interpreted when the procedure is executed. This has the advantage of creating a very flexible stored procedure language, but it creates significant run-time overhead for complex stored procedures. The DBMS must read the statements that make up the stored procedure at run-time, parse and analyze them, and determine what to do on the fly.

Because of the overhead in the interpreted approach, some DBMS brands compile stored procedures into an intermediate form that is much more efficient to execute. Compilation may be automatic when the stored procedure is created, or the DBMS may provide the ability for the user to request stored procedure compilation. The disadvantage of compiled stored procedures is that the exact technique used to carry out the stored procedure is fixed when the procedure is compiled. Suppose, for example, that a stored procedure is created and compiled soon after a database is first created, and later some useful indexes are defined on the data. The compiled queries in the stored procedure won't take advantage of these indexes, and as a result they may run much more slowly than if they were recompiled.

To deal with "stale" compiled procedures, some DBMS brands automatically mark any compiled procedures that may be affected by subsequent database changes as "in need of recompilation." The next time the procedure is called, the DBMS notices the mark and recompiles the procedure before executing it. Normally, this approach provides the best of both worlds—the performance benefits of precompilation while keeping the compiled procedure up to date. Its disadvantage is that it can yield unpredictable stored procedure execution times. When no recompile is necessary, the stored procedure may execute quickly; when a recompile is activated, it may produce a significant delay; and in most cases, the recompile delay is much longer than the disadvantage of using the "old" compiled version.

To determine the stored procedure compilation capabilities of a particular DBMS, you can examine its CREATE PROCEDURE and EXECUTE PROCEDURE statement options or look for other procedure management statements such as ALTER PROCEDURE.

System-Defined Stored Procedures

DBMS brands that support stored procedures sometimes provide built-in, system-defined stored procedures to automate database processing or management functions. Sybase SQL Server pioneered this use of system stored procedures. Today hundreds of Transact-SQL system stored procedures provide functions such as managing users, database roles, job execution, distributed servers, replication, and others. Most Transact-SQL system procedures follow this naming convention:

- *SP_ADD_something*. Add a new object (user, server, replica, and so on)
- *SP_DROP_something*. Drop an existing object
- *SP_HELP_something*. Get information about an object or objects

For example, the SP_HELPUSER procedure returns information about the valid users of the current database.

External Stored Procedures

Although stored procedures written in the extended SQL dialects of the major enterprise DBMS brands can be quite powerful, they have limitations. One major limitation is that they do not provide access to features outside the DBMS, such as the features of the operating system or other applications running on the same computer system. The extended SQL dialects also tend to be fairly high-level languages, with limited capability for the lower-level programming usually done in C or C++. To overcome these limitations, some DBMS brands provide access to external stored procedures.

An external stored procedure is a procedure written in a conventional programming language (such as C or Pascal) and compiled outside the DBMS itself. The DBMS is given a definition of the procedure's name and its parameters, along with other essential information such as the calling conventions used by the programming language in which the stored procedure was written. Once defined to the DBMS, the external stored procedure can be called as if it were a SQL stored procedure. The DBMS handles the call, turns over control to the external procedure, and then receives back any return values and parameters.

Microsoft SQL Server provides a set of system-defined external stored procedures that provide access to selected operating system capabilities. The XP_SENDMAIL procedure can be used to send electronic mail to users, based on conditions within the DBMS:

```
XP_SENDMAIL @RECIPIENTS = 'Joe', 'Sam',
            @MESSAGE = 'Customer table nearly full';
```

Similarly, the XP_CMDSHELL external procedure can be called to pass commands to the underlying operating system on which SQL Server is operating. Beyond these predefined external procedures, SQL Server allows a user-written external procedure to be stored in a dynamic linked library (DLL) and called from within SQL Server stored procedures.

Informix provides basic access to underlying operating system capabilities with a special SYSTEM statement. In addition, it supports user-written external procedures through its CREATE PROCEDURE statement. Where the statement block comprising the body of an Informix SPL procedure would appear, an EXTERNAL clause specifies the name, location, and language of the externally written procedure. With the procedure defined in this way, it can be called in the same way as "native" Informix SPL procedures. Newer versions of Oracle (Oracle 8 and later) provide the same capability, also via the `CREATE PROCEDURE` statement. IBM's DB2 database family provides the same set of capabilities.

Triggers

A trigger is a special set of stored procedure code whose activation is caused by modifications to the database contents. Unlike stored procedures created with a `CREATE PROCEDURE` statement, a trigger is not activated by a `CALL` or `EXECUTE` statement. Instead, the trigger is associated with a database table. When the data in the table is changed (by an `INSERT`, `DELETE`, or `UPDATE` statement), the trigger is "fired", which means that the DBMS executes the SQL statements that make up the body of the trigger.

Triggers can be used to cause automatic updates of information within a database. For example, suppose you wanted to set up the sample database so that any time a new salesperson is inserted into the `SALESREPS` table, the sales target for the office where the salesperson works is raised by the new salesperson's quota. Here is an Oracle PL/SQL trigger that accomplishes this goal:

```
create trigger upd_tgt
   /* Insert trigger for SALESREPS */
   before insert on salesreps
   for each row
   when (new.quota is not null)
   begin
      update offices
         set target = target + new.quota;
   end;
```

The `CREATE TRIGGER` statement is used by most DBMS brands that support triggers to define a new trigger within the database. It assigns a name to the trigger (`UPD_TGT` for this one) and identifies the table the trigger is associated with (`SALESREPS`) and the update action(s) on that table that will cause the trigger to be executed (`INSERT` in this case). The body of this trigger tells the DBMS that for each new row inserted into the table, it should execute the specified `UPDATE` statement for the `OFFICES` table. The `QUOTA` value from the newly inserted `SALESREPS` row is referred to as `NEW.QUOTA` within the trigger body.

Advantages and Disadvantages of Triggers

Triggers can be extremely useful as an integral part of a database definition. Triggers can be used for a variety of different functions, including:

- *Auditing changes*. A trigger can detect and disallow specific updates and changes that should not be permitted in the database.

- *Cascaded operations.* A trigger can detect an operation within the database (such as deletion of a customer or salesperson) and automatically cascade the impact throughout the database (such as adjusting account balances or sales targets).

- *Enforce interrelationships.* A trigger can enforce more complex interrelationships among the data in a database than those that can be expressed by simple referential integrity constraints or check constraints, such as those that require a sequence of SQL statements or IF...THEN...ELSE processing.

- *Stored procedure invocation.* A trigger can call one or more stored procedures or even invoke actions outside the DBMS itself through external procedure calls in response to database updates.

In each of these cases, a trigger embodies a set of business rules that govern the data in the database and modifications to that data. The rules are embedded in a single place in the database (the trigger definition). As a result, they are uniformly enforced across all applications that access the database. When they need to be changed, they can be changed once with the assurance that the change will be applied uniformly.

The major disadvantage of triggers is their potential performance impact. If a trigger is set on a particular table, then every database operation that attempts to update that table causes the DBMS to execute the trigger procedure. For a database that requires very high data insertion or update rates, the overhead of this processing can be considerable. This is especially true for bulk load operations, where the data may have already been prechecked for integrity. To deal with this disadvantage, some DBMS brands allow triggers to be selectively enabled and disabled, as appropriate.

Triggers in Transact-SQL

Transact-SQL provides triggers through a CREATE TRIGGER statement in both its Microsoft SQL Server and Sybase Adaptive Server dialects. Here is a Transact-SQL trigger definition for the sample database, using the example from earlier in this chapter:

```
create trigger upd_tgt
   /* Insert trigger for SALESREPS */
   on salesreps
   for insert
   as
   if (@@rowcount = 1)
      begin
         update offices
            set target = target + inserted.quota
          from offices, inserted
         where offices.office = inserted.rep_office;
      end
   else
      raiserror 23456
```

The first clause names the trigger (UPD_TGT). The second clause is required and identifies the table to which the trigger applies. The third clause is also required and tells which database update operations cause the trigger to be fired. In this case, only an INSERT statement causes the trigger to fire. You can also specify UPDATE or DELETE operations, or a combination of two or three of these operations in a comma-separated list. Transact-SQL restricts triggers so that only one trigger may be defined on a particular table for each of the three data modification operations. The body of the trigger follows the AS keyword. To understand the body of a trigger like this one, you need to understand how Transact-SQL treats the rows in the target table during database modification operations.

For purposes of trigger operation, Transact-SQL defines two "virtual tables" whose column structure is identical to the "target" table on which the trigger is defined. One of these virtual tables is named DELETED, and the other is named INSERTED. These virtual tables are populated with rows from the target table, depending on the data modification statement that caused the trigger to fire, as follows:

- *For a DELETE statement.* Each row of the target table that is deleted by the DELETE statement is placed into the DELETED table. The INSERTED table is empty.

- *For an INSERT statement.* Each row of the target table that is added by the INSERT statement is also placed into the INSERTED table. The DELETED table is empty.

- *For an UPDATE statement.* For each row of the target table that is changed by the UPDATE statement, a copy of the row *before* any modifications is placed into the DELETED table. A copy of the row *after* all modifications is placed into the INSERTED table.

These two virtual tables can be referenced within the body of the trigger, and the data in them can be combined with data from other tables during the trigger's operation. In this Transact-SQL trigger, the trigger body first tests to make sure that only a single row of the SALESREPS table has been inserted, by checking the system variable @@ROWCOUNT. If this is true, then the QUOTA column from the INSERTED virtual table is added to the appropriate row of the OFFICES table. The "appropriate" row is determined by joining the virtual table to the OFFICES table based on matching office numbers.

Here is a different trigger that detects a different type of data integrity problem. In this case, it checks for an attempt to delete a customer when there are still orders outstanding in the database for that customer. If it detects this situation, the trigger automatically rolls back the entire transaction, including the DELETE statement that fired the trigger:

```
create trigger chk_del_cust
    /* Delete trigger for CUSTOMERS */
```

```
on customers
for delete
as
/* Detect any orders for deleted cust #'s */
if (select count(*)
      from orders, deleted
    where orders.cust = deleted.cust_num) > 0
  begin
    rollback transaction
    print "Cannot delete; still have orders"
    raiserror 31234
  end
```

Transact-SQL triggers can be specified to fire on any UPDATE for a target table, or just for updates of selected columns. This trigger fires on inserts or updates to the SALESREPS table and does different processing depending on whether the QUOTA or SALES column has been updated:

```
create trigger upd_reps
   /* Update trigger for SALESREPS */
   on salesreps
   for insert, update
   if update(quota)
     /* Handle updates to quota column */
     . . .
   if update (sales)
     /* Handle updates to sales column */
     . . .
```

Triggers in Informix SPL

Informix also supports triggers through a CREATE TRIGGER statement. As in the Transact-SQL dialect, the beginning of the CREATE TRIGGER statement defines the trigger name, the table on which the trigger is being defined, and the triggering actions. Here are statement fragments that show the syntax:

```
create trigger new_sls
   insert on salesreps . . .

create trigger del_cus_chk
   delete on customers . . .
```

```
create trigger ord_upd
   update on orders . . .

create trigger sls_upd
   update of quota, sales on salesreps . . .
```

The last example is a trigger that fires only when two specific columns of the SALESREPS table are updated.

Informix allows you to specify that a trigger should operate at three distinct times during the processing of a triggered change to the target table:

- *BEFORE*. The trigger fires before any changes take place. No rows of the target table have yet been modified.

- *AFTER*. The trigger fires after all changes take place. All affected rows of the target table have been modified.

- *FOR EACH ROW*. The trigger fires repeatedly, once as each row affected by the change is being modified. Both the "old" and "new" data values for the row are available to the trigger.

An individual trigger definition can specify actions to be taken at one or more of these steps. For example, a trigger could execute a stored procedure to calculate the sum of all orders BEFORE an update, monitor updates to each ORDERS row as they occur with a second action, and then calculate the revised order total AFTER the update with a call to another stored procedure. Here is a trigger definition that does all of this:

```
create trigger upd_ord
   update of amount on orders
   referencing old as pre new as post

   /* Calculate order total before changes */
   before (execute procedure add_orders()
              into old_total;)

   /* Capture order increases and decreases */
   for each row
      when (post.amount < pre.amount)
         /* Write decrease data into table */
         (insert into ord_less
               values (pre.cust,
                       pre.order_date,
```

```
                        pre.amount,
                        post.amount)
        when (post.amount > pre.amount)
          /* Write increase data into table */
          (insert into ord_more
                values (pre.cust,
                        pre.order_date,
                        pre.amount,
                        post.amount)

    /* After changes, recalculate total */
    after (execute procedure add_orders()
              into new_total;
```

The BEFORE clause in this trigger specifies that a stored procedure named ADD_ORDERS is to be called before any UPDATE statement processing occurs. Presumably this procedure calculates the total orders and returns the total value into the local variable OLD_TOTAL. Similarly, the AFTER clause specifies that a stored procedure (in this case, the same one) is to be called after all UPDATE statement processing is complete. This time the total orders amount is placed into a different local variable, NEW_TOTAL. The FOR EACH ROW clause specifies the action to be taken as each affected row is updated. In this case, the requested action is an INSERT into one of two order tracking tables, depending on whether the order amount is being increased or decreased. These tracking tables contain the customer number, date, and both the old and new order amounts. To obtain the required values, the trigger must be able to refer to both the old (pre-change) and the new (post-change) values of each row. The REFERENCING clause provides names by which these two states of the "currently being-modified" row of the ORDERS table can be used. In this example, the pre-change values of the columns are available through the column name qualifier PRE, and the post-change values through the column name qualifier POST. These are not special names; any names can be used.

Informix is more limited than some other DBMS brands in the actions that can be specified within the trigger definition itself. These actions are available:

- An INSERT statement
- A DELETE statement
- An UPDATE statement
- An EXECUTE PROCEDURE statement

In practice, the last option provides quite a bit of flexibility. The called procedure can perform almost any processing that could be done in-line within the trigger body itself.

Triggers in Oracle PL/SQL

Oracle provides a more complex trigger facility than either the Informix or Transact-SQL facility described in the preceding sections. It uses a CREATE TRIGGER statement to specify triggered actions. As in the Informix facility, a trigger can be specified to fire at specific times during specific update operations:

■ A *statement-level trigger* fires once for each data modification statement. It can be specified to fire either before the statement is executed or after the statement has completed its action.

■ A *row-level trigger* fires once for each row being modified by a statement. In Oracle's structure, this type of trigger may also fire either *before* the row is modified or *after* it is modified.

■ An *instead-of trigger* takes the place of an attempted data modification statement. It provides a way to detect an attempted update, insert or delete operation by a user or procedure, and substitute other processing instead. You can specify a trigger should be executed instead of a statement or that it should be executed instead of each attempted modification of a row.

These trigger structures and their options provide 14 different valid Oracle trigger types (12 resulting from a choice of INSERT/DELETE/UPDATE triggers for BEFORE or AFTER processing at the ROW or STATEMENT level (3 x 2 x 2), and 2 more from INSTEAD OF triggers at the STATEMENT or ROW level). In practice, relational databases built using Oracle don't tend to use INSTEAD OF triggers; they were introduced in Oracle8 to support some of its newer object-oriented features.

Here is a PL/SQL trigger definition that implements the same processing as in the complex Informix example from the previous section. It has been split into three separate Oracle CREATE TRIGGER statements; one each for the BEFORE and AFTER statement-level triggers and one trigger that is executed for each update row.

```
create trigger bef_upd_ord
   before update on orders
   begin
     /* Calculate order total before changes */
     old_total = add_orders();
   end;
create trigger aft_upd_ord
   after update on orders
   begin
     /* Calculate order total after changes */
     new_total = add_orders();
   end;
```

```
create trigger dur_upd_ord
   before update of amount on orders
   referencing old as pre new as post

   /* Capture order increases and decreases */
   for each row
      when (post.amount != pre.amount)
         begin
            if (post.amount < pre.amount)
            then
               /* Write decrease data into table */
               insert into ord_less
                     values (pre.cust,
                              pre.order_date,
                              pre.amount,
                              post.amount;
            elsif (post.amount > pre.amount)
            then
               /* Write increase data into table */
               insert into ord_more
                     values (pre.cust,
                              pre.order_date,
                              pre.amount,
                              post.amount;
            end if;
         end;
```

Other Trigger Considerations

Triggers pose some of the same issues for DBMS processing that UPDATE and DELETE rules present. For example, triggers can cause a cascaded series of actions. A user's attempt to update a table may cause a trigger to fire. Within the body of that trigger is an UPDATE statement for another table. A trigger on that table causes the UPDATE of still another table, and so on. The situation is even worse if one of the fired triggers attempts to update the original target table that caused the firing of the trigger sequence in the first place! In this case, an infinite loop of fired triggers could result.

Various DBMS systems deal with this issue in different ways. Some impose restrictions on the actions that can be taken during execution of a trigger. Others provide built-in functions that allow a trigger's body to detect the level of nesting at which the trigger is operating. Some provide a system setting that controls whether cascaded trigger processing is allowed. Finally, some provide a limit on the number of levels of nested triggers that can fire.

One additional issue associated with triggers is the overhead that can result during very heavy database usage, such as when bulk data is being loaded into a database. Some DBMS brands provide the ability to selectively enable and disable trigger processing to handle this situation. Oracle, for example, provides this form of the `ALTER TRIGGER` statement:

```
ALTER TRIGGER BEF_UPD_ORD DISABLE;
```

A similar capability is provided within the `CREATE TRIGGER` statement of Informix.

Stored Procedures and the SQL Standard

The development of DBMS stored procedures has been largely driven by DBMS vendors and the competitive dynamics of the database industry. Sybase's initial introduction of stored procedures and triggers in SQL Server triggered a competitive response, and by the mid-1990s many of the enterprise-class systems had added their own, proprietary procedural extensions to SQL. Stored procedures were not a focus of the SQL2 standards efforts but became a part of the standardization agenda after the 1992 publication of the SQL2 standard. The work on stored procedure standards was split off from the broader object-oriented extensions that were proposed for SQL3, and was focused on a set of procedural extensions to the SQL2 language.

The result was a new part of the SQL standard, published in 1996 as SQL/Persistent Stored Modules (SQL/PSM), International Standard ISO/IEC 9075-4. The actual form of the standard specification is a collection of additions, edits, new paragraphs, and replacement paragraphs to the 1992 SQL2 standard (ISO/IEC 9075:1992). SQL/PSM is actually Part 4 of an expected multi-part structure for the ISO SQL standard. The SQL Call-Level Interface (CLI) standard, described in Chapter 19, is being treated the same way; it is Part 3 of the eventual standard.

The SQL/PSM standard addresses only stored procedures and stored functions. It explicitly does *not* provide a specification of a trigger facility for the ISO SQL standard. The standardization of trigger functions is closely tied to other object-oriented extensions proposed for SQL3 and must await the resolution of the larger issues involved with those object features.

Core Capabilities

The capabilities specified in the SQL/PSM standard parallel the core features of the proprietary stored procedure capabilities of today's DBMS systems. They include SQL language constructs to:

- Define and name procedures and functions written in the extended SQL language

- Invoke (call) a previously defined procedure or function
- Pass parameters to a called procedure or function, and obtain the results of its execution
- Declare and use local variables within the procedure or function
- Group a block of SQL statements together for execution
- Conditionally execute SQL statements (IF...THEN...ELSE)
- Repeatedly execute a group of SQL statements (looping)

The SQL/PSM standard specifies two types of "SQL-invoked routines." A SQL-procedure is a routine that does not return a value. It is called with a CALL statement:

```
CALL ADD_CUST('XYZ Corporation',2137,30000.00,50000.00,103,'Chicago')
```

A SQL-function does return a value. It is called just like a built-in SQL function within a value expression:

```
SELECT COMPANY
  FROM CUSTOMERS
 WHERE GET_TOT_ORDS(CUST_NUM) > 10000.00
```

SQL routines are objects within the SQL2 database structure. The SQL/PSM allows the creation of routines within a SQL2 schema (a "schema-level routine") where it exists along with the tables, views, assertions, and other objects in the scheme. It also allows the creation of routines within a SQL2 module, which is the SQL procedure model carried forward from the SQL1 standard.

Creating a SQL Routine

Following the practice of most DBMS brands, the SQL/PSM standard uses the CREATE PROCEDURE and CREATE FUNCTION statements to specify the definitions of stored procedures and functions. Figure 20-18 shows a simplified syntax for each of these statements. In addition to the capabilities shown in the figure, the standard provides a capability to define external stored procedures, specifying the language they are written in, whether they can or cannot read or modify data in the database, their calling conventions, and other characteristics.

Flow-of-Control Statements

The SQL/PSM standard specifies the common programming structures to control the flow of execution that are found in most stored procedure dialects. Figure 20-19 shows

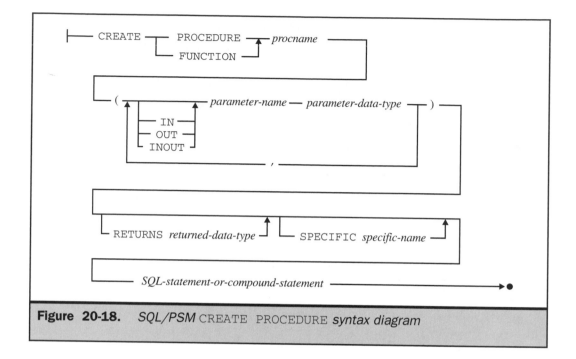

Figure 20-18. *SQL/PSM* CREATE PROCEDURE *syntax diagram*

the conditional branching and looping syntax. Note that the SQL statement lists specified for each structure consist of a sequence of SQL statements, each ending with a semicolon. Thus, explicit block structures are not required for simple multi-statement sequences that appear in an IF...THEN...ELSE statement or a LOOP statement. The looping structures provide a great deal of flexibility for loop processing. There are forms that place the test at the top of the loop and at the bottom of the loop, as well as a form that provides infinite looping and requires the explicit coding of a test to break loop execution. Each of the program control structures is explicitly terminated by an END flag that matches the type of structure, making programming debugging easier.

Cursor Operations

The SQL/PSM standard extends the cursor manipulation capabilities specified in the SQL2 standard for embedded SQL into SQL routines. The DECLARE CURSOR, OPEN, FETCH, and CLOSE statements retain their roles and functions. Instead of using application program host variables to supply parameter values and to receive retrieved data, SQL routine parameters and variables can be used for these functions.

The SQL/PSM standard does introduce one new cursor-controlled looping structure, shown in Figure 20-20. Like the similar structures in the Oracle and Informix dialects described earlier in this chapter, it combines the cursor definition, OPEN, FETCH, and CLOSE statement in a single loop definition that also specifies the processing to be performed for each row of retrieved query results.

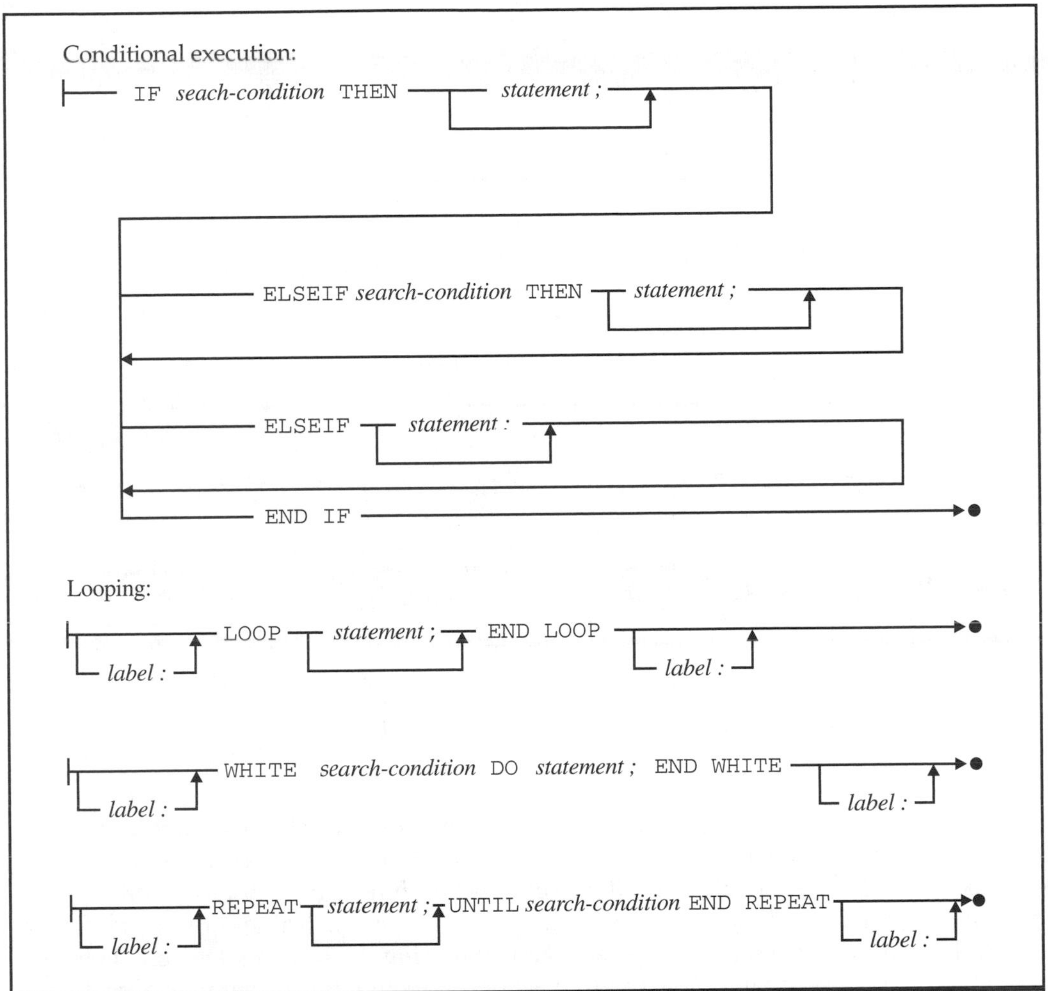

Conditional execution:

Looping:

Figure 20-19. *SQL/PSM flow-of-control statements syntax diagrams*

Block Structure

Figure 20-21 shows the block structure specified by the SQL/PSM standard. It is a quite comprehensive structure, providing the following capabilities:

- Label the block of statements with a statement label
- Declare local variables for use within the block
- Declare local user-defined error conditions
- Declare cursors for queries to be executed within the block

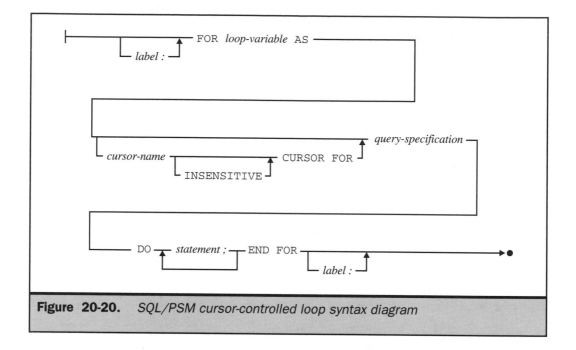

Figure 20-20. *SQL/PSM cursor-controlled loop syntax diagram*

- Declare handlers to process error conditions that arise
- Define the sequence of SQL statements to be executed

These capabilities resemble some of those described earlier in this chapter for statement blocks in the Informix and Oracle dialect stored procedure dialects.

Local variables within SQL/PSM procedures and functions (actually, within statement blocks) are declared using the DECLARE statement. Values are assigned using the SET statement. Functions return a value using the return statement. Here is a statement block that might appear within a stored function with examples of each:

```
try_again:
  begin
    /* Declare some local variables */
    declare msg_text varchar(40);
    declare tot_amt decimal(16,2);

    /* Get the order total */
    set tot_amt = get_tot_ords();
    if (tot_amt > 0)
    then
```

```
      return (tot_amt);
   else
      return (0.00);
   end if
end try_again
```

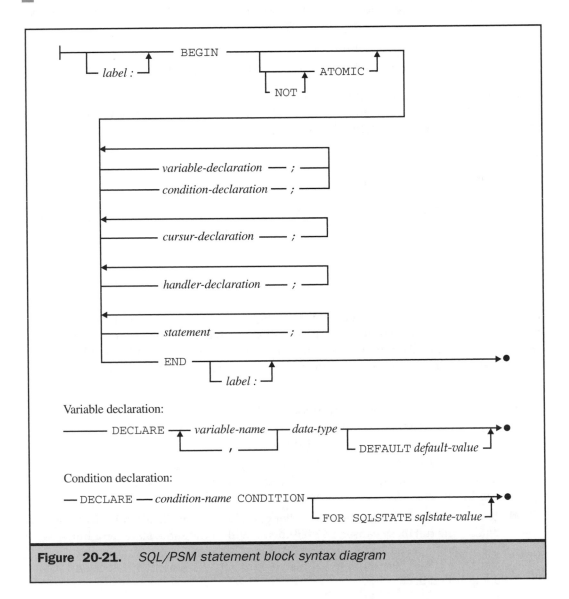

Figure 20-21.   *SQL/PSM statement block syntax diagram*

Error Handling

The block structure specified by the SQL/PSM standard provides fairly comprehensive support for error handling. The standard specifies predefined "conditions" that can be detected and handled, including:

- *SQLWARNING*. One of the warning conditions specified in the SQL2 standard
- *NOT FOUND*. The condition that normally occurs when the end of a set of query results is reached with a FETCH statement
- *SQLSTATE values*. A test for specific SQLSTATE error codes
- *User-defined conditions*. A condition named by the stored procedure

Conditions are typically defined in terms of SQLSTATE values. Rather than using numerical SQLSTATE codes, you can assign the condition a symbolic name. You can also specify your own user-defined condition:

```
declare bad_err condition for sqlstate '12345';
declare my_err condition;
```

Once the condition has been defined, you can force the condition to occur through the execution of a SQL routine with the SIGNAL statement:

```
signal bad_err;
signal sqlstate '12345';
```

To handle error conditions that may arise, SQL/PSM allows you to declare a *condition-handler*. The declaration specifies the list of conditions that are to be handled and the action to be taken. It also specifies one of four types of condition handling. The four types differ in what happens to the flow of control after the handler is finished with its work:

- *CONTINUE type*. After the condition handler completes its work, control returns to the next statement following the one that caused the condition. That is, execution *continues* with the next statement.
- *EXIT type*. After the condition handler completes its work, control returns to the *end* of the satement block containing the statement that caused the condition. That is, execution effectively *exits* the block.
- *UNDO type*. After the condition handler completes its work, all modifications to data in the database caused by statements within the same statement block as the statement causing the error are undone. The effect is the same as if a transaction had been initiated at the beginning of the statement block and was being rolled back.

Here are some examples that show the structure of the handler definition:

```
/* Handle SQL warnings here, then continue */
declare continue handler for sqlwarning
   call my_warn_routine();

/* Handle severe errors by undoing effects */
declare undo handler for user_disaster
   begin
      /* Do disaster cleanup here */
      . . .
   end;
```

Error handling can get quite complex, and it's possible for errors to arise during the execution of the handler routine itself. To avoid infinite recursion on errors, the normal condition signaling does not apply during the execution of a condition handler. The standard allows you to override this restriction with the RESIGNAL statement. It operates just like the SIGNAL statement previously described but is used exclusively within condition handler routines.

Routine Name Overloading

The SQL/PSM standard permits "overloading" of stored procedure and function names. Overloading is a common attribute in object-oriented systems and is a way to make stored routines more flexible in handling a wide variety of data types and situations. Using the overloading capability, several different routines can be given the *same* routine name. The multiple routines defined with the same name must differ from one another in the number of parameters that they accept or in the data types of the individual parameters. For example, you might define these three stored functions:

```
create function combo(a, b)
   a integer;
   b integer;
   returns integer;
   as return (a+b)

create function combo(a, b, c)
   a integer;
   b integer;
   c integer;
   returns integer;
   as return (a+b+c)
```

```
create procedure combo(a, b)
   a varchar(255);
   b varchar(255);
   returns varchar(255);
   as return (a || b)
```

The first COMBO function "combines" two integers by adding them and returns the sum. The second COMBO function "combines" three integers the same way. The third COMBO function "combines" two character strings by concatenating them. The standard allows both of these functions named COMBO to be defined at the same time within the database. When the DBMS encounters a reference to the COMBO function, it examines the number of arguments in the reference and their data types, and determines which version of the COMBO function to call. Thus, the overloading capability allows a SQL programmer to create a family of routines that logically perform the same function and have the same name, even though the specifics of their usage for different data types is different.

To simplify the management of a family of routines that share an overloaded name, the SQL/PSM standard has the concept of a *specific* name. A specific name is a second name that is assigned to the routine that *is* unique within the database schema or module. It uniquely identifies a specific routine. The specific name *is* used to drop the routine, and it is reflected in the Information Schema views that describe stored routines. The specific name is not used to call the routine; that would defeat the primary purpose of the overloaded routine name. Support for specific names is beginning to appear in commercial relational databases that support object-oriented features, such as Informix Universal Server.

Other Stored Procedure Considerations

The SQL/PSM standard adds one additional privilege to the set specified by the SQL2 standard. The EXECUTE privilege gives a user the ability to execute a stored procedure. It is managed by the GRANT and REVOKE statements in the same manner as other database privileges.

Because the stored routines defined by SQL/PSM are defined within SQL2 schemas, many routines can be defined in many different schemas throughout the database. When calling a stored routine, the routine name can be fully qualified to uniquely identify the routine within the database. The SQL/PSM standard provides an alternative method of searching for the definition of unqualified routine names through a new PATH concept.

The PATH is the sequence of schema names that should be searched to resolve a routine reference. A default PATH can be specified as part of the schema header in the CREATE SCHEMA statement. The PATH can also be dynamically modified during a SQL session through the SET PATH statement.

Summary

Stored procedures and triggers are two very useful capabilities for SQL databases used in transaction processing applications:

- Stored procedures allow you to predefine common database operations, and invoke them simply by calling the stored procedure, for improved efficiency and less chance of error.

- Extensions to the basic SQL language give stored procedures the features normally found in programming languages. These features include local variables, conditional processing, branching, and special statements for row-by-row query results processing.

- Stored functions are a special form of stored procedures that return a value.

- Triggers are procedures whose execution is automatically initiated based on attempted modifications to a table. A trigger can be fired by an INSERT, DELETE, or UPDATE statement for the table.

- There is wide variation in the specific SQL dialects used by the major DBMS brands to support stored procedures and triggers

- There is now an international standard for stored procedures (but not triggers); as one of the newer standards, it has not yet had a major impact on the actual implementation by leading DBMS vendors.

Chapter 21

SQL and Data Warehousing

One of the most important forces shaping relational database technology and the SQL language today is the rapidly growing area of data warehousing and business intelligence. The focus of data warehousing is to use accumulated data to provide information and insights for decision making. The rhetoric of data warehousing talks about an organization "treating its data as a valuable asset." The process of "data mining" involves in-depth analysis of historical and trend data to find "nuggets" of valuable insight. SQL-based relational databases are a key technology underlying data warehousing applications.

Business intelligence applications have exploded in popularity over the last decade. Corporate IS surveys show that the majority of large corporations have some type of business analysis or data warehousing projects underway. In many ways, data warehousing represents relational databases coming "full circle," back to their roots. When relational databases first appeared on the scene, the established databases (such as IBM's hierarchical IMS database) were squarely focused on business transaction processing applications. Relational technology gained popularity by focusing on "decision support" applications and their ad hoc queries. As the popularity of these applications grew, most relational database vendors shifted their focus to compete for new transaction processing applications. With data warehousing, attention has turned back to what was formerly called "decision support," albeit with new terminology and much more powerful tools than those of 15 years earlier.

Data Warehousing Concepts

One of the foundations of data warehousing is the notion that databases for transaction processing and databases for business analysis serve very different needs. The core focus of an OLTP (online transaction processing) database is to support the basic day-to-day functions of an organization. In a manufacturing company, OLTP databases support the taking of customer orders, ordering of raw materials, management of inventory, billing of customers, and similar functions. Their heaviest users are the applications used by order processing clerks, production workers, warehouse staff, and the like. By contrast, the core focus of a business intelligence (BI) database is to support business decision making through data analysis and reporting. Its heaviest users are typically product managers, production planners, and marketing professionals.

Table 21-1 highlights the significant differences in OLTP and business intelligence application profiles and the database workloads they produce. A typical OLTP transaction processing a customer's order might involve these database accesses:

- Read a row of the customer table to verify the proper customer number

- Check the credit limit for that customer

- Read a row of the inventory table to verify a product is available

- Insert a new row in an order table and an order-items table to record the customer's order

- Update the row of the inventory table to reflect the decreased quantity available

Database Characteristic	OLTP Database	Data Warehouse Database
Data contents	Current data	Historical data
Data structure	Tables organized to align with transaction structure	Tables organized to be easy to understand and query
Typical table size	Thousands of rows	Millions of rows
Access patterns	Predetermined for each type of transaction to be processed	*Ad hoc*, depending on the particular decision to be made
Rows accessed per "request"	Tens	Thousands to millions
Row coverage per access	Individual rows	Groups (summary queries)
Access rate	Many business transactions per second or minute	Many minutes or hours per query
Access type	Read, insert, and update	Almost 100 percent read
Performance focus	Transaction throughput	Query completion time

Table 21-1.   *OLTP versus Data Warehouse Database Attributes*

The workload presents a large volume of short, simple database requests that typically read, write, or update individual rows and then commit a transaction. The same type of workload is presented by all of the most frequent types of transactions, such as:

- Retrieving the price of a product
- Checking the quantity of product available
- Deleting an order
- Updating a customer address
- Raising a customer's credit limit

In contrast, a typical business analysis "transaction" (generating an order analysis report) might involve these database accesses:

- Join information from the orders, order-items, products, and customers tables
- Summarize the detail from the orders table by product in a summary query

- Compute the total order quantities for each product
- Sort the resulting information by customer

This workload presents a single, long-running query that is read-intensive. It processes many rows of the database (in this case, *every* order item) and involves computing totals and averages and summarizing data. These characteristics are typical of almost all business analysis queries, such as:

- Which regions had the best performance last quarter?
- How did sales by product last quarter compare to last year?
- What is the trend line for a particular product's sales?
- Drill down on high-growth products to see which customers are buying.
- What characteristics do those customers share?

The difference between the business intelligence and the OLTP workloads is substantial and makes it difficult or impossible for a single DBMS to serve both types of applications.

Components of a Data Warehouse

Figure 21-1 shows the architecture of a data warehousing environment. There are three key components:

- *Warehouse loading tools.* Typically a suite of programs that extract data from corporate transaction processing systems (relational databases, mainframe and minicomputer files, legacy databases), process it, and load it into the warehouse. This process typically involves substantial "cleanup" of the transaction data, filtering it, reformatting it, and loading it on a bulk basis into the warehouse.

- *A warehouse database.* Typically a relational database optimized for storing vast quantities of data, bulk loading data at high speeds, and supporting complex business analysis queries.

- *Data analysis tools.* Typically a suite of programs for performing statistical and time series analysis, doing "what if" analysis, and presenting the results in graphical form.

Vendors in the data warehousing market have tended to concentrate in one of these component areas. Several vendors build product suites that focus on the warehouse loading process and challenges. A different group of vendors have focused on data analysis. There has been some vendor consolidation in each of these areas, but both remain areas of focus for individual independent software companies, including several whose revenues are in the $100 million range.

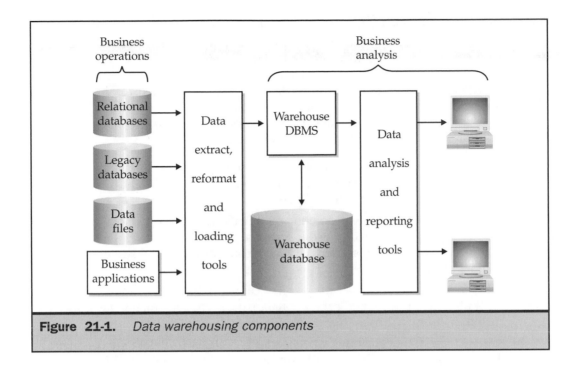

Figure 21-1.   *Data warehousing components*

Specialized warehouse databases were also the target of several startup companies early in the data warehousing market. Over time, the major enterprise DBMS vendors also moved to address this area. Some developed their own specialized warehouse databases; others added warehouse databases to their product line by acquiring smaller companies that produced them. Today the database component in the figure is almost always a specialized, SQL-based warehouse DBMS supplied by one of the major enterprise database vendors.

The Evolution of Data Warehousing

The initial focus of data warehousing was the creation of huge, enterprise-wide collections of "all" of the enterprise's accumulated data. By creating such a "warehouse" of data, almost any possible question about historical business practices could be posed. Many companies started down the road to creating warehouses with this approach, but success rates were low. Large, enterprise-wide warehouses generally proved too difficult to create, too big, and too unwieldy to use in practice.

The focus eventually turned to smaller data warehouses focused on specific areas of a business that could most benefit from in-depth data analysis. The term *data mart* was coined to describe these smaller (but still often massive) data warehouses. With the advent of multiple data marts within enterprises, a recent area of focus has been on management of distributed data marts. In particular, there is a large potential for duplication of effort in the data cleansing and reformatting process when there are multiple marts drawing data from the same production databases. The emerging answer seems to be a coordinated approach to data transformation for distributed marts, rather than a return to huge centralized warehouses.

Data warehousing, and more recently data marts, have grown to prominence in many different industries. They are most widely (and aggressively) used in industries where better information about business trends can be used to make decisions that save or generate large amounts of money. For example:

- *High-volume manufacturing.* Analysis of customer purchase trends, seasonality, and so on can help the company plan its production and lower its inventory levels, saving money for other purposes.

- *Packaged goods.* Analysis of promotions (coupons, advertising campaigns, direct mail, and so on) and the response of consumers with different demographics can help to determine the most effective way to reach prospective customers, saving millions of dollars in advertising and promotion costs.

- *Telecommunications.* Analysis of customer calling patterns can help to create more attractive pricing and promotional plans, perhaps attracting new customers from a competitor.

- *Airlines.* Analysis of customer travel patterns is critical to "yield management," the process of setting airfares and associated restrictions on available airline seats to maximize profitability.

- *Financial services.* Analysis of customer credit factors and comparing them to historical customer profiles can help to make better decisions about which customers are creditworthy.

Database Architecture for Warehousing

The structure (schema) of a warehouse database is typically designed to make the information easy to analyze, since that is the major focus of its use. The structure must make it easy to "slice and dice" the data along various dimensions. For example, one day a business analyst may want to look at sales by product category by region, to compare the performance of different products in different areas of the country. The next day, the same analyst may want to look at sales trends over time by region, to see which regions are growing and which are not. The structure of the database must lend itself to this type of analysis along several different dimensions.

Fact Cubes

In most cases, the data stored in a warehouse can be accurately modeled as an N-dimensional cube ("N-cube") of historical business facts. A simple, three-dimensional cube of sales data is shown in Figure 21-2 to illustrate the structure. The "fact" in each cell of the cube is a dollar sales amount. Along one edge of the cube, one of the "dimensions" is the month during which the sales took place. Another dimension is the region where the sales occurred. The third dimension is the type of product that was sold. Each cell in the cube represents the sales for one combination of these three dimensions. The $50,475 amount in the upper left front cell represents the sales amount for January, for Clothing, in the East region.

Figure 21-2 shows a simple three-dimensional cube, but in many warehousing applications, there will be a dozen dimensions or more. Although a 12-dimensional cube is difficult to visualize, the principles are the same as for the three-dimensional example. Each dimension represents some variable on which the data may be analyzed. Each combination of dimension values has one associated "fact" value, which is typically the historical business result obtained for that collection of dimension values.

To illustrate the database structures typically used in warehousing applications, we use a warehouse that might be found in a distribution company. The company distributes different types of products, made by various suppliers, to several hundred customers located in various regions of the country, through the efforts of its sales force. The company wants to analyze historical sales data along these dimensions, to discover

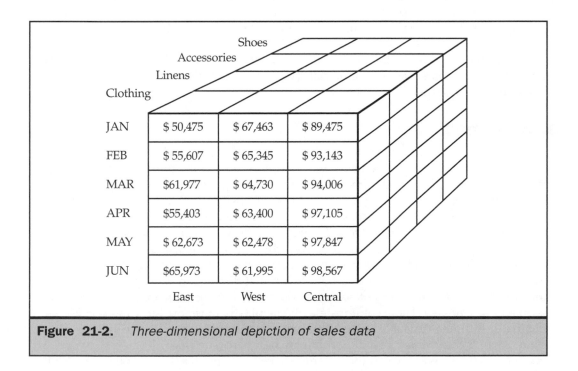

Figure 21-2.   *Three-dimensional depiction of sales data*

trends and gain insights that will help it better manage its business. The underlying model for this analysis will be a five-dimensional fact cube with these dimensions:

- *Category*. The category of product that was sold, with values such as Clothing, Linens, Accessories, and Shoes. The warehouse has about two dozen product categories.

- *Supplier*. The supplier who manufactures the particular product sold. The company might distribute products from 50 different suppliers.

- *Customer*. The customer who purchased the products. The company has several hundred customers. Some of the larger customers purchase products centrally and are serviced by a single salesperson; others purchase on a local basis and are served by local sales people.

- *Region*. The region of the country where the products were sold. Some of the company's customers operate in one region of the country only; others operate in two or more regions.

- *Month*. The month when the products were sold. For comparison purposes, the company has decided to maintain 36 months (three years) of historical sales data in the warehouse.

With these characteristics, each of the five dimensions is relatively independent of the others. Sales to a particular customer may be concentrated in a single region or in multiple regions. A specific category of product may be supplied by one or many different suppliers. The "fact" in each cell of the five-dimensional cube is the sales amount for that particular combination of dimension values. With the attributes described above, the fact cube contains over 35 million cells (24 categories × 50 suppliers × 300 customers × 3 regions × 36 months).

Star Schemas

In most data warehouses, the most effective way to model the N-dimensional fact cube is with a star schema. A star schema for the distributor warehouse in the previous example is shown in Figure 21-3. Each dimension of the cube is represented by a dimension table. There are five of them in the figure, named CATEGORIES, SUPPLIERS, CUSTOMERS, REGIONS, and MONTHS. There is one row in each dimension table for each possible value of that dimension. The MONTHS table has 36 rows, one for each month of sales history being stored. Three regions produce a three-row REGIONS table.

Dimension tables in a star schema often contain columns with descriptive text information or other attributes associated with that dimension (such as the name of the buyer for a customer, or the customer's address and phone number, or the purchasing terms for a supplier). These columns may be displayed in reports generated from the database. A dimension table always has a primary key that contains the value of the dimension. If the "values" of a dimension are numbers (such as a clothing size) or short text strings (such as a city name), the primary key may be this dimension value itself. It's more common for dimension values to be expressed in some type of "code-value."

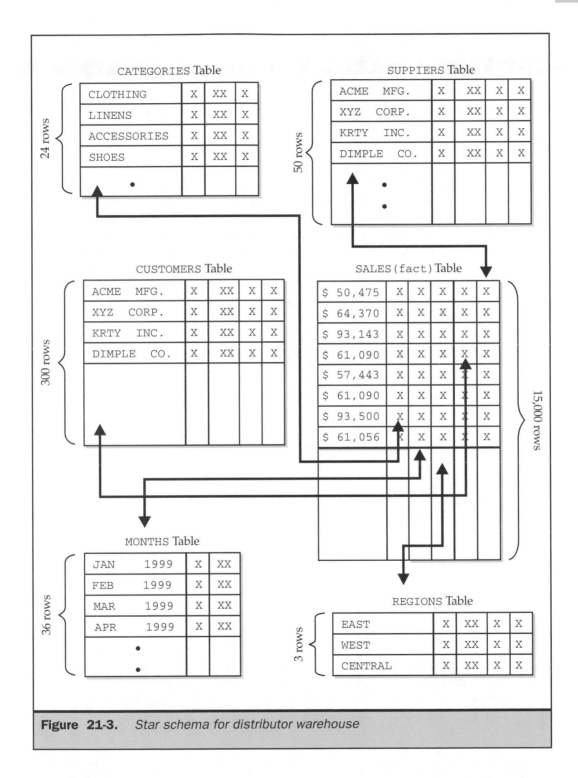

Figure 21-3. *Star schema for distributor warehouse*

Three-letter airport codes and customer numbers are typical examples. In the sample warehouse of Figure 21-3, we assume that actual values are used as primary keys for REGIONS (East, West, and so on), CATEGORIES (Clothing, Shoes, and so on), and MONTHS. The other two dimensions use coded values (CUST_CODE for CUSTOMERS, SUPP_CODE for SUPPLIERS).

The largest table in the database is the *fact table* in the center of the schema. This table is named SALES in Figure 21-3. The fact table contains a column with the data values that appear in the cells of the N-cube in Figure 21-2. In addition, the fact table contains a column (or columns) that forms a foreign key for each of the dimension tables. In this example, there are five such foreign-key columns. With this structure, each row represents the data for one cell of the N-cube. The foreign keys link the row to the corresponding dimension table rows for its position in the cube.

The fact table typically contains only a few columns, but many rows—hundreds of thousands or even millions of rows are not unusual in a production data warehouse. The "fact" column almost always contains numeric values, such as currency amounts, units shipped or received, or pounds processed. Virtually all reports from the warehouse involve summary data—totals, averages, high or low values, percentages—based on arithmetic computations on this numeric value.

The schema structure of Figure 21-3 is called a "star schema" for obvious reasons. The fact table is at the center of a "star" of data relationships. The dimension tables form the points of the star. The relationships created by the foreign keys in the fact table connect the center to the points. With the star-schema structure, most business analysis questions turn into queries that join the central fact table with one or more dimension tables. Here are some examples:

Show the total sales for Clothing in January, by region.

```
SELECT SALES_AMOUNT, REGION
  FROM SALES, REGIONS
 WHERE MONTH = 01/1999
   AND PROD_TYPE = "Clothing"
   AND SALES.REGION = REGIONS.REGION
 ORDER BY REGION
```

Show the average sales for each CUSTOMER, by SUPPLIER, for each month.

```
SELECT AVG(SALES_AMOUNT), CUST_NAME, SUPPLIER_NAME, MONTH
  FROM SALES, CUSTOMERS, SUPPLIERS
 WHERE SALES.CUST_CODE = CUSTOMERS.CUST_CODE
   AND SALES.SUPP_CODE = SUPPLIERS.SUPP_CODE
 GROUP BY CUST_NAME, SUPP_NAME
 ORDER BY CUST_NAME, SUPP_NAME, MONTH
```

Multi-Level Dimensions

In the star schema structure of Figure 21-3, each of the dimensions has only one level. In practice, multi-level dimensions are quite common. For example:

- Sales data may in fact be accumulated for each sales office. Each office is a part of a sales district, and each district is a part of a sales region.

- Sales data is accumulated by month, but it may also be useful to look at quarterly sales results. Each month is a part of a particular quarter.

- Sales data may be accumulated for individual products ordered, and the products are associated with a particular supplier.

Multi-level dimensions such as these complicate the basic star schema, and in practice there are several ways to deal with them:

- *Additional data in the dimension tables.* The geographic dimension table might contain information about individual offices, but also include columns indicating the district and region that the office belongs to. Aggregate data for these higher levels of the geographic dimension can then be obtained by summary queries that join the fact table to the dimension table and select based on the district or region columns. This approach is conceptually simple, but it means that all aggregate (summary) data must be calculated query-by-query. This likely produces unacceptably poor performance.

- *Multiple levels within the dimension tables.* The geographic dimension table might be extended to include rows for offices, districts, and regions. Rows containing summary (total) data for these higher-level dimensions are added to the fact table when it is updated. This solves the run-time query performance problem by precalculating aggregate (summary) data. However, it complicates the queries considerably. Since every sale is now included in three separate fact table rows (one each for office, district, and region), any totals must be computed very carefully. Specifically, the fact table must usually contain a "level" column to indicate the level of data summarization provided by that row, and *every* query that computes totals or other statistics must include a search condition that restricts it to rows at only a specific level.

- *Precomputed summaries in the dimension tables.* Instead of complicating the fact table, summary data may be precomputed and stored in the dimension tables (for example, summary sales for a district stored in the district's row of the geographic dimension table). This solves the "duplicate facts" problem of the previous solution, but it works only for very simple precomputed amounts. The precalculated totals don't help with queries about products by district or district results by month, for example, without further complicating the dimension tables.

■ *Multiple fact tables at different levels.* Instead of complicating the fact table, this approach creates multiple fact tables for different levels of summary data. To support cross-dimension queries (for example, district-results-by-month), specialized fact tables that summarize data on this basis are needed. The resulting pattern of dimension tables and fact tables tends to have many interrelationships, creating a pattern resembling a snowflake; hence, this type of schema is often referred to as a "snowflake schema." This approach solves the run-time performance problem and eliminates the possibility of erroneous data from a single fact table, but it can add significant complexity to the warehouse database design, making it harder to understand.

In practice, finding the right schema and architecture for a particular warehouse is a complicated decision, driven by the specifics of the facts and dimensions, the types of queries frequently performed, and other considerations. Many companies use specialized consultants to help them design data warehouses and deal with exactly these issues.

SQL Extensions for Data Warehousing

With a star schema structure, a relational database conceptually provides a good foundation for managing data for business analysis. The ability to freely relate information within the database based solely on data values is a good match for the *ad hoc*, unstructured queries that typify business intelligence applications. But there are some serious mismatches between typical business intelligence queries and the capabilities of the core SQL language. For example:

■ *Data ordering.* Many business intelligence queries deal explicitly or implicitly with data ordering—they pose questions like "what is the top 10 percent," "what are the top 10," or "which are the worst-performing." As a set-oriented language, SQL manipulates unordered sets of rows. The only support for sorting and ordering data within standard SQL is the ORDER BY clause in the SELECT statement, which is applied only at the end of all other set-oriented processing.

■ *Time series.* Many business intelligence queries compare values based on time—contrasting this year's results to last year's, or this month's results to the same month last year, or computing year-over-year growth rates, for example. It is very hard, and sometimes impossible, to get "side-by-side" comparisons of data from different time periods within a single row of standard SQL query results, depending on the structure of the underlying database.

■ *Comparison to aggregate values.* Many business intelligence queries compare values for individual entities (for example, office sales results) to an overall total, or to subtotals (such as regional results). These comparisons are difficult to express in standard SQL. A report format showing line-item detail, subtotals, and totals is impossible to generate directly from SQL, since all rows of query results must have the same column structure.

To deal with these issues, DBMS products on data warehousing have tended to extend the core SQL language. For example, the DBMS from Red Brick, one of the data warehousing pioneers and now a part of Informix's product line, features these extensions as part of its RISQL (Red Brick Intelligent SQL) language:

- *Ranking* supports queries that ask for the "top 10" and similar requests.

- *Moving totals and averages* support queries that smooth raw data for time series analysis.

- *Running totals and averages* allow query responses that show results for individual months plus year-to-date totals, and similar requests.

- *Ratios* allow queries that very simply express the ratio of individual values to a total or subtotal without the use of complex subqueries.

- *Decoding* simplifies the translation of dimension-value codes (like the supplier id in the example warehouse) into understandable names.

- *Subtotals* allow production of query results that combine detailed and summary data values, at various levels of summarization.

Other warehousing vendors provide similar extensions in their SQL implementations or provide the same capabilities built into their data analysis products. As with extensions in other areas of the SQL language, although the conceptual capabilities provided by several different DBMS brands may be similar, the specifics of the implementation differ substantially.

Warehouse Performance

The performance of a data warehouse is one of the keys to its usefulness. If business analysis queries take too long, people tend not to use the warehouse on an ad hoc basis for decision making. If it takes too long to load data into the warehouse, the corporate IS organization will probably resist frequent updates, and stale data may make the warehouse less useful. Achieving a good balance between load performance and run-time performance is one of the keys to successful warehouse deployment.

Load Performance

The process of loading a warehouse can be very time-consuming. It's not uncommon for warehouse data loads to take hours or even days for very large warehouses. Load processing typically involves these operations:

- *Data extraction*. The data to be loaded into the warehouse database typically comes from several different operational data sources. Some may be relational databases that support OLTP applications.

■ *Data cleansing*. Operational data tends to be "dirty" in the sense that it contains significant errors. For example, older transaction processing systems may not have strong integrity checks, permitting the entry of incorrect customer numbers or product numbers. The warehouse loading process typically includes data integrity and "data sanity" checks.

■ *Data cross-checking*. In many companies, the data processing systems that support various business operations have been developed at different times and are not integrated. Changes that are processed by one system (for example, adding new product numbers to an order processing application) may not automatically be reflected in other systems (for example, the inventory control system), or there may be delays in propagating changes. When data from these nonintegrated systems arrives at the warehouse, it must be checked for internal consistency.

■ *Data reformatting*. Data formats in the operational data stores may differ considerably from the warehouse database. Character data may need transformation from a mainframe's EBCDIC encoding to ASCII. Zoned decimal or packed decimal data may need reformatting. Date and time formats are another source of differences. Beyond these simple data format differences, data from one OLTP data source row may have to be broken apart into multiple warehouse tables, while data from multiple OLTP tables or files may have to be combined to create a warehouse table.

■ *Data insertion/update*. After the preprocessing, actual bulk loading of data into a warehouse database tends to be a specialized operation. High-volume data loaders typically operate in a batch-oriented mode, without transaction logic and with specialized recovery. Row loading or update rates of hundreds of megabytes per hour may be required.

■ *Index creation/update*. The specialized indexes used by the warehouse must be modified to reflect the revised warehouse contents. As with the actual data insertion and update, specialized handling is typically applied. In some cases, it is more efficient to rapidly recreate an entire index than to modify it incrementally as data rows are inserted or updated. Other index structures permit more incremental updates.

These tasks are typically performed by specialized warehouse-building programs on a batch processing basis. *Ad hoc* query access to the warehouse is turned off during the update/refresh processing, allowing it to proceed at maximum speed without competition for DBMS cycles. Despite these optimizations, warehouse load times tend to grow as the amount of accumulated data grows, so the load-time versus run-time performance tradeoff must be made on an ongoing basis. Warehouses with many indexes or precomputed summary values may offer much better run-time performance but at the expense of unacceptably long load times. Simpler structures with less loading work may increase the time required for *ad hoc* queries beyond an acceptable level. In practice, the warehouse administrator must find a good balance between loading and run-time query performance.

Query Performance

Database vendors focused on warehousing have invested considerable energy in optimizing their DBMS products to maximize query performance. As a result, warehousing performance has improved dramatically over the last several years. The growth in the size and complexity of warehouses has prevented some of this performance gain from actually being translated into perceived end-user benefit.

Several different techniques have evolved to maximize the performance of business analysis queries in a warehouse, including:

- *Specialized indexing schemes.* Typical business analysis queries involve a subset of the data in the warehouse, selected on the basis of dimension values. For example, a comparison of this month's and last month's results involves only two of the 36 months of data in the example warehouse. Specialized indexing schemes have been developed to allow very rapid selection of the appropriate rows from the fact table and joining to the dimension tables. Several of these involve bitmap techniques, where the individual possible values for a dimension (or a combination of dimensions) are each assigned a single bit in an index value. Rows meeting a selection criteria can be very rapidly identified by bitwise logical operations, which a computer system can perform more rapidly than value comparisons.

- *Parallel processing techniques.* Business analysis queries can often be broken up into parts that can be carried out in parallel, to reduce the overall time required to produce the final results. In a query joining four warehouse tables, for example, the DBMS might take advantage of a two-processor system by joining two of the tables in one process and two others in another. The results of these intermediate joins are then combined. Alternatively, the workload of processing a single table in the query might be split and carried out in parallel – for example, assigning rows for specific month-ranges to specific processes. The use of multiprocessor systems in these cases is quite different than for OLTP databases. For OLTP, the focus of multiprocessor operations is to increase overall throughput. For warehousing, the focus is usually the improvement in overall execution time in response to a single complex query.

- *Specialized optimizations.* When faced with a complex database query involving selection criteria and joins, the DBMS has many different sequences in which it can carry out the query. The optimizer for an OLTP database tends to benefit from the assumption that foreign key/primary key relationships should be exercised early in its processing, since they tend to cut down dramatically on the number of rows of intermediate results. The optimizer for a warehousing database may make a quite different decision, based on information accumulated during the load process about the distribution of data values within the database.

As with load-time performance, maximizing the run-time performance of a warehouse is an ongoing task for the database administrator. Newer revisions of DBMS software often provide performance benefits, as do higher-performance processors or more processors.

Summary

Data warehousing is a rapidly growing part of the market for SQL-based relational databases and is one with a set of specialized requirements:

- Warehouse databases are optimized for the workload of typical business analysis queries, which is quite different from OLTP workloads.

- Specialized utility programs provide high-performance loading of the warehouse and analysis tools for taking advantage of warehoused data.

- Specialized database schema structures, such as the star schema, are typically used in warehouse applications to support typical business analysis queries and optimize performance.

- SQL extensions are frequently used to support typical business analysis queries involving time series and trend analysis, rank orderings, and time-based comparisons.

- Careful design of a large warehouse is required to provide the correct balance between load-time performance and run-time performance.

Chapter 22

SQL Networking and Distributed Databases

751

One of the major computing trends through the late 1980s and late 1990s has been the move from large centralized computers to distributed networks of computer systems. With the advent of minicomputers, data processing tasks such as inventory control and order processing moved from corporate mainframes to smaller departmental systems. The explosive increase in the popularity of the personal computer brought computer power directly onto the desktops of millions of people.

With the widespread adoption of personal computers, organizations moved to connect them into local area networks (LANs), powered by hardware and software from companies like 3COM and Novell. Later, corporate IS organizations focused on interconnecting departmental LANs into large, enterprise-wide data networks, linked by routers and other network equipment from companies like Cisco Systems. The exploding popularity of the Internet added a new chapter, and a new era of growth, to computer networking. Today, the Internet creates a global, interconnected data network that is capable of linking computers and people around the world. The focus of computer networks has moved from the workgroup, to the organization, and beyond, to create a truly global network for accessing information, transmitting messages, and conducting electronic commerce.

As computers and computer networks have spread throughout and beyond organizations, computer data no longer resides on a single system under the control of a single DBMS. Instead, data within an organization is spread across many different systems, each with its own database manager. Often the various computer systems and database management systems come from different manufacturers. As companies try to interconnect their data processing systems via the Internet, the challenge becomes even greater. Even if a company has managed to standardize on a single, company-wide DBMS and on database structures, those standards won't apply to its suppliers or customers as it tries to build external links to conduct business electronically.

These trends have led to a strong focus in the computer industry and in the data management community on the problems of database management in a networked environment. This chapter discusses the challenges of managing distributed data, the variety of architectural approaches, and some of the products that DBMS vendors have offered to meet those challenges.

The Challenge of Distributed Data Management

When the foundations of relational database management and the SQL language were being laid in the 1970s, almost all commercial data processing happened on large, centralized computer systems. The company's data was stored on mass storage attached to the central system. The business programs that processed transactions and generated reports ran on the central system and accessed the data. Much of the workload of the central system was batch processing. Online users accessed the central system through "dumb" computer terminals with no processing power of their own. The central system formatted information to be displayed for the online user and accepted data typed by the user for processing.

In this environment, the roles of a relational database system and its SQL language were clear and well contained. The DBMS had responsibility for accepting, storing, and retrieving data based on requests expressed in the SQL language. The business processing logic resided *outside* the database and was the responsibility of the business programs developed and maintained by the information systems staff. The programs and the DBMS software executed on the same centralized system where the data was stored, so the performance of the system was not affected by external factors like network traffic or outside system failures.

Commercial data processing in a modern corporation has evolved a long way from the centralized environment of the 1970s. Figure 22-1 shows a portion of a computer network that you might find in a manufacturing company, a financial services firm, or a distribution company today. Data is stored on a variety of computer systems in the network:

- *Mainframes.* The company's core data processing applications, such as accounting and payroll, run on an IBM mainframe. The oldest applications, developed and maintained over the last 20 or 30 years, still store their data in hierarchical IMS databases. The company has a strategy to migrate these applications to DB2 over time, and all new mainframe applications development uses DB2 as its database manager.

- *Workstations and Unix-based servers.* The company's engineering organization uses Unix-based workstations and servers (from Sun Microsystems) for engineering design, testing, and support. Engineering test results and specifications are stored in an Oracle database. The company also uses Oracle databases running on Unix-based servers from Hewlett-Packard located in its six distribution centers to manage inventory and to process orders.

- *LAN servers.* All of the company's departments have individual PC local area networks (LANs) to share printers and files. Some of the departments also have local databases to support their work. For example, the personnel department has purchased a human resources management system software package, and it uses SQL Server on Windows NT to store its data. In the financial planning department, the data processing staff has built a custom-written corporate planning application, which uses Informix Universal Server.

- *Desktop personal computers.* All of the company's office workers use personal computers. Many of the administrative assistants and some of the senior managers maintain personal databases using Excel spreadsheets, Microsoft Access, or one of the lightweight DBMS products, such as Oracle Light. In a few cases, the databases are shared with other users, using LAN versions of these products.

- *Mobile laptop PCs.* The company recently purchased a sales force automation software package and equipped every salesperson with a laptop PC. The laptop runs sales presentations, sends and receives e-mail, and also holds a local lightweight database (SQL Anywhere from Sybase) with recent product pricing and availability data. The database also captures orders entered by the salesperson. At night, the laptop PC connects to the corporate network over a dial-up connection, transmits its orders, and receives updated information for its local copy of the products database.

- *Internet connections.* The company has an Internet Web site where customers, dealers, and distributors can find out the latest information about its products and services. At first, this was an "information-only" Web site, but competitors have recently begun accepting customer orders directly via the Internet. One of the corporate IS department's highest priorities is to respond to this competitive challenge by supporting e-commerce transactions on the company's Web site.

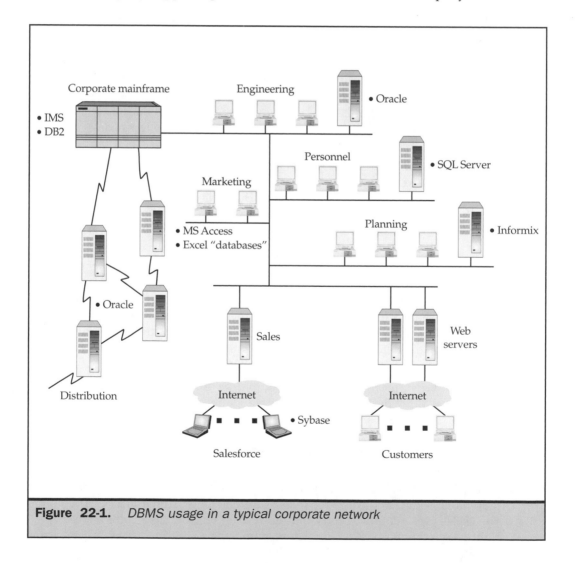

Figure 22-1.   *DBMS usage in a typical corporate network*

With data spread over many different systems, it's easy to imagine requests that span more than one database and the possibility for conflicting data among the databases:

- An engineer needs to combine lab test results (on an engineering workstation) with production forecasts (on the mainframe) to choose among three alternative technologies.

- A financial planner needs to link financial forecasts (in an Informix database) to historical financial data (on the mainframe).

- A product manager needs to know how much inventory of a particular product is in each distribution center (data stored on six Unix servers) to plan product obsolescence.

- Current pricing data needs to be downloaded daily from the mainframe to the distribution center servers, and also to all of the sales force's laptop computers.

- Orders need to be uploaded daily from the laptop systems and parceled out to the distribution centers; aggregate order data from the distribution centers must be uploaded to the mainframe so that the manufacturing plan can be adjusted.

- Salespeople may accept customer orders and make shipment date estimates for popular products based on their local databases, without knowing that other salespeople have made similar commitments. Orders must be reconciled and prioritized, and revised shipment estimates provided to customers.

- Engineering changes made in the workstation databases may effect product costs and pricing. These changes must be propagated through the mainframe systems and out to the Web site, the distribution centers, and the sales force laptops.

- Managers throughout the company want to query the various shared databases using the PCs on their desktops.

As these examples suggest, effective ways of distributing data, managing distributed data, and providing access to distributed data have become critical as data processing has moved to a distributed computing model. The leading DBMS vendors are committed to delivering distributed database management, and currently offer a variety of products that solve some of the distributed data problems illustrated by these examples. Distributed data management has also been the focus of extensive university and corporate research, and many technical articles have been published about the theory of distributed data management and the tradeoffs involved. There is general agreement among the researchers about the "ideal" characteristics that should be provided by a scheme to manage distributed databases:

- *Location transparency.* The user shouldn't have to worry about where the data is physically located. The DBMSs should present all data as if it were local and be responsible for maintaining that illusion.

- *Heterogeneous systems.* The DBMSs should support data stored on different systems, with different architectures and performance levels, including PCs, workstations, LAN servers, minicomputers, and mainframes.

- *Network transparency.* Except for differences in performance, the DBMSs should work the same way over different networks, from high-speed LANs to low-speed telephone links.

- *Distributed queries.* The user should be able to join data from any of the tables in the (distributed) database, even if the tables are located on different physical systems.

- *Distributed updates.* The user should be able to update data in any table for which the user has the necessary privileges, whether that table is on the local system or on a remote system.

- *Distributed transactions.* The DBMSs should support distributed transactions (using COMMIT and ROLLBACK) across system boundaries, maintaining the integrity of the (distributed) database even in the face of network failures and failures of individual systems.

- *Security.* The DBMSs must provide a security scheme adequate to protect the entire (distributed) database from unauthorized forms of access.

- *Universal access.* The DBMSs should provide universal, uniform access to all of the organization's data.

No current distributed DBMS product even comes close to meeting this ideal, and it's unlikely that any product ever will. In practice, formidable obstacles make it difficult to provide even simple forms of distributed database management. These obstacles include:

- *Performance.* In a centralized database, the path from the DBMS to the data has an access speed of a few milliseconds and a data transfer rate of millions of characters per second. Even on a fast local area network, access speeds lengthen to tenths of a second, and transfer rates fall to 100,000 characters per second or less. On a modem link, data access may take seconds or minutes, and a few thousand characters per second may be the maximum effective throughput. This vast difference in speeds can dramatically slow the performance of remote data access.

- *Integrity.* Distributed transactions require active cooperation by two or more independent copies of the DBMS software running on different computer systems if the transactions are to remain "all or nothing" propositions. Special "two-phase commit" transaction protocols must be used. These protocols generate a great deal of network traffic and lock parts of the databases that are participating in the distributed transaction for long periods of time.

- *Static SQL.* A static embedded SQL statement is compiled and stored in the database as an application plan. When a query combines data from two or more databases, where should its application plan be stored? Must there be two or more cooperating plans? If there is a change in the structure of one database, how do the application plans in the other databases get notified? Using dynamic SQL to solve these problems in a networked database environment almost always leads to unacceptably slow application performance, due to network overhead and delays.

- *Optimization.* When data is accessed across a network, the normal rules for SQL optimization don't apply. For example, it may be more efficient to sequentially scan an entire local table than to use an index search on a remote table. The optimization software must know about the network(s) and their speeds. Generally speaking, optimization becomes both more critical and more difficult.

- *Data compatibility.* Different computer systems support different data types, and even when two systems offer the same data type, they often use different formats. For example, a VAX and a Macintosh store 16-bit integers differently. IBM mainframes store EBCDIC character codes while minicomputers and PCs use ASCII. A distributed DBMS must mask these differences.

- *System catalogs.* As a DBMS carries out its tasks, it makes very frequent access to its system catalogs. Where should the catalog be kept in a distributed database? If it is centralized on one system, remote access to it will be slow, bogging down the DBMS. If it is distributed across many different systems, changes must be propagated around the network and synchronized.

- *Mixed-vendor environment.* It's highly unlikely that all the data in an organization will be managed by a single brand of DBMS, so distributed database access will cross DBMS brand boundaries. This requires active cooperation between DBMS products from highly competitive vendors—an unlikely prospect. As the DBMS vendors scramble to extend the capabilities of their products with new features, capabilities, and data types, the ability to sustain a cross-vendor standard is even less likely.

- *Distributed deadlocks.* When transactions on two different systems each try to access locked data on the other system, a deadlock can occur in the distributed database, even though the deadlock is not visible on either of the two systems. The DBMS must provide global deadlock detection for a distributed database. Again, this requires coordination of processing across a network and will typically lead to unacceptably slow application performance.

- *Recovery.* If one of the systems running a distributed DBMS fails, the operator of that system must be able to run its recovery procedures independent of the other systems in the network, and the recovered state of the database must be consistent with that of the other systems.

Distributing Data—Practical Approaches

Because of the formidable obstacles to realizing the "ideal" distributed database, DBMS vendors are taking a step-by-step approach to databases and networking. They have focused on specific forms of network database access, data distribution, and distributed data management that are appropriate for particular application scenarios. For example, a DBMS vendor may first provide tools to rapidly extract subset data from a "master" database and send it across a network for loading into a "slave" database. Later the vendor may enhance the tool to track updates to the master database since the last extract, and to extract and transmit only the changes to the master database. A subsequent version of the tool may automate the entire process, providing a graphical user interface for specifying the data to be extracted and scripts to automate the periodic extract process. Similarly, a DBMS may provide initial support for distributed queries by allowing a user on one system to query a database located on another system. In subsequent releases, the DBMS may allow the remote query as a subquery within a query that accesses local database tables. Still later, the DBMS may allow distributed queries that more freely intermix data from local and remote databases.

Remote Database Access

One of the simplest approaches to managing data stored in multiple locations is remote data access. With this capability, a user of one database is given the ability to "reach out" across a network and retrieve information from a different database. In its simplest form, this may involve carrying out a single query against the remote database, as shown in Figure 22-2. It may also involve performing an INSERT, UPDATE, or DELETE statement to modify the remote database contents. This type of requirement often arises when the local database is a "satellite" database (such as a database in a local sales office or distribution center) and the remote database is a central, corporate database.

In addition to the remote data access request, Figure 22-2 also shows a client/server request to the remote database from a (different) PC user. Note that, from the standpoint of the remote database, there is very little difference between processing the request from the PC client and processing the remote database access request. In both cases, a SQL request arrives across the network and the remote database determines that the user making the request has appropriate privileges and then carries it out. And, in both cases, the status of the SQL processing is reported back across the network.

The local database in Figure 22-2 must do some very different work than the process it normally uses to process local database requests, however. There are several complications for the local DBMS:

- It must determine which remote database the user wants to access, and how it can be accessed on the network.

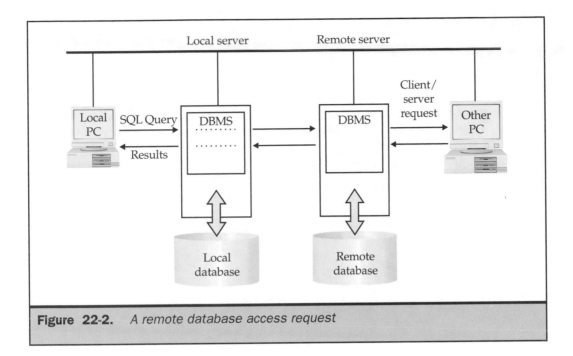

Figure 22-2. *A remote database access request*

- It must establish a connection to the remote database for carrying out remote requests.

- It must determine how the local user authentication and privilege scheme maps to the remote database. That is, does it simply pass the user name/password supplied for local database access to the remote database, or is a different "remote" user name/password supplied, or should some kind of automatic "mapping" be performed?

In effect, the local DBMS becomes an "agent" for the user making the remote access request. It becomes a client in a client/server connection to the remote DBMS.

Several of the leading enterprise DBMS vendors offer the kind of remote database access capability shown in Figure 22-2. They differ in the specific way that remote access is presented to the user and to the database administrator. In some cases, they involve extensions to the SQL language accepted by the DBMS. In others, the extra mechanisms for establishing remote access are mostly external to the SQL language.

Sybase Adaptive Server offers a simple entry-level remote database access capability as part of its Component Integration Services offering. While connected to a "local" Adaptive Server installation, the user can issue a CONNECT TO SQL statement, naming a remote server that is known to the local server. For example, if a remote server named CENTRALHOST contains a copy of the sample database, then this statement:

```
CONNECT TO CENTRALHOST
```

makes that remote server the "current" server for the session. The local server in effect enters a "passthrough" mode, sending all SQL statements to the remote server. The remote database can now be processed directly over the connection, with standard, unmodified queries and data manipulation statements:

Get the names and sales numbers of all salespeople who are already over quota.

```
SELECT NAME, QUOTA, SALES
  FROM SALESREPS
 WHERE SALES > QUOTA
```

When the remote access is completed, a companion SQL statement:

```
DISCONNECT
```

ends the passthrough mode, and the local server once again becomes the current server. Except for the CONNECT/DISCONNECT statement pair, all of the mechanism for managing remote access is external to the SQL language. The database administrator tells the local database about the existence, locations, and names of remote servers through the spaddserver() and spdropserver() system stored procedures. The current local user name and password are used by default for access to the remote server. Alternatively, the database administrator can specify a "proxy" user name/password that is used for remote server access, again through system stored procedures. Sybase offers other, more complex distributed database capabilities, but this basic capability has the advantage of maximum simplicity.

Oracle takes a somewhat different approach to remote database access, but one that is similar to the capabilities provided by other DBMS brands. It requires that Oracle's SQL*Net networking software be installed along with the Oracle DBMS on both the local and the remote system. The database administrator is responsible for establishing one or more named *database links* from the local database to remote databases. Each database link specifies:

- Network location of the target remote computer system
- Communications protocol to use
- Name of the Oracle database on the remote server
- Remote database user name and password

All remote database access occurs via a database link and is governed by the privileges of the supplied user name in the remote system. The database link thus embodies the answers to the "which database," "how to communicate," and "what privileges" questions raised earlier. The database administrator assigns the database link a name. Links can be private (created for use by a specific user of the local system) or public (available for use by multiple users of the local system).

To access a remote database over a database link, the local system user uses standard SQL statements. The name of the database link is appended to the remote table and view names, following an at sign (@). For example, assume you are on a local computer system that is connected to a copy of the sample database on a remote system over a database link called CENTRALHOST. This SQL statement retrieves information from the remote SALESREPS table:

Get the names and sales numbers of all salespeople who are already over quota.

```
SELECT NAME, QUOTA, SALES
  FROM SALESREPS@CENTRALHOST
 WHERE SALES > QUOTA
```

Oracle supports nearly all of the query capabilities that are available for the local database against remote databases (some object-oriented extensions in Oracle8 are not supported, but all of the core relational capabilities are). The only restriction is that every remote database entity (table, view, and so on) must be suffixed with the database link name. Here is a two-table join, executed on the remote Oracle database:

Get the names and office cities of all salespeople who are already over quota.

```
SELECT NAME, CITY, QUOTA, SALES
  FROM SALESREPS@CENTRALHOST, OFFICES@CENTRALHOST
 WHERE SALES > QUOTA
   AND REP_OFFICE = OFFICE
```

Oracle also supports data definition and database update operations carried out in the remote database. Here is an example:

Create a new remote table of high-credit-limit customer info in the remote database and populate it with data from the CUSTOMERS table.

```
CREATE TABLE HIGHCUST@CENTRALHOST
    (CUST_NUM INTEGER NOT NULL,
     COMPANY VARCHAR(20) NOT NULL,
     REP_NAME VARCHAR(15))
```

```
INSERT INTO HIGHCUST@CENTRALHOST
    SELECT CUST_NUM, COMPANY, NAME
      FROM CUSTOMERS@CENTRALHOST, SALESREPS@CENTRALHOST
     WHERE CREDIT_LIMIT > 50000.00
       AND CUST_REP = EMPL_NUM
```

Informix Universal Server provides capabilities that are similar to those offered by Oracle, but uses a different mechanism for identifying remote databases and a different SQL syntax extension. The Informix architecture differentiates between a remote database *server* and a remote *database* that is managed by the remote server, since it tends to provide rich support for multiple, named databases per server. Suppose an Informix copy of the sample database is called SAMPLE and it resides on a remote database server called CENTRALHOST. Then this query is equivalent to the previous Oracle and Sybase examples:

Get the names and sales numbers of all salespeople who are already over quota.

```
SELECT NAME, QUOTA, SALES
  FROM SAMPLE@CENTRALHOST:SALEREPS
 WHERE SALES > QUOTA
```

The database name appears at the *beginning* of the table name (as an additional "qualifier" before the colon). If the database is remote, then the server name appears following the at sign (@) after the database name.

Remote Data Transparency

With any of the remote database-naming conventions that extend the usual SQL table and view names, the additional qualifiers can quickly become annoying or confusing. For example, if two tables in the remote database have columns with the same names, any query involving both tables must use qualified column names—and the "tablename" qualifiers now have the remote database qualification as well. Here's a qualified Informix column name for the NAME column in the remote SALESREPS table owned by the user JOE in a remote database named SAMPLE on the remote Informix server CENTRALHOST:

```
SAMPLE@CENTRALHOST.JOE.SALESREPS.NAME
```

A single column reference has grown to half a line of SQL text! For this reason, table aliases are frequently used in SQL statements involving remote database access.

Synonyms and aliases (previously described in Chapter 16) are also very useful for providing more transparent access to remote databases. Here's an Informix synonym definition that could be established by a user or a database administrator:

```
CREATE SYNONYM REMOTE_REPS FOR SAMPLE@CENTRALHOST.JOE.SALESREPS
```

The equivalent Oracle synonym definition is:

```
CREATE SYNONYM REMOTE_REPS FOR JOE.SALESREPS@CENTRALHOST
```

With this synonym in place, the preceding qualified column name becomes simply:

```
REMOTE_REPS.NAME
```

Any query referencing the REMOTE_REPS "table" and its columns is actually a remote database query, but that fact is transparent to the user. In practice, most database installations with frequently accessed remote tables will have a set of synonyms defined for them. Most of the DBMS brands support both "public" synonyms (available to all users) and "private" synonyms that are created for a specific user or group of users. With this structure, synonyms can become an additional part of the remote access security mechanism, limited to only those users with a real need for remote access.

Several DBMS brands take the synonym capability for transparent database access one step further and permit *views* in the local database that are defined in terms of remote database tables. Here is an Oracle view definition that creates a view called EAST_REPS in the local database. The view is a subset of information from the remote sample database:

Create a local view defined in terms of two remote tables.

```
CREATE VIEW EAST_REPS AS
    SELECT EMPL_NUM, NAME, AGE, CITY
      FROM SALESREPS@CENTRALHOST, OFFICES@CENTRALHOST
     WHERE REP_OFFICE = OFFICE
       AND REP_OFFICE BETWEEN 11 AND 19
```

After this view has been defined, a user can pose queries in terms of the EAST_REPS view, without worrying about database links or remote table names. The view not only provides transparent remote access, but also "hides" from the user the remote join operation between the OFFICES and SALESREPS tables.

Transparent access to remote data, provided by views and synonyms, is usually considered a very desirable characteristic. It does have one drawback, however. Because the remote aspect of the database access is now hidden, the network overhead created by the access is also hidden. Therefore, the possibility of a user or programmer inadvertently creating a great deal of network traffic through very large queries is increased. The database administrator must make this tradeoff when deciding whether to permit remote transparent synonyms and views.

Transparent remote access also inevitably raises one additional question: since the remote tables now appear as if they are local, can the user pose queries that involve *both* remote and local tables? That is, can a join cross the database server boundaries and relate information from the remote database and the local database? Even more serious questions are posed when the SQL transaction scheme is considered. If a database permits transparent access to a remote database, then is a user allowed to update a row in the local database *and* insert a row in the remote database, and then decide to rollback the transaction? Since the remote resources have been made to appear as if they are local, the "obvious" answer to the question is: "of course—the local and remote databases together should appear as if they were just one local, integrated database."

In fact, supporting such distributed queries and transactions adds a major new level of complexity (and potentially huge network data transmission overhead) to the remote access. Because of this, although several commercial DBMS systems support distributed queries and transactions, they are not heavily used in practice. These capabilities, and their overhead implications, are more fully discussed later in this chapter. The next section discusses a practical alternative—duplicating data, or database replication—that is much more frequently used in practice.

Table Extracts

Remote database access is very convenient for small remote queries and occasional remote database access. If an application requires heavy and frequent access to a remote database, however, the communications overhead of remote database access can become large. Once remote access grows beyond a certain point, it is often more efficient to maintain a local *copy* of the remote data in the local database. Many of the DBMS vendors provide tools to simplify the process of data extraction and distribution. In its simplest form, the process extracts the contents of a table in a "master" database, sends it across a network to another system, and loads it into a corresponding "replica" table in a "slave" database, as shown in Figure 22-3. In practice, the extract is performed periodically and during off-peak times of database activity.

This approach is very appropriate when the data in the replicated table changes slowly, or when changes to the table naturally occur in a batch. For example, suppose some tables of the sample database, located on a remote central computer system, are to be replicated in a local database. The contents of the OFFICES table hardly ever change. It would be an excellent candidate for replication onto distribution center or

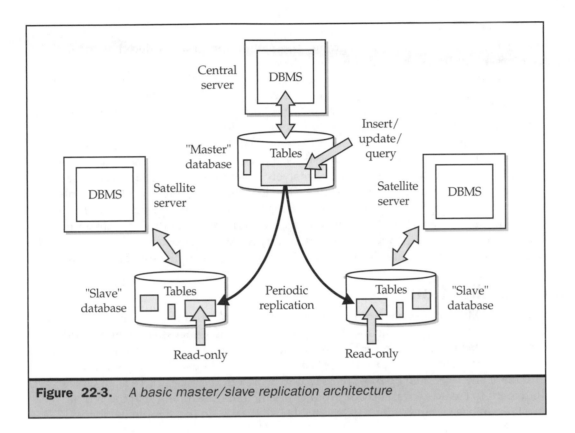

Figure 22-3.   *A basic master/slave replication architecture*

sales force automation databases. Once the initial (local) replica tables are set up and populated, they might need to be updated only once per month, or when a new sales office is opened.

The PRODUCTS table is also a good candidate for replication. Product price changes occur more frequently than office changes, but in most companies, they happen in batches, perhaps once a week or once a day. With this natural processing cycle, it would be very effective to extract a table of product price data just after each batch of updates, and send it to the distribution center databases and the sales force automation central database. The price data in these databases does not need to be tightly linked to the mainframe database to insure that it is fresh. A weekly or daily extract/update cycle will make the data just as current, with substantially less processing workload.

It's possible to implement this type of replicated-table strategy without any support from the DBMS. You could write an application program that uses SQL on the mainframe to extract the product pricing data into a file. A file transfer program could transmit the file to the distribution centers, where another application program could read its contents and generate the appropriate DROP TABLE, CREATE TABLE, and INSERT statements to populate the replicated table.

The first step toward automating this strategy was the development of high-speed data extract and data loading programs. These utility programs, offered by the DBMS vendors, typically use proprietary, lower-level database access techniques to extract the data and load the data much more rapidly than is possible through SQL SELECT and INSERT statements. More recently, software companies have targeted this area as an opportunity for standalone software packages, independent of the DBMS vendors. This category of software, called "Enterprise Application Integration" (EAI) software, focuses on linking disparate computer systems, software packages, database systems, and file formats. Linking different DBMS systems is a small part of the total solution offered by these systems, which are extensively customized to meet an individual company's needs when they are installed. The EAI systems typically offer a graphical user interface for specifying the data extraction, an array of tools for reformatting data between the source and destination systems, a messaging capability for transmitting the data, perhaps a store-and-forward capability for staging extracted data before and after transmission, and utilities for managing and monitoring the overall process.

Table Replication

Several DBMS vendors have moved beyond their extract and load utility programs to offer support for table extraction within the DBMS itself. Oracle8, for example, offers a "snapshot" facility to automatically create a local copy of a remote table. In its simplest form, the local table is a read-only replica of the remote "master" table, which is automatically refreshed by the Oracle DBMS on a periodic basis. Here is an Oracle SQL statement to create a local copy of product pricing data, assuming that the remote master database includes a PRODUCTS table like the one in the sample database:

Create a local replica of pricing information from the remote PRODUCTS table.

```
CREATE SNAPSHOT PRODPRICE
        AS SELECT MFR_ID, PRODUCT_ID, PRICE
           FROM PRODUCTS@REMOTE_LINK
```

This statement effectively creates a local Oracle table named PRODPRICE. It contains three columns, specified by the SELECT statement against the remote (master) database. The at sign and name REMOTE_LINK in the statement tell Oracle that the PRODUCTS table from which the data is to be replicated is a remote table, accessible via the Oracle database link named REMOTE_LINK. The Oracle database administrator sets up these remote database links as part of the distributed Oracle capabilities that are required to use the snapshot feature. Finally, the CREATE SNAPSHOT statement will actually cause the local PRODPRICE snapshot table to be populated with data from the remote PRODUCTS table.

With this type of read-only snapshot, users are not allowed to change the snapshot table with INSERT, UPDATE, or DELETE statements. All database updates occur in the master (remote) table and are propagated to the replicated (snapshot) table by Oracle. The database administrator can manually refresh the snapshot table as desired. The CREATE SNAPSHOT statement also includes rather comprehensive facilities for specifying automatic refreshes. Here are some examples:

Create a local replica of pricing information from the remote PRODUCTS table. Refresh the data once per week, with a complete reload of the data.

```
CREATE SNAPSHOT PRODPRICE
        REFRESH COMPLETE START WITH SYSDATE NEXT SYSDATE+7
            AS SELECT MFR_ID, PRODUCT_ID, PRICE
                FROM PRODUCTS@REMOTE_LINK
```

Create a local replica of pricing information from the remote PRODUCTS table. Refresh the data once per day, sending only changes from the master table.

```
CREATE SNAPSHOT PRODPRICE
        REFRESH FAST START WITH SYSDATE NEXT SYSDATE+1
            AS SELECT MFR_ID, PRODUCT_ID, PRICE
                FROM PRODUCTS@REMOTE_LINK
```

In the latter example, the snapshot is refreshed by transmitting only changes from the remote PRODUCTS table. Oracle implements this capability by maintaining a log of changes (a "snapshot log") on the remote system and updating the log every time an update to the PRODUCTS table would effect the snapshot replica. When the time for a refresh arrives, information from the snapshot log is used. For applications like this one, where product price changes probably affect only a small percentage of the overall table, this strategy is effective. The additional overhead of maintaining the log for the master table is more than offset by the reduced network traffic of transmitting only changed data. In other applications, where a large percentage of the rows in the master table will be modified between refreshes, it may be more efficient to simply do a complete refresh and eliminate the overhead of maintaining the snapshot log. By default, Oracle identifies rows (to determine whether they are "changed") based on their primary key. If the primary key is not part of the replicated data, this can cause confusion about which rows have been updated; in this case, Oracle uses an internal row-id number to identify the modified rows for refreshes to the snapshot.

The SELECT statement that defines the snapshot table offers a very general capability for data extraction. It can include a SELECT clause to extract only selected rows of the master table:

Create a local replica of pricing information for high-priced products from the remote PRODUCTS table. Refresh the data once per day, sending only changes from the master table.

```
CREATE SNAPSHOT PRODPRICE
        REFRESH FAST START WITH SYSDATE NEXT SYSDATE+1
            AS SELECT MFR_ID, PRODUCT_ID, PRICE
                FROM PRODUCTS@REMOTE_LINK
                WHERE PRICE > 1000.00
```

Note that this makes maintaining the snapshot log more complex. Oracle does not need to add to the log all updates to the PRODUCTS table; only those that modify rows that meet the search criterion. The snapshot can also be created as a joined table, extracting its data from two or more "master" tables in the remote database:

Create a local replica of salesperson data, refreshed weekly.

```
CREATE SNAPSHOT SALESTEAM
        REFRESH FAST START WITH SYSDATE NEXT SYSDATE+7
            AS SELECT NAME, QUOTA, SALES, CITY
                FROM SALESREPS@REMOTE, OFFICES@REMOTE
                WHERE REP_OFFICE = OFFICE
```

Adding to the complexity, the snapshot can be defined by a grouped query:

Create a local summary of customer order volume, refreshed daily.

```
CREATE SNAPSHOT CUSTORD
        REFRESH FAST START WITH SYSDATE NEXT SYSDATE+1
            AS SELECT COMPANY, SUM(AMOUNT)
                FROM CUSTOMERS@REMOTE, ORDERS@REMOTE
                WHERE CUST = CUST_NUM
```

Of course, with each level of additional complexity, the overhead of managing the snapshot and the replication process increases. Regardless of how simple or complex the definition of the snapshot, however, the overall principles remain the same. Instead of having queries against the replicated data travel across the network to the remote database, the remote data is "brought down" into the snapshot. The refreshes to the snapshot still generate network traffic, but the day-to-day queries against the snapshot data are carried out locally and do not generate network traffic. For situations where the query workload is much higher than the overhead of maintaining the snapshot, this can be an effective way to improve overall database performance.

Updateable Replicas

In the simplest implementations, a table and its replicas have a strict master/slave relationship, as shown in Figure 22-3. The central/master copy contains the "real" data. It is always up to date, and all updates to the table must occur on this copy of the table. The other slave copies are populated by periodic updates, managed by the DBMS. Between updates, they may become slightly out of date, but if the database is configured in this way, then it is an acceptable "price to pay" for the advantage of having a local copy of the data. Updates to the slave copies are not permitted. If attempted, the DBMS returns an error condition.

By default, the Oracle CREATE SNAPSHOT statement creates this type of "slave" replica of a table. The master/slave relationship is implicit in the Microsoft SQL Server structure for replication. The SQL server architecture defines the master as the "publisher" of the data and the slaves as "subscribers" to the data. In the default configuration, there is a single (updateable) publisher, and there may be multiple (read-only) subscribers. The SQL Server architecture carries this analogy one step further, supporting both the notion of "push" updates (the publisher actively sends the update data to the subscribers) and "pull" updates (where the subscribers have primary responsibility for getting updates from the publisher).

There are some applications for which table replication is an excellent technique, but where the master/slave relationship does not apply. For example, applications that demand high availability use replicated tables to maintain identical copies of data on two different computer systems. If one system fails, the other contains current data and can carry on processing. An Internet application may demand very high database access rates, and achieve this scalability by replicating a table many times on different computer systems and then spreading out the workload across the systems. A sales force automation application will probably contain one central CUSTOMER table and hundreds of replicas on laptop systems, and individual salespeople should be able to enter new customers or change customer contact information on the laptop replicas. In these configurations (and others), the most efficient use of the computer resources is achieved if *all* of the replicas can accept updates to the table, as shown in Figure 22-4.

A replicated table where multiple copies can accept updates creates a new set of data integrity issues. What happens if the same row of the table is updated in one or more replicas? When the DBMS tries to synchronize the replicas, which of the two updates should apply, or should neither apply or both? What happens if a row is deleted from one copy of the table, but it is updated in another copy of the table?

In DBMS systems that support updateable replicas, these issues are addressed by creating a set of conflict resolution rules that are applied by the replication system. For example, when replication is set up between a central CUSTOMER table and laptop versions of the table, the replication rule may say that changes to the central customer database always "win" over changes entered on a laptop system. Alternatively, the replication rule might say that the most recent update always wins. In addition to the built-in rules provided by the DBMS itself, the replication definition may include the

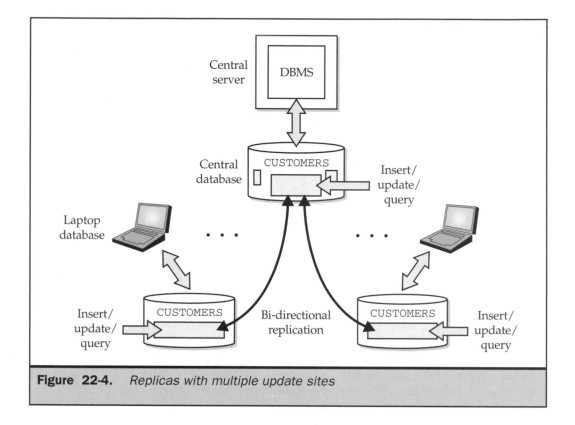

Figure 22-4. *Replicas with multiple update sites*

capability to pass conflicts to a user-written procedure (such as a stored procedure within the database) for selection of the "winner" and "loser" replicas.

Replication Tradeoffs

Practical replication strategies always involve a tradeoff between the desire to keep data as current as possible and the desire to keep network traffic down to a practical level and provide adequate performance. These tradeoffs usually involve not just technical considerations, but business practices and policies as well. For example, consider an order processing application using the sample database, and assume that order processing is distributed across five different call centers that are geographically distributed around the world. Each call center has its own computer system and database. Incoming orders are checked against the PRODUCTS table to be certain that enough inventory is on hand to fill the order. The PRODUCTS table keeps track of product-on-hand quantities for all of the company's warehouses, worldwide.

Suppose the company's policy is that the order processing clerk must be able to absolutely guarantee a customer that products can be shipped within 24 hours of the time an order is accepted. In this case, the PRODUCTS table must contain absolutely up-to-the-minute data, reflecting the inventory impact of orders taken just seconds earlier. There are only two possible designs for the database in this case. There could be a single, central copy of the PRODUCTS table, shared by all users at all five order processing sites. Alternatively, there could be a fully mirrored copy of the PRODUCTS table at each of the five sites. The fully mirrored solution is almost certainly impractical because the frequent updates to the PRODUCTS table as each order is taken will cause excessive network traffic to keep the five copies of the table in perfect synchronization.

But suppose the company believes it can still maintain adequate customer satisfaction with a policy that is slightly less strict—for example, it promises to notify any customer within 24 hours if their order cannot be filled immediately and give the customer an opportunity to cancel the order. In this case, a replicated PRODUCTS table becomes an excellent solution. Once a day, updates to the PRODUCTS table can be downloaded to the replicated copy at each of the five sites. During the day, orders are verified against the *local copy* of the PRODUCTS table, but only the local PRODUCTS table is updated. This prevents the company from taking an order for which there was not adequate stock on hand at the beginning of the day, but it does not prevent orders taken at two or three different sites from exceeding the available stock. The next night, when data communications costs are lower than they are during the day, the orders from each site are transmitted to a central site, which processes them against a central copy of the PRODUCTS table. Orders that cannot be filled from inventory are flagged, and a report of them is generated. When processing is complete, the updated PRODUCTS table, along with the "problem orders report," is transmitted back to each of the five sites to prepare for the next day's processing.

Which is the "correct" architecture for supporting the operation of this global business? As the example shows, it is not so much a database architecture question as a business policy question. The interdependence of computer systems architectures and business operations is one of the reasons why decisions about replication and data distribution inevitably make certain types of business operations easier and others harder.

Typical Replication Architectures

In many cases, it's possible to structure an application that involves replicated data so that conflicts between replica updates are avoided or greatly minimized. The DBMS conflict resolution rules are then applied as a last resort, when a conflict arises despite the design of the application. The next few sections describe some typical replicated table scenarios and the application structure that is often used in each scenario to minimize replication conflicts.

Horizontal Table Subsets

One efficient way to replicate parts of a table across a network is to divide the table horizontally, placing different rows of the table on different systems. Figure 22-5 shows

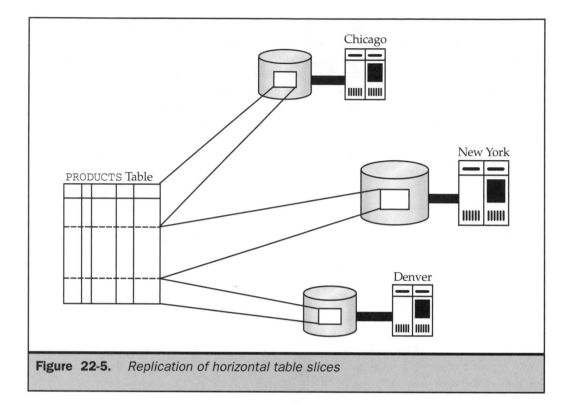

Figure 22-5. *Replication of horizontal table slices*

a simple example where a horizontal table split is useful. In this application, a company operates three distribution centers, each with its own computer system and DBMS to manage an inventory database and order processing. A central database is also maintained for production planning purposes.

To support this environment, the PRODUCTS table is split horizontally into three parts and expanded to include a LOCATION column that tells where the inventory is located. The central copy of the table contains all of the rows. The rows of the table that describe inventory in each distribution center are replicated in the local database managed by that center's DBMS.

In this case, most updates to the PRODUCTS table take place at the distribution center itself, as it processes orders. Because distribution center replicas are mutually exclusive (that is, a row from the PRODUCTS table appears in only one distribution center replica), update conflicts are avoided. The replicas in the distribution center can periodically transmit updates to the central database to keep it up to date.

Vertical Table Subsets

Another efficient way to manage table replication is to divide the table vertically, replicating different columns of the table on different systems. Figure 22-6 shows a simple example of a vertical table split. The SALESREPS table has been expanded to

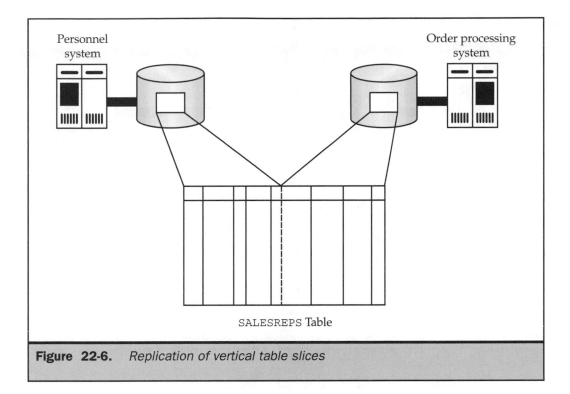

Figure 22-6. *Replication of vertical table slices*

include new columns of personnel information (phone number, marital status, and so on), and its information is needed in two databases—one in the order processing department and the other in the personnel department. Most of the activity in each department focuses on one or two columns of the table, but many queries and reports use both personnel-related and order-related columns.

To accommodate this application, the SALESREPS table is replicated on both systems, but conceptually it is split vertically into two parts. The columns of the table that store personnel data (NAME, AGE, HIRE_DATE, PHONE, MARRIED) are "owned" by the personnel system. It wins any conflicts related to updates on these columns. The other columns (EMPL_NUM, QUOTA, SALES, REP_OFFICE) are "owned" by the order processing system. It wins update conflicts related to these columns. Because the entire table is replicated on both systems, either system can be used to generate reports and handle *ad hoc* inquiries, and all of these can be processed locally. Only updates involve the replication mechanism, generate network traffic, and potentially require conflict resolution.

Mirrored Tables

When table replication is used to achieve high availability (that is, resistance to computer or database failure), the entire table is typically mirrored, as shown in Figure 22-7. The easiest way to implement this configuration is if one system is the "active"

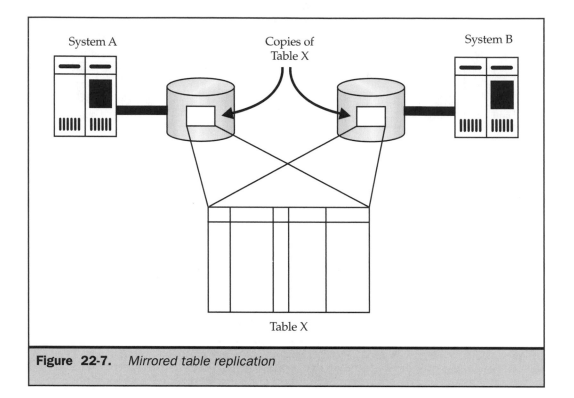

Figure 22-7. *Mirrored table replication*

system and another is a "hot standby." In this scheme, all database access normally flows to the active system (System A), which replicates any updates to the standby system (System B). Only in the event of system failure does the database access switch over to the standby system, but it has "fresh" data because of the replicated table. The disadvantage of this scheme is that it "wastes" the standby computer system under normal operation. The system must be paid for and maintained, but it doesn't add any data processing capacity.

For this reason, high-availability systems are often designed to also provide load balancing, as shown in Figure 22-8. In this configuration, some "front-end" software intercepts DBMS access requests and evenly distributes them between the two (or more) computer systems. Under normal operation, both (all) systems contribute data processing power; none is "wasted." Furthermore, it's conceptually easy to grow the data processing power, simply by adding more computer systems with a copy of the replicated table.

This type of mirrored table approach can be highly effective if the ratio of database queries to database updates is very high (for example, 95 percent read access/5 percent

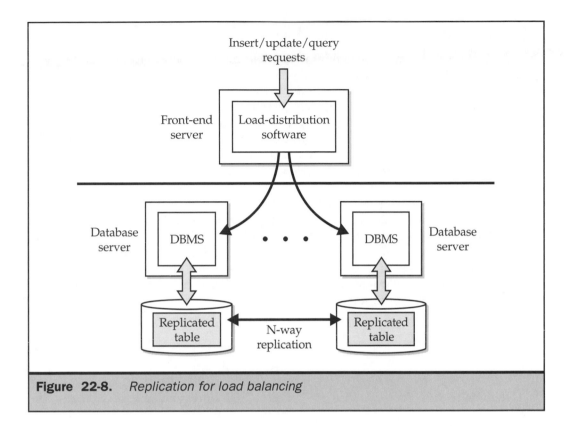

Figure 22-8.   *Replication for load balancing*

update access). If the percentage of updates is higher, the potential for conflicts and the replication overhead can diminish the effectiveness and scalability of the overall configuration. Efficiency also decreases with each increase in the number of replicated systems, since the replication overhead rises.

One common way to get more efficiency out of a mirrored table configuration like the one in Figure 22-8 is to divide updates to the table based on some rule. For example, if the mirrored table is a customer table, the primary key may be the customer name. The "front-end" load balancing software can then be written so that updates for customer names starting with "A" through "M" are routed to the one system and updates for customer names starting with "N" through "Z" are routed to the other system. This eliminates the possibility of update conflicts. Because the table remains fully replicated under this scenario, read access requests can still be distributed randomly between the two systems to balance the workload. This type of approach can be quite effective in achieving scalable database performance with replicated tables.

Distributed Database Access

Over the last several years, research into fully distributed database access has slowly but surely found its way into commercial products. Today many of the mainstream enterprise database products offer at least some level of transparent distributed database access. As noted earlier in the chapter, the performance implications of distributed database access and updates can be very substantial. Two very similar-looking queries can create massively different amounts of network traffic and overhead. A single query, carried out in a "brute force" method or an "optimized" method can create the same differences, depending on the quality of the optimization done by the DBMS.

Because of these challenges, all of the vendors have taken a step-by-step approach to delivering distributed database access. Several years ago, IBM announced its blueprint for its SQL products and has been steadily implementing it. IBM was not the first vendor to offer distributed data access, and it is not the vendor with the most advanced distributed DBMS capability today, but IBM's four stages, shown in Table 22-1, provide an excellent framework for understanding distributed data management capabilities and their implications.

Stage	Description
1. Remote request	Each SQL statement accesses a single remote database; each statement is a transaction.
2. Remote transaction	Each SQL statement accesses a single remote database; multi-statement transactions are supported for a single database.
3. Distributed transaction	Each SQL statement accesses a single remote database; multi-statement transactions are supported across multiple databases.
4. Distributed request	SQL statement may access multiple databases; multi-statement transactions are supported across multiple databases.

Table 22-1. *IBM's Four Stages of Distributed Database Access*

The IBM scheme provides a simple model for defining the distributed data access problem: a user of one computer system needs to access data stored on one or more other computer systems. The sophistication of the distributed access increases at each stage. Thus the capabilities provided by a given DBMS can be described in terms of which stage it has reached. In addition, within each stage a distinction can be made between read-only access (with the SELECT statement) and update access (with the INSERT, DELETE, and UPDATE statements). A DBMS product often provides read-only capability for a given stage before full update capability is provided.

Remote Requests

The first stage of distributed data access, as defined by IBM, is a *remote request*, shown in Figure 22-9. In this stage, the PC user may issue a SQL statement that queries or updates data in a single remote database. Each individual SQL statement operates as its own transaction, similar to the "auto-commit" mode provided by many interactive SQL programs. The user can issue a sequence of SQL statements for various databases, but the DBMS doesn't support multi-statement transactions.

Remote requests are very useful when a PC user needs to query corporate data. Usually the required data is located within a single database, such as a database of order processing or manufacturing data. Using a remote request, the PC program can retrieve the remote data for processing by a PC spreadsheet, graphics program, or desktop publishing package.

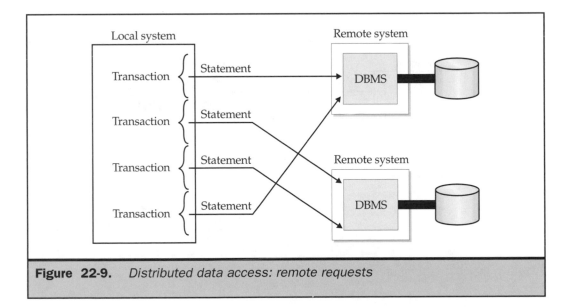

Figure 22-9. *Distributed data access: remote requests*

The remote request capability is not powerful enough for most transaction processing applications. For example, consider a PC-based order entry application that accesses a corporate database. To process a new order, the PC program must check inventory levels, add the order to the database, decrease the inventory totals, and adjust customer and sales totals, involving perhaps half a dozen different SQL statements. As explained in Chapter 11, database integrity can be corrupted if these statements do not execute as a single transaction. However, the remote request stage does not support multi-statement transactions, so it cannot support this application.

Remote Transactions

The second stage of distributed data access, as defined by IBM, is a *remote transaction* (called a "remote unit of work" by IBM), shown in Figure 22-10. Remote transactions extend the remote request stage to include multi-statement transaction support. The PC user can issue a series of SQL statements that query or update data in a remote database and then commit or roll back the entire series of statements as a single transaction. The DBMS guarantees that the entire transaction will succeed or fail as a unit, as it does for transactions on a local database. However, all of the SQL statements that make up the transaction must reference a single remote database.

Remote transactions open the door for distributed transaction processing applications. For example, in an order processing application, a PC-based order entry program can now perform a sequence of queries, updates, and inserts in the inventory database to process a new order. The program ends the statement sequence with a COMMIT or ROLLBACK for the transaction.

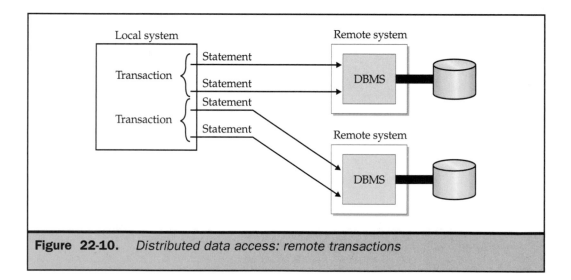

Figure 22-10. *Distributed data access: remote transactions*

Remote transaction capability typically requires a DBMS (or at least transaction processing logic) on the PC as well as the system where the database is located. The transaction logic of the DBMS must be extended across the network to ensure that the local and remote systems always have the same opinion about whether a transaction has been committed. However, the actual responsibility for maintaining database integrity remains with the remote DBMS.

Remote transaction capability is often the highest level of distributed database access provided by database gateways that link one vendor's DBMS to other DBMS brands. For example, most of the independent enterprise database vendors (Sybase, Oracle, Informix) provide gateways from their Unix-based DBMS systems to IBM's mainframe DB2 implementation. Some gateway products go beyond the bounds of remote transactions, allowing a user to join, in a single query, tables from a local database with tables from a remote database managed by a different brand of DBMS. However, these gateways do not (and cannot, without support from the remote DBMS) provide the underlying transaction logic required to support the higher stages of distributed access as defined by IBM. The gateway can ensure the integrity of the local and remote databases individually, but it cannot guarantee that a transaction will not be committed in one and rolled back in the other.

Distributed Transactions

The third stage of distributed data access, as defined by IBM, is a *distributed transaction* (a "distributed unit of work" in IBM parlance), shown in Figure 22-11. At this stage, each individual SQL statement still queries or updates a single database on a single remote computer system. However, the sequence of SQL statements within a

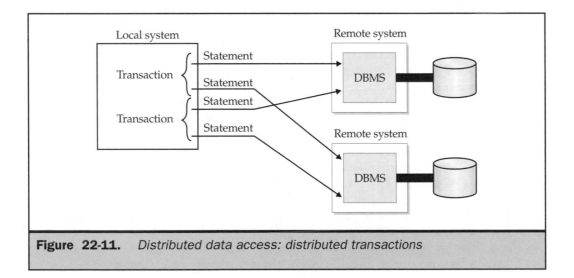

Figure 22-11. *Distributed data access: distributed transactions*

transaction may access two or more databases located on different systems. When the transaction is committed or rolled back, the DBMS guarantees that all parts of the transaction on all of the systems involved in the transaction, will be committed or rolled back. The DBMS specifically guarantees that there will not be a "partial transaction," where the transaction is committed on one system and rolled back on another.

Distributed transactions support the development of very sophisticated transaction processing applications. For example, in the corporate network of Figure 22-1, a PC order processing application can query the inventory databases on two or three different distribution center servers to check the inventory of a scarce product and then update the databases to commit inventory from multiple locations to a customer's order. The DBMS ensures that other concurrent orders do not interfere with the remote access of the first transaction.

Distributed transactions are much more difficult to provide than the first two stages of distributed data access. It's impossible to provide distributed transactions without the active cooperation of the individual DBMS systems involved in the transaction. For this reason, the DBMS brands that support distributed transactions almost always support them only for a homogeneous network of databases, all managed by the same DBMS brand (that is, an all-Oracle or all-Sybase network). A special transaction protocol, called the *two-phase commit* protocol, is used to implement distributed transactions and insure that they provide the "all-or-nothing" requirement of a SQL transaction. The details of this protocol are described later in this chapter.

Distributed Requests

The final stage of distributed data access in the IBM model is a distributed request, shown in Figure 22-12. At this stage, a single SQL statement may reference tables from two or more databases located on different computer systems. The DBMS is responsible for automatically carrying out the statement across the network. A sequence of distributed request statements can be grouped together as a transaction. As in the previous distributed transaction stage, the DBMS must guarantee the integrity of the distributed transaction on all systems that are involved.

The distributed request stage doesn't make any new demands on the DBMS transaction processing logic, because the DBMS already had to support transactions across system boundaries at the previous distributed transaction stage. However, distributed requests pose major new challenges for the DBMS optimization logic. The optimizer must now consider network speed when it evaluates alternate methods for carrying out a SQL statement. If the local DBMS must repeatedly access part of a remote table (for example, when making a join), it may be faster to copy part of the table across the network in one large bulk transfer rather than repeatedly retrieving individual rows across the network.

The relative sizes of the tables on the local and remote system are also relevant optimization factors, as well as the selectivity of any search conditions in the SELECT clause. For some queries, the search conditions may select only one or a few rows on the local system and hundreds of rows on the remote system, so they should be

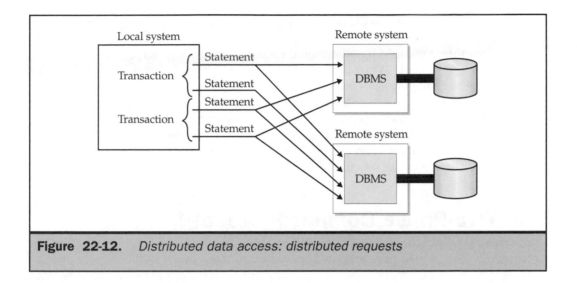

Figure 22-12. *Distributed data access: distributed requests*

applied locally first. For other queries involving the same tables, the relative selectivity may be reversed, and the remote search condition should be applied. For still other queries, the join condition itself may limit the rows that participate in both the local and remote systems, and it may be most efficient to apply it first. In each case, the "cost" of the query is not just the cost of the database access but also the cost of shipping the results of intermediate query execution steps back and forth across the network.

The optimizer must also decide which copy of the DBMS should handle statement execution. If most of the tables are on a remote system, it may be a good idea for the remote DBMS on that system to execute the statement. However, that may be a bad choice if the remote system is heavily loaded. Thus the optimizer's task is both more complex and much more important in a distributed request.

Ultimately, the goal of the distributed request stage is to make the entire distributed database look like one large database to the user. Ideally, the user would have full access to any table in the distributed database and could use SQL transactions without knowing anything about the physical location of the data. Unfortunately, this "ideal" scenario would quickly prove impractical in real networks. In a network of any size, the number of tables in the distributed database would quickly become very large, and users would find it impossible to find data of interest. The user-ids of every database in the organization would have to be coordinated to make sure that a given user-id uniquely identified a user in *all* databases. Database administration would also be very difficult.

In practice, therefore, distributed requests must be implemented selectively. Database administrators must decide which remote tables are to be made visible to local users and which will remain hidden. The cooperating DBMS copies must translate user-ids from one system to another, allowing each database to be administered autonomously while providing security for remote data access.

Distributed requests that would consume too many DBMS or network resources must be detected and prohibited before they impact overall DBMS performance.

Because of their complexity, distributed requests are not fully supported by any commercial SQL-based DBMS today, and it will be some time before even a majority of their features are available. One major step toward distributed processing across database brands has been the standardization of a distributed transaction protocol. The "XA" protocol, originally developed to coordinate among multiple transaction monitors, is being actively applied to distributed database transactions as well. It is one of the areas of work on the proposed SQL3 standard and has already been adopted by several standards bodies in its earlier forms.

The Two-Phase Commit Protocol *

A distributed DBMS must preserve the "all or nothing" quality of a SQL transaction if it is to provide distributed transactions. The user of the distributed DBMS expects that a committed transaction will be committed on all of the systems where data resides, and that a rolled back transaction will be rolled back on all of the systems as well. Further, failures in a network connection or in one of the systems should cause the DBMS to abort a transaction and roll it back, rather than leaving the transaction in a partially committed state.

All commercial DBMS systems that support or plan to support distributed transactions use a technique called *two-phase commit* to provide that support. You don't have to understand the two-phase commit scheme to use distributed transactions. In fact, the whole point of the scheme is to support distributed transactions without your knowing it. However, understanding the mechanics of a two-phase commit can help you plan efficient database access.

To understand why a special two-phase commit protocol is needed, consider the database in Figure 22-13. The user, located on System A, has updated a table on System B and a table on System C and now wants to commit the transaction. Suppose that the DBMS software on System A tried to commit the transaction by simply sending a COMMIT message to System B and System C, and then waiting for their affirmative replies. This strategy works so long as Systems B and C can both successfully commit their part of the transaction. But what happens if a problem such as a disk failure or a deadlock condition prevents System C from committing as requested? System B will commit its part of the transaction and send back an acknowledgment, System C will roll back its part of the transaction because of the error and send back an error message, and the user ends up with a partially committed, partially rolled back transaction. Note that System A can't "change its mind" at this point and ask System B to roll back the transaction. The transaction on System B has been committed, and other users may already have modified the data on System B based on the changes made by the transaction.

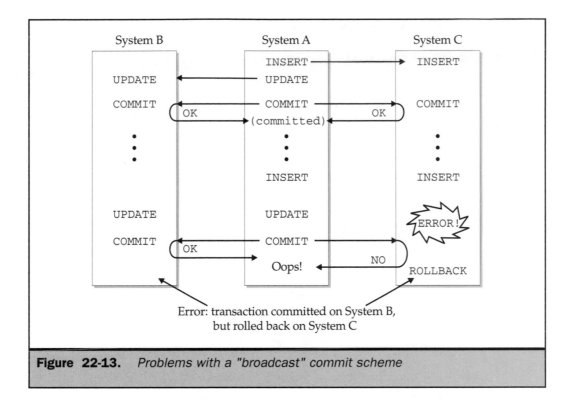

Figure 22-13. *Problems with a "broadcast" commit scheme*

The two-phase commit protocol eliminates the problems of the simple strategy shown in Figure 22-13. Figure 22-14 illustrates the steps involved in a two-phase commit:

1. The program on System A issues a COMMIT for the current (distributed) transaction, which has updated tables on System B and System C. System A will act as the *coordinator* of the commit process, coordinating the activities of the DBMS software on Systems B and C.

2. System A sends a GET READY message to both System B and System C and notes the message in its own transaction log.

3. When the DBMS on System B or C receives the GET READY message, it must either to commit or to roll back the current transaction. If the DBMS can get into this "ready to commit" state, it replies YES to System A and notes that fact in its local transaction log; if it cannot get into this state, it replies NO.

4. System A waits for replies to its GET READY message. If all of the replies are YES, System A sends a COMMIT message to both System B and System C, and

notes the decision in its transaction log. If any of the replies is NO, or if all of the replies are not received within some timeout period, System A sends a ROLLBACK message to both systems and notes that decision in its transaction log.

5. When the DBMS on System B or C receives the COMMIT or ROLLBACK message, it must do as it is told. The DBMS gave up the ability to decide the transaction's fate autonomously when it replied YES to the GET READY message in Step 3. The DBMS commits or rolls back its part of the transaction as requested, writes the COMMIT or ROLLBACK message in its transaction log, and returns an OK message to System A.

6. When System A has received all the OK messages, it knows the transaction has been committed or rolled back and returns the appropriate SQLCODE value to the program.

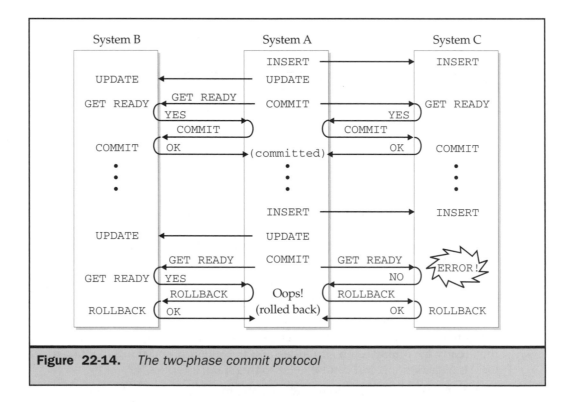

Figure 22-14. *The two-phase commit protocol*

This protocol protects the distributed transaction against any single failure in System B, System C, or the communications network. These two examples illustrate how the protocol permits recovery from failures:

- Suppose a failure occurs on System C before it sends a YES message in Step 3. System A will not receive a YES reply and will broadcast a ROLLBACK message, causing System B to roll back the transaction. The recovery program on System C will not find the YES message or a COMMIT message in the local transaction log, and it will roll back the transaction on System C as part of the recovery process. All parts of the transaction will have been rolled back at this point.

- Suppose a failure occurs on System C after it sends a YES message in Step 3. System A will decide whether to commit or roll back the distributed transaction based on the reply from System B. The recovery program on System C will find the YES message in the local transaction log but will not find a COMMIT or ROLLBACK message to mark the end of the transaction. The recovery program then asks the coordinator (System A) what the final disposition of the transaction was and acts accordingly. Note that System A must maintain a record of its decision to commit or roll back the transaction until it receives the final OK from all of the participants, so that it can respond to the recovery program in case of failure.

The two-phase commit protocol guarantees the integrity of distributed transactions, but it generates a great deal of network traffic. If there are n systems involved in the transaction, the coordinator must send and receive a total of $(4 * n)$ messages to successfully commit the transaction. Note that these messages are *in addition* to the messages that actually carry the SQL statements and query results among the systems. However, there's no way to avoid the message traffic if a distributed transaction is to provide database integrity in the face of system failures.

Because of their heavy network overhead, distributed transactions can have a serious negative effect on database performance. For this reason, distributed databases must be carefully designed so that frequently accessed (or at least frequently updated) data is on a local system or on a single remote system. If possible, transactions that update two or more remote systems should be a relatively rare occurrence.

Network Applications and Database Architecture

Innovations in computer networking have been closely linked to many of the innovations in relational database architectures and SQL over the years. Powerful minicomputers with mainframe network connections (such as Digital's VAX family) were the first popular platform for SQL-based databases. They offered a platform for decision support, based on data offloaded from mainframe systems. They also supported local data processing applications, for capturing business data and uploading it to corporate mainframe applications.

Unix-based servers and powerful local area networks (such as Sun's server products) drove another wave of DBMS growth and innovation. This era of databases and networks gave birth to the client/server architecture that dominated enterprise data processing in the late 1980s and 1990s. Later, the rise of enterprise-wide networks and applications (such as ERP) created a need for a new level of database scalability and distributed database capability. Today, the exploding popularity of the Internet is driving still another wave of innovation, as very high peak-load transaction rates and personalized user interaction drive database caching and main-memory database technologies.

Client/Server Applications and Database Architecture

When SQL-based databases were first deployed on minicomputer systems, the database and application architecture was very simple—all of the processing, from screen display ("presentation") to calculation and data processing ("business logic") to database access occurred on the minicomputer's CPU. The advent of powerful personal computers and server platforms drove a major change in that architecture, for several reasons.

The graphical user interface (GUI) of popular PC office automation software (spreadsheets, word processors, and so on) set a new standard for ease of use, and companies demanded the same style of interface from corporate applications. Supporting a GUI is processor-intensive and demands a high-bandwidth path from the processor to the display memory that holds the screen image. While some protocols emerged for running a GUI over the LAN (the X-windows protocol), the best place to run a production application's presentation-layer code was clearly on the PC itself.

Economics was also a factor. Personal computer systems were much cheaper, on a cost-per-processing-power basis, than minicomputers or Unix-based servers. If more of the processing for a business application could take place on lower-cost PCs, the overall hardware cost of deploying an application would be reduced. This was an argument for moving not just the presentation layer, but much of the business logic layer, onto the PC as well.

Driven by these and other factors, the first client/server architectures, shown in Figure 22-15 emerged. Many PC-based applications are still being deployed today using this architecture. SQL plays a key role as the client/server language. Requests are sent from the application logic (on the PC) to the DBMS (on the server) expressed in SQL statements. The answers come back across the network in the form of SQL completion status codes (for database updates) or SQL query results (for information requests).

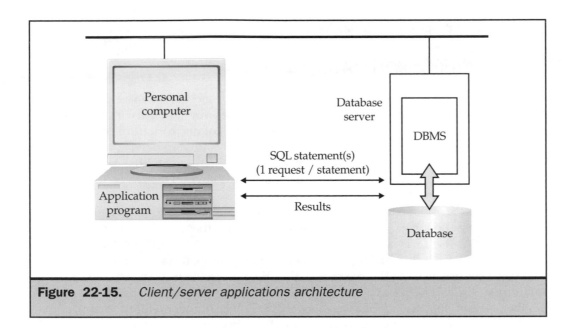

Figure 22-15.   *Client/server applications architecture*

Client/Server Applications with Stored Procedures

Whenever an application is split across two or more networked computer systems, as in Figure 22-15, one of the major issues is the interface between the two halves of the split application. Each interaction across this interface now generates network traffic, and the network is always the slowest part of the overall system, both in its data transmission capacity (bandwidth) and in round-trip messaging delays (latency). With the architecture shown in Figure 22-15, each database access (that is, each SQL statement) generates at least one round-trip across the network.

In an OLTP application, typical transactions may require as many as a dozen individual SQL statements. For example, to take a customer's order for a single product in the simple structure of the sample database, the order processing application might:

■ Retrieve the customer number based on the customer name (single-row SELECT)

■ Retrieve the customer's credit limit to verify credit-worthiness (single-row SELECT)

■ Retrieve product information, such as price and quantity available (single-row SELECT)

■ Add a row to the ORDERS table for the new order (INSERT)

- Update the product information to reflect the lower quantity available (UPDATE)
- Update the customer's credit limit, reducing the available credit (UPDATE)
- Commit the entire transaction (COMMIT)

for a total of seven round-trips between the application and the database. In a real-world application, the number of database accesses might be two or three times this amount. As transaction volumes grow, the amount of network traffic can be very significant.

Database stored procedures provide an alternative architecture that can dramatically reduce the amount of network traffic, as shown in Figure 22-16. A stored procedure within the database itself incorporates the sequence of steps and the decision-making logic required to carry out all of the database operations associated with the transaction. Basically, part of the business logic that formerly resided within the application itself has been "pushed across the network" onto the database server. Instead of sending individual SQL statements to the DBMS, the application calls the stored procedure, passing the customer name, the product to be ordered, and the quantity desired. If all goes well, the stored procedure returns successfully. If a problem arises (such as lack of available product or a customer credit problem), a returned error code and message describes it. By using the stored procedure, the network traffic is reduced to a single client/server interaction.

There are several other advantages to using stored procedures, but the reduction in network traffic is one of the major ones. It was a major selling advantage of Sybase SQL

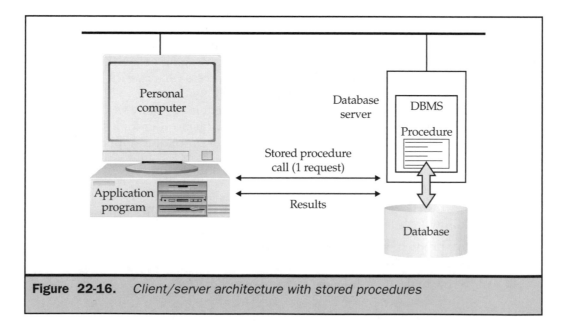

Figure 22-16.   *Client/server architecture with stored procedures*

Server when it was first introduced and helped to position Sybase as a DBMS specialized for high-performance OLTP applications. With the popularity of stored procedures, every major general-purpose enterprise DBMS now offers this capability.

Enterprise Applications and Data Caching

Today, major applications from the large packaged enterprise software vendors are all based on SQL and relational databases. Examples include large enterprise resource planning (ERP), supply chain management (SCM), human resources management (HRM), financial management, and other packages from vendors such as SAP, BAAN, PeopleSoft, Vantive, Clarify, Siebel Systems, I2 Technologies, Manugistics, and others. These large-scale applications typically run on large Unix-based server systems and place a heavy workload on the supporting DBMS. To isolate the applications and DBMS processing, and apply more total processing power to the application, they often use a three-tier architecture shown in Figure 22-17.

Even with the use of stored procedures to minimize network traffic, the network and database access demands of the most data-intensive of these enterprise applications can outstrip the available network bandwidth and DBMS transaction rates. For example, consider a supply chain planning application that helps a

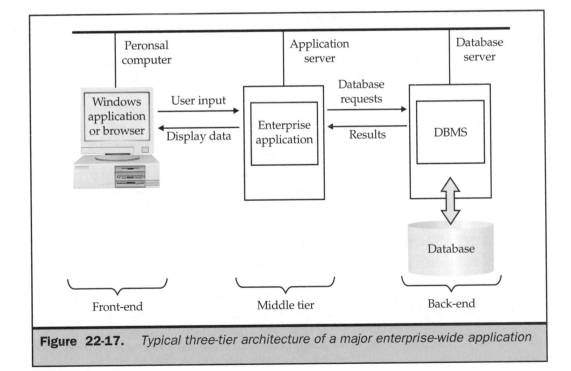

Figure 22-17. *Typical three-tier architecture of a major enterprise-wide application*

manufacturing company determine the parts that it must order from suppliers. To generate a complete plan, the application must examine *every* open order and apply the product bill-of-materials to it. A complex product might involve hundreds of parts, some of which are themselves subassemblies consisting of dozens or hundreds of parts. If written using straightforward programming techniques, the planning application must perform a database inquiry to determine the parts makeup of every product, and then every subassembly, for every order, and it will accumulate the "total-needed" information in the planning database for each of these parts. Using this technique, the application will take hours to process the hundreds of thousands of orders that may be currently on the books. In fact, the application will probably run so long that it cannot possibly complete its work during the typical overnight low-volume "batch processing" window of time during which the company normally runs such applications.

To deliver acceptable performance, all data-intensive enterprise applications employ caching techniques, pulling the data forward, out of the database server, closer to the application. In most cases, the application uses relatively primitive caching techniques. For example, it might read the bill-of-materials once and load it into main-memory data tables within the application program. By eliminating the heavily repeated product-structure queries, the program can dramatically improve its performance.

Recently, enterprise application vendors have begun to use more complex caching techniques. They may replicate the most heavily accessed data (the "hot" data) in a duplicate database table, on the same system as the application itself. Main-memory databases offer an even higher-performance alternative and are already being used where there is a relatively small amount of "hot" data (tens to hundreds of megabytes). With the advent of 64-bit operating system architectures and continuing declines in memory prices, it is becoming practical to cache larger amounts of data (several gigabytes or tens of gigabytes).

Advanced caching and replication will become more important in response to emerging business requirements. Leading-edge manufacturing companies want to move toward "real-time planning" where incoming customer orders and changes immediately impact production plans. They want to offer more customized products, in more configurations, to more closely match customer desires. These and similar trends will continue to raise the volume and complexity of database access.

High-Volume Internet Data Management

High-volume Internet applications are also driving the trend to database caching and replication in networked database architectures. For example, financial services firms are competing for online brokerage clients by offering more and more advanced real-time stock reporting and analysis capabilities. The data management to support this application involve real-time data feeds (to insure that pricing and volume information in the database is current) and peak-load database inquiries of tens of thousands of transactions per second. Similar volume demands are found in applications for managing and monitoring high-volume Internet sites. The trend to personalize Web sites (determining "on the fly" what banner ads to display, what products to feature, and so on) and measure the effectiveness of such personalization is another trend driving peak-load data access and data capture rates.

The Web has already shown an effective architecture for dealing with these types of peak-load Internet volume demands—through Web site caching. Copies of heavily-accessed Web pages are "pulled forward" in the network and replicated. As a result, the total network capacity for serving Web pages is increased, and the amount of network traffic associated with those page hits is reduced. Similar architectures are beginning to emerge for high-volume Internet database management, as shown in Figure 22-18. In this case, an Internet information services application caches "hot" data, such as the most recent news and financial information, in a very high-performance main-memory database from a vendor such as TimesTen Performance Software. It also

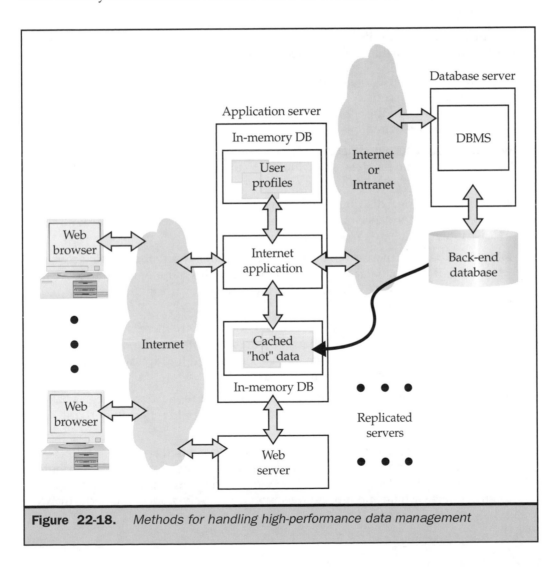

Figure 22-18. *Methods for handling high-performance data management*

stores summary user profile information in a main-memory database, which is used to personalize users' experiences as they interact with the Web site.

As Figure 22-18 shows, the methods for handling high-performance data management are beginning to follow those already established for high-performance Web page management. The issues for databases are more complex, because of database integrity issues, but the emerging techniques are similar—replication, high-volume read access, memory-resident databases, and highly fault-tolerant architectures. These demands will only grow as Internet traffic and personalization continues to increase, leading to more advanced network database architectures.

Summary

This chapter described the distributed data management capabilities offered by various DBMS products and the tradeoffs involved in providing access to remote data:

- A distributed database is implemented by a network of computer systems, each running its own copy of the DBMS software and operating autonomously for local data access. The copies of the DBMS cooperate to provide remote data access when required.

- The "ideal" distributed database is one in which the user doesn't know and doesn't care that the data is distributed; to the user, all of the relevant data appears as if it were on the local system.

- Because this ideal distributed DBMS is very difficult to provide and involves too many performance tradeoffs, commercial DBMS products are providing distributed database capability in phases.

- Remote database access can be useful in situations where the remote access is a small part of total database activity; in this case, it's more practical to leave the data in the remote location and incur the network overhead for each database access.

- Database replication is very useful in situations where there is relatively heavy access to data in multiple locations; it brings the data closer to the point-of-access, but at the cost of network overhead for replica synchronization and data that is not 100 percent up to date.

- The particular tradeoffs of remote data access and replication strategies have implications beyond technology decisions; they should reflect underlying tradeoffs in business priorities as well.

- Enterprise-wide distributed applications, Internet-based applications, data warehousing, and other trends are increasing the complexity of the distributed data management environment. The N-tier architectures they use will require smart data caching and replication strategies to deliver adequate performance.

Chapter 23

SQL and Objects

The only serious challenge to the dominance of SQL and relational database management over the last few years has come from the emergence of an equally significant trend—the growing popularity of object-oriented technologies. Object-oriented programming languages (such as C++ and Java), object-oriented development tools, and object-oriented networking (including object request brokers) have emerged as foundation technologies for modern software development. Object technologies gained much of their initial popularity for building personal computer applications with graphical user interfaces. But their impact has grown, and they are being used today to build (and more importantly, to link together) enterprise-wide network-based applications for large corporations.

In the early 1990s, a group of venture-backed "object-oriented database" companies was formed with the goal of applying object-oriented principles to database management. These companies believed that their object-oriented databases would supplant the "outdated" relational databases as surely as the relational model had supplanted earlier data models. However, they met with limited marketplace success in the face of entrenched relational technologies and SQL. In response to the object challenge, many relational database vendors moved aggressively to graft object technologies onto their relational systems, creating hybrid "object-relational" models. This chapter describes the object database challenge to SQL and the resulting object-relational features provided by some major DBMS vendors.

Object-Oriented Databases

Considerable academic research on database technology over the past decade has been focused on new, "post-relational" data models. Just as the relational model provided clear-cut advantages over the earlier hierarchical and network models, the goal of this research is to develop new data models that will overcome some of the disadvantages of the relational model. Much of this research has focused on how to merge the principles of object-oriented programming and design with traditional database characteristics, such as persistent storage and transaction management.

In addition to the academic research, in the early and mid-1990s some large venture capital investments flowed into a group of startup software companies whose goal was to build a new generation of data management technologies. These companies typically started with the object data structures used by an object-oriented program to manage its in-memory data, and extended them for disk-based storage and multi-user access. Enthusiastic supporters of these "object-oriented databases" (OODBs) firmly believed that they would mount a serious challenge to the relational model and become the dominant database architecture by the end of the decade. That scenario proved far off the mark, but the object database vendors have had a significant impact on their relational rivals.

Object-Oriented Database Characteristics

Unlike the relational data model, where Codd's 1970 paper provided a clear, mathematical definition of a relational database, there is no single definition of an object-oriented database. However, the core principles embodied in most object-oriented databases include:

- *Objects*. In an object-oriented database, everything is an object and is manipulated as an object. The tabular, row/column organization of a relational database is replaced by the notion of collections of objects. Generally, a collection of objects is itself an object and can be manipulated in the same way that other objects are manipulated.

- *Classes*. Object-oriented databases replace the relational notion of atomic data types with a hierarchical notion of classes and subclasses. For example, VEHICLES might be a class of object, and individual members ("instances") of that class would include a car, a bicycle, a train, or a boat. The VEHICLES class might include subclasses called CARS and BOATS, representing a more specialized form of vehicle. Similarly, the CARS class might include a subclass called CONVERTIBLES, and so on.

- *Inheritance*. Objects inherit characteristics from their class and from all of the higher-level classes to which they belong. For example, one of the characteristics of a vehicle might be "number of passengers." All members of the CARS, BOATS, and CONVERTIBLES classes also have this attribute, because they are subclasses of VEHICLES. The CARS class might also have the attribute "number of doors," and the CONVERTIBLES class would inherit this attribute. However, the BOATS class would not inherit the attribute.

- *Attributes*. The characteristics that an object possesses are modeled by its attributes. Examples include the color of an object, or the number of doors that it has, and its English-language name. The attributes are related to the object they describe in roughly the same way that the columns of a table relate to its rows.

- *Messages and methods*. Objects communicate with one another by sending and receiving *messages.* When it receives a message, an object responds by executing a *method,* a program stored within the object that determines how it processes the message. Thus an object includes a set of behaviors described by its methods. Usually an object shares many of the same methods with other objects in higher-level classes.

- *Encapsulation*. The internal structure and data of objects is hidden from the outside world ("encapsulated") behind a limited set of well-defined interfaces. The only way to find out about an object, or to act on it, is through its methods, whose functions and behaviors are clearly specified. This makes the object more predictable and limits the opportunities for accidental data corruption.

- *Object identity*. Objects can be distinguished from one another through unique object identifiers, usually implemented as an abstract pointer known as an object *handle*. Handles are frequently use to represent relationships among objects; an object "points to" a related object by storing the object's handle as one of its data items (attributes).

These principles and techniques make object-oriented databases well suited to applications involving complex data types, such as computer-aided design or compound documents that combine text, graphics, and spreadsheets. The database provides a natural way to represent the hierarchies that occur in complex data. For example, an entire document can be represented as a single object, composed of smaller objects (sections), composed of still smaller objects (paragraphs, graphs, and so on). The class hierarchy allows the database to track the "type" of each object in the document (paragraphs, charts, illustrations, titles, footnotes, and so on). Finally, the message mechanism offers natural support for a graphical user interface. The application program can send a "draw yourself" message to each part of the document, asking it to draw itself on the screen. If the user changes the shape of the window displaying the document, the application program can respond by sending a "resize yourself" message to each document part, and so on. Each object in the document bears responsibility for its own display, so new objects can easily be added to the document architecture.

Pros and Cons of Object-Oriented Databases

Object-oriented databases have stirred up a storm of controversy in the database community. Proponents claim that object databases are essential to create a proper match between the programming and database data models. They claim that the rigid, fixed, row/column structure of relational tables is a holdover from the punch-card era of data processing with its fixed data fields and "record" orientation. A more flexible model, where classes of objects can be similar to one another (that is, share certain attributes) but also different from one another is essential, they claim, to effectively model real-world situations. Another claim is that the multi-table joins that are an integral part of the relational data model inherently create database overhead and make relational technology unsuitable for the ever-increasing performance demands of today's applications. Finally, since objects are well-established as the in-memory data model for modern programs, the proponents claim that the only "natural" data model is one that transparently extends the in-memory model to permanent, shared, disk-based, multi-user storage.

Opponents of object-oriented databases are just as adamant in their claims that object-oriented databases are unnecessary and offer no real, substantive advantages over the relational model. They claim that the "handles" of object-oriented databases are nothing more than the embedded database pointers of pre-relational, hierarchical, and network databases, recycled with different names. They point out that, like these earlier database technologies, the object-oriented databases lack the strong underlying mathematical theory that forms the basis of relational databases. The lack of object database standards and the absence of a standardized query language like SQL are reflections of this deficiency, and have prevented the development of vendor-independent tools and applications that have been essential to the development of the database industry. In response to claims of inferior performance, they point to the use of relational technology in some of the most performance-demanding enterprise applications. They are also careful to draw a distinction between the *external* relational model of data and the underlying *implementation*, which may well contain embedded pointers for performance acceleration. Finally, they claim that any mismatch between object-oriented programming and relational databases can be addressed by technologies like JDBC and other object-to-relational interfaces.

Objects and the Database Market

In the marketplace, pure object-oriented databases have gained some success in applications with very complex data models and those where the model of classes and inheritance closely parallels the real world. However, the object database companies have had real difficulty breaking through into the mainstream. Most are still far from breaking through the $100 million annual revenue mark, and many are not yet profitable and have been through several generations of management. In contrast, the largest relational database vendors have continued to experience steady growth. The largest have annual revenues in hundreds of millions or billions of dollars per year. Relational database technology clearly continues to dominate the database market today.

Not surprisingly, the object-oriented and relational camps have had a substantial impact on one another. With the slow marketplace acceptance of object-oriented technology, the object-oriented vendors have focused on some of the factors that created the success of the relational generation two decades ago. They have formed standards groups, such as the Object Data Management Group (ODMG), to standardize object-oriented database technology. Several have added relational adapters, with standard interfaces such as ODBC and SQL, as optional layers for relational access to their databases. Several have focused on the international standards process and have worked to put strong object-oriented capabilities into the SQL3 standard. The net result has been a trend toward embracing or co-existing with the relational world, rather than competing with it.

The object-oriented challenge has had a significant impact on the relational mainstream as well. Several features that began as relational capabilities (for example, stored procedures) are now being touted as providing object-oriented advantages (for example, encapsulation). Vendors have also steadily added onto their relational databases selected object-oriented capabilities, such as abstract data types. The resulting "object-relational" databases provide a hybrid of relational and object capabilities. They stretch the relational model—some would say past the breaking point—to incorporate features such as tables-within-tables, which model the relationships between object classes.

One of the major vendors, Informix Software, gained its object-relational capabilities by acquisition, buying Illustra Software. Illustra's object-relational technology was based on the Postgres work at the University of California at Berkeley, a follow-on to the university's pioneering relational database system, Ingres. The Informix version of the Illustra product is Informix Universal Server. Another of the major vendors, Oracle Corporation, evolved its own mainstream database system to include object-relational technologies. Oracle8, introduced in 1998, embodies several years of intensive Oracle development in this area. These products represent strong examples of object-relational database technology available today. Additional vendors will no doubt introduce object-relational products or product extensions, based on the popularity of these initial offerings.

Object-Relational Databases

Object-relational databases typically begin with a relational database foundation, and add selected features that provide object-oriented capabilities. This approach simplifies the addition of object capabilities for the major RDBMS vendors, whose enterprise-class RDBMS products have been developed over the course of 15 or more years and would be tremendously costly to reproduce from scratch. It also recognizes the large installed base of relational systems and gives those customers a smoother upgrade path (not to mention an upgrade revenue stream for the vendors).

The object extensions that are commonly found in object-relational databases are:

- *Large data objects.* Traditional relational data types are small in size—integers, dates, short character strings; large data objects can store documents, audio and video clips, Web pages, and other "new media" data types.

- *Structured/abstract data types.* Relational data types are atomic and indivisible; structured data types allow groups of individual data items to be grouped into higher-level structures that can be treated as entities of their own.

- *User-defined data types.* Relational databases typically provide a limited range of built-in data types; object-oriented systems and databases emphasize the user's ability to define their own, new data types.

- *Tables-within-tables.* Relational database columns store individual data items; object-relational databases allow columns to contain complex data items, such as structured types or even entire tables. This can be used to represent object hierarchies.

- *Sequences, sets, and arrays.* In a traditional relational database, sets of data are represented by rows in their own table, linked to an "owning" entity by a foreign key; object-relational databases may allow the direct storage of collections of data items (sequences, sets, arrays) within a single column.

- *Stored procedures.* Traditional relational databases provide set-based interfaces, such as SQL, for storing, selecting, and retrieving data; object-relational databases provide procedural interfaces, such as stored procedures, that encapsulate the data and provide strictly defined interactions.

- *Handles and object-ids.* A pure relational database requires that data within the database itself (the primary key) uniquely identifies each row; object-relational databases provide built-in support for row-ids or other unique identifiers for objects.

Large Object Support

Relational databases have traditionally focused on business data processing, storing and manipulating data items that represent money amounts, names, addresses, unit quantities, dates, times, and the like. These data types are relatively simple and require small amounts of storage space, from a few bytes for an integer that holds order or inventory quantities to a few dozen bytes for a customer name, employee address, or product description. Relational databases have been optimized to manage rows containing up to a few dozen columns of this type of data. The techniques they use to manage disk storage and to index data assume that data rows will occupy a few hundred to a few thousand bytes. The programs that store and retrieve data can easily hold dozens or hundreds of these types of data items in memory, and can easily store and retrieve entire rows of data at a time through reasonably sized memory buffers. The row-at-a-time processing techniques for relational query results work well.

Many "modern" types of data have quite different characteristics from traditional business data. A single high-resolution graphical image to be displayed on a PC screen can require hundreds of thousands of bytes of storage or more. A word processing document, such as a contract or the text of this book, can take even more storage. The HTML text that defines Web pages and the PostScript files that define printed images are other examples of larger, document-oriented data items. Even a relatively short high-quality audio track can occupy millions of bytes, and video clips can run to hundreds of megabytes or even gigabytes of data. As multimedia applications have become more important, users have wanted to manage these types of data along with the other data in their databases. The ability to efficiently manage "large objects," often called "binary large objects" or BLOBs, was one of the earliest advantages claimed for object-oriented databases.

BLOBs in the Relational Model

The first approach to supporting BLOBs in relational databases was through the underlying operating system and its file system. Each individual BLOB data item was stored in its own operating system file. The name of the file was placed in a character-valued column within a table, as a pointer to the file. The table's other columns could be searched to find rows that met certain criteria. When an application needed to manipulate the BLOB content associated with one of the rows, it read the name of the file and retrieved the BLOB data from it. Management of the file input/output was the responsibility of the application program. This approach worked, but it was error-prone and required that a programmer understand *both* the RDBMS and the file system interfaces. The lack of integration between the BLOB contents and the database was readily apparent. For example, you couldn't ask the database to compare two BLOB data items to see if they were the same, and the database couldn't provide even basic text searching capability for BLOB contents.

Today, most major enterprise-class DBMS systems provide direct support for one or more types of BLOB data. You can define a column as containing one of these BLOB data types and use it in certain situations in SQL statements. There are typically substantial restrictions on the BLOB data, such as not allowing its use in a join condition or a GROUP BY clause.

Sybase Adaptive Server provides two large object data types. Its TEXT data type can store up to two billion bytes of variable-length text data. You can use a limited set of SQL capabilities (such as the LIKE text-search operator) to search the contents of TEXT columns. A companion IMAGE data type can store up to two billion bytes of variable-length binary data. Microsoft SQL Server supports these types, plus an NTEXT data type that allows up to 1 billion characters of 2-byte national language text.

IBM's DB2 provides a similar set of data types. A DB2 CLOB (character large object) type stores up to 2 billion bytes of text. A DB2 DBCLOB (double-byte character large object) type stores up to 1 billion 2-byte characters. A DB2 BLOB (binary large object) stores up to 2 billion bytes of binary data.

Oracle historically provided two large object data types. A LONG data type stored up to 2 billion bytes of text data. A LONG RAW data type stored up to 2 billion bytes of binary data. Oracle restricted the use of either LONG type to only a single column per table. With the introduction of Oracle8, support for BLOB data was expanded substantially:

- An Oracle BLOB type stores up to 4 gigabytes of binary data within the database.
- An Oracle CLOB type stores up to 4 gigabytes of single-byte character data within the database.
- An Oracle NCLOB type stores multi-byte character data as a BLOB.
- An Oracle BFILE type stores long binary data in a file external to the database.

The BLOB, CLOB, and NCLOB types are tightly integrated into Oracle's operation, including transaction support. BFILE data is managed through a pointer within the database to an external operating system file. It is not supported by Oracle transaction semantics. Special Oracle PL/SQL functions are provided to manipulate BLOB, CLOB, and NCLOB data from within PL/SQL stored procedures, as described in the next section.

Informix Universal Server's support for large object data is similar to that of Oracle8. It supports "simple large objects" and "smart large objects":

- An Informix BYTE type is a simple large object that stores binary data.
- An Informix TEXT type is a simple large object that stores text data.
- An Informix BLOB type is a smart large object that stores binary data.
- An Informix CLOB type is a smart large object that stores text (character) data.

Informix simple large objects store up to 1 gigabyte of data. The entire large object must be retrieved or stored as a unit from the application program, or it can be copied between the database and an operating system file. Smart large objects can store up to 4 terabytes of data. Special Informix functions are provided to process smart large objects in smaller, more manageable chunks. These functions provide random access to the contents of an Informix smart object, similar to the random access typically provided for operating system files. Informix also provides advanced controls over logging, transaction management, and data integrity for smart large objects.

Specialized BLOB Processing

Because BLOBs can be very large in size compared to the data items typically handled by RDBMS systems, they pose special problems in several areas:

- *Data storage and optimization*. Storing a BLOB item "in-line" with the other contents of a table's row would destroy the optimization that the DBMS performs to fit database data neatly into pages that match the size of disk pages. For this reason, BLOB data is always stored "out-of-line" in separate storage areas. Most DBMS brands that support BLOBs provide special BLOB storage options, including named storage spaces that are specified when the BLOB type column is created.

- *Storing BLOB data in the database*. Because a BLOB can be tens or hundreds of megabytes in size, most programs can't hold the entire contents of a BLOB in a memory buffer at once. They process portions of the BLOB at a time (for example, pages of a long document or individual frames of a video clip). But Embedded SQL and normal SQL APIs are designed for row-at-a-time processing (through INSERT and UPDATE statements) that store the values for all columns in the row at once. Special techniques are required to put data into a database BLOB column piece-by-piece, through multiple API calls per BLOB column.

- *Retrieving BLOB data from the database*. This is the same issue as retrieving the data, but in reverse. Embedded SQL and normal SQL APIs are designed for SELECT statement or FETCH statement processing that retrieves data values for all columns of a row at once. But because a stored BLOB value can be tens or hundreds of megabytes in size, most programs can't possibly process it all at once in a memory buffer. Special techniques are required to retrieve the database BLOB column data, piece-by-piece, so that it can be processed by the application.

- *Transaction logging*. Most DBMSs support transactions by maintaining "before" and "after" images of modified data in a transaction log. Because of the potentially large size of BLOB data, the logging overhead could be extreme. For this reason, many DBMS's don't support logging for BLOB data, or they allow logging but provide the ability to turn it on and off.

Several DBMSs address these issues through extended APIs that specifically support BLOB manipulation. These calls provide random access to individual segments of the BLOB contents, allowing the program to retrieve or store the BLOB in manageable "chunks." Oracle8 introduced this capability for manipulating its LOB data types (character and binary) within stored procedures written in the Oracle PL/SQL language. Its capabilities are similar to those provided by other object-relational databases, such as Informix Universal Server.

When a stored procedure reads an Oracle LOB column from a table, Oracle does not actually return the contents of the column. Instead, a *locator* for the LOB data (in object parlance, a "handle" for the LOB) is returned. The locator is used in conjunction with a set of nine special LOB-processing functions that the stored procedure can then use to manipulate the actual data stored in the LOB column of the database. Here is a brief description of each LOB-processing function:

- *dbms_lob.read*(*locator*, *length*, *offset*, *buffer*). Reads into the PL/SQL buffer the indicated number of bytes/characters from the LOB identified by the locator, starting at the offset.

- *dbms_lob.write*(*locator*, *length*, *offset*, *buffer*). Writes the indicated number of bytes/characters from the PL/SQL buffer into the LOB identified by the locator, starting at the offset.

- *dbms_lob.append*(*locator1*, *locator2*). Appends the entire contents of the LOB identified by *locator2* to the end of the contents of the LOB identified by *locator1*.

- *dbms_lob.erase*(*locator*, *length*, *offset*). Erases the contents of the LOB identified by the locator at *offset* for *length* bytes/characters; for character-based LOBs, spaces are inserted, and for binary LOBs, binary zeroes are inserted.

- *dbms_lob.copy*(*locator1*, *locator2*, *length*, *offset1*, *offset2*). Copies *length* bytes/characters from the LOB identified by *locator2* at *offset2* into the LOB identified by *locator1* at *offset1*.

- *dbms_lob.trim*(*locator1*, *length*). Trims the LOB identified by the locator to the indicated number of bytes/characters.

- *dbms_lob.substr*(*locator*, *length*, *offset*). Returns (as a text string return value) the indicated number of bytes/characters from the LOB identified by the locator, starting at the offset; the return value from this function may be assigned into a PL/SQL VARCHAR variable.

- *dbms_lob.getlength*(*locator*). Returns (as an integer value) the length in bytes/characters of the LOB identified by the locator.

- *dbms_lob.compare*(*locator1*, *locator2*, *length*, *offset1*, *offset2*). Compares the LOB identified by *locator1* to the LOB identified by *locator2*, starting at *offset1* and *offset2*, respectively, for *length* bytes/characters; returns zero if they are the same and nonzero if they are not.

- *dbms_lob.instr*(*locator*, *pattern*, *offset*,*i*). Returns (as an integer value) the position within the LOB identified by the locator where the *i*-th occurrence of *pattern* is matched; the returned value may be used as an offset in subsequent LOB processing calls.

Oracle imposes one further restriction on updates and modifications to LOB values that are performed through these functions. LOBs can impose an unacceptably high overhead on Oracle's transaction mechanisms, so Oracle normally does not lock the contents of a LOB data item when the row containing the LOB is read by an application program or a PL/SQL routine. If the LOB data is to be updated, the row must be explicitly locked prior to modifying it. This is done by including a FOR UPDATE clause in the SELECT statement that retrieves the LOB locator. Here is a PL/SQL fragment that retrieves a row containing a LOB that contains document text, and updates 100 characters in the middle of the LOB data:

```
declare
    lob      CLOB;
    textbuf varchar(255);

begin
    /* Put text to be inserted into buffer /

    . . .

    /* Get lob locator and lock LOB for update */
    select document_lob into lob
      from documents
     where document_id = '34218'
       for update;

    /* Write new text 500 bytes into LOB */
    dbms_lob.write(lob,100,500,textbuf);

    commit;
end;
```

Abstract (Structured) Data Types

The data types envisioned by the relational data model are simple, indivisible "atomic" data values. If a data item such as an address is actually composed of a street address, city, state, and postal code, you as a database designer have two choices. You can treat the address as four separate data items, each stored in its own column, so that you can search and retrieve the items individually. Or you can treat the address as a single unit, in which case you cannot process its individual component parts within the database. There is no "middle ground" that allows you to treat the address as a unit for certain situations and access its component parts for others.

Many programming languages (including even nonobject-oriented languages like C or Pascal) do provide such a "middle ground." They support compound data types or named data structures. The data structure is composed of individual data items or lower-level structures, which can be accessed individually. But the entire data structure can also be treated as a single unit when that is most convenient. Structured or composite data types in object-relational databases provide this same capability in a DBMS context.

Informix Universal Server supports abstract data types through its concept of *row data types.* You can think of a row type as a structured sequence of individual data items, called *fields.* Here is an Informix CREATE TABLE statement for a simple PERSONNEL table that uses a row data type to store both name and address information:

```
CREATE TABLE PERSONNEL (
    EMPL_NUM INTEGER,
        NAME ROW(
      F_NAME VARCHAR(15),
      M_INIT CHAR(1),
      L_NAME VARCHAR(20))
     ADDRESS ROW(
      STREET VARCHAR(35),
        CITY VARCHAR(15),
       STATE CHAR(2),
    POSTCODE ROW(
        MAIN INTEGER,
         SFX INTEGER)));
```

This table has three columns. The first one, EMPL_NUM, has an integer data type. The last two, NAME and ADDR, have a row data type, indicated by the keyword ROW, followed by a parenthesized list of the fields that make up the row. The NAME column's row data type has three fields within it. The ADDRESS column's row data type has four fields. The last of these four fields itself has a row data type and consists of two fields. In this simple example, the hierarchy is only two levels deep, but the capability can be (and often is) extended to additional levels.

Individual fields within the columns of the table are accessible in SQL statements through an extension of the SQL "dot" notation that is already used to qualify column names with table names and user names. Adding a dot *after* a column name allows you to specify the names of individual fields within a column. This SELECT statement retrieves the employee numbers and first and last names of all personnel with a specified main postal code:

```
SELECT EMPL_NUM, NAME.F_NAME, NAME.L_NAME
   FROM PERSONNEL
 WHERE ADDRESS.POSTCODE.MAIN = '12345';
```

Suppose another table within the database, named MANAGERS, had the same NAME structure as one of its columns. Then this query retrieves the employee numbers of employees who are also managers:

```
SELECT EMPL_NUM
   FROM PERSONNEL, MANAGERS
 WHERE PERSONNEL.NAME = MANAGERS.NAME;
```

In the first of these two queries, it makes sense to retrieve the individual fields within the NAME column. The second query shows a situation where it's more convenient to use the *entire* name column (all three fields) as the basis for comparison. It's clearly a lot more convenient to ask the DBMS to compare the two abstract data typed columns than it is to specify separate comparisons for each of the individual fields. Together, these examples show the advantages of the row data type in allowing access to the fields at any level of the hierarchy.

The row data type columns require special handling when inserting data into the database. The PERSONNEL table has three columns, so an INSERT statement for the table must have three items in its VALUES clause. The columns that have a row data type require a special ROW value-constructor to "put together" the individual data items into a row-type item that matches the data type of the column. Here is a valid INSERT statement for the table that illustrates the use of the ROW constructor:

```
INSERT INTO PERSONNEL
     VALUES (1234,
             ROW('John','J','Jones'),
             ROW('197 Rose St.','Chicago','IL',
                ROW(12345,6789)));
```

Defining Abstract Data Types

With the Informix row data type capabilities illustrated so far, each individual structured column is defined in isolation. If two tables need to use the same row data type structure, it is defined within each table. This violates one of the key principles of object-oriented design, which is reusability. Instead of having each "object" (the two columns in the two different tables) have its own definition, the row data type should be defined once and then reused for the two columns. Informix Universal Server provides this capability through its *named row type* feature. (The row data types shown in previous examples are *unnamed* row data types.)

You create an Informix named row type with the CREATE ROW TYPE statement. Here are examples for the PERSONNEL table:

```
CREATE ROW TYPE NAME_TYPE (
    F_NAME VARCHAR(15),
    M_INIT CHAR(1),
    L_NAME VARCHAR(20));

CREATE ROW TYPE POST_TYPE (
      MAIN INTEGER,
       SFX INTEGER);

CREATE ROW TYPE ADDR_TYPE (
    STREET VARCHAR(35),
      CITY VARCHAR(15),
     STATE CHAR(2),
  POSTCODE POST_TYPE);
```

Note that the definition of a named row type can depend on other, previously created named row types, as shown by the ADDR_TYPE and POST_TYPE definitions. With these row data types defined, the name and address columns in the PERSONNEL table (and any other columns holding name or address data in other tables of the database) can be defined using it. The aggressive use of abstract data types can thus help to enforce uniformity in naming and data typing within an object-relational database. Here is the new Informix definition of the PERSONNEL table, using the just-defined abstract data types:

```
CREATE TABLE PERSONNEL (
    EMPL_NUM INTEGER,
        NAME NAME_TYPE,
     ADDRESS ADDR_TYPE);
```

Figure 23-1 shows some sample data for this table and the hierarchical column/field structure created by the abstract data types.

Oracle supports abstract data types through a very similar structure, with slightly different SQL syntax. Here is the Oracle CREATE TYPE statement to create the same abstract data structure for names and addresses:

```
CREATE TYPE NAME_TYPE AS OBJECT (
    F_NAME VARCHAR(15),
```

```
     M_INIT CHAR(1),
     L_NAME VARCHAR(20));

CREATE TYPE POST_TYPE AS OBJECT (
     MAIN INTEGER,
      SFX INTEGER);

CREATE TYPE ADDR_TYPE AS OBJECT (
     STREET VARCHAR(35),
       CITY VARCHAR(15),
      STATE CHAR(2),
   POSTCODE POST_TYPE);
```

Oracle calls the abstract data type an "object" instead of a row type. In fact, the type is functioning as an "object class" in the usual object-oriented terminology. Extending the object-oriented terminology further, the individual components of an Oracle abstract data type are referred to as *attributes* (corresponding to the Informix *fields* described earlier). The addr_type type has four attributes in this example. The fourth attribute, POSTCODE, is itself an abstract data type.

Both Oracle and Informix use the "extended dot notation" to refer to individual data elements within abstract data types. With nested abstract types, it takes several levels of dot-delimited names to identify an individual data item. The main postal code within the PERSONNEL table is identified as:

```
PERSONNEL.ADDRESS.POSTCODE.MAIN
```

PERSONNEL Table

| EMPL_NUM | NAME | | | ADDRESS | | | POSTCODE | |
	F_NAME	M_INIT	L_NAME	STREET	CITY	STATE	MAIN	SFX
1234	Sue	J.	Marsh	1803 Main St.	Alamo	NJ	31948	4567
1374	Sam	F.	Wilson	564 Birch Rd.	Marion	KY	82942	3524
1421	Joe	P.	Jones	13 High St.	Delano	NM	13527	2394
1532	Rob	G.	Mason	9123 Plain Av.	Franklin	PA	83624	2643

Figure 23-1.   *PERSONNEL table using abstract data types*

If the table were owned by another user, Sam, the qualified name becomes even longer:

```
SAM.PERSONNEL.ADDRESS.POSTCODE.MAIN
```

Informix allows the use of row types to go one step beyond their role as data type "templates" for individual columns. You can use a row type to define the structure of an entire table. For example, with this row type definition:

```
CREATE ROW TYPE PERS_TYPE (
   EMPL_NUM INTEGER,
      NAME NAME_TYPE,
   ADDRESS ADDR_TYPE)
```

you can define the PERSONNEL table using the row type as a model:

```
CREATE TABLE PERSONNEL
     OF TYPE PERS_TYPE;
```

The columns of this PERSONNEL table will be exactly as they were in the previous CREATE TABLE examples, but now PERSONNEL is a "typed table." The most basic use of the typed table capability is to formalize the object structure in the database. Each object class has its own row type, and the typed table that holds objects (rows) of that class is defined in terms of the row type. Beyond this usage, typed tables are also a key component of the Informix notion of table inheritance, described in a later section.

Manipulating Abstract Data Types

Unfortunately, structured data types create new complexity for database update statements that must insert or modify their structured data values. Informix Universal Server is fairly liberal in its data type conversion requirements for unnamed row types. The data you assign into a row-type column must simply have the same number of fields, of the same data types. The ROW constructor is used, as shown in previous examples, to assemble individual data items into a row-type value for inserting or updating data.

For named row types, the requirement is more stringent; the data you assign into a named row-type column must actually have the same named row type. You can achieve this in the INSERT statement by *explicitly casting* the constructed row-value to have the NAME_TYPE data type:

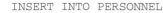
```
INSERT INTO PERSONNEL
```

```
VALUES (1234,
        ROW('John','J','Jones')::NAME_TYPE,
        ROW('197 Rose St.','Chicago','IL',
            ROW(12345,6789))));
```

The double-colon operator casts the constructed three-field row as a NAME_TYPE row and makes the VALUES clause compatible with the data types of the columns in the table.

Oracle uses a slightly different approach to constructing structured data items and inserting them into columns that have abstract data types. When you create an Oracle abstract data type (using the CREATE TYPE statement), Oracle automatically defines a *constructor method* for the type. You can think of the constructor method as a function that takes as its arguments the individual components of the abstract data type and returns an abstract data type value, with the individual components all packaged together. The constructor is used in the VALUES clause of the INSERT statement to "glue together" the individual data item values into a structured data value that matches the column definition. Here is an INSERT statement for the PERSONNEL table:

```
INSERT INTO PERSONNEL
    VALUES (1234,
            NAME_TYPE('John','J','Jones'),
            ADDR_TYPE('197 Rose St.','Chicago','IL',
                    POST_TYPE(12345,6789)));
```

The constructors (NAME_TYPE, ADDR_TYPE, POST_TYPE) perform the same functions as the ROW constructor does for Informix, and also provide the casting required to insure strict data type correspondence.

Inheritance

Support for abstract data types gives the relational data model a foundation for object-based capabilities. The abstract data type can embody the representation of an "object," and the values of its individual fields or subcolumns are its attributes. Another important feature of the object-oriented model is *inheritance*. With inheritance, new objects can be defined as being a "particular type of" an existing object type ("class") and inherit the predefined attributes and behaviors of that type.

Figure 23-2 shows an example of how inheritance might work in a model of a company's employee data. All employees are members of the class PERSONNEL, and they all have the attributes associated with being an employee (employee number, name, and address). Some employees are salespeople, and they have additional attributes (such as a sales quota and the identity of their sales manager). Other

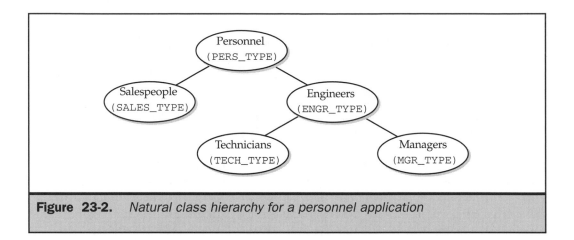

Figure 23-2. *Natural class hierarchy for a personnel application*

employees are engineers, with a different set of attributes (such as the academic degrees they hold or the current project to which they are assigned). Each of these employee types has its own class, which is a "subclass" of PERSONNEL. The subclass inherits all of the characteristics of the class above it in the hierarchy (we want to track all of the core personnel data for engineers and salespeople, too). However, the subclasses have additional information that is unique to their type of object. In Figure 23-2, the class hierarchy goes down to a third layer for engineers, differentiating between technicians, developers, and managers.

Informix Universal Server's abstract data type inheritance mechanism provides an easy way to define abstract data types (Informix row types) that correspond to the natural hierarchy in Figure 23-2. Assume that the Informix PERS_TYPE row type has already been created, as defined earlier in this chapter, and a typed table named PERSONNEL has been created based on this row type. Using the Informix inheritance capabilities, here are some CREATE ROW TYPE statements for other types in the hierarchy:

```
CREATE ROW TYPE SALES_TYPE (
    SLS_MGR INTEGER,                    /* employee number of sales mgr */
    SALARY MONEY(9,2),                  /* annual salary */
    QUOTA MONEY(9,2))
    UNDER PERS_TYPE;

CREATE ROW TYPE ENGR_TYPE (
    SALARY MONEY(9,2),                  /* annual salary */
  YRS_EXPER INTEGER                     /* years of experience */
    UNDER PERS_TYPE;
```

```
CREATE ROW TYPE MGR_TYPE (
     BONUS MONEY(9,2))                      /* annual bonus */
     UNDER ENGR_TYPE;

CREATE ROW TYPE TECH_TYPE (
  WAGE_RATE MONEY(5,2))                     /* hourly wage rate */
     UNDER ENGR_TYPE;
```

The type defined for technicians (TECH_TYPE) is a subtype ("subclass") of the engineer type (ENGR_TYPE), so it inherits all of the fields for the personnel type (PERS_TYPE) *plus* the fields added at the ENGR_TYPE level *plus* the additional field added in its own definition. A abstract type that is defined UNDER another type, and inherits its fields, is called a *subtype* of the higher-level type. Conversely, the higher-level type is a *supertype* of the lower-level types defined UNDER it.

With this type hierarchy defined, it's easy to create Informix typed tables that use them. Here are some Informix statements that create a table for engineers, separate tables for managers and technicians, and another table to hold salesperson data:

```
CREATE TABLE ENGINEERS
     OF TYPE ENGR_TYPE;
CREATE TABLE TECHNICIANS
     OF TYPE TECH_TYPE;
CREATE TABLE MANAGERS
     OF TYPE MGR_TYPE;
CREATE TABLE REPS
     OF TYPE SALES_TYPE;
```

The type hierarchy has pushed the complexity into the data type definitions and made the table structure very simple and easy to define. All other characteristics of the table can (and must) still be defined within the table definition. For example, the salesperson table contains a column that is actually a foreign key to the personnel table, so its table definitions should probably include a FOREIGN KEY clause like this:

```
CREATE TABLE REPS
     OF TYPE SALES_TYPE
  FOREIGN KEY (SLS_MGR)
   REFERENCES PERSONNEL(EMPL_NUM);
```

Type inheritance creates a relationship among the *structure* of the tables that are based on the defined row types, but the tables remain independent of one another in terms of the data that they contain. Rows inserted into the TECHNICIANS table don't automatically appear in the ENGINEERS table nor in the PERSONNEL table. Each is a table in its own right, containing its own data. A different kind of inheritance, *table inheritance*, provides a very different level of linkage between the table's contents, actually turning the tables into something much closer to object classes. It is described in the next section.

Table Inheritance—Implementing Object Classes

Informix Universal Server provides a capability called *table inheritance* that moves the table structure of a database away from the traditional relational model and makes it much closer to the concept of an object class. Using table inheritance, it's possible to create a hierarchy of typed tables ("classes"), such as the one shown in Figure 23-3. The tables are still based on a defined type hierarchy, but now the tables themselves have a parallel hierarchy.

Here is a set of CREATE TABLE statements that implements this table inheritance:

```
CREATE TABLE ENGINEERS
     OF TYPE ENGR_TYPE
        UNDER PERSONNEL;
CREATE TABLE TECHNICIANS
     OF TYPE TECH_TYPE
        UNDER ENGINEERS;
CREATE TABLE MANAGERS
     OF TYPE MGR_TYPE
        ENDER ENGINEERS;
CREATE TABLE REPS
     OF TYPE SALES_TYPE
        UNDER PERSONNEL;
```

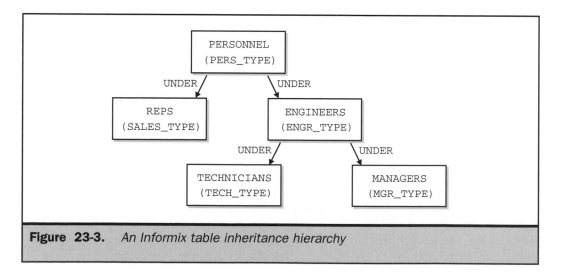

Figure 23-3. *An Informix table inheritance hierarchy*

When a table is defined in this way (as "under" another table), it inherits many more characteristics from its "supertable" than just the column structure. It inherits the foreign key, primary key, referential integrity, and check constraints of the supertable, any triggers defined on the supertable, as well as indexes, storage areas, and other Informix-specific characteristics. It's possible to override this inheritance by specifically including the overridden characteristics in the CREATE TABLE statements for the subtables.

A table type hierarchy has a profound impact on the way that the Universal Server DBMS treats the rows stored in the tables. The tables in the hierarchy now form a collection of nested *sets* of rows, as shown in Figure 23-4. When a row is inserted into the table hierarchy, it is still inserted into a specific table. Joe Jones, for example, is in the TECHNICIANS table, while Sam Wilson is in the ENGINEERS table and Sue Marsh is in the PERSONNEL table.

SQL queries behave quite differently, however. When you perform a database query on one of the tables in the hierarchy, it returns rows not only from the table itself, but from *all* of the included subtables of that table. This query:

```
SELECT *
  FROM PERSONNEL;
```

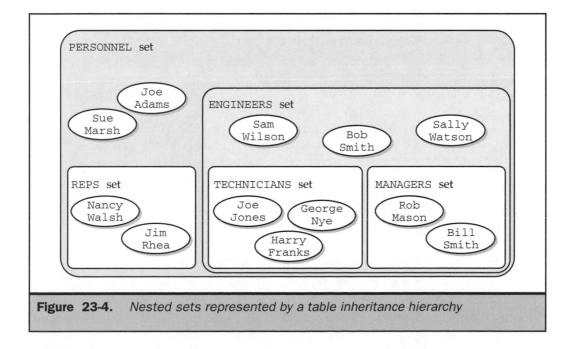

Figure 23-4.   *Nested sets represented by a table inheritance hierarchy*

returns rows from the PERSONNEL table *and* rows from the ENGINEERS, TECHNICIANS, and REPS tables. Similarly this query:

```
SELECT *
  FROM ENGINEERS;
```

returns rows from TECHNICIANS and MANAGERS in addition to ENGINEERS. The DBMS is now treating the tables as a nested collection of rows, and a query on a table (row set) applies to *all* rows included in the set. If you want to retrieve *only* the rows that appear in the top-level table itself, you must use the ONLY keyword:

```
SELECT *
  FROM ONLY(ENGINEERS);
```

The DBMS applies the same set-of-rows logic to DELETE operations. This DELETE statement:

```
DELETE FROM PERSONNEL
  WHERE EMPL_NUM = 1234;
```

successfully deletes the row for employee number 1234 *regardless* of which table in the hierarchy actually contains the row. The statement is interpreted as "delete any rows from the PERSONNEL set that match these criteria." As with the queries, if you want to delete *only* rows that appear in the ENGINEERS table of the hierarchy, but not rows from any of its subtables, you can use this statement:

```
DELETE FROM ONLY(ENGINEERS)
  WHERE EMPL_NUM = 1234;
```

The same logic holds for UPDATE statements. This one changes the employee number, regardless of which table in the hierarchy actually holds the row for the employee:

```
UPDATE PERSONNEL
   SET L_NAME = 'Harrison'
 WHERE EMPL_NUM = 1234;
```

Again the ONLY construct may be used to restrict the scope of the UPDATE operation to only rows that actually appear in the named table and not those that appear in its subtables.

Of course, when operating at a given level within the table hierarchy, your SQL statements can only reference columns that are defined at that level. You cannot use this statement:

```
DELETE FROM PERSONNEL
  WHERE SALARY < 20000.00;
```

because the SALARY column doesn't exist in the top-level PERSONNEL table (class). It is only defined for some of its subtables (subclasses). You *can* use this statement:

```
DELETE FROM MANAGERS
  WHERE SALARY < 20000.00;
```

because SALARY is defined at this level of the table (class) hierarchy.

As noted, table inheritance moves the operation of Informix Universal Server fairly far out of the relational database realm and into the object-oriented world. Relational purists point to examples like the previous ones to claim that object-relational databases bring with them dangerous inherent inconsistencies. "Why should an INSERT of a row into one table cause it to suddenly appear in two other tables?" and "Why should a searched DELETE statement that doesn't match any rows of a table cause other rows in other tables to disappear?" are typical of the questions they ask. The answer, of course, is that the table hierarchy has stopped behaving strictly as if it were a set of relational tables, and instead has taken on many of the characteristics of an object class and object class hierarchy. Whether this is "good" or "bad" depends on your point of view. It *does* mean that you must be very careful about applying relational database assumptions blindly to an object-relational implementation.

Sets, Arrays, and Collections

In a relational database, tables are the *only* database structure used to represent a "set of objects." For example, the set of engineers in our personnel database is represented by the rows in the ENGINEERS table. Suppose each engineer has a set of academic degrees (a B.S. in science from MIT, a Ph.D. in electrical engineering from Michigan, and so on) that are to be stored in the database. The number of degrees for each engineer will vary—from none for some engineers to perhaps half a dozen for others. In a pure relational database, there is only one "correct" way to add this information to the data model. A new table, DEGREES, must be created, as shown in Figure 23-5. Each row in the DEGREES table represents one individual academic degree held by one of the engineers. A column in the DEGREES table holds the employee number of the engineer holding the degree described by that particular row, and serves as a foreign key to the ENGINEERS table, linking the two tables in a parent/child relationship. The other columns in the DEGREES table describe the particulars of the degree.

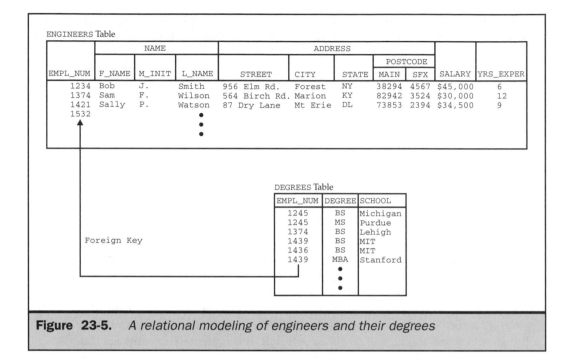

Figure 23-5. *A relational modeling of engineers and their degrees*

You have seen the type of parent/child relational table structure shown in Figure 23-5 many times in the earlier chapters of this book, and it has been a basic construct of relational databases since the beginning. However, there are some disadvantages to having this be the *only* way in which sets of data attributes can be modeled. First, the database tends to have a great many tables and foreign key relationships and becomes hard to understand. Second, many common queries need to join three, four, or more tables to get the required answers. Third, with the implementations of relational joins provided by most DBMS systems, the performance of queries will deteriorate as they involve more and more joins.

An object-oriented model of the engineers and their degrees would tend to reject the table structure of Figure 23-5. It would claim that the degrees are not substantial "objects" in their own right and deserving of their own table. Instead, they are *attributes* of the engineer holding the degrees. True, a variable number of degrees are associated with each engineer, but the object-oriented model would have no problem with representing this situation as an array or a set of data *within* the engineer object.

The object-relational databases support this object-oriented view of data by supporting sets, arrays, or other "collection" data types. A column within a table can be defined to have one of these data types. It will then contain not a single data item value but a *set* of data item values. Special SQL extensions allow a user, or more often a stored procedure, to manipulate the set of data items as a whole or to access individual members of the set.

Defining Collections

Informix Universal Server supports collections of attributes through its *collection data types*. Three different collection data types are supported:

- A *list* is an ordered collection of data items, all of which have the same type. Within a list, there is the concept of a "first" item, a "last" item, and the *n*-th item. The items in the list are *not* required to be unique. For example, a list of the first names of the employees hired in the last year, in order of hire, might be {'Jim', 'Mary', 'Sam', 'Jim', 'John'}.

- A *multiset* is an unordered collection of data items, all of which have the same type. There is no concept of a sequencing to the items in a multiset; its items have no implied ordering. The items are *not* required to be unique. The list of employee first names could be considered a multiset if you didn't care about the order of hire: {'Jim', 'Sam', 'John', 'Jim', 'Mary'}.

- A *set* is an unordered collection of unique data items, all of which have the same type. As in a multiset, there is no concept of "first" or "last"; the set has no implied ordering. The items *must* have unique values. The first names in the previous examples wouldn't qualify, but the last names might: {'Johnson', 'Samuels', 'Wright', 'Jones', 'Smith'}.

To illustrate the concept of collection data, we will expand the tables in our example object-relational database as follows:

- The REPS table will include sales targets for each of the first, second, third, and fourth quarters. The quarterly targets can naturally be represented as a list column added to the REPS table. The quarters have a natural ordering (first through fourth), the quota for each quarter has the same data type (money), and the values are not necessarily unique (that is, the quotas for the first and second quarters might be the same).

- The ENGINEERS table will include information about the academic degrees that each engineer holds. Two items of data will actually be stored about each degree—the actual degree (B.S., Ph.D., MBA, and so on) and the school. This data will be stored as a multiset column added to the ENGINEERS table, because it's possible to have two identical entries—for example, an engineer may have an B.S. degree in engineering and an B.S. degree in business from the same school.

- The TECHNICIANS table will include information about the projects to which each technician is assigned. Each technician may be assigned to two or more projects, but each project has a unique name. This data will be stored as a set column added to the TECHNICIANS table. The data values must be unique, but no particular order is associated with them.

Here are some Informix ALTER TABLE statements that implement these changes to the previously defined tables:

```
ALTER TABLE REPS
      ADD QTR_TGT LIST(MONEY(9,2));   /* four quarterly targets */

ALTER TABLE TECHNICIANS
      ADD PROJECT SET(VARCHAR(15));   /* projects assigned */

ALTER TABLE ENGINEERS (
      ADD DEGREES MULTISET(ROW(      /* degree info */
   DEGREE VARCHAR(3),
   SCHOOL VARCHAR(15));
```

These collection column types create a "row-within-a-row" structure within the table that contains them, as shown in Figure 23-6. In the case of the ENGINEERS table, the structure might more accurately be described as a "table-within-a-table." Clearly, the relational model of row/column tables with atomic data items has been "stretched" considerably by the introduction of collection data types.

Informix Universal Server allows collections to be used quite generally and intermixed with other object-relational extensions. A collection can be a field of a row data type. The items of a collection can be row data types. It's also possible to define collections-within-collections where that makes sense. For example, the projects in this example might have subprojects that must be tracked for each technician. At each level of additional complexity, the complexity of the SPL and SQL expressions that are required to manipulate the data items and process them increases accordingly.

Oracle also provides extensive support for collection-type data, through two different Oracle object-relational extensions:

- A *varying array* is an ordered collection of data items, all having the same data type. There is no requirement that the items in the array be unique. You define the maximum number of data items that can occur when you specify a varying array type for a column. Oracle provides extensions to SQL to access the individual items within the array.

- A *nested table* is an actual table-within-a-table. A column with a nested table type contains individual data items that are themselves tables. Oracle actually stores the nested table data separately from the main table that contains it, but it uses SQL extensions to process nested references to the inner table. Unlike a varying array, a nested table can contain any number of rows.

A column within a table can be declared to have a VARRAY (varying array) or TABLE OF (nested table) structure. Here are some Oracle CREATE TYPE and CREATE

REPS Table

EMPL_NUM	NAME			ADDRESS					SLS_MGR	SALARY	QUOTA	QTR_TGT
	F_NAME	M_INIT	L_NAME	STREET	CITY	STATE	POSTCODE					
							MAIN	SFX				
4267	Nancy	Q.	Walsh	• • •	• • •	• • •	• • •	• • •	2598	$35,000	$750,000	$160,000
												$190,000
												$210,000
												$190,000
4316	Jim	F.	Rea	• • •	• • •	• • •	• • •	• • •	2598	$32,000	$690,000	$120,000
												$165,000
												$190,000
												$215,000
			•									
			•									
			•									

TECHNICIANS Table

EMPL_NUM	NAME			ADDRESS					WAGE_RATE	PROJECT
	F_NAME	M_INIT	L_NAME	STREET	CITY	STATE	POSTCODE			
							MAIN	SFX		
1421	Joe	P.	Jones	• • •	• • •	• • •	• • •	• • •	$16.75	bingo
										atlas
										checkmate
1537	Harry	E.	Franks	• • •	• • •	• • •	• • •	• • •	$20.50	atlas
1618	George	W.	Nye	• • •	• • •	• • •	• • •	• • •	$19.75	gonzo
										bingo
			•							
			•							

ENGINEERS Table

EMPL_NUM	NAME			ADDRESS					SALARY	YRS_EXPER	DEGREES	
	F_NAME	M_INIT	L_NAME	STREET	CITY	STATE	POSTCODE				DEGREE	SCHOOL
							MAIN	SFX				
1234	Bob	J.	Smith	• • •	• • •	• • •	• • •	• • •	$45,000	6	BS	Michigan
		F.									MS	Purdue
1374	Sam	P.	Wilson	• • •	• • •	• • •	• • •	• • •	$30,000	12	BS	Lehigh
1439	Sally		Watson	• • •	• • •	• • •	• • •	• • •	$34,500	9	BS	MIT
											BS	MIT
											MBA	Stanford
			•									
			•									
			•									

Figure 23-6.   *Tables with collection data typed columns*

TABLE statements that use varying arrays and nested tables to achieve table structures like those shown in Figure 23-6:

```
CREATE TABLE REPS (
    EMPL_NUM INTEGER,
        NAME NAME_TYPE,
    ADDRESS ADDR_TYPE,
    SLS_MGR INTEGER,                    /* employee number of mgr */
```

```
        SALARY MONEY(9,2),                        /* annual salary */
         QUOTA MONEY(9,2),                        /* sales quota */
       QTR_TGT VARRAY(4) OF NUMBER(9,2));         /* four quarterly tgts */

CREATE TYPE DEGR_TYPE AS OBJECT ( (
    DEGREE VARCHAR(3),
    SCHOOL VARCHAR(15));

CREATE TABLE ENGINEERS (
    EMPL_NUM INTEGER,
        NAME NAME_TYPE,
     ADDRESS ADDR_TYPE,
      SALARY NUMBER(9,2),                         /* annual salary */
   YRS_EXPER INTEGER,                             /* years of experience */
     DEGREES TABLE OF DEGR_TYPE);
NESTED TABLE DEGREES STORE AS DEGREES_TABLE;
```

The quarterly target information for the REPS table is most easily represented as an Oracle varying array column. There will be exactly four quarters of information, so the maximum size of the array is known in advance. In this example, the varying array contains a simple data item as its element, but it's also common to define varying arrays whose items are themselves abstract (structured) data types.

The academic degree information for the ENGINEERS table is represented as a nested table. For a data item like this one, you could decide to place an upper limit on the number of rows and use a varying array structure instead, but in general if the maximum number of items is unknown, a nested table is the right choice. In this case the nested table has an abstract data type composed of two attributes. Each "row" of the nested table will contain information about a degree granted and the school that granted it.

Querying Collection Data

Collection-valued columns complicate the process of querying the tables that contain them. In the SELECT item list, they generate multiple data values for each row of query results. In search conditions, they don't contain individual data items, but it's sometimes convenient to treat them as sets of data. The object-relational databases typically provide a limited set of SQL extensions or extend existing SQL concepts to provide simple queries involving collection data. For more advanced queries, they require you to write stored procedure language programs with loop structures that process the collection data items one-by-one.

For query purposes, Informix treats the collection types as if they were a set of data values, like the values that might be returned by a subquery. You can match individual items within a collection using the SQL IN search condition. Here is a query that finds any technicians who work on a project named "bingo":

```
SELECT EMPL_NUM, NAME
  FROM TECHNICIANS
 WHERE 'bingo' IN (PROJECTS);
```

The name of the collection-valued column (in this case, the set-valued column PROJECTS) appears in parentheses. Informix treats the members of the collection as a set and applies the IN matching condition. In interactive SQL, you can put a collection-valued column in the select item list. Informix displays the collection of data as either a SET, LIST, or MULTISET in the displayed output. To process collection-valued data in the select list of a programmatic request (that is, from a program using ESQL or a call-level API), you must use special API extensions and/or extensions to the Informix stored procedure language.

Oracle provides additional capabilities for processing nested tables within SQL queries. A special THE keyword "flattens" the nested table, in effect producing an unnested table with one row for each row of the nested table within each row of the main table. Here's a query that shows the schools from which one of the engineers has received degrees:

```
SELECT NEST.SCHOOL
  FROM THE (SELECT DEGREES
              FROM ENGINEERS
             WHERE EMPL_NUM = 1234) NEST;
```

The query within the inner parentheses is a query against the main (ENGINEERS) table. It selects the column containing the nested table, but it could select other columns as well. The THE operation, applied to the query results, flattens them out, creating a row for each nested row within each row of the main table. This flattened table is assigned an alias (NEST in this example), and it becomes the source of candidate query results rows from the FROM clause of the main, top-level query. With this table as a source, the main query in this example is quite simple; it selects one column that originated in the nested table.

The ability to flatten nested tables in this way and process them as if they were actually joined versions of two separate tables is actually quite powerful. It allows many queries to be expressed in high-level SQL that would otherwise require you to resort to stored procedures. However, the logic behind such queries and the task of actually constructing them correctly can be extremely complicated, as even this simple example begins to show.

Manipulating Collection Data

Extensions to standard SQL syntax are used to insert new rows into a table containing collection-valued columns. Informix provides a trio of "constructors"—the SET constructor, MULTISET constructor, and LIST constructor—for this purpose. They transform a list of data items into the corresponding collections to be inserted. Here is a pair of INSERT statements that illustrates their use with the tables in Figure 23-6:

```
INSERT INTO TECHNICIANS
    VALUES (1279,
            ROW('Sam','R','Jones'),
            ROW('164 Elm St.','Highland','IL',ROW(12345,6789)),
            "SET{'atlas','checkmate','bingo'}");

INSERT INTO ENGINEERS
    VALUES (1281,
            ROW('Jeff','R','Ames'),
            ROW('1648 Green St.','Elgin','IL',ROW(12345,6789)),
            "MULTISET{ROW('BS','Michigan'),
                      ROW('BS','Michigan'),
                      ROW('PhD','Stanford')}");
```

The first statement inserts a single row into the TECHNICIANS table with a three-item set in the PROJECTS column. The second inserts a single row into the ENGINEERS table with a three-item multiset in the DEGREES column. Because the members of this particular multiset are themselves row types, the row constructor must be used for each item.

Oracle uses a different approach to constructing the collection-valued data items for insertion into the table. Recall from the discussion of Oracle abstract data types that each Oracle abstract data type automatically has an associated *constructor method* that is used to "build" a data item of the abstract type out of individual data items. This concept is extended to varying arrays and nested tables. A constructor method is automatically supplied for each varying array or nested table, and it is used in the INSERT statements:

```
INSERT INTO TECHNICIANS
    VALUES (NAME_TYPE('Sam','R','Jones'),
            ADDR_TYPE('164 Elm St.','Highland','IL',
                      POST_TYPE(12345,6789)),
            PROJECTS('atlas','checkmate','bingo'));
```

```
INSERT INTO ENGINEERS
    VALUES (NAME_TYPE('Jeff','R','Ames'),
            ADDR_TYPE('1648 Green St.','Elgin','IL',
                      POST_TYPE(12345,6789)),
            DEGREES(DEGREE_TYPE('BS','Michigan'),
                    DEGREE_TYPE('BS','Michigan'),
                    DEGREE_TYPE('PhD','Stanford'))));
```

Collections and Stored Procedures

Collections pose special problems for stored procedures that are retrieving and manipulating data in tables that contain them. Both Oracle and Informix provide special stored procedure language facilities for this purpose. In Informix, special SPL collection variables must be used. Here is an SPL stored procedure fragment that handles the PROJECTS collection column from the TECHNICIANS table:

```
define proj_coll collection;          /* holds project collection */
define a_project varchar(15);         /* holds individual project */
define proj_cnt  integer;             /* number of projects */
define empl_name name_type;           /* buffer for tech name */

/* Check how many projects the technician is supporting */
select cardinality(projects) into proj_cnt
  from technicians
 where empl_num = 1234;

/* If too many projects, then refuse to add a new one */
if (proj_cnt > 6) then . . .

/* Retrieve row, including project set for the technician */
select name, projects into empl_name, proj_coll
  from technicians
 where empl_num = 1234;

/* Add the 'gonzo' project to the list for this tech */
insert into table(proj_coll)
     values ('gonzo');

/* Search through project list one by one */
foreach proj_cursor for
 select * into a_project
   from table(proj_coll)
```

```
    if (a_project = 'atlas') then
       begin
          update table(proj_coll)(project)
             set project = 'bingo'
           where current of proj_cursor;
          exit foreach;
       end;
    end if;
end foreach;

/* Update the database row with modified project list */
update technicians
   set projects = proj_coll
 where empl_num = 1234;
```

The example shows several aspects of collection-handling in Informix SPL. First, the collection is retrieved from the database into an SPL variable as a "collection" data type. It would also be possible to retrieve it into a variable explicitly declared as having a SET type (or in other situations, a LIST or MULTSET type). The collection stored in the variable is then explicitly treated as a table for manipulating items within the collection. To add a new project, an INSERT is performed into the collection "table." To find and modify a specific project, a cursor is used to search through the collection "table," and a cursor-based UPDATE statement is used to change the value of one member of the collection. Note that the FOREACH loop retrieves each item of the collection into a variable so that the SPL routine can process it. Finally, the collection variable's contents are used to update the collection column within the table.

Oracle takes a similar approach to processing varying arrays. The individual elements of an array within an abstract data type are available through subscripted references within a structured data type. The typical Oracle PL/SQL process for accessing variable array elements is:

1. Retrieve the row from the table containing the varying array into a local variable whose data type is defined to match the row structure of the table, or of the particular columns being retrieved.

2. Execute a FOR loop with an index variable, n, that counts from 1 to the number of elements in the varying array. The number of elements is available through the value of a "special" attribute of the array column named COUNT.

3. Within the FOR loop, a subscript is used on the varying array name to access the n-th element of the varying array.

A similar technique can be used to process nested tables; however, it's usually not necessary. Instead, the THE operator is generally used to flatten the table in a SQL query, and the results are processed with a single cursor-driven FOR loop. The processing may still be complex. In particular, the stored procedure may need to detect whether a particular row coming from the query results is from the same "main table" row as the previous row and, upon detecting a change in "main table" rows, perform special processing such as computing subtotals. In this aspect, the processing of both varying arrays and nested tables begins to resemble the nested-loop processing typical of the COBOL report-writing programs of 30 years ago that handled "master" and "detail" records.

As the discussion in this section has illustrated, collection types and the processing of individual collection items tend to call for programmatic access through stored procedures rather than for *ad hoc* SQL use. One of the criticisms of object-oriented databases is that they are a regression from the simplicity of the relational model and reintroduce that need for explicit database navigation that was part of the pre-relational databases. Examples like these provide evidence that there is at least a certain amount of truth in the criticism.

User-Defined Data Types

Object-relational data management systems generally provide a mechanism through which a user can extend the built-in data types provided by the DBMS with additional, user-defined data types. For example, a mapping application might need to operate on a LOCATION data type that consists of a pair of latitude and longitude measurements, each consisting of hours, minutes, and seconds. To effectively process location data, the application may need to define special functions, such as a DISTANCE(X,Y) function that computes the distance between two locations. The meanings of some built-in operations, such as a test for equality (=) will need to be redefined for location type data.

One way that Informix Universal Server supports user-defined data types is through its OPAQUE data type. An OPAQUE data type is (not surprisingly) "opaque" to the DBMS. The DBMS can store and retrieve data with this type, but it has no knowledge of the internal workings of the type. In object-oriented terms, the data is completely encapsulated. The user must explicitly provide (in external routines, written in C or some similar programming language) the data structure for the type, code to implement the functions or operations that can be performed on the type (such as comparing two data items of the type for equality), and code to convert the opaque type between internal and external representations. Thus, OPAQUE data types represent a low-level capability to extend the core functionality of the DBMS with data types that appear as if they were built-in.

A more basic user-defined data type capability is provided by the implementation of DISTINCT data types within Informix. A DISTINCT type is useful to distinguish among different types of data, all of which use one of the DBMS built-in data types. For example, the city and company name data items in a database might both be defined with the data type VARCHAR(20). Even though they share the same underlying DBMS data type, these data items really represent quite different types of data. You would never normally compare a city value to a company name, and yet the DBMS will let you do this because the two VARCHAR(20) columns are directly comparable.

To maintain a higher level of database integrity, you could define each of these three data items as having a DISTINCT data type:

```
CREATE DISTINCT TYPE CITY_TYPE AS VARCHAR(20);
CREATE DISTINCT TYPE CO_NAME_TYPE AS VARCHAR(20);
```

Now tables can be created containing city and customer name data items in terms of the CITY_TYPE and CO_NAME_TYPE data types. If you try to compare columns with these two different data types, the DBMS automatically detects the situation and generates an error. You *can* compare them, but only by explicitly casting the data type of one item to match the data type of the other. As a result, the distinct data types assigned to the different columns help to maintain the integrity of the database and prevent inadvertent errors in programs and *ad hoc* queries that use the database.

Methods and Stored Procedures

In object-oriented languages, objects encapsulate both the data and programming code that they contain; the details of the data structures within an object and the programming instructions that manipulate those data structures are explicitly hidden from view. The only way to manipulate the object and obtain information about it is through *methods*, which are explicitly defined procedures associated with the object (or more accurately with the object class). For example, one method associated with a customer object might obtain the customer's current credit limit. Another method might provide the ability to change the credit limit. The credit limit data itself is encapsulated, hidden within the customer object.

The data within the tables of a relational database is inherently *not* encapsulated. The data and its structure are directly visible to "outside" users. In fact, one of the main advantages of a relational database is that SQL can be used to carry out *ad hoc* queries against the database. When the system catalog of a relational database is considered, the contrast with the object-oriented ideal is even more extreme. With the catalog, the database is self-describing, so that even applications that don't know the internal structure of the database in advance can use SQL queries to find out what it is!

Stored procedures provide a way for relational databases to offer capabilities that resemble those of object-oriented methods. At the extreme, all users of a relational database could be granted permission only to execute a limited set of stored procedures, and no underlying data access permissions on the base tables at all. In this case, the users' access would approach the encapsulation of the object-oriented ideal. In practice, stored procedures are often used to provide application designers with the limited database access that they need. However, the *ad hoc* capabilities of the database are almost always exploited by query tools or reporting programs.

Oracle formalizes the linkage between object methods and database stored procedures by allowing you to explicitly define a stored procedure as a *member function* of an abstract data type. Once defined in this way, the member function can be used in queries involving the abstract data type, just as if it were a built-in function of the DBMS designed to work on that type. Here is a redefinition of the ADDR_TYPE abstract data type that is used to store addresses, with a relatively simple member function, named GET_FULL_POST. The function takes the postal-code part of the address, which stores both a five-digit main postal code and a four-digit suffix as two separate numbers, and combines them into one nine-digit number, which it returns:

```
CREATE TYPE ADDR_TYPE AS OBJECT (
     STREET VARCHAR(35),
       CITY VARCHAR(15),
      STATE CHAR(2),
   POSTCODE POST_TYPE,
     MEMBER FUNCTION GET_FULL_POST(POSTCODE IN POST_TYPE)
     RETURN NUMBER,
     PRAGMA RESTRICT_REFERENCES(GET_FULL_POST, WNDS));

CREATE TYPE BODY ADDR_TYPE AS
     MEMBER FUNCTION GET_FULL_POST(POSTCODE POST_TYPE)
     RETURN NUMBER IS
       BEGIN
         RETURN((POSTCODE.MAIN * 10000) + POSTCODE.SFX);
       END;
      . . .
```

The member function is identified as such within the CREATE TYPE statement for the abstract data type, following the lines that describe the data items. The additional PRAGMA clause tells Oracle that the function does not modify the contents of the database, which is a requirement for a function that is to be used within query expressions. There are several more options, which are beyond the scope of this discussion. A separate CREATE TYPE BODY statement defines the actual procedural code for the function. After the first few words of the statement, it follows the same format as the standard CREATE PROCEDURE or CREATE FUNCTION statements. Once the member function is defined, it can be used in query expressions like this one, which finds employees living in postal code 12345-6789:

```
SELECT EMPL_NUM
  FROM PERSONNEL
 WHERE GET_FULL_POST(ADDRESS.POSTCODE) = 123456789;
```

Informix Universal Server doesn't have an extended mechanism like Oracle's to turn stored procedures into object-oriented methods. Instead, it's possible to use an Informix row type (corresponding to an Oracle "object" type) as the parameter of a stored function. When called, the function is passed a data item with the appropriate row type (such as the POSTCODE abstract data item in the preceding Oracle example) and can perform appropriate calculations on it. You could, for example, define an Informix stored function GET_FULL_POST() with a single parameter of type POST_TYPE. With that definition, the preceding Oracle SELECT statement could be used, unmodified, in the equivalent Informix database.

Another powerful feature associated with object-relational stored procedures is the *overloading* of procedure definitions to allow them to process different types of data. In an object class hierarchy, it's frequently necessary to define a method that carries out the same or very similar operations on different classes of objects. For example, you may want to define a GET_TGT_WAGES method (function) that can obtain the target total annual wages for any of the subclasses of the PERSONNEL class in our example database. The method (which will be implemented as a stored function) should return the target total wages for the employee to which it is applied. The particulars of the calculation differ, depending on the type ("class") of employee:

- For technicians, total wages are the hourly rate times a normal 40-hour week, times 52 weeks per year.
- For managers, total wages are equal to their annual salary plus bonus.
- For all other engineers, total wages are equal to their annual salary.

To solve this problem, a *different* GET_TGT_WAGES routine is defined for each class. The routine takes an object (a row of the TECHNICIANS, ENGINEERS, or MANAGERS table) as its parameter and returns the calculated amount. The three routines are identically named, which is the reason why the procedure name is said to be "overloaded"—a single name is associated with more than one actual stored procedure. When the routine is called, the DBMS looks at the particular data type of the argument (that is, the particular class of the object) and determines which of the routines is the appropriate one to call.

Informix Universal Server implements this stored procedure overloading capability without any additional object-oriented extensions. It allows you to define many different stored procedures with identical names, provided that no two of them have the identical number of arguments with identical data types. In the previous example, there would be three CREATE FUNCTION definitions like this:

```
/* Calculates target wages for a technician */
CREATE FUNCTION GET_TGT_WAGES(PERSON TECH_TYPE)
   RETURNS MONEY(9,2) AS RETURN (PERSON.WAGE_RATE * 40 * 52)
END FUNCTION;

/* Calculates target wages for a manager */
CREATE FUNCTION GET_TGT_WAGES(PERSON MGR_TYPE)
   RETURNS MONEY(9,2) AS RETURN (PERSON.SALARY + PERSON.BONUS)
END FUNCTION;

/* Calculates target wages for an engineer */
CREATE FUNCTION GET_TGT_WAGES(PERSON ENGR_TYPE)
   RETURNS MONEY(9,2) AS RETURN (PERSON.SALARY)
END FUNCTION;
```

With these definitions in place, you can invoke the GET_TGT_WAGES() function and pass it a row from the ENGINEERS, MANAGERS, or TECHNICIANS table. The DBMS automatically figures out which of the functions to use and returns the appropriate calculated value.

Stored procedures are made even more valuable for typed tables through Informix Universal Server's *substitutability* feature. If you call a stored procedure whose argument is a row type and pass it one of the rows from a typed table, Informix will first search for a stored procedure with the appropriate name whose argument data type is an exact match. For example, if you call a GET_LNAME() stored procedure to extract the last name from a TECH_TYPE row (probably from the TECHNICIANS table), Informix searches for a procedure written to process TECH_TYPE data. But if Informix doesn't find such a stored procedure, it does not immediately return with an error. Instead, it searches upwards in the type hierarchy, trying to find a procedure with the same name that is defined for a supertype of TECH_TYPE. If there is a GET_LNAME() stored procedure defined for the ENGR_TYPE type, Informix will execute that stored procedure to obtain the required information. If not, it will continue up the hierarchy, looking for a GET_LNAME() stored procedure defined for the PERS_TYPE type. Thus, substitutability means that you can define stored procedures (methods) for the highest-level type in the hierarchy to which they apply. The stored procedures are automatically available to process all subtypes of that type (that is, all subclasses inherit the method from the class).

Summary

Object-oriented databases will likely play an increasing role in specialized market segments, such as engineering design, compound document processing, and graphical user interfaces. They are not being widely adopted for mainstream enterprise data processing applications. However, hybrid object-relational databases are being offered by some of the leading enterprise DBMS vendors:

- The object-relational databases significantly extend the SQL and stored procedure languages with object-oriented statements, structures, and capabilities.

- Common object-relational structures include abstract/structured data types, tables-within-tables, and explicit support for object identifiers. These capabilities stretch the simple relational model a great deal and tend to add complexity for casual or *ad hoc* users.

- The object-relational extensions added by the various DBMS vendors are highly proprietary. There are significant conceptual differences in the approaches as well as differences in implementation approach.

- Object-relational capabilities are particularly well suited for more complex data models, where the overall design of the database may be simpler, even though individual tables/objects are more complex.

- Object-relational capabilities are a major focus of the SQL3 standards efforts, and more relational databases are likely to incorporate them in the future.

Chapter 24

The Future of SQL

SQL is one of the most important foundation technologies underpinning the computer market today. From its first commercial implementation about two decades ago, SQL has grown to become *the* standard database language. In its first decade, the backing of IBM, the blessing of standards bodies, and the enthusiastic support of DBMS vendors made SQL a dominant standard for enterprise-class data management. In its second decade, the dominance of SQL extended to personal computer and workgroup environments and to new, database-driven market segments, such as data warehousing. Today's evidence clearly shows the importance of SQL:

- The world's second-largest software company, Oracle, has been built on the success of SQL-based relational data management, through both its flagship database servers and tools and SQL-based enterprise applications.

- IBM, the world's largest computer company, offers its SQL-based DB2 product line as a common foundation across all of its product lines and for use on competitor's systems as well.

- Microsoft, the world's largest software company, uses SQL Server as a critical part of its strategy to penetrate the enterprise computing market with its Windows NT and Windows 2000 platforms.

- Every significant database company offers either a SQL-based relational database product or SQL-based access to its non-relational products.

- All of the major packaged enterprise applications (enterprise resource planning, supply chain management, financial reporting, sales force automation, customer service management, etc.) are built on SQL-based databases.

- SQL is emerging as a standard for specialized databases in applications ranging from data warehousing to mobile laptop databases to embedded applications in telecomm and data communications networks.

- SQL-based access to databases is an integral feature of Windows, available on the vast majority of personal computer systems, and it is a built-in capability of popular PC software products such as spreadsheets and report writers.

This chapter describes some of the most important current trends and developments in the database market, and projects the major forces acting on SQL and database management over the next five to ten years.

Database Market Trends

Today's market for database management products exceeds $10 billion per year in products and services revenues, up from about $3 billion per year a decade ago. On several occasions over the last decade, lower year-over-year growth in the quarterly revenues of the major database vendors have led analysts to talk about a maturing database market. Each time, a wave of new products or new data management applications has returned the market to double-digit growth. If the history of the 1990s is any indication, database technology will continue to find new applications and generate increasing revenues for years to come. The trends shaping the market bode well for its continued health and point to a continuing tension between market maturity and consolidation on the one hand and exciting new database capabilities and applications on the other.

Enterprise Database Market Maturity

Relational database technology has become accepted as a core enterprise data processing technology and relational databases have been deployed by virtually all large corporations. Because of the importance of corporate databases and years of experience in using relational technology, many, if not most, large corporations have selected a single DBMS brand as an enterprise-wide database standard. Once such a standard has been established and widely deployed within a company, there is strong resistance to switching brands. Even though an alternative DBMS product may offer advantages for a particular application or may pioneer a new, useful feature, an announcement by the "standard" vendor that such features are planned for a future release will often forestall the loss of a customer by the established vendor. The trend to corporate database standards has tended to reinforce and strengthen the market positions of the established major DBMS vendors. The existence of large direct sales forces, established customer support relationships, and multi-year volume purchase agreements has become as important as, or more important than, technology advantage. With this market dynamic, the large, established players tend to concentrate on growing their business within their existing installed base instead of attempting to take customers away from competitors. In the late 1990s, industry analysts saw and predicted this tendency at both Informix and Sybase. Oracle, with a much larger share of the market, was forced to aggressively compete for new accounts in its attempt to maintain its database license revenue growth. Microsoft, as the "upstart" in the enterprise database market, was cast in the role of challenger, attempting to leverage its position in workgroup databases into enterprise-level prototypes and pilot projects as a way to pry enterprise business away from the established players.

One important impact of the trend to corporate DBMS vendor standardization has been a consolidation in the database industry. New startup database vendors tend to pioneer new database technology and grow by selling it to early adopters. These early adopters have helped to shape the technology and identified the solution areas where it can deliver real benefits. After a few years, when the advantages of the new technology have been demonstrated, the startup vendors are acquired by large, established players. These vendors can bring the new technology into their installed base, and bring their marketing and sales muscle to bear in an attempt to win business in their competitor's accounts. The early 1990s saw this cycle play out with database vendor acquisitions of database tools vendors. In the late 1990s, the same cycle applied to mergers and acquisitions of database vendors. Informix's purchase of Illustra (a pioneering object-relational vendor) and Red Brick (a pioneering data warehousing vendor) are two examples of the pattern.

Market Diversity and Segmentation

Despite the maturing of some parts of the database market (especially the market for corporate enterprise-class database systems), it continues to develop new segments and niches that appear and then grow rapidly. For much of the 1990s, the most useful way to segment the database market has been based on database size and scale—there were PC databases, minicomputer databases, mainframe databases, and later workgroup databases. Today's database market is much more diverse and is more accurately segmented based on target application and specialized database capabilities to address unique application requirements. Market segments that have appeared and are experiencing high growth include:

■ Data warehousing databases, focused on managing thousands of gigabytes of data, such as historical retail purchase data.

■ OLAP and ROLAP databases, focused on carrying out complex analyses of data to discover underlying trends ("data mining"), allowing organizations to make better business decisions.

■ Mobile databases, in support of mobile workers such as salespeople, support personnel, field service people, consultants, and mobile professionals. Often these mobile databases are tied back to a centralized database for synchronization.

■ Embedded databases, which are an integral, transparent part of an application sold by an ISV or a VAR. These databases are characterized by small footprints and very simple administration.

■ Micro-databases, designed for appliance-type devices, such as smart cards, network computers, smart phones, and handheld PCs and organizers.

■ In-memory databases, designed for ultra-high-performance OLTP applications, such as those embedded in telecomm and data communications networks and used to support customer interaction in very high-volume Internet applications.

Packaged Enterprise Applications

A decade or two ago, the vast majority of corporate applications were developed in-house by the company's information systems department. Decisions about database technology and vendor standardization were part of the company's IS architecture planning function. Leading-edge companies sometimes took a risk on new, relatively unproven database technologies in the belief that they could gain competitive advantage by using them. Sybase's rise to prominence in the financial services sector during the late 1980s and early 1990s is an example.

Today, most corporations have shifted from "make" to "buy" strategies for major enterprise-wide applications. Examples include Enterprise Resource Planning (ERP) applications, Supply Chain Management (SCM) applications, Human Resource Management (HRM) applications, Sales Force Automation (SFA) applications, customer support applications, and others. All of these areas are now supplied as enterprise-class packaged applications, along with consulting, customization and installation services, by groups of software vendors. Several of these vendors have reached multi-hundred-million dollar annual revenues. All of these packages are built on a foundation of SQL-based relational databases.

The emergence of dominant purchased enterprise applications has had a significant effect on the dynamics of the database market. The major enterprise software package vendors have tended to support DBMS products from only two or three of the major DBMS vendors. For example, if a customer chooses to deploy SAP as its enterprise-wide ERP application, the underlying database is restricted to those supported by the SAP packages. This has tended to reinforce the dominant position of the current "top-tier" enterprise database players and make it more difficult for newer database vendors. It has also tended to lower average database prices, as the DBMS is viewed more as a component part of an application-driven decision rather than a strategic decision in its own right.

The emergence of packaged enterprise software has also shifted the relative power of corporate IS organizations and the packaged software vendors. The DBMS vendors today have marketing and business development teams focused on the major enterprise application vendors to insure that the latest versions of the applications support their DBMS and to support performance tuning and other activities. The largest independent DBMS vendor, Oracle Corporation, is playing *both* roles, supplying both DBMS software and major enterprise applications (that run on the Oracle DBMS, of course).

Hardware Performance Gains

One of the most important contributors to the rise of SQL has been a dramatic increase in the performance of relational databases. Part of this performance increase was due to advances in database technology and query optimization. However, most of the DBMS performance improvement came from gains in the raw processing power of the underlying computer systems. For example, with the introduction of one new DB2 version, IBM claimed a performance increase of 120 percent over the previous DB2 release. However, a close examination of the underlying performance data showed that DB2 software performance improved only 51 percent; the rest of the increase was due to the more powerful mainframe on which the new tests were conducted.

The performance improvements in mainframe systems were paralleled in the Unix-based and Windows-based server markets, where processing power continues to double year by year. Some of the most dramatic advances are in symmetric multiprocessor (SMP) systems, where two, four, eight, or more processors operate in parallel, sharing the processing workload. A multiprocessor architecture can be applied to OLTP applications, where the workload consists of many small, parallel database transactions. Traditional OLTP vendors, such as Tandem, have always used a multiprocessor architecture, and the largest mainframe systems have used multiprocessor designs for more than a decade. In the early 1990s, multiprocessor systems became a mainstream part of the Unix-based server market, and somewhat later, an important factor at the high end of the PC server market. With Intel's introduction of multiprocessor chipsets, SMP systems featuring 2-way and 4-way multiprocessing achieved near-commodity status in the LAN server market, and were available for well under $10,000.

SMP systems also provided performance benefits in decision support and data analysis applications. As SMP servers became more common, the DBMS vendors invested in "parallel" versions of their systems that were able to take the work of a single complex SQL query and split it into multiple, parallel paths of execution. When a DBMS with parallel query capabilities is installed on a 4-way or 8-way SMP system, a query that might have taken two hours on a single-processor system can be completed in less than an hour. Companies are taking advantage of this hardware-based performance boost in two ways: either by obtaining business analysis results in a fraction of the time previously required or by leaving the timeframe constant and carrying out much more complex and sophisticated analysis.

Operating system support for new hardware features (such as multiprocessor architectures) has often lagged the availability of the hardware capabilities—often by several quarters or even years. This has posed a special dilemma for DBMS vendors, who need to decide whether to bypass the operating system in an attempt to improve database performance. The Sybase DBMS, for example, when originally introduced, operated as a single process and took responsibility for its own task management, event handling, and input/output—functions that are usually handled by an operating system such as Unix or VMS. In the short term, this gave Sybase a major performance advantage over rival DBMS products with less parallel processing capability. But when operating system SMP support arrived, many of its benefits were "automatically" available to rival systems that had relied on the operating system for task management, while Sybase had the continuing burden of extending and enhancing its low-level performance-oriented software. This cycle has played out for SMP designs, with major database vendors now relying on operating systems for thread support and SMP scaling. But the same tradeoffs continue to apply to new hardware features as they appear and require explicit strategic decisions on the part of the DBMS vendors.

Another hardware-based market trend in the 1980s and early 1990s was the emergence of companies that combined high-performance microprocessors, fast disk drives, and multiprocessor architectures to build dedicated systems that were optimized as database servers. These vendors argued that they could deliver much better database performance with a specially designed database engine than with a general-purpose computer system. In some cases, their systems included application-specific integrated circuits (ASICs) that implement some of the DBMS logic in hardware for maximum speed. Dedicated database systems from companies such as Teradata and Sharebase (formerly Britton-Lee) found some acceptance in applications that involve complex queries against very large databases. However, they have not become an important part of the mainstream database market, and these vendors eventually disappeared or were acquired by larger, general-purpose computer companies.

Interestingly, the notion of a packaged, all-in-one "database server appliance" was rekindled at the end of the decade by Oracle Corporation and its CEO, Larry Ellison. They argue that the Internet era had seen the success of other "all-in-one" products, such as networking equipment and Web cache servers. Whether the notion of a database server appliance will catch on or not remains an open question as of this writing.

In contrast, it appears certain that continuing advances in processor technology and I/O subsystems will continue to drive database performance higher. With today's highest-performance servers featuring dozens of multi-hundred-megahertz processors, hardware advances have more than overcome the higher overhead of the relational data model, giving it performance equal to, or better than, the nonrelational databases of a decade ago. At the same time, of course, the demand for higher and higher transaction rates against larger and larger databases continues to grow. At the top end of the database market, it appears that one can never have "too much" database performance.

Benchmark Wars

As SQL-based relational databases have moved into the mainstream of enterprise data processing, database performance has become a critical factor in DBMS selection. User focus on database performance, coupled with the DBMS vendors' interest in selling high-priced, high-margin, high-end DBMS configurations, has produced a series of "benchmark wars" among DBMS vendors. Virtually all of the DBMS vendors have joined the fray at some point over the last decade. Some have focused on maximum absolute database performance. Others emphasize price/performance and the cost-effectiveness of their DBMS solution. Still others emphasize performance for specific types of database processing, such as OLTP or OLAP. In every case, the vendors tout benchmarks that show the superior performance of their products while trying to discredit the benchmarks of competitors.

The early benchmark claims focused on vendor-proprietary tests, and then on two early vendor-independent benchmarks that emerged. The Debit/Credit benchmark simulated simple accounting transactions. The TP1 benchmark, first defined by Tandem, measured basic OLTP performance. These simple standardized benchmarks were still easy for the vendors to manipulate to produce results that cast them in the most favorable light.

In an attempt to bring more stability and meaning to the benchmark data, several vendors and database consultants banded together to produce standardized database benchmarks that would allow meaningful comparisons among various DBMS products. This group, called the Transaction Processing Council, defined a series of "official" OLTP benchmarks, known as TPC-A, TPC-B, and TPC-C. The Council has also assumed a role as a clearinghouse for validating and publishing the results of benchmarks run on various brands of DBMS and computer systems. The results of TPC benchmarks are usually expressed in transactions per minute (e.g., tpmC), but it's common to hear the results referred to simply by the benchmark name (e.g.,"DBMS Brand X on hardware Y delivered 10,000 TPC-Cs").

The most recent TCP OLTP benchmark, TPC-C, attempts to measure not just raw database server performance but the overall performance of a client/server configuration. Modern multiprocessor workgroup-level servers are delivering thousands or tens of thousands of transactions per minute on the TPC-C test. Enterprise-class Unix-based SMP servers are delivering multiple tens of thousands of tpmC. The maximum results on typical commercially-available systems (a multi-million dollar 64-bit Alpha processor cluster) exceed 100,000 tpmC.

The Transaction Processing Council has branched out beyond OLTP to develop benchmarks for other areas of database performance. The TPC-D benchmark focuses on data warehousing applications. The suite of tests that comprise TPC-D are based on a database schema typical of warehousing environments, and they include more complex data analysis queries, rather than the simple database operations more typical of OLTP environments. As of this writing, development is underway on a third type of benchmark, currently called "TPC-W." This benchmark is designed to measure database performance in a typical Web-based Internet application.

Interestingly, the TPC benchmarks specify that the size of the database must increase as the claimed number of transactions per minute goes up. A TPC benchmark result of 5,000 tpmC may reflect results on a database of hundreds of megabytes of data, for example, while a result of 20,000 tpmC on the same benchmark may reflect a test on a multi-gigabyte database. This provision of the TPC benchmarks is designed to add more realism to the benchmark results since the size of database and computer system needed to support an application with demands in the 5,000 tpm range is typically much smaller than the scale required to support an application with 20,000 tpm demands.

In addition to raw performance, the TPC benchmarks also measure database price/performance. The "price" used in the calculation is specified by the council as the five-year ownership cost of the database solution, including the purchase price of the computer system, the purchase price of the database software, five years of maintenance and support costs, etc. The price/performance measure is expressed in "dollar-per-TPC" (e.g., "Oracle on a Compaq 4-way server broke through the $500-per-TPC-C barrier"). While higher numbers are better for transactions-per-minute results, lower numbers are better for price/performance measure.

Over the last several years, vendor emphasis on TPC benchmark results have waxed and waned. The existence of the TPC benchmarks, and the requirement that published TPC results be audited, have added a level of integrity and stability to benchmark claims. It appears that benchmarking and performance testing will be part of the database market environment for some time to come. In general, benchmark results can help with matching database and hardware configurations to the rough requirements of an application. On an absolute basis, small advantages in benchmark performance for one DBMS over another will probably be masked by other factors.

SQL Standardization

The adoption of an official ANSI/ISO SQL standard was one of the major factors that secured SQL's place as the standard relational database language in the 1980s. Compliance with the ANSI/ISO standard has become a checkoff item for evaluating DBMS products, so each DBMS vendor claims that its product is "compatible with" or "based on" the ANSI/ISO standard. Through the late 1980s and early 1990s, all of the popular DBMS products evolved to conform to the parts of the standard that represented common usage. Other parts, such as the module language, were effectively ignored. This produced slow convergence around a core SQL language in popular DBMS products.

As discussed in Chapter 3, the SQL1 standard was relatively weak, with many omissions and areas that are left as implementation choices. For several years, the standards committee worked on an expanded SQL2 standard that remedies these weaknesses and significantly extends the SQL language. Unlike the first SQL standard, which specified features that were already available in most SQL products, the SQL2 standard, when it was published in 1992, was an attempt to lead rather than follow the market. It specified features and functions that were not yet widely implemented in current DBMS products, such as scroll cursors, standardized system catalogs, much broader use of subqueries, and a new error message scheme. DBMS vendors are still in the process of evolving their products to support the full features of SQL2. In practice, proprietary extensions (such as enhanced support for multimedia data or stored procedures or object extensions) have often been more important to a DBMS vendor's success than higher levels of SQL2 compliance.

The work of the SQL standards groups continues, but it appears unlikely to produce a single "SQL3" standard as a large step forward. Work on "SQL3" was divided fairly early into separate, parallel efforts, focused on the core of the language, a call-level interface, persistent stored modules (stored procedures), distributed transaction capabilities, time-based data, etc. Some of these efforts have already surfaced as standards in their own right, or as enhancements to the 1992 SQL2 standard. For example, a SQL2-compatible call-level interface (CLI) standard was released in 1995.

The major thrust of the SQL3 core language work (called the "foundation" part of the standard) has been on adding object capabilities to SQL2. This has been a very controversial activity. Relational database theorists and purists have taken a strong stand against many of the proposed extensions. They claim that the proposals confuse conceptual and architectural issues (e.g., adding substructure beyond the row/column tables) with implementation issues (e.g., performance issues of normalized databases and multi-table joins). Others point to the popularity of object-oriented programming and development techniques, and insist that the rigid row/column structure of relational databases must be extended to embrace object concepts or it will be bypassed by the object revolution.

The disagreements over the core SQL language object capabilities have impacted the progress of other areas of the standard as well. The call level interface (CLI) must be extended to allow retrieval and manipulation of more complex objects beyond simple columns with scalar data types, for example. However, this work cannot be done until the object capabilities of the SQL language itself are firm. For this reason, final agreement on a collection of standards that equate to what was originally envisioned as "SQL3" seems to still be well in the future. In a market environment where major database systems have not yet achieved full SQL2 compliance, it appears likely that the DBMS vendors will pick and choose which pieces of new standards they will support, focusing on those where they can extend their competitive advantage.

In addition to the official SQL standard, IBM's and Oracle's SQL products will continue to be a powerful influence on the evolution of SQL. As the developer of SQL and a major influencer of corporate IS management, IBM's SQL decisions have always had a major impact on other vendors of SQL products. Oracle's dominant market position has given it similar clout when it has added new SQL features to its products. When the IBM, Oracle, and ANSI SQL dialects have differed in the past, most independent DBMS vendors have chosen to follow the IBM or Oracle standards.

The likely path of SQL standardization thus appears to be a continuation of the history of the last several years. The core of the SQL language will continue to be highly standard. More features will slowly become a part of the core (stored procedures are an example). Database vendors will continue to add new, proprietary features in an ongoing effort to differentiate their products and offer customers a reason to buy.

SQL in the Next Decade

Predicting the path of the database market and SQL over the next ten years is a risky proposition. The computer market is in the early stages of a major transition into a new, Internet-driven era whose impact is not yet fully understood. The emergence of the PC and its creation of the client/server era of the 1980s and 1990s illustrates how shifts in the underlying computer systems market can produce major changes in data management architectures. It's likely that the Internet will have at least as large, if not a larger, impact on the data management architectures of the next ten years. Nonetheless, several trends appear to be safe predictions for the future evolution of database management. They are discussed in the final sections of this chapter.

Distributed Databases

As more and more applications are used on an enterprise-wide basis or beyond, the ability of a single, centralized database to support dozens of major applications and thousands of concurrent users will continue to erode. Instead, major corporate databases will become more and more distributed, with dedicated databases supporting the major applications and functional areas of the corporation. To meet the higher service levels required of enterprise-wide or Internet-based applications, data must be distributed; but to insure the integrity of business decisions and operations, the operation of these distributed databases must be tightly coordinated.

Another strain on centralized database architectures will be the continuing growth of mobile personal computers and other mobile "information appliance" devices. These devices are, by their nature, more useful if they can become an integral part of a distributed network. However, by their nature they are also "occasionally-connected"—they work in a sometimes-disconnected, sometimes-connected mode, using either wired or wireless networks. The databases at the heart of mobile applications must be able to operate in this occasionally-connected environment.

These trends will drive heavy demand for data distribution, database integration, data synchronization, and distributed database technology. A "one size fits all" model of distributed data and transaction is inadequate for the highly distributed, anywhere/anytime environment that will emerge. Instead, some transactions will require absolute synchronization with a centralized master database, while others will demand support for "long-duration transactions" where synchronization may take hours or days. Developing ways to create and operate these distributed environments, without having them become a database administrator's nightmare, will be a major challenge for DBMS vendors in the next decade, and a major source of revenues for the vendors that provide practical, relatively easy-to-use solutions.

Massive Data Warehousing

The last few years have demonstrated that companies that use database technology aggressively and treat their data as a valuable corporate asset can gain tremendous competitive advantage. The competitive success of WalMart, for example, is widely attributed to its use of information technology (led by database technology) to track its inventory and sales on a daily basis, based on cash register transaction data. This allowed the company to minimize its inventory levels and closely manage its supplier relationships. Data mining techniques have allowed companies to discover unexpected trends and relationships based on their accumulated data—including the legendary discovery by one retailer that late-night sales of diapers were highly correlated with sales of beer.

It seems clear that companies will continue to accumulate as much information as they can on their customers, sales, inventories, prices, and other business factors. The databases to manage these massive quantities of data will need to support multi-level storage systems. They will need to rapidly import vast quantities of new data, and rapidly peel off large data subsets for analysis. Despite the high failure rate of data warehousing projects, the large potential payoffs in reduced operating costs and more "on-target" marketing and sales activities will continue to drive data warehousing growth.

Beyond the collection and warehousing of data, pressure will build to perform business analyses in "real-time." One IS consulting group has already coined the term "zero-latency enterprise" to describe an architecture in which customer purchases translate directly into changes in business plans with zero or very little delay. To meet this challenge, database systems will continue to take advantage of processor speed advances and multiprocessing technologies.

Ultra-High-Performance Databases

The emergence of an Internet-centric architecture is exposing enterprise data processing infrastructures to new peak-load demands that dwarf the workloads of just a few years ago. When databases primarily supported in-house applications used by a few dozen employees at a time, database performance issues may have produced employee frustration, but they did not really impact customers. The advent of call centers and other customer support applications produced a closer coupling between data management and customer satisfaction, but applications were still limited to at most hundreds of concurrent users (the people manning the phones in the call center).

With the Internet, the connection between a customer and the company's databases becomes a direct one. Database performance problems translate directly into slow customer response times. Database unavailability translates directly into lost sales. Furthermore, databases and other parts of the data processing infrastructure are no longer buffered from peak-load transaction rates. If a financial services firm offers online trading or portfolio management, it will need to prepare for peak-load volumes on days of heavy stock price movement that may be ten or twenty times the average daily volume. Similarly, an online retailer must gear up to support the heaviest end-of-year selling season, not just mid-March transaction rates.

The demands of e-commerce and "real-time" Internet information access are already producing peak-load transaction rates from the most popular Internet services that are one or two orders of magnitude higher than the fastest conventional disk-based RDBMS systems. To cope with these demands, companies will increasingly turn to distributed and replicated databases. They will pull "hot" data forward and cache it closer to the customer interaction within the network. To meet peak-load demands, they will use in-memory databases. This will in turn require new database support for deciding what data to cache, and what levels of synchronization and replication are appropriate. At first, these issues will apply only to the largest and highest-volume sites, but just as Web page caching has become an accepted and then an essential technique for maintaining adequate Web browser performance, hot data caching will become a mainstream Internet data management architecture as volumes grow.

Internet and Network Services Integration

In the Internet era, database management will increasingly become just one more network service, and one that must be tightly integrated with other services, such as messaging, transaction services, and network management. In some of these areas, standards have emerged, such as the XA standard for distributed transaction management. In others, standards have not yet emerged, making integration a more difficult problem.

The multi-tier architecture that is emerging for Internet-centric applications also poses new questions about what roles should be played by the database manager and by other components of the overall information system. For example, when network transactions are viewed from the point of distributed databases, a two-phase commit protocol, implemented in a proprietary way by a DBMS vendor, may provide a solution. When network transactions involve a combination of legacy applications (e.g., mainframe CICS transactions), relational database updates, and inter-application messages, the transaction management problem moves outside the database and external mechanisms are required.

A similar tradeoff is being created by the emergence of application servers as a middle-tier platform for executing business logic. Stored procedures have emerged as the DBMS technique for embedding business logic within the database itself. Application servers are creating an alternative platform for business logic, external to the database. It's not yet clear how these two trends will be rationalized, and whether business logic will continue its migration into the database or will settle in an application server layer. Whichever trend predominates, tighter integration between database servers and application servers will be required. Several of the DBMS vendors now produce their own application servers, and it seems likely that they will provide the best integration within their own product lines. Whether this approach will prevail against a "best-of-breed" approach remains another open question.

Embedded Databases

Relational database technology has reached into many parts of the computer industry, from small handheld devices to large mainframes. Databases underlie nearly all enterprise-class applications as the foundation for storing and managing their information. Lightweight database technology underlies an even broader range of applications. Directory services, a foundation technology for the new era of value-added data communications network services, are a specialized form of database technology. Lightweight, very high performance databases also form an integral part of telecommunications networks, enabling cellular networks, advanced billing schemes, smart messaging services and similar capabilities.

These embedded database applications have traditionally been implemented using proprietary, custom-written data management code tightly integrated with the application. This application-specific approach produced the highest possible performance, but at the expense of an inflexible, hard-to-maintain data management solution. With declining memory prices and higher-performance processors, lightweight SQL-based relational databases are now able to economically support these applications. The advantages of a standards-based embedded database are substantial. Without a serious compromise in performance, an application can be developed in a more modular fashion, changes in database structure can be handled transparently, and new services and applications can be rapidly deployed atop existing databases. With these advantages, embedded database applications appear destined to be a new area of growth potential for SQL and relational database technology.

Object Integration

The most significant unknown in the future evolution of SQL is how it will integrate with object-oriented technologies. The center of gravity of application development has clearly shifted to object-oriented techniques and tools. C++ and Java are growing in popularity, not only for client-side interaction, but for server-side business logic as well. The core row/column principles of the relational data model and SQL, however, are rooted in a much earlier COBOL era of records and fields, not objects and methods.

The object database vendors solution to the relational/object mismatch has been the wholesale discarding of the relational model in favor of pure object database structures. But the lack of standards, steep learning curve, lack of simple query facilities and other disadvantages have prevented pure object databases from having any significant market success to date. The relational database vendors have responded to the object database challenge by embracing object-oriented features, but the result has been a proliferation of non-standard, proprietary database features and SQL extensions.

It's clear that relational database technology and object technology must be more tightly integrated if relational databases are to remain an integral part of the next generation of applications. Several trends are visible today:

- Java-based interfaces to RDBMSs, such as JDBC and embedded SQL for Java, and perhaps additional interfaces more like those presented by the OODBMSs.

- Java as a standardized stored procedure language for implementing business logic within a RDBMS. Virtually all of the major DBMS vendors have announced plans to support Java as an alternative to their proprietary stored procedure languages.

- Abstract, complex data types that exhibit object-oriented capabilities such as encapsulation and inheritance. Beyond high-level agreement on the need to store "objects" within a row/column structure, the specifics (nested tables, arrays, complex columns) vary dramatically.

■ Extensions to standard SQL constructs to deal with complex data structures, including the extensions in the object-oriented parts of the proposed SQL3 standard. The diversity in SQL extensions matches the diversity in the way objects are being integrated into the relational model.

■ Message-oriented interfaces, including database triggers that produce messages external to the DBMS for integration with other applications.

Whether these extensions to SQL and the relational model can successfully integrate the worlds of RDBMS and objects remains to be seen. The object-oriented database vendors continue to maintain that object capabilities "bolted onto" an RDBMS can't provide the kind of transparent integration needed. The enterprise DBMS vendors have announced and added substantial object-relational capabilities, but it's hard to determine how many of them are actually being used. In addition, new, Internet-driven standards (such as XML, the Extensible Markup Language) provide "quasi-database" capabilities by adding database-like structure to document architecture. With all of these competing alternatives, the further integration of object technologies into the world of relational databases seems certain. The specific path that this evolution will take remains the largest unknown in the future of SQL.

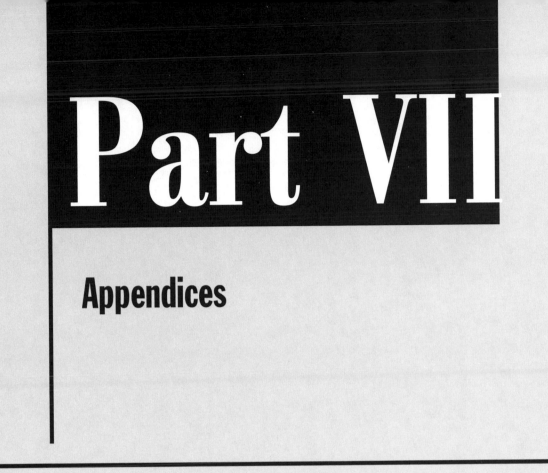

Part VII

Appendices

Appendix A

The Sample Database

Most of the examples in this book are based on the sample database described in this appendix. The sample database contains data that supports a simple order processing application for a small distribution company. It consists of five tables:

- CUSTOMERS, which contains one row for each of the company's customers.

- SALESREPS, which contains one row for each of the company's ten salespeople.

- OFFICES, which contains one row for each of the company's five sales offices where the salespeople work.

- PRODUCTS, which contains one row for each type of product that is available for sale.

- ORDERS, which contains one row for each order placed by a customer. For simplicity, each order is assumed to be for a single product.

Figure A-1 graphically shows the five tables, the columns that they contain, and the parent/child relationships among them. The primary key of each table is shaded. The five tables in the sample database can be created using the CREATE TABLE statements shown here:

```
CREATE TABLE CUSTOMERS
    (CUST_NUM INTEGER NOT NULL,
     COMPANY VARCHAR(20) NOT NULL,
     CUST_REP INTEGER,
 CREDIT_LIMIT MONEY,
  PRIMARY KEY (CUST_NUM),
  FOREIGN KEY HASREP (CUST_REP)
   REFERENCES SALESREPS
    ON DELETE SET NULL)

CREATE TABLE OFFICES
    (OFFICE INTEGER NOT NULL,
       CITY VARCHAR(15) NOT NULL,
     REGION VARCHAR(10) NOT NULL,
        MGR INTEGER,
     TARGET MONEY,
      SALES MONEY NOT NULL,
  PRIMARY KEY (OFFICE),
  FOREIGN KEY HASMGR (MGR)
   REFERENCES SALESREPS
    ON DELETE SET NULL)
```

```
CREATE TABLE SALESREPS
    (EMPL_NUM INTEGER NOT NULL,
         NAME VARCHAR(15) NOT NULL,
          AGE INTEGER,
   REP_OFFICE INTEGER,
        TITLE VARCHAR(10),
    HIRE_DATE DATE NOT NULL,
      MANAGER INTEGER,
        QUOTA MONEY,
        SALES MONEY NOT NULL,
 PRIMARY KEY (EMPL_NUM),
 FOREIGN KEY (MANAGER)
  REFERENCES SALESREPS
   ON DELETE SET NULL,
 FOREIGN KEY WORKSIN (REP_OFFICE)
  REFERENCES OFFICES
   ON DELETE SET NULL)

CREATE TABLE ORDERS
   (ORDER_NUM INTEGER NOT NULL,
   ORDER_DATE DATE NOT NULL,
         CUST INTEGER NOT NULL,
          REP INTEGER,
          MFR CHAR(3) NOT NULL,
      PRODUCT CHAR(5) NOT NULL,
          QTY INTEGER NOT NULL,
       AMOUNT MONEY NOT NULL,
  PRIMARY KEY (ORDER_NUM),
  FOREIGN KEY PLACEDBY (CUST)
   REFERENCES CUSTOMERS
    ON DELETE CASCADE,
  FOREIGN KEY TAKENBY (REP)
   REFERENCES SALESREPS
    ON DELETE SET NULL,
  FOREIGN KEY ISFOR (MFR, PRODUCT)
   REFERENCES PRODUCTS
    ON DELETE RESTRICT)
```

```
CREATE TABLE PRODUCTS
    (MFR_ID CHAR(3) NOT NULL,
 PRODUCT_ID CHAR(5) NOT NULL,
DESCRIPTION VARCHAR(20) NOT NULL,
      PRICE MONEY NOT NULL,
QTY_ON_HAND INTEGER NOT NULL,
PRIMARY KEY (MFR_ID, PRODUCT_ID))
```

Figures A-2 through A-6 show the contents of each of the five tables in the sample database. The query results in examples throughout the book are based on the data shown in these figures.

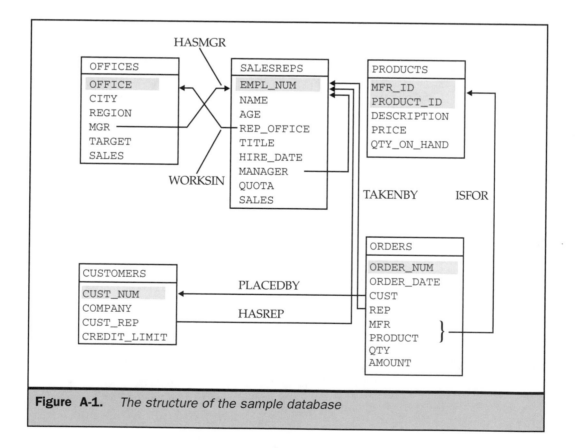

Figure A-1. *The structure of the sample database*

CUST_NUM	COMPANY	CUST_REP	CREDIT_LIMIT
2111	JCP Inc.	103	$50,000.00
2102	First Corp.	101	$65,000.00
2103	Acme Mfg.	105	$50,000.00
2123	Carter & Sons	102	$40,000.00
2107	Ace International	110	$35,000.00
2115	Smithson Corp.	101	$20,000.00
2101	Jones Mfg.	106	$65,000.00
2112	Zetacorp	108	$50,000.00
2121	QMA Assoc.	103	$45,000.00
2114	Orion Corp.	102	$20,000.00
2124	Peter Brothers	107	$40,000.00
2108	Holm & Landis	109	$55,000.00
2117	J.P. Sinclair	106	$35,000.00
2122	Three-Way Lines	105	$30,000.00
2120	Rico Enterprises	102	$50,000.00
2106	Fred Lewis Corp.	102	$65,000.00
2119	Solomon Inc.	109	$25,000.00
2118	Midwest Systems	108	$60,000.00
2113	Ian & Schmidt	104	$20,000.00
2109	Chen Associates	103	$25,000.00
2105	AAA Investments	101	$45,000.00

Figure A-2.   *The* CUSTOMERS *table*

EMPL_NUM	NAME	AGE	REP_OFFICE	TITLE	HIRE_DATE	MANAGER	QUOTA	SALES
105	Bill Adams	37	13	Sales Rep	12-FEB-88	104	$350,000.00	$367,911.00
109	Mary Jones	31	11	Sales Rep	12-OCT-89	106	$300,000.00	$392,725.00
102	Sue Smith	48	21	Sales Rep	10-DEC-86	108	$350,000.00	$474,050.00
106	Sam Clark	52	11	VP Sales	14-JUN-88	NULL	$275,000.00	$299,912.00
104	Bob Smith	33	12	Sales Mgr	19-MAY-87	106	$200,000.00	$142,594.00
101	Dan Roberts	45	12	Sales Rep	20-OCT-86	104	$300,000.00	$305,673.00
110	Tom Snyder	41	NULL	Sales Rep	13-JAN-90	101	NULL	$75,985.00
108	Larry Fitch	62	21	Sales Mgr	12-OCT-89	106	$350,000.00	$361,865.00
103	Paul Cruz	29	12	Sales Rep	01-MAR-87	104	$275,000.00	$286,775.00
107	Nancy Angelli	49	22	Sales Rep	14-NOV-88	108	$300,000.00	$186,042.00

Figure A-3.   *The* SALESREPS *table*

OFFICE	CITY	REGION	MGR	TARGET	SALES
22	Denver	Western	108	$300,000.00	$186,042.00
11	New York	Eastern	106	$575,000.00	$692,637.00
12	Chicago	Eastern	104	$800,000.00	$735,042.00
13	Atlanta	Eastern	105	$350,000.00	$367,911.00
21	Los Angeles	Western	108	$725,000.00	$835,915.00

Figure A-4. *The OFFICES table*

ORDER_NUM	ORDER_DATE	CUST	REP	MFR	PRODUCT	QTY	AMOUNT
112961	17-DEC-89	2117	106	REI	2A44L	7	$31,500.00
113012	11-JAN-90	2111	105	ACI	41003	35	$3,745.00
112989	03-JAN-90	2101	106	FEA	114X	6	$1,458.00
113051	10-FEB-90	2118	108	QSA	XK47	4	$1,420.00
112968	12-OCT-89	2102	101	ACI	41004	34	$3,978.00
113036	30-JAN-90	2107	110	ACI	4100Z	9	$22,500.00
113045	02-FEB-90	2112	108	REI	2A44R	10	$45,000.00
112963	17-DEC-89	2103	105	ACI	41004	28	$3,276.00
113013	14-JAN-90	2118	108	BIC	41003	1	$652.00
113058	23-FEB-90	2108	109	FEA	112	10	$1,480.00
112997	08-JAN-90	2124	107	BIC	41003	1	$652.00
112983	27-DEC-89	2103	105	ACI	41004	6	$702.00
113024	20-JAN-90	2114	108	QSA	XK47	20	$7,100.00
113062	24-FEB-90	2124	107	FEA	114	10	$2,430.00
112979	12-OCT-89	2114	102	ACI	4100Z	6	$15,000.00
113027	22-JAN-90	2103	105	ACI	41002	54	$4,104.00
113007	08-JAN-90	2112	108	IMM	773C	3	$2,925.00
113069	02-MAR-90	2109	107	IMM	775C	22	$31,350.00
113034	29-JAN-90	2107	110	REI	2A45C	8	$632.00
112992	04-NOV-89	2118	108	ACI	41002	10	$760.00
112975	12-OCT-89	2111	103	REI	2A44G	6	$2,100.00
113055	15-FEB-90	2108	101	ACI	4100X	6	$150.00
113048	10-FEB-90	2120	102	IMM	779C	2	$3,750.00
112993	04-JAN-89	2106	102	REI	2A45C	24	$1,896.00
113065	27-FEB-90	2106	102	QSA	XK47	6	$2,130.00
113003	25-JAN-90	2108	109	IMM	779C	3	$5,625.00
113049	10-FEB-90	2118	108	QSA	XK47	2	$776.00
112987	31-DEC-89	2103	105	ACI	4100Y	11	$27,500.00
113057	18-FEB-90	2111	103	ACI	4100X	24	$600.00
113042	02-FEB-90	2113	101	REI	2A44R	5	$22,500.00

Figure A-5. *The ORDERS table*

MFR_ID	PRODUCT_ID	DESCRIPTION	PRICE	QTY_ON_HAND
REI	2A45C	Ratchet Link	$79.00	210
ACI	4100Y	Widget Remover	$2,750.00	25
QSA	XK47	Reducer	$355.00	38
BIC	41672	Plate	$180.00	0
IMM	779C	900-lb Brace	$1,875.00	9
ACI	41003	Size 3 Widget	$107.00	207
ACI	41004	Size 4 Widget	$117.00	139
BIC	41003	Handle	$652.00	3
IMM	887P	Brace Pin	$250.00	24
QSA	XK48	Reducer	$134.00	203
REI	2A44L	Left Hinge	$4,500.00	12
FEA	112	Housing	$148.00	115
IMM	887H	Brace Holder	$54.00	223
BIC	41089	Retainer	$225.00	78
ACI	41001	Size 1 Widget	$55.00	277
IMM	775C	500-lb Brace	$1,425.00	5
ACI	4100Z	Widget Installer	$2,500.00	28
QSA	XK48A	Reducer	$177.00	37
ACI	41002	Size 2 Widget	$76.00	167
REI	2A44R	Right Hinge	$4,500.00	12
IMM	773C	300-lb Brace	$975.00	28
ACI	4100X	Widget Adjuster	$25.00	37
FEA	114	Motor Mount	$243.00	15
IMM	887X	Brace Retainer	$475.00	32
REI	2A44G	Hinge Pin	$350.00	14

Figure A-6.   *The PRODUCTS table*

The Complete Reference

Appendix B

Database Vendor Profiles

The database systems vendors profiled in this appendix have been selected because of their unique positions within the broader database industry. They include the providers of the leading enterprise-class DBMS products, some smaller companies that are leaders in new technology areas, pioneers in newer segments of the database market, and vendors that focus on embeddable database technology. Any compilation like this cannot possibly be exhaustive, and the omission of a company does not mean that its products or capabilities are inferior to those of the vendors profiled here. Collectively, these companies and their profiles as presented, illustrate the landscape of today's multi-billion-dollar database software and services market. The vendors are:

- A2i, Inc.
- Angara Database Systems
- Arbor Software (now Hyperion Solutions Corporation)
- Ardent Software
- Centura Software (SQLBase)
- Cloudscape, Inc.
- Computer Associates (Jasmine, Ingres II)
- Computer Corporation of America (Model 204)
- Empress Software
- IBM Corporation (DB2)
- Informix Software
- Microsoft Corporation (SQL Server)
- Object Design
- Objectivity
- Oracle Corporation
- Persistence Software
- Pervasive Software
- Quadbase Systems
- Raima Corporation
- Red Brick Systems (now part of Informix Software)
- Rogue Wave Software
- Sybase, Inc.
- Tache Group
- Tandem Computers (NonStop SQL)
- TimesTen Performance Software
- Versant Corporation

A2i, Inc. (www.a2i.com)

Founded in 1993, A2i develops and markets an integrated, database-driven, cross media catalog publishing system that centralizes the management of catalog data, simplifies the catalog production process, and completely automates the catalog production workflow. The system includes tools for creating, designing, and publishing both printed and electronic catalogs; supports simultaneous publishing to paper, CD-ROM and the Web from a single data source; and efficiently manages catalogs containing from hundreds to millions of items.

All of A2i's software products layer on top of a SQL-based DBMS. They include performance accelerators that improve catalog access by a factor of 10 to 1000 times that of SQL alone, and feature additional catalog-specific functionality that supports interactive browsing and sorting of large databases in ways that would otherwise be impossible using a traditional SQL-based DBMS alone. A2i's parametric search technology—an alternative to DBMS-style query forms that is intuitive, easy to use, and very, very fast—allows a user to search an entire catalog and locate any item or group of items in a matter of seconds, narrowing down from thousands or millions of items to one or several with just a few mouse clicks.

Angara Database Systems (www.angara.com)

Angara Database Systems is focused on the emerging market for in-memory database systems. The Angara main-memory data manager is planned to offer both a SQL-level interface as well as a lower-level C language API for direct access to the storage manager. For data sets that can be completely contained in a computer system's main memory, the company claims database performance of up to 40 times the speed of a disk-based RDBMS's in-memory cache.

The Angara technology is derived from main-memory database research done at Stanford University. The company was founded in 1996 to commercialize this technology. As of this writing, it is just beginning to ship its first product. Angara is a privately held, venture-backed company

Arbor Software (www.hyperion.com)

Arbor was one of the early leaders in the development of Online Analytic Processing (OLAP) databases and tools. Arbor's flagship Essbase OLAP server was first introduced in 1992 and pioneered many of the capabilities that have now become commonplace in analytic systems. Large corporations typically use the Essbase product suite to create integrated reporting, analysis, and planning systems.

Current versions of the Essbase product support both client/server and Web-based analytic processing and reporting. They support both pre-calculated data (a hallmark of most OLAP systems) and dynamic, "on the fly" calculations. Another major enhancement of the Essbase product is "distributed OLAP" capability, which allows OLAP databases to be partitioned across computer networks. Essbase supports both its own proprietary multidimensional database formats and integrates with conventional relational databases. It runs on Windows-based systems, OS/2, the leading Unix systems, and IBM's AS/400 mid-range systems.

In 1998, Arbor merged with Hyperion Solutions Corporation to create a $400 million company (annual revenue) focused on business reporting and analysis. The product line has grown to include integration products and customization services. It spans applications from single-user analysis on Windows workstations to enterprise-wide Web-based OLAP deployments for hundreds of users.

Ardent Software (www.ardentsoftware.com)

Ardent Software, headquartered in Westboro, Massachusetts, offers a family of database products and tools. Ardent's UniVerse relational database system is a SQL-based RDBMS with ODBC and ActiveX interfaces. It offers entry-level compliance with the SQL2 standard, with extensions including national language support, stored procedures, triggers, and distributed database capability. A` separate data manager, UniData, offers support for complex data management applications with a "nested relational" capability (tables-within-tables).

Other products in the Ardent suite include development tools, integration tools, and system administration tools. The DataStage product suite handles data reformatting, transformation, and cleansing tasks for creating data warehouses. The JRB (Java Relational Binding) toolkit bridges the object-oriented world of Java applications with the row/column structure of an RDBMS. Other tools extend and enhance the capabilities of the O2 object database.

Centura Software (www.centurasoft.com)

Centura Software was founded as Gupta Technologies, by a former manager of Oracle's microcomputer division. The company's initial focus was a DBMS and database development tools for PCs and PC-local area networks. Renamed Centura Software, the company now focuses on embedded database applications, primarily targeting independent software vendors and value-added resellers.

SQLBase, the company's flagship DBMS product, has evolved considerably since its origins as a standalone and client/server database for IBM PCs under MS-DOS. It has grown to support Windows NT and Netware as database servers. Centura currently targets SQLBase for applications on PCs and sub-PC devices such as handheld PCs, RISC-based information appliances (e.g., smart phones), and even smart cards. It features a small footprint, "zero-maintenance" operation, and a scalable architecture. ODBC 3.0 and JDBC interfaces are provided.

A second database engine, Centuranet.db, is targeted for building dynamic Web sites. It features automatic generation of HTML Web pages for a page-per-table view into the database contents. Associated point-and-click editing tools facilitate the creation of Web-based data input and queries. Other tools support the publishing of SQL-based databases over the Web.

Cloudscape, Inc. (www.cloudscape.com)

Cloudscape is a venture-backed, privately held database company founded by some of the principal architects of Sybase's database systems. The founders formed Cloudscape to build a 100 percent pure Java implementation of a SQL-based relational database. Because the Cloudscape DBMS itself is a set of Java routines, it can run on virtually any computer system that has a Java virtual machine. This includes devices ranging from "information appliances" such as enhanced telephones and network computers to mainframe-class systems. It also means the Cloudscape DBMS can be integrated relatively easily as an embedded DBMS within a Web browser. New or updated components of the DBMS can be transmitted over a network in the same way that Java applets are transmitted to a Web browser.

Cloudscape is targeting its DBMS to mobile computing applications running on notebook computer systems. In this configuration, Cloudscape can run as a "disconnected" DBMS to support local laptop applications. Later, when the notebook computer is connected to a central server database, the Java-based capabilities of Cloudscape make activities like data and application synchronization easier. At this writing, the Cloudscape DBMS has just recently begun to ship.

Computer Associates (www.cai.com)

Computer Associates (CA) is one of the world's largest independent software companies. Initially focused on mainframe software, the company has steadily expanded its focus to provide an extensive line of software products and services for enterprise data processing. Computer Associates has been built largely through acquisition, taking advantage of its large direct sales force and well-established relationships with senior Fortune 500 information systems executives. Through its acquisitions, it has steadily added more products to its portfolio.

Ingres, one of the earliest relational database systems to appear on the market, is now a product of Computer Associates. It was originally developed at the University of California at Berkeley as a research project under the direction of Professor Michael Stonebreaker. The research project became the foundation of an independent company, which eventually changed its name to Ingres Corporation in the 1980s. Ingres and its native QUEL query language were an early competitor to SQL, which was backed by rival Oracle Corporation. Although most analysts gave Ingres clear claim to technical leadership, Oracle's aggressive marketing and sales efforts, coupled with IBM's backing of SQL, eventually led to SQL dominance in the market. Eventually, Ingres was adapted to support SQL, which emerged as the dominant standard. In the 1990s, Ingres was sold to the ASK Group, and eventually to Computer Associates.

The current version of the product, Ingres II, is a comprehensive relational database management product suite. The core Ingres/DBMS is augmented by Ingres/ICE (Internet Commerce Enabled), a capability that links the DBMS to the Web. Networking support and standards-based ODBC access are supported by the Ingres/Net product. Distributed database support is available through Ingres/Star (a sophisticated distributed data manager) and Ingres/Replicator, which provides transparent replication. Computer Associates' OpenROAD product provides a layered development environment for Ingres with a three-layer development framework, encompassing Presentation, Business Object, and DBMS layers.

Computer Associates also offers Jasmine, a new, object-oriented DBMS. Although touted as a complete DBMS solution with a modern object-oriented architecture, two major areas of focus for Jasmine are multimedia and Internet applications. The core DBMS is heavily object-oriented, featuring multiple inheritance, instance and class methods and properties, and set-level methods. Methods for the Jasmine OODBMS can be written in C, C++, or Java. Jasmine includes an extensive class library with support for multimedia data types (images, animation sequences, audio, video, rich text, page layouts). A Jasmine Studio product provides an easy-to-use development environment.

CA is clearly positioning Jasmine as a "new-generation," pure object-oriented database. It is not positioned as having object/relational capabilities, and does not offer any SQL access to its own data management capabilities. CA does tout Jasmine's integration with back-end relational databases (Oracle, Sybase, Informix, SQL Server, DB2) and mainframe files (VSAM and CA-IDMS). The linkage to an Ingres II back-end is especially close, with tightly integrated transaction management, security, and replication management capabilities.

Computer Corporation of America (www.cca-int.com)

Computer Corporation of America (CCA) is one of the pioneering software companies, and has been involved in data management since its founding in 1965. It develops and sells one of the earliest DBMS systems: Model 204. The product has been substantially enhanced over the years, but the focus continues to be on mainframe systems.

Model 204 now features an ANSI-compliant SQL interface, even though the underlying structure is a network database architecture. The network structure is manifested in Model 204's embedded table capability—essentially a table-within-a-table structure. Although network databases fell out of favor with the advent of SQL and the relational model, some of the same capabilities provided by the network systems are now appearing in highly touted new object-relational systems. The nested table structure offered by Model 204 is an example of such a capability, which appears in object-relational systems from Informix and in Oracle's flagship Oracle 8 object-oriented extensions.

The current version of Model 204 includes multiprocessing and parallel query options for data warehousing applications. Over the years its indexing structures have become quite sophisticated and now include bit-map, hashing, b-tree, and record list schemes. Another unique feature of Model 204 is support for iterative queries—queries that are carried out against the results of previous queries. SQL-based access to mainframe Model 204 databases is available through CCA's Connect* product, which offers ODBC and OLE-DB APIs for remote database access from Windows and Unix-based client workstations.

IBM Empress Software (www.empress.com)

Empress Software produces an ANSI SQL relational database system for embedded applications. The company was founded in 1979 and is headquartered in Toronto, Canada. The Empress DBMS offers both an ODBC callable API and Embedded SQL interfaces. It also offers a low-level set of database access calls that come in "below" the SQL access layer. These calls provide direct access to the Empress storage manager layer for very high performance record insert, update, delete, and retrieve operations.

The Empress DBMS runs on many different Unix-based systems, including several Unix operating system variants that run on Intel processor-based systems. It also supports Windows, Windows NT, and a range of real-time operating systems typically used for embedded applications. It offers a rich collection of data types, plus user-definable functions and procedures. For Internet-based applications, Empress also offers script language interfaces for the popular Perl and Tcl/Tk scripting languages.

IBM Corporation (www.ibm.com)

IBM, the largest computer company in the world, is also among the largest software vendors in the world. IBM researchers pioneered the relational database concept, invented the SQL language, and produced the first relational database prototype—System/R—in the 1970s. Over the next two decades, IBM's flagship relational database—DB2—for its mainframe systems, pioneered several relational capabilities that have since found their way into mainstream RDBMS products and into generations of SQL standards. During this same time, relational database technology proliferated onto other IBM computer system platforms, including time-sharing mainframes (SQL/DS), minicomputers (AS/400), Unix-based workstations and servers (DB2/6000 on RS/6000 systems), and personal computers (OS/2 Extended Edition). In the late 1990s, IBM moved aggressively to bring all of these IBM data management products under a single umbrella (using the DB2 Universal Data Base name), and to offer its DB2 relational database technology on non-IBM platforms from other leading Unix system vendors.

Today, DB2 is a comprehensive, enterprise-class, SQL-based relational database system. DB2 implementations run on a very broad range of platforms, from desktop personal computers to the largest IBM mainframe clusters. DB2 can be characterized as a quite complete and comprehensive SQL implementation, especially in areas that have been traditional IBM strongholds, such as high-availability, reliability, maintainability, and worldwide support (international character set). Adjunct products and tools support software development, distributed database capabilities, data warehousing, data replication and distribution, and most other major areas of database activity. Although IBM has made its products available on non-IBM platforms, the vast majority of IBM DB2 installations are on IBM computer systems and are sold as part of integrated IBM-based enterprise systems.

Informix Software (www.informix.com)

Informix was one of the original leaders in the Unix-based relational database market. The company's first relational DBMS was implemented on Unix-based microcomputer systems in the early 1980s, and was known for its efficiency and compactness. In 1985, Informix was rewritten as a SQL-based DBMS and introduced as Informix-SQL. It was subsequently ported to a wide range of systems, from IBM PCs under MS-DOS to Amdahl mainframes running Unix. Informix was also one of the first database vendors to expand its product offerings beyond the core database engine to include development tools. Its Informix-4GL product family supports the development of forms-based interactive applications.

In the early 1990s, Informix expanded its product line into the office automation area, including among other products, a database-integrated spreadsheet named Wingz. This effort was not very successful against Microsoft's office suite juggernaut, and Informix refocused on its core database capabilities. One of its flagship products during the mid-1990s was Informix Parallel Server, the technology leader in so-called parallel query technology. Parallel Server splits the processing of a single complex query into multiple, parallel operations, which can take advantage of symmetric multiprocessing (SMP) servers. Later, Informix established a leadership position in object-relational technology through the acquisition of Illustra. Illustra was a venture-backed database software firm, led by Michael Stonebreaker (the same Berkeley professor who had led the development of Ingres years before). A side-effect of the Illustra acquisition was a proliferation of product lines and development teams within Informix, adding to some confusion among Informix customers.

Today, Informix is a multi-hundred-million dollar database company. It has merged its distinct product lines into a unified product line based on Informix Dynamic Server, a multithreaded database server for Unix and Windows NT-based systems. What were formerly separate product lines are now modular optional additions to the core Dynamic Server architecture. The Universal Data option adds object-relational capabilities, including the capability to develop customized plug-in "data blades" that support new data types and methods for handling them. The Advanced Decision Support Option provides capabilities for complex analytic processing, and a MetaCube ROLAP option supports multidimensional data warehousing. The Extended Parallel Option provides support for parallel queries, and a Workgroup Option provides a version of the DBMS adapted to smaller, distributed workgroup applications. The Informix databases can be accessed through Informix-4GL, and through Embedded SQL for C and Cobol and CLI call-level interfaces.

Microsoft Corporation (www.microsoft.com)

Microsoft Corporation, the world's largest personal computer software company, is also a major vendor in the SQL-based database market. Microsoft's first foray into database products came in 1987 and began as a defensive move. With the announcement of OS/2 Extended Edition, IBM tried to establish built-in database management and data communications as key components of an enterprise-class PC operating system. In 1988, Microsoft responded with SQL Server, a version of the Sybase DBMS ported to OS/2. Although Microsoft later abandoned OS/2 in favor of its own Windows NT operating system, SQL Server continued as its flagship DBMS. Today SQL Server is a major product in the workgroup database segment, and Microsoft is aggressively moving to establish it as an enterprise-class DBMS competing with Oracle and DB2.

Expanding on its early experience with SQL Server, Microsoft moved on several other fronts to expand its role as a database vendor. In the early 1990s, Microsoft acquired Foxbase Corporation, developer of the Foxbase DBMS. Foxbase had established itself as a very successful "clone" of dBASE, the most popular and widely used PC database product. Through the acquisition, Microsoft moved to challenge Borland International, which had acquired the rights to dBASE shortly before.

While the Foxbase acquisition was focused more on the PC installed base and the relatively mature market for character-based, flat file PC databases, Microsoft's internal development focused on the new, growing market for graphical lightweight relational PC databases. After several false starts and abandoned development prototypes, the result product, Microsoft Access, was introduced. Microsoft Access continues today as both a standalone lightweight database product, and a front-end for SQL-based production databases.

Microsoft also moved aggressively to enable Windows as a database access and database development platform. Its first major move in this area was the introduction of Open DataBase Connectivity (ODBC), a SQL-based API for database access. Microsoft built ODBC capability into Windows and successfully lobbied the SQL

Access Group, a database vendor association, to adopt it as a callable database API standard. This early version of ODBC eventually made its way into the formal ISO standards as the SQL Call Level Interface (CLI). Microsoft has continued to evolve ODBC and expand its capabilities.

Microsoft has also layered other database access APIs on top of ODBC. The first such step was to incorporate database access into Microsoft's Object Linking and Embedding (OLE) framework for linking applications together. The OLE/DB portion of the OLE suite provided source-independent data access, and relied on ODBC as its underlying architecture for working with relational databases. Later, with the recasting of OLE into the ActiveX component framework, another layer was added to the database access hierarchy. The Active Data Objects (ADO) set of components provide data access within Microsoft's Component Object Model (COM) architecture. Again, the ADO capabilities are layered on top of ODBC for relational database access.

Parallelling the evolution of the Windows database access capability, Microsoft has steadily expanded and enhanced the capabilities of SQL Server. SQL Server 7, introduced in 1998, represented a major step forward. Among its major features was an integrated OLAP server and Data Transformation Services, putting Microsoft squarely into competition with the data warehousing vendors and the warehouse-oriented database engine of the major database vendors. The high-end Enterprise Edition package provided fail-over clustering, multiprocessing support for up to 8-way SMP systems and much more extensive replication services for both online and offline distributed databases. The major enterprise database vendors maintain that SQL Server is still not an enterprise-scale DBMS, but in typical fashion, Microsoft continues to work, release by release, toward that goal.

Object Design (www.odi.com)

Object Design was one of the early object database vendors. The company, headquartered in Burlington, Massachusetts, was founded in 1988. The initial version of its ObjectStore object database system was shipped in 1990. Object Design is still firmly focused on a pure object-oriented database approach. It does not offer SQL-based access to ObjectStore. However, it does position ObjectStore as a front-end database technology that can access "legacy" SQL-based relational databases, such as Oracle, DB2, Sybase, and Informix, through its ObjectStore DBConnect product.

The current ObjectStore product is offered in two packages addressing two different target markets. ObjectStore Persistent Storage Engine (PSE) is a small-footprint persistent object store for Java, C++, and ActiveX applications. It is focused on embedded database applications, where the DBMS is hidden within the applications. The most recent release of ObjectStore PSE is a pure Java database for embedded use. The full-blown ObjectStore OODBMS is focused on more conventional database applications, with features such as distributed database support and replication. It also focuses on delivering improved OODBMS performance through intelligent object caching, using a so-called cache-forward architecture.

Objectivity (www.objectivity.com)

Objectivity was one of the early object-oriented database vendors, and has steadily enhanced its Objectivity OODBMS over the years. It has added fault-tolerant and data replication capabilities to its core object database engine. Access to the Objectivity OODBMS is provided from C++, Java, and Smalltalk.

Although Objectivity remains firmly focused on an object-oriented architecture, it has moved to provide SQL-based access to its object database engine. The Objectivity/SQL++ product provides both an ODBC interface and a proprietary Objectivity C++ API, and an Interactive SQL++ capability. The SQL language used through these interfaces contains many extensions to accommodate access to object database structures. Unique object-ids within the Objectivity database are automatically mapped to row-ids available via the SQL interface. Object "associations" within the OODB are available for use as SQL join criteria. Stored procedures and triggers are presented via extended SQL features. Extended SQL syntax is also provided to access elements of arrays and nested object structures, which appear as "complex columns" to the SQL user. These capabilities provide the advantages of "SQL-based" access to many of Objectivity's object-oriented capabilities, but at the expense of very non-standard SQL syntax.

Oracle Corporation (www.oracle.com)

Oracle Corporation was the first DBMS vendor to offer a commercial SQL product, preceding IBM's own announcement by almost two years. During the 1980s, Oracle grew to become the largest independent DBMS vendor. Today it is the dominant enterprise DBMS competitor, selling its products through an aggressive direct sales force and through a variety of other channels.

The Oracle DBMS was originally implemented on Digital minicomputers, but the center of gravity of Oracle system sales shifted firmly to Unix-based minicomputers and servers in the 1990s. One of the major advantages of Oracle is its portability. It is available on dozens of different computer systems, from Windows-based laptop computers through Sun, HP, and IBM Unix-based systems to IBM mainframes. Using Oracle's SQL*Net networking software, many of these Oracle implementations can participate in a distributed network of Oracle systems. With these capabilities, Oracle has targeted enterprise-wide database deployments and has been effective in leveraging its market leadership into a position as an IS-imposed corporate-wide database standard in many organizations.

The Oracle DBMS was originally based on IBM's System/R prototype, and has remained generally compatible with IBM's SQL-based products. In recent years, Oracle has been aggressively marketing the OLTP performance of its DBMS, using benchmark results from multiprocessor systems to substantiate its claim as the OLTP performance leader. In the late 1990s, it ran advertisements touting a breakthrough level of 100,000 TPC-C transactions per minute on a high-end cluster of SMP 64-bit Digital Alpha servers.

Oracle has consistently combined good technology with an aggressive sales force and high-profile marketing campaigns (including the high-profile presence of its flamboyant CEO and founder, Larry Ellison). It has expanded its product line to include not only DBMS software and database development and management tools, but also enterprise applications software for financial and business management applications. Oracle's core server products also include an application server for implementing multi-tier Internet applications. Oracle also acquired the Rdb relational database from Digital Equipment Corporation, picking up a large installed base of Digital users that it is converting to its Oracle products. Consulting services and recurring maintenance revenues have also become a major part of its revenue. It has also announced that it will make several of its products available on an outsourced basis, effectively allowing customers to use them on a fee-for-services basis. Today DBMS licensing revenues account for less than half of Oracle's annual revenues, but enterprise-class data management remains at the heart of the company's business.

Oracle8 and Oracle8i, introduced in 1998 and 1999 respectively, represent major steps forward in the evolution of the Oracle DBMS. Oracle8 includes extensive object-relational capabilities, including abstract data types, object structures (such as nested tables, arrays, and sequences), Java APIs (both embedded SQL for Java and a JDBC callable API), and specialized capabilities for high-performance OLTP on SMP systems and data warehousing. To accommodate a broad range of systems, low-end DBMS capability continues to be provided by an Oracle-Lite product for notebook systems. Oracle 8i is specifically focused on integration of the Oracle DBMS with Internet technologies, such as Web and application servers.

Oracle considers its major competitor to be Microsoft, and it embraces a network-centric enterprise computing architecture to combat Microsoft's PC-centric view. In the Oracle view, a centralized database system is the critical data store for all information within an organization, which should be accessible anytime and anywhere via the Internet. Easier central control and administration provided by this architecture are key selling points for Oracle to enterprise IS organizations.

Persistence Software (www.persistence.com)

Persistence Software was initially focused on software that bridged the gap between object-oriented development and messaging technologies (including object request brokers) and relational database technology. Its middleware products supported object-based data management structures and requests, and mapped them into relational databases stored in the major RDBMS systems. One of the primary target markets for Persistence products has been the financial services market.

More recently, Persistence has enhanced its products and repositioned them as a transactional application server. The company's PowerTier server family includes versions designed to support C++ development or Java (via Enterprise Java Beans). One of the major features of the PowerTier servers is in-memory caching of objects, which Persistence describes as in-memory caching of "current business state." Other capabilities of the servers include object transaction isolation and object triggers. The servers continue to offer database independence, integrating with the mainstream enterprise database engines of Oracle, Informix, Sybase, and Microsoft. Application development in C++, Java, and Visual Basic is supported.

Pervasive Software (www.pervasive.com)

Pervasive Software is one of the newer RDBMS companies, but it traces its roots back to the earliest days of personal computer databases. The storage manager that underlies the Pervasive products, Btrieve, was initially developed as a PC-based database for MS-DOS systems in the early 1980s. SoftCraft, the company that developed Btrieve, was acquired in 1987 by Novell Netware, the vendor of the industry's leading network operating system. As a result, Btrieve became a more tightly integrated part of the Netware OS. Layered capabilities, including Netware SQL, were developed as layers on top of the Btrieve storage manager.

In 1994, Novell decided to refocus on its core network operating system capabilities, and its database technologies were spun out into a new company, which was renamed Pervasive Software in 1996. Pervasive's focus is on cost-effective SQL-based databases for use by independent software vendors (ISVs) and value-added resellers (VARs). Packaged software for accounting, inventory control, order processing, and similar functions use it as an underlying, bundled database manager. These products are typically sold to small and medium-sized businesses, and to departments of big companies.

Pervasive's current product, Pervasive SQL, combines their Scalable SQL and Btrieve products. The emphasis is on features important to the small/medium business market. These include low database administration, scalability to support business volumes, a small DBMS footprint, and the ability to handle reasonable data volumes at low cost. Overwhelmingly, Pervasive SQL is used by an ISV or VAR and delivered as a bundled component of their software product, often invisible to the end user.

Quadbase Systems (www.quadbase.com)

Quadbase is a SQL-based client/server database system for IBM-compatible PCs. It was originally offered in the early 1990s as a DOS/Windows database with a file-server architecture. It has since evolved into a client/server database, with support for Netware, Windows, and Windows NT-based servers. The Quadbase SQL implementation is ANSI SQL-92 compliant at the Entry Level. It provides both Embedded SQL interfaces (for C, C++, and SmallTalk) and an ODBC callable API.

Quadbase supports a number of advanced SQL features including updateable scroll cursors and views. Its multi-user concurrency control offers the flexibility of multiple isolation levels for balancing database integrity requirements with performance concerns. Quadbase also supports read-only schemas that allow it to be used to create and access read-only databases on CD-ROMs.

Raima Corporation (www.raima.com)

Raima Corporation, founded in 1982, was an early database vendor focused on the IBM PC database market. Its initial db_VISTA product was first released in 1984. It has been steadily enhanced over the years and combined with an object manager to create the current Raima Database Manager++ (RDM++) product.

A newer Raima product, the Velocis Database Server, was first shipped in 1993. Velocis is a SQL-based relational database system with an ODBC interface. It is designed as an embeddable database, and the company targets it to professional application developers (ISVs and VARs) who use it as a bundled database foundation. Velocis runs on Windows, Windows NT, OS/2, and many Unix-based operating system variants.

A distinctive feature of the Velocis server is its explicit support for network data model's embedded pointers within a SQL-based database. A CREATE JOIN statement specifies an explicit relationship, implemented with network database-style pointers, which are stored within the database structure. These can then be exploited with SQL syntax, delivering very fast performance. Velocis supports C/C++, Java, Visual Basic, Delphi, and Perl language interfaces as well as the industry-standard ODBC interface.

Red Brick Systems (www.redbrick.com)

Red Brick (named after the red brick building where the company was founded in Los Gatos, California) was an early pioneer in the data warehousing market. Its founder, Ralph Kimball, remains a recognized expert in data warehousing. The company's core offering is a SQL-based DBMS which is heavily optimized for data warehousing applications.

Optimizations in the Red Brick system include high-performance data loading, with a parallel loader capability for exploiting SMP systems and high-performance data transformation, cleansing, and integrity checking. The Red Brick software also allows automatic pre-calculation of aggregate data values (sums, averages, minimum, and maximum values) during the table loading process.

The Red Brick DBMS also focused on a high-performance implementation of the "star schema" structure often found in data warehousing applications. Its STARindex technology and associated STARjoin capability implement support for star schemas within the database structure itself. The DBMS also features adaptive bitmap indexing for rapid data selection from very large tables. SQL extensions within the RISQL language handle typical decision support query structures, such as selecting the "top 3" or the "95th percentile" of rows based on some numerical measure.

Despite its early lead in the data warehousing market and several early customer successes, Red Brick found its early momentum hard to sustain. Other, much larger database vendors, including Oracle Corporation, Sybase, IBM, and eventually Microsoft, saw data warehousing as a major market opportunity and announced (sometimes with much-delayed shipment) data warehousing capabilities for their product lines. Although its products retained acknowledged technical advantages, Red Brick saw customers decide to wait for their current DBMS vendor. The company was sold to Informix Corporation in 1998, and the Red Brick data warehousing engine will be integrated into the Informix product line.

Rogue Wave Software (www.roguewave.com)

Rogue Wave Software, founded in 1989, is a provider of object-oriented software components. The company's products include component object parts that can be combined and reused to build enterprise-class applications. Other products are development tools for building user interfaces and other application elements using object-oriented techniques.

Rogue Wave's database tools are designed to bridge the gap between object-oriented software development techniques and relational database systems. Its DbTools suite is designed for use in C++ applications. The DBTools.J suite provides the same capabilities for Java-based development. The DBTools.J product also forms the database access part of the company's comprehensive StudioJ suite of JavaBeans components and classes.

Sybase, Inc. (www.sybase.com)

Sybase was a hot mid-1980s DBMS startup company, funded by tens of millions of dollars in venture capital. The company's founding team and many of its early employees were alumni of other DBMS vendors, and for most of them, Sybase represented the second or third relational DBMS they had built. Sybase quite effectively positioned its product as "the relational DBMS for on-line applications," and stressed the technical and architectural features that distinguished it from contemporary SQL-based DBMS products. These features included the following:

- A client/server architecture, with client software running on Sun and VAX workstations and IBM PCs and the server running on VAX/VMS or Sun systems

- A multi-threaded server that handled its own task management and input/output for maximum efficiency

- A programmatic API, instead of the embedded SQL interface used by most other DBMS vendors at the time

- Stored procedures, triggers, and a Transact-SQL dialect that extended SQL into a complete programming language for building substantial parts of an application within the database itself

Aggressive marketing and a first-class roster of venture capital backers gained Sybase the attention of industry analysts, but it was a subsequent OEM deal with Microsoft (the leading PC software vendor) and Ashton-Tate (the leading PC database vendor) that positioned the company as an up-and-coming DBMS vendor. Renamed SQL Server, the Sybase DBMS was ported to OS/2 (at the time, both IBM's and Microsoft's strategic future PC operating system) to be marketed to computer systems vendors by Microsoft and through retail computer channels by Ashton-Tate. Sales from the alliance never met early expectations, but it propelled Sybase into the DBMS market as a serious player. Today, SQL Server (several generations later) continues to be Microsoft's strategic DBMS for Windows NT; Microsoft has split from Sybase, pursuing its own development path. Sybase remains a major DBMS vendor, but the positive impact of its formative alliance with Microsoft has long since passed.

The innovations that made the Sybase product unique in the late 1980s were eventually copied by the other DBMS vendors. Sybase's early lead cemented its leadership position in market segments that demanded high-performance OLTP, including especially financial services applications—these niches remain Sybase strongholds today. During the 1990s, Sybase expanded its product line to include development tools through a merger with PowerSoft, one of the leading DBMS tools vendors. Other mergers and acquisitions brought consulting services and other data management technologies.

Sybase's current product line has three distinct database engines, focused on three different segments of the database market:

- Sybase Adaptive Server IQ is focused on data warehousing. It features complex query optimization techniques that are claimed to improve performance by 100 times over conventional RDBMSs.

- Sybase Adaptive Server Anywhere is focused on mobile computing. It features a small footprint and integrated support for Java classes and objects as well as Java stored procedures.

■ Sybase Adaptive Server Enterprise is the successor to the Sybase SQL Server products, optimized for OLTP workloads. It features flexible locking strategies and query performance improvements.

Together with the Sybase application server, other middleware products, database development tools, and consulting services, these product lines make Sybase a multi-hundred-million-dollar database supplier.

Tache Group (www.tachegroup.com)

The Tache Group is the vendor of CQL++, a SQL and B-tree/ISAM data management package. CQL++ offers both single-user and client/server operation. It is a layered product, providing database access both at the SQL level and at the lower, ISAM record-oriented level. CQL++ is designed for embedded applications. A unique feature is that it includes complete C++ source code for the DBMS, which allows the user to extend the core database and ISAM capabilities. CQL++ is available on Linux, HP, Silicon Graphics, and Solaris Unix-based systems, and on Windows and Windows NT platforms.

Tandem Computers (www.tandem.com)

Tandem was an early leader in the market for fault-tolerant minicomputer systems and remains a major competitor in this market. Many Tandem systems are sold to financial services and transportation companies for use in online transaction processing applications that demand 24 hours/day, 7 days/week non-stop operation. Tandem's older systems run the proprietary TXP operating system, and fault-tolerant applications are generally written in the proprietary Tandem Application Language (TAL). More recent Tandem systems are based on Unix operating systems. In 1997, Tandem was acquired by Compaq Computer Corporation, a leading vendor of personal computer systems and workgroup servers, as part of its move to become a major enterprise computer systems vendor. Tandem has since announced that its future fault-tolerant systems will be based on the Digital Alpha 64-bit processor and Digital Unix. (Digital Computer, once a leading independent minicomputer vendor, was itself acquired by Compaq in 1998, continuing Compaq's push into enterprise data processing.)

Database management for non-stop applications on Tandem systems has been provided for many years by a SQL-based Tandem-developed RDBMS called Non-Stop SQL. Because of Tandem's heavy OLTP emphasis, Non-Stop SQL has pioneered several special techniques, such as disk mirroring. It also takes advantage of the inherent

Tandem multi-processor architecture and provides distributed database capabilities. The programmatic interface to Non-Stop SQL is through embedded SQL.

During the 1980s and early 1990s, virtually every minicomputer vendor had its own proprietary SQL-based implementation (Digital with Rdb/VMS, Hewlett-Packard with Allbase/SQL, Data General with DG-SQL, etc.). Over the years, all of the other systems vendors have concluded that the high cost of maintaining their own RDBMS with competitive features was prohibitive. They also had difficulty managing the dual roles of competing with the independent DBMS vendors (such as Oracle) and also working with them as ISV partners on their platforms. As a result, Tandem is the only remaining major system vendor (except for IBM) with its own proprietary SQL-based RDBMS.

TimesTen Performance Software (www.timesten.com)

TimesTen is a venture-backed database company focused on delivering ultra-high-performance main-memory database systems. The company was formed as a spinoff of a main-memory database project at Hewlett-Packard, and its underlying technology has been shipping as an embedded component of HP telecommunications systems since 1996. TimesTen's version of the technology began shipments in early 1998. It features an ODBC API and industry-standard SQL, and runs on Windows NT and Unix-based servers from HP, Sun Microsystems, and IBM.

The TimesTen main-memory data manager is targeted at applications with high performance requirements in telecomm/datacomm systems and high-volume Internet applications such as information services and e-commerce. It has been deployed as a standalone data manager within cellular networks and datacomm applications. It has also been used as a high-performance data cache front-ending conventional disk-based RDBMS systems in Internet applications.

For typical OLTP applications, the TimesTen engine delivers at least ten times (1000 percent) the performance of a fully-cached conventional RDBMS. TimesTen 3.0, which began shipment in December 1998, supports 64-bit database addressing, allowing in-memory databases of tens of gigabytes. In addition to its RDBMS features, TimesTen offers N-way data replication capabilities for high-availability and load-sharing configurations. The company's main-memory database products have been measured at transaction rates exceeding 1.5 million SQL read operations (read based on primary key) per minute on SMP Windows NT servers.

Versant Corporation (www.versant.com)

Versant was one of the early object database vendors. Its first OODBMS product shipped in September 1990. The current version of its database product offers Java,

C++, and Smalltalk interfaces. The object database engine is multi-session and multi-threaded and runs on Windows NT and Unix platforms. One of its distinguishing characteristics is fault-tolerant capability with automatic failover.

Like all of the pure object database vendors, Versant initially presented itself as a next generation DBMS system, rejecting the relational vendors and their systems as "yesterday's technology." More recently, the company has opened its OODBMS to the relational world through the Versant SQL suite, providing SQL access and an ODBC API. The SQL facility, and a corresponding Interactive SQL utility, are available for Versant servers on Solaris, AIX, HP-UX, and Windows NT platforms

The philosophy of the Versant SQL suite is to automatically present as much of the OODBMS capabilities in a relational model as possible. It automatically maps the Versant database's object schema to a corresponding SQL schema: for example, it transforms two object classes with many-to-many relationship into two base tables and intersection table to represent relationships. SQL schema information is available through virtual SYSTABLES, SYSCOLUMNS, and SYSINDEXES catalog views. Embedded pointers within the object schema are exploited transparently to enhance query performance. In addition to the programmatic (ODBC) and interactive SQL interfaces, the SQL suite includes data loading and extraction tools to move information between the Versant OODBMS and conventional RDBMS systems.

Appendix C

Company and Product List

This appendix contains a list of companies and products in the DBMS marketplace, most of which are mentioned in this book. The majority of the products listed are SQL-based database management systems or database tools. The companies appear in alphabetical order. Key products for each company appear in italics.

A2i, Inc.
1925 Century Park East, Suite 255
Los Angeles, CA 90067
phone: 310-286-2220
fax: 310-286-2221
e-mail: info@a2i.com
Web: **www.a2i.com**
Cross-Media Catalog Publishing System

Angara Database Systems
3045 Park Boulevard
Palo Alto, CA 94306
phone: 650-321-2700
fax: 650-462-9752
e-mail: info@angara.com
Web: **www.angara.com**
Angara Data Server

Arbor Software (now Hyperion Solutions Corporation)
1344 Crossman Avenue
Sunnyvale, CA 94089
phone: 408-744-9500
fax: 408-744-0400
e-mail: info@hyperion.com
Web: **www.hyperion.com**
Essbase

Ardent Software, Inc.
50 Washington Street
Westboro, MA 01581
phone: 508-366-3888
fax: 508-366-3669
e-mail: info@ardentsoftware.com
Web: **www.ardentsoftware.com**
UniVerse, UniData

Centura Software Corporation
975 Island Drive
Redwood Shores, CA 94065
phone: 650-596-3400
fax: 650-596-4900
e-mail: info@centurasoft.com
Web: **www.centurasoft.com**
SQLBase

Cloudscape, Inc.
180 Grand Avenue, Suite 300
Oakland, CA 94612
phone: 510-239-1900
fax: 510-239-1909
e-mail: info@cloudscape.com
Web: **www.cloudscape.com**
Cloudscape

Computer Associates International, Inc.
One Computer Associates Plaza
Islandia, NY 11788
phone: 516-342-5224
fax: 516-342-5329
e-mail: info@cai.com
Web: **www.cai.com**
Ingres II, Jasmine

Computer Corporation of America
500 Old Connecticut Path
Framingham, MA 01701
phone: 508-270-6666
fax: 508-270-6688
e-mail: info@cca-int.com
Web: **www.cca-int.com**
Model 204

Empress Software Inc.
6401 Golden Triangle Drive
Greenbelt, MD 20770
phone: 301-220-1919
fax: 301-220-1997
e-mail: sales@empress.com
Web: **www.empress.com**
Empress

IBM Corporation
One New Orchard Road
Armonk, NY 10504
phone: 914-499-1900
fax: 914-765-6021
e-mail: info@ibm.com
Web: **www.ibm.com**
DB2, SQL/DS

Informix Software, Inc.
4100 Bohannon Drive
Menlo Park, CA 94025
phone: 650-926-6300
fax: 650-926-6593
e-mail: info@informix.com
Web: **www.informix.com**
Informix Dynamic Server

Microsoft Corporation
One Microsoft Way
Redmond, WA 98052
phone: 425-882-8080
fax: 425-936-7329
e-mail: info@microsoft.com
Web: **www.microsoft.com**
SQL Server

Object Design, Inc.
25 Mall Road
Burlington, MA 01803
phone: 781-674-5000
fax: 781-674-5010
e-mail: webmaster@objectdesign.com
Web: **www.odi.com**
ObjectStore

Objectivity Inc.
301B East Evelyn Ave.
Mountain View, CA 94041
phone: 650-254-7100
fax: 650-254-7171
e-mail: info@objectivity.com
Web: **www.objectivity.com**
Objectivity/SQL++

Oracle Corporation
500 Oracle Parkway
Redwood Shores, CA 94065
phone: 650-506-7000
fax: 650-506-7200
e-mail: info@oracle.com
Web: **www.oracle.com**
Oracle

Persistence Software Inc.
1720 South Amphlett Blvd., Suite 300
San Mateo, CA 94402
phone: 650-372-3600
fax: 650-341-8432
e-mail: info@persistence.com
Web: **www.persistence.com**
PowerTier

Pervasive Software
12365 Riata Trace Pkwy, Bldg. II
Austin, TX 78727
phone: 512-231-6000
fax: 512-231-6010
e-mail: info@pervasive.com
Web: **www.pervasive.com**
Pervasive SQL

Quadbase Systems, Inc.
2855 Kifer Road, Suite 203
Santa Clara, CA 95051
phone: 408-982-0835
fax: 408-982-0838
e-mail: info@quadbase.com
Web: **www.quadbase.com**
Quadbase-SQL

Raima Corporation
4800 Columbia Center
701 Fifth Avenue
Seattle, WA 98104
phone: 206-515-9477
fax: 206-748-5200
e-mail: sales@raima.com
Web: **www.raima.com**
Velocis Database Server

Red Brick Systems, Inc. (now part of Informix Software)
4100 Bohannon Drive
Menlo Park, CA 94025
phone: 650-926-6300
fax: 650-926-6593
e-mail: webmaster@redbrick.com
Web: **www.redbrick.com**
Red Brick Warehouse

Rogue Wave Software, Inc.
5500 Flatiron Pkwy.
Boulder, CO 80301
phone: 303-473-9118
fax: 303-447-2568
e-mail: info@roguewave.com
Web: **www.roguewave.com**
DBTools.J

Sybase, Inc.
6475 Christie Avenue
Emeryville, CA 94608
phone: 510-922-3500
fax: 510-922-3210
e-mail: info@sybase.com
Web: **www.sybase.com**
Sybase Adaptive Server

Tache Group, Inc.
One Harbor Place, Suite 810
1901 South Harbor City Boulevard
Melbourne, FL 32901
phone: 407-768-6050
fax: 407-768-1333
e-mail: info@tachegroup.com
Web: **www.tachegroup.com**
CQL++

Tandem Computers (a Compaq company)
19333 Vallco Parkway
Cupertino, CA 95014
phone: 408-285-6000
fax: 408-285-0112
e-mail: info@tandem.com
Web: **www.tandem.com**
Non-Stop SQL

TimesTen Performance Software
2085 Landings Drive
Mountain View, CA 94043
phone: 650-526-5100
fax: 650-526-5199
e-mail: info@timesten.com
Web: **www.timesten.com**
TimesTen

Versant Corporation
6539 Dumbarton Circle
Fremont, CA 94555
phone: 510-789-1500
fax: 510-789-1515
e-mail: info@versant.com
Web: **www.versant.com**
Versant

Appendix D

SQL Syntax Reference

T he ANSI/ISO SQL standard specifies the syntax of the SQL language using a formal BNF notation. Unfortunately, the standard is difficult to read and understand for several reasons. First, the standard specifies the language bottom-up rather than top-down, making it difficult to get the "big picture" of a SQL statement. Second, the standard uses unfamiliar terms (such as *table-expression* and *predicate*). Finally, the BNF in the standard is many layers deep, providing a very precise specification but masking the relatively simple structure of the SQL language.

This appendix presents a complete, simplified BNF for "standard" SQL as it is commonly implemented in the products of most DBMS vendors. Specifically:

- The language described generally conforms to that required for entry-level conformance to the SQL2 standard, plus those intermediate-level and full-level conformance features that are commonly found in the major DBMS products.

- The module language is omitted because it is replaced in virtually all SQL implementations by embedded SQL or a SQL API.

- Components of the language are referred to by the common names generally used in DBMS vendor documentation, rather than by the technical names used in the standard.

The BNF in this appendix uses the following conventions:

- SQL keywords appear in all UPPERCASE MONOSPACE characters.

- Syntax elements are specified in *italics*.

- The notation *element-list* indicates an *element* or a list of *elements* separated by commas.

- Vertical bars (|) indicate a choice between two or more alternative syntax elements.

- Square brackets ([ ]) indicate an optional syntax element enclosed within them.

- Braces ({ }) indicate a choice among required syntax elements enclosed within them.

Data Definition Statements

These statements define the structure of a database, including its tables and views and the DBMS-specific "objects" that it contains:

```
CREATE TABLE table ( table-def-item-list )

DROP TABLE table [ drop-options ]
```

```
ALTER TABLE table alter-action

CREATE VIEW view [ ( column-list ) ]
   AS query-spec
 [ WITH CHECK OPTION ]

DROP VIEW view [ drop-options ]

CREATE db-object-type db-object-name [ db-object-spec ]

DROP db-object-type [ drop-options ]

ALTER db-object-type alter-action

GRANT { ALL PRIVILEGES | privilege-list }
   ON { table | db-object-type db-object-name }
   TO { PUBLIC | user-list }
 [ WITH GRANT OPTION ]

REVOKE { ALL PRIVILEGES | privilege-list }
   ON { table | db-object-type db-object-name }
   FROM { PUBLIC | user-list }
 [ WITH GRANT OPTION ]
```

The keywords used to specify database objects (*db-object-type*) depend on the specific DBMS. Typical "database objects" with associated privileges include TABLE, VIEW, SCHEMA, PROCEDURE, DOMAIN, INDEX, and the named storage areas maintained by the DBMS. The SQL syntax used to specify these objects is specific to the DBMS that supports them. The specific set of *alter-actions* that are supported are also DBMS-specific and object type-specific.

The language elements that are used in the CREATE, DROP, ALTER, GRANT, and REVOKE statements are:

Language Element   Syntax

Language Element	Syntax
table-def-item	*column-definition*	*table-constraint*

column-definition	*column data-type*
	    [DEFAULT { *literal*
		USER	NULL }]
			    [*column-constraint-list*]

Language Element	Syntax
column-constraint	[CONSTRAINT *constraint-name*] { NOT NULL | *uniqueness* | *foreign-key-ref* | *check-constr* } [*constraint-timing*]
table-constraint	[CONSTRAINT *constraint-name*] { *uniqueness* | *foreign-key-constr* | *check-constr* } [*constraint-timing*]
uniqueness	UNIQUE (*col-list*) | PRIMARY KEY (*col-list*)
foreign-key-constr	FOREIGN KEY (*col-list*) *foreign-key-ref*
foreign-key-ref	REFERENCES *table* [(*col-list*)] [MATCH FULL | PARTIAL] [ON DELETE *ref-action*]
ref-action	CASCADE | SET NULL | SET DEFAULT | NO ACTION
check-constr	CHECK (*search-condition*)
constraint-timing	[INITIALLY IMMEDIATE | INITIALLY DEFERRED] [[NOT] DEFERRABLE]

Privilege	SELECT |
	  DELETE |
	  UPDATE [(*colmn-list*)]
	  INSERT [(*colmn-list*)]

drop-options	CASCADE | RESTRICT

Basic Data Manipulation Statements

The "singleton SELECT" statement retrieves a single row of data into a set of host variables (embedded SQL) or stored procedure variables:

```
SELECT [ ALL | DISTINCT ] { select-item-list | * }
   INTO variable-list
   FROM table-ref-list
 [ WHERE search-condition ]
```

The "interactive SELECT" statement retrieves any number of rows of data in an interactive SQL session (multi-row retrieval from embedded SQL or stored procedures requires cursor-based statements):

```
SELECT [ ALL | DISTINCT ] { select-item-list | * }
   INTO host-variable-list
```

```
     FROM table-ref-list
   [ WHERE search-condition ]
   [ GROUP BY column-ref-list ]
   [ HAVING search-condition ]
   [ ORDER BY sort-item-list ]
```

These statements modify the data in the database:

```
INSERT INTO table [ ( column-list ) ]
  { VALUES ( insert-item-list ) | query-expr }

DELETE FROM table [ WHERE search-condition ]

UPDATE table SET set-assignment-list [ WHERE search-condition ]
```

Transaction Processing Statements

These statements signal the end of a SQL transaction:

```
COMMIT [ WORK ]

ROLLBACK [ WORK ]
```

Cursor-Based Statements

These programmatic SQL statements support data retrieval and positioned update of data:

```
DECLARE cursor [ SCROLL ] CURSOR FOR query-expr
  [ ORDER BY sort-item-list ]
  [ FOR { READ ONLY | UPDATE [ OF column-list ] } ]

OPEN cursor

CLOSE cursor

FETCH [ [ fetch-dir ] FROM ] cursor INTO variable-list

DELETE FROM table WHERE CURRENT OF cursor

UPDATE table SET set-assignment-list WHERE CURRENT OF cursor
```

The optional fetch direction (*fetch-dir*) is specified as the following; and *row-nr* can be specified as a variable or a literal.

```
NEXT | PRIOR | FIRST | LAST | ABSOLUTE row-nr | RELATIVE row-nr
```

Query Expressions

The SQL2 standard provides a rich set of expressions for specifying queries, from simple queries to more complex query expressions that use relational database operations to combine the results of simpler queries.

The basic query specification has the form:

```
SELECT [ ALL | DISTINCT ] { select-item-list | * }
    FROM  table-ref-list
  [ WHERE  search-condition ]
  [ GROUP BY  column-ref-list ]
  [ HAVING  search-condition ]
```

The table references (*tbl-ref*) in the FROM clause can be:

- A *simple table reference*, consisting of a (possibly qualified) *table name*.

- A *derived table reference*, consisting of a subquery (see the text that follows) that produces a table-valued result. Not all DBMS brands allow table-valued subqueries to appear in the FROM clause.

- A *joined table reference* (see the text that follows) that combines data from two or more tables using relational OUTER JOIN, INNER JOIN, or other join operators. Not all DBMS brands allow join specifications to appear in the FROM clause.

Joined tables are specified according to the SQL2 standard as follows; in practice, there is wide variation in the specific types of joins supported by individual DBMS brands and the syntax used to specify various join types:

Join Type	Syntax
joined-table	*inner-join* | *outer-join* | *union-join* | *cross-join* | (*joined-table*)

Join Type	Syntax
inner-join	*table-ref* [NATURAL] [INNER] JOIN *table-ref* | *table-ref* [INNER] JOIN *table-ref* [*join-spec*]
outer-join	*table-ref* [NATURAL] [LEFT|RIGHT|FULL] OUTER JOIN *table-ref* | *table-ref* [LEFT|RIGHT|FULL] OUTER JOIN *table-ref* [*join-spec*]
union-join	*table-ref* UNION JOIN *table-ref*
cross-join	*table-ref* CROSS JOIN *table-ref*
join-spec	ON *search-condition* | USING (*col-list*)

The SQL2 standard allows basic query specifications to be combined with one another using the set-oriented relational operations UNION, EXCEPT, and INTERSECT. The resulting *query-expression* provides the full relational set-processing power of the standard. Enclosed in parentheses, a query-expression becomes a subquery that can appear in various positions within SQL statements (for example, within certain search conditions in the WHERE clause).

Not all DBMS brands support all of these operations. A simplified form of the SQL2 syntax for the operations (without the details of operator precedence) is given by:

Expression	Syntax
query-expr	*Simple-table* | *joined-table* | *union-expr* | *except-expr* | *intersect-expr* | (*query-expr*)
union-expr	*query-expr* UNION [ALL] [*corresponding-spec*] *query-expr*
except-expr	*query-expr* EXCEPT [ALL] [*corresponding-spec*] *query-expr*
Intersect-expr	*query-expr* INTERSECT [ALL] [*corresponding-spec*] *query-expr*
corresponding-spec	CORRESPONDING [BY (*col-list*)]
subquery	(*query-expr*)

Search Conditions

These expressions select rows from the database for processing:

Language Element	Syntax
search-condition	*search-item* | *search-item* { AND | OR } *search-item*
search-item	[NOT] { *search-test* | (*search-condition*) }
search-test	*comparison-test* | *between-test* | *like-test* | *null-test* | *set-test* | *quantified-test* | *existence-test*
comparison-test	*expr* { = | <> | < | <= | > | >= } { *expr* | *subquery* }
between-test	*expr* [NOT] BETWEEN *expr* AND *expr*
like-test	*column-ref* [NOT] LIKE *value* [ESCAPE *value*]
null-test	*column-ref* IS [NOT] NULL
set-test	*expr* [NOT] IN { *value-list* | *subquery* }
quantified-test	*expr* { = | <> | < | <= | > | >= } [ALL | ANY | SOME] *subquery*
existence-test	EXISTS *subquery*

Expressions

These expressions are used in SQL select lists and search conditions:

Language Element	Syntax
expr	*expr-item* | *expr-item* { + | − | * | / } *expr-item*
expr-item	[+ | −] [*value* | *column-ref* | *function* | (*expr*) }
value	*literal* | USER | *host-variable* | *stored-proc-variable*
host-variable	*variable* [[INDICATOR] *variable*]
function	COUNT(*) | *distinct-fcn* | *all-fcn*
distinct-function	{ AVG | MAX | MIN | SUM | COUNT } (DISTINCT *column-ref*)
all-function	{ AVG | MAX | MIN | SUM | COUNT } ([ALL] *expr*)

Statement Elements

These elements appear in various SQL statements:

Language Element	Syntax
set-assignment	*column* = { *expr* | NULL | DEFAULT }
sort-item	{ *column-ref* | *integer* } [ASC | DESC]
insert-item	{ *value* | NULL }
select-item	*expr*
table-ref	*table* [*table-alias*]
column-ref	[{ *table* | *alias* } .] *column*

Simple Elements

These following are the basic names and constants that appear in SQL statements:

Language Element	Description
table	Table name
column	Column name
user	Database user name
variable	Host language or stored procedure variable name
literal	Number or a string literal enclosed in quotes
integer	Integer number
data-type	SQL data type
alias	SQL identifier
cursor	SQL identifier

Appendix E

SQL Call Level Interface

This appendix describes the collection of routines that comprise the ISO/IEC standard SQL Call Level Interface (CLI). The routines are presented here in their C-language forms. The names of the routines presented are identical to the names used in the standard. They should be used in exactly this form to call the routines in a CLI-compliant library.

For clarity, the routines are presented here with two differences from the standard. The names of the parameters of the routines are abbreviated in this appendix to make the routine headers easier to read, and in some cases, to clarify their function. In actual calls to the routines from an application program, you should use the names of the application program variables to be used as input and output parameters instead of the parameter names. Also for clarity, the data types of the parameters are stated here in terms of the actual C-language data types (e.g., `long`, `short`, `*char`). The standard defines the parameters using defined symbolic constants (#define's in the C language) to represent these data types.

Appendix A.1 of the standard (ISO/IEC 9075-3:1995) is a C-language header file that defines symbolic constants for all of the constants and codes specified in the standard, and uses the full parameter variable names specified in the standard. The following is a summary of the routines, organized by function:

`AllocHandle()`	Allocates resources for environment, connection, descriptor, or statement
`FreeHandle()`	Frees previously allocated resources
`AllocConnect()`	Allocates resources for a database connection
`FreeConnect()`	Frees resources for a database connection
`Connect()`	Establishes a database connection
`Disconnect()`	Ends an established database connection
`DataSources()`	Gets a list of available SQL servers to which connection may be made
`AllocEnv()`	Allocates resources for a SQL environment
`FreeEnv()`	Frees resources for a SQL environment
`SetEnvAttr()`	Set attribute value for a SQL environment
`GetEnvAttr()`	Retrieves attribute value for a SQL environment
`AllocStmt()`	Allocates resources for a SQL statement
`FreeStmt()`	Frees resources for a SQL statement
`SetStmtAttr()`	Set descriptor area to be used for a SQL statement
`GetStmtAttr()`	Get descriptor area for a SQL statement
`ExecDirect()`	Directly executes a SQL statement

Prepare()	Prepares a SQL statement for subsequent execution
Execute()	Executes a previously-prepared SQL statement
EndTran()	Ends a SQL transaction
Cancel()	Cancels execution of a SQL statement
GetDescField()	Gets value of a descriptor field
SetDescField()	Sets value of a descriptor field
GetDescRec()	Gets values from a descriptor record
SetDescRec()	Sets values in a descriptor record
CopyDesc()	Copies descriptor area values
NumResultCols()	Determines the number of query results columns
DescribeCol()	Describes result column of a query
ColAttribute()	Gets attribute of a query results column
BindParam()	Binds program location to a parameter value
ParamData()	Processes deferred parameter values
PutData()	Provides deferred parameter value or portion of a character string value
SetCursorName()	Sets the name of a cursor
GetCursorName()	Obtains the name of a cursor
Fetch()	Fetches a row of query results
FetchScroll()	Fetches a row of query results with scrolling
GetData()	Obtains the value of a query results column
CloseCursor()	Closes an open cursor
Error()	Obtains error information
GetDiagField()	Gets value of a diagnostic record field
GetDiagRec()	Gets value of the diagnostic record
RowCount()	Gets number of rows affected by last SQL statement
GetFunctions()	Gets information about supported features of a SQL implementation
GetInfo()	Gets information about supported features of a SQL implementation
GetTypeInfo()	Gets information about supported data types

CLI Return Values

Every CLI routine returns a `short` value with one of the following values and meanings:

CLI Return Value	Meaning
0	Statement completed successfully
1	Successful completion with warning
	No data found (when retrieving query results)
99	Data needed (required dynamic parameter missing)
-1	Error during SQL statement execution
-2	Error—invalid handle supplied in call

General Handle Management Routines

These routines are used to allocate a handle for use by the CLI, and to free a previously-allocated handle that is no longer needed. The allocation routine accepts an argument indicating what type of handle is to be allocated. In general, it may be preferable to use the routines that create and free the specific types of handles, described in their respective sections. These routines must be used to allocate and free application program descriptor handles.

```
/* Allocate a handle for use in subsequent CLI calls */
short SQLAllocHandle (
    short     hdlType,     /* IN:  integer handle type code */
    long      inHdl,       /* IN:  env or conn handle */
    long     *rtnHdl)      /* OUT: returned handle */
```

```
/* Free a handle previously allocated by SQLAllocHandle() */
short SQLFreeHandle (
    short  hdlType,   /* IN:  integer handle type code */
    long   inHdl)     /* IN:  handle to be freed */
```

SQL Environment Management Routines

These routines are used to allocate a handle a new SQL-environment, to free an environment handle when it is no longer needed, and to retrieve and set the value of attributes associated with the SQL-environment.

```
/* Allocate a handle for a new SQL-environment */
short SQLAllocEnv (
   long  *envHdl)      /* OUT: returned env handle */


/* Free an environment handle previously allocated */
short SQLFreeEnv (
   long  envHdl)       /* IN:  environment handle */


/* Obtain the value of a SQL-environment attribute */
short SQLGetEnvAttr(
   long   envHdl,     /* IN:  environment handle */
   long   AttrCode,   /* IN:  integer attribute code*/
   void  *rtnVal,     /* OUT: return value */
   long   bufLen,     /* IN:  length of rtnVal buffer */
   long  *strLen)     /* OUT: length of actual data */


/* Set the value of a SQL-environment attribute */
short SQLSetEnvAttr(
   long   envHdl,     /* IN:  environment handle */
   long   AttrCode,   /* IN:  integer attribute code*/
   void  *attrVal,    /* IN:  new attribute value */
   long  *strLen)     /* IN:  length of data */
```

SQL Connection Management Routines

These routines are used to create, terminate, and manage a connection to a SQL-server. They allocate and free the handles used to maintain connection status, setup and terminate connections, manage the attributes associated with a connection, and obtain a list of the SQL-servers available for connection.

```
/* Allocate a handle for a new SQL-connection */
short SQLAllocConnect (
   long   envHdl,      /* IN:  environment handle */
   long  *connHdl)     /* OUT: returned connection handle */


/* Free a connection handle previously allocated */
short SQLFreeConnect (
   long   connHdl)     /* IN:  connection handle */
```

```
/* Initiate a connection to a SQL-server */
short SQLConnect(
    long    connHdl,     /* IN:  connection handle */
    char    *svrName,    /* IN:  name of target SQL-server */
    short   svrnamlen,   /* IN:  length of SQL-server name */
    char    *userName,   /* IN:  user name for connection */
    short   usrnamlen,   /* IN:  length of user name */
    char    *passwd,     /* IN:  connection password */
    short   pswlen)      /* IN:  password length */
```

```
/* Disconnect from a SQL-server */
short SQLDisconnect(
    long    connHdl)     /* IN:  connection handle */
```

```
/* Get the name(s) of accessible SQL-servers for connection */
short SQLDataSources (
    long    envHdl,      /* IN:  environment handle */
    short   direction,   /* IN:  indicates first/next rqst */
    char    *svrname,    /* OUT: buffer for server name */
    short   buflen,      /* IN:  length of server name buffer */
    short   *namlen,     /* OUT: actual length of server name */
    char    *descrip,    /* OUT: buffer for description */
    short   buf2len,     /* IN:  length of description buffer */
    short   *dsclen)     /* OUT: actual length of description */
```

```
/* Obtain the value of a SQL-connection attribute */
short SQLGetConnectAttr(
    long    connHdl,     /* IN:  connection handle */
    long    AttrCode,    /* IN:  integer attribute code*/
    void    *rtnVal,     /* OUT: return value */
    long    bufLen,      /* IN:  length of rtnVal buffer */
    long    *strLen)     /* OUT: length of actual data */
```

```
/* Set the value of a SQL-connection attribute */
short SQLSetConnectAttr(
    long    connHdl,     /* IN:  connection handle */
    long    AttrCode,    /* IN:  integer attribute code*/
    void    *attrVal,    /* IN:  new attribute value */
    long    *strLen)     /* IN:  length of data */
```

SQL Statement Management Routines

These routines are used to allocate and free the handle associated with a SQL statement, to pass SQL statement text for execution, and to request preparation and actual execution of the statement via the CLI.

```
/* Allocate a handle to manage processing of SQL statement(s) */
short SQLAllocStmt (
    long    envHdl,      /* IN:  environment handle */
    long   *stmtHdl)     /* OUT: statement handle */


/* Free a statement handle previously allocated */
short SQLFreeStmt (
    long    stmtHdl,     /* IN:  statement handle */
    long    option)      /* IN:  cursor & unbind options */


/* Bind a SQL statement parameter to a program data area */
short SQLBindParam (
    long    stmtHdl,     /* IN:  statement handle */
    short   parmnr,      /* IN:  parameter number (1,2,3...) */
    short   valtype,     /* IN:  data type of value supplied */
    short   parmtype,    /* IN:  data type of parameter */
    short   colsize,     /* IN:  column size */
    short   decdigits,   /* IN:  number of decimal digits */
    void   *value,       /* IN:  pointer to parm value buffer */
    long   *lenind)      /* IN:  ptr to length/indicator buffer */


/* Obtain the value of a SQL-statement attribute */
short SQLGetStmtAttr(
    long    stmtHdl,     /* IN:  statement handle */
    long    AttrCode,    /* IN:  integer attribute code*/
    void   *rtnVal,      /* OUT: return value */
    long    bufLen,      /* IN:  length of rtnVal buffer */
    long   *strLen)      /* OUT: length of actual data */


/* Set the value of a SQL-statement attribute */
short SQLSetStmtAttr(
    long    stmtHdl,     /* IN:  statement handle */
    long    AttrCode,    /* IN:  integer attribute code*/
    void   *attrVal,     /* IN:  new attribute value */
    long   *strLen)      /* IN:  length of data */
```

SQL Statement Execution Routines

These routines are used to pass SQL statement text to the CLI and to request SQL statement execution, either immediately or after being prepared. They also control the execution of SQL transactions and the cancellation of currently operating statements.

```
/* Pass SQL statement text and request its execution */
short SQLExecDirect (
   long   stmtHdl,    /* IN:  statement handle */
   char  *stmttext,   /* IN:  SQL statement text */
   short  textlen)    /* IN:  statement text length */


/* Prepare a SQL statement, passing it in SQL text form */
short SQLPrepare (
   long   stmtHdl,    /* IN:  statement handle */
   char  *stmttext,   /* IN:  SQL statement text */
   short  textlen)    /* IN:  statement text length */


/* Execute a previously-prepared SQL statement */
short SQLExecute (
   long   stmtHdl)    /* IN:  statement handle */


/* COMMIT or ROLLBACK a SQL transaction */
short SQLEndTran (
   short  hdltype,    /* IN:  type of handle */
   long   txnHdl,     /* IN:  env, conn or stmt handle */
   short  compltype)  /* IN:  txn type (commit/rollback) */


/* Cancel a currently-executing SQL statement */
short SQLCancel (
   short  stmtHdl)    /* IN:  statement handle */
```

Query Results Processing Routines

These routines are used to retrieve rows of query results and to specify the application program data areas that are to receive the returned query results.

```
/* Advance the cursor to the next row of query results */
short SQLFetch (
   long    stmtHdl)    /* IN:  statement handle */
```

```
/* Scroll the cursor up or down through the query results */
short SQLFetchScroll (
   long    stmtHdl,    /* IN:  statement handle */
   short   fetchdir,   /* IN:  direction (first/next/prev) */
   long    offset)     /* IN:  offset (number of rows) */
```

```
/* Get the data for a single column of query results */
short SQLGetData (
   long    stmtHdl,    /* IN:  statement handle */
   short   colnr,      /* IN:  column number to be retrieved */
   short   tgttype,    /* IN:  data type to return to program */
   void    *value,     /* IN:  ptr to buffer for column data */
   long    buflen,     /* IN:  length of program buffer */
   long    *lenind)    /* OUT: actual length and/or NULL ind */
```

```
/* Close a cursor to end access to query results */
short SQLCloseCursor (
   long    stmtHdl)    /* IN:  statement handle */
```

```
/* Establish a cursor name for an open cursor */
short SQLSetCursorName (
   long    stmtHdl,    /* IN:  statement handle */
   char    cursname,   /* IN:  name for cursor */
   short   namelen)    /* IN:  length of cursor name */
```

```
/* Retrieve the name of an open cursor */
short SQLGetCursorName (
   long    stmtHdl,    /* IN:  statement handle */
   char    cursname,   /* OUT: buffer for returned name */
   short   buflen,     /* IN:  length of buffer */
   short   *namlen)    /* OUT: actual length of returned name */
```

```
/* Bind a query results column to a program data area */
short SQLBindCol (
   long    stmtHdl,    /* IN:  statement handle */
   short   colnr,      /* IN:  column number to be bound */
   short   tgttype,    /* IN:  data type of program data area */
   void    value,      /* IN:  pointer to program data area */
   long    buflen,     /* IN:  length of program buffer */
   long    lenind)     /* IN:  ptr to length/indicator buffer */
```

Query Results Description Routines

These routines are used to obtain a description of the results of a query, including the number of columns of query results, the data type, and other attributes of each column.

```
/* Determine the number of result columns in a query */
short SQLNumResultCols (
   long    stmtHdl,     /* IN:  statement handle */
   short *colcount)     /* OUT: returned number of columns */
```

```
/* Determine the characteristics of a column of query results */
short SQLDescribeCol (
   long    stmtHdl,     /* IN:  statement handle */
   short   colnr,       /* IN:  number of column to describe */
   char   *colname,     /* OUT: name of query results column */
   short   buflen,      /* IN:  length of column name buffer */
   short *namlen,       /* OUT: actual column name length */
   short *coltype,      /* OUT: returned column data type code */
   short *colsize,      /* OUT: returned column data length */
   short *decdigits,    /* OUT: returned # digits in column */
   short *nullable)     /* OUT: can column have NULL values */
```

```
/* Obtain detailed info about a column of query results */
short SQLColAttribute (
   long    stmtHdl,     /* IN:  statement handle */
   short   colnr,       /* IN:  number of column to describe */
   short   attrcode,    /* IN:  code of attribute to retrieve */
   char   *attrinfo,    /* OUT: buffer for attribute info */
   short   buflen,      /* IN:  length of col attribute buffer */
   short *actlen)       /* OUT: actual attribute info length */
```

Query Results Descriptor Management Routines

These routines are used to obtain a description of the results of a query using the CLI descriptor mechanism, and to manipulate the descriptors to manage the return of query results into application program data areas.

```
/* Retrieve frequently-used info from a CLI descriptor */
short SQLGetDescRec (
   long    descHdl,     /* IN:  descriptor handle */
   short   recnr,       /* IN:  descriptor record number */
   char   *name,        /* OUT: name of item being described */
   short   buflen,      /* IN:  length of name buffer */
   short  *namlen,      /* OUT: actual length of returned name */
   short  *datatype,    /* OUT: data type code for item*/
   short  *subtype,     /* OUT: data type subcode for item */
   short  *length,      /* OUT: length of item */
   short  *precis,      /* OUT: precision of item, if numeric */
   short  *scale,       /* OUT: scale of item, if numeric */
   short  *nullable)    /* OUT: can item have NULL values */


/* Obtain detailed info for an item described by a CLI descriptor */
short SQLColAttribute (
   long    descHdl,     /* IN:  descriptor handle */
   short   recnr,       /* IN:  descriptor record number */
   short   attrcode,    /* IN:  code of attribute to describe */
   void   *attrinfo,    /* OUT: buffer for attribute info */
   short   buflen,      /* IN:  length of col attribute buffer */
   short  *actlen)      /* OUT: actual attribute info length */


/* Set frequently-used info in a CLI descriptor */
short SQLSetDescRec (
   long    descHdl,     /* IN:  descriptor handle */
   short   recnr,       /* IN:  descriptor record number */
   short   datatype,    /* IN: data type code for item*/
   short   subtype,     /* IN: data type subcode for item */
   short   length,      /* IN: length of item */
   short   precis,      /* IN: precision of item, if numeric */
   short   scale,       /* IN: scale of item, if numeric */
   void   *databuf,     /* IN: data buffer address for item */
   short   buflen,      /* IN: data buffer length */
   short  *indbuf)      /* IN: indicator buffer addr for item */


/* Set detailed info about an item described by a CLI descriptor */
short SQLColAttribute (
   long    descHdl,     /* IN:  descriptor handle */
   short   recnr,       /* IN:  descriptor record number */
   short   attrcode,    /* IN:  code of attribute to describe */
   void   *attrinfo,    /* IN:  buffer with attribute info */
   short   buflen)      /* IN:  length of attribute info */
```

```
/* Copy a CLI descriptor contents into another descriptor */
short SQLCopyDesc (
    long   indscHdl,    /* IN:  source descriptor handle */
    long   outdscHdl)   /* IN:  destination descriptor handle */
```

Deferred Dynamic Parameter Processing Routines

These routines are used to process deferred parameters when their values are requested by the CLI during execution of a SQL statement containing them.

```
/* Get param-tag for next required dynamic parameter */
short SQLParamData (
    long   stmtHdl,     /* IN:  stmt handle w/ dynamic params */
    void  *prmtag)      /* OUT: buffer for rtn param-tag value */
```

```
/* Obtain detailed info for an item described by a CLI descriptor */
short SQLPutData (
    long   stmtHdl,     /* IN:  stmt handle w/ dynamic params */
    void  *prmdata,     /* IN:  buffer with data for param */
    short  prmlenind)   /* IN:  param length or NULL ind */
```

Error, Status, and Diagnostic Routines

These routines are used to determine the reason for an error condition returned by the CLI, to determine the number of rows affected by successful statement execution, and to obtain detailed diagnostic information about error conditions.

```
/* Retrieve error information associated with a previous CLI call */
short SQLError (
    long   envHdl,      /* IN:  environment handle */
    long   connHdl,     /* IN:  connection handle */
    long   stmtHdl,     /* IN:  statement handle */
    char  *sqlstate,    /* OUT: five-character SQLSTATE value */
    long  *nativeerr,   /* OUT: returned native error code */
    char  *msgbuf,      /* OUT: buffer for err message text */
    short  buflen,      /* IN:  length of err msg text buffer */
    short *msglen)      /* OUT: returned actual msg length */
```

```
/* Determine number of rows affected by previous SQL statement */
short SQLRowCount (
    long   stmtHdl,     /* IN:  statement handle */
    long  *rowcnt)      /* OUT: number of rows */
```

```
/* Retrieve info from one of the CLI diagnostic error records */
short SQLGetDiagRec (
    short   hdltype,      /* IN:  handle type code */
    long    inHdl,        /* IN:  CLI handle */
    short   recnr,        /* IN:  requested err record number */
    char   *sqlstate,     /* OUT: returned 5-char SQLSTATE code */
    long   *nativeerr,    /* OUT: returned native error code */
    char   *msgbuf,       /* OUT: buffer for err message text */
    short   buflen,       /* IN:  length of err msg text buffer */
    short  *msglen)       /* OUT: returned actual msg length */


/* Retrieve a field from one of the CLI diagnostic error records */
short SQLGetDiagField (
    short   hdltype,      /* IN:  handle type code */
    long    inHdl,        /* IN:  CLI handle */
    short   recnr,        /* IN:  requested err record number */
    short   diagid,       /* IN:  diagnostic field id */
    void   *diaginfo,     /* OUT: returned diagnostic info */
    short   buflen,       /* IN:  length of diag info buffer */
    short  *actlen)       /* OUT: returned actual info length */
```

CLI Implementation Information Routines

These routines return information about the specific CLI implementation, including the CLI calls, statements, and data types that it supports.

```
/* Retrieve info about capabilities of a CLI implementation */
short SQLGetInfo (
    long    connHdl,      /* IN:  connection handle */
    short   infotype,     /* IN:  type of info requested */
    void   *infoval,      /* OUT: buffer for retrieved info */
    short   buflen,       /* IN:  length of info buffer */
    short  *infolen)      /* OUT: returned info actual length */


/* Determine number of rows affected by previous SQL statement */
short SQLGetFunctions (
    long    connHdl,      /* IN:  connection handle */
    short   functid,      /* IN:  function id code */
    short  *supported)    /* OUT: whether function supported */
```

```
/* Determine information about supported data types */
short SQLGetTypeInfo (
    long    stmtHdl,    /* IN:  statement handle */
    short   datatype)   /* IN:  ALL TYPES or type requested */
```

CLI Parameter Value Codes

These codes are passed to or returned by the CLI as parameter values, to indicate handle types, data types, statement types, etc.

Code	Value
Handle Type Codes:	
SQL-environment handle	1
SQL-connection handle	2
SQL-statement handle	3
SQL-descriptor handle	4
SQL Implementation Data Type Codes:	
CHARACTER	1
NUMERIC	2
DECIMAL	3
INTEGER	4
SMALLINT	5
FLOAT	6
REAL	7
DOUBLE	8
DATETIME	9
INTERVAL	10
VARCHAR	12
BIT	14
Implementation-defined	< 0
Application program language data type codes:	
CHARACTER	1
NUMERIC	2

Code	Value
DECIMAL	3
INTEGER	4
SMALLINT	5
FLOAT	6
REAL	7
DOUBLE	8
Implementation-defined	< 0

DateTime subcodes for SQL data types:

DATE	1
TIME	2
TIMESTAMP	3
TIME w/ ZONE	4
TIMESTAMP w/ ZONE	5

DateTime interval codes for SQL *DateTime* types:

YEAR	1
MONTH	2
DAY	3
HOUR	4
MINUTE	5
SECOND	6
YEAR TO MONTH	7
DAY TO HOUR	8
DAY TO MINUTE	9
DAY TO SECOND	10
HOUR TO MINUTE	11
HOUR TO SECOND	12
MINUTE TO SECOND	13

Code	Value
Transaction termination codes:	
COMMIT	0
ROLLBACK	1
FreeStmt() processing option codes:	
CLOSE CURSOR	0
FREE HANDLE	1
UNBIND COLUMNS	2
UNBIND PARAMS	3
Fetch orientation codes:	
NEXT	1
FIRST	2
LAST	3
PRIOR	4
ABSOLUTE	5
RELATIVE	6
GetData() Data Type Codes:	
CHARACTER	1
INTEGER	4
SMALLINT	5
REAL	7
DOUBLE	8
CLI Routine Codes for GetFunction() *Call:*	
AllocConnect	1
AllocEnv	2
AllocHandle	1001
AllocStmt	3
BindCol	4
BindParam	1002
Cancel	5

Code	Value
CloseCursor	1003
ColAttribute	6
Connect	7
CopyDesc	1004
DataSources	57
DescribeCol	8
Disconnect	9
EndTran	1005
Error	10
ExecDirect	11
Execute	12
Fetch	13
FetchScroll	1021
FreeConnect	14
FreeEnv	15
FreeHandle	1005
FreeStmt	16
GetConnectAttr	1007
GetCursorName	17
GetData	43
GetDescField	1008
GetDescRec	1009
GetDiagField	1010
GetDiagRec	1011
GetEnvAttr	1012
GetFunctions	44
GetInfo	45
GetStmtAttr	1014
GetTypeInfo	47
NumResultCols	18

Code	Value
ParamData	48
Prepare	19
PutData	49
RowCount	20
SetConnectAttr	1016
SetCursorName	21
SetDescField	1017
SetDescRec	1018
SetEnvAttr	1019
SetStmtAttr	1020

Concise Data Type Codes:

CHARACTER	1
NUMERIC	2
DECIMAL	3
INTEGER	4
SMALLINT	5
FLOAT	6
REAL	7
DOUBLE	8
VARCHAR	12
BIT	14
VARBIT	15
DATE	91
TIME	92
TIMESTAMP	93
TIME w/ ZONE	94
TIMESTAMP w/ ZONE	95
INTERVAL YEAR	101
INTERVAL MONTH	102
INTERVAL DAY	103

Code	Value
INTERVAL HOUR	104
INTERVAL MINUTE	105
INTERVAL SECOND	106
INTERVAL YEAR TO MONTH	107
INTERFAL DAY TO HOUR	108
INTERVAL DAY TO MINUTE	109
INTERVAL DAY TO SECOND	110
INTERVAL HOUR TO MINUTE	111
INTERVAL HOUR TO SECOND	112
INTERVAL MINUTE TO SECOND	113

Appendix F

SQL Information Schema

Standard

This appendix describes the Information Schema views specified by the SQL2 standard. These views must be supported by any database system claiming Intermediate-Level or Full conformance to the standard; they are not required for Entry-Level conformance. The views make a SQL2-compliant database self-describing. By querying them, a user can determine relevant information about all of the database objects (schemas, tables, columns, views, constraints, domains, character sets, etc.) accessible to him or her.

Information about schemas, tables, and columns:

SCHEMATA	Describes all schemas owned by the current user
TABLES	Describes all tables accessible to the current user
COLUMNS	Describes all columns of those tables owned/accessible to the current user

Information about views:

VIEWS	Describes all views accessible to the current user
VIEW_TABLE_USAGE	Describes tables on which those views depend
VIEW_COLUMN_USAGE	Describes columns on which those views depend

Information about constraints (unique, primary keys, foreign keys, check constraints, assertions):

TABLE_CONSTRAINTS	Describes all constraints on tables owned by user
REFERENTIAL_CONSTRAINTS	Describes all foreign key constraints owned by user
CHECK_CONSTRAINTS	Describes all check constraints owned by user
KEY_COLUMN_USAGE	Describes keys defined by the current user
ASSERTIONS	Describes all assertions owned by the current user
CONSTRAINT_TABLE_USAGE	Describes all tables used by constraints
CONSTRAINT_COLUMN_USAGE	Describes columns used by constraints

Information about privileges:

TABLE_PRIVILEGES	Describes privileges on tables
COLUMN_PRIVILEGES	Describes privileges on columns
USAGE_PRIVILEGES	Describes privileges on other database objects

Information about domains:

DOMAINS	Describes domains accessible to the user
DOMAIN_CONSTRAINTS	Describes constraints that define those domains
DOMAIN_COLUMN_USAGE	Describes columns based on those domains

Information about character sets:

CHARACTER_SETS	Describes character sets
COLLATIONS	Describes collating sequences
TRANSLATIONS	Describes translations between character sets

Information about supported programming languages:

SQL_LANGUAGES	Describes supported languages and SQL APIs

The specific contents of each Information Schema view are described on the following pages.

SCHEMATA View

The SCHEMATA view contains one row for each schema that is owned by the current user. Its structure is shown in the following table:

Column Name	Data Type	Description
CATALOG_NAME	VARCHAR(*len*)	Name of catalog containing this schema
SCHEMA_NAME	VARCHAR(*len*)	Name of schema described by this row

Column Name	Data Type	Description
SCHEMA_OWNER	VARCHAR(*len*)	Name of schema's creator
DEFAULT_CHARACTER_ SET_CATALOG	VARCHAR(*len*)	Catalog of default character set for this schema
DEFAULT_CHARACTER_ SET_SCHEMA	VARCHAR(*len*)	Schema of default character set for this schema
DEFAULT_CHARACTER_ SET_NAME	VARCHAR(*len*)	Name of default character set for this schema

VARCHAR(*len*) is the data type for SQL identifiers; *len* is the maximum length defined by the SQL implementation.

TABLES View

The TABLES view contains one row for each table defined in the current catalog that is accessible to the current user. Its structure is shown in the following table:

Column Name	Data Type	Description
TABLE_CATALOG	VARCHAR(*len*)	Name of catalog containing this table definition
TABLE_SCHEMA	VARCHAR(*len*)	Name of schema containing this table definition
TABLE_NAME	VARCHAR(*len*)	Name of the table
TABLE_TYPE	VARCHAR(*maxlen*)	Type of table (BASE TABLE / VIEW / GLOBAL TEMPORARY / LOCAL TEMPORARY)

VARCHAR(*len*) is the data type for SQL identifiers; *len* is the maximum length defined by the SQL implementation.

VARCHAR(*maxlen*) is a VARCHAR data type with the largest maximum length permitted by the SQL implementation.

COLUMNS View

The COLUMNS view contains one row for each column of each table defined in the current catalog that is accessible to the current user. Its structure is shown in the following table:

Column Name	Data Type	Description
TABLE_CATALOG	VARCHAR(*len*)	Name of catalog containing table definition containing this column
TABLE_SCHEMA	VARCHAR(*len*)	Name of schema containing table definition containing this column
TABLE_NAME	VARCHAR(*len*)	Name of table containing this column
COLUMN_NAME	VARCHAR(*len*)	Name of the column
ORDINAL_POSITION	INTEGER > 0	Position of the column within this table
COLUMN_DEFAULT	VARCHAR(*maxlen*)	Text representation of default value for column
IS_NULLABLE	VARCHAR(*maxlen*)	May column contain NULL values? (YES/NO)
DATA_TYPE	VARCHAR(*maxlen*)	SQL2 data type of column (text representation)
CHARACTER_MAXIMUM_LENGTH	INTEGER > 0	Maximum length, in characters, for variable-length columns
CHARACTER_OCTET_LENGTH	INTEGER > 0	Maximum length, in bytes, for variable-length columns
NUMERIC_PRECISION	INTEGER > 0	Precision for numeric data type columns
NUMERIC_PRECISION_RADIX	INTEGER > 0	Radix of the precision

Column Name	Data Type	Description
NUMERIC_SCALE	INTEGER > 0	Scale for numeric data type columns
DATETIME_PRECISION	INTEGER > 0	Precision for DateTime data type columns
CHARACTER_SET_CATALOG	VARCHAR(*len*)	Catalog containing character set definition for this column
CHARACTER_SET_SCHEMA	VARCHAR(*len*)	Schema containing character set definition for this column
CHARACTER_SET_NAME	VARCHAR(*len*)	Name of character set for this column, if any
COLLATION_CATALOG	VARCHAR(*len*)	Catalog containing collation definition for this column
COLLATION_SCHEMA	VARCHAR(*len*)	Schema containing collation definition for this column
COLLATION_NAME	VARCHAR(*len*)	Name of collation for this column, if any
DOMAIN_CATALOG	VARCHAR(*len*)	Catalog containing domain definition for this column
DOMAIN_SCHEMA	VARCHAR(*len*)	Schema containing domain definition for this column
DOMAIN_NAME	VARCHAR(*len*)	Name of domain for this column, if any

VARCHAR(*len*) is the data type for SQL identifiers; *len* is the maximum length defined by the SQL implementation.

VARCHAR(*maxlen*) is a VARCHAR data type with the largest maximum length permitted by the SQL implementation.

VIEWS *View*

The VIEWS view contains one row for each view defined in the current catalog that is accessible to the current user. Its structure is shown in the following table:

Column Name	Data Type	Description
TABLE_CATALOG	VARCHAR(*len*)	Name of catalog containing this view definition

Column Name	Data Type	Description
TABLE_SCHEMA	VARCHAR(*len*)	Name of schema containing this view definition
TABLE_NAME	VARCHAR(*len*)	Name of the view
VIEW_DEFINITION	VARCHAR(*maxlen*)	Text of the SQL SELECT statement defining the view
CHECK_OPTION	VARCHAR(*maxlen*)	Check option for this view (CASCADED/LOCAL/NONE)
IS_UPDATABLE	VARCHAR(*maxlen*)	Whether the view is updateable (YES/NO)

VARCHAR(*len*) is the data type for SQL identifiers; *len* is the maximum length defined by the SQL implementation.

VARCHAR(*maxlen*) is a VARCHAR data type with the largest maximum length permitted by the SQL implementation.

VIEW_TABLE_USAGE *View*

The VIEW_TABLE_USAGE view contains one row for each table on which a view defined in the current catalog by the current user depends. Its structure is shown in the following table:

Column Name	Data Type	Description
VIEW_CATALOG	VARCHAR(*len*)	Name of catalog containing the view definition
VIEW_SCHEMA	VARCHAR(*len*)	Name of schema containing the view definition
VIEW_NAME	VARCHAR(*len*)	Name of the view
TABLE_CATALOG	VARCHAR(*len*)	Catalog containing the definition of the table on which the view depends
TABLE_SCHEMA	VARCHAR(*len*)	Schema containing the definition of the table on which the view depends
TABLE_NAME	VARCHAR(*len*)	Name of the table on which the view depends

VARCHAR(*len*) is the data type for SQL identifiers; *len* is the maximum length defined by the SQL implementation.

VIEW_COLUMN_USAGE *View*

The VIEW_COLUMN_USAGE view contains one row for each column on which a view defined in the current catalog by the current user depends. Its structure is shown in the following table:

Column Name	Data Type	Description
VIEW_CATALOG	VARCHAR(*len*)	Name of catalog containing the view definition
VIEW_SCHEMA	VARCHAR(*len*)	Name of schema containing the view definition
VIEW_NAME	VARCHAR(*len*)	Name of the view
TABLE_CATALOG	VARCHAR(*len*)	Catalog containing the definition of the column on which the view depends
TABLE_SCHEMA	VARCHAR(*len*)	Schema containing the definition of the column on which the view depends
TABLE_NAME	VARCHAR(*len*)	Name of the table containing the column on which the view depends
COLUMN_NAME	VARCHAR(*len*)	Name of the column on which the view depends

VARCHAR(*len*) is the data type for SQL identifiers; *len* is the maximum length defined by the SQL implementation.

TABLE_CONSTRAINTS *View*

The TABLE_CONSTRAINTS view contains one row for each table constraint defined for tables in the current catalog owned by the current user. Its structure is shown in the following table:

Column Name	Data Type	Description
CONSTRAINT_CATALOG	VARCHAR(*len*)	Name of catalog containing the constraint definition
CONSTRAINT_SCHEMA	VARCHAR(*len*)	Name of schema containing the constraint definition
CONSTRAINT_NAME	VARCHAR(*len*)	Name of the constraint
TABLE_CATALOG	VARCHAR(*len*)	Name of catalog containing the table definition

Column Name	Data Type	Description
TABLE_SCHEMA	VARCHAR(*len*)	Name of schema containing the table definition
TABLE_NAME	VARCHAR(*len*)	Name of the table being constrained
CONSTRAINT_TYPE	VARCHAR(*maxlen*)	Type of constraint (UNIQUE / PRIMARY KEY / FOREIGN KEY / CHECK)
IS_DEFERRABLE	VARCHAR(*maxlen*)	Is constraint deferrable? (YES/NO)
INITIALLY_DEFERRED	VARCHAR(*maxlen*)	Is constraint initially deferred? (YES/NO)

VARCHAR(*len*) is the data type for SQL identifiers; *len* is the maximum length defined by the SQL implementation.

VARCHAR(*maxlen*) is a VARCHAR data type with the largest maximum length permitted by the SQL implementation.

REFERENTIAL_CONSTRAINTS *View*

The REFERENTIAL_CONSTRAINTS view contains one row for each referential constraint (foreign key / primary key relationship) defined for tables in the current catalog owned by the current user. Its structure is shown in the following table:

Column Name	Data Type	Description
CONSTRAINT_CATALOG	VARCHAR(*len*)	Name of catalog containing the constraint definition
CONSTRAINT_SCHEMA	VARCHAR(*len*)	Name of schema containing the constraint definition
CONSTRAINT_NAME	VARCHAR(*len*)	Name of the constraint
UNIQUE_CONSTRAINT_ CATALOG	VARCHAR(*len*)	Name of catalog containing the unique or primary key constraint definition for the "parent" table
UNIQUE_CONSTRAINT_ SCHEMA	VARCHAR(*len*)	Name of schema containing the unique or primary key constraint definition for the "parent" table

Column Name	Data Type	Description
UNIQUE_CONSTRAINT_ NAME	VARCHAR(*len*)	Name of the unique or primary key constraint definition for the "parent" table
MATCH_OPTION	VARCHAR(*maxlen*)	Type of partial foreign-key matching (NONE/PARTIAL/FULL)
UPDATE_RULE	VARCHAR(*maxlen*)	Update rule for the referential constraint (CASCADE / SET NULL / SET DEFAULT / NO ACTION)
DELETE_RULE	VARCHAR(*maxlen*)	Delete rule for the referential constraint (CASCADE / SET NULL / SET DEFAULT / NO ACTION)

VARCHAR(*len*) is the data type for SQL identifiers; *len* is the maximum length defined by the SQL implementation.

VARCHAR(*maxlen*) is a VARCHAR data type with the largest maximum length permitted by the SQL implementation.

CHECK_CONSTRAINTS *View*

The CHECK_CONSTRAINTS view contains one row for each check constraint (check constraint, domain check constraint, or assertion definition) defined in the current catalog that is owned by the current user. Its structure is shown in the following table:

Column Name	Data Type	Description
CONSTRAINT_CATALOG	VARCHAR(*len*)	Name of catalog containing the constraint definition
CONSTRAINT_SCHEMA	VARCHAR(*len*)	Name of schema containing the constraint definition
CONSTRAINT_NAME	VARCHAR(*len*)	Name of the constraint
CHECK_CLAUSE	VARCHAR(*maxlen*)	Text of the SQL search condition that defines the check constraint

VARCHAR(*len*) is the data type for SQL identifiers; *len* is the maximum length defined by the SQL implementation.

VARCHAR(*maxlen*) is a VARCHAR data type with the largest maximum length permitted by the SQL implementation.

KEY_COLUMN_USAGE *View*

The KEY_COLUMN_USAGE view contains one row for each column that participates in a key defined in the current catalog by the current user. Its structure is shown in the following table:

Column Name	Data Type	Description
CONSTRAINT_CATALOG	VARCHAR(*len*)	Name of catalog containing the key constraint definition
CONSTRAINT_SCHEMA	VARCHAR(*len*)	Name of schema containing the key constraint definition
CONSTRAINT_NAME	VARCHAR(*len*)	Name of the key constraint
TABLE_CATALOG	VARCHAR(*len*)	Name of catalog containing the definition of the table containing the key
TABLE_SCHEMA	VARCHAR(*len*)	Name of schema containing the definition of the table containing the key
TABLE_NAME	VARCHAR(*len*)	Name of the table containing the key column
COLUMN_NAME	VARCHAR(*len*)	Name of the column
ORDINAL_POSITION	INTEGER > 0	Position of the column within the key

VARCHAR(*len*) is the data type for SQL identifiers; *len* is the maximum length defined by the SQL implementation.

ASSERTIONS *View*

The ASSERTIONS view contains one row for each assertion defined in the current catalog that are owned by the current user. Its structure is shown in the following table:

Column Name	Data Type	Description
CONSTRAINT_CATALOG	VARCHAR(*len*)	Name of catalog containing the assertion definition
CONSTRAINT_SCHEMA	VARCHAR(*len*)	Name of schema containing the assertion definition
CONSTRAINT_NAME	VARCHAR(*len*)	Name of the assertion

Column Name	Data Type	Description
IS_DEFERRABLE	VARCHAR(*maxlen*)	Is assertion deferrable? (YES/NO)
INITIALLY_DEFERRED	VARCHAR(*maxlen*)	Is assertion initially deferred? (YES/NO)

VARCHAR(*len*) is the data type for SQL identifiers; *len* is the maximum length defined by the SQL implementation.

VARCHAR(*maxlen*) is a VARCHAR data type with the largest maximum length permitted by the SQL implementation.

CONSTRAINT_TABLE_USAGE *View*

The CONSTRAINT_TABLE_USAGE view contains one row for each table used by a constraint (referential constraint, unique constraint, check constraint, or assertion) defined in the current catalog by the current user. Its structure is shown in the following table:

Column Name	Data Type	Description
TABLE_CATALOG	VARCHAR(*len*)	Name of catalog containing the table definition
TABLE_SCHEMA	VARCHAR(*len*)	Name of schema containing the table definition
TABLE_NAME	VARCHAR(*len*)	Name of the table
CONSTRAINT_CATALOG	VARCHAR(*len*)	Catalog containing the definition of the constraint
CONSTRAINT_SCHEMA	VARCHAR(*len*)	Schema containing the definition of the constraint
CONSTRAINT_NAME	VARCHAR(*len*)	Name of the constraint

VARCHAR(*len*) is the data type for SQL identifiers; *len* is the maximum length defined by the SQL implementation.

CONSTRAINT_COLUMN_USAGE *View*

The CONSTRAINT_COLUMN_USAGE view contains one row for each column used by a constraint (referential constraint, unique constraint, check constraint or assertion) defined in the current catalog by the current user. Its structure is shown in the following table:

Column Name	Data Type	Description
TABLE_CATALOG	VARCHAR(*len*)	Name of catalog containing the column definition
TABLE_SCHEMA	VARCHAR(*len*)	Name of schema containing the column definition
TABLE_NAME	VARCHAR(*len*)	Name of the table containing the column
COLUMN_NAME	VARCHAR(*len*)	Name of the column
CONSTRAINT_CATALOG	VARCHAR(*len*)	Catalog containing the definition of the constraint
CONSTRAINT_SCHEMA	VARCHAR(*len*)	Schema containing the definition of the constraint
CONSTRAINT_NAME	VARCHAR(*len*)	Name of the constraint

VARCHAR(*len*) is the data type for SQL identifiers; *len* is the maximum length defined by the SQL implementation.

TABLE_PRIVILEGES *View*

The TABLE_PRIVILEGES view contains one row for each privilege on tables defined in the current catalog that has been granted to the current user, been granted to all users, or has been granted by the current user. Its structure is shown in the following table:

Column Name	Data Type	Description
GRANTOR	VARCHAR(*len*)	Authorization-id of user granting the privilege
GRANTEE	VARCHAR(*len*)	Authorization-id of user being granted the privilege
TABLE_CATALOG	VARCHAR(*len*)	Name of catalog containing this view definition
TABLE_SCHEMA	VARCHAR(*len*)	Name of schema containing this view definition

Column Name	Data Type	Description
TABLE_NAME	VARCHAR(*len*)	Name of the view
PRIVILEGE_TYPE	VARCHAR(*maxlen*)	Type of privilege (SELECT/INSERT/DELETE/UPDATE/REFERENCES)
IS_GRANTABLE	VARCHAR(*maxlen*)	Is privilege granted WITH GRANT OPTION? (YES / NO)

VARCHAR(*len*) is the data type for SQL identifiers; *len* is the maximum length defined by the SQL implementation.

VARCHAR(*maxlen*) is a VARCHAR data type with the largest maximum length permitted by the SQL implementation.

COLUMN_PRIVILEGES *View*

The COLUMN_PRIVILEGES view contains one row for each privilege on columns defined in the current catalog that has been granted to the current user, been granted to all users, or has been granted by the current user. Its structure is shown in the following table:

Column Name	Data Type	Description
GRANTOR	VARCHAR(*len*)	Authorization-id of user granting the privilege
GRANTEE	VARCHAR(*len*)	Authorization-id of user being granted the privilege
TABLE_CATALOG	VARCHAR(*len*)	Name of catalog containing the table definition containing this column
TABLE_SCHEMA	VARCHAR(*len*)	Name of schema containing the table definition containing this column
TABLE_NAME	VARCHAR(*len*)	Name of the table containing this column
COLUMN_NAME	VARCHAR(*len*)	Name of the column
PRIVILEGE_TYPE	VARCHAR(*maxlen*)	Type of privilege (SELECT/INSERT/DELETE/UPDATE/REFERENCES)

Column Name	Data Type	Description
IS_GRANTABLE	VARCHAR(*maxlen*)	Is privilege granted WITH GRANT OPTION? (YES/NO)

VARCHAR(*len*) is the data type for SQL identifiers; *len* is the maximum length defined by the SQL implementation.

VARCHAR(*maxlen*) is a VARCHAR data type with the largest maximum length permitted by the SQL implementation.

USAGE_PRIVILEGES *View*

The USAGE_PRIVILEGES view contains one row for each privilege on objects defined in the current catalog that has been granted to the current user, been granted to all users, or has been granted by the current user. Its structure is shown in the following table:

Column Name	Data Type	Description
GRANTOR	VARCHAR(*len*)	Authorization-id of user granting the privilege
GRANTEE	VARCHAR(*len*)	Authorization-id of user being granted the privilege
OBJECT_CATALOG	VARCHAR(*len*)	Name of catalog containing the object definition
OBJECT_SCHEMA	VARCHAR(*len*)	Name of schema containing the object definition
OBJECT_NAME	VARCHAR(*len*)	Name of the object
OBJECT_TYPE	VARCHAR(*maxlen*)	Type of object (DOMAIN / CHARACTER SET / COLLATION / TRANSLATION)
PRIVILEGE_TYPE	VARCHAR(*maxlen*)	Type of privilege (always the literal USAGE)
IS_GRANTABLE	VARCHAR(*maxlen*)	Is privilege granted WITH GRANT OPTION? (YES/NO)

VARCHAR(*len*) is the data type for SQL identifiers; *len* is the maximum length defined by the SQL implementation.

VARCHAR(*maxlen*) is a VARCHAR data type with the largest maximum length permitted by the SQL implementation.

DOMAINS *View*

The DOMAINS view contains one row for each domain defined in the current catalog that is accessible to the current user. Its structure is shown in the following table:

Column Name	Data Type	Description
DOMAIN_CATALOG	VARCHAR(*len*)	Name of catalog containing this domain definition
DOMAIN_SCHEMA	VARCHAR(*len*)	Name of schema containing this domain definition
DOMAIN_NAME	VARCHAR(*len*)	Name of the domain
DATA_TYPE	VARCHAR(*maxlen*)	SQL2 data type on which the domain definition is based (text representation)
CHARACTER_MAXIMUM_LENGTH	INTEGER > 0	Maximum length, in characters, for variable-length character types
CHARACTER_OCTET_LENGTH	INTEGER > 0	Maximum length of variable-length data type, in bytes
COLLATION_CATALOG	VARCHAR(*len*)	Catalog containing the definition of the collation for this domain
COLLATION_SCHEMA	VARCHAR(*len*)	Schema containing the collation for this domain
COLLATION_NAME	VARCHAR(*len*)	Name of collation for this domain
CHARACTER_SET_CATALOG	VARCHAR(*len*)	Catalog containing the definition of the character set for this domain
CHARACTER_SET_SCHEMA	VARCHAR(*len*)	Schema containing the definition of the character set for this domain
CHARACTER_SET_NAME	VARCHAR(*len*)	Name of the character set for this domain
NUMERIC_PRECISION	INTEGER > 0	Precision if this domain is based on a numeric data type
NUMERIC_PRECISION_RADIX	INTEGER > 0	Radix of the precision
NUMERIC_SCALE	INTEGER > 0	Scale if this domain is based on a numeric type
DATATIME_PRECISION	INTEGER > 0	Precision if this domain is based on a DateTime data type

Column Name	Data Type	Description
DOMAIN_DEFAULT	VARCHAR(*maxlen*)	Text representation of the default value for the domain

VARCHAR(*len*) is the data type for SQL identifiers; *len* is the maximum length defined by the SQL implementation.

VARCHAR(*maxlen*) is a VARCHAR data type with the largest maximum length permitted by the SQL implementation.

DOMAIN_CONSTRAINTS *View*

The DOMAIN_CONSTRAINTS view contains one row for each domain constraint for a domain defined in the current catalog that is accessible to the current user. Its structure is shown in the following table:

Column Name	Data Type	Description
CONSTRAINT_CATALOG	VARCHAR(*len*)	Name of catalog containing this constraint definition
CONSTRAINT_SCHEMA	VARCHAR(*len*)	Name of schema containing this constraint definition
CONSTRAINT_NAME	VARCHAR(*len*)	Name of the constraint
DOMAIN_CATALOG	VARCHAR(*len*)	Name of catalog containing the domain definition to which constraint applies
DOMAIN_SCHEMA	VARCHAR(*len*)	Name of schema containing the domain definition to which constraint applies
DOMAIN_NAME	VARCHAR(*len*)	Maximum length of variable-length data type, in octets
IS_DEFERRABLE	VARCHAR(*maxlen*)	Is constraint deferrable? (YES/NO)
INITIALLY_DEFERRED	VARCHAR(*maxlen*)	Is constraint initially deferred? (YES/NO)

VARCHAR(*len*) is the data type for SQL identifiers; *len* is the maximum length defined by the SQL implementation.

VARCHAR(*maxlen*) is a VARCHAR data type with the largest maximum length permitted by the SQL implementation.

DOMAIN_COLUMN_USAGE *View*

The DOMAIN_COLUMN_USAGE view contains one row for each column used by a domain defined in the current catalog by the current user. Its structure is shown in the following table:

Column Name	Data Type	Description
DOMAIN_CATALOG	VARCHAR(*len*)	Catalog containing the definition of the domain
DOMAIN_SCHEMA	VARCHAR(*len*)	Schema containing the definition of the domain
DOMAIN_NAME	VARCHAR(*len*)	Name of the domain
TABLE_CATALOG	VARCHAR(*len*)	Name of catalog containing the column definition
TABLE_SCHEMA	VARCHAR(*len*)	Name of schema containing the column definition
TABLE_NAME	VARCHAR(*len*)	Name of the table containing the column
COLUMN_NAME	VARCHAR(*len*)	Name of the column

VARCHAR(*len*) is the data type for SQL identifiers; *len* is the maximum length defined by the SQL implementation.

CHARACTER_SETS *View*

The CHARACTER_SETS view contains one row for each character set defined in the current catalog that is accessible to the current user. Its structure is shown in the following table:

Column Name	Data Type	Description
CHARACTER_SET_ CATALOG	VARCHAR(*len*)	Name of catalog containing the character set definition
CHARACTER_SET_ SCHEMA	VARCHAR(*len*)	Name of schema containing the character set definition
CHARACTER_SET_ NAME	VARCHAR(*len*)	Name of the character set
FORM_OF_USE	VARCHAR(*len*)	Form-of-use of the character set

Column Name	Data Type	Description
NUMBER_OF_ CHARACTERS	INTEGER > 0	Number of characters in the character set
DEFAULT_COLLATE_ CATALOG	VARCHAR(*len*)	Catalog containing the default collation definition for this character set
DEFAULT_COLLATE_ SCHEMA	VARCHAR(*len*)	Schema containing the default collation definition for this character set
DEFAULT_COLLATE_ NAME	VARCHAR(*len*)	Name of default collation for this character set

VARCHAR(*len*) is the data type for SQL identifiers; *len* is the maximum length defined by the SQL implementation.

VARCHAR(*maxlen*) is a VARCHAR data type with the largest maximum length permitted by the SQL implementation.

COLLATIONS *View*

The COLLATIONS view contains one row for each collation (sorting sequence) defined in the current catalog that is accessible to the current user. Its structure is shown in the following table:

Column Name	Data Type	Description
COLLATION_CATALOG	VARCHAR(*len*)	Name of catalog containing the collation definition
COLLATION_SCHEMA	VARCHAR(*len*)	Name of schema containing the collation definition
COLLATION_NAME	VARCHAR(*len*)	Name of the collation
CHARACTER_SET_ CATALOG	VARCHAR(*len*)	Catalog containing the character set definition on which the collating sequence is defined
CHARACTER_SET_ SCHEMA	VARCHAR(*len*)	Schema containing the character set definition on which the collating sequence is defined
CHARACTER_SET_NAME	VARCHAR(*len*)	Name of the character set on which the collating sequence is defined

Column Name	Data Type	Description
PAD_ATTRIBUTE	VARCHAR(*maxlen*)	Character padding (PAD SPACE / NO PAD)

VARCHAR(*len*) is the data type for SQL identifiers; *len* is the maximum length defined by the SQL implementation.

VARCHAR(*maxlen*) is a VARCHAR data type with the largest maximum length permitted by the SQL implementation.

TRANSLATIONS *View*

The TRANSLATIONS view contains one row for each translation (conversion from one character set to another) defined in the current catalog that is accessible to the current user. Its structure is shown in the following table:

Column Name	Data Type	Description
TRANSLATION_CATALOG	VARCHAR(*len*)	Name of catalog containing the translation definition
TRANSLATION_SCHEMA	VARCHAR(*len*)	Name of schema containing the translation definition
TRANSLATION_NAME	VARCHAR(*len*)	Name of the translation
SOURCE_CHARACTER_SET_CATALOG	VARCHAR(*len*)	Catalog containing the character set definition from which the translation occurs
SOURCE_CHARACTER_SET_SCHEMA	VARCHAR(*len*)	Schema containing the character set definition from which the translation occurs
CHARACTER_SET_NAME	VARCHAR(*len*)	Name of the character set from which translation occurs
TARGET_CHARACTER_SET_CATALOG	VARCHAR(*len*)	Catalog containing the character set definition to which the translation occurs
TARGET_CHARACTER_SET_SCHEMA	VARCHAR(*len*)	Schema containing the character set definition to which the translation occurs
TARGET_CHARACTER_SET_NAME	VARCHAR(*len*)	Name of the character set to which translation occurs

VARCHAR(*len*) is the data type for SQL identifiers; *len* is the maximum length defined by the SQL implementation.

SQL_LANGUAGES *View*

The SQL_LANGUAGES view contains one row for each ANSI-standard language supported by this SQL implementation. Its structure is shown in the following table:

Column Name	Data Type	Description
SQL_LANGUAGE_ SOURCE	VARCHAR(*maxlen*)	Text identifying source of language standard (e.g., ISO 9075)
SQL_LANGUAGE_ YEAR	VARCHAR(*maxlen*)	Year in which standard was approved (e.g., 1987)
SQL_LANGUAGE_ CONFORMANCE	VARCHAR(*maxlen*)	Conformance level (1/2)
SQL_LANGUAGE_ INTEGRITY	VARCHAR(*maxlen*)	Integrity (YES/NO) or NULL
SQL_LANGUAGE_ IMPLEMENTATION	VARCHAR(*maxlen*)	Implementation-defined character string or NULL
SQL_LANGUAGE_ BINDING_STYLE	VARCHAR(*maxlen*)	Binding style (e.g., EMBEDDED/MODULE/DIRECT)
SQL_LANGUAGE_ PROGRAMMING_ LANGUAGE	VARCHAR(*maxlen*)	Name of the supported programming language (e.g., ADA/C/COBOL/ FORTRAN/PASCAL/PLI)

VARCHAR(*maxlen*) is a VARCHAR data type with the largest maximum length permitted by the SQL implementation.

The Complete Reference

Appendix G

CD-ROM Installation Guide

937

T he Bonus CD that accompanies this book includes full-function Windows 95/NT versions of all five of the leading brands of SQL-based DBMS:

- Microsoft SQL Server 7
- Oracle8
- Informix
- Sybase
- IBM DB2

These are *not* incomplete "demo" versions of the DBMS products. Rather, they are full-capability *evaluation* versions* of the latest software from these five leading database vendors, allowing you to learn SQL using a live DBMS, test out and compare each product, and find a SQL DBMS that best suits your specific needs.

The CD also includes data files that you can use to populate the DBMS products with the five tables of the sample database so that you can easily run the example queries in the book. The files reside in the root directory of the CD and are named:

- CUSTOMERS.DAT
- OFFICES.DAT
- ORDERS.DAT
- PRODUCTS.DAT
- SALESREPS.DAT

Finally, the CD includes a simple DBMS installation program that you can use to automatically install any or all of the five products. The program resides in the root directory of the CD and is named SQLINSTALL.EXE.

Enjoy this unique CD that is available only with *SQL: The Complete Reference*, the most comprehensive book on SQL with the most comprehensive collection of valuable SQL DBMS software from the leading DBMS vendors.

---

*The products are subject to restricted use licenses, are for evaluation purposes only, and, in some cases, include expiration mechanisms that cause the software to cease operation 60 or 120 days after installation. See the tables in the sections that follow for specific details on each product.

Installing the SQL DBMS Software

When you insert the Bonus CD into your CD-ROM drive, Windows automatically launches the DBMS installation program on the CD. The program prompts you to accept the Osborne/McGraw-Hill license agreement and then allows you to select a DBMS for installation as shown here:

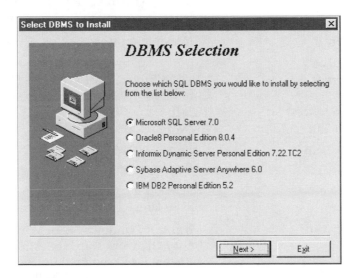

The sections that follow contain detailed instructions for installing each brand of SQL DBMS.

Microsoft SQL Server 7

The following table lists details and facts about the product and the company.

Product name	SQL Server 7.0
First shipment	1988
Platform	Windows 95/NT
DBMS version	7.0
Installation program	\SQLSERVER7\AUTORUN.EXE
Software limitations	Expires 120 days after installation
Vendor	Microsoft Corporation
Founded	1975
Annual sales	$15.3 billion

Hardware and Software Requirements

Microsoft SQL Server requires the following hardware and software:

Category	Requirements
Computer	Intel or compatible (Pentium 166MHz or higher, Pentium PRO, or Pentium II)
Memory (RAM)	32MB minimum
Hard disk space[1]	
SQL Server	180MB (full), 170MB (typical), 65MB (minimum), 90MB (management tools only)
OLAP Services[2]	50MB
English Query	12MB
Operating system	Windows 95/98 or Windows NT Workstation 4.0 or later[3] with SP4 or later[3]
Internet software	Microsoft Internet Explorer version 4.01 with SP1 or later[4]
Network software	Microsoft Windows NT or Windows 95/98 built-in network software. Additional network software is not required unless you are using Banyan VINES or AppleTalk ADSP. Novell NetWare client support is provided by NWLink.
Clients supported	Windows 95/98, Windows NT Workstation, Unix[5,4] Macintosh[5,4] and OS/2[5]

[1]These figures are the maximum hard disk space required. Setup installs a number of components that can be shared by other applications and may already exist on the computer.
[2]Enter the 10-digit CD Key "111-1111111" when installing OLAP Services.
[3]Windows NT SP4 is included on the CD.
[4]Internet Explorer is required for Microsoft Management Console (MMC) and HTML Help. A minimal installation is sufficient, and your default browser need not be Internet Explorer. Internet Explorer 4.01 with SP1 is included on the CD.
[5]Requires ODBC client software from a third-party vendor.

SQL Server Services User Accounts

Under Windows NT, you must assign a user account for each of the Microsoft SQL Server services during installation. You may also specify whether the services should start automatically whenever you restart the computer. The SQLServerAgent service is dependent on the MSSQLServer service. You can autostart the SQLServerAgent service only if you autostart the MSSQLServer service as well.

You may enter one user account for all of the services or specify an account for each. The default account is the domain user account currently logged into the computer.

SQL Server 7.0 Installation

Perform the following steps to install SQL Server 7.0:

1. Under Windows NT, log on to the system as a member of the Administrators group.

2. If you are installing SQL Server 7.0 on the same computer alongside SQL Server 6.x, back up your Microsoft SQL Server 6.x installation, and do *not* install SQL Server 7.0 in the same directory as SQL Server 6.x.

3. If necessary, shut down all services dependent on SQL Server. This includes any service that is using ODBC, such as Microsoft Internet Information Services (IIS).

4. If necessary, shut down Microsoft Windows NT Event Viewer and REGEDT32.EXE.

5. Insert the Bonus CD into your CD-ROM drive.

6. Windows automatically launches the DBMS installation program on the CD. If the installation program does not launch automatically, double-click **SQLINSTALL.EXE** in the root directory of the CD to launch it manually.

7. The installation program displays a dialog prompting you to accept the Osborne/McGraw-Hill license agreement. Indicate your acceptance of the agreement, and click **Next**.

8. The installation program displays the DBMS selection dialog. Select **Microsoft SQL Server 7** from the list of DBMS choices, and click **Next**. This invokes the SQL Server Autorun application as shown here:

9. Autorun displays the entry screen. Click **Install SQL Server 7.0 Components**.

10. Autorun displays the next set of choices. Click **Database Server – Standard Edition or Database Server – Desktop Edition**. Under Windows 95/98 or Windows NT Workstation, you must select **Desktop Edition**.

11. Under Windows NT, the Setup Install Method dialog appears. Select **Local Install**, and click **Next**.

12. The Welcome dialog appears. Click **Next** to continue.

13. The Software License Agreement dialog appears. Click **Yes** to accept the agreement.

14. The User Information dialog appears. Enter your name and company if they are different than the default values indicated, and click **Next**.

15. If you have an earlier version of SQL Server installed on your system, the Convert Existing SQL Server Data dialog may appear and ask if you want to upgrade your existing SQL Server databases. Do *not* check the box to upgrade at this time. Click **Next** to continue.

16. The Setup Type dialog appears. Select **Typical**. The dialog also indicates the default directories into which the SQL Server files will be copied. Accept the defaults or click **Browse** to specify different directories, and click **Next**.

17. Under Windows NT, the Services Accounts dialog appears. Enter an existing user name and password to use for the SQL Server service, or select **Use the Local System account** and click **Next**. Note that the SQLServerAgent service defaults to the same account entered for the MSSQLServer service unless you specify another account.

18. The Start Copying Files dialog appears. Click **Next** to continue.

19. Autorun installs SQL Server on your hard disk. This may take several minutes.

20. When installation is complete, the Setup Complete dialog appears. If this is the first time you have ever installed SQL Server on your system, Autorun prompts you to reboot your computer. Select **Yes**, and click **Finish** to exit Autorun and automatically reboot. If you have previously installed SQL Server, you do not have to reboot your computer at this time, and Autorun will not prompt you to do so. Click **Finish** to return to the Autorun entry screen and **Exit** to return to Windows.

Starting SQL Server 7.0

After you install SQL Server for the first time, you must reboot your computer before you can begin to use the software.

Under Windows 95, after you reboot, double-click on the **Service Manager** icon in the Windows system tray, and then click on the green **Start/Continue** icon to start the

MSSQLServer service. Also check the Auto-start service when OS starts box so that SQL Server is started automatically each time you subsequently reboot your computer.

Under Windows NT, SQL server is started automatically after you reboot and each time you start your computer after that.

Stopping SQL Server 7.0

Perform the following steps to shut down SQL Server 7.0:

1. Stop all SQL Server services (if any are running). To do this…

    Under Windows 95:

    - Double-click on the **Service Manager** icon in the Windows system tray.

    - Click on the red **Stop** icon to shut down any service that is running.

    - Click on the **Close** button to close the SQL Server Service Manager.

    Under Windows NT:

    - Choose **Start | Settings | Control Panel** from the Windows taskbar.

    - Double-click on the **Services** application.

    - Click on the **Stop** icon to shut down any SQL Server service (such as MSSQLServer and SQLServerAgent) that has the status Started.

    - Click **Close** to exit the Services application.

2. Shut down the SQL Server Service Manager (if it is running). To do so, right-click on the **Service Manager** icon in the Windows system tray, and select **Exit**.

Uninstalling SQL Server 7.0

Perform the following steps to uninstall SQL Server 7.0:

1. Stop all SQL Server services, and close all SQL Server applications.

2. Choose **Start | Programs | Microsoft SQL Server 7.0 | Uninstall SQL Server 7.0** from the Windows taskbar.

3. The Confirm File Deletion dialog appears and asks you to confirm that you want to uninstall the program. Click **Yes** to continue.

4. The Remove Shared Files? dialog appears and asks you to confirm that you want to remove shared files that are no longer being used. Click **Yes to All** to remove these files, and click **Yes** when the second confirmation dialog appears. The Uninstall program removes all SQL Server 7.0 programs from your system.

Oracle8

The following table provides a variety of miscellaneous details about the product and the company:

Product name	Oracle8 Personal Edition
First shipment	1979
Platform	Windows 95/NT
DBMS version	8.0.4
Installation program	\TEMP\ORACLE8\SETUP.EXE (after decompression)
Software limitations	None (subject to 30-day trial license)
Vendor	Oracle Corporation
Founded	1977
Annual sales	$7.52 billion

Products Included on the CD

You'll find the following products on the CD-ROM included with this book:

Product	**Version**
Assistant Common Files	1.0.1.0.0
Java Runtime Environment	1.1.1.0.0
Oracle Call Interface	8.0.4.0.0
Oracle Data Migration Assistant	8.0.4.0.0
Oracle Database Assistant (for Windows NT only)	2.0.0.0.1
Oracle Documentation	8.0.4.0.0
Oracle Installer	3.3.0.1.3
Oracle Migration Assistant for Microsoft Access	8.0.4.0.0
Oracle Net8 Add-on	8.0.4.0.0
Oracle Net8 Assistant	8.0.4.0.3
Oracle Net8 Client	8.0.4.0.2c

Product	Version
Oracle LU6.2 Protocol Adapter (for Windows NT only)	8.0.4.0.0
Oracle Named Pipes Protocol Adapter	8.0.4.0.0
Oracle SPX Protocol Adapter	8.0.4.0.0
Oracle TCP/IP Protocol Adapter	8.0.4.0.2
SQL*Net Add-on (Patch) (for Windows 95 only)	2.2.2.1.1
Oracle LU6.2 Protocol Adapter (for Windows NT only)	2.3.4.0.0
Oracle Named Pipes Protocol Adapter	2.3.4.0.0
Oracle SPX Protocol Adapter	2.3.4.0.0
Oracle TCP/IP Protocol Adapter	2.3.4.0.0
SQL*Net Add-on	2.3.4.0.2
SQL*Net Client	2.3.4.0.2
Oracle Objects for OLE	2.2.2.2.0
Oracle Patch Assistant	1.0.0.0.1
Oracle Web Publishing Assistant (for Windows NT only)	2.0.0.0.0
Oracle7 Utilities	7.3.4.0.0
Oracle8 JDBC Drivers	8.0.4.0.0
Oracle8 Navigator	8.0.4.0.0
Online Help	8.0.4.0.0
Oracle8 ODBC Driver	8.0.4.0.0
Oracle8 Personal Edition	8.0.4.0.0
Oracle8 Database	8.0.4.0.0
Oracle8 Utilities	8.0.4.0.1
Oracle8 Personal Edition Release Notes	8.0.4.0.0
Required Support Files	7.3.4.1.1
Required Support Files	8.0.4.0.4
SQL*Plus	8.0.4.0.0

Hardware and Software Requirements

Oracle8 Personal Edition requires the following hardware and software:

Category	Requirements
Computer	Pentium-based personal computer
Memory (RAM)	32MB for standard starter database 48MB for replication starter database
Hard disk space	134MB (Application Developer with standard database) 149MB (Application Developer with replication database)[1] 100MB (Runtime with standard database) 115MB (Runtime with replication database)[1] 163MB (Custom installation)[2]
Operating system	Windows 95 or Windows NT 4.0
Network software	If you want to use the distributed features of Oracle8 Personal Edition, install one of the following network transport protocols: TCP/IP, SPX, Named Pipes LU6.2 (under Windows NT only), a frames and Java-enabled Web browser

[1]Use of advanced replication (for example, updateable snapshots) requires a remote database configured for advanced replication.
[2]The amount of hard disk space required for the Custom installation varies according to which components you select.

Installing on a Windows 95 Compressed Drive

In general, Oracle8 does not support use of disk compression software with database files. You can install Oracle8 on a compressed disk drive under Windows 95. However, the starter database that is installed when you perform the software installation must be installed on a noncompressed disk drive.

If you choose to install the Oracle8 software on a compressed drive, you are asked to install the starter database on a noncompressed disk drive of your choice.

If all your disk drives are compressed, then you must adjust the free space allocated between the compressed drive and the noncompressed host drive. The disk compression utility provides information on this procedure.

If you need to resize a compressed drive, use the utility provided with the disk compression software. Adjust the free space allocated between the compressed drive and the noncompressed host drive to gain enough noncompressed disk space on the host drive for the starter database. Then, specify the host drive as the noncompressed disk drive on which to install your starter database. Please refer to the disk compression utility's online help for more information on how to adjust free space.

You need 40MB of noncompressed disk space to install the starter database with support for advanced replication. Otherwise, you need 20MB of noncompressed disk space.

Under Windows NT, installation of Oracle8 on an NTFS compressed drive is not supported.

Additional Windows 95 Disk Space Requirements

Oracle8 Personal Edition for Windows 95 requires 20MB of free disk space on the disk drive where the Windows 95 Virtual Memory page file is located (usually the C: drive). This space is required in addition to the space needed for Oracle8 program files.

Windows 95 Known Problems

The Universal Naming Convention (UNC) for filenames and directory paths is not supported. This has two implications:

- When providing a directory path or filename, use the standard DOS naming convention. The directory path or filename must be no longer than eight characters and the extension must be no longer than three characters.

- Use of the \ \ notation to represent the start of a directory path is not supported.

Products Available for Installation

When you run the Oracle installation program, a dialog box displays several product installation options. The Custom option enables you to selectively install from a list of *all* available products. By contrast, the Application Developer (Complete) and Runtime (Database Only) options automatically install a group of products as follows:

Product	Application Developer	Runtime
Oracle8 Personal Edition	✓	✓
Oracle8 Navigator	✓	
Oracle8 Utilities	✓	
Oracle Net8 Assistant	✓	
Oracle8 Database	✓	
Oracle Net8 Add-On	✓	✓
Oracle Net8 Client	✓	✓

Product	Application Developer	Runtime
SQL*Plus	✓	
Oracle Call Interface	✓	
Oracle Objects for OLE	✓	
Oracle8 ODBC Driver	✓	
Oracle Documentation	✓	
Oracle8 Personal Edition Release Notes	✓	✓
Assistant Common Files	✓	✓
Oracle Trace Collection Services	✓	✓
Java Runtime Environment	✓	✓
Oracle Installer	✓	✓
Oracle Data Migration Assistant	✓	✓
Oracle Home Selector	✓	
Oracle Database Assistant	✓	
Oracle Web Publishing Assistant	✓	
Oracle Patch Assistant	✓	
Oracle Migration Assistant Microsoft Access	✓	
Required Support Files	✓	✓

Oracle8 Personal Edition Installation

Perform the following steps to install Oracle8 Personal Edition:

1. Under Windows NT, log on to the system as a member of the Administrators group.

2. Insert the Bonus CD into your CD-ROM drive.

3. Windows automatically launches the DBMS installation program on the CD. If the installation program does not launch automatically, double-click **SQLINSTALL.EXE** in the root directory of the CD to launch it manually.

4. The installation program displays a dialog prompting you to accept the Osborne/McGraw-Hill license agreement. Indicate your acceptance of the agreement, and click **Next**.

5. The installation program displays the DBMS selection dialog. Select **Oracle8 Personal Edition** from the list of DBMS choices, and click **Next**.

6. Due to the size of the Oracle distribution, it must first be decompressed into a temporary directory on your hard disk before installation begins. The DBMS installation program prompts you for the name of the temporary directory. Verify the name of the directory, and click **Next**.

7. The Oracle files are decompressed onto the temporary directory. This may take ten or fifteen minutes. When decompression is complete, the installation program invokes the Oracle Setup application as shown here:

8. Setup displays the Oracle Installation Settings dialog and indicates the default values for Company Name, Oracle Home Name, Oracle Home Location, and Oracle Home Language. Accept the default values or specify different values, and click **OK**.

9. The Select Installation Options dialog appears. Select **Application Developer (Complete)**, and click **OK**.

10. The Select a Starter Database Configuration dialog appears. Select **Standard**, and click **OK**.

11. The Installing Oracle Documentation dialog appears. Select **Hard Drive** if you would like to install the Oracle HTML documentation on your hard drive. Click **OK** to continue.

12. Setup installs Oracle on your hard disk. This may take several minutes.

13. When installation is complete, the Installation Completed dialog appears. Click **Yes** to view the documentation or **No** to exit Setup and return to Windows.

Starting Oracle8 Personal Edition

After you install Oracle8 Personal Edition, you must start Oracle8 before you can begin to use the software.

Under Windows 95, choose **Start | Programs | Oracle8 Personal Edition | Start Database** from the Windows taskbar. Rebooting is not necessary.

Under Windows NT, Oracle8 is started automatically after you reboot the machine and each time you start your computer after that.

Stopping Oracle8 Personal Edition

Perform the following steps to shut down Oracle8 Personal Edition:

1. Choose **Start | Programs | Oracle8 Personal Edition | Stop Database** from the Windows taskbar.

2. Under Windows NT, stop all Oracle8 services (if any are running). To do this:

   ■ Choose **Start | Settings | Control Panel** from the Windows taskbar.

   ■ Double-click on the **Services** application.

   ■ Click on the **Stop** icon to shut down any Oracle service that has the status Started.

   ■ Click **Close** to exit the Services application.

Uninstalling Oracle8 Personal Edition

Perform the following steps to uninstall Oracle8 Personal Edition:

1. Stop all Oracle services and close all Oracle applications.

2. Choose **Start | Programs | Oracle for Windows XX | Oracle Installer** from the Windows taskbar, where *XX* is either 95 or NT.

3. The Software Asset Manager dialog appears. Select the product(s) you want to remove from the Installed Products list on the right side, and click **Remove**.

4. The Confirmation dialog appears. Click **Yes** to continue.

5. The Dependencies dialog appears warning you that other products are dependent on Required Support Files. Click **Yes** to continue.

6. The Remove Database dialog appears asking if you want to remove the Oracle database. Click **Yes** to continue.

7. The Database Files dialog appears informing you that the additional databases you created will not be removed automatically by deinstallation. Click **OK** to continue. Oracle Installer removes the specified Oracle Personal Edition programs from your system.

8. The General Information dialog appears. Click **OK**, click **Yes** when the confirmation dialog appears, and click **Exit** to exit the Software Asset Manager and return to Windows.

Informix

The following table provides a variety of miscellaneous details about the product and the company:

Product name	Informix Dynamic Server Personal Edition
First shipment	1981
Platform	Windows 95/NT
DBMS version	7.22.TC2
Installation program	\INFORMIX\SETUP.EXE

License information
    Serial number
    Key
	
	AAC#A524494
	BDQGIP

Software limitations	None
Vendor	Informix Software, Inc.
Founded	1980
Annual sales	$700 million

Hardware and Software Requirements

Informix Personal Edition requires the following hardware and software:

Category	Requirements
Computer	Pentium-based personal computer
Memory (RAM)	16MB required, 32MB recommended
Hard disk space	72MB
Operating system	Windows 95 or Windows NT 4.0 with SP3 or earlier[1]
Network software	TCP/IP (Microsoft version)
User account	Under Windows NT, you must be a member of the Windows Administrators group to install or upgrade Informix Personal Edition and the Administration tools on your system. Use the Windows User Manager to assign yourself this role.

[1]Informix Personal Edition does not run on Windows NT 4.0 with SP4 or later.

Informix User Accounts

Under Windows NT, the installation program creates a user account called informix and an administrative group called Informix-Admin. Users in the Informix-Admin group can administer, back up and restore, modify tables, and modify dbspaces for the database server.

The installation program automatically assigns the current user and user informix accounts to the Informix-Admin group. Informix Personal Edition runs under the user informix account. The user informix owns and is the default user for this database server.

Informix Personal Edition Installation

Perform the following steps to install Informix Personal Edition:

1. Under Windows NT, log on to the system as a member of the Administrators group.

2. Insert the Bonus CD into your CD-ROM drive.

3. Windows automatically launches the DBMS installation program on the CD. If the installation program does not launch automatically, double-click **SQLINSTALL.EXE** in the root directory of the CD to launch it manually.

4. The installation program displays a dialog prompting you to accept the Osborne/McGraw-Hill license agreement. Indicate your acceptance of the agreement, and click **Next**.

5. The installation program displays the DBMS selection dialog. Select **Informix Dynamic Server Personal Edition** from the list of DBMS choices, and click **Next**.

6. The installation program displays a dialog prompting you to accept the Informix Software license agreement. Indicate your acceptance of the agreement, and click **Next**. This invokes the Informix Setup application as shown here:

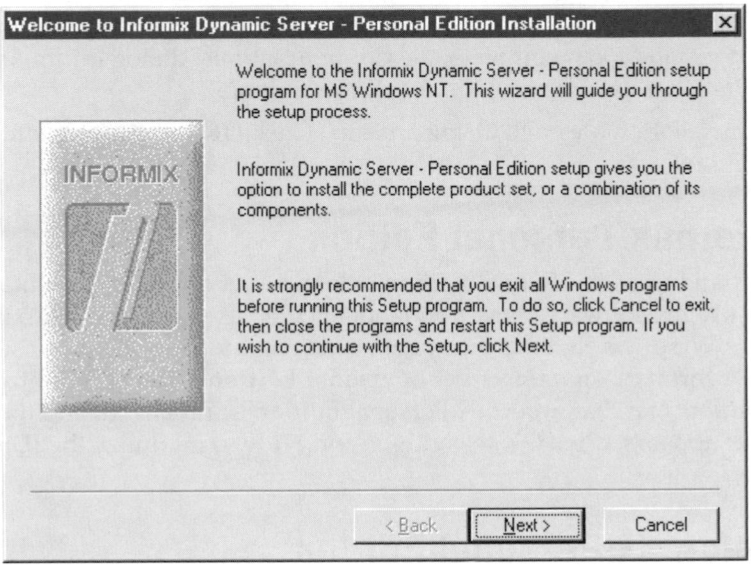

7. Setup displays the Welcome dialog. Click **Next** to continue.

8. The Select Installation Preference dialog appears. Select **Express Installation**, and click **Next**.

9. The Setup Information dialog appears and indicates the destination directory into which the Informix Personal Edition files will be copied. Accept the default, or specify a different directory. Also, enter your name and company if they are different than the default values indicated. Finally, you must enter the following software license information:

   ■ Serial Number: AAC#A524494

   ■ Key: BDQGIP

   Click **Next** to continue.

10. Setup installs Informix Personal Edition on your hard disk. This may take several minutes.

11. Under Windows NT, the Password dialog might appear if you have a user informix on your computer from a previous installation. Confirm the password if this dialog appears.

12. During installation, a series of status dialogs appear, including one with the message "Your Informix Dynamic Server - Personal Edition is being initialized." Under Windows NT 4.0 with Service Pack 4 (and possibly Service Pack 3 as well), this message may appear indefinitely (for several minutes or more). If this occurs, the installation has failed. Click **Cancel** to continue. Unfortunately, you cannot successfully install Informix Personal Edition on your system.

13. When installation is complete, the Congratulations! dialog informs you that the installation was successful. Click **OK** to continue.

14. The Installation Message dialog appears. Click **OK** to exit Setup and return to Windows.

Starting Informix Personal Edition

After you install Informix Personal Edition, you must reboot your computer before you can begin to use the software. After you reboot, log on as user informix to the Informix DBMS (under Windows 95) or to the system (under Windows NT), and choose **Start | Programs | Informix Dynamic Server - Personal Edition | IDS-PE Control Panel** from the Windows taskbar. Informix Personal Edition is initialized, and the IDS-PE Control Panel appears. Click **OK** to continue and **Hide** to minimize the IDS-PE control panel.

Stopping Informix Personal Edition

Perform the following steps to shut down Informix Personal Edition:

1. Log on as user informix to the Informix DBMS (under Windows 95) or to the system (under Windows NT).

2. Maximize the IDS-PE control panel. To do so, either:

   - Double-click on **IDS-PE control panel** on the Windows taskbar, or

   - Choose **Start | Programs | Informix Dynamic Server - Personal Edition | IDS-PE Control Panel** from the Windows taskbar.

3. Click **Shut Down**, and then click **OK** to confirm.

4. Under Windows NT, stop all Informix services (if any are running). To do this:

- Choose **Start** | **Settings** | **Control Panel** from the Windows taskbar.

- Double-click on the **Services** application.

- Click on the **Stop** icon to shut down any Informix service that has the status Started.

- Click **Close** to exit the Services application.

Troubleshooting Installation Problems

Installation problems that you might encounter with the Informix Personal Edition installation are listed here:

Problem	**Solution**
You install Informix Personal Edition under Windows NT and the installation program displays the following error: Install failed to add OnLine service	Make sure that you are a local Administrator on your Windows NT computer when you run the installation program. You must also be a Windows NT administrator. To assign yourself Administrator privileges, use the Windows User Manager.
You attempt to install Informix Personal Edition. The IDS-PE control panel and the online.log display the following error message: -930 Cannot connect to database server servername	Make sure that your TCP/IP setup is correct. Try to ping machine_name where machine_name is the name of your computer.
When you install Informix Personal Edition, you are unable to install the product in a directory such as: C:\Program Files\Informix.	Your destination directory contains a space. Your destination directory name should only contain letters, numbers, and underscores.

Uninstalling Informix Personal Edition

Perform the following steps to uninstall Informix Personal Edition:

1. Log on to the system as user informix.

2. Stop all Informix Personal Edition services, and close all **Informix Personal Edition** applications.

3. Choose **Start | Programs | Informix Dynamic Server - Personal Edition | Uninstall** from the Windows taskbar.

4. Select the items to uninstall, and click **OK**.

5. The program asks you to confirm that you want to uninstall the specified items. Click **Yes** to continue. Uninstall removes the specified Informix items from your system.

Sybase

The following provides a variety of miscellaneous details about the product and the company:

Product name	Sybase Adaptive Server Anywhere
First shipment	1987
Platform	Windows 95/NT
DBMS version	6.0
Installation program	\SYBASE\SETUP.EXE
Software limitations	Expires 60 days after installation
Vendor	Sybase, Inc.
Founded	1984
Annual sales	$858 million

Hardware and Software Requirements

Sybase Adaptive Server Anywhere requires the following hardware and software:

Category	Requirements
Computer	Pentium-based personal computer
Memory (RAM)	16MB required, 32MB recommended. Adaptive Server Anywhere can run in as little as 3MB of memory. If you use Java in the database, Adaptive Server Anywhere requires an additional 8MB of memory. Your computer must have this much memory in addition to the requirements for the operating system.
Hard disk space	40MB

Category	Requirements
Operating system	Windows 95 or Windows NT 4.0
Network software	If you are running a Sybase Adaptive Server Anywhere network server, you must have appropriate networking software installed and running. The Sybase Adaptive Server Anywhere network server is available for Windows 95, Windows NT, Novell NetWare, OS/2, and Unix operating systems. It is not available for Windows 3.x. Sybase Adaptive Server Anywhere supports the following network protocols: TCP/IP, IPX (not Unix operating systems), and NetBIOS (not Unix operating systems)

Sybase Adaptive Server Anywhere Installation

Perform the following steps to install Sybase Adaptive Server Anywhere:

1. Insert the Bonus CD into your CD-ROM drive.
2. Windows automatically launches the DBMS installation program on the CD. If the installation program does not launch automatically, double-click **SQLINSTALL.EXE** in the root directory of the CD to launch it manually.
3. The installation program displays a dialog prompting you to accept the Osborne/McGraw-Hill license agreement. Indicate your acceptance of the agreement, and click **Next**.
4. The installation program displays the DBMS selection dialog. Select **Sybase Adaptive Server Anywhere** from the list of DBMS choices, and click **Next**. This invokes the Sybase Adaptive Server Anywhere Setup application as shown here:

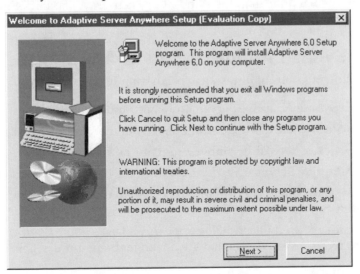

5. Setup displays the Welcome dialog. Click **Next** to continue.

6. The Software License Agreement dialog appears. Click **Yes** to accept the agreement.

7. The Choose Destination Location dialog appears and indicates the default directory into which the Sybase Adaptive Server Anywhere files will be copied. Accept the default or specify a different directory, and click **Next**.

8. The Setup Type dialog appears. Select **Personal Server**, and click **Next**.

9. The Select Components dialog appears. Select **Adaptive Server Anywhere** and **Sybase Central**, and click **Next**.

10. The Start Copying Files dialog appears. Click **Next** to continue.

11. Setup installs Sybase Adaptive Server Anywhere on your hard disk. This may take several minutes.

12. When installation is complete, the Setup Complete dialog appears. Click **Finish** to exit Setup and return to Windows.

Starting Sybase Adaptive Server Anywhere

After you install Sybase Adaptive Server Anywhere, choose **Start | Programs | Sybase | Adaptive Server Anywhere 6.0 | Personal Server Sample** from the Windows taskbar. This starts a personal server running the sample database. The server displays as an icon in the Windows system tray at the opposite end of the taskbar from the Start button.

Stopping Sybase Adaptive Server Anywhere

To shut down the Sybase Adaptive Server Anywhere server (if it is running), double-click on the **Server** icon in the Windows system tray, and click **Shutdown**. The window closes, and the Sybase server stops.

Uninstalling Sybase Adaptive Server Anywhere

Perform the following steps to uninstall Sybase Adaptive Server Anywhere:

1. Close all Sybase Adaptive Server Anywhere applications.

2. Choose **Start | Settings | Control Panel** from the Windows taskbar.

3. Double-click on the **Add/Remove Programs** application.

4. Select **Adaptive Server Anywhere 6.0** from the list, and click **Add/Remove**.

5. Windows asks you to confirm that you want to uninstall the program. Click **Yes** to continue.

6. The Remove Shared Files? dialog appears and asks you to confirm that you want to remove shared files that are no longer being used. Click **Yes to All** to

remove these files, and click **Yes** when the second confirmation dialog appears. Windows removes all Sybase Adaptive Server Anywhere programs from your system.

IBM DB2

The following provides a variety of miscellaneous details about the product and the company:

Product name	DB2 Universal Database Personal Edition
First shipment	1985
Platform	Windows 95/NT
DBMS version	5.2
Installation program	\IBMDB2\DB2\WINNT95\EN\DB2INST.EXE
Software limitations	Expires 60 days after installation
Vendor	IBM Corporation
Founded	1911
Annual sales	$80.3 billion

Hardware and Software Requirements

IBM DB2 Personal Edition requires the following hardware and software:

Category	Requirements
Computer	Pentium-based personal computer
Memory (RAM)	32MB—the minimum required to accommodate an average size database while using the full set of graphical tools. The amount of memory you need on your system depends on the size of your databases. If you want to access data in remote DB2 servers, you will not need additional memory.
Hard disk space	70MB
Operating system	Windows 95 4.00.950 or later, Windows NT 3.51, or Windows NT 4.0 or later

Category	**Requirements**
Network software	For DB2 Personal Edition to act as a client to other servers, the following communications software is required: Under Windows 95: IPX/SPX, Named Pipes, NetBIOS, or TCP/IP. The Windows 95 base operating system provides NetBIOS, IPX/SPX, TCP/IP, and Named Pipes connectivity. Under Windows NT: APPC, IPX/SPX, Named Pipes, NetBIOS, or TCP/IP. The Windows NT base operating system provides NetBIOS, IPX/SPX, TCP/IP, and Named Pipes connectivity. For APPC connectivity, you require one of the following products: IBM Communications Server for Windows NT 5.0, Microsoft SNA Server 2.11 or later on the LAN, or PCOMM AS/400 and 3270 V4.1 or later.
Other	If you have the IBM Antivirus program installed on your computer, it must be version 3.0 or later.

DB2 User Accounts

During installation, you will be asked to provide a user name and password that will be used by the Administration Server to log on to the system and to start itself as a service.

Under Windows 95, the user name must simply be a valid DB2 user name (eight characters or less and compliant with DB2's naming rules).

Under Windows NT, the user name must belong to the Administrators group and also be a valid DB2 user name, or have the "Act as part of the operating system" advanced user right. If this user name does not comply with DB2's naming rules but has the Act as part of the operating system advanced user right, the Setup program will create the user name db2admin to perform the installation. This user name will be removed from the system when the installation is complete unless it will be used by the Administration Server.

By default, the Setup program will fill the Username, Password, and Confirm Password fields with db2admin. You can accept these default values or provide your own. Setup will check to see if the user name specified for the Administration Server exists. If it does not exist, it will be created. If it does exist, Setup will verify that the user name is a member of the Administrators group and also that the password is valid, provided that the user name used to install DB2 has the Act as part of the operating system advanced user right.

When Setup creates the db2admin user name, it also makes it a member of the Administrators group. If you did not change the default password for this user name, you should change its password using the User Manager function of Administration

Tools; you should also change the password for the DB2-DB2DAS00 service to match the new password that you specified for the db2admin user name.

DB2 Personal Edition Installation

Perform the following steps to install DB2 Universal Database Personal Edition:

1. Under Windows NT, log on to the system as a user that meets the requirements for installing DB2. For more information, see the previous section "DB2 User Accounts."

2. If a DB2 version 5 product is already installed on the system, you must install this product on the same drive and in the same directory.

3. Insert the Bonus CD into your CD-ROM drive.

4. Windows automatically launches the DBMS installation program on the CD. If the installation program does not launch automatically, double-click **SQLINSTALL.EXE** in the root directory of the CD to launch it manually.

5. The installation program displays a dialog prompting you to accept the Osborne/McGraw-Hill license agreement. Indicate your acceptance of the agreement, and click **Next**.

6. The installation program displays the DBMS selection dialog. Select **IBM DB2 Personal Edition** from the list of DBMS choices, and click **Next**.

7. The installation program displays a dialog prompting you to accept the IBM Corporation license agreement. Indicate your acceptance of the agreement, and click **Next**. This invokes the DB2 Personal Edition Setup application as shown here:

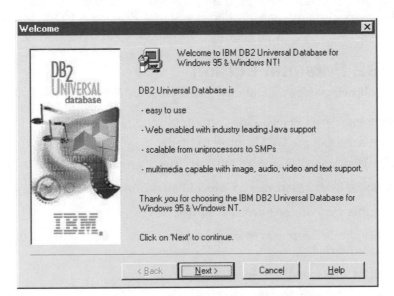

8. Setup displays the Welcome dialog. Click **Next** to continue.

9. The Select Products dialog appears. Select **DB2 Universal Database Personal Edition**, and click **Next**.

10. The Select Installation Type dialog appears. Select **Typical Install** by clicking on the corresponding graphic pushbutton.

11. The Select Destination Directory dialog appears and indicates the default directory into which the IBM DB2 Personal Edition files will be copied. Accept the default or specify a different directory, and click **Next**.

12. Under Windows NT, the Enter Username and Password dialog appears. Accept the default db2admin user name and password, and click **Next**.

13. The Start Copying Files dialog appears. Click **Install** to continue.

14. Setup installs DB2 Personal Edition on your hard disk. This may take several minutes.

15. When installation is complete, the Setup Complete dialog appears. Select **Yes**, and click **Finish** to exit Setup and automatically reboot your computer. If you used the default user name db2admin, remember to change the default password for this user name.

Starting DB2 Personal Edition

After you install DB2 Personal Edition, you must reboot your computer before you can begin to use the software. DB2 is started automatically after you reboot and each time you start your computer after that.

The DB2 First Steps application executes automatically the first time you reboot after installing the software. You can use First Steps to create the sample database. First Steps can be invoked at any time by choosing **Start | Programs | DB2 for Windows XX | First Steps** from the Windows taskbar, where *XX* is either 95 or NT.

Stopping DB2 Personal Edition

Perform the following steps to shut down DB2 Personal Edition:

1. If necessary, exit the DB2 First Steps application.

2. If necessary, exit the DB2 Control Center.

3. Under Windows NT, stop all DB2 services (if any are running). To do this:

   - Choose **Start | Settings | Control Panel** from the Windows taskbar.

   - Double-click on the **Services** application.

   - Click on the **Stop** icon to shut down any DB2 service that has the status Started.

   - Click **Close** to exit the Services application.

Verifying the Installation

You can verify that DB2 is installed correctly by creating the DB2 sample database on your system and accessing data from it by performing the following steps:

1. Log on to the system with a valid DB2 username.

2. Create the sample database by clicking on **Create the SAMPLE Database** in the main panel of First Steps.

3. Once the database is created, click on **View the SAMPLE Database** on the main panel of First Steps to select data from the SAMPLE database. This starts the Command Center allowing you to use the supplied script that shows some of the data from the database. Click on the **Execute** icon to begin the query.

4. Click on **Work with the SAMPLE Database** on the main panel of First Steps to start the Control Center. This allows you to see the tables that are in the SAMPLE database and enables you to perform actions on them.

After you have verified the installation, you can remove the sample database to free up disk space. Issue the **drop database sample** command from the command-line processor to remove the sample database.

Troubleshooting Installation Problems

For information on errors encountered during product installation, see the DB2.LOG file. The DB2.LOG file stores general information and error messages resulting from installation and uninstall activities. By default, the DB2.LOG file is located in the $X:\DB2LOG$ directory; where $X:$ is the drive on which your operating system is installed.

Uninstalling DB2 Personal Edition

Perform the following steps to uninstall DB2 Personal Edition:

1. Stop all IBM DB2 services, and close all IBM DB2 applications.

2. Choose **Start | Programs | DB2 for Windows *XX* | Uninstall** from the Windows taskbar, where *XX* is either 95 or NT.

3. The Confirm DB2 Deletion dialog appears and asks you to confirm that you want to uninstall the program. Click **Yes** to continue. The Uninstall program removes all IBM DB2 Personal Edition programs from your system.

Index

D

U